Lecture Notes in Computer Science

Edited by G. Goos, Karlsruhe and J. Hartmanis, Ithaca

1

GI
Gesellschaft für Informatik e. V.

3. Jahrestagung
Hamburg, 8.–10. Oktober 1973

Herausgegeben im Auftrag
der Gesellschaft für Informatik
von Wilfried Brauer

Springer-Verlag Berlin Heidelberg GmbH 1973

AMS Subject Classifications (1970): 68-02, 68 A 05, 68 A 10, 68 A 15, 68 A 20, 68 A 25, 68 A 30, 68 A 35, 68 A 45, 68 A 50, 68 A 55

ISBN 978-3-662-40668-7　　　　ISBN 978-3-662-41148-3 (eBook)
DOI 10.1007/978-3-662-41148-3

Offsetdruck: Julius Beltz, Hemsbach/Bergstr.

Die Jahrestagungen der Gesellschaft für Informatik sollten dazu
dienen

- eine Übersicht über den Stand der Informatik-Forschung zu vermitteln
  und dabei vor allem auch die Kontakte zwischen den verschiedenen Teil-
  gebieten der Informatik (für die die Fachausschüsse der GI regelmäßig
  Fachtagungen veranstalten) zu stärken

- die Anwendung der Informatik in anderen Wissenschaften sowie in Wirt-
  schaft, öffentlicher Verwaltung, Gesundheitswesen, Bildungswesen etc.
  zu fördern und die Zusammenarbeit zwischen Forschern und Anwendern
  zu intensivieren,

- die Beziehungen zwischen Forschung und Lehre sowie Fragen der Informatik-Ausbildung zu erörtern.

Entsprechend dem Charakter der GI, eine nicht nur rein deutsche Gesellschaft zu sein, sondern Mitglieder verschiedener Nationalität zu besitzen,
fanden alle GI-Tagungen mit internationaler Beteiligung statt. Ich freue
mich daher besonders, daß unsere Bitte um Vortragsanmeldung eine starke
Resonanz nicht nur im Inland sondern auch im Ausland gefunden hat und
daß wir eine Reihe ausländischer Wissenschaftler für die Hauptvorträge
und als Diskussionsredner gewinnen konnten, so daß 22 der 58 Vortragenden
aus 12 europäischen und außereuropäischen Staaten kommen werden.

Der Programmausschuß, dem die Herren

W. Brack, Mannesmann-Datenverarbeitung, Lintorf
W. Brauer, Universität Hamburg
H. Görling, Siemens-Zentrallabor, München
G. Krüger, Gesellschaft für Kernforschung, Karlsruhe
H. Langmaack, Universität Saarbrücken
G. Meyer-Brötz, AEG-Telefunken, Ulm
P.L. Reichertz, Medizinische Hochschule, Hannover
K. Samelson, Technische Universität München
H. Tzschach, IBM, Stuttgart

angehörten, hat sich bemüht, aus den vielen Vortragsanmeldungen diejenigen Vorträge herauszufinden, die die interessantesten und wichtigsten Ergebnisse zu enthalten versprachen - Vorträge, die im wesentlichen nur Pläne oder Produktbeschreibungen enthielten wurden nicht angenommen. Obwohl wir etwas darauf achteten, eine angemessene Verteilung der Themen auf die verschiedenen Gebiete zu erhalten, spiegelt die Verteilung der angenommenen Vorträge ziemlich genau die der Anmeldungen wider. Zwar wurde eine größere Zahl von Anwendern außerhalb des Bereichs der Hochschulen und der Forschungsinstitute gezielt über die GI-Tagung informiert, dennoch blieb die Zahl der Vorträge aus diesem Bereich im Verhältnis zu gering. Es ist zu hoffen, daß die großen Anstrengungen der deutschen Universitäten und Fachhochschulen auf dem Gebiet der Informatik-Ausbildung und die von den GI-Tagungen ausgehenden Impulse dieses Verhältnis verbessern werden.

Das Tagungsprogramm enthält zusätzlich zu den Vorträgen eine Podiumsdiskussion über das Thema

"What point is there to formal semantics?",

an der, unter der Leitung von M. Paul, Technische Universität München, die Herren J. de Bakker, Mathematisch Centrum, Amsterdam; H.Langmaack, Universität Saarbrücken; M. Nivat, Université Paris VII; D. Scott, University of Oxford; M. Sintzoff, MBLE Research Laboratory, Brüssel teilnehmen werden.

Außerhalb des wissenschaftlichen Programms werden parallel zu den Kurzvorträgen Hard- und Software-Hersteller über ihre Produkte referieren, und es wird ein Informations- und Diskussionsabend über das Informatikstudium in Deutschland stattfinden.

Einige Manuskripte der angemeldeten Vorträge sind leider nicht rechtzeitig eingegangen. Ich habe mich daher kurzfristig, und ohne die Autoren fragen zu können, entschlossen, die dem Programmausschuß vorgelegten Kurzfassungen in den Tagungsband aufzunehmen.

Allen, die zum Zustandekommen und Gelingen dieser Tagung beigetragen
haben bzw. noch beitragen werden, sei herzlichst gedankt, insbesondere

dem Bundesminister für Forschung und Technologie
der Universität Hamburg
den Firmen

> AEG-Telefunken
> Digital Equipment
> IBM
> Siemens
> Telefunken Computer

den Mitgliedern des Programmausschusses
den Angehörigen des Instituts für Informatik der Universität Hamburg,
vor allem dem Organisationskomitee unter Leitung von E. Jessen
und, nicht zuletzt, allen Vortragenden und Diskussionsteilnehmern.

Ferner ist dem Springer-Verlag sehr dafür zu danken, daß er auch diesen
GI-Tagungsband veröffentlicht und zwar in so kurzer Frist, daß er den
Tagungsteilnehmern noch vor Beginn der Tagung zugesandt werden kann.

Für ihre Mithilfe bei der Herausgabe dieses Bandes bin ich meiner
Sekretärin, Frau E. Faulborn, und meinem Mitarbeiter M. Opp sehr dankbar.

Allen Tagungsteilnehmern wünsche ich einen angenehmen und anregenden
Tagungsverlauf und hoffe, daß das vorzeitige Erscheinen dieses Bandes
nicht,wie es bei Vorlesungsskripten der Fall sein soll, dazu verleitet,
Vorträge zu schwänzen.

Hamburg, Anfang Juli 1973

W. Brauer

INHALTSVERZEICHNIS
==================

---

 *) Manuskript spät eingegangen, siehe Seite 489
**) Manuskript nicht eingegangen

HAUPTVORTRÄGE

ON COVERS AND PRECEDENCE ANALYSIS[*]

Michael A. Harrison

INTRODUCTION

The notion of one grammar "covering" another has been introduced in a number of places by a number of people [1,10,11,16,17]. There are often significant differences in the various definitions used in these studies. With the definition to be used here, it will turn out that G' "covers" G when the ability to parse G' allows one to parse G by "table lookup techniques." The formal definitions will be more complicated than this because of some practical considerations such as the desire to exclude productions which have no semantic significance. We will justify our definition and use it to prove some "positive results," e.g. any Λ-free context free grammar can be covered by a grammar in operator normal form [5]. On the other hand, a typical negative result is that there are grammars which cannot be covered by any grammar in Greibach form [12].

Attention is then turned to the class of bottom up parsing methods. Bottom up parsing may be regarded as the iteration of a two step process: detecting a phrase and then reducing it. It is shown that each step may be trivialized at the expense of the other. It is shown that every $LR(k)$ grammar [1,13,15] may be covered by a grammar which is precedence detectable and $LR(k)$ reducible. A similar result holds when "$LR(k)$" is replaced by "bounded right context" [1,6,8,9,13,15].

We now begin to list some of the formal definitions which are required.

<u>Definition</u>. A <u>context free grammar</u> is a 4-tuple $G = (V,\Sigma,P,S)$ where:

    (i) V is a finite non-empty set (<u>vocabulary</u>).

    (ii) $\Sigma \subseteq V$ is a finite non-empty set (<u>terminal symbols</u>).

    (iii) $N = V - \Sigma$ is the set of <u>variables</u> and $S \in N$.

    (iv) P is a finite subset[(1)] of $N \times V^*$ and we write $u \rightarrow v$ in P instead of $(u,v) \in P$. P is the set of <u>productions</u>.

It is convenient to introduce a general notation concerning relations.

<u>Definition</u>. Let ρ be a binary relation on a set X, i.e., $\rho \subseteq X \times X$. Define

$$\rho^0 = \{(a,a) \mid a \in X\}$$

---

[*]Research supported by the National Science Foundation NSF GJ-474.

[(1)]Let X and Y be sets of words. Write $XY = \{xy \mid x \in X, y \in Y\}$ where xy is the concatenation of x and y. Define $X^0 = \{\Lambda\}$ where Λ is the null word. For each $i \geq 0$, define $X^{i+1} = X^i X$ and $X^* = \underset{i \geq 0}{\cup} X^i$. Let $X^+ = X^* X$ and let $\emptyset$ denote the empty set. Finally, if x is a string, let $lg(x)$ denote the length of x which is the number of occurrences of symbols in x.

and for each[2] $i \geq 0$

$$\rho^{i+1} = \rho^i \rho \quad .$$

Lastly,

$$\rho^* = \bigcup_{i \geq 0} \rho^i$$

and

$$\rho^+ = \rho^* \rho \quad .$$

For a binary relation ρ on X, ρ^* is the <u>reflexive-transitive closure</u> of ρ while ρ^+ is the <u>transitive closure</u> of ρ.

Next, we can define the rules for rewriting strings.

<u>Definition</u>. Let $G = (V, \Sigma, P, S)$ be a context free grammar and let $u, v \in V^*$. Define $u \Rightarrow v$ if there exist words $x, y, w \in V^*$ and $A \in N$ so that $u = xAy$, $v = xwy$, and $A \to w$ is in P. If $y \in \Sigma^*$, we write $u \underset{R}{\Rightarrow} v$. Furthermore, define

$$\overset{*}{\Rightarrow} = (\Rightarrow)^*$$
and
$$\underset{R}{\overset{*}{\Rightarrow}} = (\underset{R}{\Rightarrow})^* \quad .$$

A string $x \in V^*$ is said to be a <u>sentential form</u> if $S \overset{*}{\Rightarrow} x$ and a <u>canonical sentential form</u> if $S \underset{R}{\overset{*}{\Rightarrow}} x$. Not every sentential form is canonical.

The set $L(G) = \{x \in \Sigma^* \mid S \overset{*}{\Rightarrow} x\}$ is the <u>language generated by</u> G. Two grammars G and G' are <u>equivalent</u> if $L(G) = L(G')$.

We now mention some similar but notationally different definitions of derivations.

If $u_0 \Rightarrow u_1 \Rightarrow \cdots \Rightarrow u_r$ then we say that the sequence $(u_0, \ldots, u_r)$ is a <u>derivation</u> of u_r from u_0. If $u_0 \underset{R}{\Rightarrow} u_1 \underset{R}{\Rightarrow} \cdots \underset{R}{\Rightarrow} u_r$ the derivation is said to be a <u>canonical derivation</u>. If for each $0 \leq i < r$ in a canonical derivation, if $u_i = v_i A_i w_i$, $u_{i+1} = v_i y_i w_i$, and u_{i+1} may be obtained from u_i by using production $\pi_i = A_i \to y_i$, we say that $(\pi_0, \ldots, \pi_{r-1})$ is a <u>canonical derivation of</u> u_r <u>from</u> u_0. Any particular derivation also corresponds to a labelled directed tree, called the <u>parse tree</u>.

If the sequence $(u_0, \ldots, u_r)$ is a derivation of u_r from u_0 then $(u_r, \ldots, u_0)$ is said to be a <u>parse</u> of u_r to u_0. If the derivation is canonical then the parse is said to be <u>canonical</u>. If u_0 is not mentioned then we assume that $u_0 = S$.

---

[2] The operation is a <u>composition</u> of relations which is defined as follows: if $\rho \subseteq X \times Y$ and $\sigma \subseteq Y \times Z$, define

$$\rho\sigma = \{(x,z) \mid (x,y) \in \rho \text{ and } (y,z) \in \sigma \text{ for some } y \in Y\} \quad .$$

Observe that $\rho\sigma \subseteq X \times Z$.

If $(s_1,\ldots,s_n)$ is any sequence, it may be denoted by $(s_i)_{i=1}^n$. If P is some predicate defined on the s_i then the subsequence of those s_i satisfying P is denoted by

$$(s_i \mid P(s_i))_{i=1}^n \quad .$$

If f is a function on the s_i then the sequence $(f(s_1),\ldots,f(s_n))$ is denoted by

$$(f(s_i))_{i=1}^n \quad .$$

If we have a canonical derivation

$$S \overset{*}{\underset{R}{\Rightarrow}} \alpha A w \underset{R}{\Rightarrow} \alpha \beta w = \gamma$$

where $\alpha, \beta, \gamma \in V^*$, $A \in N$ and $w \in \Sigma^*$, then the designated β is said to be a _simple phrase_ of γ. Moreover the pair $(A \to \beta, \, \lg(\alpha\beta))$ is said to be a _handle_ of γ.

Let Σ and Δ be two alphabets and suppose f is a function from Σ into Δ^*. f may be extended (uniquely) to a monoid _homomorphism_ from Σ^* into Δ^* by the conditions

$$f(\Lambda) = \Lambda$$
$$f(a_1 \ldots a_n) = f(a_1) \ldots f(a_n)$$

for $a_i \in \Sigma$ for $1 \leq i \leq n$. If $L \subseteq \Sigma^*$, define $f(L) = \{f(x) \mid x \in L\}$. If L is context free (regular) and f is a homomorphism then $f(L)$ is context free (regular) [1,7,14].

We will be considering a number of special properties of grammars and we now list some of these. Many of these definitions are in standard textbooks on language theory [1,7,14].

Definition. A context free grammar $G = (V,\Sigma,P,S)$ is said to be
    (i)   _Λ-free_ if $P \subseteq N \times V^+$.
    (ii) _chain free_[3] if $P \cap (N \times N) = \emptyset$.
  (iii) _reduced_ if
        (a) for each $A \in V$, there exist $x, y \in V^*$ so that $S \overset{*}{\Rightarrow} xAy$,
and   (b) for each $A \neq S$ there exists $x \in \Sigma^*$ so that $A \overset{*}{\Rightarrow} x$.
    (iv) in _operator form_ if $P \subseteq N \times (V^* - V^*N^2V^*)$.
    (v) in _canonical two form_ if $P \subseteq N \times (\{\Lambda\} \cup V \cup N^2)$.
    (vi) in _Greibach form_ if $P \subseteq N \times \Sigma V^*$.

The following results are well known:
(a) Every context free language not containing Λ has a Λ-free grammar.

---

[3] A derivation $Z_0 \Rightarrow \cdots \Rightarrow Z_r$ is said to be a _chain_ if $r > 0$ and $Z_i \in N$ for $0 \leq i \leq r$.

(b) Every context free language has a context free grammar which is chain free.

(c) Every context free language has a reduced context free grammar.

(d) Every context free language has a grammar in operator form [12].

(e) Every context free language has a grammar in canonical two form. See [1] for a related result.

(f) Every context free language not containing Λ has a context free grammar in Greibach form [12].

These results may be combined into pairs (i.e., a grammar may be assumed to satisfy an arbitrary pair of the properties) except that pairs (d,e) and (e,f) are incompatible.

I. BASIC RESULTS

There have been a number of definitions of "cover" proposed in the literature [1,10,17]. In [10], these definitions are enumerated and it is argued that the following definition is appropriate for applications to programming languages.

Before presenting our notion of covering, we must generalize the idea of generation because of the following practical considerations. In most formal treatments of parsing, the parser must enumerate <u>all</u> the nodes of the parse tree. In programming practice, certain nodes of the parse tree have no semantic significance and do not need to be present in a similar grammar. For example, a generation tree for $A \leftarrow B$ in EULER [18] involves 23 productions, only 5 of which have semantic significance. Cf. [10] for a diagram of the tree. For the purpose of code generation, it would suffice to have the "semantically significant subsequence" of the parse.

We can formalize these notions by assuming that, independent of context, a production either does or does not have semantic significance. If it does not, it may be omitted from the parse. In what follows, think of H as the set of those productions of G with semantic significance and $P-H$ as those productions with no semantic significance.

<u>Definition</u>. Let $G = (V,\Sigma,P,S)$ be a grammar and let $H \subseteq P$. Let $D = (A_i \rightarrow x_i)_{i=1}^n$ be a canonical derivation in G. Then the corresponding <u>H-sparse</u> <u>derivation</u> is

$$D_H = (A_i \rightarrow x_i \mid A_i \rightarrow x_i \text{ is in } H)_{i=1}^n \quad .$$

Let $\underline{CD(G,H)}$ denote the set of all such H-sparse derivations in G.

Note that if $H = \emptyset$, D_H is the null sequence. In general D_H is not a derivation; it is simply the subsequence of steps of D involving productions of H. As usual, by inverting the index i, one obtains parses from derivations. In particular $(A_i \rightarrow x_i \mid A_i \rightarrow x_i \text{ is in } H)_{i=n}^1$ will be called the corresponding canonical <u>H-sparse</u> parse of x.

We can now reformulate the parsing problem as follows: Given a grammar G and a set $H \subseteq P$, produce a parser which, for each $x \in \Sigma^*$, enumerates all canonical H-sparse parses with respect to G.

In this light, parsing G' will be as good as parsing G if for some $H' \subseteq P'$ one can easily construct all canonical H-sparses in G for x from all canonical H'-sparse parses of x in G'.

We are finally ready to present our definition of cover.

<u>Definition</u>. Let $G = (V, \Sigma, P, S)$ and $G' = (V', \Sigma, P', S')$ be context free grammars. Let $H \subseteq P$ and $H' \subseteq P'$. Let φ be a map from H' into H. For any canonical derivation $D = (A_i \to x_i)_{i=1}^{n}$ in G' of some $x \in \Sigma^*$, define the <u>image of</u> D <u>under</u> φ to be $\varphi(D) = (\varphi(A_i \to x_i) \mid A_i \to x_i$ is in $H')_{i=1}^{n}$. $\varphi(D)$ is an element of H^*. (G', H') is said to <u>cover</u> (G, H) <u>under</u> φ iff

    (a) $L(G) = L(G')$

and (b) for each $x \in L(G)$

        (i) if D is an H-sparse derivation of x in G then there is an H'-sparse derivation D' of x in G' so that

$$\varphi D' = D$$

and   (ii) if D' is an H'-sparse generation of x in G' then φD is an H-sparse generation of x in G.

    G' is said to <u>cover</u> (G, H) if some H' and φ exist such that (G', H') covers (G, H) under φ. If G' covers (G, P) we say G' <u>completely covers</u> G.

We remark immediately that these relations are reflexive and transitive but not symmetric in general; thus they are not equivalence relations. We now summarize some of the simple properties of covers.

<u>Proposition</u>.
    (a) G' covers $(G, \emptyset)$ if and only if G and G' are equivalent.
    (b) If (G', P') covers (G, P) under φ which is one-to-one then the degree[4] of ambiguity in G' and G on any string $x \in \Sigma^*$ is the same.
    (c) If (G'', H'') covers (G', H') under φ' and (G', H') covers (G, H) under φ then (G'', H'') covers (G, H) under $\varphi\varphi'$.

Thus covers provide a spectrum of relationships as H and H' vary.

One might think that if G covers G' and if G' covers G then G and G' are very similar. Consider the following two grammars.

---

[4] Let $G = (V, \Sigma, P, S)$ be a grammar and $x \in \Sigma^*$. The <u>degree of ambiguity</u> of x is the number of canonical derivations of x in G.

$$G: \qquad\qquad\qquad\qquad\qquad G':$$
$$S \rightarrow Ab \qquad\qquad\qquad\qquad S \rightarrow aB$$
$$A \rightarrow a \qquad\qquad\qquad\qquad B \rightarrow b$$

Clearly G covers G' and G' covers G yet G and G' are not "isomorphic." Indeed the trees are quite different. Many other examples of this type exist and when null rules are used, the trees may differ radically.

<u>Open Problem</u>. Suppose we have two grammars G and G' which cover each other. Characterize such grammars. What relations can be expected to hold among their trees?

Before using covers in a treatment of bottom up parsing we first explore the relationship between grammars and some of their normal forms.

<u>Theorem 1.1</u>. Each context free grammar G is completely covered by a grammar G' which is in canonical two form.

We omit the proof of this result which is available in [10].

Another commonly encountered normal form is the operator normal form grammar. It plays an important role in precedence analysis [4,5,11]. Greibach [12] originally showed that every grammar could be transformed to an equivalent grammar in operator normal form. However it is known that this transformation drastically changes the structure of the parse tree. It was conjectured that the reason that Floyd's precedence scheme is weaker than the scheme of Wirth and Weber was that it was impossible to get covering grammars that are in operator normal form. This conjecture proved to be false as the next result shows. One should consult [11] for a further discussion of this point.

<u>Theorem 1.2</u>. Every Λ-free grammar is completely covered by a grammar in operator normal form.

<u>Proof</u>. We present a proof of this result as an example of a typical argument involving covers.

Let $G' = (V,\Sigma,P,S)$ be a context free grammar. We may assume, without loss of generality, that G is in canonical two form by using Theorem 1.1 and the transitivity of covers.

Let $G = (V',\Sigma,P',S)$ where $V' = \{S\} \cup \Sigma \cup (N \times \Sigma)$ and define $P' = P_1 \cup P_2 \cup P_3 \cup P_4$ as follows:

$P_1 = \{S \rightarrow (S,a)a \mid a \in \Sigma\}$,

$P_2 = \{(A,a) \rightarrow \Lambda \mid A \in N, a \in \Sigma, A \rightarrow a \text{ in } P\}$,

$P_3 = \{(A,a) \rightarrow (B,a) \mid A, B \in N; a \in \Sigma, A \rightarrow B \text{ in } P\}$,

$P_4 = \{(A,a) \rightarrow (B,b)b(C,a) \mid A, B, C \in N; a, b \in \Sigma; A \rightarrow BC \text{ in } P\}$.

Next we define $H' = P_2 \cup P_3 \cup P_4$ and φ is defined by cases.

$\varphi((A,a) \rightarrow \Lambda) = A \rightarrow a$ if $(A,a) \rightarrow \Lambda$ is in P_2,

$\varphi((A,a) \rightarrow (B,a)) = A \rightarrow B$ if $(A,a) \rightarrow (B,a)$ is in P_3,

$\varphi((A,a) \rightarrow (B,b)b(C,a)) = A \rightarrow BC$ if $(A,a) \rightarrow (B,b)b(C,a)$ is in P_4.

We must show that (G',H') covers (G,P) under φ. To do this, we establish a claim.

<u>Claim.</u> For each $a \in \Sigma$, $x \in \Sigma^*$, $A \in N$, $(A,a) \overset{*}{\Rightarrow} x$ in G' by a canonical derivation $(\pi_i')_{i=1}^n$ if and only if $A \overset{*}{\Rightarrow} xa$ in G by canonical derivation $\varphi((\pi_i')_{i=1}^n)$.

<u>Proof.</u> The argument is an induction on n.

<u>Basis.</u> If $n = 1$, then $x = \Lambda$ and $(A,a) \rightarrow \Lambda$ is in P'. This holds if and only if $A \rightarrow a$ is in P which completes the basis.

<u>Induction Step.</u> Assume the result for $1 \leq n < k$ and consider the case $n = k$. Since $n = k > 1$, $\pi_1' \in P_3 \cup P_4$. There are two cases depending on whether $\pi_1' \in P_3$ or $\pi_1' \in P_4$. We will give the details only in case $\pi_1' \in P_4$ and leave the (easier) case of $\pi_1' \in P_3$ to the reader. If $\pi_1' = (A,a) \rightarrow (B,b)b(C,a)$ then $\varphi(\pi_1') = A \rightarrow BC$ by construction. There is some j so that $(\pi_i')_{i=2}^j$ is a canonical derivation of $(C,a) \overset{*}{\underset{R}{\Rightarrow}}^{G'} x_2$ and $(\pi_i')_{i=j+1}^n$ is a canonical derivation of $(B,b) \overset{*}{\underset{R}{\Rightarrow}}^{G'} x_1$ where $x = x_1 b x_2$. By the induction hypothesis, these canonical derivations exist if and only if $\varphi((\pi_i')_{i=2}^j)$ is a canonical derivation of $C \overset{G*}{\underset{R}{\Rightarrow}} x_2 a$ and $\varphi((\pi_i')_{i=j+1}^n)$ is a canonical derivation of $B \overset{G*}{\underset{R}{\Rightarrow}} x_1 b$. Combining these results

$$(A,a) \overset{G'}{\Rightarrow} (B,b)b(C,a) \overset{G'*}{\underset{R}{\Rightarrow}} x_1 b x_2$$

if and only if

$$A \overset{G}{\Rightarrow} BC \overset{G*}{\underset{R}{\Rightarrow}} x_1 b x_2 a \quad .$$

This extends the induction and completes the proof of the claim.

From the claim it follows that for any $x \in \Sigma^*$; $a \in \Sigma$;

$$S \Rightarrow (S,a)a \overset{*}{\Rightarrow} xa \quad \text{in} \quad G'$$

by derivation $(\pi_i')_{i=1}^n$ if and only if $S \overset{*}{\Rightarrow} xa$ in G' by canonical derivation $\varphi(\pi_i')_{i=1}^n$. This shows that $L(G') = L(G)$ and that φ is a map from $CD(G',H')$ onto $CD(G,P)$. Therefore G' covers G under φ. $\square$

We note that a slightly more complex construction for G' would yield a Λ-free grammar. The strongest result we can state is that every Λ-free grammar is completely covered by a Λ-free operator grammar. Furthermore, this construction preserves Floyd precedence relations [5,11].

The statement of the previous theorem immediately suggests the question of whether the hypothesis of Λ-freeness can be dropped. We will now show that it cannot be omitted and this will be our first real result of a negative character.

Theorem 1.3. There is a context free grammar G which is not covered by any operator normal form grammar.

Proof. Let G be the grammar whose rules are:

$$S \to SS|\Lambda \quad .$$

It is shown in [10] that G cannot be covered by any operator normal form grammar.

We now state another negative result by exhibiting a grammar which cannot be covered by any grammar in Greibach form. Thus the elimination of left recursive changes the structure of a grammar sufficiently that it cannot have a covering grammar.

Theorem 1.4. Let G be the following context-free grammar:

$$S \to S0|S1|0|1 \quad .$$

There is no grammar $G' = (V',\Sigma',P',S')$ in Greibach normal form such that (G',H') covers (G,P) under φ for any $H' \subseteq P'$ and φ mapping H' into P.

The proof of this result is nontrivial and is omitted. Full details may be found in [10].

We now turn to the study of an important property of grammars used in programming language description.

Definition. A context free grammar $G = (V,\Sigma,P,S)$ is said to be <u>invertible</u> if $A \to w$ and $B \to w$ in P implies $A = B$.

This property is very important in some bottom up parsing schemes because once a simple phrase of a sentential form in an invertible grammar has been found, then the lefthand side of the production is uniquely and simply found.

Our first result says that for any grammar, there is an equivalent invertible grammar. This result was obtained independently by Graham [8,9].

Theorem 1.5. For each context-free grammar $G = (V,\Sigma,P,S)$ there is an invertible context-free grammar $G' = (V',\Sigma,P',S')$ so that $L(G') = L(G)$. Moreover, if G is Λ-free then so is G'.

We will not prove this result here but refer the reader to [10].

It is easy to see that the invertibility condition is compatible with conditions (a) through (e) and not compatible with (f) in Section 1. It is interesting to note that for any grammar G, one can find an equivalent grammar G' which is invertible and chain free. On the other hand, there are grammars G for which there do not exist equivalent grammars which are invertible, chain free and Λ-free. An example of such a grammar is:

$$S \rightarrow A|b$$
$$A \rightarrow aA|a$$

[To prove this, suppose that G' is such a grammar. One can easily show by induction that for each $i \geq 1$, $a^i \in L(G')$ implies $S \rightarrow a^i$ is in P'. For $L(G')$ to equal $L(G)$ it must follow that P' is infinite which is a contradiction.]

The grammar G' of Theorem 1.5 does not necessarily cover G. For example if G is the grammar:

$$S \rightarrow A|B$$
$$A \rightarrow a$$
$$B \rightarrow a$$

then G' is:

$$\{S\} \rightarrow \{A,B\}$$
$$\{A,B\} \rightarrow a$$

which cannot cover G since φ must be a function. However the grammar:

$$S \rightarrow A|B$$
$$A \rightarrow a$$
$$B \rightarrow aL$$
$$L \rightarrow \Lambda$$

does completely cover G. Generalizing this result we obtain the following theorem.

<u>Theorem 1.6</u>. Let $G = (V,\Sigma,P,S)$ be a Λ-free context-free grammar. Then G is completely covered by an invertible grammar G'.

<u>Proof</u>. We simply present the construction. Index the elements of N by the integers[5] $1,2,\ldots,|N|$. Let the index of $A \in N$ be denoted $I(A)$. Let L be a new symbol and construct $G' = (V',\Sigma,P',S)$ as follows:

$$N' = N \cup \{L\}$$
$$P' = \{A \rightarrow xL^i|\ A \rightarrow x \in P \text{ and } I(A) = i\} \cup \{L \rightarrow \Lambda\}$$

Then (G',H) covers (G,P) under φ where $H = P' - \{L \rightarrow \Lambda\}$ and where $\varphi: H \rightarrow P$ is defined by $\varphi(A \rightarrow xL^i) = (A \rightarrow x)$ for each $A \in N$, $i = I(A)$, $(A \rightarrow xL^i) \in H$. $\square$

It is easy to see that the grammar:

$$S \rightarrow A|B$$
$$A \rightarrow a$$
$$B \rightarrow a$$

---

[5] For any set X, the cardinality of X is denoted by $|X|$.

cannot be completely covered by any invertible grammar which is Λ-free.

These results indicate theoretical applications of covers. The difference between Theorems 1.5 and 1.6 is quite illuminating. Theorem 1.6 does give a covering while Theorem 1.5 does not. On the other hand, the construction of Theorem 1.6 leads to a resulting grammar G' which has Λ-rules even when G does not.

Although the construction given in Theorem 1.2 uses Λ-rules in a similar way, null rules can be eliminated by a more complex construction. Cf. the remarks following Theorem 1.2.

Theorems 1.2 and 1.4 are quite surprising in a number of ways. First it is surprising to be able to prove that the Greibach normal form (elimination of left recursion) alters parse trees so significantly that no covering grammar can exist. [This is as much of a consequence of our definition of covering as it is of the normal form.] In light of Theorem 1.4, Theorem 1.2 is even more surprising. The previous operator normal form construction [12] had first constructed the Greibach normal form of the grammar and then gone to an operator form. Theorem 1.4 shows that such transformations can never be expected to lead to a covering but we have seen that a simple direct construction will work for Λ-free grammars.

II. BOTTOM UP PARSING

Bottom up parsing methods are usually described as algorithms which scan an input stream while computing with a pushdown store and a bounded amount of additional memory. At each stage, the algorithm performs one of the following actions:

(1)　reads an input symbol onto the stack. This continues until a simple phrase resides in the stack.

or　(2)　replaces the simple phrase in the stack by a nonterminal which generated it.

The first action is called <u>phrase detection</u> while the second operation is called <u>phrase reduction</u>. The entire algorithm can be represented by a flow chart:

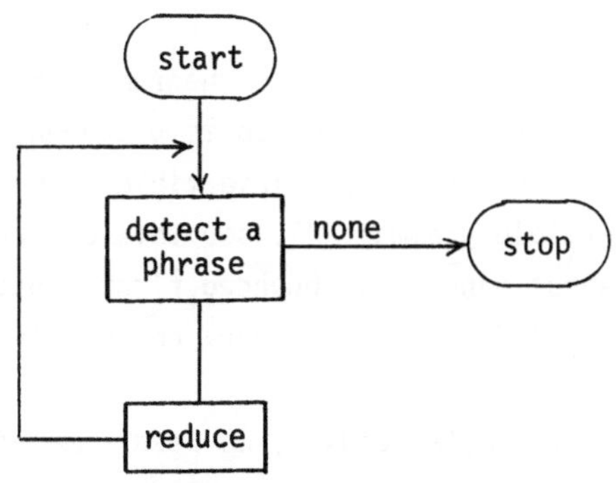

Flow chart of a bottom up parser

Figure 2.1

For example, Wirth and Weber [18] present a bottom up parsing scheme for invertible simple precedence grammars.[6] They do reduction using dictionary lookup and they detect phrases using simple precedence relations. It is known [4] that the above class [simple precedence detection and invertible reduction] is not powerful enough to parse all context free languages. In our more general framework, it is natural to inquire about the potency of simple precedence detection and of invertible reduction for particular grammars.

Is invertible reduction powerful enough to parse every context free grammar? The answer to this question depends on one's notion of adequate. If one requires that every grammar be equivalent to an invertible grammar then the answer is YES by virtue of Theorem 1.5. In the previous section, we argued that adequacy is essentially the ability to cover, i.e., parsing G' is as good as parsing G if and only if G' covers G. If our definition of adequacy is that every grammar be completely covered by an invertible grammar then we must examine Theorem 1.6. We know that we can completely cover a Λ-free grammar G by an invertible grammar G'. But the proof of Theorem 1.6 reveals that although G is Λ-free, G' has null rules (and is more complicated to parse than G in that respect at least). We have already seen (cf. remarks after Theorem 1.6) that there are $(\Lambda$-free) grammars which cannot be completely covered by any invertible Λ-free grammar. In light of this, the answer to our original question can be taken to be NO.

In some sense this means that the reduction phase of a general parser must be nontrivial. Surprising enough we shall now show that all the "work" in bottom up parsing can be done by the reduction phase.

What does it mean to shift all the work in parsing to the reduction phase? Since simple precedence is the simplest form of phrase detection, we ask whether every grammar may be completely covered by a simple precedence grammar. The (surprising (?)) answer is yes. In fact, we can say much more; we can cover grammars of type X by simple precedence grammars and reduce them by techniques appropriate for type X grammars. Some examples of these results follow the present discussion.

Lest the reader try to formulate the theorem "for all X, every grammar of type X can be covered by a grammar which is precedence detectable and X reducible" we point out that not every invertible grammar is covered by a precedence detectable invertible grammar. To see this observe that precedence detection plus invertibility cannot handle all bounded right context languages [4,13,15]. On the other hand, Theorem 1.6 shows that every context free language has an invertible grammar.

In order to prove our main results, we need some additional concepts.

----

[6] In this introduction, we will discuss a number of special types of grammars such as simple precedence grammars. Formal definitions occur in this paper before the mathematical use of each concept. Definitions for concepts which are discussed but are not used in theorems may be found in [1,10,11].

<u>Definition</u>. A context free grammar $G = (V,\Sigma,P,S)$ is said to be <u>chain</u> <u>reduced</u> if G is reduced and if for any $A \in N$ it is not the case that $A \overset{+}{\Rightarrow} A$.

If a grammar is not chain reduced then it is ambiguous. One can easily decide whether a grammar is chain reduced and if it is not, one can remove the "cycles" by a straight forward construction and then reduce it. Note that a chain reduced grammar may have chains but they are of bounded length.

Before we can state the next result, we must recall the formalism for $LR(k)$ grammars [13,15].

<u>Definition</u>. Let $G = (V,\Sigma,P,S)$ be a context free grammar with no derivations of the form $S \overset{+}{\underset{R}{\Rightarrow}} S$; also let $k \geq 0$. G is <u>$LR(k)$ detectable</u> if for each $w, w', x \in \Sigma^*$; $\alpha, \alpha', \beta, \beta' \in V^*$; $A, A' \in N$

if $\qquad S \overset{*}{\underset{R}{\Rightarrow}} \alpha A w \underset{R}{\Rightarrow} \alpha\beta w \qquad$ has handle $(A \to \beta,\ \lg(\alpha\beta))$,

if $\qquad S \overset{*}{\underset{R}{\Rightarrow}} \alpha'A'x \underset{R}{\Rightarrow} \alpha'\beta'x = \alpha\beta w' \quad$ has handle $(A' \to \beta',\ \lg(\alpha'\beta'))$,

and[7] if $\qquad\qquad\qquad\qquad {}^{(k)}w = {}^{(k)}w'$

then $\lg(\alpha'\beta') = \lg(\alpha\beta)$ and $\beta = \beta'$.
    Note that $A = A'$ is not necessarily true.

<u>Definition</u>. Let $G = (V,\Sigma,P,S)$ be a context free grammar with no derivations of the form $S \overset{+}{\underset{R}{\Rightarrow}} S$ and let $k \geq 0$. G is <u>$LR(k)$ reducible</u> if for each $w, w', x \in \Sigma^*$; $\alpha, \alpha', \beta \in V^*$; $A, A' \in N$

if $\qquad\qquad S \overset{*}{\underset{R}{\Rightarrow}} \alpha A w \underset{R}{\Rightarrow} \alpha\beta w \qquad$ has handle $(A \to \beta,\ \lg(\alpha\beta))$,

if $\qquad\qquad S \overset{*}{\underset{R}{\Rightarrow}} \alpha'A'x \Rightarrow \alpha'\beta x = \alpha\beta w' \quad$ has handle $(A' \to \beta,\ \lg(\alpha\beta))$,

and if $\qquad\qquad\qquad {}^{(k)}w = {}^{(k)}w'$

then $A = A'$.

Finally the two previous definitions can be combined.

<u>Definition</u>. Let $G = (V,\Sigma,P,S)$ be a context free grammar with no derivations of the form $S \overset{+}{\underset{R}{\Rightarrow}} S$ and let $k \geq 0$. G is <u>$LR(k)$</u> if G is $LR(k)$ detectable and $LR(k)$ reducible, i.e. for each $\alpha, \alpha', \beta, \beta' \in V^*$; $w, w', x \in \Sigma^*$, $A, A' \in N$

if $\qquad\qquad S \overset{*}{\underset{R}{\Rightarrow}} \alpha A w \underset{R}{\Rightarrow} \alpha\beta w \qquad$ has handle $(A \to \beta,\ \lg(\alpha\beta))$,

if $\qquad\qquad S \overset{*}{\underset{R}{\Rightarrow}} \alpha'A'x \underset{R}{\Rightarrow} \alpha'\beta'x = \alpha\beta w' \quad$ has handle $(A' \to \beta',\ \lg(\alpha'\beta'))$,

and if $\qquad\qquad\qquad {}^{(k)}w = {}^{(k)}w'$

---

[7] For any $k \geq 0$ and any $\alpha = a_1 \cdots a_n$, $a_i \in V$ for $1 \leq i \leq n$, if $k \geq n$, define ${}^{(k)}\alpha = \alpha$. If $k < n$, then ${}^{(k)}\alpha = a_1 \cdots a_k$.

then $(A \to \beta, \lg(\alpha\beta)) = (A' \to \beta', \lg(\alpha'\beta'))$.

<u>Example</u>. Consider the grammar G_1 shown below

$$S \to Ab \mid Bc$$
$$A \to Aa \mid \Lambda$$
$$B \to Ba \mid \Lambda$$

G_1 is not LR(k) reducible for any k but G_1 is LR(1) detectable. On the other hand, let G_2 be

$$S \to A$$
$$A \to AA \mid \Lambda$$

G_2 is LR(0) reducible because it is invertible, but is not LR(k) detectable for any k.

Our next result, while interesting in its own right, is intended as a device to help prove Theorem 2.2.

<u>Theorem 2.1</u>. Every LR(k) grammar G can be completely covered by an LR(k) canonical two form grammar G'. If G is chain-reduced and Λ-free so is G'.

Before stating our main result, we need the following concepts about precedence analysis. The reader is referred to [11] which presents this theory in greater detail and generality. Also see [1,2,3,4,5,8,9].

<u>Definition</u>. Let $G = (V, \Sigma, P, \lfloor S \rfloor)$ be a context free grammar with delimiter.[8]
Define the following binary relations on V:

$\lambda = \{(A,B) \mid A \to By$ is in P for some $y \in V^*\}$,

$\rho = \{(A,B) \mid B \to xA$ is in P for some $x \in V^*\}$,

$\alpha = \{(A,B) \mid C \to xABz$ is in P for some $x, z \in V^*\} \cup \{(\lfloor,S),(S,\rfloor)\}$.

Finally, define

$\lessdot = \alpha\lambda^+$,

$\doteq = \alpha$,

$\gtrdot = (\rho^+\alpha\lambda^*) \cap (V \times \Sigma)$.

The reader who is familiar with the general theory of canonical precedence will note that this is the special case where $T = V$ so that G is Λ-free, $\alpha = \gamma$ and $\lambda = \delta$ and $\rho = \omega$.

Now we can give the following definition.

---

[8] At this point, we use context free grammars with delimiters. Formally, the conventions are that $\lfloor \in \Sigma$, $\lfloor S \rfloor$ is the start string and $P \subseteq (V-\Sigma) \times (V-\{\lfloor\})^*$. All of the previous theorems are true with minor modifications for grammars with delimiters. Cf. [11].

<u>Definition</u>. A context free grammar $G = (V, \Sigma, P, \lfloor S \rfloor)$ is said to be a <u>precedence detectable</u> <u>grammar</u> if

(a) G is Λ-free,

and (b) the relations $<\cdot$, $\doteq$, and $\cdot>$ are pairwise disjoint.

We can now state and prove the main result of this section.

<u>Theorem 2.2</u>. If G is a Λ-free chain reduced $LR(k)$ grammar in canonical two form, then G is covered by a simple precedence detectable, $LR(k)$ reducible grammar G'.

Combining these results leads immediately to our main theorem, which was independently obtained by Graham [8,9].

<u>Theorem 2.3</u>. Every Λ-free chain reduced $LR(k)$ grammar is covered by a precedence detectable, $LR(k)$ reducible grammar.

<u>Proof</u>. The result follows immediately from Theorem 2.1, Theorem 2.2, and the transitivity of covers. $\square$

By analogous techniques, one can show the following result, also obtained by Graham [8,9].

<u>Theorem 2.4</u>. Every Λ-free chain reduced $BRC(n,m)$ grammar is covered by a precedence detectable, $BRC(n+r,m)$ reducible grammar for some integer r.

III. <u>SUMMARY AND CONCLUSIONS</u>

Past work in the areas of normal forms and of classes of parsers has focussed primarily on the existence of a certain normal form for a grammar or the existence of a recognizer for a language. Often the proof is by a construction which mutilates the structure of the original grammar or produces an impractically large grammar. In an attempt to define and examine these properties one is led to the concept of grammatical covering. The definition of covering, although intuitively quite simple, is formally complex and gives rise to rather lengthy proofs. However, the definition yields some interesting results.

It shows, as expected, that the canonical two form is a useful normal form and that any conceivable Greibach normal form construction significantly changes the shape of the parse trees of some grammars. Surprisingly there exist constructions for the operator normal form which do not significantly change the shape and labelling of the parse trees. Similarly there exist constructions for the invertible form of a grammar which do not significantly change the shape of the parse trees.

Perhaps a word of caution is appropriate here. The constructions presented work as claimed. However the resulting grammars are typically considerably larger than the original [Theorem 1.1 yields an EULER [18] grammar two times larger,

Theorem 1.2 yields a grammar 1600 times larger, Theorem 1.5 yields a grammar 2^{40} times larger, and Theorem 2.2 yields a grammar 16 times larger.]. The theorems present certain tricks which apply uniformly to the entire grammar. However, in practical situations, they should be used incrementally and with discretion to repair local anomalies in a grammar. The substance of any particular theorem is that there is (is not) hope of going from grammar G to a covering normal form grammar.

For example, fast parsers have been constructed which use a precedence detection scheme and LR(k) reduction. Theorem 2.2 indicates that such techniques can handle all LR(k) grammars. By employing the constructions of Theorem 1.1 and Theorem 2.1 it is possible to convert any Λ-free and chain free LR(k) grammar G to a grammar G' which is precedence detectable and LR(k) reducible. Further, this new grammar completely covers the original grammar. Thus one can build a parser for G which uses precedence detection and LR(k) reduction on G' and translates G' parses to G parses by dictionary lookup at each step of the parse.

In conclusion, we mention that there are a number of questions which are open. Can other normal form theorems be strengthened to be covers? For instance, there are some very strong results in [9] which may be "covering theorems." Claims of this type have been made by Mickunas and Schneider [16] but we have not seen their proofs. Are covers a better device for classifying grammars than the theory of transductions. Cf. [1] for general background.

ACKNOWLEDGEMENT

This work was done jointly with J.N. Gray and most of the material is drawn from a joint paper [10].

REFERENCES

1. Aho, A.V. and Ullman, J.D., _The Theory of Parsing, Translation, and Compiling,_ Vols. I and II, Prentice Hall Inc., Englewood Cliffs, N.J., 1972-1973.

2. Colmerauer, A., _Precedence, Analyse Syntaxique, et Langages de Programmation,_ Thesis, University of Grenoble, 1967.

3. Feldman, J. and Gries, D., "Translator Writing Systems," _Communications of the Association for Computing Machinery,_ Vol. 11, pp. 77-113, 1968.

4. Fischer, M.J., "Some Properties of Precedence Languages," _Proceedings of the Symposium on Theory of Computing,_ pp. 181-190, May 1969.

5. Floyd, R.W., "Syntactic Analysis and Operator Precedence," _Journal of the Association for Computing Machinery,_ Vol. 10, pp. 316-333, 1963.

6. Floyd, R.W., "Bounded Context Syntactic Analysis," _Communications of the Association for Computing Machinery,_ Vol. 7, pp. 62-66, 1964.

7. Ginsburg, S., _The Mathematical Theory of Context Free Languages,_ McGraw-Hill Book Co., New York, 1966.

8. Graham, S.L., "Extended Precedence Languages, Bounded Right Context Languages and Deterministic Languages," _Proceedings IEEE 11th Annual Symposium on Switching and Automata Theory_, pp. 175-180, Oct. 1970.

9. Graham, S.L., _Precedence Languages and Bounded Right Context Languages_, Ph.D. Thesis, Department of Computer Science, Stanford University, July 1971.

10. Gray, J.N. and Harrison, M.A., "On the Covering and Reduction Problems for Context-Free Grammars," _Journal of the Association for Computing Machinery_, Vol. 19, pp. 675-698, 1972.

11. Gray, J.N. and Harrison, M.A., "Canonical Precedence Schemes," _Journal of the Association for Computing Machinery_, Vol. 20, pp. 214-234, 1973.

12. Greibach, S.A., "A New Normal Form Theorem for Context Free Phrase Structure Grammars," _Journal of the Association for Computing Machinery_, Vol. 12, pp. 42-52, 1965.

13. Harrison, M.A. and Havel, I.M., "On the Parsing of Deterministic Languages," submitted for publication.

14. Hopcroft, J.E. and Ullman, J.D., _Formal Languages and their Relation to Automata_, Addison Wesley Publishing Co., Reading, Mass., 1969.

15. Knuth, D.E., "On the Translation of Languages from Left to Right," _Information and Control_, Vol. 8, pp. 607-639, 1965.

16. Mickunas, M.D. and Schneider, V., oral communication.

17. Reynolds, J.C. and Haskell, R., "Grammatical Coverings," unpublished manuscript.

18. Wirth, N. and Weber, H., "Euler: A Generalization of ALGOL and its Formal Definition," _Communications of the Association for Computing Machinery_, Vol. 9, pp. 11-23, 89-99, 1966.

COMPUTER ARCHITECTURE
COMMENTS ON THE STATE-OF-THE ART

C. Gordon Bell

Various authors and computer designers (computer architects) have defined computer architecture in several ways: Amdahl, Blauuw and Brooks (1964) in the article, "Architecture of the IBM System/360", define architecture:

> "The term architecture is used here to describe the attributes of a system as seen by the programmer, i.e., the conceptual structure and functional behavior, as distinct from the organization and data flow and control, the logical design and the physical implementation."

Caxton Foster (1970) states that architecture is:

> "...the art of designing a machine that will be a pleasure to work with."

Also, Yaohan Chu has, in the SIGARCH-IEEE Computer Architecture Group News (1972), conjectured:

> "Computer Architecture is an emerging discipline as a result of recent rapid technical advances in computer technology. Instead of merely studying the hardware structural and algorithmic features of a computer system, the scope of computer architecture is being broadened to the conceptual formation and specification of computer systems. Full recognition of and the formal training in computer architecture will hasten computer application to new horizons. Before the end of this decade, a new breed of professionals, computer architects, will arise. Computer architects practice computer architecture just as building architects practice building architecture."

Taking a view relatively close to those above, it must be added that computer architecture is not another art form measured qualitatively. Quantitative measures and methods of analysis exist and must be applied, including those to guarantee that computers operate reliably. No doubt there have been and will be many machines that are a pleasure to use (e.g., have a nice facade), but cannot be justified because the added pleasure is not worth the high cost or poor performance. It is not clear that every user can afford an architect, especially when computer costs are very small, nor is it clear that one can stand the unreliability of one-of-a-kind computers. The activity of building an information processing system will more likely be collecting computer components, the associated basic operating systems and programming languages, and then interconnecting them and programming the resulting structure in terms of the components--exactly as we do now within applications areas. Computer architects who specify computer structures to carry out highly specialized tasks (i.e., for communications networks, automobiles, etc.) may possibly be justified, and perhaps will exist.

Computer architecture can be thought of as the satisfaction of constraints imposed by technologists (component providers), implementers (logical designers and system programmers), and market-user-buyer-programmer (problem being solved).

The user, however, may view this instead as a sequential process, with no feedback, consisting of:

technology——⟶design (architecture)——⟶system programs——⟶user programs——⟶use

There is assuredly feedback (via the market mechanism), but nevertheless it is difficult to get out of the sequence of invent, develop, and use. Therefore, it appears
to take too long for use to affect machine structure. The evolution of the architect
as an all-knowing mediator to create a globally optimum system for each application
may not occur.

Over the last 2 decades of computer evolution, basic component and organization
technology has contributed to an annual effective increase in cost effectiveness,
which we have recently measured at 1.25-1.40; thus for a given cost, the performance
yield since 1946 has been a factor of about 10^8 instead of the less conservative
$(1.25 \sim 1.40)^{27}$ or $4 \sim 9 \times 10^3$. The following observations about the structures we
build is based on a simple model of a product with a completely elastic demand. That
is, for every application, there is a given price and number of buyers for that
facility. In general, looking at <u>all</u> computation as a whole, there is a completely
elastic demand--thus for $\emptyset$ cost computation, an infinite number of buyers exist.
Therefore, in a very gross sense, computer structure evolution represents an excur-
sion along the demand curve.

Alternatively, computer architecture, if more broadly defined, could be similar to
conventional architecture. Thus the architect would take native materials, user
constraints and regulations to provide aesthetically pleasant structures. The trends,
therefore, in computer architecture are dictated by technology. This technology is
not just the single logic technology dimension which we use to measure computer
generations (i.e. first-vacuum tubes 1946-1960; second-transistors 1960-1966; third-
transistor integrated circuits 1966-1973; and fourth-transistor large scale integrated circuits 1973-) but consists of several inter-related technologies.

Each technology is at a different stage of evolution, thus their performance/cost
improvements vary at different rates. The dominant basic technologies for computers
are below listed in order of decreasing rates (roughly corresponding to their tech-
nological age):

1. Logic (e.g. transistors, integrated circuits)
2. Magnetic-recording for primary, secondary, and tertiary storage (e.g. cores,
    disks, tape)
3. Electro-optical recording
4. Communications
5. Terminals for direct communications
6. Packaging (e.g. discrete components, printed circuits)
7. Paper handling (e.g. cards, printing)

For example, if logic technology improves by 30%/year, and magnetic recording using
cores improves only at 20%, we know that the former technology can eventually replace
the later. These replacements are difficult to predict because they can be stimu-
lated or retarded depending on production rates, and rate of introduction.

To further increase the complexity, the basic user techniques also affect the
designs. For example, while processor cost dominates a design, program techniques
are developed to minimize processing at the expense of memory size whereas higher
memory cost stimulates better encoding and cause the space-time tradeoff considerations to be on space. Now the trend may be reversing. Also, the design considerations now favor user convenience, thereby requiring more capability (and size).

In most cases a new technology replaces an existing technology (e.g. vacuum tubes
were replaced by transistors, which in turn are able to be replaced by larger scale
integrated circuits...). Each technology has a maximum capability in terms of cost,
speed, heat dissipation, environment, packing density, reliability, etc., which
ultimately limits its applicability. Thus, we progress for a while to the limit of a
given technology, and phase over to a competing technology--when there is one. Often,
the new rival is not driven by the computer industry, but instead derives by-product
advantages. For example, integrated circuit technology was initiated for aerospace
requirements, and is now being used in consumer electronics. This basic improvement

translates into 3 types of computer structures. The first two are main line
evolution and the third is more experimental and may eventually influence the evolution.

1. Hold cost constant (i.e. computing budget) and use the resulting increased
    performance. General purpose computation sales is predicated on this principal.
    In essence, a given human organization cost is fixed, fixing the relative amount
    available to be spent on computation. Therefore, there is a match between the
    organization's ability to increase its computing load and the technological gain.
    Whether the budget, problem solving ability, or computational ability is the
    constraint, varies over time for a given group supplying computation.

2. Hold performance constant and use the lower performance resulting structure to
    move up the demand curve and discover new applications. The minicomputer has
    been the vehicle for this excursion since it was initially the minimal computer
    that could be constructed for a given technology. Each year, as the price of the
    minimal computer continues to decrease, new applications are economically
    feasible, since the total system price is the important variable.

    The minimal processor-on-a-chip, (microprocessor) hence the computer-on-a-
    printed-circuit-board, represents a new technology which again provides alterna-
    tives to solve problems. Often significant overhead is required in the computer
    to carry out a similar function. With these computers, powerful, low cost desk
    calculators are possible, being integrated into a terminal.

3. Advance the state of the art. Build a completely new structure which solves
    problems in a fashion that would otherwise be considered infeasible. Usually,
    there are two motivations (justifications) for operating ahead of the state of
    the art: the technology will eventually be there, thus it is important to do
    the preliminary research which will make these applications ultimately feasible;
    and defense--an essentially infinite amount of money, because the benefit (not
     annihilation) is infinite.

    Many of the early computers were designed for research, and there have been high
    performance special systems for defense. The research-directed computers have
    required longer times than anticipated, and occasionally are obsolete before they
    operate, since the wrong technology was selected--i.e. technology has passed them
    by.

Current State of Architecture

Table 1 presents the current status of various computer structures and components.
These are grouped according to PMS computer component types roughly in order of
decreasing complexity (see Bell and Newell, 1971). This attempts to show the current
and leading edge of computer technology together with the urierlying research needed
to carry out the (r)evolution.

Rather than dwelling on the current state-of-the-art and the leading edge structure,
the bibliography lists articles which provide more details. Underlying all
structures is a basic need to understand parallelism; i.e. given a problem, how can
it be solved in different ways using parallel processing of some form.

Currently, four distinctly evolving structures based on increased parallelism can be
seen:

1. Computer networks operating on multiple tasks. Usually the nodes are physically
    dispersed interconnected by relatively low data-rate links (e.g. the ARPA net-
    work, ASP, and loop schemes).

2. Computer networks operating on a single task. A Computer Module (CM) which is physically small (1/2"x8"x16") has been postulated. The structures (links and ports) are of concern because they effect the applications.

3. Single computers with multiple processors (e.g. CMU C.mmp, UC/Berkeley PRIME).

4. Parallel-type processors such as STAR (pipeline), STARAN (array), PEPE (array), and ILLIAC-IV (array). These single instruction stream processors all operate on multiple data items in either a strictly array or pipelined form of parallelism.

<u>A View of the Fourth Generation</u>

Each of the previous generations has permitted a certain sized module to be fabricated. These modules in turn become the components for forming larger computer structures. Each previous generation and the corresponding primitive modules are:

<u>Generation</u>	<u>Technology</u>	<u>Primitive Modules</u>
First	Vacuum tubes	Single flip flop; 1 6 gates.
Second	Single transistors	Few flip flops or gates.
Third	Small $\sim$ medium scale integrated circuits.	Same as above but packaged into bit sliced or functional registers and operation.
Fourth	Large scale integrated circuits	Registers; read-only and read-write memories; functional components (e.g. processors)

Thus, at the current level of integration (1973) with 1000 $\sim$ 10,000 gates per single integrated circuit, it is necessary to have components which can be commonly used for many applications. The type of components include: read-only and read-write memories, complete arithmetic units with general purpose capability, and finally the processor-on-a-chip, or microprocessor. This technology forces us to think about the algorithm, not the details of implementation. Finally, by having very low cost computers of this form, the interconnection scheme becomes the main component. It is important to note that with this type of design, the emphasis on design is at registers and algorithms <u>not</u> the customary combinational and sequential circuits common to the first, second, and third generation design.

Because densities of Large Scale Integration increase slowly, microcomputer processors are the first to appear. In fact, according to the minicomputer definition that states a minicomputer is the smallest (minimal) computer that can be built with a given technology, they are precisely minicomputers. That is, at the 1000 to 10,000 gates per single integrated circuit package, it is possible to provide a single, relatively slow, byte-oriented processor. Yet, using this approach, which gives a significant decrease in cost, we may conclude: new structures will emerge (e.g. powerful single user desk calculators dedicated to a single language such as BASIC can be embedded in a display or typewriter console; new applications are feasible (e.g. hand-held inventory taking devices that require some amount of logical and arithmetic capability); and finally, due to the decreased cost, lower cost components can be combined to give an increase in cost effectiveness through parallelism. This later structure (see Bell, et al 1973), which is a structure composed as a set of interconnected (micro) computers, we call Computer Modules is the subject of research into parallelism. The modules are combined in the following ways:

1. Networks to form a conventional computer. Each computer controls (manages) a
    part of what is currently a separate function (e.g. a card reader, terminal,
    disk).

2. Process control--a given application is broken into a number of independent
    tasks. In some types of process control, this is relatively easy, since a
    number of control loops are independent with only slight interaction among
    variables.

3. Parallel Computation--highly parallel computation can be carried out on certain
    data types and data operations, such as Matrices and Fast Fourier Transforming.

4. Conventional Language Interpretation--a given machine such as Fortran, which
    includes program preparation, compilation, and interpretation can be broken
    into independent tasks for pipeline execution.

All these structures focus on the links, which provide for the intercommunication of
information among the modules.

Conclusions

Several observations about the current state of the art in computer structures have
been made. In an earlier paper by myself, Allen Newell (1971), we listed several
points about design:

1. Computer design is still driven by the changes in technology, especially in the
    varying trade-offs.

2. Distinct regions in the space of trade-offs lead to qualitatively different
    designs.

3. These designs have to be discovered by computer designers, and this can happen
    only after the trade-off characteristics of a new region become reasonably well
    understood.

4. Thus, our designs always lag the technology seriously. Those that are reaching
    for the new technology are extremely crude. Those that are iterations on exist-
    ing designs, hence more polished, fail to be responsive to the newly emerging
    trade-offs.

5. Since the development cycle on new total systems is still of the order of years,
    the only structures that can be predicted with even minimal confidence are those
    already available in nascent form.

6. The design tools that we have for discussing (and discovering) appropriate de-
    signs are weak, especially in the domain over which the structures under consid-
    eration here have changed--essentially the PMS level.

7. In particular, there is no really useful language for expressing the trade-offs
    in a rough and qualitative way, yet precisely enough so that the design conse-
    quences can be analyzed.

8. In particular (as well), design depends ultimately on having conceptual compon-
    ents of the right size relative to the system to be constructed: small enough
    to permit variety, large enough to permit discovery. The transient character
    of the underlying space (the available space of computer structures) reinforces
    the latter requirement.

TABLE 1 – STATE OF THE ART OF COMPUTER STRUCTURES

STRUCTURES	CURRENT	PREDICTED--LEADING EDGE	RESEARCH/PROBLEMS
Networks	Dual; duplicated; 1-level tree (central node)	ARPA network (store and forward message switching), loops	OR-type; protocol; analysis; exploitation of parallelism
Computers	gp: 2 Pc; Pipelined: CDC STAR and TI ASC	C.mmp	Analysis + multiprocessors + computability.
	mini: Microprocessors on a chip		Interconnected nets.
	special: ILLIAC IV; Goodyear STARAN		Exploitation of parallelism.
	reliable: JPL-STAR; Hamming code memory+data path; TMR and duplex, Instruction re-try.		Reliability theory; diagnosable.
Processors	Parallelism: pipeline, set, array, assoc. (e.g. PEPE), microprogrammed (e.g. B1700), GP emulation (360/370)	Extensive cache use; language based; FFT & specialized; large array.	Exploitation of parallelism; semantic notations for general interpretation; virtual systems
Memory	LSI (fast + slow) $\rightarrow$ cache (hierarchies)	Content addressable memories (e.g. STARAN)	Memory hierarchies.
	Disks + tape (density increase)	Solid-state, magnetic domain + photo non-mechanical, optical	Photo storage
Switches	Bus-based computers; rings		Analysis; reliability.
Links	50 Khz	1 ∼ 4 Mhz	Relationship to cable TV. Comm. syntax + protocol.
Transducers (terminals)	Typewriters	Word processing typewriters	Non-impact, quiet print.
	Scopes; optical character readers, special terminals for: production, order entry, point of sale.	Image processing; real time animation + solid figures; lower cost; color; higher resolution with graphics.	Human factors.
	Speech synthesis--limited vocabulary.	Elimination of punched cards, tactile I/O, portable.	Speech recognition.
K(controls)	Hardwire, microprogram, modular structures (e.g. macromodules, PDP-16); processor on a chip.	gp modules	Interconnectability, specification.
Technology: LSI	Large scale gp functions (microprocessors, comm. transceivers, queues, etc.) MOS (>1000 gates/chip)	gp modules; iterative structures. CMOS, TTL? ECL?	Easier design and fabrication process. What are right primatives?

Bibliography and References

Amdahl, G.M., G.A. Blaauw and F.P. Brooks, "Architecture of the IBM System/360," IBM J. Res. and Dev., Vol. 8, No.2, pp. 87-101, April 1964. (Classic article on 360, outlining 360 design goals and 360 architecture. Early use of "computer architecture".)

Baer, J.C. "A Survey of Some Theoretical Aspects of Multiprocessing", Computer Surveys, pp.31-80, Vol. 5, No. 5, March 1973.

Bell, C.G. and A. Newell,"Computer Structures--Past, Present and Future", 1971 FJCC, pp. 387-394 (Postulates several multiprocessor and cache memory structures.)

Bell, C.G., J. Grason and A. Newell, Designing Computers and Digital Systems Using PDP-16 Register Transfer Modules, Digital Press, Maynard, Mass., 1972 (Modular design at the register transfer level.)

Bell, C.G., R. Chen and S. Rege, "The Effect of Technology on Near Term Computer Structures", Computer, Vol. 5., No. 2, March/April 1972. (Tutorial on technology. Describes ILLIAC IV, CDC STAR, and Goodyear STARAN.)

Bell, C.G., R.C. Chen, S.H. Fuller, J. Grason, S. Rege, and D.P. Siewiorek, "The Architecture and Application of Computer Modules: A Set of Components for Digital Sy stems Design", pp. 177-180 IEEE COMPCON, 1973 (Large computer networks.)

Bell, C.G. and A. Newell, Computer Structures: Readings and Examples, McGraw Hill, 1971. (650 pages, 44 computers) (See Computing Reviews, May 1972, by F.P. Brooks.)

CDC STAR--(100 Mhz operation rate), see papers IEEE COMPCON 1971 and 1972.

Chu, Yaohan, Computer Organization and Microprogramming, Prentice-Hall, 1972. (Emphasis on implementation and descriptive language CDL.)

Coury, Fred, "Minicomputer Applications", IEEE Reprints, 1972. (A collection of papers covering structures, applications and software.)

Farber, D.J., J. Feldman, F.R. Heinrich, M.D. Hopwood, K.C. Larson, D.C. Loomis, L.A. Rowe, "The Distributed Computing System", pp. 31-34, IEEE COMPCON 1973.

Foster, Caxton, Computer Architecture, Van Nostrand, 1971 (Introductory.)

Lapidus, Gerald, "MOS/LSI Launches the Low Cost Processor," IEEE Spectrum, pp.33-40, November 1972. (Overview of several microcomputers on single LSI chips.)

Roberts, L.G., The Advanced Research Projects Agency (ARPA) Network, six papers, 1970 SJCC, with follow-on evaluation papers, 1972 SJCC. Also IEEE COMPCON 1973. (Excellent set of papers on a structure we will all eventually use.)

Rustin, Randall, editor, "Computer Networks", Courant Computer Science Symposium 3, Prentice Hall. (Collection of papers.)

Slotnick, D.L., "The Fastest Computer", Scientific American, pp. 76-88, No. 2, Vol. 224, February 1971. (Good on applications of parallelism to computers--ILLIAC IV)

Wulf, W. and C.G. Bell; C.mmp--A Multi-Mini-Processor Computer, pp. 765-777, FJCC 1972.

A SURVEY OF MATHEMATICAL RESULTS IN FLOW-TIME SCHEDULING FOR COMPUTER SYSTEMS

E. G. COFFMAN, JR.

Introduction

In a broad sense the problems most central to the design of operating systems are
sequencing problems. This is reflected in the term, operating systems, itself.
These problems include sequencing to ensure mutually exclusive use of a resource,
determinacy, avoidance of deadlocks, or synchronized execution of tasks; sequencing
to make efficient use of memory and input/output resources; and sequencing task
executions to optimize performance measures such as schedule-length and mean finishing time. (A mathematical treatment of these classes of problems can be found in
$\begin{bmatrix} 1 \end{bmatrix}$). Clearly, the first objective in the study of these problems has been and
is the discovery of algorithms that are optimal in some desirable sense, or if
optimality implies an excessive implementation cost, heuristic algorithms that are
easily implemented and whose performance is reasonably close to the optimal. The
frequently difficult mathematics associated with these studies is concerned with
proofs of optimality, general complexity analyses, and the analysis of the performance of algorithms.

Mathematical approaches to performance analysis have been of two types $\begin{bmatrix} 1 \end{bmatrix}$:
Combinatorial analysis of static (or deterministic) models and the analysis of
probability models. In the majority of cases the latter approach is more realistic
simply because the randomness attributable to certain aspects of human behavior and
the tasks they submit to computer systems can be modeled directly. The requirement
of mathematical tractability severely limits the generality of the models that can
be successfully analyzed using probability models. Short of simulation, results can
frequently be obtained through the study of deterministic models. These results
are often limited in scope but they normally provide valuable insight into the
combinatorial nature of sequencing problems.

The purpose of this paper is to survey important mathematical results in deterministic scheduling theory. The coverage is inevitably limited by the author's
ability to remain current in a field integral to so many academic disciplines
(computer science, industrial engineering, operations research, management science,
and applied mathematics generally), and in a field in which so much activity has
recently emerged. Our presentation will focus primarily on flow-time results
obtained within the last 5 or 6 years. Our point of departure, then, will be the
text by Conway, Maxwell, and Miller $\begin{bmatrix} 2 \end{bmatrix}$ in 1967, in which one finds a rather
complete mathematical treatment of single-processor sequencing problems and job-
shop problems, and Graham's survey $\begin{bmatrix} 3 \end{bmatrix}$ last year in which the problems of

scheduling anomalies and processor-minimization under schedule-length deadlines were emphasized.

Preliminaries

The basic scheduling model consists of a set $\mathcal{T} = \{T_1, \ldots, T_n\}$ of n tasks, a partial order $\prec$ on $\mathcal{T}$ and a mapping $\mu: \mathcal{T} \to (0, \infty)$, where $\mu(T_i)$ is the execution time of T_i. The partial order represents operational precedence in the sense that if $(T_i, T_j) \in \prec$, also written $T_i \prec T_j$, then T_i must complete before T_j begins. We use m to denote the number of processors. In general, the processors $P_1, P_2, \ldots,$ P_m may not be identical in terms of their speed or the operations they can perform.

The tasks, being our unit of computation or operation, may be variously interpreted as CPU programs, channel programs, subroutines, operations, microprogram commands, etc. depending on the application. If $\prec$ defines a collection of chains of tasks then we may also call such chains, jobs. If $\prec = \varphi$ (no precedence constraints) we say that the tasks are independent.

A schedule for a system $(\mathcal{T}, \prec, \mu, m)$ is conveniently described by a timing diagram as shown in Fig. 1. (For our purposes this informal notion of a schedule is sufficient*, although it is not difficult to formalize a schedule as a suitable mapping.) The schedule in Fig. 1 is nonpreemptive in the sense that once tasks are begun they execute to completion. Figure 2 illustrates a preemptive schedule for the system shown in the figure. In reality preempting tasks normally incurs costs (time delays) which may not be negligible. However, results to date have been restricted to the assumption that preemption costs are zero, the main reason being the obvious one of mathematical tractability. Hence, we shall make this assumption hereafter when discussing preemptive scheduling.

We shall let S be the basic symbol representing schedules. The finishing time of T_i in schedule S will be denoted $f_i(S)$. Examples are shown in Fig. 2. We define the schedule length or maximum flow-time of S

$$\omega(S) = \max_i \{f_i(S)\}$$

and the mean flow time of S

$$\bar{\omega}(S) = \frac{1}{n} \sum_{i=1}^{n} f_i(S)$$

---

* We shall not always provide these so-called Gantt [4] charts with our examples but the interested reader will no doubt want to draw them for himself in order to better perceive schedule structure.

When fixed deferral costs w_i $(1 \leq i \leq n)$ are associated with the tasks we have the mean weighted flow-time

$$\bar{\omega}(S) = \frac{1}{n} \sum_{i=1}^{n} w_i f_i(S)$$

The above notation will be simplified by eliminating the explicit dependence on the schedule S, whenever the schedule is clear in the context of the discussion. Subscripts will normally be used in an obvious way to indicate specific scheduling algorithms.

When dealing with nonpreemptive scheduling we shall be concerned primarily with the specific class, $\mathcal{L}$, of algorithms called list scheduling algorithms, which work as follows. First, a list (permutation) of the tasks in $\mathcal{T}$ is constructed according to a rule which identifies the algorithm. The list $L = \{T_{i_1}, T_{i_2}, \dots, T_{i_n}\}$ is then scanned linearly from left-to-right, each time a processor becomes available for assignment, until the first task T is found which has not yet been assigned to a processor and whose predecessors (all T' such that $T' < T$) have all completed execution. The task T is then assigned. If more than one processor becomes available at the same time we assume that they are assigned tasks in the order of their indices (i.e. P_1 before P_2 before P_3, etc.). A list corresponding to S in Fig. 1 is $L = (T_1 \ T_2, \dots, T_9)$.

When dealing with independent tasks (i.e. when $< = \phi$) the constraints inherent in the structure of list scheduling do not produce any loss in capability with respect to obtaining optimal schedules. We shall illustrate later that this is not generally the case when $< \neq \phi$

Important list scheduling algorithms for the case when $< = \phi$ includes:
 i) the largest-processing-time-first (LPT) rule whereby the list L is in
    non-increasing order with respect to $\mu(T_i)$. The symbols ω_L and $\bar{\omega}_L$ will
    denote the maximum and mean flow time, respectively, of LPT schedules.

ii) the subclass $\mathcal{L}_S$ of algorithms defined as follows. First, assume n = km for
    k an integer. If this is not the case we augment $\mathcal{T}$ with zero-length tasks
    so that it is the case; it will be obvious that this artifice will have no
    effect on the schedule properties relative to the non-null tasks. Now partition
    $\mathcal{T}$ into k blocks $\pi_1, \pi_2, \dots, \pi_k$ of m tasks each so that $T_i \in \pi_r$, $T_j \in \pi_s$
    and $r < s$ imply $\mu(T_i) \leq \mu(T_j)$ for all i and j and $r \neq s$. An algorithm is in $\mathcal{L}_S$
    if L is such that in the resulting schedule the ith task assigned to P_j (for all
    $j, 1 \leq j \leq m$) is in π_i. For a given system use ω_{S^*} to denote the length of the
    minimal-length schedule schieved by algorithms in $\mathcal{L}_S$. If L is in non-
    decreasing order by $\mu(T_i)$ then we have that algorithm in $\mathcal{L}_S$ called the

shortest-processing-time-first (SPT) rule. The notation ω_S and $\bar{\omega}_S$ will have the obvious meaning.

Before proceeding with a summary of results we must describe some of the recent work that has been done in establishing the complexity of certain classes of problems. Specifically, we refer to recent studies of the class of polynomial complete problems. This work has had a considerable impact on the study of sequencing problems, primarily in directing the researcher away from those approaches to these problems which are very unlikely to prove fruitful.

In order to define the class of "polynomial complete problems", a number of concepts that are basic to any discussion in language theory must be assumed on the part of the reader. For the necessary definitions see $[8]$, for example.

Let Σ be some alphabet. Let P (NP) be the class of languages over Σ , accepted by polynomial time bounded deterministic (nondeterministic) Turing machines. P is clearly a subset of NP, but it is not known whether P = NP.

Just as languages accepted by Turing machines are defined, it is possible to define the "function computed" by a Turing machine. (See $[9]$, for instance.) Let Π be the class of functions from Σ^* into Σ^* computed by polynomial time bounded deterministic Turing machines. Let M_1 and M_2 be languages. M_1 is said to be <u>reducible</u> to M_2, if there exists a function $f \in \Pi$, such that $f(x)$ is in M_2 if and only if x is in M_1. M_1 is called (<u>polynomial</u>) <u>complete</u> if M_1 is in NP, and every language in NP is reducible to M_1. Either all complete languages are in P, or none of them is. The former alternative holds if and only if P = NP $[9]$.

Demonstrating that all languages in NP are reducible to a given language M is facilitated by a theorem due to Cook $[10]$. Informally, Cook showed that acceptance of a string in any language in NP is reducible to determining if a formula in the propositional calculus is satisfiable.

Generally, in our informal terminology a "problem" corresponds to a language M and a string in M to some encoding of the information defining some instance of the problem; e.g. this would include the graph in a traveling salesman problem. Moreover, such problems must be recast in such a way that acceptance of the string (tape) occurs if and only if the problem has a solution. For example, in a knapsack problem a set S of integers and an additional integer b can be encoded on the tape of an appropriately defined Turing machine, which then accepts the input if and only if some subset of S has a sum equal to b.

Now the knapsack problem is polynomial complete [9]. Hence, the point of the earlier definitions is that if a deterministic, polynomial time bounded (in terms of tape length) Turing machine can be found for this problem then by the reductions in [9] we can find Turing machines with similar properties for the other polynomial complete problems, including for example determining whether P = NP, finding the chromatic number of a graph and solving the traveling salesman problem.

It should be noted that instead of speaking of a time bound which is expressible as a polynomial in the length of a Turing machine tape on which some instance of a problem is encoded, we will restate this as a time bound of some characteristic of the problem (e.g. the number of vertices in a graph); but it must be assumed that an encoding is expressible as a polynomial in this characteristic. In particular, for polynomial complete scheduling problems we may consider a polynomial in the number of tasks when we assume some fixed bound on the number of bits needed to express the $\mu(T_i)$.

<u>Scheduling Independent Tasks to Reduce Schedule-length</u>

The problem of (non-preemptively) sequencing independent tasks on $m \geqslant 2$ identical processors has received a fair amount of attention in the last few years, largely because of its broad applicability and interest. Despite its tantalizing simplicity, particularly for $m = 2$, this problem has been shown to be polynomial complete. Nevertheless a number of interesting results have been obtained in bounding the performance of efficient but sub-optimal algorithms. In particular, for given m, $\mathcal{T}$ and μ it is rather easily shown that the ratio ω/ω' of the schedule lengths corresponding to <u>any</u> two arbitrary list scheduling algorithms is bounded by

$$(1) \qquad \frac{\omega}{\omega'} \leq 2 - \frac{1}{m}$$

In fact, this is a special case of a more general result [5] that we describe later. Of course, (1) is not generally a best bound. An important example of this fact is provided by the specialization to a comparison of LPT and optimal scheduling. We have [5]

$$(2) \qquad \frac{\omega_L}{\omega_0} \leq \frac{4}{3} - \frac{1}{3m}$$

and this is a best bound. The worst-case in (2) is achieved by $n = 2m + 1$

$$\mu(T_i) = \begin{cases} 2m - \left\lfloor \frac{i+1}{2} \right\rfloor ; & 1 \leq i \leq 2m \\ m ; & i = 2m + 1 \end{cases}$$

However, (1) is indeed a best bound [6] for ω_{S*}/ω_0 and ω_{S*}/ω_L as shown by $n = m(m-1)k + 1$

$$\mu(T_i) = \begin{cases} m \, ; & i = 1 \\ 1/k \, ; & 2 \leq i \leq n \end{cases}$$

In general, the ratio for this class of examples is $\omega_{S*}/\omega_0 = 2 - 1/m - 1/km$ which approaches the bound (1) as k becomes large. Clearly, $2 - 1/m$ must also be a best bound for ω_S/ω_L and ω_S/ω_0. It is also readily verified by examining the reverse of SPT schedules that $\omega_S/\omega_L \geq 1$ for all choices of m, $\mathcal{J}$ and μ But this is not true for ω_{S*}/ω_L. It has been conjectured [6] that

$$(3) \qquad \frac{\omega_L}{\omega_{S*}} \leq \frac{5m-2}{4m-1}$$

although it has only been proved for m = 2. The ratio $(5m - 2)/(4m - 1)$ is achieved by $n = 2m+1$

$$\mu(T_i) = \begin{cases} 3m-1-i \, ; & 1 \leq i \leq m \\ 3m-i \, ; & m+1 \leq i \leq 2m \\ m \, ; & i = 2m+1 \end{cases}$$

A number of other approximate methods have been considered in trying to arrive at algorithms which have a desirable balance in their complexity and the schedule-lengths they produce. One such method optimally schedules the largest k tasks (i.e. by producing an optimal list L_k for these tasks) and then scheduling the remaining tasks according to an arbitrary (remaining) list of the remaining tasks. If $\omega(k)$ denotes the schedule length produced from a list so formed we have as a best bound [3]

$$\frac{\omega(k)}{\omega_0} \leq 1 + \frac{1 - 1/m}{1 + \lfloor k/m \rfloor}$$

Note that (4) reduces to (1) for k = 0. Clearly, the goodness of the schedule desired is obtained at the cost of finding, by some form of enumeration, the optimal schedule for sufficiently high k. An example showing that (4) is a best bound is given by

$$\mu(T_i) = \begin{cases} m \, ; & 1 \leq i \leq k+1 \\ 1 \, ; & k+2 \leq i \leq n = k+1 + m(m-1) \end{cases}$$

with the list $L = \{T_1, \ldots, T_k, T_{k+2}, \ldots, T_n, T_{k+1}\}$. A similarly motivated result, as yet unpublished [7], has shown how to obtain schedules within 1/k of the optimal using an algorithm whose complexity is $O(n^k)$.

The following result [3] shows that if the total execution requirement is large relative to individual execution times then ω cannot be too far from ω_0.

Specifically, if

$$\max \mu(T_i) \Big/ \sum_{i=1}^{n} \mu(T_i) \;\leq\; \beta$$

then

(5)
$$\frac{\omega}{\omega_0} \;\leq\; 1 + m\beta$$

Finally, suppose we adopt a procedure which takes an arbitrary Gantt chart and performs pair-wise interchanges of tasks on different processors which decrease the schedule-length. If this procedure is iterated until no further decreases can be made a best bound on the length of the resulting schedule-length is [3]

(6)
$$\frac{\omega}{\omega_0} \;\leq\; 2 - 2/(m+1) \;=\; \frac{2m}{m+1}$$

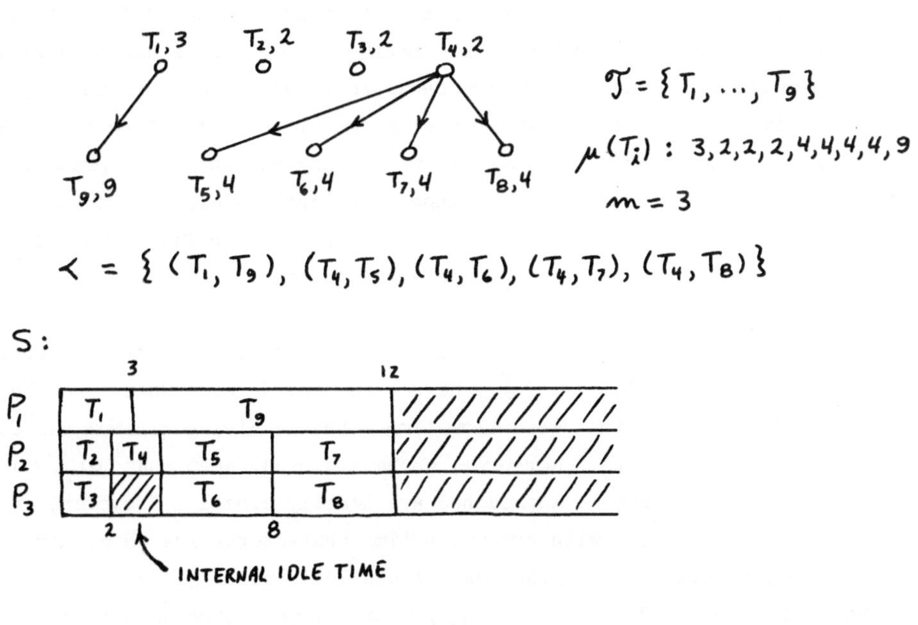

Figure 1 - Example System and Schedule

For the minimal solution (noting that $\bar{\omega}(n) \geq 2\bar{\omega}(1)/(m+1)$ from the above bound) we have the bounds

$$\frac{m+n}{m(n+1)}\,\bar{\omega}(1) \leq \bar{\omega}(m) < \frac{1}{m}\,\bar{\omega}(1) + \frac{m-1}{m}\,\bar{\omega}(n)$$

The upper bound can be shown to be best in terms of the parameters in which it is expressed. A more elaborate, but best lower bound in terms of the same parameters of the upper bound is given by

$$\bar{\omega}(m) \geq \max\left\{ \bar{\omega}(n), \frac{1}{m}\,\bar{\omega}(1) + \frac{m-1}{2m}\,\bar{\omega}(n)\right\}$$

Suppose that we consider minimizing the mean flow time (returning to the assumption $w_i = 1$ $(1 \leq i \leq n)$) when the processors are not assumed identical. Let $\mu_i(T_j)$ denote the execution time of T_j on P_i. A non-enumerative solution to this problem has also been shown to exist [6] by showing that it can be approached as a special case of the classical transportation problem [12].

Clearly, the discovery of efficient algorithms that produce schedules with favorable performance in terms of both mean and maximum flow time is highly desirable. In the former case we provide a performance appreciated directly by the user and in the latter case we provide a performance of immediate interest to the manager desiring high system throughput. However, we quickly encounter the problem that strict SPT sequencing has poor schedule-length performance along with its optimal mean flow-time property, and LPT scheduling has a <u>worst</u> mean flow-time property along with its favorable schedule-length characteristics.

At this point two approaches have been made to this problem. First, the schedule-length properties of algorithms in $\mathcal{L}_S$ have been considered. Unfortunately, the problem of finding that optimal mean flow-time schedule giving minimum schedule-length is polynomial complete. Moreover, we have already seen that ω_{S*}/ω_L has a bound $2 - 1/m$ that can be approached arbitrarily closely. However, an efficient algorithm in $\mathcal{L}_S$ with execution time characteristics which may be good on the average (especially under the assumptions leading to (5)) can be described as follows. The blocks $\pi_1, \pi_2, \ldots, \pi_{n/m}$ of the partition used in defining the $\mathcal{L}_S$ algorithms are scheduled simply by assigning tasks in π_2 in LPT fashion after those in π_1, then assigning tasks in π_3 in LPT fashion after those in π_2 have been assigned, and so on.

Another approach to the problem is simply to use the left-justified reverse of the LPT schedule, which we shall call the RPT schedule. Although for any given $M > 0$ a $\mathcal{T}$ and μ can be found such that $\bar{\omega}_L/\bar{\omega}_0 > M$, it is not difficult to show that for RPT scheduling we have the bound for all $\mathcal{T}$ and μ [6]

The problem of preemptive scheduling to minimize schedule length for sets of
independent tasks is a simple one. In particular, the lower bound

$$(7) \qquad \omega_{min} = \max \{ \max \mu(T_i), \; (1/n) \sum_{i=1}^{n} \mu(T_i) \}$$

is always achievable by a rather simple algorithm [11] . Assuming max
$\mu(T_i) \leq (1/n)\sum_{i=1}^{n} \mu(T_i)$ the algorithm simply assigns tasks in order on P_1
then P_2, etc., terminating the assignment on a processor at the point when
$(1/n) \sum_{i=1}^{n} \mu(T_i)$ is reached. Tasks not completely assigned at this point
have their remaining requirement assigned to the next processor. Figure 2 shows
an example. For the case max $\mu(T_i) > (1/n)\sum_{i=1}^{n} \mu(T_i)$ the algorithm is
trivially amended.

A problem of interest here is the ordering of the tasks to be used in the above
procedure, for use of the proper ordering will yield a minimal number of
preemptions. On the other hand, it is not difficult to see the connection of this
problem with the bin packing problem and hence its polynomial completeness [3].

Scheduling Independent Tasks to Reduce Mean Flow Time

The principal result for $\prec = \emptyset$ and arbitrary m is that every algorithm in $\mathcal{L}_S$
minimizes the mean flow time. This result is not difficult to prove [2, 6] and
illustrates the inherent greater simplicity of this problem relative to the
corresponding maximum flow-time problem, which as we have already indicated is
polynomial complete. However, suppose we want to minimize the mean weighted flow-
time

$$(8) \qquad \bar{\omega} = \frac{1}{n} \sum_{i=1}^{n} w_i f_i$$

This problem has recently been shown to be polynomial complete [6] . The proof
essentially amounts to showing that the knapsack problem reduces to a maximum flow
time problem equivalent to the problem of minimizing (8) for m = 2. On the other
hand, for m = 1 an efficient solution exists [11] : We simply sequence the tasks
in any non-increasing order of the ratios $w_i / \mu(T_i)$. For arbitrary m
bounds have been computed for the mean weighted flow time [19] . Given $\mathcal{T}$ and μ
let $\bar{\omega}(m)$ denote the minimum mean weighted flow time for m processors. Clearly,
$\bar{\omega}(1)$ and $\bar{\omega}(n)$ are easily computed as $(1/n) \sum_j \sum_{i \leq j} w_j \mu(T_i)$
and $(1/n) \sum_i w_i \mu(T_i)$ respectively, where n is the number of tasks
as usual, and where we assume that the tasks are indexed so that $i > j$
implies $w_i / \mu(T_i) \leq w_j / \mu(T_j)$. We have for an <u>arbitrary</u> schedule the following
lower bound on $\bar{\omega}$

$$\bar{\omega} \geq \frac{1}{m} \left[\bar{\omega}(1) - \frac{1}{2} \bar{\omega}(n) \right] + \frac{1}{2} \bar{\omega}(n)$$

(9)
$$\frac{\overline{\omega}_R}{\overline{\omega}_0} \leq m$$

This bound can be approached arbitrarily closely as can be seen by the example

$$\mu(T_i) = \begin{cases} 1 \; ; & 1 \leq i \leq k \\ k \; ; & k+1 \leq i \leq n = m+k+1 \end{cases}$$

for which

$$\frac{\overline{\omega}_R}{\overline{\omega}_0} = m \; \frac{k + (2m-1)}{k + (2m^2+m-2)}$$

The tasks on individual processors in an RPT schedule are in non-decreasing (SPT) order, and therefore one might expect that the (worst-case) bound in (9) is not very informative. In fact, as numerical studies have shown with geometric-type distributions for task execution times, $\overline{\omega}_R/\overline{\omega}_0 \approx 1.02$ as a conservative approximation with a very small variance. Hence, RPT scheduling would appear to be an efficient algorithm for the purpose of providing low, if not optimal, mean and maximum flow times.

Sequencing with Precedence Constraints

Clearly, with the assumption of arbitrary partial orders the class of problems that we have already found difficult become even more so. The questions that have been successfully answered are correspondingly simpler. The results for minimum length (non-preemptive) schedules, which we discuss first, have depended on the assumption that task execution times are all equal. Under this assumption the only efficient optimal algorithm that has been found for arbitrary partial orders is for the case m = 2. Actually, two such algorithms have been found. The first [13] , whose execution time is $O(n^3)$, is based on a matching algorithm for bipartite graphs [14] . The second [15] , whose execution time is $O(n^2)$, is presented below. Note that this latter algorithm must possess maximal efficiency in the sense that $O(n^2)$ arcs may be expected in an arbitrary partial order.

We specify the algorithm as a list scheduling algorithm. To define the list we first label the vertices of the graph G corresponding to $<$ according to the following algorithm. Let $\ell(T_i)$ denote the (integer) label of T_i and let

$$\underline{s}(T_i) = [\ell(T_{i_1}), \ell(T_{i_2}), \ldots, \ell(T_{i_n})]$$

where the $\ell(T_{i_j})$ are in decreasing order and where $\{T_{i_j}\}$ is precisely the set of immediate successors of T_i. (See Fig. 3 for examples.)

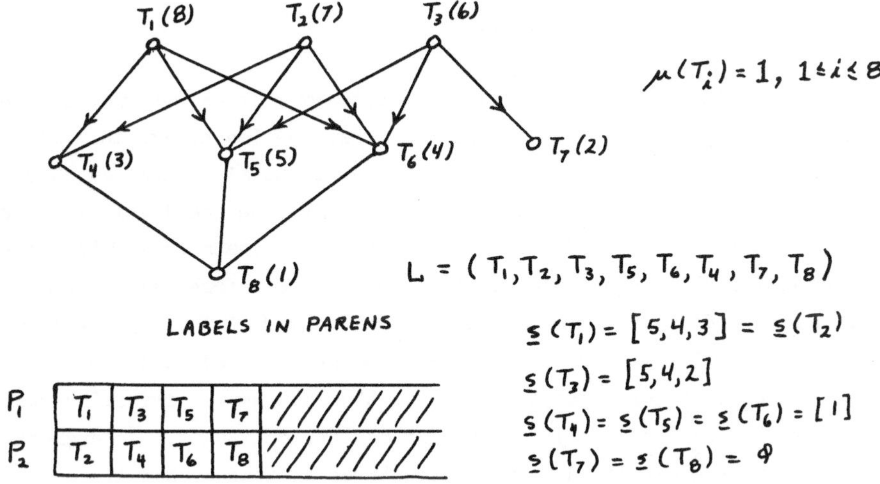

Figure 2 – Illustrating Preemptive Scheduling

Figure 3 – Example for Nonpreemptive Scheduling

<u>Labeling algorithm</u>

1. Label the (say k) terminal tasks of G with the integers 1 through k in any order.
2. Determine the set U of unlabeled tasks all of whose successors are already labeled. Pick a T in U whose $\mathscr{s}$(T) is lexicographically least of all those tasks in U and make ℓ(T) the next higher integer. Repeat this step until all tasks are labeled. (It is not difficult to show that this algorithm can be performed in time $O(n^2)$.)

Figure 3 shows an example. The list to be formed simply consists of that permutation of $\mathcal{T}$ for which the corresponding task labels are in decreasing order. The basic result is that the corresponding list scheduling algorithm produces a minimal length schedule for m = 2.

The above algorithm is also optimal for arbitrary m if we restrict G to be a tree (the arcs are directed towards the root so that the leaves are initial tasks and the root is the single terminal task). However, the algorithm can be much more simply stated under these circumstances. Let λ(T) be the level of a vertex T in a tree G; i.e. the number of vertices in the (unique)path from T to the root of G. Then any list L which orders tasks at higher levels before all tasks at lower levels corresponds to a minimal length schedule $[16]$. The algorithm is trivially revised to optimally schedule forests and to optimally schedule forests in which arcs are directed towards the leaves (i.e. the root is the initial vertex and the leaves the terminal vertices). Note that the optimality of this highest-level-first criterion can be generalized to such structures as graphs that are each a con-catenation of trees. The notion of concatenation here requires that every task of one tree must complete before any task in a subsequent tree can begin.

It should be noted at this point that with arbitrary systems $(\mathcal{T}, \prec, \mu, m)$ the optimal list schedule is not always an optimal nonpreemptive schedule. This follows basically because list scheduling does not allow processors to be idle while tasks are available for assignment. This notion is illustrated in Fig. 4.

Moreover, list scheduling is subject to some rather curious anomalies $[5]$, which tend to be undesirable. For example, we can find systems $(\mathcal{T}, \prec, \mu, m)$ such that <u>removal</u> of certain constraints in $\prec$, <u>decreases</u> of execution times defined by μ , or an <u>increase</u> in m can cause the schedule length to <u>increase</u>. Such a system is shown in Fig. 1 with the list $(T_1, T_2, \ldots, T_9)$. As can be readily verified, either the removal of (T_4, T_5) and (T_4, T_6), decreasing all execution times by 1, or increasing m from 3 to 4 causes the schedule length to increase.

Let ω denote the schedule length of a system $(\mathcal{T}, \prec, \mu, m)$ and let ω' denote the schedule length of a system $(\mathcal{T}, \prec', \mu', m')$ derived from the former system by any one or more of the general changes indicated above. It has been shown [5] that the possible effect of anomalies is bounded by

$$(10) \qquad \frac{\omega'}{\omega} \leq 1 + \frac{m-1}{m'}$$

which reduces to (1) when $m = m'$. Furthermore, examples can be given which show that (10) is a best bound for the anomaly produced by any one of the changes indicated above [5] .

Under the same sets of assumptions as above, except that now execution times may be arbitrary[*], efficient algorithms also exist for minimizing schedule-lengths when preemptions are allowed. Consider the following algorithm for an arbitrary graph in which each task is labeled with its level, where the level of a task T is now defined as the sum of task execution times in a path from T to a terminal task for which this sum is maximal.

Compute the set S_1 of highest level tasks in the graph and provide each of them an equal execution time in the interval $(0, t_1)$ where t_1 is the least time such that either of the following events occurs.
  i) A task in S_1 completes, or
  ii) one or more tasks in S_1 have had their level reduced (in the graph remaining) to a point where some task not in S_1 has the same level.

Now compute S_2 for the remaining graph and compute the time interval (t_1, t_2), where t_2 is defined as above. Then provide tasks in S_2 with equal execution time in (t_1, t_2). This process is repeated until all tasks in G have been completed.

Note that the process of providing equal execution time over any interval for tasks in S_i can always be done by the method discussed in connection with Fig. 2 for preemptive scheduling when $\prec = \phi$. An example of the application of the algorithm is shown in Fig. 5. The principal result concerning this algorithm is that it produces minimal length schedules when either G is a tree [17] or m = 2 [18] . Figure 6 shows an example for which the above algorithm is not optimal

---

[*] Actually, we require them to be mutually commensurable; i.e. there exists a number in terms of which each execution time can be expressed as some multiple. This is clearly a restriction of no real importance from a practical point of view.

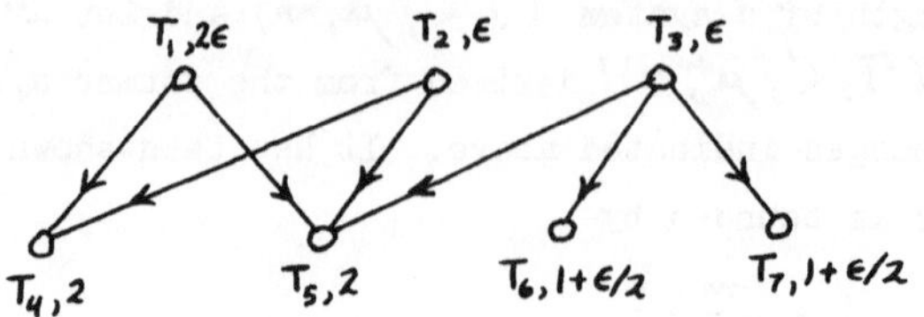

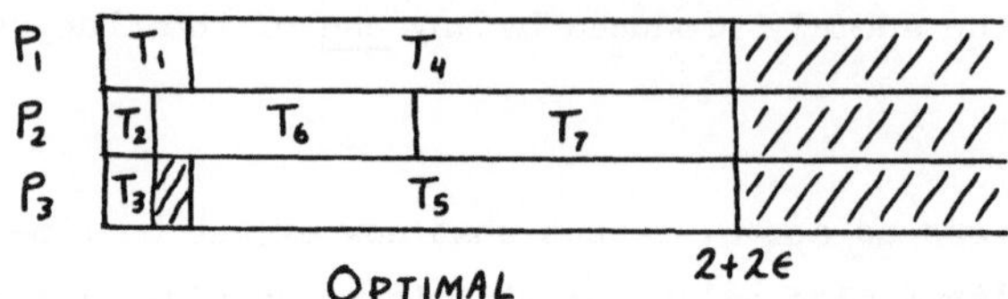

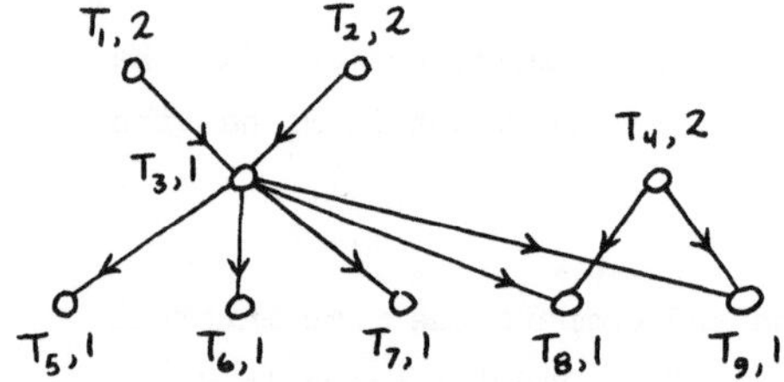

Figure 4 - Introducing Idle Time

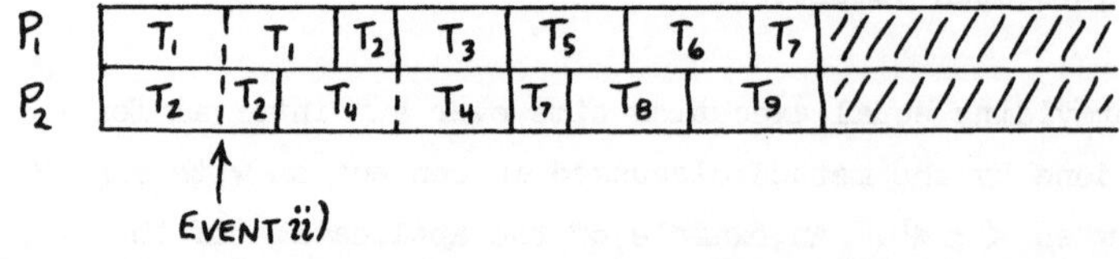

Figure 5 - Optimal Preemptive Scheduling

when neither of the above conditions is met.

Counterexamples are also easily provided to show that the nonpreemptive scheduling algorithm presented earlier is not optimal when $m > 2$ or when it is not the case that $\mu(T_i) = \mu(T_j)$ for all i and j. Figure 7(a) shows such an example for $m = 3$ and Fig. 7(b) shows such an example when we allow $\mu(T_i)$ to be either 1 or 2 units in length.

Quite recently, it has been demonstrated [21] that certain of the obvious extensions to the optimality results above constitute polynomial complete problems. In particular, for the nonpreemptive case with m a parameter the equal execution time problem is polynomial complete*. The reductions in the proof commence with the satisfiability problem. Similarly, it has been shown that the following problems are polynomial complete:
  i) the nonpreemptive scheduling problem for $m = 2$ but with execution times allowed to be either 1 or 2 times units in length,
  ii) the general preemptive scheduling problem

It is easily verified that compared to nonpreemptive scheduling preemptive scheduling provides shorter schedule-lengths in general. (Consider the simple examples in (14) below, for example.) For a given system $(\mathcal{J}, \prec, \mu, m)$ let ω_P, ω_N, and $\omega_\mathcal{L}$ denote the optimal schedule lengths for preemptive, non-preemptive, and list scheduling, respectively. It has been shown that [15]

$$(11) \qquad \frac{\omega_\mathcal{L}}{\omega_P} \leq 2 - 1/m$$

and that [20]

$$(12) \qquad \frac{\omega_N}{\omega_P} \leq \frac{2m}{m+1}$$

and that these bounds cannot be improved. Examples verifying this last assertion are given, respectively, by

$$\mu(T_i) = \begin{cases} \epsilon ; & 1 \leq i \leq m-1 \\ 2\epsilon ; & i = m \\ 1 ; & m+1 \leq i \leq 2m \\ m-1 ; & 2m+1 \leq i \leq n = 3m \end{cases}$$

---

*However, it should be noted that this result does not rule out the possibility that for some specific m an algorithm producing optimal schedules can be found.

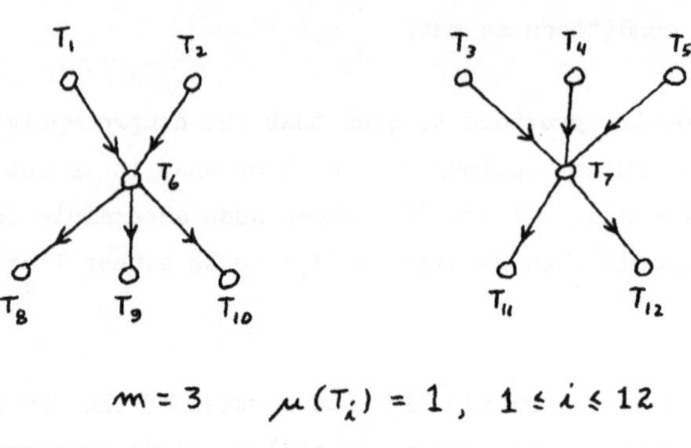

Figure 6 - Counterexample: Preemptive Scheduling

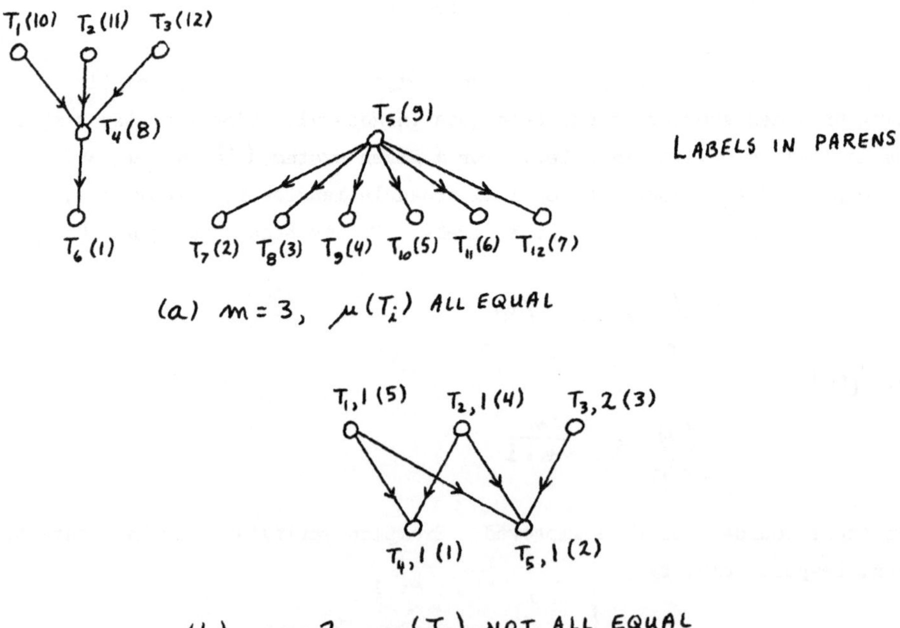

Figure 7 - Counterexamples: Nonpreemptive Scheduling

$$\prec' = \{ (T_1, T_{m+1}), \ldots, (T_1, T_{2m}), (T_2, T_{m+1}), \ldots, (T_2, T_{2m}) \ldots$$

(13)
$$\ldots (T_m, T_{m+1}), \ldots, (T_m, T_{2m}), (T_{m+1}, T_{2m+1}), \ldots, (T_{2m}, T_{2m+1}) \}$$

where $\prec$ is the transitive closure of $\prec'$, and

(14)
$$\mu(T_i) = 1; \quad 1 \le i \le n = m+1, \quad \prec = \phi$$

In the example of (13) we get $\omega_g / \omega_p = (2m - 1 + \epsilon)/(m + 2\epsilon)$ which can be made to approach the bound in (11) arbitrarily closely.

If we now consider distinct processors and chains of tasks requiring execution on different processors we arrive at the flow-shop or more general job-shop problems. Specifically, in the general job-shop problem each task in $\mathcal{T}$ carries three identifiers (indices): one indicating the task-chain to which it belongs, one indicating its sequence number (position in the chain), and one indicating the processor on which it must execute. The general problem of finding the minimal length schedule with such systems is known to be polynomial complete [9] (and this can be inferred, of course, from the special cases which we have already noted as polynomial complete.) However, efficient algorithms for m = 2 have been found which are important in the computer application.

The principal result is the solution of the two-processor flow-shop problem in which the task-chains (jobs) are of length two, the first task of a job having to be executed on P_1 and the second on P_2. Let $\mu_i(J_j)$ be the execution time of job J_j on P_i, i = 1 or 2 and $1 \le j \le k$. That is, $\mu_1(J_j)$ (respectively $\mu_2(J_j)$) is the execution time of the first (respectively second) task on P_1 (respectively P_2). Suppose we order the jobs on P_1 and P_2 so that J_i precedes J_j whenever min $(\mu_1(J_i), \mu_2(J_j)) < $ min $(\mu_2(J_i), \mu_1(J_j))$. (Except for ties, which can be resolved arbitrarily, this criterion can be shown to linearly order the jobs.) Note that this __job__ ordering implies that the ith tasks on P_1 and P_2 constitute the ith job scheduled. It has been shown that this schedule has minimal length [22] .

Under certain restrictions this result can be generalized to the three-processor flow-shop in which a job must first execute a task on P_1, then a task on P_2, and finally a task on P_3. In particular, a similar result can be derived if the maximum execution time of any job on P_2 does not exceed the execution time of any job on P_1, or if the minimum execution time of any job on P_2 is no less than the execution time of any job on P_3 [22] . With minor

modifications the two-processor flow-shop result can be applied to optimally
schedule the two-processor job-shop in which jobs can consist of at most two
tasks [23] . The reader is referred to [2] for an extended discussion of these
problems, including approximate methods that have been used, and to [31] for more
recent specialized results.

For m $\geqslant$ 2 very little is known about optimally sequencing tasks with precedence
structure in order to minimize mean flow time. No general efficient algorithms
have appeared, even for interesting special cases [2] . For the case m = 1 the
most general result currently known is restricted to tree-structured precedence
structures [24, 25] . The algorithm is as follows.

For each task of the tree G compute the sum of the execution times of the tasks in
the subtree of which it is the root. Label each task T with its corresponding sum
divided by the number of tasks in the corresponding subtree. Find a task (say T)
in G whose label is minimal, and then assign to the processor the tasks of the
subtree defined by T. If this subtree consists of more than one task (i.e. not
just T alone) then recursively apply the procedure being described in order to
determine the order in which the tasks of this subtree are to be sequenced. Next,
remove from G the subtree defined by T and recompute the task labels, as necessary.
The process is then repeated on the resulting tree G' to augment the sequence
determined so far and to determine a new labeled tree G'' . The procedure continues
in this way until the root of G is finally assigned.

For the purpose of assessing the performance of approximate methods through
numerical studies, lower bounds on ω_0 have been calculated [16, 26, 28] ; in this
approach we avoid the cost of enumerating schedules to find ω_0, and sacrifice an
accuracy which is measured by the tightness of the bound used. One such bound,
which is relatively easily computed for a given system ($\mathcal{T}, \prec, \mu$) and which is
as tight a bound as has been proposed to-date is described as follows.

For convenience let the $\mu(T_i)$ be integers and let ω_c be the length (sum of the
execution times) in a longest path in G; i.e. the minimum time that $\mathcal{T}$ can be
scheduled assuming m as large as we like. Define the multi-set $\underline{S}$ (respectively
$\bar{S}$) for a given (integer) interval $\Delta = (t_1, t_2) \in [0, \omega_c]$ as the set of tasks
which cannot be executing earlier than t_1 (respectively later than t_2) in any
schedule of length ω_c satisfying precedence constraints. A task is repeated in
one of these multisets as many times as it receives units of service in Δ (t_1 and
t_2 are integers). It has been shown that [26]

$$\omega_0 \geqslant \omega_c + \left\lceil \max_{\Delta \in I} \left[\frac{1}{m} \left| \underline{S} \wedge \bar{S} \right| - |\Delta| \right] \right\rceil$$

where I is the set of all intervals $\Delta = (t_1, t_2)$ in $[0, \omega_c]$ with t_1 and t_2 integers. Algorithms have been proposed to efficiently compute these bounds and similarly derived but looser bounds that can be computed more efficiently. An example of this latter type [16] for equal (unit) length tasks is provided by

$$\omega_0 \geq \max_{0 \leq k \leq \omega_c} (k + \Lambda(k)/m)$$

where $\Lambda(k)$ is the number of tasks in G having a level strictly greater than k. This bound has been generalized in a simple way to preemptive scheduling [27].

Open Problems

The results presented in the previous sections point up a host of open problems. Consider first the problems of determining efficient algorithms for finding optimal schedules. Examples include:

1. Is there a fixed m such that the m-processor equal execution time problem is polynomial complete? If so, find if possible polynomial time algorithms for the problem with 3, 4,..., m - 1 processors. [21]

2. Are there combinations of integers k and m such that the problem of preemptively scheduling m processors with tasks requiring 1, 2,...,k time units is of polynimial complexity, or alternatively, polynomial complete?

3. Is the general problem of scheduling arbitrary task systems on $m \geq 1$ processors to minimize mean flow time polynomial complete?

Our presentation has also pointed up the significant amount of activity in studying heuristic methods for sequencing problems most of which have been shown to be polynomial complete. Obvious desirable extensions include the derivations of similar bounds for cases in which $\prec \neq \phi$. Some work has appeared in the study of critical path algorithms [3] but further work is indicated in seeking heuristics with tighter worst-case bounds and heuristics for reducing mean flow times.

Finally, the important general problems of finding algorithms which provide favorable performance in terms of more than one measure have received very little attention. Besides both flow-time measures other performance measures include storage utilization [28] (which, however, is not completely independent of the mean flow time performance [2]). Significant work appearing along the above line [32] has concentrated on efficient techniques for identifying classes of (schedule-length) optimal schedules. These results help provide a basis for searching a class of schedules optimal in one sense for a schedule that exhibits favorable performance in one or more other respects.

Our presentation has confined itself to flow-time sequencing problems. A number
of closely related research areas are also rich sources of intriguing problems.
The problem of finding the minimum number of processors to execute a given task
system under a deadline constraint dates back to 1968 $\begin{bmatrix} 29 \end{bmatrix}$ and has received,
very recently, considerable attention $\begin{bmatrix} 3, 26 \end{bmatrix}$. The general, and related due-date
sequencing problems discussed in $\begin{bmatrix} 2 \end{bmatrix}$ should also be mentioned in this regard. For
a broad survey of mathematical problems and results connected with multiprocessing
see the recent survey in $\begin{bmatrix} 30 \end{bmatrix}$.

References

1. Coffman, E. G. and P. J. Denning, _Operating Systems Theory_, Prentice-Hall, July 1973.

2. Conway, R. W., W. L. Maxwell, and L. W. Miller, _Theory of Scheduling_, Addison-Wesley, 1967.

3. Graham, R. L., "Bounds on Multiprocessing Anomalies and Related Packing Algorithms", _AFIPS Conference Proceedings_, Vol. 40, 1972, pp. 205-217.

4. Clark, W., _The Gantt Chart_, (3rd Edition), Pitman and Sons, Ltd., London, 1952.

5. Graham, R. L., "Bounds on Multiprocessing Timing Anomalies", _SIAM J. on Applied Math._, Vol. 17, No. 2, March 1969, pp. 416-429.

6. Bruno, J. L., E. G. Coffman, and R. Sethi, "Scheduling Independent Tasks to Reduce Mean Finishsng Time", Tech. Rep., Computer Science Dept, Pennsylvania State Univ. 1973.

7. Horowitz, Ellis, Computer Science Dept., Cornell University (private communication).

8. Hopcroft, J. E. and J. D. Ullman, _Formal Languages and Their Relation to Automata_, Addison-Wesley, 1969.

9. Karp, R. M., "Reducibility among Combinatorial Problems", Tech. Rep. No. 3 Computer Science Dept., Univ. of California, Berkeley, 1972.

10. Cook, S. A., "The Complexity of Theorem-Proving Procedures", _Third Ann. ACM Symp. on Theory of Computing_, May 1971, pp. 151-158.

11. McNaughton, R., "Scheduling with Deadlines and Loss Functions", _Management Science_, Vol. 12, No. 1, Oct. 1959.

12. Ford, F. L. and D. R. Fulkerson, _Flows in Networks_, Princeton Univ. Press, 1962.

13. Fujii, M., T. Kasami, and K. Ninomiya, "Optimal Sequencing of Two Equivalent Processors", _SIAM J. of Applied Math._, Vol. 17, No. 3, 1969, pp. 784-789 (Erratum. Vol. 20, No. 1, 1971, p. 141.)

14. Edmonds, J., "Path, Trees, and Flowers", _Can. J. of Math._ Vol. 17, 1965, pp. 449-467.

15. Coffman, E. G. and R. L. Graham, "Optimal Scheduling for Two-Processor Systems", _Acta Informatica_, Vol. 1, No. 3, 1972, pp. 200-213.

16. Hu, T. C., "Parallel Sequencing and Assembly Line Problems", _Operations Research_, Vol. 9, No. 6, Nov. 1961, pp. 841-848.

17. Muntz, R. R. and E. G. Coffman, "Preemptive Scheduling of Real-Time Tasks on Multiprocessor Systems", _J. of the ACM_, Vol. 17, No. 2, April 1970, pp. 324-338.

18. Muntz, R. R. and E. G. Coffman, "Optimal Preemptive Scheduling on Two-Processor Systems", _IEEE Trans. on Computers_, Vol. C-18, No. 11, Nov. 1969, pp. 1014-1020.

19. Eastman, W. L., S. Even, and I. M. Isaacs, "Bounds for the Optimal Scheduling of n jobs on m Processors", _Management Science_, Vol. 11, No. 2, 1964, pp. 268-279.

20. Liu, C. L., "Optimal Scheduling on Multiprocessor Computing Systems", _Proc., Sw. and Auto. Theory Symp._, Oct. 1972.

21. Ullman, J. D., "Polynomial Complete Scheduling Problems", Tech. Rep. No. 9, Computer Science Dept., Univ. of California, Berkeley, March 1973.

22. Johnson, S. M., "Optimal Two and Three Stage Production Schedules with Set-up Times Included", _Nav. Res. and Log. Quart._, Vol. 1, No. 1, March 1954.

23. Jackson, J. R., "An Extension of Johnson's Results on Job-Lot Scheduling", _Nav. Res. and Log. Quart._, Vol. 3, No. 3, Sept. 1956.

24. Horn, W. A., "Single-Machine Job Sequencing with Tree-Like Precedence Ordering and Linear Delay Penalties", _SIAM J. of Applied Math._, Vol. 23, No. 2, Sept. 1972, pp. 189-202.

25. Sydney, J. B., "One Machine Sequencing with Precedence Relations and Deferral Costs", Working Paper No. 125, Fac. of Commerce and Bus. Ad., Univ. of British Columbia, 1972.

26. Fernandez, E. and B. Bussell, "Bounds on the Number of Processors and Time for Multiprocessor Optimal Schedule", Tech. Rep. Computer Science Dept., Univ. of California, Los Angeles, 1973.

27. Muntz, R. R., _Scheduling of Computations on Multiprocessor Systems: The Preemptive Assignment Discipline_, Ph.D. Thesis, Elect. Eng. Dept., Princeton Univ., 1969.

28. Chen, Y. E. and D. L. Epley, "Memory Requirements in a Multiprocessing Environment", _Journal of the ACM_, Vol. 19, No. 1, Jan. 1972.

29. Barskiy, A. B., "Minimizing the Number of Computing Devices Needed to Realize a Computational Process within a Specified Time", _Eng. Cybernetics_ (USSR), No. 6, pp. 59-63 (translation from Russian) 1968.

30. Baer, J. L., "A Survey of Some Theoretical Aspects of Multiprocessing", _ACM Comp. Surveys_, Vol. 5, No. 1, March 1973, pp. 31-80.

31. Shen, V. Y. and Y. E. Chen, "A Scheduling Strategy for the Flow-Shop Problem in a System with Two Classes of Processors", _Proc. 6th Ann. Conf. Info. Sys. and Sci._ March 1972, Elect. Eng. Dept., Princeton Univ.

32. Schindler, S. and W. Simonsmeier, "The Class of All Optimal Schedules for Two-Processor Systems", _Proc. 7th Ann. Conf. on Info. Sys. and Sci._, Elect. Eng. Dept., Princeton Univ., March 1973.

AUTOMATENTHEORIE

CONTROLLABILITY-OBSERVABILITY TYPE DUALITY RELATIONS OF FINITE-STATE MACHINES

GERHARD F. BECKHOFF[*]

ZUSAMMENFASSUNG

Die Begriffe der Erreichbarkeit, Kontrollierbarkeit, Beobachtbarkeit und Rekonstruierbarkeit in der linearen Regelungstechnik werden auf sequentielle Maschinen uebertragen, wobei die Dualitätsbeziehungen erhalten bleiben. Diese Begriffe werden charakterisiert, und Algorithmen angegeben, die es ermöglichen, (a) für eine gegebene sequentielle Maschine die grössten Untermaschinen und Quotientenmaschinen zu finden, die obige Eigenschaften besitzen, (b) initiale Zustandsuntermengen und terminale Zustandspartitionen zu finden, die einem gegebenen Automaten diese Eigenschaften geben und (c) besondere Eingangsfolgen (synchronierende, diagnosierende und homing) und deren duale Folgen zu finden. Diese Algorithmen sind eng verknüpft mit der Existenz und Anzahl der wahren maximalen und minimalen Ideen und Kongruenzen eines Automaten.

INTRODUCTION

It has been generally recognized by people working in coding theory, control theory and other areas and also by researchers trying to lay a general foundation of systems theory that there exist fruitful interrelations between Linear Systems Theory and Sequential Machine Theory. In this paper we explore another interesting connection between these two disciplines. The concepts of controllability and observability, so important in Linear Systems Theory, will be extended to sequential machines. Previous attempts at this problem, noticeably by Arbib and Zeiger [2] and more recently by Y. Kambayashi [5] lack the duality aspects. Two notions of duality are available for systems, the automaton-theoretic, given a limited formulation by Rabin-Scott [8] and extended by Arbib [1], and the linear system notion given weight by Kalman's work relating reachability of a system to observability of its dual. We discard the Rabin-Scott duality formulation and define two submodels of a sequential machine called the initial and the terminal automaton, which are dual to each other in a certain sense. Following Kalman [6], we then define reachability, controllability of an initial automaton and their duals, observability and reconstructibility of a terminal automaton. The duality exists between sets and partitions and could be rigorously shown by category theoretical means; however, we prefer to use instead automaton theoretical methods. To this end we define four associate automata of a given automaton A, whose state sets are either all the subsets or all the partitions of the state set of A. We characterize the concepts of reachability and controllability and their duals, observability and reconstructibility. We give algorithms for finding subautomata and quotient automata, respectively, having these properties. We also develop algorithms for selecting an initial state set or a terminal partition, in order that a given automaton attains these properties. Finally, we state algorithms for finding synchronizing, diagnosing and homing sequences and their dual sequences. It is hoped that this research is a step towards a theoretical foundation for the fault diagnosis of digital systems.

[*]This research was supported by the National Research Council of Canada under grant A4141.

ASSOCIATE AUTOMATA

A sequential machine is a septuple $\mathcal{M}$ = $(Q,I,R,Z,\delta,\rho,\lambda)$ where
Q,I,R,Z are finite sets, the sets of states, input, reset and output
symbols, respectively, and $\delta : Q \times I \to Q$, $\rho : R \to Q$, $\lambda : Q \to Z$ are functions, called, respectively, the transition, reset and output function.
The reset function is assumed to be injective and the output function
is assumed to be surjective. The domain of the transition function δ
is extended to I^*, the free monoid generated by I, in the following
recursive way: $\delta(q,\Lambda) = q$ (Λ is the identity (empty word) of I^*)
$\delta(q,xi) = \delta(\delta(q,x),i)$ $(\forall i \epsilon I)$ $(\forall x \epsilon I^*)$. We also consider the function
$\delta_x : Q \to Q$, defined by $\delta_x(q) = \delta(q,x)$.

The following submodels of a sequential machine are important
tools in our subsequent investigation. The triple $A = (Q,I,\delta)$ is
called a (finite) automaton. The quintuples $M = (Q,I,Z,\delta,\lambda)$ and
$N = (Q,I,R,\delta,\rho)$ are called output (or Moore) machine and reset machine
respectively. These latter two submodels play in a certain sense a
dual role. They can be replaced by modified automata models. Setting
$\rho(R) = Q_0$ we define the initial automaton $A(Q_0) = (Q,I,\delta)$ to be one
which can start only in one of the states of Q_0, the initial state
set. Similarly, letting θ be the equivalence kernel of λ (e.g.,
$q \theta q' \Longleftrightarrow \lambda(q) = \lambda(q')$), we define the terminal automaton
$A(\theta) = (Q,I,\delta)$ to be one which indicates in which block of θ it
terminates after having processed an input string.

To show duality, we associate four different automata with any
given automaton A. These are

(i) $\mathcal{R}(A) = (\mathcal{R}(Q),I,\mathcal{R}(\delta) = \mathbf{f})$

(ii) $\mathcal{R}^+(A) = (\mathcal{R}(Q),I,\mathcal{R}^+(\delta) = \mathbf{f}^+)$

(iii) $P(A) = (P(Q),I,P(\delta) = f)$

(iv) $P^+(A) = (P(Q),I,P^+(\delta) = f^+)$

where $\mathcal{R}(Q)$ and $P(Q)$ are the set of all subsets of Q and the set of
all partitions[*] on Q, respectively. The transition functions of the
associate automata are defined as follows:

For $i \epsilon I$, $x \epsilon I^*$, $Q' \epsilon \mathcal{R}(Q)$, $\pi \epsilon P(Q)$

(i) $\mathbf{f}(Q',\Lambda) = Q'$, $\mathbf{f}(Q',xi) = \mathbf{f}(\mathbf{f}(Q',x),i)$
$\mathbf{f}(Q',x) = \{q \epsilon Q \mid (\exists q' \epsilon Q') \; \delta(q',x) = q\}$

(ii) $\mathbf{f}^+(Q',\Lambda) = Q'$, $\mathbf{f}^+(Q',ix) = \mathbf{f}^+(\mathbf{f}^+(Q',x),i)$
$\mathbf{f}^+(Q',x) = \{q \epsilon Q \mid (\exists q' \epsilon Q') \; q' = \delta(q,x)\}$

(iii) $f(\pi,\Lambda) = \pi$, $f(\pi,xi) = f(f(\pi,x),i)$

$$q f(\pi,x) q' \Longleftrightarrow \delta_x^{-1}(q) \; \pi \; \delta_x^{-1}(q')$$

(iv) $f^+(\pi,\Lambda) = \pi$, $f^+(\pi,ix) = f^+(f^+(\pi,x),i)$

$$q f(\pi,x) q' \Longleftrightarrow \delta(q,x) \; \pi \; \delta(q',x).$$

---

[*]Partitions and equivalence relations are used interchangeably and
denoted by the same symbol.

Note that the automata $\mathcal{P}^+(A)$ and $P^+(A)$ read from right to left. To
put them in line with the more common left-to-right reading automata,
we have to feed them the mirror image of the input string.

Some properties of the above transition functions have been
stated in [3]. The functions $\mathbf{f}_x$ and f_x are residuated functions [4]
and $\mathbf{f}_x^+$, f_x^+ are their residuals, respectively. The mapping $\mathbf{f}_1$ and f_1
can be obtained directly from the given state table, whereas the
mappings $\mathbf{f}_1^+$ and f_1^+ can be found immediately from the state predeces-
sor table or inverted state table.

<h2 style="text-align:center"><u>BASIC DEFINITIONS</u></h2>

We extend now concepts from linear control theory to sequential
machines. The distinction between original and dual definitions,
problems and propositions has been made by differing their numbering
only in the last digit which is either a 1 (for original) or a 2 (for
dual) and off-setting this digit by a decimal point.

<u>Definition 1.1</u>. A state q of an initial automaton $A(Q_0)$ is said to
be reachable (or reduced) if

$(\exists q_0 \; \varepsilon \; Q_0) \; (\exists x \varepsilon I^*) \; \delta(q_0,x) = q.$

$A(Q_0)$ is said to be reachable (or reduced) if every state of $A(Q_0)$ is
reachable. In this case Q_0 is called a generating set. A generating
set Q_0 is said to be minimal or m-generating if for every generating
set $Q_0' \subseteq Q$ the property holds $Q_0' \subseteq Q_0 \Rightarrow Q_0' = Q_0.$

<u>Definition 2.1</u>. A state q of an initial automaton $A(Q_0)$ is said to
be controllable if
$(\exists x \varepsilon I^*) \; \delta(q,x) \varepsilon Q_0$

$A(Q_0)$ is said to be controllable if every state of $A(Q_0)$ is controllable. In this case, Q_0 is called an accessible set. An accessible
set Q_0 is said to be minimal or m-accessible if for any accessible
set $Q_0' \subseteq Q$ the property holds $Q_0' \subseteq Q_0 \Rightarrow Q_0' = Q_0.$ The complement $\overline{Q}_0$
is called inaccessible.

The next two statements define the dual concepts.

<u>Definition 1.2</u>. Two states q and q' of a terminal automaton $A(\theta)$ are
said to be unobservable (or indistinguishable, or equivalent) if
$(\forall x \varepsilon I^*) \; \delta(q,x) \; \theta \delta(q',x).$
The states q and q' are called observable or distinguishable if they
are not unobservable. The terminal automaton $A(\theta)$ is said to be
observable (or reduced) if every pair of distinct states of $A(\theta)$
is observable. In this case θ is called a future-distinguishing or a
diagnosing partition. A diagnosing partition θ is said to be maximal
or M-diagnosing if for any diagnosing partition θ' the property holds
$\theta' \geq \theta \Rightarrow \theta' = \theta.$

<u>Definition 2.2</u>. Two states q and q' of a terminal automaton $A(\theta)$ are
said to be non-reconstructible if

$(\forall x \varepsilon I^*) \quad \delta_x^{-1}(q) \; \theta \; \delta_x^{-1}(q').$

The states q and q' are called reconstructible if they are not non-reconstructible. The terminal automaton $A(\theta)$ is said to be reconstructible if every pair of distinct states of $A(\theta)$ is reconstructible. In this case θ is called a past-distinguishing or, for short, a distinguishing partition. A distinguishing partition θ is said to be maximal or M-distinguishing if for any distinguishing partition θ' the property holds $\theta' > \theta \Rightarrow \theta' = \theta$. The complement of a distinguishing partition will be called indistinguishing.

Finally we state the definitions for a synchronizing, diagnosing and homing sequence and their corresponding dual sequences.

Definition 3.1.   Let $x\epsilon I^*$ be an input sequence and $P(x) = \{y\epsilon I^* | (\exists\, z\epsilon I^*)\ x = yz\}$ be the set of prefixes of x.

(a) $x\epsilon I^*$ is said to be a synchronizing sequence for the automaton
      $A = (Q,I,\delta)$ if
      $(\forall\, q,q'\epsilon Q)\ \ \delta(q,x) = \delta(q',x)$

(b) $x\epsilon I^*$ is called a diagnosing sequence for the terminal automaton
      $A(\theta) = (Q,I,\delta)$ if
      $(\forall\, q,q'\epsilon Q)\ (\forall\, y\epsilon P(x))\ \delta(q,y)\ \theta\ \delta(q',y) \Rightarrow q=q'$

(c) $x\epsilon I^*$ is called a homing sequence for the terminal automaton
      $A(\theta) = (Q,I,\delta)$ if
      $(\forall\, q,q'\epsilon Q)\ (\forall\, y\epsilon P(x))\ \delta(q,y)\ \theta\ \delta(q',y) \Rightarrow \delta(q,x) = \delta(q',x)$

Definition 3.2.   Let $x\epsilon I^*$ be an input sequence and $S(x) = \{z\epsilon I^* | (\exists\, y\epsilon I^*)\ x = yz\}$ be the set of all suffixes of x.

(a) $x\epsilon I^*$ is said to be a dual synchronizing sequence for the automaton
     $A = (Q,I,\delta)$ if
     $(\exists\, q_x\epsilon Q)\ (\forall\, q\epsilon Q)\ \ \delta(q,x) = q_x$

(b) $x\epsilon I^*$ is called a dual diagnosing sequence for the initial automaton $A(Q_0) = (Q,I,\delta)$ if
     $(\forall\, q\epsilon Q)\ (\exists\, z\epsilon S(x))\ (\exists\, q_0\epsilon Q_0)\ \delta(q_0,z) = q$

(c) $x\epsilon I^*$ is called a dual homing sequence for the initial automaton $A(Q_0) = (Q,I,\delta)$ if
     $(\forall\, q\epsilon Q)\ (\exists\, z\epsilon S(x))\ (\exists\, q_0\epsilon Q_0)\ \delta(q_0,z) = \delta(q,x)$

<u>STATEMENT OF PROBLEMS</u>

We assume that the automata under consideration have a finite state set. The following problems will be dealt with

Problem 1.1.   Given the initial automaton $A(Q_0)$, find the maximal reachable subautomaton $A'(Q_0)$

Problem 2.1.   Given the finite automaton A, find an m-generating set Q_0 for A.

Problem 3.1.   Given a reachable (or reduced) initial automaton $A(Q_0)$ find a shortest dual diagnosing sequence for $A(Q_0)$ (if it exists).

Problem 4.1.   Given the finite automaton A, find an m-accessible set Q_0 for A.

<u>Problem 5.1.</u> Given a controllable initial automaton $A(Q_0)$, find a shortest dual homing sequence for $A(Q_0)$.

The dual problems are:

<u>Problem 1.2.</u> Given the terminal automaton $A(\theta)$, find the maximal observable quotient automaton $A'(\theta')$.

<u>Problem 2.2.</u> Given the finite automaton A, find an M-diagnosing partition θ for A.

<u>Problem 3.2.</u> Given an observable (or reduced) terminal automaton $A(\theta)$, find a shortest diagnosing sequence for $A(\theta)$ (if it exists).

<u>Problem 4.2.</u> Given the finite automaton A, find an M-distinguishing partition θ for A.

<u>Problem 5.2.</u> Given an observable (or reduced) terminal automaton $A(\theta)$, find a shortest homing sequence for $A(\theta)$.

<u>SOLUTIONS AND ALGORITHMS</u>

We consider first problem 1.1 and its dual problem 1.2.

<u>Proposition 1.1.</u> Let $A(Q_0) = (Q,I,\delta)$ be an initial automaton and $Q' \in \mathcal{P}(Q)$. Then the following statements are equivalent:

(i) Q' is the smallest ideal containing Q_0

(ii) $Q' = \{\delta(q_0,x)\mid q_0 \in Q_0,\ x \in I^*\}$

(iii) $Q' = \bigcup_{x \in I^*} f(Q_0,x)$

(iv) $Q' = f_I^*(Q_0)$

where $f_I(Q_0) = \bigcup_{i \in I} f(Q_0,i)$

$f(Q_0,i)$ is the transition function of $\mathcal{P}(A)$

$f_I^* = f_I^0 \cup f_I \cup f_I^2 \cup \ \cdots$

f_I^0 is the identity function on $\mathcal{P}(Q)$, $f_I^n = f_I \circ f_I^{n-1}$

Knowing Q', it is a simple matter to construct the subautomaton $A' = A\mid Q' = (Q',I,\delta' = \delta\mid Q')$.

We next give an algorithm to find Q'

<u>Proposition 2.1.</u> Let $A(Q_0) = (Q,I,\delta)$ be an initial automaton. The minimal ideal generated by Q_0 can be found recursively as follows:

$Q_0 = Q_0$

$Q_k = Q_0 \cup f_I(Q_{k-1}) \qquad k=1,2,\ldots$

$Q_n = Q_{n+1} \Rightarrow Q_n = Q'$

The dual propositions solve problem 1.2.

__Proposition 1.2.__   Let $A(\theta) = (Q,I,\delta)$ be a terminal automaton and $\pi \in P^-(Q)$. Then the following conditions are equivalent:

(i) π is the greatest congruence smaller or equal to θ

(ii) $q\pi q' \Leftrightarrow \delta(q,x) \, \theta \, \delta(q',x) \quad (\forall x \in I^*)$

(iii) $\bigwedge_{x \in I^*} f^+(\theta,x) = \pi$

(iv) $f_I^{+*}(\theta) = 0$

$\quad$ where $f_I^+(\theta) = \bigwedge_{i \in I} f^+(\theta,i)$,

$\quad$ $f^+(\theta,i)$ is the transition function of $P^+(A)$

$\quad$ $f_I^{+*} = f_I^{+0} \wedge f_I^+ \wedge f_I^{+2} \wedge \; \cdots$

$\quad$ f_I^{+0} is the identity function on $P(Q)$, $f_I^{+n} = f_I^+ \circ f_I^{+(n-1)}$

__Proposition 2.2.__   Let $A(\theta) = (Q,I,\delta)$ be a terminal automaton. The largest congruence $\pi \leq \theta$ can be found recursively as follows:

$\pi_0 = \theta$

$\pi_k = \theta \wedge f_I^+(\pi_{k-1}) \quad k=1,2,\ldots$

$\pi_n = \pi_{n+1} \Rightarrow \pi_n = \pi$

We now turn our attention to problems 2.1, 3.1, and their duals 2.2 and 3.2. The set Q of all states of a given automaton A is clearly a generating and also an accessible set. Since A is finite, Q contains at least one m-generating subset and also at least one m-accessible subset. The set Q is the only generating and accessible set iff every state is isolated (that is, $(\forall q \in Q)(\forall i \in I) \; \delta(q,i) = q$). In analogy with category theory, such an automaton is called skeleton automaton. It should also be noted that the empty set can never be a generating or accessible set for any non-empty automaton.

The following proposition characterizes generating sets.

__Proposition 3.1.__   Let $A = (Q,I,\delta)$ be a finite automaton ($Q \neq \phi$), $Q_0 \subseteq Q$, and $\{Q_\gamma^{max} \mid \gamma \in \Gamma\}$ be the set of all proper maximal ideals of A. Then the following statements are equivalent:

(i) Q_0 is a generating set

(ii) $\bigcup_{x \in I^*} f(Q_0,x) = Q$

(iii) $f_I^*(Q_0) = Q$

(iv) $(\forall \gamma \in \Gamma) \; Q_0 \nsubseteq Q_\gamma^{max}$

(v) $(\forall \gamma \in \Gamma) \; Q_0 - Q_\gamma^{max} \neq \phi$

Next we characterize m-generating sets.

<u>Proposition 4.1.</u> Let $A = (Q,I,\delta)$ be a finite automaton ($Q \neq \phi$), $Q_0 \subseteq Q$ be a generating set of A, and $\{Q_\gamma^{max} | \gamma \epsilon \Gamma\}$ be the set of all proper maximal ideals of A. Then the following statements are equivalent:

  (i) Q_0 is an m-generating set

  (ii) $q \epsilon Q_0$ and $\delta(q,x) \epsilon Q_0 \Rightarrow q = \delta(q,x)$

(iii) $(\forall \gamma \epsilon \Gamma)$ $|Q_0 - Q_\gamma^{max}| = 1$

Furthermore, any two m-generating sets have the same cardinality which is equal to the number of proper maximal ideals of A.

From statement (iii) of the last proposition follows that a generating set is composed of exactly one element of each of the disjoint complement sets $\overline{Q}_\gamma^{max}$. In addition, we can state

<u>Corollary 4.1</u> [7] An automaton A is cyclic (or connected) iff it contains a unique proper maximal ideal. A is simple (or strongly connected) if the proper maximal ideal of A is the empty set (that is, the only ideals of A are Q and ϕ). In this case, every element of Q is a generating set.

We now characterize accessible sets. To expose more clearly the converse relations, we must use inaccessible sets. The corresponding statements for accessible sets have been added in parenthesis.

<u>Proposition 5.1.</u> Let $A = (Q,I,\delta)$ be a finite automaton ($Q \neq \phi$), $Q_0 \subseteq Q$, and $\{Q_\gamma^{min} | \gamma \epsilon \Gamma\}$ be the set of all proper minimal ideals of A. Then the following conditions are equivalent.

  (i) $\overline{Q}_0$ is an inaccessible set (Q_0 is an accesible set)

  (ii) $\bigcap\limits_{x \epsilon I*} f^+(\overline{Q}_0,x) = \phi$ $(\bigcup\limits_{x \epsilon I*} f^+(Q_0,x) = Q)$

(iii) $f_I^{+*}(\overline{Q}_0,x) = \phi$

  (iv) $(\forall \gamma \epsilon \Gamma)$ $\overline{Q}_0 \not\supseteq Q_\gamma^{min}$ $(Q_0 \not\supseteq \overline{Q}_\gamma^{min})$

  (v) $(\forall \gamma \epsilon \Gamma)$ $Q_\gamma^{min} - \overline{Q}_0 \neq \phi$ $(Q_\gamma^{min} \cap Q_0 \neq \phi)$

<u>Proposition 6.1.</u> Let $A = (Q,I,\delta)$ be a finite automaton ($Q \neq \phi$), $Q_0 \subseteq Q$ be an accessible set and $\{Q_\gamma^{min} | \gamma \epsilon \Gamma\}$ be the set of all proper minimal ideals of A. Then the following conditions are equivalent:

  (i) Q_0 is an m-accessible set

  (ii) $q \epsilon Q_0$ and $\delta(q,x) \epsilon Q_0 \Rightarrow q = \delta(q,x)$

(iii) $(\forall \gamma \epsilon \Gamma)$ $|Q_0 \cap Q_\gamma^{min}| = 1$

It is clear from statement (iii) of proposition 6.1, that the m-accessible set is composed of just one element from each minimal ideal of A.

Corollary 6.1.   An automaton A is simple iff every state of A is an accessible set. We now state conditions under which a given initial automaton can be both reachable and controllable.

Proposition 7.1.   Let $A = (Q, I, \delta)$ be an automaton and $Q_0 \subseteq Q$. Then

(i) Q_0 is an m-generating set implies

$$\bigcap_{x \in I^*} f^+(\overline{Q}_0, x) = \bigcap_{\gamma \in \Gamma} Q_\gamma^{max}$$

(ii) Q_0 is an m-accessible set implies

$$\bigcup_{x \in I^*} f(Q_0, x) = \bigcup_{\gamma \in \Gamma} Q_\gamma^{min}$$

It is immediately seen from propositions 7.1, 3.1 and 5.1 that the following holds.

Proposition 8.1.   An initial automaton $A(Q_0) = (Q, I, \delta)$ is both controllable and reachable iff

$$\bigcap_{\gamma \in \Gamma} Q_\gamma^{max} = \phi \text{ and } \bigcup_{\gamma \in \Gamma} Q_\gamma^{min} = Q.$$

We turn now to the dual problems 2.2 and 3.2. Generally speaking, there is a basic difference between the lattices $\mathcal{R}(Q)$ and $P(Q)$ in that the former is distributive and the latter is not. Although any element of $\mathcal{R}(Q)$ or $P(Q)$ has a complement, distributivity implies that the complement in $\mathcal{R}(Q)$ is unique, whereas any element in $P(Q)$ with the exception of the extreme points (0 and u) has several complements. Hence we have to take special care in the dualization process whenever we encounter complements.

The equality partition 0 of the state set Q of a given automaton A is clearly a diagnosing and also a distinguishing partition. Since A is finite, there exists at least one M-diagnosing partition and at least one M-distinguishing partition. The equality partition is the only diagnosing and distinguishing partition iff A is a skeleton automaton. Furthermore, the universal partition can never be a diagnosing or distinguishing partition for any automaton with $|Q| > 1$ states.

We now characterize diagnosing partitions.

Proposition 3.2.   Let $A = (Q, I, \delta)$ be a finite automaton ($|Q| > 1$), θ be a partition of Q and $\{\pi_\gamma^{min} | \gamma \in \Gamma\}$ be the set of all proper minimal congruences of A. Then the following conditions are equivalent:

(i) θ is a diagnosing partition

(ii) $\bigwedge_{x \in I^*} f^+(\theta, x) = 0$

(iii) $f_I^{+*}(\theta) = 0$

(iv) $(\forall \gamma \in \Gamma)$ $\theta \nleq \pi_\gamma^{min}$

56

An M-diagnosing partition θ can be formally found in the following way. For every $\gamma\varepsilon\Gamma$ find the set $\overline{C}_\gamma$ of co-atoms which are not in π_γ^{min} and form their intersection. If $\theta \in \bigcap_{\gamma\varepsilon\Gamma} \overline{C}_\gamma \neq \phi$, then θ is M-diagnosing; if the intersection is empty, then for any $k\varepsilon\Gamma$ take $\bigcap_{\gamma\varepsilon\Gamma-\{k\}} \overline{C}_\gamma$. If there is some k for which this intersection is non-empty then $\theta = \theta' \cap \theta''$ is M-diagnosing, where $\theta' \in \bigcap_{\gamma\varepsilon\Gamma-\{k\}} \overline{C}_\gamma$ and $\theta'' \varepsilon \overline{C}_k$ are chosen in such a way that the number of blocks of θ becomes minimal. Usually, an M-diagnosing partition with only two blocks can be found.

We now characterize the distinguishing partitions. This is done indirectly by characterizing their complements, the indistinguishing partitions.

<u>Proposition 5.2.</u>   Let $A = (Q,I,\delta)$ be a finite automaton ($|Q| > 1$), $\overline{\theta}$ be a partition of Q and $\{\pi_\gamma^{max}|\gamma\varepsilon\Gamma\}$ be the set of all proper maximal congruences of A. Then the following statements are equivalent:

(i) $\overline{\theta}$ is an indistinguishing partition

(ii) $\bigvee_{x\varepsilon I^*} f(\overline{\theta},x) = u$

(iii) $f_I^*(\overline{\theta}) = u$

(iv) $(\forall \gamma\varepsilon\Gamma)\ \overline{\theta} \nleqq \pi_\gamma^{max}$

An M-distinguishing partition can be found in the following way: For every $\gamma\varepsilon\Gamma$ find the set $\overline{A}_\gamma$ of all atoms which are not in π_γ^{max} and form the intersection of these sets. If $\overline{\theta} \in \bigcap_{\gamma\varepsilon\Gamma} \overline{A}_\gamma \neq \phi$, then its complement θ is an M-distinguishing partition. If the inter-section is empty, then for any $k\varepsilon\Gamma$ form $\bigcap_{\gamma\varepsilon\Gamma-\{k\}} \overline{A}_\gamma$. If there is some k for which this intersection is non-empty a complement of $\overline{\theta} = \overline{\theta}' \cup \overline{\theta}''$ is M-diagnosing, where $\overline{\theta}' \in \bigcap_{\gamma\varepsilon\Gamma-\{k\}} \overline{A}_\gamma$ and $\overline{\theta}'' \varepsilon \overline{A}_k$ are chosen in such a way that the size of the biggest block of $\overline{\theta}$ becomes minimal. Usually, the maximal size does not exceed more than 2 elements.

SPECIAL SEQUENCES

We first state briefly algorithms for finding the synchronizing diagnosing and homing sequences by use of partitions only. For more detail and examples, applied to Mealy-type sequential machines, see [3].

<u>Proposition 10.1.</u>   Let $A = (Q,I,\delta)$ be a finite automaton ($|Q| > 1$) and $x\varepsilon I^*$ be an input sequence to A. Then the following statements are equivalent:

(i) $x\varepsilon I^*$ is a synchronizing sequence for A

(ii) $f^+(0,x) = u$

(iii) $x \in I^*$ is a dual synchronizing sequence for A

(iv) $f(Q,x) = \{q_x\}$

    The above proposition states that the property: "x is synchronizing for A" is self-dual. To find the shortest (dual) synchronizing sequence (if it exists), we start the associate automaton $P^+(A) = (P(Q),I,f^+)$ in state 0 (equality partition) and develop the response tree. A has a synchronizing sequence x if according to condition (ii) we have $f^+(0,x) = u.$(Remember that in the response tree x has to be read from the leaf to the root). Equally well we can start the associate automaton $R(A) = (R(Q),I,f)$ in state Q. Then according to statement (iv), the sequence $x \in I^*$ is synchronizing if $f(Q,x) = \{q_x\}$; in other words, $R(A)$ must terminate in a singleton set.

    We turn now our attention to the problem of finding a diagnosing sequence.

<u>Proposition 11.1.</u> Let $A(\theta) = (Q,I,\delta)$ be a terminal automaton $(|Q| > 1)$ $x \in I^k$ be an input sequence to $A(\theta)$ for some positive integer k and $P(x) = \{y \in I^* \,|\, (\exists z \in I^*)\ x = yz\}$ be the set of all prefixes of x. Then the following statements are equivalent:

(i) $x \in I^k$ is a diagnosing sequence for $A(\theta)$

(ii) The map $\delta_x^* : Q \to [Q/\theta]^{k+1}$ is injective, where

$$\delta_{i_1 \ldots i_n}^*(q) = ([q]_\theta, [\delta(q,i_1)]_\theta, [\delta(q,i_1 i_2)]_\theta, \ldots [\delta(q,i_1 \ldots i_n)]_\theta)$$

(iii) $\bigwedge_{y \in P(x)} f^+(\theta,y) = 0$

(iv) $\hat{f}^+(\theta,x) = 0$

    where $\hat{f}^+(\pi,x) = \hat{f}^+(\pi,x) \wedge \theta$ $(\forall x \in I^*)$.

    To find a diagnosing sequence (if it exists), start the automaton $\hat{P}^+(A) = (P(Q),I,\hat{f}^+)$ in state θ and develop the response tree. Then according to statement (iv), x is diagnosing if $\hat{f}^+(\theta,x) = 0$.

<u>Proposition 12.1.</u> Let $A(\theta) = (Q,I,\delta)$ be a terminal automaton $(|Q| > 1)$, $x \in I^k$ be an input sequence to $A(\theta)$ for some positive integer k and $P(x) = \{y \in I^* \,|\, (\exists z \in I^*)\ x = yz\}$ be the set of all prefixes of x. Then the following statements are equivalent:

(i) $x \in I^k$ is a homing sequence for $A(\theta)$

(ii) There is a map $\chi_x : [Q/\theta]^{k+1} \to Q$ such that

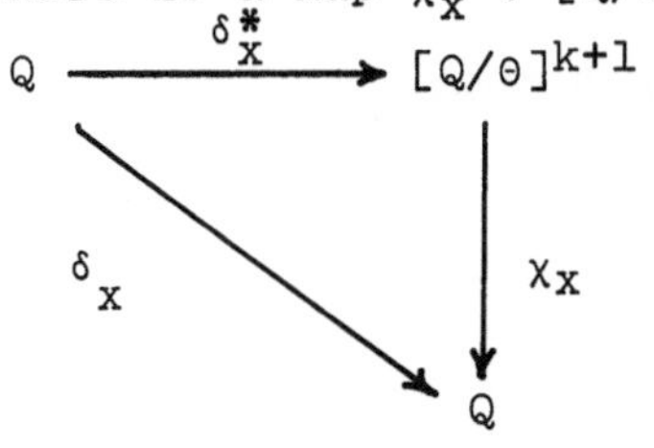

$$\chi_x \circ \delta_x^* = \delta_x$$

(iii) $\bigwedge\limits_{y \in P(x)} f^+(\theta,y) \leq f^+(0,x)$

(iv) $\hat{f}^+(\theta,x) \leq f^+(0,x)$

A homing sequence can be recognized by the direct product $\overline{A}$ of two automata, one able to recognize synchronizing sequences and the other able to recognize diagnosing sequences; $\overline{A} = \hat{A} \times A = (P(Q) \times P(Q), I, \overline{f}^+)$, where $\overline{f}^+(q,q',x) = (\hat{f}^+(q,x), f^+(q',x)) = (f^+(q,x) \wedge \theta, f^+(q',x))$. Start $\overline{A}$ in the initial state $(\theta,0)$ and develop the response tree. Then according to statement (iv), x is a homing sequence if there is a state (π,π') such that $\pi \leq \pi'$.

The dual diagnosing and homing sequence can be found by the dual algorithms, where partitions have to be substituted by subsets, meet by union, 0 by Q, etc. We will state only two dual propositions:

<u>Proposition 11.2.</u>   Let $A(Q_0) = (Q,I,\delta)$ be an initial automaton $(Q \neq \phi)$, $x \in I^k$ be an input sequence to $A(\theta)$ for some positive integer k and $S(x) = \{z \in I^* | (\exists\, y \in I^*)\ x=yz\}$ be the set of all suffices of x.   Then the following statements are equivalent:

(i) $x \in I^k$ is a dual diagnosing sequence for $A(\theta)$

(ii)   The map $\delta_x^{\#} : Q_0 \times [k] \to Q$ is surjective, where $[k] = \{0,1,\ldots,k\}$

$\delta^{\#}_{i_1 \ldots i_n}(q_0,0) = \delta(q_0,\Lambda) = q_0$

$\delta^{\#}_{i_1 \ldots i_n}(q_0,r) = (q_0, i_{n-r+1}, i_{n-r+2} \cdots, i_n) \qquad 1 \leq r \leq n$

(iii) $\bigcup\limits_{y \in S(x)} f(Q_0,y) = Q$

(iv) $\hat{f}(Q_0,x) = Q$

where $\hat{f}(Q',x) = f(Q',x) \cup Q_0$

Note that $Q \times [k]$ is in 1:1 correspondence with the direct union $\overset{\cup}{\underset{k+1}{}} Q_0$.

<u>Proposition 12.2.</u>   Let $A(Q_0) = (Q,I,\delta)$ be an initial automaton $(Q \neq \phi)$, $x \in I^k$ be an input sequence to $A(\theta)$ for some positive integer k and $S(x) = \{z \in I^*)(\exists\, y \in I^*)\ x=yz\}$ be the set of all suffixes of x.   Then the following statements are equivalent.

(i) $x \in I^k$ is a dual homing sequence

(ii) There exists a map $\psi_x : Q_0 \to Q \times [k]$ such that

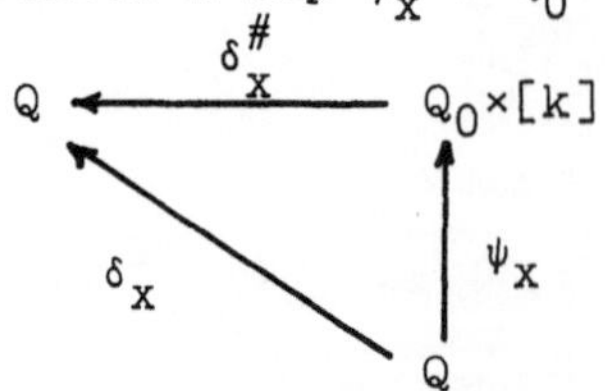

(iii) $\bigcup\limits_{y \in S(x)} f(Q_0, y) \supseteq f(Q, x)$

(iv) $\hat{f}(Q_0, x) \supseteq (Q, x)$

REFERENCES

1. ARBIB, M.A. : A common framework for automata theory and control theory. J. SIAM, Control, Ser. A., 3, (1965).

2. ARBIB, M.A., ZEIGER, H.P. : On the relevance of abstract algebra to control theory. Automatica, 5, 589-606 (1969).

3. BECKHOFF, G.F. : Experiments on sequential machines, Proc. Tenth Annual Allerton Conf. on Circuit and System Theory, 10, 471-480 (1972).

4. BLYTH, T.S., JANOWITZ, M.F. : Residuation Theory, Pergamon Press, London (1972).

5. KAMBAYASHI, YAHIKO : Controllability of sequential machines, Infor. Contr., 21, 306-328 (1972).

6. KALMAN, R.E., FALB, P.L., ARBIB, M.A. : Topics in mathematical system theory, McGraw-Hill, New York (1969)

7. PERROT, J.F. : Contribution à l' étude des monoïdes syntactiques et de certains groups associés aux automates finis. Thèse de doctorat d'état es Sciences, Université de Paris VI (1972).

8. RABIN, M.O., SCOTT, D. : Finite automata and their decision problems, IBM J. Res. Dev., 3, 114-125 (1959).

9. THIERRIN, G. : Theory of automata, Class notes (1972).

ON THE PROBLEM OF AUTOMATA SET REPRESENTATION

Jerzy W. Grzymala-Busse

The main studied problem is: When for the given set $\mathcal{A}$ of finite automata there exists another finite automaton A such that for each automaton A' in $\mathcal{A}$ there exist a subautomaton A" of A (we restrict our attention to a special class of subautomata) and a homomorphism f of A" into A' .

1. Basic definitions and formulation of problems

Following $[2,3]$ we define a <u>finite</u> <u>automaton</u> (or briefly <u>automaton</u>) as a pair (S,J) , where S is a finite set (state set) and J is a set of functions of S into S. The set J , together with the operation of superposition, generates a semigroup $\langle J \rangle$ of functions of S into S. An element f in $\langle J \rangle$ will be written as a right operator. For f,f' in $\langle J \rangle$ we have

$$s(ff')=(sf)f' .$$

Let $A=(S_A,J_A)$ and $B=(S_B,J_B)$ be automata and let h_1 and h_2 be functions of S_A into S_B and J_A into J_B , respectively. Both

h_1 and h_2 will be written as left operators. If for each s in S_A and f in J_A we have

$$h_1(sf)=h_1(s)h_2(f)$$

the the pair (h_1,h_2) will be called a __homomorphism__ __of__ A __into__ B. The set of all homomorphisms of A into B will be denoted by $\mathrm{Hom}(A \longrightarrow B)$.

Let K be a set of functions of S into S . We assume here that the pair (S,K) is said to be a __subautomaton__ __of__ __the__ __automaton__ (S,J) if and only if $K \subseteq \langle J \rangle$.

Let i be a positive integer. For i we define the set J^i as the set

$$\left\{ f_1 f_2 \cdots f_i \; : \; f_1,f_2,\ldots,f_i \in J \right\}$$

and the set J_d^i as the set

$$\left\{ ff\cdots f = f^i \; : \; f \in J \right\} .$$

Then $A^i=(S,J^i)$ and $A_d^i=(S,J_d^i)$ are subautomata of $A=(S,J)$. In the following we consider only such subautomata. For some properties of A^i and A_d^i see $[7\text{-}9]$.

Subautomata A^i and A_d^i of A could be called subautomata of A, associated with the change of operating time of A, since automaton A^i may be replaced by the automaton A in which functions in $\langle J \rangle$ act at moments $1,2,3,\ldots$ of time, but the states of A are observed at moments $1,i+1,2i+1,\ldots$ of time, and automaton A_d^i may be replaced by the automaton A in which any function in $\langle J \rangle$ acts i-fold, i.e. it is constant from moment 1 until i , from moment $i+1$ until $2i, \ldots$ and the states of A are observed also at moments $1,i+1,$ $2i+1, \ldots$ of time. Under different names, restricted or extended concepts related to such subautomata were mainly studied in $[1,4]$.

Now we state our main problems

__First Problem.__ Let $\mathcal{A}$ $=\left\{ A_1=(S_1,J_1), \; A_2=(S_2,J_2), \; \ldots \right\}$ __be__ __a__ __set__ of automata. Does there exist an automaton $A=(S,J)$ such that for each $A_j \in \mathcal{Q}$ there exists a subautomaton $A^i=(S,J^i)$ of A such that $\text{Hom }(A^i \longrightarrow A_j) \neq \emptyset$?

Second Problem. Does there exist an automaton $A=(S,J)$ such that for each $A_j \in \mathcal{Q}$ there exists a subautomaton $A_d^i=(S,J_d^i)$ of A such that $\text{Hom }(A_d^i \longrightarrow A_j) \neq \emptyset$?

Using a realization approach $[10]$, we may generalize these problems for automata with outputs. Roughly speaking, it may be done by replacing the condition that the set of homomorphisms is nonempty by the condition of the existence of an assignment.

All these problems - in a general form - are still open, although a particular case of the First Problem is solved in $[9]$. Such problems have applications in the physical realization of automata, since the set of subautomata of A is obtained in a simple way by means of an additional multichannel clock with different channel frequencies. In the case of positive solution of one of the above problems, any automaton in $\mathcal{Q}$ is simulated by just one automaton A.

Our problems motivate the study of homomorphisms of a subautomaton of A into automaton B.

2. Algorithm for determining homomorphisms

First we introduce some additional notions.

Let $A=(S_A,J_A)$ and $B=(S_B,J_B)$ be automata. Then by a state homomorphism of A into B, associated with the function h_2 of J_A into J_B we mean any function of the set

$$\{h_1 \; : \; (h_1,h_2) \in \text{Hom}(A \longrightarrow B)\}.$$

The set of all state homomorphisms of A into B, associated with h_2, will be denoted by $\text{SHom}_{h_2}(A \longrightarrow B)$.

Let $A=(S,J)$ be an automaton and let $f \in \langle J \rangle$. Then an automaton $(S,\{f\})$ is said to be an <u>autonomous factor of</u> A, <u>associated with the function</u> f, and it will be denoted by A_f (cf. [6,11]).

We obtain easily the following modification of Theorem from [6]

<u>Theorem 1.</u> <u>Let</u> $A=(S_A,J_A)$ <u>and</u> $B=(S_B,J_B)$ <u>be automata. Then</u>

$$\mathrm{SHom}_{h_2}(A \longrightarrow B) = \bigcap_{f \in J_A} \mathrm{SHom}_{h_2}(A_f \longrightarrow B_{h_2(f)}).$$

Thanks to this theorem, the determining all homomorphisms of A into B is reduced to a computation, step by step, for each function h_2 of J_A into J_B and $f \in J_A$ state homomorphisms of A_f into $B_{h_2(f)}$ associated with h_2, since

$$\mathrm{Hom}(A \longrightarrow B) = \bigcup_{h_2 \in J_B^{J_A}} \mathrm{SHom}_{h_2}(A \longrightarrow B).$$

The algorithm for determining $\mathrm{SHom}_{h_2}(A_f \longrightarrow B_{h_2(f)})$ was given in [6].

Note that for automata with outputs, for which homomorphisms are defined as function triples, where the first and second functions are defined as our functions h_1 and h_2, and the third function is defined as a function of the output set of the first automaton into the output set of the second one, an algorithm for determining such homomorphisms of automata with outputs directly follows from the algorithm for determining homomorphisms of our automata, since determining the third function for any pair (h_1,h_2) is independent from the determination of such a pair.

3. Conditions for $\mathrm{Hom}(A \longrightarrow B) \neq \emptyset$

In our problems we are interested when $\mathrm{Hom}(A \longrightarrow B) \neq \emptyset$, and hence in all that follows we shall consider this question.

Let $A_f=(S,\{f\})$ be an autonomous factor of $A=(S,J)$. Then by

A_f^c we denote a pair $(S_f^c, \{f\})$, where S_f^c is the maximal subset of S such that f restricted to S_f^c is a permutation. We have

Theorem 2. Let $A=(S_A, J_A)$ and $B=(S_B, J_B)$ be automata and let $f \in J_A$. Then for any function h_2 of J_A into J_B the following conditions are equivalent:

i) $\mathrm{SHom}_{h_2}(A_f \longrightarrow B_{h_2(f)}) \neq \emptyset$,

ii) $\mathrm{SHom}_{h_2}(A_f^c \longrightarrow B_{h_2(f)}^c) \neq \emptyset$,

and

iii) for each cycle C_A of the permutation given as f restricted to $(S_A)_f^c$ there exists a cycle C_B of the permutation given as $h_2(f)$ restricted to $(S_B)_{h_2(f)}^c$ such that the length of C_B is a divisor of the length of C_A .

Proof. Thanks to Lemmas 2 and 3 from $[6]$, the proof is obvious.

Corollary 1. Let $A=(S_A, J_A)$ and $B=(S_B, J_B)$ be automata. If for each function h_2 of J_A into J_B there exists $f \in J_A$ such that

$$\mathrm{SHom}_{h_2}(A_f^c \longrightarrow B_{h_2(f)}^c) = \emptyset$$

then

$$\mathrm{Hom}\,(A \longrightarrow B) = \emptyset \ .$$

Theorem 3. Let $A=(S_A, J_A)$ and $B=(S_B, J_B)$ be automata. Then

i) $\mathrm{Hom}\,(A_d^i \longrightarrow B) = \emptyset$ implies $\mathrm{Hom}\,(A^i \longrightarrow B) = \emptyset$,

ii) $\mathrm{Hom}\,(A \longrightarrow B^i) = \emptyset$ implies $\mathrm{Hom}\,(A \longrightarrow B_d^i) = \emptyset$.

Proof. i) Let h_2 be a function of $(J_A)_d^i$ into J_B and let h_2' be a function of $(J_A)^i$ into J_B such that for each $f \in (J_A)_d^i$ we have $h_2'(f)=h_2(f)$, i.e. h_2' is an extension of h_2 . Then

$$\bigcap_{f \in (J_A)_d^i} \mathrm{SHom}_{h_2'}(A_f \longrightarrow B_{h_2'(f)}) = \bigcap_{f \in (J_A)_d^i} \mathrm{SHom}_{h_2}(A_f \longrightarrow B_{h_2(f)})$$

and hence

$$\bigcap_{f \in (J_A)^i} \mathrm{SHom}_{h_2'}(A_f \longrightarrow B_{h_2'(f)}) \subseteq \bigcap_{f \in (J_A)^i_d} \mathrm{SHom}_{h_2}(A_f \longrightarrow B_{h_2(f)}).$$

Thus, thanks to Theorem 1, i) is proved.

ii) The set of all functions of J_A into $(J_B)^i_d$ is included in the set of all functions of J_A into $(J_B)^i$, hence if for each $h_2 \colon J_A \longrightarrow (J_B)^i$ we have

$$\bigcap_{f \in J_A} \mathrm{SHom}_{h_2}(A_f \longrightarrow B_{h_2(f)}) = \emptyset \; ,$$

then for each $h_2' \colon J_A \longrightarrow (J_B)^i_d$ we have

$$\bigcap_{f \in J_A} \mathrm{SHom}_{h_2'}(A_f \longrightarrow B_{h_2'(f)}) = \emptyset \; .$$

Regarding Theorem 1, ii) is also proved.

From i) of Theorem 3 follows that the Second Problem is more general than the First Problem, since if there is no solution of the Second Problem, there is no solution of the First Problem.

It is possible that for an automaton A and a positive integer i there is $\mathrm{Hom}(A^i_d \longrightarrow A) = \mathrm{Hom}(A \longrightarrow A^i) = \emptyset$. Hence, neither $\mathrm{Hom}(A \longrightarrow B) = \emptyset$ implies $\mathrm{Hom}(A^i \longrightarrow B) = \emptyset$ nor $\mathrm{Hom}(A \longrightarrow B^i) = \emptyset$ implies $\mathrm{Hom}(A \longrightarrow B) = \emptyset$. Furthermore, there exist examles showing that $\mathrm{Hom}(A \longrightarrow B) = \emptyset$ does not imply $\mathrm{Hom}(A \longrightarrow B^i_d) = \emptyset$ and $\mathrm{Hom}(A^i_d \longrightarrow B) = \emptyset$ does not imply $\mathrm{Hom}(A \longrightarrow B) = \emptyset$.

A <u>state diagram</u> $\Gamma(A)$ of the automaton $A = (S, J)$ is an oriented graph defined as follows: To each $s \in S$ corresponds a <u>vertex</u> of $\Gamma(A)$ denoted by s , and to each $s \in S$ and $f \in J$ corresponds a <u>branch</u> of $\Gamma(A)$ oriented from s to sf and denoted by f . A finite connected sequence of branches of $\Gamma(A)$ which can be traced on $\Gamma(A)$ will be called a <u>chain</u>. A <u>length of the chain</u> with the first vertex s and the last vertex s' is the difference between the number of consistent and opposite branches examined along

the chain from s to s' . A chain for which the first vertex is e-
qual to the last will be called a _circuit_. A _cycle_ is a circuit along
which all branches are consistently oriented. If the branches of a cycle are all distinct then the cycle is said to be _simple_. An automaton A=(S,J) is said to be _connected_ if and only if for all s,s'∈ S
there exists a chain in Γ(A) with the first vertex s and the
last vertex s' .

For any automaton A there exists the maximal number D_A such
that each circuit of Γ(A) has the circuit length equal to a multiple of D_A . If A is a connected automaton then in Γ(A)   there
exists a circuit with the circuit length equal to D_A . We have the
following generalization of Corollary 2 from [5] :

Theorem 4. _Let_ A _and_ B _be_ _automata_ _and_ _let_ Hom(A $\longrightarrow$ B)≠∅.
Then D_B _is_ _a_ _divisor_ _of_ D_A .

Proof. It is easy to see that the homomorphic image of a circuit
C of Γ(A) , i.e. the circuit of Γ(B) the vertices of which are
subsequently images of vertices of C under the function h_1 and the
branches of which are denoted by the images of branches of C under
the function h_2 , where (h_1,h_2)∈ Hom(A $\longrightarrow$ B) , has the length e-
qual to a divisor of the length of C . From this directly follows
our theorem.

From Theorem 4 and the fact that D_{A^i} is a divisor of D_A follows:

Corollary 2. _If_ _for_ _set_ $\mathcal{A}$ =$\{A_1,A_2,...\}$ _of_ _automata_ _there_
exists _an_ _automaton_ A _such_ _that_ _for_ _each_ A_j ∈ $\mathcal{A}$ _there_ _exists_
_a_ _subautomaton_ A^i _of_ A _such_ _that_ Hom(A^i $\longrightarrow$ A_j) ≠ ∅ _then_
D_A _is_ _a_ _multiple_ _of_ D_{A_1} , D_{A_2} ,... .

4. k-asynchronous and permutation automata

An automaton $A=(S,J)$ will be called <u>k-asynchronous</u> if and only if for each $s \in S$ and $f \in J$ we have

$$sf^k = sf^{k+1} \ .$$

1-asynchronous automata will be called directly <u>asynchronous</u>. Some properties of k-asynchronous automata were studied in $[7,8]$. We have additional results to present.

<u>Theorem 5</u>. <u>For each automaton</u> $A=(S,J)$ <u>there exists a positive integer</u> i <u>such that</u> $A_d^i=(S,J_d^i)$ <u>is asynchronous</u>.

<u>Proof</u>. Let $\mathscr{E}$ be a set of all simple cycles of all the state diagrams in the set $\{\Gamma(A_f) : f \in J\}$. Let i be the least common multiple of all the lenghts of cycles from set $\mathscr{E}$. Then there exists a positive integer k such that for all $s \in S$ and $f \in J$ we have

$$sf^{ki} = sf^{2ki} \ ,$$

i.e. A_d^{ki} is asynchronous.

If h_2 is onto, then a homomorphic image of k-asynchronous automaton under homomorphism (h_1,h_2) is k'-asynchronous for $k' \leqslant k$.

<u>Theorem 6</u>. <u>Let</u> A <u>be an asynchronous automaton and let</u> B <u>be an automaton. Then if</u> $\mathrm{Hom}(A \longrightarrow B)=\emptyset$ <u>then</u> $\mathrm{Hom}(A^i \longrightarrow B)=\emptyset$.

<u>Proof</u>. It follows from the fact that $J=J_d^i$ and Theorem 3.

Moreover, for an asynchronous automaton A we have

$$\mathrm{SHom}_{h_2'}(A^i \longrightarrow B) \subsetneq \mathrm{SHom}_{h_2}(A \longrightarrow B) \ ,$$

where h_2' is an extension of h_2 .

Automaton $A=(S,J)$ is said to be a <u>permutation automaton</u> if and only if $\langle J \rangle$ is a group. Automaton $A=(S,J)$ is <u>strongly</u>

<u>connected</u> if and only if for each $s,s' \in S$ there exists $f \in J$ such that

$$sf=s' \ .$$

We have easily

<u>Lemma</u>. <u>Let</u> $A=(S_A,J_A)$ <u>be an automaton, let</u> $B=(S_B,J_B)$ <u>be a strongly connected automaton, let</u> $(h_1,h_2) \in \mathrm{Hom}(A \longrightarrow B)$, <u>and let</u> h_2 <u>be onto. Then</u> h_1 <u>is also onto</u>.

<u>Theorem 7</u>. <u>Let</u> $A=(S_A,J_A)$ <u>be a permutation automaton and let</u> $B=(S_B,J_B)$ <u>be a strongly connected non-permutation automaton. Let</u> h_2 <u>be a function of</u> $(J_A)^i_d$ <u>onto</u> J_B . <u>Then</u>

$$\mathrm{SHom}_{h_2}(A^i_d \longrightarrow B) = \emptyset \ .$$

<u>Proof</u>. If h_2 is onto then - by Lemma - also h_1 is onto. Let f $(J_A)^i_d$ and let $h_2(f)$ be such that in $\Gamma(B_{h_2(f)})$ there exists a vertex s' not belonging to any cycle. State s' is an image of state in the cycle of $\Gamma(A_f)$ under h_1 , and this is a contradiction, by Lemma 2 of $[6]$.

<u>Corollary 3</u>. <u>Let</u> $A=(S_A,J_A)$ <u>be a permutation</u> <u>automaton and let</u> $B=(S_B,J_B)$ <u>be a strongly connected asynchronous automaton with</u> $|S_B|>1$, <u>where</u> $|S_B|$ <u>denotes the cardinality of set</u> S_B . <u>Let</u> i,j <u>be positive integers and let</u> h_2 <u>be a function of</u> $(J_A)^i_d$ <u>onto</u> $(J_B)^j$. <u>Then</u>

$$\mathrm{SHom}_{h_2}(A^i_d \longrightarrow B^j) = \emptyset \ .$$

<u>Proof</u>. It follows from the fact that B^j_d is strongly connected and asynchronous, and hence B^j is strongly connected and non-permutable.

<u>Theorem 8</u>. <u>Let</u> $A=(S_A,J_A)$ <u>be a k-asynchronous automaton and let</u> $B=(S_B,J_B)$ <u>be a strongly connected permutation automaton with</u> $|S_B|>1$. <u>Let</u> h_2 <u>be a function of</u> $(J_A)^i_d$ <u>onto</u> J_B . <u>Then</u>

$$\text{SHom}_{h_2}(A_d^1 \longrightarrow B) = \emptyset .$$

__Proof__. Thanks to Lemma, h_1 is onto. Hence for any h_2 there exists $f \in (J_A)_d^1$ such that in $\Gamma(B_{h_2(f)})$ there exists a cycle C of a length greater than 1. Let $s \in S_A$ be such that $h_1(s)$ is in C. Such s belongs to a component of $\Gamma(A_f)$, the cycle of which has the length equal to 1, since A is k-asynchronous. Thus we get a contradiction, by Lemma 3 of [6].

References

1. Ajzerman, M.A., Gusev, L.A., Rozonoer, L.I., Smirnova, I.M., Tal', A.A.: Logic, Automata, Algorithms, Moscow, Fizmatgiz 1963 (in Russian)

2. Brauer, W.: Gruppentheoretische Untersuchungen bei endlichen Automaten. __Z. Angew. Math. Mech__. 48, T113-T115 (1968).

3. Deussen, P.: On the algebraic theory of finite automata. __ICC Bull__. 4, 231-264 (1966).

4. Gill, A.: Single-channel and multichannel finite-state machines. __IEEE Trans. Computers__ C-19, 1073-1078 (1970).

5. Grzymala-Busse, J.W.: On the endomorphisms of finite automata. __Math. Syst. Theory__ 4, 373-384 (1970)

6. Grzymala-Busse, J.W.: Operation-preserving functions and autonomous factors of finite automata. __J. Comput. Syst. Sci__.5, 465-474 (1971).

7. Grzymala-Busse, J.W.: Subautomata of finite automata, associated with the change of operating time, Technical U. Poznan, Rep. 46, 1972 (in Polish).

8. Grzymala-Busse, J.W.: Generalized endomorphisms, congruences, and subautomata associated with the change of operating time of finite automata. Submitted for publication.

9. Grzymala-Busse, J.W.: Problems of time-invariance of finite automata. Submitted for publication.

10. Hartmanis, J., Stearns, R.E.: Algebraic Structure Theory of Sequential Machines, Englwood Cliffs, N.J., Prentice-Hall, Inc.1966.

11. Hotz, G.: On the mathematical theory of linear sequential networks, in Switch. Theory Space Technol. (Aiken, Main, Eds.), Stanford, Calif., Stanford University Press 1963.

On oriented hypergraphs and on dynamics of some discrete systems

Václav Rajlich   (Kurzfassung)[+]

In the early 60's there was a surge of papers dealing with growth, self-reproduction, self-repair, etc., of automata. These notions were often discussed in the framework of the "classical" theory of automata, i.e. theory which deals with automata whose inputs and outputs are considered to be words over certain finite alphabet. In other cases, special frameworks for this purpose were created, namely tessalations, and many results were obtained in this way. However both these approaches had certain limitations and it is now apparent that a new, more general framework, is needed.

In this paper, we attempted to generalize both the theory of automata and of tessalations. The basic mathematical structure used is that of oriented hypergraphs with labeled edges. This structure can be alternatively thought of as a set and some set of relations on it. This structure is well suited for our purposes, namely for its intuitive appeal, immense generality and flexibility, and also for its potential in description of the real world, consisting of interrelated objects.

It is also necessary to represent time and change. For this purpose, we adopted the so-called "productions", which are capable of representing "local" change in a hypergraph, i.e. a change affecting finite number of nodes and edges at any given time. System is defined by an original hypergraph and a set of such productions.

It is demonstrated that Turing machines, context-free grammars, and tessalations can be simulated by systems. Several unsolvability results are derived in this way.

Next a configuration is defined, i.e. a part of a hypergraph with certain properties. Several related and important notions are investigated: interaction, growth, self-reproduction, etc. Several algorithms and complexity estimates are given.

[+] Manuskript nicht eingegangen

EFFIZIENTE ALGORITHMEN

OPTIMALE ALGORITHMEN ZUM TRANSPONIEREN QUADRATISCHER MATRIZEN

Wolfgang J.Paul

Abstract: Eine nxn-Matrix M_o,die aus lauter verschiedenen Elementen besteht,soll in möglichst wenigen Schritten transponiert werden.
In einem Schritt wird folgendes getan:

  i) man nimmt k Zeilen aus der Matrix heraus

  ii) genau aus den Elementen dieser Zeilen bildet man k neue
  Zeilen

  iii) man fügt die neuen Zeilen an Stelle der alten in die
  Matrix ein

Es sei $T_k(n)$ die minimale Zahl von Schritten,mit denen man M_o
transponieren kann.In $[II]$ wurde gezeigt:

Satz 1: $$T_k(n) \geqslant \frac{n\log n}{k\log k}$$

Satz 2: $\quad T_k(k^y) = yk^{y-1} \qquad$ für $y \in IN$

Überall,wo im Beweis von Satz 1 " $\geqslant$ " oder " $\leqslant$ " abgeschätzt
wird,muß bei Algorithmen,die die Schranke dieses Satzes annehmen,Gleichheit gelten.Ziel dieser Arbeit ist,hieraus eine an-
schauliche Charakterisierung aller optimalen Algorithmen zum
Transponieren von k^yxk^y-Matrizen zu gewinnen.

1.Definitionen und Hilfssätze:

M_o sei eine nxn-Matrix,die aus lauter verschiedenen Elementen besteht.
Eine nxn-Matrix M heißt <u>Rearrangement von M_o</u>,wenn sie aus den gleichen
Elementen wie M_o besteht.

$R:= \{M \mid M$ ist Rearrangement von $M_o \}$

Es seien M,M' $\in$ R.Für den Sachverhalt,daß M' aus M in einem Schritt
(wie im Abstract definiert) hervorgeht,schreiben wir: M $\rightarrow$ M'
Eine Folge $D = \{M_t\}_{t=o}^{T}$ mit

  i) $M_t \in R$ für alle $t \in [o:T]$

  ii) $M_{t-1} \rightarrow M_t$ für alle $t \in [1:T]$

heißt <u>Rechnung</u> der Länge T.Die Rechnung <u>transponiert</u> M_o,falls $M_T = M_o^t$.

$\qquad T_k(n) := \min \{T \mid$ es gibt eine Rechnung der Länge T,die M_o transponiert $\}$

Die Zeilen,der Matrix,die schrittweise umgeformt wird,seien von 1
bis n durchnumeriert.

$\qquad z:= \{I \mid I \subseteq [1:n]$ und $card(I)=k \}$

Mit einem Element $I \in Z$ kann man beschreiben,auf welche Zeilen man in
einem Schritt zugegriffen hat.Eine Abbildung $F:[1:T] \rightarrow Z$ heißt <u>Z-Folge</u>.
Ist $D = \{M_t\}_{t=o}^{T}$ eine Rechnung, dann heißt $F:[1:T] \rightarrow Z$ <u>Z-Folge von D</u>,

wenn für alle $t \in [1:T]$ gilt: beim Umformen von M_{t-1} in M_t wird auf die Zeilen mit Nummern $i \in F(t)$ zugegriffen.

Wir geben ohne Beweis die folgenden Hilfssätze an:

<u>Hilfssatz 1</u>: Es seien $x_1, \ldots, x_k \geq 0$; dann gilt

(a) $$\sum_{i=1}^{k} x_i \log x_i \leq (\sum_{i=1}^{k} x_i) \log (\sum_{i=1}^{k} x_i)$$

(b) Gleichheit gilt in (a) genau dann wenn höchstens ein x_i von Null verschieden ist

<u>Hilfssatz 2</u>: Es seien $x_1, \ldots, x_k \geq 0$; dann gilt

(a) $$(\frac{1}{k}\sum_{i=1}^{k} x_i) \log (\frac{1}{k}\sum_{i=1}^{k} x_i) \leq \frac{1}{k}\sum_{i=1}^{k} x_i \log x_i$$

(b) Gleichheit gilt in (a) genau dann wenn $x_1 = \ldots = x_k$

Bemerkungen: i) hier wie im folgenden ist $0 \log 0 := 0$ zu nehmen.

ii) Hilfssatz 2 ist generell für streng konvexe Funktionen richtig ($x \log x$ ist streng konvex).

<u>2.Eine untere Schranke für $T_k(n)$</u>:

<u>Satz 1</u>: $$T_k(n) \geq \frac{n \log n}{k \log k}$$

Dieser Satz wurde zuerst für $k=2$ von R.W.Floyd $[I]$ bewiesen.In $[II]$ wird Satz 1 als Anwendung eines allgemeineren Satzes gezeigt.In $[IV]$ zeigt H.J.Stoß eine modifizierte Fassung:wenn man in einem Schritt auf k Zeilen zugreift und dann alle möglichen Zeilen,die sich aus den Zeichen dieser k Zeilen bilden lassen,abspeichert,braucht man mindestens $(n \log n)/(k \log(3k^2))$ Schritte,um eine nxn-Matrix zu transponieren.

Wir geben jetzt einen direkten Beweis von Satz 1,auf den wir später zurückgreifen.

Jedem $M \in R$ wird eine nxn-Matrix $A(M)$ und eine <u>Komplexität</u> $K(M)$ zugeordnet durch:

$A_{ij}(M) :=$ Zahl der Zeichen in Zeile i von M,die bei M_0 in Zeile j standen.

$$K(M) := \sum_{j=1}^{n} \sum_{i=1}^{n} A_{ij}(M) \log A_{ij}(M)$$

Ist $D = \{M_t\}_{t=0}^{T}$ eine Rechnung,dann nennen wir die Folge $\{A(M_t)\}_{t=0}^{T}$ die <u>A-Folge von D</u>.

Man stellt fest:

$$A_{ij}(M_0) = \begin{cases} n & \text{falls } i=j \\ 0 & \text{sonst} \end{cases} \quad ; \quad A_{ij}(M_0^t) = 1 \quad (1 \leq i,j \leq n)$$

also: $K(M_0) = n^2 \log n$; $K(M_0^t) = 0$

Wir zeigen

<u>Hilfssatz 3</u>: Es seien $M, M' \in R$ und es gelte $M \longrightarrow M'$

dann ist $K(M) - K(M') \leq nk\log k$

Hiermit beweist man sofort Satz 1. Es sei etwa $\{M_t\}_{t=0}^{T}$ eine Rechnung, die M_o transponiert. Dann ist

$$n^2 \log n = K(M_o) - K(M_o^t) = \sum_{t=1}^{T} (K(M_{t-1}) - K(M_t)) \leq T\, nk\,\log k$$

Das ist offenbar die Behauptung.

Beweis von Hilfssatz 3:

M' möge aus M hervorgehen, indem man die Zeilen mit Nummern $i_1, \ldots, i_k$ neu arrangiert. $I := \{i_1, \ldots, i_k\}$ sei die Menge dieser Zeilennummern. Es ist abzuschätzen

$$C := K(M) - K(M') = \sum_{j=1}^{n} \sum_{i=1}^{n} (A_{ij}(M)\log A_{ij}(M) - A_{ij}(M')\log A_{ij}(M'))$$

Da nur die Elemente in den Zeilen mit Nummern $i_1, \ldots, i_k$ ihre Plätze ändern, gilt: $A_{ij}(M') = A_{ij}(M)$ für $i \notin I$

also $\quad C = \sum_{j=1}^{n} \sum_{i \in I} (A_{ij}(M)\log A_{ij}(M) - A_{ij}(M')\log A_{ij}(M'))$

$$\leq \sum_{j=1}^{n} \Big[\, (\sum_{i \in I} A_{ij}(M))\log(\sum_{i \in I} A_{ij}(M))$$

$$- (\sum_{i \in I} A_{ij}(M'))\log(\tfrac{1}{k}\sum_{i \in I} A_{ij}(M')\,)\,\Big]$$

wegen Hilfssatz 1 (a) und 2 (a).

Nun ist $\sum_{i \in I} A_{ij}(M)$ die Gesamtzahl von Zeichen in den Zeilen mit Nummern $i \in I$, die ursprünglich in Zeile j standen. Diese Zahl ändert sich in einem Schritt nicht; d.h. $\sum_{i \in I} A_{ij}(M) = \sum_{i \in I} A_{ij}(M')$

Damit erhält man

$$C \leq \sum_{j=1}^{n} \sum_{i \in I} A_{ij}(M)\log k = \sum_{i \in I} \sum_{j=1}^{n} A_{ij}(M)\log k$$

$\sum_{j=1}^{n} A_{ij}(M)$ ist die Gesamtzahl von Zeichen in Zeile i:

$$C \leq \sum_{i \in I} n\log k = nk\log k$$

<u>3. Eine optimale Rechnung für $n = k^y$ $(y \in IN)$</u>:

<u>Satz 2</u>: $\quad T_k(k^y) = yk^{y-1} \quad\quad (y \in IN)$

Beweis durch Induktion über y:

Eine kxk-Matrix (y=1) kann offenbar in einem Schritt transponiert werden.
Zum Schluß von y auf y+1 verwenden wir

$$M^t = \begin{pmatrix} M_{11} & \cdots & M_{1k} \\ \cdot & & \cdot \\ \cdot & & \cdot \\ \cdot & & \cdot \\ M_{k1} & \cdots & M_{kk} \end{pmatrix}^t = \begin{pmatrix} M_{11}^t & \cdots & M_{k1}^t \\ \cdot & & \\ \cdot & & \\ \cdot & & \\ M_{1k}^t & \cdots & M_{kk}^t \end{pmatrix}$$

wobei die M_{ij} k^yxk^y-Teilmatrizen der zu transponierenden
k^{y+1}xk^{y+1}-Matrix M sind.

Nach Induktionsannahme ist es möglich, jede Teilmatrix M_{ij} in yk^{y-1}
Schritten zu Transponieren, wobei man einen Schritt als das Neuarrangie-
ren von k Zeilen der Länge k^y zu verstehen hat. Da wir aber beim Transponieren von M k-mal so lange Zeilen der Länge k^{y+1} in einem Schritt
verarbeiten, können wir für festes i die Teilmatrizen M_{ij} ($1 \le j \le k$) parallel in yk^{y-1} Schritten transponieren.
Nach $k(yk^{y-1})$ Schritten ist

$$\begin{pmatrix} M_{11} & \cdots & M_{1k} \\ \cdot & & \cdot \\ \cdot & & \cdot \\ \cdot & & \cdot \\ M_{k1} & \cdots & M_{kk} \end{pmatrix}^t \quad \text{in} \quad \begin{pmatrix} M_{11}^t & \cdots & M_{1k}^t \\ \cdot & & \cdot \\ \cdot & & \cdot \\ \cdot & & \cdot \\ M_{k1}^t & \cdots & M_{kk}^t \end{pmatrix} \qquad \text{überführt.}$$

Um diese Matrix in M^t zu überführen, bringe man zunächst die ersten Zeilen der M_{ij}^t an ihren endgültigen Platz - das geht in einem Schritt - ,
dann die zweiten Zeilen etc. Insgesamt braucht man noch k^y Schritte:

$$T_k(k^{y+1}) = k(yk^{y-1}) + k^y = (y+1)k^{(y+1)-1}$$

Durch den Beweis ist gleichzeitig ein optimales Verfahren definiert.

4. Eine Charakterisierung der optimalen Rechnungen zum Transponieren von k^yxk^y-Matrizen:

Schreibt man sich als Beispiel irgendeine Rechnung, die dem Verfahren
aus dem 3. Abschnitt folgt, auf und schreibt man dazu die zugehörige
A-folge auf, dann stellt man folgendes fest: die Rechnung versucht, die
Matrix so schnell wie möglich durcheinanderzubringen bis in jeder Zeile
je ein Zeichen aus jeder Zeile der ursprünglichen Matrix steht. Das äußert
sich in folgender Weise:

(E1) Wird beim Übergang von M_{t-1} nach M_t auf die Zeilen $i_1, \ldots, i_k$ zu-
      gegriffen und in Zeile i_s von M_{t-1} stehen Zeichen, die in Zeile j
      von M_o standen ($A_{i_s j}(M_{t-1}) \ne o$), dann steht in keiner der Zeilen i_r
      mit $i_r \ne i_s$ ein solches Zeichen ($A_{i_r j}(M_{t-1}) = o$).

(E2) Stehen in Zeile i_s von M_{t-1} gerade $x \neq o$ Zeichen,die bei M_o in Zeile j standen ($A_{i_s j}(M_{t-1})=x$),dann stehen in jeder der Zeilen i_r von M_t ($r \in [1:k]$) gerade x/k dieser Zeichen ($A_{i_r j}(M_t)=x/k$);d.h. die Zeichen werden gleichmäßig über die Zeilen,auf die zugegriffen wurde,verteilt.

(E3) Man erreicht,indem man nur Schritte der eben beschriebenen Art ausführt,daß schließlich in jeder Zeile je ein Zeichen aus jeder Zeile der ursprünglichen Matrix steht.

Wir werden nun zeigen,daß diese Eigenschaften die optimalen Rechnungen zum Transponieren von $k^y x k^y$-Matrizen charakterisieren.Aus dem Beweis von Satz 1 folgert man schnell,daß diese Bedingungen notwendig sind:

<u>Satz 3</u>: Es sei $D = \{M_t\}_{t=o}^T$ eine optimale Rechnung zum Transponieren einer $k^y x k^y$-Matrix M_o.

$\{A^t\}_{t=o}^T := \{A(M_t)\}_{t=o}^T$ sei die A-Folge von D.

F: $[1:T] \longrightarrow Z$ sei die Z-Folge von D.

Dann ist folgendes richtig:

(Z1) Für alle $t \in [1:T]$ und $j \in [1:k^y]$ gilt:
Es gibt höchstens ein $i_s \in F(t)$ so daß $A_{i_s j}^{t-1} \neq o$

(Z2) Für alle $t \in [1:T]$ und $j \in [1:k^y]$ gilt:
Sind $f,g \in F(t)$ so ist
$$A_{fj}^t = A_{gj}^t = \frac{1}{k} \sum_{i \in F(t)} A_{ij}^{t-1}$$

(Z3) $A_{ij}^T = 1$ für alle $i,j \in [1:k^y]$

(Z4) Für alle $t \in [1:T]$ und $j \in [1:k^y]$ gilt:
$A_{ij}^t = A_{ij}^{t-1}$ für $i \notin F(t)$

(Z5) $$A_{ij}^o = \begin{cases} k^y & \text{falls } i=j \\ o & \text{sonst} \end{cases}$$

<u>Bemerkung</u>: (Z1) bis (Z3) entsprechen genau den Eigenschaften (E1) bis (E3). (Z4) und (Z5) sind triviale Folgerungen davon,daß $\{A^t\}_{t=o}^T$ und F A-Folge bzw. Z-Folge irgendeiner Rechnung der Länge T sind.(Z4) und (Z5) werden aus technischen Gründen benötigt,um die Umkehrung von Satz 3 zeigen zu können.

Beweis von Satz 3:

Zu zeigen sind noch (Z1) bis (Z3).Die Rechnung D transponiert M_o; daraus folgt sofort (Z3).D ist optimal;zusammen mit Satz 2 folgt daraus: $T=yk^{y-1}$ und D nimmt die Schranke von Satz 1 an.Aus dem Beweis von Satz 1 folgt nun,daß für alle $t \in [1:T]$ gilt: $K(M_{t-1}) - K(M_t) = nk\log k$

Notwendig hierfür ist nach dem Beweis von Hilfssatz 3,daß für alle
$t \in [1:T]$ und alle $j \in [1:k^y]$ gilt:

$$\sum_{i \in F(t)} A_{ij}(M_{t-1}) \log A_{ij}(M_{t-1}) = (\sum_{i \in F(t)} A_{ij}(M_{t-1})) \log (\sum_{i \in F(t)} A_{ij}(M_{t-1}))$$

$$\sum_{i \in F(t)} A_{ij}(M_t) \log A_{ij}(M_t) = (\sum_{i \in F(t)} A_{ij}(M_t)) \log (\frac{1}{k} \sum_{i \in F(t)} A_{ij}(M_t))$$

Nach Hilfssatz 1 (b) gilt die erste Gleichheit genau dann,wenn höchstens
eins der $A_{ij}(M_{t-1})$ von Null verschieden ist.Daraus folgt (Z1).
Nach Hilfssatz 2 (b) gilt die zweite Gleichheit genau dann,wenn für alle
$f,g \in F(t)$ gilt: $A_{fj}(M_t) = A_{gj}(M_t)$

Weiter hatten wir im Beweis von Hilfssatz 3 gesehen,daß für jedes j
gilt:

$$\sum_{i \in F(t)} A_{ij}(M_t) = \sum_{i \in F(t)} A_{ij}(M_{t-1})$$

Es sei $f \in F(t)$.Nach dem eben gezeigten ist dann

$$k A_{fj}(M_t) = \sum_{i \in F(t)} A_{ij}(M_{t-1})$$

Damit ist auch (Z3) bewiesen.

Bevor wir nun die Umkehrung von Satz 3 zeigen,noch eine

<u>Bemerkung</u>: Auf eine Zeile wird im Laufe einer Rechnung i.A. mehrmals zu-
gegriffen.Die Reihenfolge,in der die Zeichen in der Zeile
stehen ist dabei nur vor dem ersten und nach dem letzten Zugriff von Bedeutung.So ist auch eine Rechnung im wesentlichen
dadurch bestimmt,welche Zeichen nach welchem Schritt in welcher Zeile stehen.Die Reihenfolge der Zeichen innerhalb der
Zeilen ist unwesentlich.

<u>Satz 4</u>: Es sei $F: [1:T] \longrightarrow Z$ eine Z-Folge.
$\{A^t\}_{t=0}^T$ sei eine Folge von $k^y \times k^y$-Matrizen.
Für F und $\{A^t\}_{t=0}^T$ seien (Z1) bis (Z5) erfüllt.
M_0 sei eine $k^y \times k^y$-Matrix.

Dann ist $T = y k^{y-1}$ und es gibt - bis auf Reihenfolge von Zeichen
innerhalb der Zeilen - genau eine Rechnung D,für die gilt:
D transponiert M_0, $\{A^t\}_{t=0}^T$ ist A-Folge von D und F ist Z-Folge
von D.

Beweis:

Durch Induktion über t zeigt man zunächst mit (Z1) und (Z2),daß alle
A_{ij}^t gleich Null oder Potenzen von k sind ($t \in [1:T]$,$i,j \in [1:k^y]$). (Z5)
dient als Verankerung.Beim Induktionsschritt muß man die Fälle $i \in F(t)$
und $i \notin F(t)$ unterscheiden.Hier kommt (Z4) ins Spiel.

Durch Induktion zeigt man auch,daß für alle $t \in [0:T]$ gilt:

$$\sum_{j=1}^{k^Y} A_{ij}^t = k^Y \qquad (1 \leq i \leq k^Y)$$

Nun zeigt man leicht

<u>Hilfssatz 4</u>: Unter den Voraussetzungen von Satz 4 ist folgendes richtig:
Ist $S \in [1:T]$,$D' = \{M_t\}_{t=0}^{S-1}$ eine Rechnung mit Z-Folge
$F\big|_{[1:S-1]}$ und es gelte für alle $t \in [o:S-1]$: $A(M_t)=A^t$,
dann kann man D' so zu einer Rechnung $\{M_t\}_{t=0}^{S}$ mit Z-Folge
$F\big|_{[1:S]}$ fortsetzen,daß gilt: $A(M_S)=A^S$.

Beweis: man greift auf die Zeilen mit Nummern $i \in F(S)$ zu.Nun konstruiert
man aus M_{S-1} irgendein M_S gemäß (E1) und (E2) -nach dem oben gesagten
ist gesichert,daß man diesen Schritt ausführen kann - und überzeugt sich
daß $A(M_S)=A^S$ gilt.

Man erhält eine Rechnung D' mit A-Folge $\{A^t\}_{t=0}^{T}$ und Z-Folge F,indem
man mit M_o startet und T mal Hilfssatz 4 anwendet.Wegen (Z3) steht in
jeder Zeile der erzeugten Matrix M_T je ein Zeichen aus jeder Zeile der
ursprünglichen Matrix M_o.Es gibt also zu je zwei Zeilen i und j ein Zeichen,das von der Zeile i in die Zeile j gewandert ist.Da aber kein Zeichen einer Zeile vor einem anderen ausgezeichnet ist,kann man zu jedem
Paar (i,j) das Zeichen,das von Zeile i in Zeile j wandert so wählen,daß
M_o transponiert wird.

Wir zeigen jetzt,daß die so konstruierte Rechnung bis auf Reihenfolge
der Zeichen innerhalb der Zeilen eindeutig bestimmt ist.

<u>Definition</u>: Es seien $i,j \in [1:k^Y]$ Nummern von Zeilen.Eine Abbildung
$w: [o:T] \rightarrow [1:k^Y]$ heißt <u>Weg von i nach j</u> falls
   i) $w(o)=i$
   ii) $w(T)=j$
   iii) für alle $t \in [1:T]$ gilt: $w(t) \in \begin{cases} F(t) & \text{falls } w(t-1) \in F(t) \\ \{w(t-1)\} & \text{sonst} \end{cases}$

Man kann ein Zeichen,das in Zeile i steht in die Zeile j bringen,wo-
bei es jeweils nach dem t-ten Schritt in Zeile w(t) steht.Die Eindeutig-
keit ist gezeigt,wenn wir beweisen,daß es zu je zwei $i,j \in [1:k^Y]$ höchstens einen Weg von i nach j gibt.Hierzu zeigen wir

<u>Hilfssatz 5</u>: Unter den Voraussetzungen von Satz 4 ist folgendes richtig:
Ist $w: [o:T] \rightarrow [1:k^Y]$ ein Weg von i nach j,dann ist für alle
$t \in [o:T]: A_{w(t)i}^t \neq o$

Beweis durch Induktion:
Für t=o ist $A_{w(o)i}^o = A_{ii}^o = k^Y \neq o$

Beim Induktionsschritt hat man wieder zwei Fälle zu unterscheiden:
1.Fall: $w(t-1) \notin F(t)$;dann ist $A_{w(t)i}^t = A_{w(t-1)i}^t \neq o$

2.Fall: $w(t-1) \in F(t)$ und damit $w(t) \in F(t)$; dann ist

$$A^t_{w(t)i} = \frac{1}{k} \sum_{g \in F(t)} A^{t-1}_{gi} = \frac{1}{k} A^{t-1}_{w(t-1)i} \neq 0$$

Es gebe nun im Gegensatz zur Behauptung $i,j \in [1:k^y]$ und zwei verschiedene Wege w,w' von i nach j.Dann gibt es ein $r \in [1:T]$ so daß

$w(T-r) = w'(T-r)$ aber

$w(T-r-1) \neq w'(T-r-1)$

Daraus folgt: $w(T-r-1),w'(T-r-1) \in F(T-r)$.Nach Hilfssatz 5 sind aber $A^{T-r-1}_{w(T-r-1)i}$ und $A^{T-r-1}_{w'(T-r-1)i}$ beide von Null verschieden,und das ist ein Widerspruch zu (Z1).

Wir schließen den Beweis von Satz 4 ab,indem wir zeigen:$T=yk^{y-1}$. Aus (Z1),(Z2),den Hilfssätzen 1(b) und 2(b) sowie dem Beweis von Hilfssatz 3 folgt,daß für alle $t \in [1:T]$ gilt:

$$\sum_{i,j} A^{t-1}_{ij} \log A^{t-1}_{ij} - \sum_{i,j} A^t_{ij} \log A^t_{ij} = k^y k \log k$$

(die Summationen sind von 1 bis k^y auszuführen).Es folgt:

$$(k^y)^2 y \log k = \sum_{i,j} A^o_{ij} \log A^o_{ij} - \sum_{i,j} A^T_{ij} \log A^T_{ij}$$

$$= \sum_{t=1}^{T} (\sum_{i,j} A^{t-1}_{ij} \log A^{t-1}_{ij} - \sum_{i,j} A^t_{ij} \log A^t_{ij})$$

$$= Tk^{y+1} \log k$$

Satz 4 ist damit vollständig bewiesen.Als nächstes interessiert nun die Frage: wie sehen alle Folgen$\{A^t\}^T_{t=0}$ und F aus,die (Z1) bis (Z5) erfüllen? Konkret heißt das: wie kann man (Z3) abschwächen?Es zeigt sich nämlich,daß man beim Konstruieren solcher Folgen leicht in Sackgassen gerät,sodaß man (Z3) nicht mehr erfüllen kann,ohne (Z1) und (Z2) zu verletzen.

Wir geben jetzt eine Klasse solcher Folgen an,müssen aber die generelle Antwort auf die eben gestellte Frage offen lassen.

<u>Satz 5:</u>

    (a) Es gibt mindestens eine Z-Folge und eine A-Folge,die die Voraussetzungen von Satz 4 erfüllen.

    (b) $F:[1:T] \to Z$ und $\{A^t\}^T_{t=0}$ mögen die Voraussetzungen von Satz 4 erfüllen. $\pi:[1:T] \to [1:T]$ sei eine Permutation.Die Z-Folge F_π und die Folge $\{A^{\pi t}\}^T_{t=0}$ seien erklärt wie folgt: Ist $F(t) = \{i_1,\ldots,i_k\}$,dann ist $F_\pi(t)=\{\pi^{-1}(i_1),\ldots,\pi^{-1}(i_k)\}$, und $A^{\pi t}_{ij} = A^t_{\pi(i)\pi(j)}$. Dann erfüllen auch diese Folgen die Voraussetzungen von Satz 4.

Beweis: (a) folgt direkt aus Satz 2 und Satz 3.

      (b) hier hat man (Z1) bis (Z5) für F_π und $\left\{A^{\pi t}\right\}_{t=0}^{T}$ nachzurechnen indem man benutzt,daß jeweils die entsprechende Eigenschaft für F und $\left\{A^{t}\right\}_{t=0}^{T}$ gilt.

5.Literatur:

I   R.W.Floyd: Permuting information in idealized two level storage; Preprint 1971

II   W.J.Paul : Über die Zeit,die benötigt wird,um endliche Mengen umzuordnen; erscheint in Acta Informatica

III   H.J.Stoß : Rangierkomplexität von Permutationen; Acta Informatica $\underline{2}$,8o-96 (1973)

IV   H.J.Stoß : Zur Komplexität von Sortierproblemen; Preprint 1973

EIN TEST DER EINBETTBARKEIT MARKIERTER GRAPHEN
UNTER VERWENDUNG EINER HASH-CODIERUNG

H.J. Schneider/D. Weber

In den letzten Jahren sind eine Reihe von mehrdimensionalen Verallgemeinerungen formaler Grammatiken (Web-Grammatiken, Array-Grammatiken)
untersucht worden. Bei ihrem praktischen Einsatz muß eine vorgegebene mehrdimensionale Symbolanordnung daraufhin untersucht werden, ob
sie linke oder rechte Seiten aus einer ebenfalls vorgegebenen Menge
von Produktionen enthält. Beschränkt man sich auf den Fall markierter
Graphen [8,9,10] (Web-Grammatiken), so handelt es sich um die Frage,
ob der gegebene Graph Teilgraphen enthält, die isomorph Graphen aus
einem bestimmten Vorrat sind. Aus der graphentheoretischen Literatur
ist bekannt, daß dieser Test sehr aufwendig ist. [2,6,11]

Die zitierte Fragestellung zeichnet sich jedoch gegenüber dem allgemeinen Fall dadurch aus, daß die Entscheidung in fast allen Fällen
negativ ausfällt. Der Aufwand läßt sich erheblich reduzieren, wenn
man einen möglichst großen Teil der negativen Fälle vorab dadurch aus-
scheidet, daß man auf der Menge der markierten Graphen G eine Signatur sign(G) und auf der Menge dieser Signaturen eine Relation $\leq_s$ so
definiert, daß gilt

$$G_1 \leq G_2 \quad \Rightarrow \quad \text{sign}(G_1) \leq_s \text{sign}(G_2).$$

Aus Gründen der Effizienz muß eine solche Signatur folgenden Anforderungen genügen:

(a) sign muß einigermaßen einfach zu berechnen sein,
(b) sign muß genügend Informationen über die Struktur eines markier-
    ten Graphen enthalten,
(c) $\leq_s$ muß mit wenigen Maschinenbefehlen zu testen sein.

Die Idee, vorgegebene Strukturen zunächst in Mengen von Unterstrukturen zu zerlegen und diese Mengen dann geeignet zu codieren, wurde bereits in anderen Zusammenhängen angewandt ⌈1,3,5,7⌉. Wesentlich ist
dabei, daß die Unterstrukturen so gewählt werden, daß sie die vorgegebene Struktur überdecken. In dem vorliegenden Aufsatz, der auf der
Diplomarbeit des zweitgenannten Autors beruht [12], werden als Unterstrukturen Pfade verschiedener Länge (k-Pfade) und Verzweigungen mit

verschiedener Anzahl von Fortsetzungen (m-Büschel) betrachtet.

Die bei Berücksichtigung der Markierung große Anzahl der möglichen
k-Pfade und m-Büschel würde immer noch eine sehr umfangreiche Signatur erfordern. Entsprechend [5,7] kann jedoch eine Hash-Codierung erfolgen, bei der verschiedene k-Pfade oder m-Büschel der gleichen Bi-
närstelle eines Maschinenwortes entsprechen und somit beim Vergleich
nicht unterschieden werden.

1. Grundlegende Definitionen

Wir beschränken uns auf den Fall, daß die Kanten der betrachteten
Graphen alle mit dem gleichen Symbol markiert sind, so daß wir auf
diese Markierung verzichten können. (Lassen wir verschieden markierte
Kanten zu, so erhalten wir keine prinzipiell neuen Ergebnisse.)

Definition 1: Ist A ein endliches Alphabet, so verstehen wir unter
einem mit Symbolen aus A markierten Graphen, kurz: A-Graphen,
ein Tripel $G = (K, \rho, \beta)$ mit
(a) K ist eine endliche Menge (Knoten),
(b) $\rho \subseteq K \times K$ (Kanten),
(c) $\beta: K \to A$ (Markierungsabbildung)
Die Menge aller A-Graphen werde mit $\mathfrak{D}(A)$ bezeichnet.

Für die in der Einleitung genannten Anwendungen spielt nur die Markierung der Knoten, nicht aber die zu ihrer Identifizierung dienende
Bezeichnung eine Rolle:

Definition 2: Sind $G_1 = (K_1, \rho_1, \beta_1)$ und $G_2 = (K_2, \rho_2, \beta_2)$ zwei A-Graphen,
so heißen sie dann und nur dann äquivalent: $G_1 \equiv G_2$, wenn es ein
bijektives $f: K_1 \to K_2$ gibt mit
(a) $f \times f(\rho_1) = \rho_2$
(b) $\beta_1 = \beta_2 f$
Die Elemente von $\mathfrak{D}(A)/_\equiv$ heißen Diagramme über A oder
A-Diagramme.

Aufgabe des Verfahrens ist es festzustellen, ob ein A-Diagramm in
einem anderen enthalten ist oder nicht. Wir definieren:

Definition 3: G_1 heißt Teilgraph von G_2: $G_1 \subseteq G_2$ genau dann,
wenn gilt:

(a) $K_1 \subseteq K_2$
(b) $\rho_1 = \rho_2 \cap (K_1 \times K_1)$
(c) $\beta_1 = \beta_2 | K_1$

G_1 soll demnach __alle__ Kanten enthalten, die in G_2 zwischen zu G_1 gehörenden Knoten existieren.

__Definition 4__: G_1 heißt __einbettbar__ in G_2: $G_1 \leq G_2$ genau dann, wenn es ein G_1' gibt mit

$$G_1' \subseteq G_2 \wedge G_1 \equiv G_1'$$

Die Einbettbarkeit entspricht der Unterdiagramm-Beziehung aus [10].

2. k-Pfade und m-Büschel

Wie in der Einleitung erwähnt, wollen wir k-Pfade und m-Büschel zur Charakterisierung der Graphen verwenden:

__Definition 5__: Ist $G = (K, \rho, \beta) \in \mathfrak{D}(A)$, so heißt ein A-Graph

$P = (K_P, \rho_P, \beta_P) \in \mathfrak{D}(A)$ __k-Pfad in G__ genau dann, wenn

(a) $K_P = \{i_0, i_1, \ldots, i_k\} \subseteq K$
(b) $\rho_P = \{(i_{j-1}, i_j) : 1 \leq j \leq k\} \subseteq \rho$
(c) $\beta_P = \beta | K_P$

Solange zyklen- und schlingenfreie A-Graphen betrachtet werden, gilt: $j \neq 1 \Rightarrow i_j \neq i_1$.

__Definition 6__: Ist $G = (K, \rho, \beta) \in \mathfrak{D}(A)$, so heißt ein A-Graph

$T = (K_T, \rho_T, \beta_T)$
__m-Büschel in G__ genau dann, wenn

(a) $K_T = \{i_0, i_1, \ldots, i_m\} \subseteq K$
(b) $\rho_T = \{(i_0, i_h) : 1 \leq h \leq m\} \subseteq \rho$
(c) $\beta_T = \beta | K_T$

Im folgenden verwenden wir die Bezeichnungen

$$P^k(G) := \{P : P \text{ ist k-Pfad in } G\}$$
$$\,^m T(G) := \{T : T \text{ ist m-Büschel in } G\}.$$

Dann gilt für alle A-Graphen

$$P^0(G) = {}^0T(G) =: V(G)$$

$$P^1(G) = {}^1T(G) =: E(G),$$

wobei $V(G)$ die Menge der Knoten einschließlich ihrer Markierung und $E(G)$ die Menge der Kanten einschließlich Quellen- und Zielknoten und deren Markierung bezeichne.

<u>Bemerkung</u>: Als Alternativlösung ist es denkbar, die Büschel durch die nach i_0 hinführenden Kanten zu ergänzen. In diesem Fall kann die Betrachtung von $P^2(G)$ entfallen.

In Abb. 1 sind ein A-Graph G und die $P^k(G)$ und ${}^mT(G)$ angegeben. Dabei sind die Markierungen in die Knoten eingetragen, während zur Knoten – identifizierung die jeweils neben dem Knoten stehenden Ziffern dienen. Man beachte, daß in den Mengen $P^k(G)$ und ${}^mT(G)$ äquivalente A-Graphen auftreten können.

Die Bestimmung der k-Pfade und m-Büschel ist nicht schwer. Speichert man die A-Graphen in Form verketteter Ringstrukturen [13], wobei jeder Knoten auf einen Ring der ihn verlassenden Kanten und jedes Ringelement (Kante) auf den Knoten zeigt, der Ziel dieser Kante ist, so sind die m-Büschel gerade die m-elementigen Teile dieser Ringe, und die k-Pfade erhält man durch Verkettung über die von den Kanten angezeigten Nachfolgerknoten.

Wir definieren auf der Menge der A-Graphen zwei Scharen von Relationen:

<u>Definition 7</u>: Für alle $G_1, G_2 \in \mathfrak{D}(A)$ gelte

    (a) $G_1 \; {}^0\!\leq \; G_2 :\Leftrightarrow {}^0T(G_1) \leq {}^0T(G_2)$

    $G_1 \; {}^m\!\leq \; G_2 :\Leftrightarrow {}^mT(G_1) \leq {}^mT(G_2) \wedge G_1 \; {}^{m-1}\!\leq \; G_2$ für $m \geq 1$

    (b) $G_1 \leq^0 G_2 :\Leftrightarrow P^0(G_1) \leq P^0(G_2)$

    $G_1 \leq^k G_2 :\Leftrightarrow P^k(G_1) \leq P^k(G_2) \wedge G_1 \leq^{k-1} G_2$ für $k \geq 1$

Dabei bedeutet $P^k(G_1) \leq P^k(G_2)$, daß man jedem k-Pfad in G_1 eindeutig einen äquivalenten in G_2 zuordnen kann. Äquivalente k-Pfade in G_1 sind entsprechend ihrer Häufigkeit zu zählen. Analog sei ${}^mT(G_1) \leq {}^mT(G_2)$ zu verstehen.

<u>Bemerkung</u>: Die rekursive Definition ist erforderlich, da die $P^k(G)$ und ${}^mT(G)$ bei festem k oder m i.a. keine Überdeckung von G liefern

Abb. 1

G:

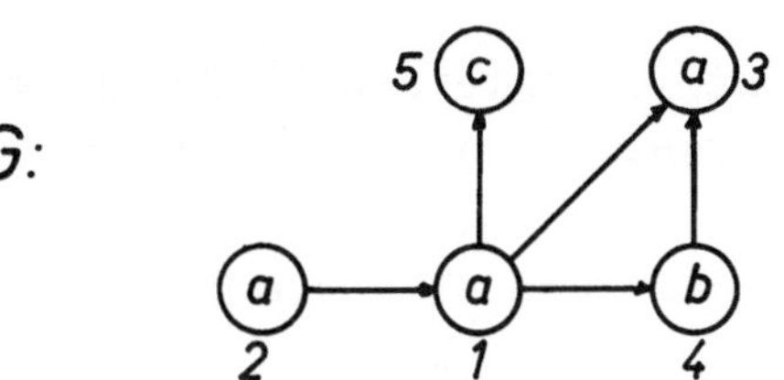

$P^0(G)$:

$P^1(G)$:

$P^2(G)$:

$P^3(G)$:

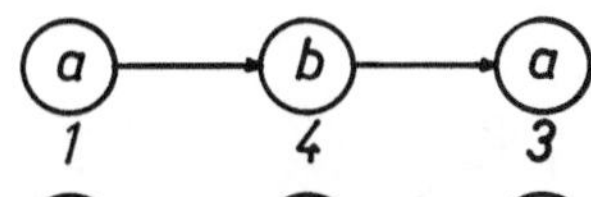

${}^2T(G)$:

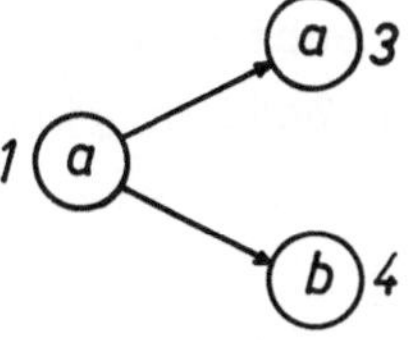

${}^3T(G)$:

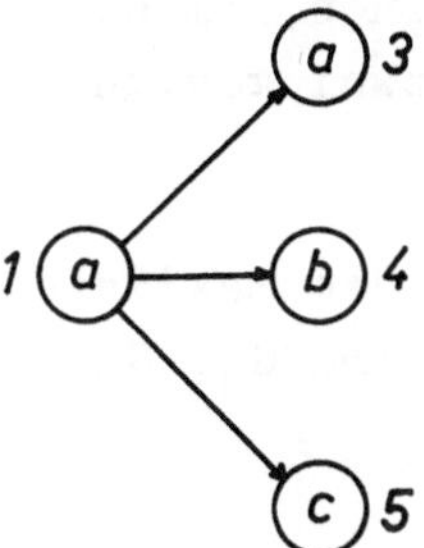

und daher zu schwach sind. (Vergleiche $P^3(G)$ in Abb. 1.) im Fall linearer Zeichenketten liefert $P^k(G)$ stets eine Überdeckung.

<u>Satz 1</u>: Für alle G_1, $G_2 \in \mathcal{D}(A)$ und alle $k, m \in \mathbb{N}_0$ gilt:

$$G_1 \leq G_2 \Rightarrow G_1 \,{}^m\!\leq G_2 \wedge G_1 \leq^k G_2$$

Der Beweis folgt aus der Definition von ${}^m\!\leq$ und $\leq^k$, die also ein notwendiges Kriterium für die Einbettbarkeit von G_1 in G_2 liefern. Soll ein brauchbares Paar (m,k) für den Test bestimmt werden, so ist die Kenntnis der gegenseitigen Beziehungen der ${}^m\!\leq$ und $\leq^k$ zweckmäßig. Die folgenden Aussagen dienen diesem Ziel:

<u>Lemma</u>: Es gilt ${}^0\!\leq \,=\, \leq^0$ und ${}^1\!\leq \,=\, \leq^1$.

Beweis: trivial.

<u>Satz 2</u>: Für beliebige k, $m \geq 2$ gilt:

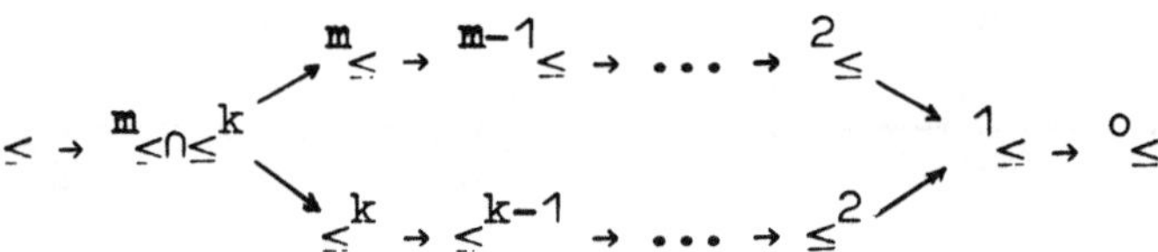

wobei jeder Pfeil von einer feineren zu einer gröberen Relation zeigt.

Beweis: Die obere und die untere Zeile des Diagramms folgen aus Def.7, die linke Seite aus Satz 1 und die rechte aus dem Lemma. Eine weitergehende Beziehung zwischen den beiden Zeilen gilt nicht:

<u>Satz 3</u>: Für alle $k, m \in \mathbb{N}_0$ gilt:

$$ {}^m\!\leq \,\not\subseteq\, \leq^k \;\wedge\; \leq^k \,\not\subseteq\, {}^m\!\leq $$

Es gibt also A-Graphen, die zwar in der einen, nicht aber in der anderen Relation stehen. Zum Beweis gebe man zwei geeignete Paare von A-Graphen an und verwende:

<u>Lemma</u>: Ist G zyklen- und schlingenfrei, p die maximale Pfadlänge in G, q der maximale Grad von G und sind G_1, G_2 beliebige A-Graphen, so gilt

(a) $G \,{}^q\!\leq G_1 \Rightarrow (\forall m \geq q) \,(G \,{}^m\!\leq G_1)$

(b) $G \leq^p G_2 \Rightarrow (\forall k \geq p) \,(G \leq^k G_2)$

Die obere und untere Zeile im Diagramm von Satz 2 sind also unvergleichbar, d.h. es ist i.a. nicht sinnvoll, einen Test nur mit Pfaden oder nur mit Büscheln durchzuführen.

<u>Satz 4</u>: Für alle $k, m \in \mathbb{N}_0$ gilt:

$$\overset{m}{\leq} \;\cap\; \overset{k}{\underset{\not\equiv}{\leq}} \;\leq$$

Der Beweis erfolgt auch hier durch Angabe eines geeigneten Beispiels. Der Satz ist insofern von Bedeutung, als die Übereinstimmung im Fall der Zeichenketten (das sind total geordnete A-Graphen) durch genügend große Wahl von k erreichbar ist [5].

Der Satz besagt, daß der erste Pfeil im Diagramm von Satz 2 eine echte Vergröberung darstellt. Für die übrigen Pfeile ist dies trivial.

3. Hash-Codierung von A-Graphen in (m,k)-Signaturen

Um den im 2. Abschnitt entwickelten Test anzuwenden, müssen wir die Mengen $P^k(G_1)$ bzw. $^mT(G_1)$ mit $P^k(G_2)$ bzw. $^mT(G_2)$ vergleichen. Sei P^k_A die Menge aller über A bildbaren, nicht äquivalenten k-Pfade und ^mT_A analog die der m-Büschel. Dann kann der Vergleich dadurch geschehen, daß man jedes $P^k(G)$ bzw. $^mT(G)$ durch einen Vektor der Dimension $|P^k_A|$ bzw. $|^mT_A|$ codiert, dessen Komponenten eindeutig den Elementen von P^k_A bzw. ^mT_A zugeordnet sind und angegeben, wie häufig dieses Element in $P^k(G)$ bzw. $^mT(G)$ auftritt. Der Nachteil dieser Methode besteht in der großen Anzahl der Komponenten. Mit $|A| = n$ ergibt sich:

$$|P^k_A| = n^{k+1} \qquad |^mT_A| = n \,\binom{n+m-1}{m}$$

Als Alternative bietet sich statt der 1-1-Codierung eine Hash-Codierung an, wie sie auch in ähnlichen Fällen angewandt wurde [5,7].

Bezeichne B^{is} die Binärfolge $(b_1, b_2, \ldots, b_s)$ der Länge s, die an der i-ten Stelle eine 1 und an allen anderen Stellen eine 0 besitzt.

<u>Definition 8</u>: Sind $\text{hash}^k_s: \; P^k_A \to \{B^{is}: 1 \leq i \leq s\}$ und

$^m_t\text{hash}: \; ^mT_A \to \{B^{it}: 1 \leq i \leq t\}$ Abbildungen, so sind Hash-Codierungen von $P^k(G)$ bzw. $^mT(G)$ definiert durch

$$\text{hash}_s(P^k(G)) := \bigvee_{P \in P^k(G)} \text{hash}^k_s(P/_\equiv)$$

$$_t\text{hash}(^mT(G)) := \bigvee_{T \in {}^mT(G)} {}^m_t\text{hash}(T/_\equiv)$$

Dabei ist $\bigvee$ bitweise zu interpretieren.

<u>Bemerkung</u>: Da die Definitionsbereiche disjunkt sind, kann auf k und m hier verzichtet werden.

<u>Definition 9</u>: Als <u>(m,k)-Signatur</u> $^m\text{sign}^k(G)$ eines A-Graphen G definieren wir eine Folge von m+k Binärfolgen $b^0,\ b^1,\ b^2,\ \ldots,$ $b^k,\ ^2b,\ ^3b,\ \ldots,\ ^mb$, so daß

$$b^i := \text{hash}_{s_i}(P^i(G)) \qquad \text{für } i := o,\ \ldots,\ k$$

$$^jb := \ _{t_j}\text{hash}(^jT(G)) \qquad \text{für } j := 2,\ \ldots,\ m$$

Definiert man für Binärfolgen

$$b' \leq b :\Leftrightarrow (\forall 1\leq i\leq s)\ (b_i' \leq b_i)$$

und für (m,k)-Signaturen: $^m\text{sign}^k(G_1) \leq\ ^m\text{sign}^k(G_2)$

$$:\Leftrightarrow (\forall o\leq i\leq k)(\text{hash}_{s_i}(P^i(G_1)) \leq \text{hash}_{s_i}(P^i(G_2)))$$

$$\wedge\ (\forall 2\leq j\leq m)(_{t_j}\text{hash}(^jT(G_1)) \leq\ _{t_j}\text{hash}(^jT(G_2)))$$

so gilt aufgrund der Definition und Satz 1:

<u>Satz 5</u>: Für alle $k,m\in\mathbb{N}_0$ und alle $^m\text{sign}^k$ gilt:

$$G_1 \leq G_2 \Rightarrow\ ^m\text{sign}^k(G_1) \leq\ ^m\text{sign}^k(G_2)$$

Zur Wahl der Parameter sei folgendes gesagt:

1. Es ist weder sinnvoll, m bzw. k größer zu wählen als den maximalen Grad oder die maximale Pfadlänge der betrachteten Graphen, noch m=k=1. Dazwischen hängt die Wahl wesentlich vom Umfang der P_A^k und ^mT_A ab.

2. Prinzipiell können alle s_i, t_j verschieden gewählt werden. (Im Hinblick auf $|P_A^k|$ und $|^mT_A|$ kann dies sogar sinnvoll sein.) Andererseits spricht einiges dafür, ein Maschinenwort zu betrachten. Im wesentlichen hängt die Wahl jedoch von der Fehlerwahrscheinlichkeit ab: Ist nur in ganz wenigen Fällen mit $G_1\leq G_2$ zu rechnen, so lohnt es sich, durch größere s_i, t_j die Wahrscheinlichkeit dafür zu verringern, daß $^m\text{sign}^k(G_1) \leq\ ^m\text{sign}^k(G_2)$ gilt, aber nicht $G_1 \leq G_2$.

Verwenden wir eine Binärfolge B der Länge s und setzen wir voraus, daß ein Element von P_A^k bzw. ^mT_A mit der Wahrscheinlichkeit s^{-1} auf eine bestimmte Komponente abgebildet wird, so ist die Wahrscheinlichkeit dafür, daß ein 1-elementiges $P^k(G)$ oder $^mT(G)$ an einer bestimm-

ten Stelle von B eine 1 erzeugt $1-(1-s^{-1})^1$. Die Wahrscheinlichkeit
für q oder mehr leere Binärstellen ist [4, p.58]

$$\binom{s}{q} \sum_{i=o}^{s-q} (-1)^i \binom{s-q}{i} (1- \frac{q+i}{s})^1 \frac{q}{q+i}$$

Daraus kann unmittelbar die Wahrscheinlichkeit $p_{s-q}^{(1)}$ für genau s-q
besetzte Binärstellen berechnet werden. Enthält $P^k(G_1)$ w Elemente,
$P^k(G_2)$ l Elemente und soll $G_1 \leq G_2$ getestet werden, so ist die Wahrscheinlichkeit, daß $\text{hash}_s(P^k(G_1)) \leq \text{hash}_s(P^k(G_2))$ ist, gegeben durch

$$\sum_{j=1}^{s} p_j^{(w)} \left[1 - (1 - \frac{1}{s})^1 \right]^j$$

Für s = 32, l = 1,...,20, w = 1,...,6 ist diese Funktion in Abb. 2
tabelliert.

Betrachten wir den Graphen G

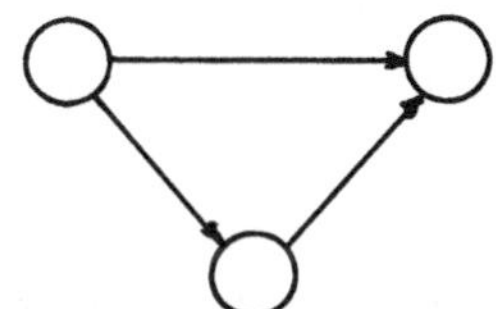

mit beliebiger Markierung, also

$$|P^0(G)| = |P^1(G)| = 3 \quad |P^2(G)| = |{}^2T(G)| = 1,$$

und einen Graphen G' mit

$$|P^0(G')| = 11 \quad |P^1(G')| = 10 \quad |P^2(G')| = 8 \quad |{}^2T(G')| = 5 \quad (*)$$

(was z.B. auf binäre Bäume zutrifft, die G nicht enthalten können),
so ist die Wahrscheinlichkeit, daß der Test ${}^2\text{sign}^2(G) \leq {}^2\text{sign}^2(G')$
liefert:

$$0,0314 \times 0.0253 \times 0.2243 \times 0.1468 \approx 2.6 \times 10^{-5}.$$

Dabei ist jedoch nicht berücksichtigt, daß nicht alle Mengen P^0, P^1,
P^2, ${}^2T$ mit (*) einen Graphen darstellen.

	1	2	3	4	5	6
1	0.0313	0.0019	0.0001	0.0000	0.0000	0.0000
2	0.0615	0.0056	0.0006	0.0000	0.0000	0.0000
3	0.0909	0.0108	0.0015	0.0002	0.0000	0.0000
4	0.1193	0.0175	0.0029	0.0006	0.0001	0.0000
5	0.1468	0.0255	0.0050	0.0011	0.0002	0.0000
6	0.1734	0.0346	0.0076	0.0018	0.0005	0.0001
7	0.1993	0.0447	0.0110	0.0029	0.0008	0.0002
8	0.2243	0.0557	0.0150	0.0043	0.0013	0.0004
9	0.2485	0.0676	0.0198	0.0062	0.0020	0.0007
10	0.2720	0.0802	0.0253	0.0084	0.0030	0.0011
11	0.2948	0.0934	0.0314	0.0112	0.0042	0.0016
12	0.3168	0.1071	0.0383	0.0144	0.0056	0.0023
13	0.3382	0.1213	0.0458	0.0181	0.0075	0.0032
14	0.3588	0.1360	0.0540	0.0224	0.0096	0.0043
15	0.3789	0.1509	0.0628	0.0272	0.0122	0.0056
16	0.3983	0.1661	0.0722	0.0325	0.0152	0.0073
17	0.4171	0.1816	0.0821	0.0384	0.0186	0.0092
18	0.4353	0.1972	0.0926	0.0449	0.0224	0.0115
19	0.4530	0.2129	0.1035	0.0518	0.0267	0.0141
20	0.4701	0.2287	0.1149	0.0593	0.0315	0.0171

Abb. 2

<u>Literatur</u>

[1] A. Brookstein: On Harrison's substring testing Technique
Commun. Assoc. Comp. Mach. <u>16</u>, 3 (1973), p. 180-181

[2] D.G. Corneil/C.C. Gotlieb: An efficient algorithm for graph
isomorphism
J. Assoc. Comp. Mach. <u>17</u>, 1 (1970), p. 51-64

[3] E. Depero: A particular representation of algebraic
structures
Preprints Int. Comp. Symp., Venice, 1972, p. 507-515

[4] W. Feller: An introduction to probability theory and its
applications
2nd edition, Wiley, New York, 1957

[5] M.C. Harrison: Implementation of the substring test by
hashing
Commun. Assoc. Comp. Mach. <u>14</u>, 12 (1971), p. 777-779

[6] W. Knödel: Ein Verfahren zur Feststellung der Isomorphie von
endlichen, zusammenhängenden Graphen
Computing 8 (1971), p. 329-334

[7] W.A. Martin: Determining the equivalence of algebraic
expressions by hash-coding.
J. Assoc. Comp. Mach. $\underline{18}$, 4 (1971), p. 549-558

[8] J.L. Pfaltz/A. Rosenfeld: Web grammars
Proc. Int. Joint Conf. Artif. Intell., Washington,
1969, p. 609-619

[9] H.J. Schneider: Chomsky-Systeme für partielle Ordnungen
Arbeitsber. Inst. Math. Masch. Datenverarb. Univ. Erlangen,
vol. III, No. 3

[10] H.J. Schneider: A necessary and sufficient condition for
Chomsky-productions over partially ordered symbol sets
Lect. Notes Econ. Math. Syst., vol 78, p. 90-98,
Springer, Berlin, 1973

[11] S.H. Unger: GIT – a heuristic program for testing pairs of
directed line graphs for isomorphism
Commun. Assoc. Comp. Mach. $\underline{7}$, 1 (1964), p. 26-34

[12] D. Weber: Ein Test der Einbettbarkeit von A-Graphen
Dipl.arbeit, Lehrst. f. Informatik II, Univ. Erlangen

[13] J. Encarnaçao: Datenstrukturen für graphische Informationsverarbeitung
Gesellsch. f. Informatik, Bericht No. 2 (1971), p. 15-49

SYNTAX VON PROGRAMMIERSPRACHEN

TOWARDS AN AUTOMATIC GENERATION OF INTERPRETERS

G. AGUZZI · F. CESARINI · R. PINZANI · G. SODA · R. SPRUGNOLI

1. Introduction

In a precedent paper (Aguzzi 1973) we defined a formal system (APS) designed, es
sentially, in order to formally define, in an interpretative way, syntax and semantics
of programming languages.

APS consists of a set of structural transformation rules acting on a set of object
strings. The applicability of each rule is determined by examining the structure of
some of the object strings by means of a recursive procedure based on the belongings
of substrings to assigned recursive languages and on the satisfiability of given pre
dicates.

The transformation operated by an applicable rule is accomplished by manipulating
the substrings matching the above mentioned structure, possibly using some given recur
sive functions.

Later we investigated the possibility of using APS as an interpreter writing sys
tem (Aguzzi 1973). The aim of this work was to achieve an universal interpretative al
gorithm whose inputs are the following strings:
a) a description of the syntax of the particular programming language to be interpre
   ted and consisting of a formal description of the used classes (languages);
b) a description of the functions and predicates used in the transformation rules of
   c);
c) a set of transformation rules (APS algorithm) constituting the description of the
   semantics of the programming language being interpreted;
d) a program written in the programming language being interpreted and its input data.

The outputs of such an algorithm are strings describing the results of the appli
cation of the program mentioned in d) to its data.

We used APL as a first approach to the implementation of this system. Obviously
in this context we had to solve many problems concerning, among other things, syntax a
nalysis.

The emphasis of the present paper is just on the description of the algorithms we
defined in order to check the applicability of a transformation rule.

2. Statement of the problem

The main problem concerning APS implementation lies, as above mentioned, in syn
tactic analysis.

Let A be our basic alphabet, L a set of recursive languages on A, B a set of sym
bols disjoint from A and μ a mapping from B into L; a *name* of a language $L \epsilon L$ is a sym
bol $L \epsilon B$ such that $\mu L = L$. Let $B° = B \times N$, where N is the set of natural (nonnegative inte
gers) numbers; an element $(L,n) \epsilon B°$ will be simply indicated by L_n.
A *B-structure* on A (or simply a *structure*) is a word $\alpha \epsilon (A \cup B°)^+$; a word $w \epsilon A^*$ *has the
structure* $\alpha = \alpha_1 \alpha_2 \ldots \alpha_k$ $(\alpha_i \epsilon A \cup B°, i=1,2,\ldots,k)$ iff there exists a decomposition $w = w_1 w_2 \ldots w_k$ such that:

S1) $\alpha_i = \alpha_j$ implies $w_i = w_j$ $\forall i,j = 1,2,\ldots,k$

S2) $\alpha_i \epsilon A$ implies $w_i = \alpha_i$ $\forall i = 1,2,\ldots,k$

S3) $\alpha_i = L_n \epsilon B°$ implies $w_i \epsilon \mu L$ $\forall i = 1,2,\ldots,k$

The decompositions of w into k subwords can be ordered by means of the rule:
we say that $w = w_1 w_2 \ldots w_k$ *precedes* $w' = w'_1 w'_2 \ldots w'_k$ iff

$$\exists i : |w_i| < |w'_i| \text{ and } \forall j < i \ w'_j = w_j$$

where $|w|$ represents the length of the word w.

A decomposition $w = w_1 w_2 \ldots w_k$ for which w has the structure α is called an α-*decom
position* of w; the first α-decomposition of w, in the above defined order, is called
the *canonical* α-decomposition of w.

The syntactic problem is then the following: given a word $w \in A^*$ and a structure α, determine whether w has the structure α.

In this paper we present our solution of the problem and the criteria we adopted to speed up, as far as possible, the answer.

3. The general solution

As a first approach to the problem, we can divide it into two separated subproblems: 1) given a word $w \in A^*$ with $|w|=n$, to decompose it into k subwords, if the structure under consideration has k symbols, and 2) to check whether the k subwords satisfy conditions S1),S2),S3) above. If we have a method to get all the possible decompositions of w into k subwords in the above specified order, the first decomposition satisfying the three mentioned conditions is the one we are looking for (the canonical α-decomposition).

First of all let us count these decompositions:

Theorem 1 There exist $C(n+k-1,n)=(n+k-1)!/n!(k-1)!$ decompositions of a word $w \in A^*$, $|w|=n$, into k subwords.

Proof We are considering also the case in which some subwords may be empty. We proceed by induction, proving that the function $f: N \times N \to N$ such that $f(n,k)$ is the number of the decompositions of w into k subwords is equal to $C(n+k-1,n)$.

1) If $n=0$, that is $w=\lambda$, there exists only 1 decomposition $\lambda=\lambda_1 \lambda_2 \ldots \lambda_k$, so that $f(0,k)=C(k-1,0)=1 \quad \forall k>0$.

2) If $k=1$ (we do not consider empty structures) there is only one possible decomposition $w=w_1$, for every $w \in A^*$, so that $f(n,1)=C(n,n)=1$.

3) If $n>0$ and $k>1$ and $w=w_1 w_2 \ldots w_k$ is a decomposition of w, then $w'=w_2 \ldots w_k$ is a decomposition into k-1 subwords of a word, the length of which is $n-|w_1|$; conversely, to every decomposition of a tail w' of w into k-1 subwords there corresponds a unique decomposition of w into k subwords, obtained adding as a first subword the head of w lacking from w'. Thus we have:
$$f(n,k)=\sum_{0i}^{n} f(i,k-1)=f(n,k-1)+\sum_{0i}^{n-1} f(i,k-1)$$
but since $f(n-1,k)=\sum_{0i}^{n-1} f(i,k-1)$ we have
$$f(n,k)=f(n,k-1)+f(n-1,k)$$

which equals the recurrence formula for $C(n+k-1,n)$:
$$C(n+k-1,n)=C(n+k-2,n)+C(n+k-2,n-1)$$

simply obtained from the well known $C(n,k)=C(n-1,k)+C(n-1,k-1)$.

Obviously, for the first part of our problem, we are not concerned with the letters of a word, but only with its length and in the lengths of the subwords which constitute some possible decomposition of w. If $|w|=n$, for fixed k, a *n-k-vector* of w is a vector $a=(a_1,a_2,\ldots,a_k)$ such that $\Sigma_{i=1}^{k} a_i=n$; it is related, in a 1-1 correspondence, to the decomposition $w=w_1 w_2 \ldots w_k$ such that $|w_i|=a_i$, $\forall i=1,2,\ldots,k$.

We remark that the formula given in theorem 1 could have been derived from this fact, since it is well known (Sansone 1958) that the number of n-k-vectors, i.e. the number of solutions of $a_1+a_2+\ldots+a_k=n$, is $C(n+k-1,n)$.

The order of decompositions of w corresponds to the following order in the set of n-k-vectors:
$$(a_1,a_2,\ldots,a_k)<(a_1',a_2',\ldots,a_k') \quad \text{iff} \quad \exists i : a_i<a_i' \text{ and } \forall j<i \quad a_j'=a_j.$$

We have the following

Theorem 2 Let $a=(a_1,a_2,\ldots,a_k)$ be a n-k-vector and define the n-k-vector $\bar{a}=(\bar{a}_1,\bar{a}_2,\ldots,\bar{a}_k)$:
if j is the greatest subscript for which $a_j>0$ then

a) $\bar{a}_{j-1}=a_{j-1}+1$

b) $\bar{a}_i=a_i \quad \forall i \neq j$ and $i \neq k$ and $i \neq j-1$

c) $\bar{a}_j=0$

d) $\bar{a}_k = a_j - 1$

Then $\bar{a}$ is the first n-k-vector following a in the specified order.

Proof First of all we remark that $\bar{a}$ is a n-k-vector, in that $\bar{a}_1 + \bar{a}_2 + \ldots + \bar{a}_k = n$; secondly $a < \bar{a}$ in that $\bar{a}_i = a_i$ for every $i < j-1$ and $a_{j-1} < \bar{a}_{j-1}$; thirdly, let us suppose that there exists a n-k-vector b such that $a \leq b \leq \bar{a}$; then for every $i < j-1$ we must have $b_i = a_i = \bar{a}_i$; now, it will be $b_{j-1} = a_{j-1}$ or $b_{j-1} = \bar{a}_{j-1}$, since $\bar{a}_{j-1} = a_{j-1} + 1$.

1) Suppose $b_{j-1} = a_{j-1}$; since j is the greatest subscript for which $a_j > 0$, in order that $b \geq a$ we must have $b_j = a_j$ and so $b_i = 0$ for every $i > j$, and this means $a = b$.
2) Suppose $b_{j-1} = \bar{a}_{j-1}$; since $\bar{a}_i = 0$ for $j \leq i < k$, in order that $b \leq \bar{a}$, we must have $b_i = 0$ for $j \leq i < k$, hence $b_k = \bar{a}_k$ and so $b = a$.

The construction given in theorem 2 allows us to construct an algorithm to obtain all the possible decompositions of a word w, $|w| = n$, into k subwords, in the specified order. In fact, we can state:

Theorem 3 Starting with the n-k-vector $(0,0,\ldots,0,n)$ and applying successively theorem 2 until we obtain the n-k-vector $(n,0,\ldots,0,0)$ we obtain all the possible n-k-vectors in the desidered order.

Proof It suffices to show that $(0,0,\ldots,0,n)$ is the first n-k-vector and $(n,0,\ldots,0,0)$ is the last one in the defined order. Supposing $b \leq (0,0,\ldots,0,n)$ we have $b_i = 0$ for every $i < k$ and so $b_k = n$, which shows $b = (0,0,\ldots,0,n)$. Analogously, if we suppose $(n,0,\ldots,0,0) \leq b$, we can show $(n,0,\ldots,0,0) = b$.

The algorithm gives a general solution to our problem, since, given a particular n-k-vector, we can get the corresponding decomposition of a word and then verify conditions S1),S2),S3) by means of a syntactic recognizer for languages of the set L.

This approach, however, is extremely inefficient, expecially in the case that the word w has not a given structure; in fact, we must make all the C(n+k-1,n) decompositions of w and verify that all of them are not α-decompositions of w.

4. An improved solution

The general solution does not take into account the peculiarities of the structure α; for example, if a symbol α_i in α is a letter of the basic alphabet, only n-k-vectors with $a_i = 1$ correspond to possible decompositions of a word w, matching structure α.

Given a structure $\alpha = \alpha_1 \alpha_2 \ldots \alpha_k$, we introduce an *inf-vector* $u = (u_1, u_2, \ldots, u_k)$ and a *sup-vector* $U = (U_1, U_2, \ldots, U_k)$ with the properties:

a) if $\alpha_i \in A$ then $u_i = U_i = 1$;

b) if $\alpha_i = L_n \in B°$ then u_i is the minimal length of the words in L and U_i is the maximal one.

We remark that, from an operational point of view, once the actual length, n, of a word w is known, we can substitute to every U_i :

$$\min(U_i, p) \qquad \text{where} \quad p = n - \sum_{\substack{j=1 \\ j \neq i}}^{k} u_j$$

We can also introduce a *repetition-vector* $r = (r_1, r_2, \ldots, r_k)$ with the property that $r_i = r_j$ iff $\alpha_i = \alpha_j$.

Then we have:

Theorem 4 A n-k-vector $a = (a_1, a_2, \ldots, a_k)$ corresponds to a possible decomposition of a word w, with $|w| = n$, if and only if we have:

a) $u_i \leq a_i \leq U_i \qquad \forall i = 1, 2, \ldots, k$

b) $r_i = r_j \Rightarrow a_i = a_j \qquad \forall i, j = 1, 2, \ldots, k$

Proof In fact, condition a) follows from S2) and S3), and condition b) follows from S1).

Now, we remark that if $u_i = U_i$ the corresponding value a_i is fixed and its presence in the vector a is inessential.

We can now introduce a *reduced* structure b and an associated *weigth* vector p in the following algorithmic way:

1) set p to the empty vector and b=λ; set i=0;

2) set i=i+1 and exit if i>k;

3) if α_i is an element for which $u_i=U_i$, go to step 2), otherwise if α_i equals some b_j in the reduced structure then set $p_j=p_j+1$ and go to step 2), otherwise set $b=b\alpha_i$ and add to p a new component 1, then go to step 2).

Now, let h be the number of symbols in the reduced structure and $m=n-\Sigma\{u_i \mid u_i=U_i\}$; we can consider the m-h-vectors associated with the reduced structure and the corres_ ponding inf-vectors and sup-vectors, and give the modified algorithm to obtain the m-h-vector successive to a given one and corresponding to a possible decomposition of a word w such that $|w|=n$.

Theorem 5 Let $a=(a_1,a_2,\ldots,a_h)$ be a reduced m-h-vector, that is a vector such that $p_1a_1+p_2a_2+\ldots+p_ha_h=m$ and let us proceed as follows:

1) set j to the greatest subscript for which $a_i>u_i$;

2) if $a_{j-1}\geq U_{j-1}$ go to step 4), otherwise set :
$$\bar{a}_i=a_i \quad \forall i\leq j-1$$
$$\bar{a}_{j-1}=a_{j-1}+1$$
$$\bar{a}_i=u_i \quad \forall i\geq j$$
$$\bar{a}_h=[(m-\textstyle\sum_{i=1}^{h-1}p_i\bar{a}_i)/p_h]$$

3) if $u_h\leq\bar{a}_h\leq U_h$ and $\sum_{i=1}^{h}p_i\bar{a}_i=m$ then exit, otherwise set $a=\bar{a}$ and go to step 1);

4) if j>1 then set j=j-1 and go to step 2), otherwise no other reduced m-h-vector exi_ sts.

Then $\bar{a}=(\bar{a}_1,\bar{a}_2,\ldots,\bar{a}_h)$ immediately follows a in the defined order.

Proof The construction follows the one given in theorem 2, and takes into account the conditions given in theorem 4, directly for what concerns condition a) and indirec_ tly, by means of the weigth vector, for condition b).

The algorithm given in theorem 5 improves the performance of the one given in theo_ rem 2) in two directions: first, it takes into account the limitations imposed by the_ orem 4) and, secondly, it restricts the use of the syntactic recognizer to those de_ compositions which satisfy the above limitation.

5. Separation criteria

In the general solution of our problem we have completely ignored the nature of the languages of L; in the improved solution we have used the minimal and maximal len_ gths of the words in each language.

Considering other properties of the languages of L we can still improve our solu_ tion, in such a way that, in many cases, we can apply the syntactic recognizer to a single decomposition and know whether a string has the given structure.

Let $\alpha=\alpha_1\alpha_2\ldots\alpha_k$ be a structure; a symbol α_i is *isolated* or *separated* iff, once the position in the word of the first character of the subword corresponding to the sym_ bol itself is known, it is possible to know, a priori, where the same subword ends.

This definition is clearly related to a left-to-right parsing of the word: let us suppose, for example, that we have already established which subwords $w_1,w_2,\ldots w_{i-1}$ correspond to symbols $\alpha_1,\alpha_2,\ldots\alpha_{i-1}$ of the given structure; moreover let us suppose that the language, the name of which is α_i, is $\{a\}^*$ and $\alpha_{i+1}=b\in A$, where a and b are characters in the basic alphabet, then we are able to isolate or separate the subwords w_i simply selecting all the characters in the string up to the first "b"; if a charac_ ter, different from "a", is encountered, we can be sure that the original string w has not the structure α; otherwise we can go on with our analysis.

A *separation criterium* is some algorithm which enables us to establish, from an analysis of the structure α and not knowing the word w, which symbols in α are isola_ ted.

In order to present the three main separation criteria we studied, we introduce the following terminology: the set of *terminal characters* of a symbol α_i in α is a subset $T(\alpha_i)\subseteq A$ so defined:

a) if $\alpha_i\in A$ then $T(\alpha_i)=\{\alpha_i\}$;

b) if $\alpha_i = L_n \in B°$ then $T(\alpha_i)$ is the set of terminal characters of μL.

Analogously, the set $L(\alpha_i)$ of *leftmost (terminal) characters* of a symbol α_i in α is defined:

a) if $\alpha_i \in A$ then $L(\alpha_i) = \{\alpha_i\}$;

b) if $\alpha_i = L_n \in B°$ then $L(\alpha_i)$ is the set of terminal characters of μL which can be heads of the words in μL itself.

In the same way we define the set $R(\alpha_i)$ of *rightmost characters* of a symbol α_i in α, and, finally, the set $C(\alpha_i)$ of *paired characters* of α_i is the subset of the cartesian product $T(\alpha_i) \times T(\alpha_i)$ of all the couples $t_1 t_2$ such that t_2 may follow t_1 in the words of μL, if $\alpha_i = L_n \in B°$; if $\alpha_i \in A$ then $C(\alpha_i) = \emptyset$.

Now, the three above mentioned criteria are:

C1) a symbol α_i is isolated in α iff $T(\alpha_i) \cap T(\alpha_{i+1}) = \emptyset$;

C2) a symbol α_i is isolated in α iff $T(\alpha_i) \cap L(\alpha_{i+1}) = \emptyset$;

C3) a symbol α_i is isolated in α iff $C(\alpha_i) \cap (R(\alpha_i) \times L(\alpha_{i+1})) = \emptyset$.

Other criteria can also be considered, for example a $C[m,n]$ criterium of this sort: suppose $\alpha_i = L_h$, $\alpha_{i+1} = M_k$ and consider the set $T_m(\alpha_i)$ of the tails of the words in μL of length m, the set $H_n(\alpha_{i+1})$ of the heads of the words in μM of length n, and the set $W(\alpha_i)$ of the subwords of length m+n of the words in μL; then α_i is isolated in α iff $W(\alpha_i) \cap (T_m(\alpha_i) \cdot H_n(\alpha_{i+1})) = \emptyset$. This is a simple generalization of criteria C2 and C3 above, which correspond to $C[0,1]$ and $C[1,1]$ respectively. Note that n must be different from 0.

A partial ordering can be introduced in the set of separation criteria: a criterium C_1 is (*properly*) *weaker* of C_2, and we shall write $(C_1 < C_2)$ $C_1 \leq C_2$ iff for every structure α, if a symbol α_i is separated in α according to C_1, then it is separated also according to C_2 (and there is a structure α and a symbol α_i in α for which α_i is isolated in α according to C_2, but not according to C_1).

For example, it is easily seen that $C[n,m] \leq C[n+1,m]$ and $C[n,m] \leq C[n,m+1]$, and we can give the following:

Theorem 6 For the three criteria C1, C2, C3 above introduced, we have C1<C2<C3.

Proof Since $L(\alpha_{i+1}) \subseteq T(\alpha_{i+1})$ then C1≤C2; moreover, $T(\alpha_i) \cap L(\alpha_{i+1}) = \emptyset$ is equivalent to $(T(\alpha_i) \times T(\alpha_i)) \cap (T(\alpha_i) \cap L(\alpha_{i+1})) = \emptyset$, as it is easily seen taking the cartesian product of both sides by $T(\alpha_i)$; but $C(\alpha_i) \subseteq T(\alpha_i) \times T(\alpha_i)$ and $R(\alpha_i) \subseteq T(\alpha_i)$ so that C2≤C3.

In order to see that C1 is properly weaker than C2, let us consider the structure
$$\text{<number><identifier>}$$
where <number> is a name of the language γ^*, γ being the set of decimal digits, and <identifier> is a name of the language $\alpha \cdot (\alpha \cup \gamma)^*$, α being the set of all the letters.

Then $T(\text{<number>}) \cap T(\text{<identifier>}) = \gamma \neq \emptyset$, but $T(\text{<number>}) \cap L(\text{<identifier>}) = \gamma \cap \alpha = \emptyset$.

In order to see that C2<C3 consider the structure
$$\text{<real number>}_1 + \text{<real number>}_2$$
where <real number> is a name of the language of the finite representations of real numbers, possibly containing an exponent part of the form "E±<number>"; in this case criterium C2 fails for $\alpha_i = \text{<real number>}_1$, in that $T(\alpha_i) \cap L(\alpha_{i+1}) = \{+\} \neq \emptyset$, but C3 succeeds since: $C(\alpha_i) = \{(\gamma,\gamma),(\gamma,E),(E,+),(E,-),(+,\gamma),(-,\gamma)\}$ and $R(\alpha_i) \times L(\alpha_{i+1}) = \{(\gamma,+)\}$ so that $C(\alpha_i) \cap (R(\alpha_i) \times L(\alpha_i)) = \emptyset$.

6. The basic algorithm

Programming languages are usually designed in such a way that some separation criterium generally succeeds; however, sometimes it may fail, so that we have been forced to conceive an algorithm taking into account every possible situation which can arise in the analysis of some structure.

In what follows we make two assumptions: 1) the languages in L do not possess the empty word as an element, an 2) given the structure α and the word w we look for a subword w' of w which has the structure α (that is, we enlarge α to a structure $A_1 \alpha A_2$, where A is a name of the language A^*).

In our algorithm (the basic algorithm we have implemented for APS), we use a three elements stack, that is a stack which, at every moment, has three pieces of informa tion at its top. Let us suppose to have a word $w=t_1t_2...t_m$ ($t_i \in A$, $\forall i=1,2,...,m$) and a structure $\alpha=\alpha_1\alpha_2...\alpha_k$ ($\alpha_i \in A \cup B°$, $\forall i=1,2,...,k$); we proceed as follows:

1) set $j=-1$ and $i=0$;

2) set $j=j+1$ and exit with a negative answer if $j>m$;

3) determine in w the first character t_p after t_j such that $t_p \in L(\alpha_1)$;

4) set $j=p-1,v=-1$ and push i,j,v into the stack;

5) set $i=i+1$ and exit with a positive answer if $i>k$;

6) consider the following cases for the symbol α_i:
   a) $\alpha_i \in A$; if $t_{j+1}=\alpha_i$ set $p=1$ and go to step 7, else go to step 8;
   b) $\alpha_i=\alpha_r=L_n$ and $r<i$, let $q=|w_r|$; if $w_q=t_{j+1}...t_{j+q}$ then set $p=q$ and go to step 7, else go to step 8;
   c) $\alpha_i=L_n$ is separated; then use some separation criterium to isolate the subword $w_i=t_{j+1}...t_{j+p}$; if $w_i \in \mu L$ then go to step 7, else go to step 8;
   d) α_i is not separated, then set $v=0$ and go to step 9;

7) set $j=j+p$ and go to step 5;

8) pop up the stack resuming the old values of i,j,v; if $v<0$ then go to step 2, else go to step 9 ;

9) push the current values of i,j,v into the stack;

10) let $\bar{\alpha}=\alpha_{i+1}...\alpha_h$ be the substructure of α such that α_h is the first symbol after α_i for which: i) α_{h+1} is a character in A, or ii) $\alpha_{h+1}=\alpha_r=L_n$ for some $r<i$, or iii) α_h is isolated, or iv) $h=k$;

11) determine the substring $\bar{w}=t_{j+1}...t_{j+q}$ in such a way that $j+q$ is the least subscript after $j+v$ for which: in case i) above $t_{j+q+1}=\alpha_{h+1}$; in case ii) if $s=|w_r|$ then $w_r=t_{j+q+1}...t_{j+q+s}$; in case iii) t_{j+q} is the last character possibly belonging to α according to the separation criterium; in case iv) $q=u_{i+1}+u_{i+2}+...+u_h$, if we are coming from step 6 and $q=v+1$ if we are coming from step 8;

12) if this procedure fails pop up the stack without resuming values and go to step 8; else store q into the stack as the value of v and apply the improved procedure to determine whether the string $\bar{w}$ has the structure $\bar{\alpha}$;

13) if this procedure succeeds then set $i=h$, $j=j+q$ and go to step 5, else pop up the stack without resuming values and go to step 8.

More informally, we can say that the algorithm uses the stack for backtracking in the following sense: once determined where the analysis of the string must begin, it stores in the stack the current positions in the string and in the structure and uses the v-component as a flag, setting it to -1; then it looks for non separated classes, each time storing into the stack the current positions in the string and in the structure and the length of the substring which has been anlyzed by means of the improved procedure.

When a failure occurs, the backtracking takes place: since subwords corresponding to separated classes cannot be changed in the backtracking if their starting position is not changed, backtracking can take place only from non separated classes, and the v-component in the stack is used to lengthen out the subword associated to the substructure to be used with the improved procedure. During backtracking we can get to the leftmost symbol in the structure: this is recognized by the flag and we move forward the pointer j.

7. The dependence order

The present implementation of APS accepts the definition of the languages in L in BNF (Backus Normal Form), that is all the languages in L are context-free; actually, as we shall later see, for efficiency sake, only precedence languages, as defined in (Colmerauer 1970), are considered; the following considerations, however, are in a large part independent of this last remark.

Let us suppose that there are n elements in B; by abuse of language, from now on, we shall speak of languages with reference to the elements of B.

The relation LdM, which is true iff M is present in the productions defining L, is then introduced among languages; the relation LdipM is the transitive closure of LdM and we can define:

$$\text{LcycM} \quad \text{iff} \quad (L{=}M) \vee ((\text{LdipM}) \wedge (\text{MdipL}))$$

Clearly, cyc is reflexive and symmetric and there is no trouble to show that it is also transitive; then cyc is an equivalence relation on B; the set B/cyc of the equivalence classes [L] of B according to cyc can be totally ordered in several ways in such a manner that

01) $[L]<[M]$ iff $\sim\text{LdipM}$

The relation < is well defined, since if $L{\neq}M$ and LdipM it cannot be MdipL, otherwise it would be $[L]{=}[M]$. If $[L]{\neq}\{L\}$, that is [L] contains at least two elements, the languages in [L] are said to constitute a *cycle*.

From a computational point of view it is easy to determine the ordering <; we begin building the boolean nxn-matrix of the relation d by a simple inspection to the definition of the languages in B; then we use Warshall algorithm (Warshall 1962) in order to determine the boolean matrix of the transitive closure dip, and, from this, we get at once the equivalence relation cyc and the total ordering <, by means of the following algorithm:

<u>Theorem 7</u> Setting $\alpha{=}\text{dip}$, consider the algorithm:

1) set $\alpha_{ii}{=}0$, $\forall i{=}1,2,\ldots,n$;

2) for every not yet marked language L_i set $v_i{=}\Sigma_{j=1}^{n}\alpha_{ij}$;

3) let $M{=}\max v_i$;

4) let $I{=}\{i_1,i_2,\ldots,i_k\}$ be the set of subscripts for which $M{=}v_i$;

5) if $M{=}0$, then $[L_j]{=}\{L_j\}$, $\forall j{\in}I$; else if $M{>}0$ then there is an h for which $k{=}(M{+}1)h$ and there exist exactly h equivalence classes, each containing M+1 languages;

6) set $\alpha_{hj}{=}0$, $\forall h{=}1,2,\ldots,n$ and $\forall j{\in}I$;

7) mark the languages L_j, $\forall j{\in}I$, and go to step 2 unless all the languages in B are all marked; in this case, exit.

Then the obtained equivalence classes are those corresponding to cyc, and the order in which they are constructed satisfies condition 01) above.

<u>Proof</u> We erase every self-reference of languages by setting the diagonal values of α to zero; summing up the rows, means to compute the number of languages on which a given one depends. If the sum is zero, then the language does not depend on any other language (it could have been self-dependent, i.e. recursive, but this is cancelled by step 1); thus, every one of such languages is the only element of its own equivalence class. On the other hand, if $M{>}0$ every language L_j ($j{\in}I$) depends on M languages, and, since the languages on which it depends, but that do not constitute a cycle with it, are not considered because of steps 6 and 7, then it must belong to some cycle. This means that $\alpha_{jj}{=}1$ before step 1, since every language in a cycle must depend on itself too, so that the cycle has M+1 elements; they can be simply found by looking at the j-th row. Once the languages in $[L_j]$ have been eliminated, there can be or not some other L_m for which $v_m{=}M$; if not, the procedure is over, else, by the same considerations, we can find out another cycle with M+1 elements, and so on. Steps 6 and 7 allow us to ignore already considered languages, which could also have been ignored simply erasing from α rows and columns $i_1,i_2,\ldots,i_k$.

By construction, rule 01) is surely satisfied.

Any ordering of B/cyc satisfying 01) will be called a *dependence order*; theorem 7 gives a constructive way to find a particular dependence order.

We remark that a dependence order allows us to consider the languages of B in a linear arrangement, instead of having them simply related in the graph corresponding to the relation (boolean matrix) dip.

8. Minimal and maximal lengths

We are now in a position to give simple algorithms to compute the minimal and maximal lengths of the elements of the languages in B; moreover, for finite languages, we need, as we shall later see, the number of words in every language.

We start defining a language as *infinite* iff it depends on itself or on an infinite language; a language is then *finite* iff it is not infinite. A simple algorithm to determine finite and infinite languages is given by:

<u>Theorem 8</u> Let $I=\{i_1,i_2,\ldots,i_k\}$ be the set of subscripts for which $\underline{dip}_{ii}=1$ and let $v_i=V_{j\in I}\underline{dip}_{ij}$; then L_i is finite iff $v_i=0$.

<u>Proof</u> Let us consider language L_i; if $i\in I$ then $v_i=1$ since $\underline{dip}_{ii}=1$ by hypothesis; in this case L_i depends on itself and hence it is infinite. Moreover, if $i\notin I$ and $v_i=1$, then there exists some $j\in I$ such that $\underline{dip}_{ij}=1$, hence L_i depends on an infinite language and it is infinite too. On the other hand, if $v_i=0$ then for every $j\in I$ we have $\underline{dip}_{ij}=0$, hence L_i does not depend on any infinite language.

For finite languages we can give:

<u>Theorem 9</u> If L is a finite language, there exist straightforward formulas which give the minimal and maximal lengths of words in L.

<u>Proof</u> Let us suppose $L::=w_1|w_2|\ldots|w_k$ be the definition of L in BNF, and $w_i=\alpha_{i1}\alpha_{i2}\cdot\cdot\cdot\cdot\alpha_{ih}$, with $\alpha_{ij}\in A\cup B$. If we set $p_{ij}=1$ if $\alpha_{ij}\in A$ and $p_{ij}=p_M$, the number of the elements of language M, if $\alpha_{ij}=M$, then we have:

$$p_L=\Sigma_{i=1}^k p_i \qquad \text{where} \qquad p_i=\Pi_{j=1}^h p_{ij}$$

Analogously, if we set $u_{ij}=U_{ij}=1$ if $\alpha_{ij}\in A$ and $u_{ij}=u_M$ and $U_{ij}=U_M$, the minimal and maximal lengths of the words in M, if $\alpha_{ij}=M$, we have:

$$(\star) \qquad \begin{aligned} u_L=\min_{i=1}^k u_i \qquad &\text{where} \qquad u_i=\Sigma_{j=1}^h u_{ij}\\ U_L=\max_{i=1}^k U_i \qquad &\text{where} \qquad U_i=\Sigma_{j=1}^h U_{ij} \end{aligned}$$

First we remark that a finite language cannot belong to a cycle, that is, if $L\underline{cyc}M$ and L is finite, then L=M, otherwise L would depend on itself. Hence, if we proceed to the evaluation of p_L, u_L, U_L following the dependence order, and we find $\alpha_{ij}=M$, for some language M, then M was already considered (by O1)), so that p_M, u_M, U_M are known and the above formulas can be directly applied.

If a language L is infinite, the number and the maximal lengths of its elements are also infinite. For the minimal lengths there exist two cases; if $[L]=\{L\}$ and we proceed following the dependence order, formula $(\star)$ of theorem 9 holds, with the restriction that alternatives w_i containing the language L itself must be ignored. If L belongs to some cycle, then we must determine the minimal lengths of the words of the languages in [L] all at a time. Always following the dependence order we can give two methods to get the desired results.

Let us suppose that the definitions of the languages in [L] are

$$L_i::=w_{i1}|w_{i2}|\ldots|w_{ik_i} \qquad \forall L_i\in[L] \qquad \text{with} \qquad w_{ij}=\alpha_{ij}^1\alpha_{ij}^2\ldots\alpha_{ij}^r \qquad \text{and} \qquad \alpha_{ij}^h\in A\cup B$$

We set $\overline{w}_{ij}=\Sigma_{h=1}^r\overline{\alpha}_{ij}^h$, where $\overline{\alpha}_{ij}^h=1$ if $\alpha_{ij}^h\in A$, $\overline{\alpha}_{ij}^h=u_M$ if $\alpha_{ij}^h=M\notin[L]$ and $\overline{\alpha}_{ij}^h=M$ if $\alpha_{ij}^h=M\in[L]$;

in this way $\overline{w}_{ij}$ is a formal expression possibly containing a number and some symbols taken from the names in [L].

Then we get the system

$$(\star\star) \qquad L_i=\min(\overline{w}_{i1},\overline{w}_{i2},\ldots,\overline{w}_{ik_i}) \qquad\qquad L_i\in[L]$$

of m equations in m variables, if m is the number of the languages in [L]. Let us call *primary* every $\overline{w}_{ij}$. This system can be solved by means of repeated applications of the following five rules:

R1) (elimination) A primary can be eliminated from an equation if it contains a term equal to the left hand member;

R2) (substitution) A formal term L_j in a primary can be substituted by the right hand member of the j-th equation;

R3) (distributivity) $\min(x,y)+z=\min(x+z,y+z)$;

R4) (associativity) $\min(x,\min(y,z))=\min(x,y,z)$;

R5) (idempotency) For every formal term L_j : $L_j+L_j=L_j$

these rules, together with the more obvious rules of min and +, can be used in order to operate a sort of Gaussian elimination of variables; in fact, by R1), once the j-th equation has been chosen, the symbol L_j is not present in the right hand member, so we can substitute, by rule R2), L_j by its right hand member in the other equations; now we use rules R3), R4), R5) to reduce every equation to the original form (**), that is a min operation applied to several primaries. In this way, if the system has a solution, we get an explicit value for a language L_h; and going back substituting values we get the complete solution.

This method is very elegant, but it is difficult to implement it on a computer because primaries may be expressions containing formal terms. So we actually used the following:

Theorem 10 Let [L] be as above and, in the BNF definition of languages in [L], let us consider only those alternatives which do not contain any language in [L]. Let $\bar{L}_j$, $\forall L_j \in [L]$, be these "reduced" languages, the minimal lengths of which can be computed using formulas given in theorem 9, and let $\bar{u}$ be the smallest of their minimal lengths. Then, if $\bar{u}$ is the minimal length of languages $\bar{L}_{j1},\ldots,\bar{L}_{jh}$ then it is also the minimal length of languages $L_{j1},\ldots,L_{jh}$.

Proof Let us call u the smallest of the minimal lengths of the languages in [L]; since the reduced language $\bar{L}_j$ is a sublanguage of L_j, $\forall L_j \in [L]$, it is clear that $\bar{u} \le u$. On the other hand, alternatives containing some $L_j \in [L]$ give a contribution of at least u, and alternatives not containing any L give exactly a contribution $\bar{u}$, by construction; thus $u = \min(u,\bar{u})$, that is $u \le \bar{u}$ and we conclude that $u = \bar{u}$. Finally, since this can be repeated for every language $L_{j1},\ldots,L_{jh}$, the theorem is completely proved.

This theorem gives the following solution to our problem:
1) determine the minimal lengths of languages $L_{j1},\ldots,L_{jh}$ in [L] by means of theorem 10;
2) set $[L]=[L]-\{L_{j1},\ldots,L_{jh}\}$;
3) if $[L]=\emptyset$ then exit, else go to step 1.

From a computational point of view, we must remark that the former method requires only one inspection to the BNF definition of languages, whilst the latter requires so many inspections how many are the cycles in preceding algorithm.

Theorems 8, 9 and 10 completely solve the problem of finding the number, the minimal and maximal lengths of the words in the languages in B; we proceed following the dependence order and we apply theorem 9 if $[L]=\{L\}$ (only the formula for u_L if L is infinite) and theorem 10 if [L] contains at least two languages.

9. Syntactic recognizers

Coming back to a structure $\alpha=\alpha_1\ldots\alpha_k$ and to a word w, once a decomposition $w=w_1\ldots w_k$ has been found, we need a syntactic recognizer in order to see whether $w_i \in L$, in the case that $\alpha_i = L_n$, for some $L \in B$.

In the present implementation of APS we use up to six different recognizers, in order to "optimize" the performances of any APS algorithm. Each recognizer is associated to a particular type of grammar, and a language, defined by means of that type of grammar, is parsed by the proper recognizer.

To be more explicit, all the languages used by an APS algorithm must be written in BNF, but according to their nature they are automatically subdivided in:
1) character languages, i.e. those languages L for which $L \subseteq A$;
2) finite languages with less than n_1 words;
3) finite languages with not less than n_1, but less than n_2 words;
4) all other finite languages;
5) right regular languages, that is regular languages defined by means of a right linear grammar;
6) left regular languages;
7) total precedence languages (Colmerauer 1970);
other context-free languages are not presently considered, but we are studying the possibility of introducing a general context-free parser or, alternatively, of using the method proposed in (Mc Afee 1972) to reduce languages to simple precedence ones.

The classification of languages is simple:
1) for a character language L we have $u_L=U_L=1$;
2) for a finite language L we have $p_L<n_1$ or $n_1 \le p_L<n_2$ or $p_L \ge n_2$;
3) for a right or left linear language L we proceed to a simple analysis of the BNF definition of L;
4) for any other language L we build up the precedence matrix, refusing L if the matrix

contains some conflict.

We remark that, if we examine languages following the dependence order, the algo rithm to determine the type of each language is quite straightforward.

For what concerns recognizers, we have:

1) character languages are recognized by a marking method;
2) finite languages with less than n_1 words are recognized by direct inspection in a table containing the words;
3) for finite languages with p words, $n_1 \leq p < n_2$, we enter these words in a hash table of appropriate size and then we use available hash methods as recognizers;
4) for other finite languages we use a finite state automaton or precedence relations, according to the fact that their definition can be considered a linear grammar or not;
5) for right or left regular languages we use the (possibly non-deterministic) finite state automaton that recognizes the language; see for example (Ginsburg 1966, Gri es 1971);
6) for other languages we use precedence relations.

We remark that in the construction of the finite state automaton for a regular language we used character languages as terminal symbols in order to reduce the size of the table of the automaton and to consider in a simple manner cases like:

<identifier>::=<letter>|<identifier><letter>|<identifier><digit>

The language <identifier> is recognized as a regular language and the corresponding automaton contains two states (<identifier> and an initial state) and it accepts two terminals (<letter> and <digit>). Since a terminal character may be present in the state transition matrix several times (e.g. it stands for itself and belongs to one or more character languages) the automaton may be non-deterministic also in this sen se: the successive state must contain all the states which are the successive states for the considered character, in that it stands for itself and/or belongs to one or more character languages accepted as input by the automaton.

References

G.Aguzzi, R.Pinzani, R.Sprugnoli - An Algorithmic Approach to the Semantics of Pro gramming Languages, in "Automata, Languages and Programming" (M.Nivat ed.), North-Holland Pub. Co., Amsterdam (1973)

G.Aguzzi, F.Cesarini, R.Pinzani, G.Soda, R.Sprugnoli - An APL Implementation of an Interpreter Writing System, in "APL 73", North-Holland Pub. Co., Amsterdam (1973)

A.Colmerauer - Total Precedence Relations, J.A.C.M., vol.17 n.1 (1970)

S.Ginsburg - "The Mathematical Theory of Context-free Languages", McGraw-Hill Book Co. New York (1966)

D.Gries - "Compiler Construction for Digital Computers", J.Wiley and Sons, New York (1971)

J.McAfee, L.Presser - An Algorithm for the Design of Simple Precedence Grammars, J.A.C.M., vol.19 n.3 (1972)

G.Sansone, R.Conti - "Lezioni di Analisi Matematica", CEDAM, Padova (1958)

S.Warshall - A Theorem on Boolean Matrices, J.A.C.M., vol.9 n.1 (1962)

IMPROVEMENTS TO EARLEY'S CONTEXT-FREE PARSER

by M. Bouckaert[*], A. Pirotte, M. Snelling[†]
MBLE Research Laboratory, Brussels, Belgium

1. Summary

This paper is devoted to the presentation of a two-parameter family M_k^t of parsers for general context-free grammars ; the algorithms have a top-down structure, in which all the possible candidate parses are investigated in parallel. Backtracking is avoided by keeping track of the stage reached in all parses in a set of "states". The integer parameters t and k describe tests performed on strings of terminals, of length t and k respectively, to the right of the point currently reached in the analysis of an input string. The tests involving parameter k enhance the performance of the parser on grammars with LR(k) characteristics, whereas those involving parameter t are most suited for grammars showing LL(t)-type conditions. However, the use of parallelism enables the algorithm to work on any CF-grammar.

Extensive comparison is made between the M_k^t parsers and algorithms proposed by Earley |3,4| which are the M_k^o members of the M_k^t family.

Theoretical comparisons are made on time bounds. It is shown that M_k^t is always at least as good as M_k^o. When M_k^t recognizes a string of length n as a sentence of some grammar G, then the time needed by the algorithm is at most proportional to n^3. Time is proportional to n^2 for unambiguous grammars and linear grammars and proportional to n for LR(k) grammars. It is also proved that M_o^t performs at most in time n for LR(t) and LL(t) grammars.

Extensive experimental comparisons show a definite superiority in time performances for M_o^1 over M_o^o, M_1^o and M_1^1, especially on large grammars which correspond to realistic examples. Only a single, very peculiar, example was found for which M_1^1 is better (i.e. takes less time) than M_o^1, but it is sufficient to preclude the possibility of discovering stronger theoretical results which would express the superiority of M_o^t.

In practice, as a parser for general context-free grammars, M_o^1 was found much more efficient than Earley's parser and it is used as the syntactic component of a general compiling system built in our laboratory (Bouckaert et al. | 1 |).

2. Definitions

2.1. Context-free grammars

A context-free grammar is a quadruple G=(V,T,P,R) where V is a finite set of symbols, the vocabulary ; T⊂V is the set of terminal symbols, N=V-T is the set of nonterminal symbols, R∈N is a distinguished nonterminal called the root of the grammar and P is a finite set of context-free productions written :

---

[*] Now at the University of Louvain, Louvain-la-Neuve, Belgium.
[†] Now at the University of Lille, France.

$$D_p \rightarrow C_p^1 \ldots C_p^{\bar{p}} \qquad (1 \leqslant p \leqslant d-1)$$

with $D_p \in N$ and $C_p^i \in V$ for $1 \leqslant i \leqslant \bar{p}$.

If α and β are strings in V^*, then $\alpha \Rightarrow \beta$ expresses that there exist $\gamma, \delta, \eta \in V^*$ and $A \in V-T$ such that $\alpha = \gamma A \delta$, $\beta = \gamma \eta \delta$ and $A \rightarrow \eta$ is a production in P. The symbol $\overset{*}{\Rightarrow}$ denotes the transitive closure of $\Rightarrow$.

A sentential form is a string $\alpha \in V^*$ such that $R \overset{*}{\Rightarrow} \alpha$.

A sentence is a sentential form consisting entirely of terminals.

The language L(G) defined by a grammar G is the set of its sentences.

The sentence input into the algorithm will be written $X_1 \ldots X_n$. To describe M_k^t two changes are made :

 - if $h = \max(k,t)$ and if $\vdash$ is a new terminal (i.e. does not belong to V), then the rule $D_0 \rightarrow R \vdash^h$ is added to the set P of productions,

 - the sentence $X_1 \ldots X_n$ is transformed into $X_1 \ldots X_n X_{n+1} \ldots X_{n+h}$ where $X_{n+i} = \vdash$ for $1 < i < h$,

 - the modified input is thus a sentence for the modified grammar.

2.2. Additional conventions

Let α and γ be strings in V^*, k be a nonnegative integer, A be any nonterminal and E a set of strings :

 - $|\alpha|$ is the length of α,
 - $k{:}\alpha$ = <u>if</u> $|\alpha| \geqslant k$ <u>then</u> the first k characters of α <u>else</u> α,
 - $k{:}E$ = $\{k{:}\alpha \mid \alpha \in E\}$,
 - <u>first (k,γ)</u> = $\{k{:}\alpha \mid \gamma \overset{*}{\Rightarrow} \alpha$ and $\alpha \in T^*\}$ is the set of all k-symbol terminal strings which can begin some sentential form derived from γ,
 - <u>follow (k,A)</u> = $\{k{:}\alpha \mid \alpha \in T^*$ and $\exists \beta \in V^*$ such that $R \overset{*}{\Rightarrow} \beta A \alpha\}$ is the set of all k-symbol terminal strings which can follow an occurrence of A in a sentential form of G.

Let β be a string in follow (j,A) :

 - <u>follow (k,A,β)</u> = <u>if</u> $j \geqslant k$ <u>then</u> $\{k{:}\beta\}$ <u>else</u> $\{\alpha \in$ follow (k,A) $\mid j{:}\alpha = \beta\}$ is the subset of follow (k,A) whose elemnts begin with the j-symbol string β.

   Let H be a set of strings (H $\subset V^*$). The following set will often be encountered :

 -   <u>first (k,γH)</u> which is written for $\bigcup_{h \in H}$ first (k, γh).

Remarks : The algorithms to be described ensure that first (k,γ) or follow (k,A,β) cannot be called with a null string γ or β.

Algorithms for computing the sets "first" and "follow" may be found in Wood $|6|$.

2.3. States

For the description of the different steps of the parse the algorithm M_k^t builds states ; a state is a quintuple $\langle p,j,f,\alpha,i \rangle$ where $p,j,f,i \in \mathcal{N}$, $\alpha \in T^k$ and

(a) p $(0 \leqslant p < d)$ is the number of a grammar rule,

(b) j $(0 \leqslant j \leqslant \bar{p})$ points to a definite item in the right part of the rule numbered p,

(c) f $(0 \leqslant f \leqslant i)$ and i $(0 \leqslant i \leqslant n)$ are pointers in the input string ; they indicate that $C_p^1 \ldots C_p^j \overset{*}{\Rightarrow} X_{f+1} \ldots X_i$,

(d) $\alpha \in$ follow (k, Dp) is called the "lookahead". It will be distinguished from the "context" which is the string $X_{i+1} \ldots X_{i+t}$.

3. The algorithm

3.0. Presentation

The algorithm consists of three rules, each of which acts on a state in a state set S and creates $0, 1$ or more new states. The new states are added to S only if they are not already present. S initially contains the state $<0,0,0,\vdash^k,0>$ or $<D_0 \to .R\vdash, 0,\vdash^k,0>$ indicating that parses are sought for the root. Then the states in S are selected systematically and the generation rules are applied whenever possible. The easiest selection strategy consists in processing all the states with the same i, then those with $i+1$ and so on until $n+1$: the algorithm thus treats all the possible parses in parallel, automatically abandoning a subparse for which a state produces no new state. Backtracking is therefore unnecessary.

3.1. The algorithm $M_k^t(G,X)$

3.1.1. Initialization : let S contain the state $<0,0,0,\vdash^k,0>$.

3.1.2. To every state $<p,j,f,\alpha,i>$ in S, apply one of the following operations :

PREDICTOR : if C_p^{j+1} is a nonterminal, then $\forall r$ such that $D_r = C_p^{j+1}$ and $\forall \beta \in$ first $(k, C_p^{j+2} \ldots C_p^{\bar{p}} \alpha)$, if $X_{i+1} \ldots X_{i+t} \in$ first $(t, C_r^1 \ldots C_r^{\bar{r}}$ follow $(t,D_r,\beta))$ then generate the state $<r,0,i,\beta,i>$.

SCANNER : if C_p^{j+1} is a terminal then if $t=0$ and $X_{i+1} = C_p^{j+1}$ or if $t \neq 0$ and $X_{i+2} \ldots X_{i+t+1} \in$ first $(t, C_p^{j+2} \ldots C_p^{\bar{p}}$ follow $(t,D_p,\alpha))$ then generate the state $<p,j+1,f,\alpha,i+1>$.

COMPLETER : if $j = \bar{p}$, then if $X_{i+1} \ldots X_{i+k} = \alpha$, for any $<p',j',f',\alpha',f> \in S$ such that $C_{p'}^{j'+1} = D_p$, if $X_{i+1} \ldots X_{i+t} \in$ first $(t, C_{p'}^{j'+2} \ldots C_{p'}^{\bar{p}'}$ follow $(t,D_{p'},\alpha))$ then generate the state $<p',j'+1,f',\alpha',i>$.

A generated state is added to S in the sense of set theory, i.e., if it is not already in S.

3.1.3. Termination

If $<0,1,0,\vdash^k,n>$ is added to S, then $X_1 \ldots X_n$ is a valid sentence for G, that is, $R \overset{*}{\Rightarrow} X_1 \ldots X_n$. Otherwise, i.e. if there exists an $i \leqslant n$ such that no state $<p,j,f,\alpha,i>$ can be generated, or if $<0,1,0,\vdash^k,n>$ is not added to S, $X_1 \ldots X_n$ does not belong to $L(G)$.

For $\langle p,j,\alpha,i\rangle$ or $\langle p,j,f,i\rangle \in S$	$-$IF $C_p^{j+1} \in$ V$-$T then PREDICTOR	IF $C_p^{j+1} \in$ T then SCANNER	IF $j=\bar{p}$ then COMPLETER
M_0^0	For any ℓ such that $D_\ell = C_p^{j+1}$, gen. $\langle \ell,0,i,i\rangle$	IF $X_{i+1} = C_p^{j+1}$, gen. $\langle p,j+1,f,i+1\rangle$.	For any $\langle p',j',f',f\rangle \in S$, such that $C_{p'}^{j'+1} = D_{p'}$, gen. $\langle p',j'+1,f',i\rangle$.
M_1^0	For any ℓ such that $D_\ell = C_p^{j+1}$, For any $\beta \in \mathrm{First}(1,C_p^{j+2}\ldots C_p^{\bar{p}})$, gen. $\langle \ell,0,i,\beta,i\rangle$.	IF $X_{i+1} = C_p^{j+1}$ gen. $\langle p,j+1,f,\alpha,i+1\rangle$.	For any $\langle p',j',f',\alpha',f\rangle \in S$, such that $C_{p'}^{j'+1} = D_{p'}$, IF $X_{i+1} = \alpha'$, gen. $\langle p',j'+1,f',\alpha', i\rangle$.
M_1^1	For any ℓ such that $D_\ell = C_p^{j+1}$, For any $\beta \in \mathrm{First}(1,C_p^{j+2}\ldots C_p^{\bar{p}}\alpha)$, IF $X_{i+1} \in \mathrm{First}(1,C_\ell^1 \ldots C_\ell^{\ell}\beta)$, gen. $\langle \ell,0,i,\beta,i\rangle$.	IF $X_{i+2} \in \mathrm{First}(1,C_p^{j+2}\ldots C_p^{p}\alpha)$, gen. $\langle p,j+1,f,\alpha,i+1\rangle$.	For any $\langle p',j',f',\alpha',f\rangle \in S$, such that $C_{p'}^{j'+1} = D_{p'}$, IF $X_{i+1} \in \mathrm{First}(1, C_{p'}^{j'+2} \ldots C_{p'}^{\bar{p}'} \alpha)$, gen. $\langle p',j'+1,f',\alpha',i\rangle$.
M_0^1	For any ℓ such that $D_\ell = C_p^{j+1}$, IF $X_{i+1} \in \mathrm{First}(1,C_\ell^1\ldots C_\ell^{\ell}$ Follow $(1,D_\ell))$, gen. $\langle \ell,0,i,1\rangle$.	IF $X_{i+2} \in \mathrm{First}(1,C_p^{j+2}\ldots C_p^{\bar{p}}$ Follow$(1,D_p))$, gen. $\langle p,j+1,f,i+1\rangle$.	For any $\langle p',j',f',f\rangle \in S$, such that $C_{p'}^{j'+1} = D_{p'}$, IF $X_{i+1} \in \mathrm{First}(1,C_{p'}^{j'+2}\ldots C_{p'}^{\bar{p}'}$ Follow$(1,D_{p'}))$, gen. $\langle p',j'+1,f',i\rangle$.

Fig. 1. : predictor, scanner, and completer in the particular cases M_0^0 , M_1^0, M_1^1, M_0^1 .

3.3. Comments.

The principal interest of the algorithms lies in their generality ($M_k^t(G,X)$ can parse any sentence X of any context-free grammar) and in their time bounds, as measured by the number of states generated during the search for a correct parse (see section 4). From a practical point of view, the relative interest of the various members of the M_k^t family is also appreciated by the amount of computation that a particular algorithm M_k^t has to perform when a grammar G is entered and before any sentence can be parsed : the sets 'first' and 'follow' have to be computed a priori in all the possible cases that the algorithm might need. This computation becomes completely unpractical for large values of k and t, considering the amount of time and space required. From this point of view, only M_0^0, M_0^1 , M_1^0 and M_1^1 are interesting. The categories of grammars that these parsers accept is the same as for any other M_k^t ; only the time bounds are affected when t and k are changed. It will be seen in section 4 that M_k^t performs best on grammars not more complicated than LR(max(t,k)) and LL(max(t,k)), and that the best value for k and t are 0 and 1 even if the grammar is not LR(1) or LL(1).

Fig. 1 gives the definition of predictor, scanner and completer for M_0^0, M_1^0, M_0^1 and M_1^1 . Despite their clumsy definition, the tests on first and follow remain simple ; for t and k⩽1, they merely consist in the verification that a given terminal belongs to a computed-in-advance subset of T.

3.4. Proof of correctness

Proving the algorithm correct amounts to proving that $R \overset{\textbf{x}}{\Rightarrow} X_1 \ldots X_n$ if and only if $<0,1,0,\vdash^k,n> \in S$. The proof, which is not very complicated, is omitted here for brevity. It can be found in Bouckaert et al. $|2|$.

4. Comparisons

4.1. Theoretical comparisons

Earley $|3,4|$ suggests a method for computing theoretical bounds for the time performance of his algorithms applied to various classes of grammars. Time bounds are expressed as a function of the length n of a sentence. Thus M_k^0 is proved to work in time n^3 for general context-free grammars, in time n^2 for linear grammars and in time n for LR(k) grammars.

A similar study is made in Bouckaert et al.$|2|$for the M_k^t algorithms. Time bounds are evaluated by computing $\#M_k^t(G,X)$, which is the number of states "generated" by M_k^t when recognizing X as a sentence of L(G) (to "generate" a state is the action of adding a state to the state set or attempting to add one which is already present). The following results are obtained (Bouckaert et al. $|2|$):

(1) *For any context-free grammar G and any sentence X of L(G), if t'>t then*
$$\# M_k^t(G,X) \;\geqslant\; \# M_k^{t'}(G,X).$$

In particular : $\#M_k^t(G,X) \leq \#M_k^0(G,X)$ for any t. This result implies that all the time bounds of M_k^0 are also valid for M_k^t.

(2) If G is LR(max(t,k)), then $\#M_k^t(G,X)$ is at most a linear function of the length n of X.

(3) With a small change in the algorithm, it is also proved that *if G is LL(k), then* $\#M_0^k(G,X) \leq \#M_k^0(G,X)$.

4.2. Experimental comparisons

Upper time bounds are interesting for comparing the M_k^t algorithms with other general algorithms. However these results introduce few differences among the various members of the M_k^t family.

Results of running M_0^0, M_1^0, M_1^1 and M_0^1 on some grammars are displayed below, and marked differences are exhibited. The figures give the number of generated states, that is, are proportional to the time needed by the algorithms to parse the sentences.

Earley's results (Earley |3,4|) are different from our results for M_0^0 : the reason is that his data presumably are numbers of *stored* states while ours are numbers of *generated* states.

EXAMPLES

Sentences	Length of sentences	Numbers of states			
		M_0^0	M_1^0	M_1^1	M_0^1
Grammar GRE :	$X \rightarrow a \mid Xb \mid Ya$				
	$Y \rightarrow e \mid YdY$				
ededea	6	43	81	58	35
ededeab^4	10	51	97	70	42
ededeab^{10}	16	63	121	88	55
ededeab^{200}	206	443	881	658	435
edeabb	6	31	57	40	25
(ed)^{4}eabb	12	101	197	146	89
(ed)^{8}eabb	20	325	645	474	305
Grammar UBDA :	$A \rightarrow AA \mid a$				
a	1	12	20	9	7
aaa	3	37	70	41	26
aaaaaa	6	122	240	159	102

Grammar RR : $A \to xA \mid x.$

x^n	n	$\dfrac{n^2}{2} + \dfrac{7n}{2} + 4$	$5n+3$	$4n+1$	$4n+1$

Grammar ILDF $C \to cbc \mid dAc \mid cAa$

$A \to E$	$L \to M$	$G \to H$	$P \to Q$	
$E \to F$	$M \to N$	$H \to I$	$Q \to R$	
$F \to G$	$N \to P$	$I \to K$	$R \to B$	
		$K \to L$	$B \to b$	

cbc	3	38	24	22	36
dbc	3	36	36	34	34
cba	3	38	38	36	36

Propositional calculus grammar :

$F \to C \mid S \mid P \mid U$ $C \to U \supset U$

$U \to (F) \mid {\sim}U \mid L$ $S \to U{\vee}S \mid U \vee U$

$L \to L' \mid p \mid q \mid r$ $P \to U{\wedge}P \mid U \wedge U$

P	1	46	85	38	24
$(p \wedge q)$	5	119	223	97	59
$(p'{\wedge}q)\vee r \vee p \vee q'$	13	225	380	173	111
$((p{\wedge}q) \vee (q{\wedge}r) \vee (r{\wedge}p'))\supset {\sim}((p'{\vee}q') \wedge (r' \vee p'))$	38	653	1144	490	306
$p \supset ((q \supset {\sim}(r'{\vee}(p{\wedge}q))) \supset (q'{\vee}r))$	26	439	755	318	204

Arithmetic expression grammar :

$G \to bBe$ $E \to T \mid E+T \mid E-T$

$B \to A \mid B,A$ $T \to P \mid T{\times}P \mid T/P$

$A \to i=E$ $P \to i \mid j \mid k \mid (E)$

$bi=i+ie$	7	70	276	176	52
$bi=i,i=(i+i)e$	13	135	548	354	105
$bi(i+(i{\times}i)),\ i=i,\ i=i\ e$	21	216	880	560	163
$bi=i+(k{\times}((i+j{\times}i)+j)),\ i=i+i\ e$	27	299	1229	751	208
$bi=i+(j/j+i{\times}j-j/i+(i-i{\times}i+i{\times}((i/j)-j)-j)-i)e$	43	448	1865	1063	298

Grammar GRE exhibits two kinds of phenomena : a linear growth of the number of generated states with the number of b's in 'ededeab^n' and a cubic growth with the number of (ed)'s in '(ed)^{n}eabb'. For the latter behavior, 8 different values of n were tried and the figures obtained are distributed on the following curves :

$$M_0^0: n^3/6+5n^2/2+22n/3+21 \qquad\qquad M_1^1 : n^3/6+9n^2/2+28n/3+26$$

$$M_1^0: N^3/3+5n^2+44n/3+37 \qquad\qquad M_0^1 : n^3/6+5n^2/2+16n/3+17$$

Grammar UBDA produces highly ambiguous sentences, and it works in a time proportional to n^3. The following curves were obtained by fitting six sentences :

$$M_0^0 : n^3/6+ 3n^2/2 + 13n/3 + 6 \qquad\qquad M_1^1 : n^3/6+3n^2+11n/6+4$$

$$M_1^0 : n^3/6+3n^2+ 26n/3+8 \qquad\qquad M_0^1 : n^3/6+ 3n^2+4n/3+4$$

Grammar RR is a right recursive LR(1) grammar : it verifies the theoretical results for LR grammars, namely, linear growth except for M_0^0. The curves were obtained for six sentences.

The ILDF grammar was constructed to make clear that the context used by Earley within the states may give better results than our use of context in a predictive manner. The need of keeping track of the right context in the states is only harmful when the values of the _first_ - function (see section 2.2) have more than one element, since more than one state is to be created in these situations. Furthermore, when the _follow_ function cannot discriminate enough, testing the lookahead instead of the context can lead to unnecessary completions : if the derivation chain is long enough, we obtain the situation depicted by ILDF. It is, however, a very artificial grammar. The last two grammars listed in the examples are the most interesting from a practical point of view : they are parts of the large grammars one can expect to find in using the algorithms in any practical situation, and were not chosen for particular theoretical aspects. They show very clearly the improvement that can be expected in most situations from the use of predictive type tests, that is, about a five-to-one ratio in favor of the M_0^1 algorithm against the M_1^0 one.

7. Conclusion

The theoretical results of section 4.1 are illustrated by the examples above. In general M_0^1 appears to be the best algorithm, followed by M_0^0, M_1^1 and M_1^0 in that order.

Increasing the length of the lookahead does not, in general, improve the time performance of the algorithm. Instead, the benefit of earlier detection of dead ends among the candidate subparses is often offset by the fact that the number of irrelevant states generated by the predictor increases with the length of the lookahead. In a sense, M_k^0 performs part of its forward tests "a posteriori", that is, the test that a candidate subparse is compatible with the next k terminals in the input sentence is not done entirely during the generation of the subparse. More specifically, every predictor operation initiates a search for a particular instance of a

production rule to be included in the parse tree. At the same time the predictor
makes a hypothesis about the k-terminal string that follows the particular occurrence of the production rule in the input sentence ; this hypothesis is not recon-
sidered before the completer operation ending the search for the occurrence of the
production rule. For any 'realistic' grammar indeed, the rule appears to be :
'the longer the lookahead, the worse the parser'. We have no general expression
of this fact so far.

The M_1^0 parser thus appears to be the best one, except for some special grammars; its states are simpler than those of both M_1^1 and M_1^0, and its _a priori_ tests
are simple and easy to perform.

We implemented another version of the analyzer, in which the test using
"follow" in the completer is replaced by successive calls of the completer itself,
in a recursive fashion. This trick dramatically improves the performance of the
parser, at least as far as space is concerned, but the time bounds become larger for
right-recursive grammars. The algorithm thus gets a hybrid structure, acting still
in parallel when doing top-down predictions, but using the recursion stack for
backtracking at completion time.

Moreover, a new way of processing ambiguities and recursivities has been stu-
died |5|. This leads to still better theoretical bounds but the algorithm is a
little more complicated.

The parsers described in this paper are _not_ very efficient, when compared to
specialized ones, especially designed for some subclass of the CF-grammars. But they
run fairly well on LL or LR grammars, while still being able to parse any CF-G. Our
impression is that this generality is not obtained at too high a cost.

References

|1| M. BOUCKAERT, A. PIROTTE, M. SNELLING, _SOFT : a tool for writing software,_
IEE Conference on Software Engineering for Telecommunication
Switching Systems, Colchester (1973), Proceedings published by
IEE (London).

|2| M. BOUCKAERT, A. PIROTTE, M. SNELLING, _Efficient parsing algorithms for general
context-free grammars,_ Information Sciences (to appear).

|3| J. EARLEY, _An efficient context-free parsing algorithm,_ Thesis, Dept. of computer
science, Carnegie-Mellon University (1968).

|4| J. EARLEY, _An efficient context-free parsing algorithm,_ CACM 13-2, 94-102 (1970)

|5| M. SNELLING, _General context-free parsing in time n^2,_ ACM Int. Computing Symp.
1973 (Davos, Switzerland), Proceedings to be published by North-
Holland.

|6| D. WOOD, _The theory of left-factored languages,_ The Computer Journal 12, 349-356
(1969) and 13, 55-62 (1970.)

THE BOOLEAN CLOSURES OF THE DETERMINISTIC AND NONDETERMINISTIC CONTEXT-FREE LANGUAGES *

Detlef Wotschke

Abstract

The Boolean closure of the deterministic context-free languages is properly contained in the intersection-closure of the context-free languages and the latter is properly contained in the Boolean closure of the context-free languages. The class of context-free languages and the Boolean closure of the deterministic context-free languages are incomparable in the sense that neither one is contained in the other. The intersection-closures of the deterministic and nondeterministic context-free languages are not principal AFDL's.

I. Introduction

It has been known for quite some time that the family of context-free languages properly contains the family of deterministic context-free languages. There are several ways to prove this fact. It has been shown that neither of the context-free languages $\{a^n b^n / n \geqslant 1\} \cup \{a^n b^{2n} / n \geqslant 1\}$ and $\{w\, w^R / w \in \Sigma *\}$ (for any finite alphabet Σ containing at least two symbols) is deterministic context-free (/5/,/3/), and that the family of deterministic context-free languages is closed under the operations of complementation, "Min" and "Max" whereas the family of context-free languages is not closed under any of these three operations (/5/).

The main goal of this paper is to investigate the relationships between the class of deterministic context-free languages, its union-, intersection- and Boolean closures and the class of context-free languages, its intersection- and Boolean closures. Moreover the relationships of these classes to the concept of AFDL's and principal AFDL's will be discussed.

Before we start a preview of the following sections let us briefly recall and introduce some definitions.

---

* The research in this paper was supported in part by the National Science Foundation under Grant GJ-803 .

114

<u>Definition I.1:</u> Let Σ be a finite set of symbols. Then $\Sigma *$ is the free monoid over Σ , $\Sigma^+ = \Sigma * - \{e\}$, where e denotes the empty word.

<u>Definition I.2:</u> A language L is <u>co-context-free</u> if and only if there is a finite alphabet Σ such that $L \subset \Sigma *$ and the language $\Sigma * - L$ is context-free.

<u>Definition I.3:</u> Let CF denote the set of all context-free languages, DCF denote the set of all deterministic context-free languages and let COCF denote the set of all co-context-free languages.

<u>Definition I.4:</u> Let $\mathcal{F}$ be a family of languages. Then $\mathcal{F}$ is <u>closed under complementation</u> if for any language $L \in \mathcal{F}$ and any finite alphabet Σ with $L \subset \Sigma *$ we have $(\Sigma * - L) \in \mathcal{F}$; $\mathcal{F}$ is <u>closed under finite union</u> (<u>finite intersection</u>) if for any finite number of languages $L_1,\ldots,L_n \in \mathcal{F}$ we have $L_1 \cup \ldots \cup L_n \in \mathcal{F}$ $(L_1 \cap \ldots \cap L_n \in \mathcal{F})$.

Let us briefly recall the definitions of Boolean closure, union- and intersection-closure of a family of languages.

<u>Definition I.5:</u> Let $\mathcal{F}$ be a family of languages. The <u>Boolean closure of $\mathcal{F}$</u> (denoted by BoCl($\mathcal{F}$)) is the least family of languages containing $\mathcal{F}$ and closed under the operations of complementation, finite union and intersection. The <u>union-closure of $\mathcal{F}$</u> (denoted by $\sqcup (\mathcal{F})$) and <u>intersection-closure of $\mathcal{F}$</u> (denoted by $\sqcap (\mathcal{F})$) are the least families of languages containing $\mathcal{F}$ and closed under finite union and finite intersection respectively.

Several results in this paper deal with hierarchies of families of languages defined by the number of times the operations of union and/or intersection are applied. We therefore define:

<u>Definition I.6:</u> For any $k \geqslant 1$, the k-union-closure of a family $\mathcal{F}$ of languages -denoted by $\sqcup_k(\mathcal{F})$- (k-intersection-closure of $\mathcal{F}$ -denoted by $\sqcap_k(\mathcal{F})$-) is the set of languages expressible as the union (intersection) of any k or fewer members of $\mathcal{F}$.

In section II we will show that the intersection-closure of the context-free languages is properly contained in the Boolean closure of the context-free languages.

In section III we will see that the Boolean closure of the deterministic context-free languages is properly contained in the Boolean closure of the context-free languages. As a consequence we obtain that there are context-free languages which are not in the Boolean closure of the deterministic context-free languages. An implication of these results for LR(k)-parsers with a finite number of runs will be discussed briefly.

In section IV we will show that the intersection-closures of the context-free and deterministic context-free languages are not principal AFDL's. Some interesting (and surprising) relationships between k-union- and k-intersection-closures of deterministic and nondeterministic context-free languages will be discussed.

In /5/ it has been remarked that the language $\{w\, w^R\, /\, w \in \Sigma^*\}$ (for any finite alphabet Σ containing at least two symbols) is not in the union-closure of the deterministic context-free languages. The results in sections III and IV of this paper will yield two quite different proofs of the fact that the union-closure of the deterministic context-free languages is properly contained in the class of context-free languages.

Section V will briefly refer to the notions of Cutpoint-pda- and Weighted-pda-languages. An open problem will be reemphasized.

II. COCF is not contained in $\Pi(\,CF\,)$

In this section we will exhibit a co-context-free language which is not expressible as the finite intersection of (nondeterministic) context-free languages, i.e. which is not in $\Pi(CF)$. We will see that the language $L = \{w\, c\, w\, /\, w \in \Sigma^*,\, c$ a new symbol$\}$ for any finite alphabet Σ containing at least two symbols is such a language. As an immediate consequence we obtain that the intersection-closure of the context-free languages is not closed under complementation and is therefore properly contained in the Boolean closure of the context-free languages.

Let us first recall some well-known facts:

<u>Theorem II.1:</u> Let Σ be a finite alphabet containing at least two symbols. The language $L = \{w\, c\, x\, /\, w,\, x \in \Sigma^*,\, w \neq x$ and c a new symbol$\}$ is context-free, but not co-context-free and so not deterministic context-free.

<u>Corollary:</u> Let Σ be a finite alphabet containing at least two symbols. The language $L = \{w\, c\, w\, /\, w \in \Sigma^*$ and c a new symbol$\}$ is co-context-free, but not context-free; L is in the Boolean closure of the context-free languages, i.e. $L \in BoCl(CF)$.

In order to prove that $L = \{w\, c\, w\, /\, w \in \Sigma^*\}$ is not in $\Pi(CF)$ we need quite a complicated machinery, provided by /8/, where an infinite hierarchy of intersections of context-free languages has been established. Let us quote a definition from /8/:

<u>Definition II.1:</u> For any integer $k \geqslant 1$, the language $L^{(k)}$ is defined as $L^{(k)} = \left\{ a_1^{i_1} a_2^{i_2} \ldots a_k^{i_k} a_1^{i_1} \ldots a_k^{i_k} \ / \ i_j \in N \ \text{ for } \ 1 \leq j \leq k \right\}$, where N is the set of positive integers and $a_i \neq a_j$ whenever $i \neq j$.

We quote Lemma 1 from /8/:

<u>Lemma II.1:</u> For any $k \geqslant 1$, $L^{(k)} \in \Pi_k(CF)$.

For the following sections of this paper it is important that we mention the following stronger result as a corollary:

<u>Corollary:</u> For any $k \geqslant 1$, $L^{(k)}$ is in $\Pi_k(DCF)$.

Let us now cite the main result in /8/:

<u>Theorem II.2:</u> For any $k \geqslant 2$, $L^{(k)}$ is not a member of $\Pi_{(k-1)}(CF)$, i.e. $L^{(k)}$ is not expressible as the intersection of any $(k-1)$ or fewer context-free languages.

<u>Corollary 1:</u> For any $k \geqslant 1$, $\Pi_k(CF)$ is properly contained in $\Pi_{(k+1)}(CF)$.

Thus the following hierarchy has been established in /8/:

$$CF \subsetneq \Pi_2(CF) \subsetneq \ldots \subsetneq \Pi_k(CF) \subsetneq \Pi_{(k+1)}(CF) \subsetneq \ldots \subsetneq \Pi(CF) .$$

The proof of the above theorem is quite complicated and uses facts about bounded context-free languages (cf. /4/) and dimensions of affine manifolds. For the remaining sections of this paper we state the following two immediate results as corollaries:

<u>Corollary 2:</u> For any $k \geqslant 2$, $L^{(k)}$ is not a member of $\Pi_{(k-1)}(DCF)$.

<u>Corollary 3:</u> For any $k \geqslant 1$, $\Pi_k(DCF)$ is properly contained in $\Pi_{(k+1)}(DCF)$.

Hence we obtain the following infinite hierarchy:

$$DCF \subsetneq \Pi_2(DCF) \subsetneq \ldots \subsetneq \Pi_k(DCF) \subsetneq \Pi_{(k+1)}(DCF) \subsetneq \ldots \subsetneq \Pi(DCF) .$$

Clearly $DCF \subsetneq CF$. The immediate question arises whether there is any k such that $\Pi_k(DCF) = \Pi_k(CF)$. Later (in section IV) we will see that the answer is no. More strongly we will see that for any $k \geqslant 1$ $\Pi_k(\sqcup(DCF)) \subsetneq \Pi_k(CF)$. But strangely enough, for any $k \geqslant 1$, $\Pi_k(DCF)$ is not contained in $\Pi_n(CF)$ for any $n < k$.

Let us define the following language:

<u>Definition II.2:</u> For any integer $k \geqslant 1$, the language $L_c^{(k)}$ is defined
as $\quad L_c^{(k)} = \left\{ a_1^{i_1} a_2^{i_2} \ldots a_k^{i_k}\, c\, a_1^{i_1} a_2^{i_2} \ldots a_k^{i_k} \;/\; i_j \in \mathbb{N} \text{ for } 1 \leq j \leq k \right\}$,
where $a_i \neq a_j$ whenever $i \neq j$ and $c \neq a_i$ for $1 \leq i \leq k$.

The following lemma is obvious:

<u>Lemma II.2:</u> For any $k \geqslant 1$, $L_c^{(k)}$ is a member of $\bigsqcap_k(CF)$ and more
strongly $L_c^{(k)}$ is a member of $\bigsqcap_k(DCF)$.

Extending and simulating the proof for theorem 8 in /8/ we
obtain:

<u>Theorem II.3:</u> For any $k \geqslant 2$, $L_c^{(k)} \notin \bigsqcap_{(k-1)}(CF)$ and therefore
$\qquad L_c^{(k)} \notin \bigsqcap_{(k-1)}(DCF)$.

Using this last theorem we can prove:

<u>Theorem II.4:</u> For any finite alphabet Σ containing at least two sym-
bols, the language $L = \left\{ w\, c\, w \;/\; w \in \Sigma^* \text{ and } c \text{ a new symbol} \right\}$ is not
contained in the intersection-closure of the context-free languages,
i.e. $L \notin \bigsqcap(CF)$ and therefore $L \notin \bigsqcap(DCF)$.

The proof merely uses Theorem II.3 and the fact that for any k
$\bigsqcap_k(CF)$ is closed under inverse homomorphism and intersection with
regular sets. The following three consequences are important enough to
state as corollaries:

<u>Corollary 1:</u> COCF is not contained in $\bigsqcap(CF)$.

<u>Corollary 2:</u> $\bigsqcap(CF)$, which is closed under finite union and inter-
section, is not closed under complementation.

<u>Corollary 3:</u> $\bigsqcap(CF)$ is properly contained in $BoCl(CF)$.

III. <u>BoCl(DCF) is properly contained in BoCl(CF)</u>

In this section we will prove that the Boolean closure of the deterministic context-free languages is properly contained in the intersection-closure of the context-free languages and thus is properly contained in the Boolean closure of the context-free languages. As a consequence we obtain that the union-closure of the deterministic context-
free languages is properly contained in the class of context-free languages. Furthermore there are context-free languages, e.g. for any finite alphabet Σ with at least two symbols the following language

$\{$ w c x $/$ w, x $\in \Sigma^*$, w $\neq$ x and c a new symbol $\}$, which are not in the Boolean closure of the deterministic context-free languages. A practical application for LR(k)-compilers with a finite number of runs will be discussed briefly.

The class of deterministic context-free languages is closed under complementation. So we obtain the following lemma:

<u>Lemma III.1:</u> $\text{BoCl(DCF)} = \sqcap (\sqcup (\text{DCF}))$ and
$\text{BoCl(DCF)} = \sqcup (\sqcap (\text{DCF}))$.

<u>Remark:</u> Since $\sqcup(\text{DCF}) \subsetneq \text{BoCl(DCF)}$ (because of $\{ a^n b^n c^n / n \geqslant 1 \}$), $\sqcap(\text{DCF})$ is properly contained in BoCl (DCF) .

Since the class of context-free languages is closed under union clearly $\sqcup$(DCF) is contained in CF. Hence we obtain:

<u>Lemma III.2:</u> BoCl(DCF) is contained in $\sqcap$(CF) .

BoCl(DCF) is a Boolean Algebra whereas $\sqcap$(CF) is not. Therefore we have:

<u>Theorem III.1:</u> The Boolean closure of the deterministic context-free languages is properly contained in the intersection-closure and hence in the Boolean closure of the context-free languages.

Combining Lemma III.1 and Theorem III.1 we state as a corollary:

<u>Corollary:</u> The union-closure of the deterministic context-free languages is properly contained in the class of context-free languages.

The immediate question arises whether the class of context-free languages is contained in the Boolean closure of the deterministic context-free languages. The answer is "no" by the following reasons: Since the language $L_1 = \{$ w c w $/$ w $\in \Sigma^* \}$ (for any finite alphabet Σ containing at least two symbols) is not a member of $\sqcap$(CF) it is also not a member of BoCl(DCF) and hence the context-free language $L_2 = \{$ w c x $/$ w $\neq$ x and w, x $\in \Sigma^* \}$ is also not a member of BoCl(DCF). Therefore CF is not contained in BoCl(DCF). On the other hand clearly BoCl(DCF) is not contained in CF. Let us state this fact as a theorem:

<u>Theorem III.2:</u> The class of context-free languages and the Boolean closure of the deterministic context-free languages are incomparable.

It is known that the class of deterministic context-free languages and the class of LR(k) languages are identical (/7/). The languages recognized by a LR(k)-parser (-compiler) with a finite number of runs is defined as the finite union and/or intersection of the languages recognized in each single run. Since $BoCl(DCF) = \sqcap (\sqcup (DCF))$ the above results show that e.g. programming languages which -vaguely speaking- contain a "w c w"- or "w c x"-structure cannot be compiled by any LR(k) - compiler with any finite number of runs.

IV. $\sqcap(DCF)$ and $\sqcap(CF)$ are not principal AFDL's

In this section we will give an alternative proof of the fact that $\sqcup(DCF)$ is properly contained in CF, which does not depend on the fact that $\{w \ c \ w \ / \ w \in \Sigma^*\}$ is not in $\sqcap(CF)$, but merely uses an immediate result from section II and a result by S.A.Greibach (/6/). Moreover we will see that $\sqcap(DCF)$ and $\sqcap(CF)$ are not principal AFDL's.

The notion of an Abstract Family of Deterministic Languages (AFDL) has been suggested by Chandler (/2/) as a model for classes of deterministic automata. Let us recall the definition of an AFDL:

<u>Definition IV.1:</u> An <u>AFDL</u> is a nonempty family of languages closed under inverse gsm mappings, marked union, marked star and removal of endmarkers. The least AFDL containing L is denoted by $\mathcal{F}_d(L)$ and is called a <u>principal</u> AFDL, L is called a <u>generator</u> of $\mathcal{F}_d(L)$.

For the notions of <u>inverse gsm mappings</u>, <u>marked union</u>, <u>marked star</u> and <u>removal of endmarkers</u> confer /2/,/4/ and /6/.

<u>Definition IV.2:</u> A <u>restricted AFDL</u> (ReAFDL) is an AFDL which is closed under inverse gsm mappings, marked union and removal of endmarkers.

It is obvious that:

<u>Lemma IV.1:</u> For any $k \geqslant 1$, $\sqcup_k(DCF)$ is a ReAFDL.

Using Corollary 3 to Theorem II.2 we can prove:

<u>Lemma IV.2:</u> For any $k \geqslant 1$, $\sqcup_k(DCF)$ is properly contained in $\sqcup_{(k+1)}(DCF)$.

Hence $\sqcup(DCF)$ is equal to the union of a strictly increasing chain of ReAFDL's. It is now easy to prove:

<u>Theorem IV.1:</u> $\sqcup(DCF)$ is not a principal ReAFDL.

S.A.Greibach (/6/) has shown that CF is a principal AFDL and more strongly is a principal ReAFDL. So we have once again:

<u>Corollary:</u> $\sqcup$(DCF) is properly contained in CF.

We have seen in section II that for any $k \geqslant 1$ $\sqcap_k$(DCF) is properly contained in $\sqcap_{(k+1)}$(DCF) and $\sqcap_k$(CF) is properly contained in $\sqcap_{(k+1)}$(CF). DCF and CF are both AFDL's. Therefore (by a result of Chandler (/2/)) $\sqcap_k$(DCF) and $\sqcap_k$(CF) are AFDL's for any $k \geqslant 1$. Hence $\sqcap$(DCF) and $\sqcap$(CF) are equal to the union of strictly ascending chains of AFDL's. Therefore we can prove:

<u>Theorem IV.2:</u> The intersection-closures of the deterministic context-free languages and the context-free languages are not principal AFDL's.

We have seen in section III that $BoCl(DCF) = \sqcap(\sqcup(DCF))$ is properly contained in $\sqcap$(CF). Therefore:

<u>Lemma IV.3:</u> For any $k \geqslant 1$, $\sqcap_k(\sqcup(DCF))$ is properly contained in $\sqcap_k$(CF) and hence $\sqcap_k$(DCF) is properly contained in $\sqcap_k$(CF).

With respect to the last lemma it is important to mention that although $BoCl(DCF) \subsetneq \sqcap$(CF), $BoCl(DCF)$ is not contained in $\sqcap_k$(CF) and $\sqcap$(DCF) is not contained in $\sqcap_k$(CF) for any k . This illustrates a strange and probably unexpected relationship between the intersection-closure and Boolean closure of the deterministic context-free languages on one side and the intersection-closure of the context-free languages on the other.

V. Conclusion and an open problem

In /9/ the notions of Cutpoint-pda-languages and Weighted-pda-languages have been introduced. Without going into any details let us briefly recall from /9/ that the class of Cutpoint-pda-languages is contained in the class of Weighted-pda-languages and that the latter is contained in the Boolean closure of the context-free languages. It is an open problem whether the last sentence still holds if we replace "contained" by "properly contained". It can easily be seen that both the Cutpoint-pda-languages and Weighted-pda-languages are not contained in the intersection-closure of the context-free languages. It is an open problem whether the intersection-closure of the context-free languages is contained (and then it would be properly contained) in the class of Cutpoint-pda- and/or Weighted-pda-languages.

It seems appropriate to reemphasize an old problem. The family Q of quasi-realtime languages is equal to $\mathcal{H}(\Pi_3(CF))$, where $\mathcal{H}(\Pi_3(CF))$ denotes the closure of $\Pi_3(CF)$ under length-preserving homomorphism, and Q is also equal to $\mathcal{H}(\Pi(CF))$ (/1/). We have seen that $\Pi(CF)$ is not a principal AFDL and S.A.Greibach (/6/) has shown that $Q = \mathcal{H}(\Pi (CF))$ is a principal AFDL. It is an open question whether $Q = \mathcal{H}(\Pi_2(CF))$. With respect to the results in this paper this problem becomes even more interesting since - intuitively speaking - the "$\mathcal{H}$-operation" breaks down the infinite hierarchy $CF \subsetneq \ldots \ldots \subsetneq \Pi_k(CF) \subsetneq \Pi_{(k+1)}(CF) \subsetneq \ldots \subsetneq \Pi(CF)$ to $\mathcal{H}(\Pi(CF)) = \mathcal{H}(\Pi_3(CF))$. If "$\mathcal{H}$" is so powerful why can't we break down $\mathcal{H}(\Pi(CF))$ to $\mathcal{H}(\Pi_2(CF))$, and if we cannot _why_ has "$\mathcal{H}$" to stop at the point $\mathcal{H}(\Pi(CF)) = \mathcal{H}(\Pi_3(CF))$?

<u>Acknowledgement:</u> I wish to thank Professor Sheila A. Greibach for several helpful discussions.

<u>REFERENCES</u>

/1/ Book, R.V. and Greibach, S.A., "Quasi-Realtime Languages", <u>Mathematical Systems Theory</u>, 4 (1970), 97 - 111.

/2/ Chandler, W.J., "Abstract Families of Deterministic Languages", SDC Technical Report, TM-738/052/00, Santa Monica, California, (1969).

/3/ Cole, S.N., "Deterministic Pushdown Store Machines and Real-Time Computation", <u>JACM</u>, 18 (1971), 306 - 328.

/4/ Ginsburg, S., <u>The Mathematical Theory of Context-Free Languages</u>, McGraw-Hill, New York, (1966).

/5/ Ginsburg, S. and Greibach, S.A., "Deterministic Context-Free Languages", <u>Information and Control</u>, 9 (1966), 602 - 648.

/6/ Greibach, S.A., "Jump PDA's, Deterministic Context-Free Languages, Principal AFDL's and Polynomial Time Recognition", <u>Proceedings of Fifth Annual ACM Symposium on Theory of Computing</u>, Austin, Texas, 1973, 20 - 28.

/7/ Knuth, D.E., "On the Tranlation of Languages from Left to Right", <u>Information and Control</u>, 8 (1965), 607 - 639.

/8/ Liu, L.Y. and Weiner, P., "An Infinite Hierarchy of Intersections of Context-Free Languages", <u>Mathematical Systems Theory</u>, 7 (1973).

/9/ Wotschke, D., "A Characterisation of Boolean Closures of Families of Languages", will appear in <u>Lecture Notes in Computer Science</u>, Springer-Verlag, New York, (1973).

SEMANTIK VON PROGRAMMIERSPRACHEN

EINE THEORIE DER SEMANTIK VON

PROGRAMMIERSPRACHEN

Herbert Kopp

Einleitung:

Die bisher bekannten Ansätze zu einer Theorie der Programmiersprachen beachten oft nicht in genügendem Maße die Wechselbeziehungen, die zwischen Programm und Daten während der Interpretation bestehen. Dies führt dazu, daß sich manche Programmiertechniken, wie zum Beispiel Laufanweisungen oder dynamische Datenstrukturen im Rahmen dieser Theorien nicht oder nur schwer darstellen lassen.

Im folgenden soll nun ein Semantikbegriff entwickelt werden, der sich auch zur Beschreibung komplizierterer Programmiertechniken eignet. Wir behandeln dabei Programm und Daten weitgehend gleich, was insbesondere Programmodifikationen während der Rechnung zuläßt. Die Semantik eines solchen aus einem Programmteil, einem Datenteil und einem Organisationsteil bestehenden Programmiersystems fassen wir als eine mathematische Maschine im Sinne der Automatentheorie auf.

Zunächst untersuchen wir einen Teilaspekt der Semantik genauer, nämlich die Interpretation von Zuordnungen mit Ausdrücken, die den "assignment statements" von ALGOL entsprechen. Dazu gehen wir von einem axiomatischen Modell für Ausdruckssprachen aus und beschreiben deren Interpretation weitgehend funktoriell.

Aufbauend auf der Interpretation von Zuordnungen mit Ausdrücken können wir die Semantik von Programmiersprachen mit Hilfe der von E. Engeler und G. Hotz zuerst benutzten Markentechnik formal vollständig definieren.

Schließlich lassen sich mit Hilfe des geschilderten Modells theoretische Untersuchungen anstellen. Die Formalisierung der Befehlsorganisation führt zu einem Minimalitätsbegriff für Programme, dessen Entscheidbarkeit gezeigt werden kann. Der in der Automatentheorie verwendete Begriff der Simulation einer mathematischen Maschine durch eine andere liefert einen Übersetzungsbegriff, der zum Vergleich verschiedener Programmiersysteme sowie zur Konstruktion und zum Nachweis der Korrektheit von Übersetzern verwendet werden kann. Korrektheitsbeweise für Übersetzer lassen sich dadurch vereinfachen, daß man einen Übersetzer in mehrere hintereinandergeschaltete Stufen zerlegen kann.

I. Syntax und Semantik von Ausdruckssprachen

Zu den wichtigsten syntaktischen Grundbausteinen der meisten Programmiersprachen gehören Ausdruckssprachen, etwa zur Beschreibung von Boole'schen oder arithmetischen Ausdrücken. Im folgenden soll nun ein axiomatisches Modell für solche Ausdruckssprachen angegeben werden, das unabhängig von der speziellen syntaktischen Form der Ausdrücke ist.

Von G. Hotz wurde in [4] vorgeschlagen, die Struktur der freien X-Kategorien zur Beschreibung der Syntax von Ausdruckssprachen heranzuziehen. Die Semantik konnte dann in natürlicher Weise durch einen Funktor in eine zweite Kategorie $\mathcal{C}$ angegeben werden, deren Objekte die Zustandsmengen von Speicherplätzen und deren Morphismen die Abbildungen zwischen diesen Zustandsmengen repräsentieren. Dieser Semantikbegriff für Ausdruckssprachen konnte dann zu einem Semantikbegriff für Programmiersprachen erweitert werden.

Es stellte sich jedoch heraus, daß dieses Vorgehen Einschränkungen bewirken würde, die in realen Programmiersprachen nicht immer erfüllt sind, da die Struktur von Ausdruckssprachen nicht immer die gleiche ist wie die der X-Kategorien. Vor allem erschien es notwendig, die Komposition von Morphismen allgemeiner zu fassen und die Semantik von Ausdrücken in einen funktoriellen und einen nicht funktoriellen Teil aufzuspalten. Dies führte zu einer Modifikation der Axiome der X-Kategorien, die wir im folgenden kurz darstellen werden.

Zur Bezeichnungsweise der kategorientheoretischen Grundbegriffe sei auf [3] verwiesen.

<u>Definition 1</u>: Ein Sechstupel $\mathcal{H} = \langle O, M, Q, Z, o, < \rangle$ heißt eine Kategorie mit Halbordnung oder eine H-Kategorie, falls die folgenden Axiome erfüllt sind:

H 1: O und M sind Mengen und $Q: M \longrightarrow O$ und $Z: M \longrightarrow O$ sind Abbildungen. O heißt die Objektmenge und M heißt die Morphismenmenge von $\mathcal{H}$.

H 2: $(O, <)$ ist eine Halbordnung.

H 3: $o: M \times M \longrightarrow M$ ist eine partielle binäre Operation auf M und für alle $f, g \in M$ ist das Produkt $f o g$ genau dann definiert, wenn $Z(g) < Q(f)$ ist. Alsdann gilt:

$$Q(f o g) = Q(g)$$
$$Z(f o g) = Z(f)$$

H 4: o ist assoziativ, d.h. für alle $f, g, h \in M$ ist $(f o (g o h))$ genau dann definiert, wenn auch $((f o g) o h)$ definiert ist und in diesem Fall gilt

$$(f o (g o h)) = ((f o g) o h)$$

H 5 : Zu jedem $A \in O$ gibt es ein Element $1_A \in M$ mit der Eigenschaft, daß

$$A = Q(1_A) = Z(1_A)$$

und für alle $g , h \in M$ gilt, falls $A = Q(h) = Z(g)$ ist :

$$1_A \circ g = g$$

$$h \circ 1_A = h$$

<u>Definition 2 :</u>   Ein Siebentupel $\mathcal{H} = \langle O , M , Q , Z , \circ , \times , < \rangle$ heißt eine X-Ka-
tegorie mit Halbordnung oder HX-Kategorie, falls
$\langle O , M , Q , Z , \circ , < \rangle$ eine H-Kategorie ist und falls außerdem
die folgenden Axiome erfüllt sind :

HX 1 : $(O , \times)$ und $(M , \times)$ sind Monoide und die Halbordnung $<$ ist mit dem
Monoidprodukt $\times$ auf O verträglich, d.h. für alle $A, B, C, D \in O$
gilt :

$$A < B \wedge C < D \implies A \times C < B \times D$$

HX 2 : Für alle $f_1, f_2, g_1, g_2 \in M$ mit $Q(f_i) = Z(g_i)$ gilt :

$$(f_1 \times f_2) \circ (g_1 \times g_2) = (f_1 \circ g_1) \times (f_2 \circ g_2)$$

HX 3 : Für alle Objekte $A , B \in O$ gilt

$$1_{A \times B} = 1_A \times 1_B$$

<u>Bemerkung :</u> Die Begriffe 'HX-Funktor' , 'Unter-HX-Kategorie' , 'freie HX-Ka-
tegorie usw. ergeben sich nun in naheliegender Weise analog zu den klassischen
kategorientheoretischen Begriffen. Die Widerspruchsfreiheit des Axiomensystems
kann man durch einen konstruktiven Beweis nachprüfen.

Die Struktur der HX-Kategorien ist nun zur Beschreibung von Ausdruckssprachen
geeignet. Die einzelnen Schritte unseres Vorgehens können hier nur kurz angedeutet werden :

1.   Zunächst betrachten wir Operationsausdrücke auf Typen. Dazu sei T eine
endliche Menge von Typen und $<$ sei eine Halbordnung auf T. Wir geben
eine HX-Kategorie $\mathcal{H}$ an, deren Struktur das Operatorengerüst der Ausdrücke
beschreibt. Die Objektmenge sei

$$O(\mathcal{H}) = \left\{ A \in \mathcal{P}(T^*) \;\middle|\; \begin{array}{l} \text{für alle } w_1, w_2 \in A \\ \text{ist } |w_1| = |w_2| \end{array} \right\}$$

Dabei ist $|w|$ die Länge des Wortes w in der Faktorzerlegung über T.

Durch $<$ wird auf $O(\mathcal{H})$ eine Halbordnung $\sqsubseteq$ induziert, wenn man festsetzt :

$$A \sqsubseteq B \quad \longleftrightarrow \quad \text{für alle } a \in A \text{ existiert ein}$$
$$b \in B \text{ mit } a < b \text{ oder } a = b$$

2. Die Morphismenmenge der HX-Kategorie $\mathcal{H}$ erzeugen wir durch eine Menge von Operationssymbolen $\mathbb{E}$ und diesen Operationssymbolen ordnen wir durch Abbildungen

$$Q : \mathbb{E} \longrightarrow O(\mathcal{L})$$
$$Z : \mathbb{E} \longrightarrow O(\mathcal{H})$$

als Quelle und Ziel Mengen von Typwörtern zu. Dadurch wird festgelegt, von welchem Typ die Operanden und das Resultat einer Operation sein können. Mit diesen Festsetzungen bilden wir die freie HX-Kategorie

$$\mathcal{H} = \mathcal{H}\left\langle O(\mathcal{H}), \mathbb{E}\right\rangle$$

Ihre Morphismen nennen wir Operationsausdrücke.

3. Über $\mathcal{H}$ konstruieren wir nun eine freie T-D-Kategorie $\mathcal{F}$, deren Objekte Wörter über einem typisierten Variablenalphabet sind, und deren Morphismen von Zuordnungen der Form $x := \mu\, y$ erzeugt werden, wobei x, y Objekte geeigneten Typs und μ ein Operationsausdruck aus $M(\mathcal{H})$ ist.

Damit haben wir ein axiomatisches Modell für Ausdruckssprachen in der Hand, das alle wesentlichen Eigenschaften der in realen Programmiersprachen verwendeten Ausdruckssprachen besitzt, insbesondere lassen sich Operationssymbole mit mehreren Bedeutungen (je nach dem Typ der Operanden) verwenden.
Es läßt sich ein Strukturisomorphismus zwischen der hier axiomatisch eingeführten Struktur der HX-Kategorien und den durch Grammatiken definierten Ausdruckssprachen angeben.

Die Semantik von Zuordnungen mit Ausdrücken, also der Morphismen der freien T-D-Kategorie $\mathcal{F}$ ist wieder in mehreren Schritten definiert, was einer Aufspaltung in einen funktoriellen und einen nicht funktoriellen Anteil entspricht :

1. Die Verankerung der Semantik besteht aus einer Interpretationsvorschrift für 'elementare Zuordnungen' der Form

$$x := \mu\, y \qquad\qquad \text{mit } \mu \in \mathbb{E}$$

und für die Transfermorphismen der freien T-D-Kategorie $\mathcal{F}$.

2. Allgemeine Zuordnungen sind von der Form

$$x := \mu\, y \qquad\qquad \text{mit } \mu \in M(\mathcal{H})$$

Ihre Interpretation erfolgt in der Weise, daß man den Operationsausdruck μ zerlegt und gleichzeitig in $M(\mathcal{F})$ einen Morphismus aufbaut, der aus elementaren Zuordnungen besteht. Dies ist im Grunde eine formale Beschreibung des Analysealgorithmus für Ausdrücke, die unabhängig von der speziellen syntaktischen Form der Ausdrücke ist, und die nur von den Zerlegungseigenschaften der Ausdrücke abhängt.

3. Der funktorielle Teil der Semantik von Zuordnungen mit Ausdrücken besteht nun wie früher in einer Interpretation der Morphismen von $\mathcal{F}$ durch einen Funktor in die oben beschriebene Kategorie $\mathcal{K}$.

Damit dürfte ein befriedigendes Modell für die Syntax und Semantik von Ausdruckssprachen gefunden sein.

II. Programmiersysteme

Wir gehen von der folgenden noch sehr allgemeinen Vorstellung aus : In Anlehnung an die Automatentheorie vertehen wir unter einer mathematischen Maschine eine Abbildung $\delta : K \longrightarrow K$. Ist nun Π eine formale Sprache über einem Alphabet A, dann betrachtet man eine Menge von mathematischen Maschinen

$$\left\{ \delta_\pi : K_\pi \longrightarrow K_\pi \mid \pi \in \Pi \right\}$$

Die Parametermenge kann man dann mit gewissem Recht eine Programmiersprache und $\pi \in \Pi$ ein Programm nennen. Außerdem hat die Zuordnung

$$\delta : \Pi \longrightarrow \left\{ \delta_\pi : K_\pi \longrightarrow K_\pi \mid \pi \in \Pi \right\}$$
$$\pi \longmapsto \delta_\pi : K_\pi \longrightarrow K_\pi$$

die Funktion einer Semantik für die Sprache Π.

Diese Auffassung entspricht einer strikten Trennung von Programm und Daten in den bisherigen Ansätzen zu einer Theorie der Programmiersprachen [1] , [4] . Das geschilderte Konzept bietet nun jedoch eine Erweiterung des Semantikbegriffs an, welche es erlaubt auch die eingangs erwähnten höheren Programmiertechniken wie Laufanweisungen u.a. zu erfassen.

Es sei $\Pi \subset A^{*}$ eine formale Sprache und K sei eine Menge. Dann verstehen wir unter einer Semantik von Π für den Bereich K eine mathematische Maschine

$$\sigma : \Pi \times K \longrightarrow \Pi \times K$$

eine solche Maschine nennen wir auch ein Programmiersystem, und unter einer Berechnung des Systems $(\sigma , \Pi \times K)$ verstehen wir eine Folge

$$(\pi_0, k_0) , (\pi_1, k_1) , \ldots.$$

mit $\qquad (\pi_{i+1}, k_{i+1}) = \sigma(\pi_i, k_i) \qquad$ für alle $i \in \mathbb{N}$

Es stellt sich nun die Aufgabe, ein Programmiersystem $(\sigma, \Pi \times K)$ vollständig formal zu definieren. Dabei erweist sich die Aufteilung der Konfigurationenmenge $\Pi \times K$ in eine Programm- und eine Datenkomponente als nicht ausreichend.

Aus Kostengründen müssen moderne Rechenanlagen nämlich so konstruiert sein, daß die Änderung des Speicherinhaltes bei einem Rechenschritt stets nur von wenigen Speicherzellen abhängt [5]. Selbst bei Maschinen mittlerer Größenordnung sind dies nur etwa 10 Speicherworte. Damit ist klar, daß bei jedem Rechenschritt nur ein relativ kurzer Programmabschnitt interpretiert werden kann und es liegt nahe, die Programme schon von vornherein aus solchen Abschnitten aufzubauen.

Diese Programmabschnitte sind in vielen Programmiersprachen die Programmzeilen. Aus ihnen kann man dann höhere syntaktische Einheiten, zum Beispiel Blöcke und Unterprogramme zusammenfügen. Von G. Hotz wurde in [4] vorgeschlagen, aus den Zeilen zunächst eine reguläre Grundstruktur aufzubauen, etwa mit Hilfe von Kleene'schen Ausdrücken, und dann Zusatzbedingungen zu stellen, die von den korrekten Programmen erfüllt sein müssen. Diese Bedingungen sind sehr einfach zu handhaben : Man untersucht einfache Relationen zwischen Teilwörtern, die sich durch Homomorphismen aus den Programmen gewinnen lassen.

Aus den gleichen Gründen ist es zweckmäßig, die Datenkonfiguration K des Programmiersystems in ein direktes Produkt von Datenmengen zu zerlegen, die man als Zustandsmengen von Speicherzellen auffassen kann.

Darüber hinaus wird es notwendig, in die Konfigurationenmenge des Programmiersystems eine Organisationskomponente Ω aufzunehmen, die zur formalen Beschreibung der Rechnerorganisation dient. Wir betrachten daher nur Programmiersysteme der Form $(\sigma, \Pi \times K \times \Omega)$ mit den genannten Eigenschaften.

In [8] wurde ein Programmiersystem formal vollständig definiert, das etwa die Möglichkeiten von ALGOL oder PASCAL bietet. Insbesondere besitzt dieses System algolähnliche Blockstruktur mit dynamischer Speicherverwaltung, rekursive Unterprogrammtechniken, Adressenmodifikationen, dynamische Felder und Laufanweisungen.

Die Semantik der dort definierten Sprache wurde in der in I beschriebenen Weise auf den Zuordnungen mit Ausdrücken verankert und dann mit Hilfe der formalen Beschreibung der Rechnerorganisation in der Konfigurationenkomponente Ω auf die ganze Sprache fortgesetzt.

III. Minimalität von Programmen

Eine auch für die Praxis interessante Fragestellung ist, ob ein Programm überflüssige Zeilen enthält. Ein solches Programm könnte man minimal nennen. Für das in [8] definierte Programmiersystem wurden dort verschiedene Minimalitätsbegriffe definiert und deren Entscheidbarkeit untersucht. Als ein wesentliches Hilfsmittel wurde dabei die formale Fassung der Befehlsorganisation benutzt. Wir können daher hier nur eine informelle Übersicht über die Resultate angeben.

1. Der statische Minimalitätsbegriff : Wir denken uns einem Programm einen gerichteten Graphen zugeordnet, in dessen Knoten je eine Programmzeile steht. Die von einem Knoten ausgehenden Kanten verbinden ihn mit den Nachfolgerzeilen der in ihm stehenden Zeile.
ein Programm nennen wir dann statisch minimal, wenn dieser Graph zusammenhängend ist. Es gilt der

<u>Satz</u> : Statische Minimalität von Programmen ist entscheidbar.

2. Der dynamische Minimalitätsbegriff : Wir nennen ein Programm minimal im dynamischen Sinne, wenn es zu jeder Zeile eine geeignete Startkonfiguration gibt und eine damit beginnende Berechnungsfolge, derart daß diese Zeile während dieser Berechnung interpretiert wird. Es gilt der Satz

<u>Satz</u> : Dynamische Minimalität von Programmen ist nicht entscheidbar.

IV. Übersetzungen

Wir gehen von dem in der Automatentheorie verwendeten Begriff der Simulation einer mathematischen Maschine durch eine andere aus :

Sind (δ, K) und (δ', K') mathematische Maschinen, so nennen wir eine Abbildung $\Sigma : K \longrightarrow K'$ eine Simulation von (δ, K) auf (δ', K'), falls für alle $k_o \in K$ das folgende Diagramm kommutativ ist :

$$
\begin{array}{ccccccccc}
k_o & \xrightarrow{\delta} & k_1 & \xrightarrow{\delta} & k_2 & \xrightarrow{\delta} & \;----\; & \xrightarrow{\delta} & k_r & \xrightarrow{\delta} \\
\Sigma\downarrow & & \Sigma\downarrow & & \Sigma\downarrow & & & & \Sigma\downarrow \\
k'_o & \xRightarrow{\delta'} & k'_1 & \xRightarrow{\delta'} & k'_2 & \xRightarrow{\delta'} & \;----\; & \xRightarrow{\delta'} & k'_r & \xRightarrow{\delta'}
\end{array}
$$

Dabei bedeuten $\quad k_i \xrightarrow{\delta} k_{i+1}$: $\quad k_{i+1} = \delta(k_i)$

$\qquad\qquad\qquad k'_i \xRightarrow{\delta'} k'_{i+1}$: $\quad$ es gibt ein $j \in \mathbb{N}$ mit $\delta'^{\,j}(k'_i) = k'_{i+1}$

Die Maschine (δ', K') simuliert also jeden Rechenschritt der Maschine (δ, K) durch eine Folge solcher Schritte.

Da wir die Semantik einer Programmiersprache als eine mathematische Maschine
aufgefaßt haben, liegt es nahe, diesen Begriff der Simulation zur Präzisierung
des Übersetzungsbegriffs zu verwenden. Dazu werden jedoch noch einige zusätzliche Überlegungen notwendig: Bei der Simulation eines Programmiersystems
durch ein anderes ist es im allgemeinen nicht notwendig, die Konfigurationen-
folge vollständig zu simulieren. Meist wird nur ein Teil davon interessieren,
den man durch eine Projektionsabbildung herausfiltern kann. Wir definieren:

<u>Definition 3</u>: (δ, K) und (δ', K') seien mathematische Maschinen und

$$p : K \longrightarrow K$$
$$p': K' \longrightarrow K'$$

seien Abbildungen mit $p^2 = p$ und $p'^2 = p'$. Eine Abbildung $\Sigma : K \longrightarrow K'$
heißt eine partiell treue Simulation von (δ, K) auf (δ', K') bezüglich p
und p' falls die folgenden drei Bedingungen erfüllt sind:

1. Für jedes $k_o \in K_o$ und jedes $k'_o \in K'_o$ mit $\Sigma(p(k_o)) = p'(k'_o)$ ist
   das folgende Diagramm kommutativ:

   ($K_o \subset K$ und $K'_o \subset K'$ sind dabei vorgegebene Mengen von Startkonfigurationen)

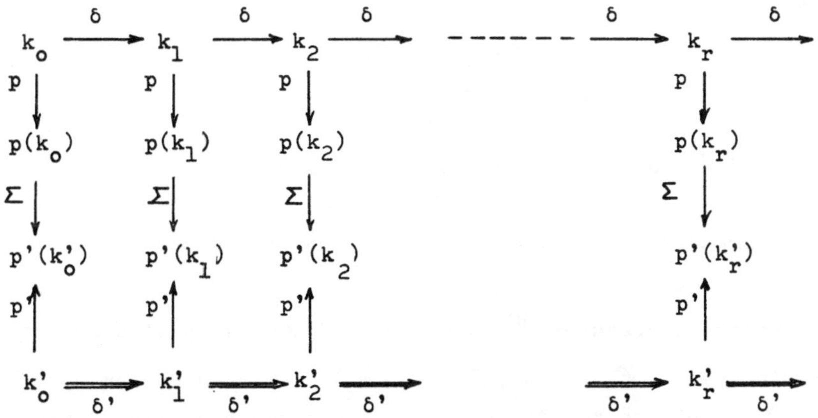

2. Die eingeschränkte Abbildung $\Sigma : p(K) \longrightarrow p'(K')$ ist bijektiv.

3. Für alle $k \in K$ und alle $k' \in K'$ mit $\Sigma(p(k)) = p'(k')$ gilt

$$\delta(k) = k \iff \delta'(k') = k'$$

<u>Bemerkung</u>: Die Projektionsabbildungen p und p' blenden aus den Kofigura-
tionen also die störenden Teile aus. Wir nennen sie daher Masken und ein Tripel (δ, K, p) eine maskierte mathematische Maschine. Auf der Menge der mas-
kierten Maschinen $\mathcal{M}$ definieren wir eine Äquivalenzrelation wie folgt:

<u>Definition 4</u> : Die maskierten Maschinen (δ,K,p) und (δ',K',p') heißen simulationsäquivalent, wenn es eine Folge auf $\mathcal{M}$ gibt :

$$(\delta,K,p) = (\delta_o,K_o,p_o) , \ldots , (\delta_n,K_n,p_n) = (\delta',K',p')$$

und eine Folge von partiell treuen Simulationen bezüglich der Masken p_i , die das folgende Diagramm erfüllen :

Man kann nun zeigen, daß sich jedes Simulationsdiagramm von der obigen Art verkürzen läßt zu einem Diagramm mit höchstens zwei partiell treuen Simulationen :

<u>Satz</u> : Die folgenden Aussagen sind äquivalent :

    i) (δ,K,p) und (δ',K',p') sind simulationsäquivalent .

    ii) Es gibt eine Maschine (δ_o,K_o,p_o) und ein Simulationsdiagramm von der Gestalt

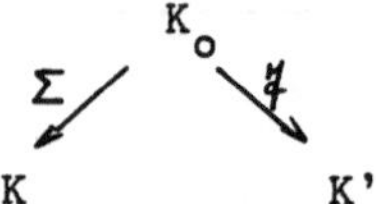

        wobei Σ und $\mathcal{T}$ partiell treue Simulationen sind.

Damit haben wir die Voraussetzungen geschaffen, um den Übersetzungsbegriff zu präzisieren :

<u>Definition 5</u> : Ein Programmiersystem $\mathcal{P}_1 = (\sigma_1, \Pi_1 \times K_1 \times \Omega_1)$ heißt übersetzbar in das Programmiersystem $\mathcal{P}_2 = (\sigma_2, \Pi_2 \times K_2 \times \Omega_2)$, falls es Masken p_1 für $\mathcal{P}_1$ und p_2 für $\mathcal{P}_2$ gibt, so daß die Programmiersysteme bezüglich dieser Masken simulationsäquivalent sind.

Sind $S_1 \subset \Pi_1 \times K_1 \times \Omega_1$ und $S_2 \subset \Pi_2 \times K_2 \times \Omega_2$ Mengen von "Startkonfigurationen", dann heißt eine Abbildung $\ddot{U} : S_1 \longrightarrow S_2$ eine Übersetzung von $\mathcal{P}_1$ in $\mathcal{P}_2$, wenn es eine Maschine (σ, K, p) gibt, so daß das folgende Simulationsdiagramm erfüllt ist :

$$\Pi_1 \times K_1 \times \Omega_1 \quad \overset{\sigma \swarrow \ \overset{K}{} \ \searrow \mathcal{T}}{\qquad} \quad \Pi_2 \times K_2 \times \Omega_2$$

und falls außerdem gilt : $\ddot{U} = \mathcal{T} \circ \sigma^{-1} /_{S_1} : S_1 \longrightarrow S_2$

$$\text{und} \qquad S_1 \subset p_1(K_1) \qquad \text{und} \qquad S_2 \subset p_2(K_2)$$

Wir stellen nun noch kurz die wesentlichen Eigenschaften dieses Übersetzungsbegriffs heraus :

1. Die Übersetzung besteht aus je nach Wahl der Masken in einer Transformation der Daten, des Programms oder der Organisation.

2. Der Satz über die Verkürzung von Simulationsketten läßt sich zur Vereinfachung von Korrektheitsbeweisen heranziehen : Man zerlegt einen vorgegebenen Übersetzer in einzelne Stufen, deren Korrektheit sich getrennt überprüfen läßt und muß dann nur die Korrektheit dieser Stufen zeigen,was i.a.
einfacher ist.

In [8] wurde für die dort definierte Sprache die Korrektheit einer Übersetzung
nachgewiesen, die Blockstruktur der Programme auflöst und von einer dynamischen Speicherverwaltung zu einer statischen Speicherorganisation übergeht.
Dabei hat sich die Zerlegung des Übersetzers in Stufen als nützlich erwiesen.

Literatur :

[1] Engeler, E. (Herausgeber) : Symposium on Semantics of Algorithmic
Languages, Springer Lect. Notes 188

[2] Engeler, E. : Algorithmic Approximations, JCSS 5 (67 - 82) 1971

[3] Hotz, G. , Claus, V. : Automatentheorie und formale Sprachen III
BI Hochschulskripten 823

[4] Hotz, G.:Grundlagen einer Theorie der Programmiersprachen I , II
Berichte des Math. Instituts und des Instituts
für Angew. Math. der Universität des Saarlandes

[5] Kaufholz, G. : Über die Vernetzungsstruktur von Maschinen
Dissertation an der Univ. des Saarlandes (1973)

[6] Kopp, H. : Rekursive Unterprogrammtechniken

[7] Kopp, H. : Programmierbare Funktionen
beides : Berichte des Math. Instituts und des
Inst. für Angew. Math. der Univ. des Saarlandes

[8] Kopp, H. : Beiträge zur Theorie der Programmiersprachen
Dissertation an der Universität des Saarlandes
(1973)

INDUCTION PRINCIPLES FOR CONTEXT-FREE LANGUAGES

Ward Douglas Maurer

INTRODUCTION

In proving assertions about programs, it is necessary to use induction principles in one form or another. Recursion induction was introduced by McCarthy [4] for the purpose of proving assertions about functions, in particular, functions defined by recursive conditional expressions. Structural induction was introduced by Burstall [1] for proving assertions about structures, such as lists and trees. The induction principles which we shall introduce here are useful for proving assertions about context-free languages and their semantic attributes, as this term is used by Knuth [3]. We shall introduce these principles informally and use them to prove the equivalence of two syntactic definitions of an unsigned integer, the equivalence of Knuth's two examples of synthesized and inherited attributes, and the validity of Hoare's first axiom (also known as the "back substitution rule") for a large class of programming languages.

A SIMPLE EXAMPLE

Consider the BNF rules ⟨alpha⟩ ::= ⟨digit⟩ | ⟨alpha⟩ ⟨digit⟩ and ⟨beta⟩ ::= ⟨digit⟩ | ⟨digit⟩ ⟨beta⟩. We wish to prove that ⟨alpha⟩ and ⟨beta⟩ are the same -- that is, that every alpha is a beta, and vice versa. Intuitively this is clear, because an alpha is defined here as a non-empty sequence of digits, and so is a beta, although in a different way. Our proof of this trivial fact will serve to give a simple example of the method of proof; more complex examples follow.

As a lemma, we first prove that ⟨beta⟩ ⟨digit⟩ ⊂ ⟨beta⟩ -- that is, "Every beta followed by a digit is again a beta." The symbol ⊂ denotes inclusion of sets, as usual. The set of all digits is denoted by ⟨digit⟩ and the set of all betas by ⟨beta⟩. Concatenation is denoted by a blank, and this operator extends to sets in the usual way; that is, X Y is the set of all x y , for all x, y in the sets X, Y.

The rule defining ⟨beta⟩ may clearly be rewritten, using this notation, as ⟨beta⟩ = ⟨digit⟩ ∪ ⟨digit⟩ ⟨beta⟩, where = denotes set equality and where concatenation binds more strongly than union. Thus the statement of the lemma is equivalent to the two statements ⟨digit⟩ ⟨digit⟩ ⊂ ⟨beta⟩ and ⟨digit⟩ ⟨beta⟩ ⟨digit⟩ ⊂ ⟨beta⟩. The first of these is obvious -- a digit followed by a digit is always a beta. (Formally, we might write ⟨digit⟩ ⟨digit⟩ ⊂ ⟨digit⟩ ⟨beta⟩ ⊂ ⟨beta⟩, where the two steps

are justified respectively by the two alternatives in the definition of ⟨beta⟩.) It is
in the second of these statements that we use our induction principle. Note that the
left side is a special case of ⟨beta⟩ ⟨digit⟩, the left side of the statement of the
lemma -- but it also contains a "smaller" ⟨beta⟩ ⟨digit⟩ (which is preceded by a digit). By induction, then, the conclusion -- that is, the statement of the lemma --
may be assumed to hold for this smaller ⟨beta⟩ ⟨digit⟩, and the result is ⟨digit⟩
⟨beta⟩ ⟨digit⟩ ⊂ ⟨digit⟩ ⟨beta⟩ (where we use the obvious fact that the associativity
of concatenation extends naturally to set-concatenation). Since we already know that
⟨digit⟩ ⟨beta⟩ ⊂ ⟨beta⟩ by the definition of ⟨beta⟩, the lemma follows.

We are now ready to prove that ⟨alpha⟩ ⊂ ⟨beta⟩ -- that is, "Every alpha is a
beta." (The converse will then follow by symmetry.) As before, we rewrite the BNF
rule for ⟨alpha⟩ as ⟨alpha⟩ = ⟨digit⟩ ∪ ⟨alpha⟩ ⟨digit⟩, which shows us that ⟨alpha⟩
⊂ ⟨beta⟩ is equivalent to ⟨digit⟩ ⊂ ⟨beta⟩ and ⟨alpha⟩ ⟨digit⟩ ⊂ ⟨beta⟩. The first
of these follows immediately from the definition of ⟨beta⟩. As for the second, using
our induction principle exactly as before, we find that we may assume that ⟨alpha⟩
⟨digit⟩ ⊂ ⟨beta⟩ ⟨digit⟩. However, by the lemma, we know that ⟨beta⟩ ⟨digit⟩ ⊂
⟨beta⟩. Therefore ⟨alpha⟩ ⟨digit⟩ ⊂ ⟨beta⟩, completing the proof.

THE EQUIVALENCE OF KNUTH'S TWO EXAMPLES

Simple context-free induction may easily be extended in two ways: to prove several assertions at once (multiple context-free induction) and to prove assertions
about the semantic attributes of a program (semantic induction). As an example of
both of these, we shall show the equivalence of the two ways of defining the value of
a number as given in [3] to illustrate the ideas of synthesized and inherited attribute.

We shall use a notation for semantic attributes which was first expounded in
[6]; this notation is illustrated as follows. Let q^v denote the value of the digit q;
let z^v denote the value of the string z of digits, considered as an integer in some
base β. The syntactic rule ⟨string of digits⟩ ::= ⟨digit⟩ | ⟨string of digits⟩ ⟨di-
git⟩ then implies that concat(z, q) (the concatenation of the strings z and q) is
also a string of digits. Let us introduce labels into this rule, as follows:

⟨string of digits⟩ x ::= ⟨digit⟩ p; y ::= ⟨string of digits⟩ z ⟨digit⟩ q

In other words, "A string of digits, x, may be a digit p; a string of digits, y, may
be a string of digits z followed by a digit q; and these are the only possibilities."
Thus concat(z, q) = y, and, if y^v denotes the value of y, then $y^v = \beta \cdot z^v + q^v$ (this
is essentially the definition of base-β values). Clearly the value of the string of
digits x is just the value of the digit p. These rules define the value of a string
of digits as a semantic attribute, in terms of the value of a digit (which is likewise assumed to be a semantic attribute); we may write

$\langle$string of digits$\rangle$ $\underline{x}$ ::= $\langle$digit$\rangle$ $\underline{u}$; $\underline{y}$ ::= $\langle$string of digits$\rangle$ $\underline{z}$ $\langle$digit$\rangle$ $\underline{q}$
　　　$\langle$value$\rangle$ $x^v = p^v$; $y^v = \beta \cdot z^v + q^v$

(here $\langle$value$\rangle$ is simply a label, giving the intuitive meaning of this attribute). In this notation, Knuth's first example becomes

$\langle$bit$\rangle$ $\underline{a}$ ::= '0'; $\underline{b}$ ::= '1'
　　　$\langle$value$\rangle$ $a^v = 0$; $b^v = 1$
$\langle$list of bits$\rangle$ $\underline{x}$ ::= $\langle$bit$\rangle$ $\underline{u}$; $\underline{y}$ ::= $\langle$list of bits$\rangle$ $\underline{z}$ $\langle$bit$\rangle$ $\underline{v}$
　　　$\langle$value$\rangle$ $x^v = u^v$; $y^v = 2z^v + v^v$
　　　$\langle$length$\rangle$ $x^n = 1$; $y^n = z^n + 1$
$\langle$number$\rangle$ $\underline{x}$ ::= $\langle$list of bits$\rangle$ $\underline{a}$; $\underline{y}$ ::= $\langle$list of bits$\rangle$ $\underline{b}$ '.' $\langle$list of bits$\rangle$ $\underline{c}$
　　　$\langle$value$\rangle$ $x^v = a^v$; $y^v = b^v + c^v/\exp(2, c^n)$

where $\exp(p, q)$ stands for p^q. Thus the value of '1101.01' is $13\frac{1}{4}$.

Knuth's second example involves an inherited attribute called the $\underline{scale}$ of a bit or of a list of bits. When a number is of the form L or L.M, where L and M are lists of bits, the scale of L is zero and the scale of M is the negative of its length. For a list of bits of the form B or LB, where B is a bit and L is a sublist, the scale of B is the scale of the entire list, while the scale of L is one more than the scale of the entire list. (Intuitively, the scale of a bit is its distance from the decimal point, which is assumed to be on the right if it is not present.) The value of a one-bit is then 2^s, where s is its scale, and the value of a number is simply the sum of the values of all its component bits. These rules may be expressed as:

$\langle$bit$\rangle$ $\underline{a}$ ::= '0'; $\underline{b}$ ::= '1'
　　　$\langle$value$\rangle$ $a^v = 0$; $b^v = \exp(2, b^s)$
　　　$\langle$scale$\rangle^s$
$\langle$list of bits$\rangle$ $\underline{x}$ ::= $\langle$bit$\rangle$ $\underline{u}$; $\underline{y}$ ::= $\langle$list of bits$\rangle$ $\underline{z}$ $\langle$bit$\rangle$ $\underline{v}$
　　　$\langle$value$\rangle$ $x^v = u^v$; $y^v = z^v + v^v$
　　　$\langle$length$\rangle$ $x^n = 1$; $y^n = z^n + 1$
　　　$\langle$scale$\rangle^s$
　　　$u^s = x^s$; $z^s = y^s + 1$; $v^s = y^s$
$\langle$number$\rangle$ $\underline{x}$ ::= $\langle$list of bits$\rangle$ $\underline{a}$; $\underline{y}$ ::= $\langle$list of bits$\rangle$ $\underline{b}$ '.' $\langle$list of bits$\rangle$ $\underline{c}$
　　　$\langle$value$\rangle$ $x^v = a^v$; $y^v = b^v + c^v$
　　　$a^s = 0$; $b^s = 0$; $c^s = -c^n$

Here $\langle$scale$\rangle^s$ under $\langle$bit$\rangle$ is again simply a label, specifying that a bit has a scale denoted by the superscript s, and similarly for $\langle$scale$\rangle^s$ under $\langle$list$\rangle$.

Since the two examples have the same syntax and the same rules for defining length, and since, in fact, the only two corresponding semantic attributes that differ in them are the two notions of value, we shall combine the two definitions into one, and denote the two kinds of value by "value-1" and "value-2":

1. $\langle$bit$\rangle$ $\underline{a}$ ::= '0'; $\underline{b}$ ::= '1'

2. $\qquad$ $\langle$value-1$\rangle$ $a^V = 0$; $b^V = 1$

3. $\qquad$ $\langle$value-2$\rangle$ $a^W = 0$; $b^W = \exp(2, b^S)$

4. $\qquad$ $\langle$scale$\rangle^S$

5. $\langle$list of bits$\rangle$ $\underline{x}$ ::= $\langle$bit$\rangle$ $\underline{u}$; $\underline{y}$ ::= $\langle$list of bits$\rangle$ $\underline{z}$ $\langle$bit$\rangle$ $\underline{v}$

6. $\qquad$ $\langle$value-1$\rangle$ $x^V = u^V$; $y^V = 2z^V + v^V$

7. $\qquad$ $\langle$value-2$\rangle$ $x^W = u^W$; $y^W = z^W + v^W$

8. $\qquad$ $\langle$length$\rangle$ $x^n = 1$; $y^n = z^n + 1$

9. $\qquad$ $\langle$scale$\rangle^S$

10. $\qquad$ $u^S = x^S$; $z^S = y^S + 1$; $v^S = y^S$

11. $\langle$number$\rangle$ $\underline{x}$ ::= $\langle$list of bits$\rangle$ $\underline{a}$; $\underline{y}$ ::= $\langle$list of bits$\rangle$ $\underline{b}$ '.' $\langle$list of bits$\rangle$ $\underline{c}$

12. $\qquad$ $\langle$value-1$\rangle$ $x^V = a^V$; $y^V = b^V + c^V/\exp(2, c^n)$

13. $\qquad$ $\langle$value-2$\rangle$ $x^W = a^W$; $y^W = b^W + c^W$

14. $\qquad$ $a^S = 0$; $b^S = 0$; $c^S = -c^n$

(The numbers 1–14 are for identification only, and are referenced in the proof.)

We wish to prove that the value-1 of any number is the same as its value-2. In order to prove this, we shall have to prove more; namely, that the value-2 of a bit, or of a list of bits, is its value-1 times 2^S, where s is its scale. Formally,

$\langle$bit$\rangle$ $\underline{b}$	15. $b^W = b^V \cdot \exp(2, b^S)$
$\langle$list of bits$\rangle$ $\underline{x}$	16. $x^W = x^V \cdot \exp(2, x^S)$
$\langle$number$\rangle$ $\underline{n}$	17. $n^W = n^V$

The proofs of these are divided into cases, as before. For example, consider the bit '0', denoted by $\underline{a}$; we must prove that $a^W = a^V \cdot \exp(2, a^S)$. In fact, this follows from $a^W = 0$ (first part of step 3, above) and $a^V = 0$ (first part of step 2). We will write

$$a^W = 0 = 0 \cdot \exp(2, a^S) = a^V \cdot \exp(2, a^S) \qquad (3a, 2a)$$

Here the first, second, third, etc., alternatives within a rule are denoted by a, b, c, etc. In this style, the proof of statement 15 above proceeds as follows:

$\langle$bit$\rangle$ a, b:

18. $\quad a^W = 0 = 0 \cdot \exp(2, a^S) = a^V \cdot \exp(2, a^S)$ $\qquad$ (3a, 2a)

19. $\quad b^W = \exp(2, b^S) = 1 \cdot \exp(2, b^S) = b^V \cdot \exp(2, b^S)$ $\qquad$ (3b, 2b)

The first line here lists the labels (in this case $\underline{a}$ and $\underline{b}$) of the alternative definitions of $\langle$bit$\rangle$. The proof of statement 16 is now:

$\langle$list of bits$\rangle$ x, y:

20. $\quad x^W = u^W = u^V \cdot \exp(2, u^S) = u^V \cdot \exp(2, x^S) = x^V \cdot \exp(2, x^S)$ $\qquad$ (7a, 15, 10a, 6a)

21. $\quad y^W = z^W + v^W = z^V \cdot \exp(2, z^S) + v^V \cdot \exp(2, v^S) = z^V \cdot \exp(2, y^S+1) + v^V \cdot \exp(2, y^S)$

$\qquad = \exp(2, y^S) \cdot (2z^V + v^V) = y^V \cdot \exp(2, y^S)$ $\qquad$ (7b, 16(*), 15, 10b, 10c, 6b)

Here we have used not only steps 6, 7, and 10 of what was given, but also step 15, which has just been proved, as well as step 16 (recursively). Recursive use of a step is marked by (*). The final conclusion, step 17, is now proved as follows:

⟨number⟩ x, y:

22. $x^w = a^w = a^v \cdot \exp(2, a^s) = a^v = x^v$ (13a, 16, 14a, 12a)

23. $y^w = b^w + c^w = b^v \cdot \exp(2, b^s) + c^v \cdot \exp(2, c^s) = b^v + c^v \cdot \exp(2, -c^n)$

       $= b^v + c^v / \exp(2, c^n) = y^v$ (13b, 16, 16, 14b, 14c, 12b)

This completes the proof.

A byproduct of constructions like these, as with any mathematical proof, arises from checking through it to see whether all the assumptions have been used. In this case, nowhere have we ever used step 8 -- in other words, the equivalence of value-1 and value-2 is entirely independent of the definition of the length of a list of bits! Even if we do something completely ridiculous like defining the length of every list of bits to be -4, so that the value-1 of '1101.01' comes out 29 instead of 13¼, we can be assured that the value-2 of '1101.01' will likewise come out 29.

THE VALIDITY OF HOARE'S FIRST AXIOM

We shall now define, syntactically and semantically, a class of programming languages, and show that, for any language in the class, that if the assertion P_0 is true before initiation of the assignment x:=f, then P will be true on its completion, where P_0 is obtained from P by substituting f (actually, in this context, (f)) for all occurrences of x. This is known as the Axiom of Assignment (see Hoare [2]).

Consider the following syntactic rule and associated semantic attribute:

1. ⟨string⟩ _x_ ::= ⟨string element⟩ _u_; _y_ ::= ⟨string⟩ _z_ ⟨string element⟩ _v_

2.   ⟨substituted string⟩ $x^u(p, q)$ = _if_ u=p _then_ concat('(', q, ')') _else_ u;

     $y^u(p, q)$ = concat($z^u(p, q)$, _if_ v=p _then_ concat('(', q, ')') _else_ v)

The substituted string $s^u(p, q)$ is meant to be the result of substituting (q) for p throughout the string s. (Compare the LISP [5] function subst(q, p, s).) We shall be using this definition of the substituted string in investigating the validity of the Axiom of Assignment. First we need a lemma.

LEMMA. _If_ ⟨string⟩ _and_ ⟨substituted string⟩ _are defined as above, then_

3. ⟨string⟩ _x_ ⟨string⟩ _y_ ⊂ ⟨string⟩ _z_

4. $z^u(p, q)$ = concat($x^u(p, q)$, $y^u(p, q)$)

That is, the concatenation of any two strings x and y is a string z whose substituted string, for any p and q, is the concatenation of the corresponding substituted strings of x and y.

PROOF. As before, we give the proof as a sequence of steps. This proof differs from the preceding two in that we are proving both a syntactic fact and a semantic fact. Consequently, we use labels (_x_, _y_, _z_, etc.) on the quantities appearing in the syntactic proof, and these labels are then referenced in the semantic proof. We apply the above definition of a string to the string $\underline{y}$; steps 5 and 6 treat the first alternative definition, while steps 7 and 8 treat the second alternative. In each case the string $\underline{x}$ is appended at the front, just as it appears in step 3 (the syntactic statement to be proved).

5. $\langle$string$\rangle$ $\underline{x}$ $\langle$string$\rangle$ $\underline{y}$ ::= $\langle$string$\rangle$ $\underline{x}$ $\langle$string element$\rangle$ $\underline{e}$ $\subset$ $\langle$string$\rangle$ $\underline{z}$ (1a, 1b)

6. $\quad z^u(p, q) = \mathrm{concat}(x^u(p, q), \underline{\text{if}}\ e{=}p\ \underline{\text{then}}\ \mathrm{concat}(\text{'('}, q, \text{')'})\ \underline{\text{else}}\ e)$
$\qquad\qquad = \mathrm{concat}(x^u(p, q), y^u(p, q))$ (2b, 2a)

7. $\langle$string$\rangle$ $\underline{x}$ $\langle$string$\rangle$ $\underline{y}$ ::= $\langle$string$\rangle$ $\underline{x}$ $\langle$string$\rangle$ $\underline{a}$ $\langle$string element$\rangle$ $\underline{b}$ $\subset$ $\langle$string$\rangle$ $\underline{c}$
$\qquad$ $\langle$string element$\rangle$ $\underline{b}$ $\subset$ $\langle$string$\rangle$ $\underline{z}$ (1b, 3(*), 1b)

8. $\quad z^u(p, q) = \mathrm{concat}(c^u(p, q), \underline{\text{if}}\ b{=}p\ \underline{\text{then}}\ \mathrm{concat}(\text{'('}, q, \text{')'})\ \underline{\text{else}}\ b)$
$\qquad = \mathrm{concat}(\mathrm{concat}(x^u(p, q), a^u(p, q)), \underline{\text{if}}\ b{=}p\ \underline{\text{then}}\ \mathrm{concat}(\text{'('}, q, \text{')'})$
$\qquad \underline{\text{else}}\ b) = \mathrm{concat}(x^u(p, q), \mathrm{concat}(a^u(p, q), \underline{\text{if}}\ b{=}p\ \underline{\text{then}}$
$\qquad \mathrm{concat}(\text{'('}, q, \text{')'})\ \underline{\text{else}}\ b)) = \mathrm{concat}(x^u(p, q), y^u(p, q))$ (2b,4(*),2b)

The labels in step 5 are referenced in (semantic) step 6; the labels in step 7 are referenced in step 8. Labels are repeated when they refer to the same quantity; thus the string x appears twice in step 5 and twice in step 7, and likewise the string element b appears twice in step 7. The use of (*) to denote induction and of a and b to denote the first and second alternative, respectively, is as before.

     We are now ready to state our main result.

     THEOREM. $\underline{\text{Let}}$ $\underline{\text{the}}$ $\underline{\text{following}}$ $\underline{\text{production}}$ $\underline{\text{rules}}$ $\underline{\text{be}}$ $\underline{\text{given}}$ $\underline{\text{as}}$ $\underline{\text{part}}$ $\underline{\text{of}}$ $\underline{\text{the}}$ $\underline{\text{definition}}$ $\underline{\text{of}}$ $\underline{\text{a}}$ $\underline{\text{grammar}}$:

1. $\langle$assignment$\rangle$ $\underline{a}$ ::= $\langle$variable$\rangle$ $\underline{v}$ ':=' $\langle$expression$\rangle$ $\underline{e}$

2. $\quad$ $\langle$effect$\rangle$ $a^e(S) = S'$, where $S'(v) = e^v(S)$, $S'(z) = S(z)$ for $z \neq v$

3. $\langle$relation$\rangle$ $\underline{r}$ ::= $\langle$expression$\rangle$ $\underline{u}$ $\langle$relational operator$\rangle$ $\underline{o}$ $\langle$expression$\rangle$ $\underline{v}$

4. $\quad$ $\langle$value$\rangle$ $r^v(S) = o^o(u^v(S), v^v(S))$

5. $\langle$expression$\rangle$ $\underline{x}$ ::= $\langle$term$\rangle$ $\underline{u}$; $\underline{y}$ ::= $\langle$adding operator$\rangle$ $\underline{a}$ $\langle$term$\rangle$ $\underline{v}$; $\underline{z}$ ::=
$\qquad$ $\langle$expression$\rangle$ $\underline{e}$ $\langle$adding operator$\rangle$ $\underline{b}$ $\langle$term$\rangle$ $\underline{w}$

6. $\quad$ $\langle$value$\rangle$ $x^v(S) = u^v(S)$; $y^v(S) = a^u(v^v(S))$; $z^v(S) = b^b(e^v(S), w^v(S))$

7. $\langle$term$\rangle$ $\underline{x}$ ::= $\langle$factor$\rangle$ $\underline{u}$; $\underline{y}$ ::= $\langle$term$\rangle$ $\underline{z}$ $\langle$multiplying operator$\rangle$ $\underline{o}$ $\langle$factor$\rangle$ $\underline{v}$

8. $\quad$ $\langle$value$\rangle$ $x^v(S) = u^v(S)$; $y^v(S) = o^o(z^v(S), v^v(S))$

9. $\langle$factor$\rangle$ $\underline{x}$ ::= $\langle$constant$\rangle$ $\underline{k}$; $\underline{y}$ ::= $\langle$variable$\rangle$ $\underline{v}$; $\underline{z}$ ::= '(' $\langle$expression$\rangle$ $\underline{e}$ ')'

10. $\quad$ $\langle$value$\rangle$ $x^v(S) \equiv k^v$; $y^v(S) = S(v)$; $z^v(S) = e^v(S)$

11. $\langle$string element$\rangle$ ::= $\langle$constant$\rangle$ | $\langle$variable$\rangle$ | $\langle$adding operator$\rangle$ | $\langle$multiplying
$\qquad$ operator$\rangle$ | $\langle$relational operator$\rangle$ | '(' | ')' | ':='

12. $\langle$string$\rangle$ $\underline{x}$ ::= $\langle$string element$\rangle$ $\underline{u}$; $\underline{y}$ ::= $\langle$string$\rangle$ $\underline{z}$ $\langle$string element$\rangle$ $\underline{v}$

13. $\quad$ $\langle$substituted string$\rangle$ $x^u(p, q) = \underline{\text{if}}\ u{=}p\ \underline{\text{then}}\ \mathrm{concat}(\text{'('}, q, \text{')'})\ \underline{\text{else}}\ u$;
$\qquad y^u(p, q) = \mathrm{concat}(z^u(p, q), \underline{\text{if}}\ v{=}p\ \underline{\text{then}}\ \mathrm{concat}(\text{'('}, q, \text{')'})\ \underline{\text{else}}\ v)$

$\underline{\text{Here}}$ $\underline{\text{the}}$ $\underline{\text{following}}$ $\underline{\text{conditions}}$ $\underline{\text{are}}$ $\underline{\text{assumed}}$ $\underline{\text{to}}$ $\underline{\text{hold}}$:

     A. $\underline{\text{The}}$ $\underline{\text{definition}}$ $\underline{\text{of}}$ $\langle$string$\rangle$ $\underline{\text{is}}$ $\underline{\text{unambiguous}}$; $\underline{\text{that}}$ $\underline{\text{is}}$, $\underline{\text{the}}$ $\underline{\text{eight}}$ $\underline{\text{alternative}}$ $\underline{\text{definitions}}$ $\underline{\text{of}}$ $\underline{\text{a}}$ $\underline{\text{string}}$ $\underline{\text{element}}$ $\underline{\text{are}}$ $\underline{\text{mutually}}$ $\underline{\text{exclusive}}$.

B. Each constant k has a value k^v which is a member of a set D of values.

C. Each adding operator o has an associated unary operator o^u: $D \to D$ and an associated binary operator o^b: $D \times D \to D$.

D. Each multiplying operator m has an associated binary operator m^o: $D \times D \to D$.

E. Each relational operator r has an associated operator r^o: $D \times D \to \{true, false\}$.

F. In the semantic rules, S denotes a state vector, whose domain is the set of all variables and whose range is D, while p denotes a variable and q an expression.

Then Hoare's first axiom holds. Specifically, each relation r is a string whose substituted string is again a relation, and the value of the relation obtained by substituting (q) for p, when applied to an arbitrary state vector S, is the same as the value of the original relation r when applied to the new state vector after the assignment p:=q. Symbolically:

$$\langle relation \rangle \ \underline{r} \subset \langle string \rangle \ \underline{s}$$
$$s^u(p, q) \in \langle relation \rangle$$
$$(s^{u'}(p,q))^v(S) = r^v((p:=q)^e(S))$$

(Note that we must write $s^u(p, q)$ rather than $r^u(p, q)$, since the production rules 1–13 above do not define the substituted string of a relation.)

Before proving the theorem, we examine its form and a few generalizations.

The syntactic and semantic rules given in the statement of the theorem constitute a programming language schema, or abstraction of the concept of a programming language, since the form of the constants, variables, and operators is left unspecified. Such a schema resembles the "abstract syntax" of McCarthy [4], except that McCarthy also leaves unspecified the order of the components of each alternative, whereas we, for example, have required that all our binary operators be infix. The need for a slightly lower level of abstraction may be seen by noting that there exist properties of programming languages which do, in fact, depend on whether operators are prefix, infix, or suffix, although not necessarily on the form of the terminals.

The current state of the computation is represented by a state vector S, viewed as a function from variables to their current values. Expressions, terms, factors, and relations are presumed to have values which are dependent upon the current state vector; an assignment has an effect, which is a function giving the new state vector after the assignment in terms of the current state vector before the assignment. The values of a relation are true and false, depending on whether that relation is or is not (currently) satisfied; the values of expressions, terms, and factors are presumed to be drawn from the same set D as are the values of constants.

Since a^e denotes the effect of the assignment a, $(p:=q)^e$ denotes the effect of the specific assignment p:=q where p is a variable and q is an expression. (See [6].)

The relation of our symbolic statement of Hoare's first axiom to its usual statement is as follows. If $P^v(S)$ denotes the current value of the predicate P when the current state vector is S, while $Q^e(S)$ denotes the next state vector after the execution of Q with current state vector S, then Hoare's first axiom is equivalent to "If $P^v(S) = true$, then $R^v(Q^e(S)) = true$," where R is our relation r, which is a string s; P is the substituted string s^u(p, q); and Q is the assignment p:=q. We actually prove the stronger statement P^v(S) = R^v(Q^e(S)); in other words, R is true after Q is executed <u>if</u> <u>and</u> <u>only</u> <u>if</u> P is true beforehand.

The theorem suggests a number of generalizations. The form of a relation may be generalized; exponential and other operators may be introduced; even side effects may be introduced, as long as they are carefully controlled. We have purposely not attempted to define a "most general" language schema for which Hoare's first axiom holds, and indeed it is doubtful whether such a schema exists. Our proof method is readily susceptible to computer-aided treatment, allowing us to construct and test syntactic and semantic definitions of subsets of FORTRAN, ALGOL 60, and so forth.

PROOF. As before, we shall need to prove more than what is stated. In fact, we shall prove that the given assertion about the values of a relation before and after an assignment holds for expressions, terms, and factors, as well as relations. We lay out the statements to be proved, as follows:

14. ⟨factor⟩ <u>f</u> ⊂ ⟨string⟩ <u>s</u>

15. s^u(p, q) ∈ ⟨factor⟩

16. $(s^u(p, q))^v$(S) = f^v($(p{:=}q)^e$(S))

17. ⟨term⟩ <u>t</u> ⊂ ⟨string⟩ <u>s</u>

18. s^u(p, q) ∈ ⟨term⟩

19. $(s^u(p, q))^v$(S) = t^v($(p{:=}q)^e$(S))

20. ⟨expression⟩ <u>e</u> ⊂ ⟨string⟩ <u>s</u>

21. s^u(p, q) ∈ ⟨expression⟩

22. $(s^u(p, q))^v$(S) = e^v($(p{:=}q)^e$(S))

23. ⟨relation⟩ <u>r</u> ⊂ ⟨string⟩ <u>s</u>

24. s^u(p, q) ∈ ⟨relation⟩

25. $(s^u(p, q))^v$(S) = r^v($(p{:=}q)^e$(S))

Here, as before, p is an arbitrary variable, q an expression, and S a state vector.

The proof now proceeds as follows:

26. ⟨factor⟩ <u>x</u> ::= ⟨constant⟩ <u>k</u> ⊂ ⟨string element⟩ <u>e</u> ⊂ ⟨string⟩ <u>s</u>   (9a, 11a, 12a)

27. s^u(p, q) = (<u>if</u> k=p <u>then</u> concat('(', q, ')') <u>else</u> k) = k = x ∈ ⟨factor⟩ (13a,A)

28. $(s^u(p, q))^v$(S) = x^v(S) = k^v = x^v($(p{:=}q)^e$(S))   (27, 10, 10)

29. ⟨factor⟩ <u>y</u> ::= ⟨variable⟩ <u>v</u> ⊂ ⟨string element⟩ <u>e</u> ⊂ ⟨string⟩ <u>s</u>   (9b, 11b, 12a)

30. s^u(p, q) = (<u>if</u> v=p <u>then</u> concat('(', q, ')') <u>else</u> v) ∈ ⟨factor⟩ (13a, 9c, 9b)

31. $(s^u(p, q))^v$(S) = (<u>if</u> v=p then $(concat('(', q, ')'))^v$(S) <u>else</u> v^v(S)) = (<u>if</u> v=p <u>then</u> q^v(S) <u>else</u> S(v))= $((p{:=}q)^e$(S))(v) = y^v($(p{:=}q)^e$(S)) (13a, 10c, 10b, 2, 10b)

32. ⟨factor⟩ <u>z</u> ::= '(' ⟨expression⟩ <u>e</u> ')' ⊂ ⟨string element⟩ <u>a</u> ⟨string⟩ <u>b</u> ⟨string element⟩<u>c</u>⊂⟨string⟩ <u>u</u> ⟨string⟩<u>v</u>⊂⟨string⟩<u>s</u> (9c, 11f, 20(*), 11g, 12a, 12b, LEMMA)

33. s^u(p, q) = concat(u^u(p, q), v^u(p, q)) = concat(<u>if</u> a=p <u>then</u> concat('(', q, ')') <u>else</u> a, concat(b^u(p, q), <u>if</u> c=p <u>then</u> concat('(', q, ')') <u>else</u> c)) = concat('(', concat(b^u(p, q), ')')) ∈ '(' ⟨expression⟩ <u>e</u> ')' ⊂ ⟨factor⟩ (LEMMA, 13a, 13b, A, A, 21(*), 9c)

34. $(s^u(p, q))^v$(S) = $(concat('(', concat(b^u(p, q), ')')))^v$(S) = $(b^u(p, q))^v$(S) = e^v($(p{:=}q)^e$(S)) = z^v($(p{:=}q)^e$(S))   (33, 10c, 22(*), 10c)

(This completes the analysis for statements 14, 15, and 16)

35. ⟨term⟩ $\underline{x}$ ::= ⟨factor⟩ $\underline{u}$ ⊂ ⟨string⟩ $\underline{s}$ (7a, 14)

36. $s^u(p, q)$ ∈ ⟨factor⟩ ⊂ ⟨term⟩   (15, 7a)

37. $(s^u(p, q))^v(S) = u^v((p:=q)^e(S)) = x^v((p:=q)^e(S))$ (16, 8a)

38. ⟨term⟩ $\underline{y}$ ::= ⟨term⟩ $\underline{z}$ ⟨multiplying operator⟩ $\underline{o}$ ⟨factor⟩ $\underline{v}$ ⊂ ⟨string⟩ $\underline{a}$ ⟨string
           element⟩ $\underline{b}$ ⟨string⟩ $\underline{c}$ ⊂ ⟨string⟩ $\underline{d}$ ⟨string⟩ $\underline{c}$ ⊂ ⟨string⟩ $\underline{s}$
           (7b, 17(*), 11d, 14, 12b, LEMMA)

39. $s^u(p, q)$ = concat($d^u(p, q)$, $c^u(p, q)$) = concat(concat($a^u(p, q)$, $\underline{if}$ o=p $\underline{then}$
     concat('(',q,')') $\underline{else}$ o),$c^u(p, q)$) = concat(concat($a^u(p, q)$, o), $c^u(p, q)$)
     ∈ ⟨term⟩⟨multiplying operator⟩⟨factor⟩ ⊂ ⟨term⟩ (LEMMA,13b,A,18(*),15,7b)

40. $(s^u(p, q))^v(S)$ = (concat(concat($a^u(p, q)$, o), $c^u(p, q)$))$^v(S) = o^o((a^u(p,$
          $q))^v(S)$, $(c^u(p, q))^v(S)) = o^o(z^v((p:=q)^e(S))$, $v^v((p:=q)^e(S)))$
          $= y^v((p:=q)^e(S))$ (39, 8b, 19(*), 16, 8b)

    (This completes the analysis for statements 17, 18, and 19)

41. ⟨expression⟩ $\underline{x}$ ::= ⟨term⟩ $\underline{u}$ ⊂ ⟨string⟩ $\underline{s}$ (5a, 17)

42. $s^u(p, q)$ ∈ ⟨term⟩ ⊂ ⟨expression⟩   (18, 5a)

43. $(s^u(p, q))^v(S) = u^v((p:=q)^e(S)) = x^u((p:=q)^e(S))$ (19, 6a)

44. ⟨expression⟩ $\underline{y}$ ::= ⟨adding operator⟩ $\underline{a}$ ⟨term⟩ $\underline{v}$ ⊂ ⟨string element⟩ $\underline{b}$ ⟨string⟩ $\underline{d}$
       ⊂ ⟨string⟩ $\underline{c}$ ⟨string⟩ $\underline{d}$ ⊂ ⟨string⟩ $\underline{s}$ (5b, 11c, 17, 12a, LEMMA)

45. $s^u(p, q)$ = concat($c^u(p, q)$, $d^u(p, q)$) = concat($\underline{if}$ a=p $\underline{then}$ concat('(', q,
       ')') $\underline{else}$ a, $d^u(p, q)$) = concat(a, $d^u(p, q)$) ∈ ⟨adding operator⟩ ⟨term⟩
       ⊂ ⟨expression⟩   (LEMMA, 13a, A, 18, 5b)

46. $(s^u(p, q))^v(S)$ = (concat(a, $d^u(p, q)$))$^v(S) = a^u((d^u(p, q))^v(S))$
          $= a^u(v^v((p:=q)^e(S))) = y^v((p:=q)^e(S))$ (45, 6b, 19, 6b)

47. ⟨expression⟩ $\underline{z}$ ::= ⟨expression⟩ $\underline{e}$ ⟨adding operator⟩ $\underline{b}$ ⟨term⟩ $\underline{w}$ ⊂ ⟨string⟩ $\underline{a}$
          ⟨string element⟩ $\underline{c}$ ⟨string⟩ $\underline{d}$ ⊂ ⟨string⟩ $\underline{g}$ ⟨string⟩ $\underline{d}$
          ⊂⟨string⟩ $\underline{s}$ (5c, 20(*), 11c, 17, 12b, LEMMA)

48. $s^u(p, q)$ = concat($g^u(p, q)$, $d^u(p, q)$) = concat(concat($a^u(p, q)$, $\underline{if}$ b=p $\underline{then}$
          concat('(', q, ')') $\underline{else}$ b), $d^u(p, q)$) = concat(concat($a^u(p,$
          q), b), $d^u(p, q)$) ∈ ⟨expression⟩ ⟨adding operator⟩ ⟨term ⟩
          ⊂ ⟨expression⟩   (LEMMA, 13b, A, 21(*), 18, 5c)

49. $(s^u(p, q))^v(S)$ = (concat(concat($a^u(p, q)$, b), $d^u(p, q)$))$^v(S) = b^b((a^u(p,$
          $q))^v(S)$, $(d^u(p, q))^v(S)) = b^b(e^v((p:=q)^e(S))$, $w^v((p:=q)^e(S)))$
          $= z^v((p:=q)^e(S))$ (48, 6c, 22(*), 19, 6c)

    (This completes the analysis for statements 20, 21, and 22)

50. ⟨relation⟩ $\underline{r}$ ::= ⟨expression⟩ $\underline{u}$ ⟨relational operator⟩ $\underline{o}$ ⟨expression⟩ $\underline{v}$ ⊂
          ⟨string⟩ $\underline{a}$ ⟨string element⟩ $\underline{b}$ ⟨string⟩ $\underline{c}$ ⊂ ⟨string⟩ $\underline{d}$
          ⟨string⟩ $\underline{c}$ ⊂ ⟨string⟩ $\underline{s}$ (3, 20, 11e, 20, 12b, LEMMA)

51. $s^u(p, q)$ = concat($d^u(p, q)$, $c^u(p, q)$) = concat(concat($a^u(p, q)$, <u>if</u> o=p <u>then</u> concat('(', q, ')') <u>else</u> o), $c^u(p, q)$) = concat(concat($a^u(p, q)$, o), $c^u(p, q)$)   expression   relational operator   expression   relation   (LEMMA, 13b, 21, 21, 3)

52. $(s^u(p, q))^v(S)$ = (concat(concat($a^u(p, q)$, o), $c^u(p, q)$))$^v(S)$
        = $o^o((a^u(p, q))^v(S)$, $(c^u(p, q))^v(S))$ = $o^o(u^v((p{:=}q)^e(S))$,
        $v^v((p{:=}q)^e(S)))$ = $r^v((p{:=}q)^e(S))$ (51, 4, 22, 22, 4)

    (This completes the analysis for statements 23, 24, and 25)   <u>Q. E. D.</u>

A few remarks are in order about the form of the proof. The statement A in the hypothesis of the theorem is used during the proof to show that expressions of the form <u>if</u> x=p <u>then</u> concat('(', q, ')') <u>else</u> x must in fact be equal to x if x is a constant (step 27), an adding operator (steps 45 and 48), a multiplying operator (step 39), a relational operator (step 51), or a left or right parenthesis (step 33). The reason, of course, is that "x=p" must be false, since p represents a variable and statement A says that variables and the other quantities mentioned here are distinct. It is also necessary to note carefully that variables, and not the individual characters in variable identifiers, are taken as elements of strings. If we were to treat characters as string elements, the definition of the substituted string would have to be considerably more complex, because we would have to be careful not to replace substrings of an identifier. We do not wish to change "alpha" into "al(q)ha" when substituting (q) for p, for example.

ACKNOWLEDGMENT

This research was partially supported by National Science Foundation Grant GJ-31612. The author is grateful to Ralph London, Michael Megas, Nori Suzuki, and Raymond Wong for their helpful comments and suggestions.

REFERENCES

1. Burstall, R. M., <u>Proving properties of programs by structural induction</u>, Computer J. 12, 41–48 (1969).

2. Hoare, C. A. R., <u>An axiomatic basis for computer programming</u>, Communications of the ACM 12, 576–580 and 583 (1969).

3. Knuth, D. E., <u>Semantics of context-free languages</u>, Math. Systems Theory 2, 127–145 (1968).

4. McCarthy, J., <u>Towards a mathematical science of computation</u>, Information Processing 1962, Proc. of IFIP Congress 62, North-Holland, Amsterdam, 21–28 (1963).

5. McCarthy, J., et al., <u>LISP 1.5 Programmer's Manual</u>, MIT Press (1962).

6. Maurer, W. D., <u>A semantic extension of BNF</u>, International J. of Computer Math., Section A, Vol. 3, 157–176 (1972).

ABOUT THE COMPLETENESS OF APL

Bernard J.ROBINET

1. Introduction

The idea of completeness of a programming language is a very important one, but at present it is impossible to prove that any language is complete. However, if one finds a language which describes all the algorithms known, one may feel some confidence that this language is, in fact, complete ; we can consult Nolin (1969) about this topic.

For APL, the Iverson's language (1962), the situation is quite different : this paper attempts to show the completeness of APL as an adequate linguistic tool to express every mixed function of manipulation on arrays.

To do this, the concepts of an array and its operators are based on the notions of abstraction and application of functions and we make use of a typed combinatory system about which we informally summarize a number of facts in the section 2 ; all notation used is introduced in this section, thus making the paper self-contained, for more details see Robinet (1972 a). These facts are reffered in section 3 to give the APL expressions for the usual distinguished constants of pure λ-calculus, say $S = \lambda a \; \lambda b \; \lambda c \; (ac)(bc)$ and $K = \lambda a \; \lambda b \; a$. Thus, we are able to prove that every APL function which manipulates arrays is expressible in APL with a finite set of basic functions.

2. Combinators with types

The presented system allow us to interpret easily terms as functions ; we assume that there are given certain basic types, each of which is intented to represent à particular set.

2.1. *The two languages*

Let A be the language generated by the grammar :

$A \to C_A$, $A \to V_A$, $A \to (AA)$ where C_A and V_A respectively are an infinite set of constants and an infinite set of variables.

The usual combinators S and K are two distinguished elements of C_A .
Let T be the language such as :

$$T \to C_T \quad , \quad T \to V_T \quad , \quad T \to FTT$$

<u>notations</u> : latin letters denote applications, elements of A and greek letters will denote types, elements of T ; we shall sometimes use the abreviations *(F α β)* for F α β and $F_n \, \alpha_1 \ldots \alpha_n \, \beta$ for $F\alpha_1(F\alpha_2(\ldots(F_n\alpha \, \beta)\ldots))$.

2.2. *Definition of typed combinatory terms*

Let θ be a relation such as :

- θ[S,FFαFβγFFαβFαγ] for all α , β ; γ in T ;

- θ[K , FαFβα] for all α, β in T ;

- if X ∈ A and θ[X,Fαβ] , Y ∈ A and θ[Y,α] then *(XY)* ∈ A and θ[*(XY)*,β].

<u>notation</u> : denoting $|X|_b$ the number of occurences of b in X ∈ A , we suppose, $\forall b, \ |X|_b \geq 1 \ \Rightarrow \ b \in \{a_1,\ldots,a_n\}$ and $\theta[a_i , \alpha_i]$, $\forall i \in [1:n]$ and also θ[X,β] .

We use the notation :

$$t(a_i) = \alpha_i \quad , \quad t(X) = \beta$$

$$t_{a \ldots a_n} X = [\alpha_1,\ldots,\alpha_n , \beta]$$

2.3. *Properties of the θ-relation*

There exists an algorithm to compute $t_{a_1 \ldots a_n} X$ for any X ∈ A and for any $a = \{a,\ldots,a_n\} \subset V_A$ such as $|X|_{V_A - a} = 0$; this algorithm can be found in Robinet (1972 b).

It is important to observe that in the definition of the θ-relation, we may substitute any elements of T in place of α,β,γ ; more formally, the rule of assignment of type is, with the new notation :

if $t(X) = F\alpha\beta$ and $t(Y) = \gamma$ with α,β,γ ∈ T then $t(XY) = \delta$; δ is obtained by substitutions, i.e :

$$\delta = Sub^{\beta_1 \ldots \beta_n}_{\alpha_1 \ldots \alpha_n} \beta = Sub^{\beta_1}_{\alpha_1}(\ldots(Sub^{\beta_n}_{\alpha_n} \beta))$$

where $Sub^{\beta_i}_{\alpha_i} \nu$ denotes the substitution of α_i to β_i in ν ; the β_i are the variables of T which belong to α and β and the α_i are obtained by solving the equation α = γ if possible.

example :

$$t(\textbf{S}) = FF\ \alpha'\ F\ \beta'\ \gamma'\ FF\ \alpha'\ \beta'\ F\alpha'\gamma'$$

$$t(\textbf{K}) = FF\ \alpha''\ F\ \beta''\ \alpha''$$

so

$$\alpha \equiv F\ \alpha'\ F\ \beta'\ \gamma'\ ,\qquad \beta = FF\alpha'\beta'F\ \alpha'\gamma'\qquad \gamma = F\ \alpha''\ F\ \beta''\ \alpha''\ ;$$

$\{\beta_i\} = \{\alpha',\beta',\gamma'\}$; the equation to solve is

$$F\ \alpha'F\ \beta'\gamma' = F\alpha''\ F\beta''\ \alpha''\quad \text{and the solutions}$$

are :

$$\alpha' = \alpha''\quad ,\quad \beta' = \beta''\quad ,\quad \gamma' = \alpha''\quad .$$

Thus

$$\delta = Sub^{\alpha'\beta'\gamma'}_{\alpha''\beta''\alpha''}\ FF\alpha'\beta'F\alpha'\gamma' = FF\alpha''\beta''F\ \alpha''\alpha''$$

and

$$t(\textbf{SK}) = FF\alpha\beta F\alpha\alpha\quad \text{for any}\quad \alpha,\beta,\epsilon\ T\quad .$$

2.4. *equivalence relations*

We say that $X \equiv_1 Y$ holds iff $t_{a_1\ldots a_n}X = t_{a_1\ldots a_n}Y$.

Let $\equiv_2$ be the least equivalence relation such that, for all X , Y , $Z \in T$ and variables a , the following will be derivable :

$$\bullet\ ((\textbf{S}X)Y)Z\ \equiv_2\ (XZ)(YZ)$$

$$\bullet\ (\textbf{K}X)Y\ \equiv_2\ X$$

$$\bullet\ Xa\ \equiv_2\ Ya\ \text{and}\ |(XY)|_a = 0\ \text{implie}\ X\ \equiv_2\ Y\quad .$$

We say that $X \equiv Y$ iff $X \equiv_1 Y$ and $X \equiv_2 Y$.

2.5. *theorem of completeness*

$$X \equiv_1 Y\ ,\ |(XY)|_a = 0\quad ,\quad Xa \equiv_2 Ya \Rightarrow X \equiv Y$$

This theorem is an important one ; that is our versus of extensionnal equality ; among other things, it shows that X and Y intuitively represent the same function, see Nolin (1971) for a proof.

2.6. *some interesting words*

The basic combinators $\int$ and K give us a systematic way of construction for each expression involving x a notation for the corresponding function of x ; but it is clear that their use is not always easy.

So we introduce the words :

$$I = (\int K)K \quad , \quad B = (\int (K\int))K \quad ,$$

$$C = \int ((BB)\int)(KK) \quad \text{and} \quad W = (\int\int)(KI) \; ;$$

it is easy to prove the following :

$$I X \equiv X \qquad\qquad t(I) = F\alpha\alpha$$

$$B XYZ \equiv X(YZ) \qquad\qquad t(B) = FF\beta\gamma FF\alpha\beta F\alpha\gamma$$

$$C XYZ = (XZ)Y \qquad\qquad t(C) = FF\alpha F\beta\gamma F\beta F\alpha\gamma$$

$$W XY = (XY)Y \qquad\qquad t(W) = FF\alpha F\alpha\beta F\alpha\beta$$

for any α, β, γ in T and X, Y, Z in A .

3. Combinators and their expressions

It is clear that in our system, like in usual combinatory logic discussed by Curry and Feys (1968), the result of applying a function f to the argument x is denoted by fx ; now, an array H being conceived in term of function of cartesian product in a set, its type is $F_n \alpha_1 \ldots \alpha_n \beta$; thus, if i_k has type α_k for $k = 1, \ldots, n$, $Hi_1 \ldots i_n$ has type β and represents indexing of H by a family of indices ; a formal definition of arrays and indexing is given in Robinet (1972a) : in this paper, we suppose arrays being conceived in term of combinators, that is to say, arrays are elements of the language A .

3.1. *expressions of $\int$ and K*

The types of $\int$ and K are respectively $FF_2 \alpha\beta\gamma\, FF\alpha\beta F\alpha\gamma$ and $F\alpha F\beta\alpha$; we know that, by remark 2.3.,

$$t(\int) = FF_n\alpha_1\ldots.\alpha_n\gamma\, FF\alpha_1\alpha_2\, F_{n-1}\alpha_1\alpha_3\ldots\alpha_n\,\gamma$$

$$t(K) = FF_n\alpha_1\ldots.\alpha_n\gamma\, F_{n+1}\alpha_1\alpha_1\ldots\alpha_n\,\gamma$$

Let us consider some operands for $\int$ and K :

- a rank-n array H with type $F_n N_1 \dots N_n \, \gamma$,

  $N_k = [1:p_k]$ for $k = 1,\dots,n$;

- a vector V with type $F_1 N_1 N_2$;

- $\{i_k\}$, an indices-family such as $i_k \in N_k$; the N_k are basic types as assumed in section 2 .

Then

$$\int H\, V i_1 i_3 \dots i_n \;\equiv\; H i_1 (V i_1) i_3 \dots i_n$$

$$\mathsf{K} H\, i_1 i_1 i_2 \dots i_n \;\equiv\; i_1 i_2 \dots i_n$$

<u>Proof</u> :

The proof is in two parts ; we give it for the first identity.

    1) prove the $\equiv_2$ relation ; it is trivial.

    2) prove the $\equiv_1$ relation ; the successive steps are :

$$t(\textstyle\int H) = FFN_1 N_2 F_{n-1} N_1 N_3 \dots N_n \, \gamma$$

$$t(\textstyle\int HV) = F_{n-1} N_1 N_3 \dots N_n \, \gamma$$

$$t(\textstyle\int HV i_1 i_3 \dots i_n) = \gamma \quad ;$$

but

$$t(H i_1) = F_{n-1} N_2 \dots N_n \, \gamma \quad \text{and} \quad t(V i_1) = N_2 \; ; \text{ thus}$$

$$t(H i_1 (V i_1) i_3 \dots i_n) = \gamma \; ; \text{ this achieves the proof for the } \equiv_1$$
équivalence.

<u>Interpretation</u>

Let H and V the APL-arrays, interpretations of H and V ; indexing of H , say $H_{i_1} (V i_1) i_3 \dots i_n$, is expressed in APL by $H[I1; V[I1] \; ; \; I3 \; ;\dots;IN]$.

By definition of indexing, we know that :

$$H[I1 \; ; \; V[I1] \; ; \; I3 \; ;\dots;IN] = (H[;V;\dots;])[I1;I1;I3;\dots;IN] \quad ;$$

but the APL-operator of <u>*dyadic transposition*</u> , for references see Pakin (1968) or

Robinet (1971), allow us to write :

$$(H[;V;\ldots;])[I1;I1;I3;\ldots;IN]=(1,1,3,\ldots,N \; \lozenge \; H[;V;\ldots;])[I1;I3;\ldots;IN]$$

So, the APL expression of $\quad HVi_1 i_3 \ldots i_n \quad$ is

$$((1,\iota N-1) \; \lozenge \; H[;V;\ldots;])[I1 \; ; \; I3 \; ;\ldots;IN]$$

Denoting $[[K]] \; HV$ for $H[;\ldots;V;\ldots;]$ where V is at the k-th position, and by the theorem of completeness, we can assume, without loos of generality, that :

$$\int \equiv (1,\iota N-1) \; \lozenge \; [[2]]$$

with N rank of the first argument of $\int$. For the combinator K , we remark that the APL operators of *size* and *reshape* allow us to write :

$$(((\rho H)[1], \; \rho H)\rho H) \; [I1;I1;\ldots;IN] = H[I1;..,IN] \quad ;$$

so, the APL-expression for $\quad KHi_1 i_1 i_2 \ldots i_n \quad$ is

$$(((\rho H)[1], \; \rho H) \; \rho H)[I1 \; ; \; I1 \; ;\ldots;IN] \quad .$$

If R is the size of the first argument of K , we can write :

$$K \equiv (R[1] \; , \; R) \; \rho$$

3.2. *some other combinators and some remarks*

It is easy to give the expression of usuals combinators ; for instance, we have seen, at the end of section 2, that $t(W) = FF\alpha F\alpha\beta F\alpha\beta$; by remark 2.3.,

$$t(W) = FF_n \alpha_1 \alpha_1 \alpha_3 \ldots \alpha_n \; \gamma \; F_{n-1} \alpha_1 \alpha_3 \ldots \alpha_n \gamma \; , \text{ so, considering a rank-n array}$$

H with type $F_n N_1 N_1 N_3 \ldots N_n \; \gamma \quad$, it should be demonstrate that

$$W \equiv (1,\iota N-1) \; \lozenge \quad .$$

and for the other combinators :

$$C \equiv (2 \; 1 \; , \; 2 + \iota \; N-2) \; \lozenge$$

$$B \equiv [[1]]$$

For I , we see that $I \equiv WK$; it suffices to show that $WK\alpha \equiv_2 K\alpha\alpha \equiv_2 \alpha$ and , since $t(W) = FF_2\alpha'\alpha'\beta'F\alpha'\beta'$ and $t(K) = F\alpha F\beta\alpha$, $t(WK) = F\alpha\alpha$;so , in APL , the identity operator of manipulation is :

$$I \equiv (1,\iota(\rho\rho H)-1) \, \varnothing \, ((\rho H)[1],\rho H)\rho$$

It does not stand to reason, but it is easy to prove these results :

$$\int \equiv W[[2]]$$

$$\int H \ \iota(\rho H)[2] \equiv W H$$

$$W[[2]]H\iota(\rho H)[2] \equiv W H$$

$$BC \equiv (1 \ 3 \ 2 \ , \ 4 + \iota \ N{-}4) \, \varnothing$$

4. Conclusion

It has been shown that it is possible by formal approach to prove that every APL operator which manipulates arrays is expressible in APL with a finite set of basic operators by composition, identity, adjunction, cancelling and permutation of arguments : in this sense, APL is complete.

References

Curry, H.B. and Feys R. (1968)   *Combinatory Logic.* North Holland.

Iverson, K.E.(1962) .   *A programming language.* Wiley

Nolin, L. (1968).   *Formalisation des notions de machine et de programme.* Gauthier-Villars.

Nolin, L. (1971).   *Logique combinatoire et algorithmes.* CRAS tome 2,série A,pp.1435-1438 and 1485-1488.

Pakin, S. (1968).   *APL/360. Reference Manual* . SRA

Robinet, B. (1971).   *Le langage APL.* Technip.

Robinet, B. (1972a).   *Sémantique des tableaux : application au langage APL.* Thesis. Université de Paris 6.

Robinet, B. (1972b).   *Semantique des langages de programmation.* Publications de l'Institut de Programmation n° 11 . Université de Paris 6.

MAIN DEGREES OF COMPLEXITY OF COMPUTER PROGRAMS
AND COMPUTABLE FUNCTIONS

Karel Čulík

(Kurzfassung)[+]

A <u>computer program</u> is a finite sequence $P=(K^{(1)},\ldots,K^{(N)})$ of labelled commands $K^{(i)}=\langle b^{(i)},C^{(i)}\rangle$, where $b^{(i)}$ is a <u>label</u> and $C^{(i)}$ is a <u>command</u> (see e.g. [1]), such that $b^{(i)}\neq b^{(j)}$ if $i\neq j$.

A finite sequence $\ell b=(K_1,\ldots,K_q)$ of labelled commands of P is called <u>consistent stopped labelled branch</u> of P if certain conditions are satisfied (e.g. if $K_1=K^{(1)}$, $C_q=$STOP, etc.). The <u>length</u> $L(\ell b)$ of ℓb is the integer $q\geqslant 1$, and the <u>width</u> $W(\ell b)$ of ℓb is the number of different variables which occur in the commands of ℓb. Let B_P be the set of all consistent stopped labelled branches of P. There are three main degrees of complexity of computer programs according to the following three possibilities for each program P:

1. <u>restricted</u> (=finite) <u>time</u> (of computation): if
$$\max_{\ell b\in B_P} L(\ell b) < \infty \quad \text{(then also} \quad \max_{\ell b\in B_P} W(\ell b) < \infty \text{);}$$

2. <u>unrestricted time</u> but <u>restricted</u> (=finite) space (of storage):
$$\text{if} \quad \max_{\ell b\in B_P} L(\ell b)= \infty \quad \text{and} \quad \max_{\ell b\in B_P} W(\ell b)< \infty \text{ ;}$$

3. <u>unrestricted space:</u> if $\quad \max\limits_{\ell b\in B_P} W(\ell b)= \infty$ (then also
$$\max_{\ell b\in B_P} L(\ell b)= \infty \text{).}$$

If there exists a flow-diagram of P then P requires only restricted space in all interpretations of P and for all their input states.

If there are no cycles in the flow-diagram of P then P requires only restricted time in all interpretations and for all their input states.

If P contains a complete set of procedures, which requires recursive calls, then there exists an interpretation of P such that P requires unrestricted space.

[+] Manuskript nicht eingegangen

A <u>macrocommand</u> is a string $Q(x_1,\ldots,x_m)=:(y_1,\ldots,y_n)$, where x_i, y_j are variables and $Q \in \text{SymbProc}^{(m/n)}$ is a new symbol without interpretation. A <u>macroprogram</u> is a program in which also macrocommands may occur. A set $\tilde{R}$ of macroprograms is called <u>complete set of macroprocedures</u> if there exists a one-to-one mapping τ of $\tilde{R}$ into SymbProc such that:

    (i) $|\text{Inp}_R| = m$ and $|\text{Outp}_R| = n \Rightarrow \tau(R) \in \text{SymbProc}^{(m/n)}$ for each $R \in \tilde{R}$;

    (ii) if the symbol $Q \in \text{SymbProc}$ occurs in a macrocommand of a macroprogram $R \in \tilde{R}$, then there exists $R' \in \tilde{R}$ such that $\tau(R')=Q$;

    (iii) if $R=(L^{(1)},\ldots,L^{(M)}) \in \tilde{R}$, where $L^{(i)}= \langle c^{(i)}, D^{(i)} \rangle$, then $D^{(M)}=\text{STOP}$ and $D^{(i)} \neq \text{STOP}$ for each $i=1,2,\ldots,M-1$;

    (iv) if $R,R' \in \tilde{R}$ and $R \neq R'$ then R,R' have no label in common.

If a fixed mapping τ , satisfying (i-iv), is choosen then $[\tilde{R},\tau]$ is called <u>complete set of declared macroprocedures</u> and $\text{Dcl}_{\tilde{R}} = \{ \tau(R)=_{df}R;\ R \in \tilde{R}\}$ is the <u>set of procedure declarations</u>.

$[\tilde{R},\tau]$ requires a <u>recursive call of procedures</u> if there exists a sequence of procedure declarations $\tau(R_{i_1})=_{df}R_{i_1}$, $\tau(R_{i_2})=_{df}R_{i_2}$, $\ldots$, $\tau(R_{i_k})=_{df}R_{i_k}$ such that a) the symbol $\tau(R_{i_j})$ occurs in $R_{i_{j-1}}$ for $j=2,3,\ldots,k$, and b) there exists index h such that $1 \leqslant h < k$ and $\tau(R_{i_h})= \tau(R_{i_k})$.

Besides the commands required in $[1]$ the following commands are added.

                                                    <u>semantics</u>

(constant input	$x \equiv :y$	in the new state the object x will be stored at the location y;
(direct 2-jump)	$\text{GOTO } \gamma(w)$	if ρ is the current state then $\rho(w)$ is the label of the next command;
(occupation)	$\underline{\text{ocp}}\ [a_1,\ldots,a_p]\ b$	starting with the command labelled by b as the first, the i-th command, where $1 \leqslant i \leqslant p$ having the form either $x=:y$ or $x \equiv :y$, is changed to the form either $a_i =:y$ or $a_i \equiv :y$;

(modification) $\quad\quad\quad\quad$ $\underline{\text{Mod}}$ (s) $[a_1,\dots,a_p]$ $\quad$ starting with the next command as the first, the i-th command, where $1 \leqslant i \leqslant p$, having the form either $a_i =: {}_o w_j$ or ${}_o w_j =: a_i$, is changed to the form either $a_i =: {}_k w_j$ or ${}_k w_j =: a_i$, where $k = \mathcal{M}(s)$ is an integer (counting the calls), $\mathcal{M}$ is the current state, and an unrestricted stack (push down) of locations is assumed:

$$
\begin{aligned}
&{}_1 w_1, \dots, {}_1 w_p, \\
&{}_2 w_1, \dots, {}_2 w_p, \\
&\quad\vdots \qquad\quad \vdots \\
&{}_k w_1, \dots, {}_k w_p, \\
&\quad\vdots \qquad\quad \vdots
\end{aligned}
$$

Using these commands the macroprogram P and macroprocedures $\mathcal{R}$ are modified to a program $P^* \cup \mathcal{R}^*$ with procedures, in which no macrocommand occur.

(1) $\quad$ K. Čulík: Structural similarity of programs and some concepts of algorithmic method, 249–280, Lecture Notes in Economics and Mathematical Systems 75, Springer 1972

PROGRAMMIER- UND DIALOGSPRACHEN

KONTEXT-SENSITIVE GENERIERUNG BEIM
PROGRAMMIEREN DURCH AUSWÄHLEN

Hans-Jürgen Hoffmann und Gerhard Winkler

1. ZUSAMMENFASSUNG

Beim *Programmieren durch Auswählen*, einer Methode der Programmformulierung unter Verwendung einer Datensichtstation in einem Dialogsystem,
wird der Programmierer vom System straff geführt; das bedeutet, daß er
im Spielraum seiner Entscheidungen gegenüber der üblichen, freien Formulierung geeignet eingeschränkt ist. Der Programmierer kann in jedem
Dialogschritt nur unter *syntaktisch richtigen* Formulierungen wählen.
Das System vollzieht darauf die Generierung eines Programms als Satz
einer formalen Sprache und zwar entsprechend der Phrasenstrukturgramma-
tik der Sprache top-down durch sukzessives Ersetzen je eines Phrasensymbols der erreichten Satzform durch die rechte Seite aus einer vom
Programmierer ausgewählten Produktion dieses Phrasensymbols.

In einer kontext-freien Grammatik läßt sich die Reihenfolge der Ersetzungen von Phrasensymbolen nicht vom System bestimmen; es muß dem Programmierer die Wahl der Reihenfolge überlassen bleiben. Im vorliegenden
Bericht wird gezeigt, wie das Verwenden einer *kontext-sensitiven Grammatik* es erlaubt, den Programmierer auch hinsichtlich der Reihenfolge
der Ersetzungen zu führen, und wie dadurch (in einem zu definierenden
Sinne) auch *semantisch richtige* Formulierungen erreicht werden können.

Die von verschiedenen Autoren vorgeschlagenen restriktiven Regeln in
der Anwendung von der Form nach kontext-freien Produktionen, bei deren
Beachtung sich eine Ausweitung zur nicht-kontextfreien Sprachklasse einstellt, erweisen sich für eine Systemimplementierung als vorteilhaft.
Als Beispiel wird die Überprüfung, ob eine Variablenbezeichnung vereinbart ist oder nicht, nach den Regeln einer *programmierten Grammatik*
vorgestellt.

2. PROGRAMMIEREN DURCH AUSWÄHLEN,
ALS METHODE DES PROGRAMMIERENS BETRACHTET

Die gebräuchliche Methode des Programmierens, bei der ein Programmierer
die Formulierung eines Programms als Niederschrift auf einem Blatt Papier (das als Ablochvorlage dient) oder unmittelbar durch Eingabe über
die Tastatur eines Datenendgeräts vornimmt, gibt keine Sicherheit gegen
formale Fehler, die aus Unwissenheit oder Unachtsamkeit zur Verletzung
einer syntaktischen Regel (einer kontext-freien Grammatik) der verwendeten Programmiersprache führen; auch Auslassungen und Unverträglichkeiten, die sich auf das entstehende Programm sinnentstellend auswirken,
semantische Fehler also, sind nicht auszuschließen. Obwohl bei dieser
Methode regelmäßig weit ausgebaute Programmiersysteme auf einer Rechenanlage den Programmierer beim Beseitigen solcher Fehler *unterstützen*
- z.B. durch Fehlermeldungen, eventl. vorgeschlagene oder gar vollzoge-
ne Fehlerkorrekturen, auch durch Dateiführung und -editierung -, wird
der Programmierer nicht, wie wir es nennen, *geführt*. Das bedeutet, daß
ihm vom System die Beachtung von Formalien nicht abgenommen, und er zu
einer vollständigen, in sich verträglichen Programmformulierung nicht
unumgehbar angehalten wird, so daß er sich allein auf die korrekte Darstellung des von ihm zur Lösung einer Programmieraufgabe ausgedachten
Algorithmus konzentrieren könnte. *Strukturiertes Programmieren*, wie es
von Dijkstra [5] und anderen vorgeschlagen wird, bringt zwar - als intel-
lektuelle Disziplin - die von uns geforderte Führung des Programmierers,
allerdings - da nicht "systematisiert" - ohne ihre Befolgung gewährlei-
sten und bei ihrem Gebrauch das Auftreten von formalen und sinnentstellenden Fehlern grundsätzlich ausschließen zu können. Diese Feststellun-
gen sind für unerfahrene wie auch erfahrene Programmierer zutreffend.

Eine Methode, die wir *Programmieren durch Auswählen* nennen, versucht,
hier eine entscheidende Verbesserung zu bringen. Die dem Programmierer
durch ein Programmiersystem gebotene Unterstützung geht über das Führen
einer Datei mit dem entstehenden Programm hinaus. Es wird vielmehr der
Programmierer veranlaßt, im Dialog über ein Datensichtgerät an ihn gestellte Fragen, die eine Auswahl unter möglichen Fortsetzungen der bis
zu dem betrachteten Dialogschritt erreichten Formulierung eines Programms erfordern, allein aufgrund von Struktur und Eigenschaften des
von ihm ausgedachten Algorithmus zu beantworten. Das Angebot möglicher
Fortsetzungen wird vom System so aufbereitet, daß Formalien nicht verletzt werden können und Sinnentstellungen vermieden werden. Als alternativ werden nur solche Fortsetzungen angesehen, bei deren Befolgen

sich eine algorithmische Alternative im späteren Ablauf des Programms
einstellt. Die Programmformulierung schreitet von der groben Festlegung
der umfassenden Struktur des Algorithmus zur detaillierten Festlegung
der Eigenschaften einzelner Schritte im Algorithmus fort. Die intellek-
tuelle Disziplin, die beim strukturierten Programmieren erforderlich
ist, wird somit zu einer systematisierten Führung des Programmierers
während der Programmformulierung im Dialog umgesetzt.

An dieser Stelle sei noch erläutert, was wir unter dem zur Semantik eines Programms in Beziehung stehenden Begriff *sinnentstellend* erfassen
wollen. Die Definition des Begriffs der *semantischen Richtigkeit* kann
damit einhergehen. Wir betrachten zwei Arten der Sinnenstellung und
erläutern sie anhand von Beispielen.

a) Ein Programm ist eine sinnentstellende Darstellung eines Algorithmus
   und daher semantisch nicht richtig, wenn es nicht alle Eigenschaften
   eines Schritts in einem Algorithmus im erforderlichen Detail festlegt. Diese Definition ist hierarchisch strukturiert anzuwenden.
   Beispiel (Ausschnitt aus umfassenderem Programm):

```
begin S := O;                         begin
for I := 1 step 1 until N do          for I := 1 step 1 until N do
    S := S + A [I]                        S := S + A [I]
end                                   end
```

oder generell:

```
<Iteration> ::=                       <Iteration> ::=
    begin <Initialisierung>;              begin
    for <Iterationsvorschrift> do         for <Iterationsvorschrift> do
        <Anweisung>                           <Anweisung>
    end                                   end
```

Die Programmformulierung rechts ist im Gegensatz zu der links eine
sinnentstellende Darstellung des algorithmischen Schrittes der Sum-
mierung von N Komponenten eines Vektors; das gleiche gilt für die
Ersetzungsregel (als Produktion einer formalen Sprache) der algorithmischen Struktur einer Iteration durch die Detaileigenschaften dieser
Strukturen rechts, nämlich nur Iterationsvorschrift und zu iterieren-
de Anweisung mit fehlender Initialisierung der Iteration.

b) Ein Programm ist eine sinnentstellende Darstellung eines Algorithmus
   und daher semantisch nicht richtig, wenn es unverträgliche Elemente
   enthält. Hierunter fallen vor allem Artunverträglichkeiten, d.h.
   fehlende oder unzutreffende Vereinbarung, aber auch unterschiedliche
   Anzahl von Parametern zwischen Vereinbarung und Aufrufen einer Funk-

tionsprozedur u.ä.. Wir dehnen diese Art der Sinnentstellung auch auf nachstehendes Beispiel aus (Ausschnitt aus umfassenderem Programm):

```
begin real S;                          begin
if N = -1 then S := 0                  if N =-1 then T := 0
else begin S := 0;                     else begin S := 0;
     for I := 1 step 1 until N do           for I := 1 step 1 until N do
         S := S + A[I]                           S := S + A[I]
     end;                                  end;
PRINT (S)                              PRINT (S)
end                                    end
```

$$\text{oder generell}^+:$$

```
⟨Resultatausgabe⟩ ::=                  ⟨Resultatausgabe⟩ ::=
begin ⟨Vereinbarung von Y⟩;            begin
⟨Wertbestimmung für Y⟩;                ⟨Wertbestimmung⟩ ;
PRINT (⟨Y⟩)                            PRINT (⟨Variable⟩)
end                                    end
```

Die Programmformulierung rechts hat in den beiden Zweigen der bedingten Anweisung unverträgliche Wertbestimmungen für zwei, nicht nur für eine Variable; in der Ersetzungsregel wird der mangelnde Zwang zu einer verträglichen Formulierung deutlich.

Einer der Verfasser hat diese Gedankengänge in einem anderen Bericht (Hoffmann [8]) ins einzelne gehender dargestellt.

3. DIALOGSYSTEM "PAD"

In der Literatur sind einige wenige Systeme beschrieben worden, die Programmieren durch Auswählen bieten:

a) Cameron, Ewing und Liveright [3] mit "DIALOG".

b) Hansen [7] mit "EMILY", dem System, das am engsten zu unseren Vorstellungen paßt.

c) Diel, Grunefeld und Menzel [4].

d) Levy [9] mit "SCARABEE" (nur nach Auftreten eines nicht korrigierbaren Syntaxfehlers).

Keines dieser Systeme hat die für die Programmiermethode charakteristische Führung des Programmierers erreicht; die Systeme gehören aber nach Handhabung und Implementierung zur Methode des Programmierens durch Auswählen.

+ Y betrachte man als Parameter der Ersetzungsregel, der an allen Stellen, an denen er auftritt, gleich zu ersetzen ist. Eine kontext-freie Produktion reicht bekanntermaßen nicht aus, um diesen Sachverhalt zu erreichen. Man beachte die Vereinbarung von Y als lokale Variable dieses Blocks.

Mit dem Dialogsystem "PAD" versuchen die Autoren[+], diese Methode voll
einsatzfähig zu machen. Es existiert eine arbeitsfähige Implementierung,
die gegen syntaktische Fehler Sicherheit bietet; an einer Verbesserung,
die auch semantische Fehler (der im 2. Abschnitt erläuterten Arten) verhindern soll, wird gearbeitet. Im Folgenden wird zunächst die Arbeitsweise von PAD erläutert, soweit sie jetzt feststeht (eine detailliertere
Erläuterung findet sich in Hoffmann [8]).

Das Dialogsystem PAD vollzieht unter der Kontrolle einer kontext-freien
Grammatik (Σ, Π, P, Π_o) die Generierung eines Programms als Satz einer formalen Sprache. Die Grammatik enthält Produktionen nach zwei Scha-
blonen (siehe Müller[10]):

a) *1-Produktionen*. Diese werden verwendet statt Produktionengruppen,
   die zu einer angereihten Struktur führen (z.B. Anweisungsfolgen,
   Parameterlisten). Dadurch wird die für die algorithmische Strukturierung eines Programms nichtssagende rekursive Definition von Phrasensymbolen (d.h. "Nonterminals") vermieden (Bock und Schinzel[2]).
   Statt den (das gleiche ausdrückenden) Produktionengruppen für ein
   $\tau \in \Pi$ (mit λ als leere Symbolkette), $\omega \in (\Pi \cup \Sigma)^* - \{\lambda\}$:

   $$\tau ::= \lambda \quad , \quad \tau ::= \tau\omega \qquad \text{bzw.} \quad \tau ::= \lambda , \quad \tau ::= \omega\tau$$

   sagt die (einzige) 1-Produktion aus, daß τ durch Anreihung (in beliebiger Anzahl) von ω entsteht; zwischen den Anreihungen einzuschie-
   bende Trennsymbole (z.B. ";" oder ",", aber auch ⟨Arithm.Operator⟩)
   können angegeben werden.

b) *s-Produktionen*. Alle Alternativen eines Phrasensymbols $\sigma \in \Pi$ werden
   in einer Gruppe von s-Produktionen zusammengefaßt:
   $$\sigma ::= \tau_1, \quad \sigma ::= \tau_2, \ldots \sigma ::= \tau_n. \quad \text{Es ist } \tau_i \in \Pi \cup (\Sigma^* - \{\lambda\}).$$
   Ist ein
   $\tau_i \in \Pi$, wird dieses τ_i (in der Regel) durch genau eine 1-Produktion
   definiert.

Das System PAD arbeitet in zwei Takten:

a) *Positionierungstakt*. Aus dem am Datensichtgerät angebotenen Programm-
   ausschnitt, das den erreichten Stand der Programmformulierung als
   Satzform wiedergibt, wird die Position vom Programmierer bestimmt,
   an der die nächste Ersetzung vorzunehmen ist. Dadurch wird die *Reihenfolge der Ersetzungen* festgelegt. Die Position kann entweder an einem Phrasensymbol - es sei σ - sein (Fall b1) oder an einem (speziellen) Anreihungsindikator für ein Phrasensymbol - es sei τ - (Fall
   b2).

+ Zur Gruppe, die das Projekt bearbeitet, gehören weiter:
  M. Biallas, A. Müller, D. Muth.

b) *Ersetzungstakt*. Es sind zwei Fälle zu unterscheiden:

b1) Es werden dem Programmierer alle τ_i der s-Produktionen von σ zur Auswahl angeboten. Um die geforderte Führung des Programmierers zu erreichen, sind die τ_i mit einer *algorithmischen Bedeutung* versehen. Nach erfolgter Auswahl eines τ ersetzt die rechte Seite der 1-Produktion von τ in der Satzform das σ an der im vorangehenden Positionierungstakt bestimmten Position. Die rechte Seite der 1-Produktion enthält Anreihungsindikatoren für τ .

b2) An der Position des im vorangehenden Positionierungstaktes bestimmten Anreihungsindikator für τ wird in die Satzform eine "Kopie" von τ eingesetzt. Eventl. erforderliche Trennsymbole, aus der 1-Produktion von τ ersichtlich, werden ebenfalls eingesetzt. Der Anreihungsindikator bleibt erhalten.

Im Ersetzungstakt wird - ähnlich wie in EMILY - jeweils genau eine kontext-freie Produktion angewandt. Im Fall b1) ist das direkt einsichtig. Im Fall b2) bedeutet das eine Erhöhung der "Rekursionstiefe" von τ aufgrund $\tau ::= \tau\omega$ um Eins. *Syntaktische Fehler* sind ausgeschlossen. In jedem *Dialogschritt* wiederholen sich diese beiden Takte, ausgehend von der Satzform π_o, das ist $\langle \text{Programm} \rangle$. Der Zerlegungsbaum, der für eine Satzform bzw. schließlich für das formulierte Programm gilt, wird vom System mitgeführt (siehe Muth[11]).

4. KONTEXT-SENSITIVE GENERIERUNG IN "PAD"

Die von uns angestrebte straffe Führung des Programmierers beinhaltet mehr als die durch ein System überwachte Erstellung des Zerlegungsbaums für eine kontext-freie Grammatik. Einen wichtigen Schritt darüber hinaus bedeutet die Verwendung syntaktischer Gebilde, die semantisch richtig (s.Abschnitt 2) sind, d.h. algorithmisch sinnvolle Strukturen darstellen. Die Tatsache, daß kontext-freie Grammatiken die bekannten algorithmischen Programmiersprachen aber nur unvollständig beschreiben (für ALGOL 60 s.Floyd[6]) und ein Teil der Regeln umgangsprachlich formuliert werden muß, führt zwangsläufig dazu, daß das PAD-System bei hinterlegter kontext-freier Grammatik eine Überwachung dieser Regeln nicht bieten kann. Es sind dies im wesentlichen solche Regeln, die eine Beziehung zwischen verschiedenen Elementen der Sprache betreffen, so z.B.:

a) Eine im Programm auftretende Variable muß vereinbart sein (ALGOL).

b) Eine dimensionierte Variable muß in einer Dimensionierungsanweisung vereinbart sein (Fortran, ALGOL).

c) Zwei "Common"-Variable dürfen nicht durch "Equivalence" verknüpft werden (Fortran).

d) Innerhalb einer Laufanweisung darf der Laufindex nicht verändert
   werden (Fortran).

Ein Verstoß gegen diese Regeln führt zu einer sinnentstellenden Darstellung eines Algorithmus (nach der Definition von Abschnitt 2, Art b).
Die Regeln betreffen den Kontext, in dem gewisse Produktionen anwendbar
sind. Für das PAD-System formuliert, besagen sie, daß bei einem Positionierungstakt nur ein Teil der Phrasensymbole (oft nur ein einziges) und
im Ersetzungstakt nur ein Teil aller dafür existierenden Produktionen
auswählbar ist. Die grammatikalische Eigenschaft der Kontextabhängig-
keit gewisser Regeln läßt sich also in ganz natürlicher Weise ausdrük-
ken als zusätzliche Führung des Programmierers. Grammatikformulierungen,
die dieser Forderung entsprechen, sind solche, bei denen die formale
Gestalt der Regeln (des "Kerns") kontextfrei bleibt, aber die Anwendbarkeit der Regeln eingeschränkt ist (z.B. Matrixgrammatiken - Abraham [1] -, Grammatiken mit Kontrollsprache - Salomaa [13] -, Programmierte
Grammatiken - Rosenkrantz [12] -). Ein Großteil dieser Grammatikformulierungen ist äquivalent in bezug auf die durch sie erzeugte Sprachklasse.
Die Formulierung als Programmierte Grammatik erscheint uns am besten
angepaßt an den dynamischen Vorgang der Programmerstellung mit dem PAD-
System.
Die Gestalt der Regeln einer Programmierten Grammatik ist:

Nr.	Regel aus dem Kern	Erfolgsfeld	Fehlerfeld
i	kontextfreie Regel	Menge von Regelnummern	Menge von Regelnummern

Genauer: Es sei $\mathcal{J}$ die Menge der Regelnummern. Als Angabe im Erfolgs-
bzw. Fehlerfeld ist zugelassen:
a) Jedes $\iota \in 2^{\mathcal{J}} - \emptyset$ ($\emptyset$= leere Menge) - Menge von Regelnummern -.
b) X - keine Angabe, Feld wird bei richtiger Grammatik nicht ange-
   sprochen -.
c) stop.
Kontextfreie Grammatiken entsprechen Programmierten Grammatiken, bei denen Erfolgs- und Fehlerfeld bei allen Regeln aus allen Regelnummern der
Grammatik bestehen. Das bedeutet, daß bei jedem Positionierungstakt das
Herausdeuten jedes in der erreichten Satzform vorhandenen Phrasensymbols
möglich ist. Bei Programmierten Grammatiken ist die Zahl der ausdeutba-
ren Phrasensymbole geringer.

5. IMPLEMENTIERUNG IN "PAD"

Zunächst einige Definitionen:

a) Der kontextfreie Kern der Programmierten Grammatik sei eine kontext-
freie Grammatik $G = (\Sigma, \pi, P, \pi_o)$. γ_i sei die Anzahl von Symbolen auf der
rechten Seite der i-ten Produktion.

b) $\sigma = \sigma_1 \sigma_2 \ldots \sigma_k \ldots \sigma_K$, $1 \le k \le K$ sei die vom PAD-System bis zum betrachteten Schritt erreichte Satzform, $\sigma_k \in \Sigma \cup \pi$.
Also: $\pi_o \overset{*}{\underset{G}{\Rightarrow}} \sigma$.

c) $n(\Delta)$ sei die Anzahl des Auftretens eines Phrasensymbols $\Delta \in \pi$ in σ.

d) *Positionieren* eines Phrasensymbols Δ bedeutet das Bestimmen einer
Stelle k der Satzform, an der das $\Delta \in \pi$ auftritt:
d1) falls $n(\Delta) > 1$, k vom Programmierer bestimmt,
d2) falls $n(\Delta) = 1$, k vom System bestimmt,
d3) falls $n(\Delta) = 0$, vom System unpositioniert gelassen.

e) E_i sei die Menge der Regelnummern im Erfolgsfeld und F_i die Menge
der Regelnummern im Fehlerfeld der i-ten Regel der Programmierten
Grammatik.

f) M sei die Menge der Regelnummern der im nächsten Schritt des Systems
anwendbaren Regeln; $m = \#(M)$ (die Anzahl der anwendbaren Regeln).
$\widetilde{M} \subseteq M$.

g) *Anwenden* der i-ten Regel mit Kern $\Delta_i \rightarrow \gamma_i$ bedeutet
g1) für $n(\Delta_i) > 0$: Ersetzen von Δ_i durch γ_i in σ an der Stelle k;
Verringern von $n(\Delta_i)$ um 1; für alle Δ', die in γ_i vorkommen,
Erhöhen von $n(\Delta')$ um 1; Erhöhen von K um $\gamma_i - 1$. E_i ergibt M.
g2) für $n(\Delta_i) = 0$ (hierbei ist Δ_i unpositioniert): σ bleibt unverändert. F_i ergibt M.

h) Q sei die Menge aller Phrasensymbole, die auf der linken Seite im
Kern der Produktionen auftreten, deren Nummern in M sind; $q = \#(Q)$
(die Anzahl der Phrasensymbole).

i) *Auswählen eines Phrasensymbols* bedeutet (bei $q > 1$) die Bestimmung
eines Δ aus Q, das der Programmierer als nächstes zu ersetzen wünscht.
Dadurch wird M auf $\widetilde{M}$ eingeengt.

j) *Auswählen einer Alternative* bedeutet (bei $m > 1$) die Bestimmung einer
Produktion mit Regelnummer i aus $\widetilde{M}$ durch den Programmierer, mit der
er als nächstes das ausgewählte Phrasensymbol zu ersetzen wünscht.

Das PAD-System stellt am Anfang die Satzform $\sigma = \pi_o$ her, also z.B.
$\sigma = \langle program \rangle$. Es ist $n(\langle program \rangle) = 1$ und $n(\Gamma) = 0$ für alle $\Gamma \in \pi$, $\Gamma \ne$
$\langle program \rangle$; es ist K=k=1; es ist $M = \{1\}$; es ist i=1. Das System beginnt
mit Schritt 1.

<u>Schritt 1</u>: *Anwenden* der Regel i mit Kern $\Delta_i \to \gamma_i$ an der Stelle k. Schritt 2.

<u>Schritt 2</u>: a) falls M=$\{$stop$\}$: Ende der Generierung ist erreicht.

          b) falls M$\neq\{$stop$\} \wedge$ q > 1: Schritt 3.

          c) falls M$\neq\{$stop$\} \wedge$ q = 1: $\tilde{M}$ ergibt M. Schritt 4.

<u>Schritt 3</u>: *Auswählen eines Phrasensymbols* $\tilde{\Delta}$. Streichen aller Regelnummern in M, deren Kern nicht $\tilde{\Delta}$ links hat; es ergibt sich $\tilde{M} \subseteq M$, m = $\#$ ($\tilde{M}$). Schritt 4.

<u>Schritt 4</u>: (Δ sei das als nächstes zu ersetzende Phrasensymbol) *Positionieren* des Phrasensymbols Δ. Schritt 5.

<u>Schritt 5</u>: a) falls m=1: Regelnummer in $\tilde{M}$ ergibt i. Schritt 1.

          b) falls m>1: *Auswählen einer Alternative*. Schritt 1.

Das PAD-System arbeitet aus der Sicht des Programmierers am Bildschirm nicht mehr in dem strengen Wechseltakt Positionieren-Auswählen. Vielmehr bestimmt der Aufbau der Programmierten Grammatik, in welcher Reihenfolge Fragen zum Positionieren bzw. Auswählen an den Programmierer zu stellen sind.

6. EINE PROGRAMMIERTE GRAMMATIK MIT KONTEXTFREIEM KERN ZUR OBERWACHUNG DER KONTEXTBEDINGUNG:

"Eine im Programm auftretende Variable muß vereinbart sein"

Nr.	Regel des Kerns	Erfolgsfeld	Fehlerfeld
1	<program> $\to$ <u>begin</u><proglist><u>end</u>	2	X
2	<proglist> $\to$<decllist>;<statlist>	3,4	X
3	<decllist> $\to$<typ><typlist>;<decllist>	5,6	X
4	<decllist> $\to$<typ><typlist>	5,6	X
5	<typ> $\to$ <u>integer</u>	6	9,10
6	<typ> $\to$ <u>real</u>	5	9,10
7.1	<typlist> $\to$<n.id$_1$>,<typlist>	$\{15.j\}$,$\{14.j\}$	X
7.j	<typlist> $\to$<n.id$_j$>,<typlist>	$\{15.j\}$,$\{14.j\}$	X
8.1	<typlist> $\to$<n.id$_1$>	$\{15.j\}$,$\{14.j\}$	X
8.j	<typlist> $\to$<n.id$_j$>	$\{15.j\}$,$\{14.j\}$	X
9	<statlist> $\to$<statement>;<statlist>	$\{11.j\}$	17.1
10	<statlist> $\to$<statement>	$\{11.j\}$	17.1
11.1	<statement> $\to$<id$_1$>:= <arithausdr>	16.1	9,10

$\vdots$	$\vdots$	$\vdots$	$\vdots$
11.j	$\langle statement\rangle \rightarrow \langle id_j\rangle := \langle arithausdr\rangle$	16.j	9,10
$\vdots$	$\vdots$	$\vdots$	$\vdots$
12	$\langle arithausdr\rangle \rightarrow \langle term\rangle + \langle arithausdr\rangle$	$\{15.j\}, \{14.j\}$	$\{11.j\}$
13	$\langle arithausdr\rangle \rightarrow \langle term\rangle$	$\{15.j\}, \{14.j\}$	$\{11.j\}$
14.1	$\langle term\rangle \rightarrow \langle id_1\rangle * \langle term\rangle$	16.1	12,13
$\vdots$	$\vdots$	$\vdots$	$\vdots$
14.j	$\langle term\rangle \rightarrow \langle id_j\rangle * \langle term\rangle$	16.j	12,13
$\vdots$	$\vdots$	$\vdots$	$\vdots$
15.1	$\langle term\rangle \rightarrow \langle id_1\rangle$	16.1	12,13
$\vdots$	$\vdots$	$\vdots$	$\vdots$
15.j	$\langle term\rangle \rightarrow \langle id_j\rangle$	16.j	12,13
$\vdots$	$\vdots$	$\vdots$	$\vdots$
16.1	$\langle n.id_1\rangle \rightarrow \langle n.id_1\rangle$	$\{15.j\}, \{14.j\}$	7.1
$\vdots$	$\vdots$	$\vdots$	$\vdots$
16.j	$\langle n.id_j\rangle \rightarrow \langle n.id_j\rangle$	$\{15.j\}, \{14.j\}$	7.j
$\vdots$	$\vdots$	$\vdots$	$\vdots$
17.1	$\langle n.id_1\rangle \rightarrow \langle id_1\rangle$	17.1	17.2
$\vdots$	$\vdots$	$\vdots$	$\vdots$
17.j	$\langle n.id_j\rangle \rightarrow \langle id_j\rangle$	17.j	stop

Bemerkung: Eine Angabe $\{z.j\}$ im Erfolgs- bzw. Fehlerfeld ist eine Abkürzung für die Menge $\{z.1, z.2,...\}$ von Regelnummern mit Gruppennummer z. Die Bestimmung einer Regelnummer i im Schritt 5 (siehe Abschnitt 5) durch Auswählen einer Alternative ist ersetzt durch eine Aufforderung an den Programmierer: Gebe $\langle id_j\rangle$. Damit ist auch das Phrasensymbol $\langle n.id_j\rangle$ in allen über j zugeordneten Produktionen bestimmt.

7. BEISPIEL: ERSTELLUNG EINES PROGRAMMS IN PAD

Es werde das folgende Programm formuliert und der zugehörige Zerlegungsbaum hergestellt:

```
begin real a,b;
      integer c,d;
      b := b + c * d;
      a := b
end
```

Nach Anwendung der Produktionen 1,2,3,4, - hier wird $\langle typ\rangle$ positioniert- 5,6,9 und 11.2 - Wahl von $\langle id2\rangle$ = b unterstellt - ergibt sich:

Satzform σ   *Zerlegungsbaum mit Schritt-nummern an den Knoten*

```
begin real <typlist>;
      integer <typlist>
         b := <arithausdruck>;
         <statlist>
end
```

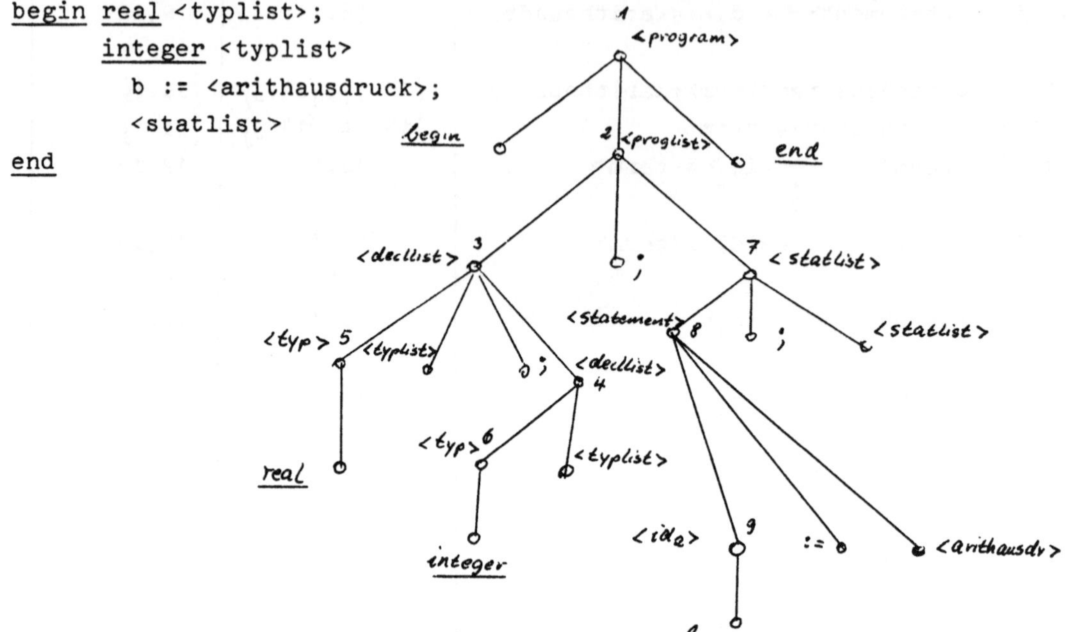

Über die "Steuerungs"-produktion 16.2 geht es weiter mit 7.2 - Positionierung auf <typlist> im Typ <u>real</u> und Einsetzen von < n.b > - und mit 12,14.2, 16.2. Weil <n.b> bereits vorhanden und <term> nicht in σ vorkommt, folgt 13 und weiter über 14.3 - Wahl von <id3> = c unterstellt - nach 16.3, und 7.3 zu:

Satzform σ

```
begin real <n.b>,<typlist>;
      integer <n.c>,<typlist>;
            b := b + c * <term>;
            <statlist>
end
```

Weiter geht es mit 15.4 - Wahl von <id4> = d unterstellt -, 16.4 zu 8.4 usw. ... bis nach 17.1, 17.2, 17.3, 17.4 bei "stop" das fertig formulierte Programm vorliegt.

An dem grob dargestellten Beispiel, dessen genauen Nachvollzug wir dem Leser überlassen, sieht man, daß die meisten der bei kontextfreien Grammatiken notwendigen Positionierungstakte entfallen. Außerdem taucht bei geeigneter Behandlung von Listenverlängerung und Listenabschluß, wie das mit Hilfe von 1-Produktionen in PAD geschieht, im gegebenen Beispiel neben den selbstverständlich unumgänglichen Alternativen im

Aufbau der beiden Wertzuweisungen nur noch eine einzige echte Alternative im Ersetzungstakt auf, nämlich die Wahl zwischen <u>real</u> und <u>integer</u>, wenn in einem Programm nur eine Typvereinbarung auftritt.

LITERATURANGABEN

[1] Abraham, S.: Some Questions of Phrase Structure Grammars I; Comp.Ling.4, 61-70 (1965)

[2] Bock, H., Schinzel, B.: Strukturgetreue Syntaxkompression und zugehörige Parserprozeduren; 2. Fachtagung über Programmiersprachen, Gesellschaft für Informatik, 141-163 (1972)

[3] Cameron, S.H., Ewing, D., Liveright, M.: DIALOG, A Conversational Programming System with a Graphical Orientation; Comm.ACM 10, 349-357 (1967)

[4] Diel, H., Grunefeld, K., Menzel, P.: Integrated Syntax and Semantic Prompting; IBM Techn.Disclosure Bull. 15,5,1634-1638 (1972)

[5] Dijkstra, E.W.: Structured Programming; APIC Studies in Data Processing, Nr. 8,1-82 (1971)

[6] Floyd, R.W.: On the Nonexistence of a Phrase Structure Grammar for ALGOL 60; Comm.ACM 5, 483-484 (1962)

[7] Hansen, W.J.: Creation of Hierarchic Text with a Computer Display; Argonne Natl.Laborat., Illinois, Applied Mathematics Division, ANL-7818, June 1971
Hansen, W.J.: Graphic Editing of Structured Text; Proc.Computer Graphics 1970 Internatl.Symp.,Brunell Univ.,Uxbridge,v3,s7 (1970)

[8] Hoffmann, H.-J.: Programming by Selection; to appear in Proc.Intl. Computing Symp 1973, Davos   (1973)

[9] Lévy, J.-P.: Automatic Handling of Syntax-Errors in SCARABEE, an Interactive System; Centre d'Enseignement Superieur des Affaires, Jouy-en-Josas, Frankreich, Cahier de Recherche 2/1973 (1973)

[10] Müller, A.: Eine Methode der kompakten Syntaxbeschreibung; Berichte der Informatik-Forschungsgruppen, TH Darmstadt, Fachbereich Informatik, Darmstadt, PU1R2/73 (1973)

[11] Muth, D.: Aufbau und Handhabung des Zerlegungsbaums durch "PAD"; Berichte der Informatik-Forschungsgruppen, TH Darmstadt, Fachbereich Informatik, Darmstadt, PU1R3/73 (1973)

[12] Rosenkrantz, D.J.: Programmed Grammars and Classes of Formal Languages; Journal ACM 16, 107-131 (1969)

[13] Salomaa, A.: On Grammars with Restricted Use of Productions; Ann. Ac.Sci.Fermic.454,1-32 (1969)

ZUR CHARAKTERISIERUNG VON DIALOGSPRACHEN

Ingbert Kupka

1. Aspekte der Kommunikation zwischen Mensch und Computer

Zur Grundmotivation der Informatik gehört das Bestreben, informationsverarbeitende Prozesse zu automatisieren. Konsequenterweise müssen hier auch solche Prozesse einbezogen werden, die der computergerechten Informationsaufbereitung dienen. Wo diese im Wechselspiel zwischen Mensch und Computer ablaufen, bedeutet dies die Entwicklung des Computers zum Dialogpartner für den Menschen. Diese Zielsetzung hat drei wesentliche und in ihrer jeweiligen Problematik sehr unterschiedliche Aspekte: Der technische Aspekt betrifft die Anpassung des Computers samt seiner Ausrüstung an die Erfordernisse der Kommunikation mit Menschen, der menschlich-psychologische Aspekt bezieht die Verhaltensweisen des Benutzers mit ein und der sprachliche Aspekt zielt auf das Medium der Kommunikation.

Auf der technischen Seite ist die Entwicklung am weitesten fortgeschritten. So wurden wichtige Voraussetzungen für praktikable Dialoge in den Teilnehmersystemen geschaffen. Hochspezialisierte Konsolgeräte kennzeichnen die Anpassung an vielfältige Benutzeranforderungen. Einen allgemeinen Überblick hierzu geben Bell, Gold (1972), S. 194 ff. Eine erwähnenswerte Sonderentwicklung ist das sog. AMTRAN-Terminal mit zwei Bildschirmen, einem zur Dialogführung und einem für graphische Ausgabe, einer Tastatur mit einer relativ großen Anzahl von Funktionssymbolen, einem Fernschreiber für Protokollzwecke und einer Hardcopy-Einrichtung zum Ablichten erzeugter Bilder, siehe Reinfelds et al. (1966).

Der Rolle des Benutzers im Dialog wird bei der praktischen Entwicklung von Dialogsystemen große Bedeutung beigemessen, vgl. Bennett (1972) und Fried (1968). Typische Fragestellungen dieses Aspekts sind die nach der Lernfähigkeit, der Gedächtnisleistung, nach dem Verhalten bei Irrtum, dem Einfluß der Wartezeiten und so fort. Die bisher implementierten interaktiven Sprachen berücksichtigen zwar Fähigkeiten und Verhalten des Benutzers, jedoch auf unterschiedliche Weise. Die Erforschung dieses Problemkreises befindet sich weitgehend noch im Stadium des Experimentierens. Auch statistische Untersuchungen über das Benutzerverhalten können vorerst nur bedingt zu einer objektiven Beurteilung führen, da die technische und die sprachliche Seite bei solchen Untersuchungen nicht hinreichend variiert werden können.

Wenig erforscht ist bislang der sprachliche Aspekt von Dialogen. Grundsätzlich werden auch natürliche Sprachen als Kommunikationsmittel in Betracht gezogen, vgl. Bennett (1972), S. 170. Da es hierbei weniger auf die äußere Form als vielmehr auf den semantischen Gehalt und seine Verarbeitung ankommt, ist ein solches Ziel kurzfristig sicher nicht erreichbar. In der Praxis wurden fehlende dialogspezifische Sprachkonzepte durch Kombinationen aus Programmiersprachen für Stapelverarbeitung

und Konsol-Kommandosprachen ersetzt. Ansätze zu einem Dialogsprachenbegriff, der den
gegenwärtigen Realisierungsmöglichkeiten Rechnung trägt, finden sich in den Konzep-
ten zu einzelnen interaktiven Sprachen, zum Beispiel zu JOSS, siehe die Beschreibung
von Smith (1970), LCC, siehe Van Zoeren (1969), und AMTRAN, siehe Reinfelds (1972).
Ein systematischer Vergleich der wichtigsten Dialogsprachenkonzepte führt zu einer
vorläufigen Charakterisierung von Dialogsprachen, die im Folgenden näher erläutert
wird.

2. Konsolaktivitäten und sprachliche Medien

Im weitesten Sinne könnte man jedes sprachliche Medium für die Kommunikation an
der Konsole als Dialogsprache bezeichnen. Die großen Unterschiede der sprachlichen
Anforderungen bei den verschiedenen Aktivitäten an der Konsole sprechen jedoch eher
dafür, in einem engeren Begriff die Dialogsprachen von speziellen Anwendungssprachen
mit anders gelagerter Problematik abzugrenzen. Der Anwendungsbereich der Dialogsprachen im engeren Sinn ist die problemorientierte Dialogprogrammierung, er ist
also vergleichbar mit dem der höheren Programmiersprachen. Typische Konsolaktivitä-
ten in diesem Bereich sind

1. die Tischrechnerfunktion,

2. die interaktive Programmentwicklung,

3. die Konsolsteuerung vorgespeicherter Programme,

4. die Programmierung an der Konsole,

5. das interaktive Erlernen der Programmierung.

Mit Tischrechnerfunktion wird die partielle Verwendung des Rechners nach der Art
eines komfortablen Tischrechners bezeichnet. In APL\360, siehe Falkoff, Iverson
(1968), und in JOSS gehört die Tischrechnerfunktion zu den Grundlagen des Sprachkonzepts, ebenso bei den JOSS-Abkömmlingen wie LCC.

Bei der interaktiven Programmentwicklung werden die Erstellung und das Austesten
von Programmen interaktiv und mit Rechnerunterstützung vorgenommen. Hierfür eignen
sich Sprachen, die einerseits die Möglichkeiten üblicher Programmiersprachen und
andererseits Sprachelemente zur Programm-Manipulation, wie z. B. für Korrekturen und
Neustart von Programmen, besitzen. Beispiele sind QUIKTRAN, eine Kurzbeschreibung
hierzu gibt Sammet (1969), S. 226-229, sowie NAPSS, siehe Symes, Roman (1969), und
auch Kombinationen aus Programmiersprachen und Kommandosprachen. Von gänzlich anderer Qualität ist die interaktive Programmentwicklung, welche Floyd (1972) in einem
fiktiven Dialogbeispiel schildert. Dort wird die axiomatische Methode (von Floyd)
der Korrektheitsüberprüfung von Programmen interaktiv zum Aufbau von Programmen benutzt. Der Benutzer formuliert Prämissen und die logische Form der Ergebnisse und
der Computer überprüft die Verträglichkeit derselben und steuert die Zergliederung
der Aufgabe in Teilaufgaben bis ein Programm vom Computer aufgestellt werden kann.
Wenn auch noch nicht alle hierbei auftretenden Probleme gelöst sind, so kann man
doch erwarten, daß sich die Dialogprogrammierung unter anderem in einer solchen

Richtung fortentwickelt.

Die <u>Konsolsteuerung vorgespeicherter Programme</u>, das heißt der Ablauf von Programmen unter der interaktiv ausgeübten Kontrolle des Benutzers, bedeutet einen weiteren
und entscheidenden Zuwachs an Flexibilität und Effektivität. Im Einzelnen handelt es
sich dabei um folgende Möglichkeiten zur Steuerung sogenannter <u>Tasks</u>, d. h. der
Laufformen ausführbarer Objekte:

  a) <u>Unterbrechung der Ausführungsphase</u>

    i)   vorprogrammiert,

    ii) im Fehlerfall,

    iii) durch Eingriff von außen,

  b) <u>Fortsetzung an der Unterbrechungsstelle</u> mit

    i)   Dateneingaben,

    ii) direkt eingegebenen Anweisungen,

    iii) neu zu startenden Tasks,

    iv) im Unterbrechungszustand wartenden Tasks,

  c) <u>Aufgabe (Löschen) von Tasks</u>,

  d) <u>Auf- und Abbau von Unterbrechungshierarchien und Verändern der Environments</u>,
    d. h. der Umgebungen zugehöriger Objekte, bei Start, Unterbrechung und Be-
    endigung von Tasks.

Mittels Kommandosprachen lassen sich diese Möglichkeiten nur teilweise und unvoll-
kommen realisieren. In Dialogsprachen gibt es recht komfortable Konzepte für die
Unterbrechungssteuerung, z. B. in LCC.

Wenn die Sprache ausführbare Objekte, Tasks und Environments kennt, wird der
Begriff "Programm" entbehrlich. Unter <u>Programmierung an der Konsole</u> (on-line
programming) verstehen wir eine Arbeitsweise unter diesen Bedingungen, welche die
Tischrechnerfunktion, die interaktive Entwicklung ausführbarer Objekte und die
Möglichkeiten der Konsolsteuerung einschließt. Damit ist gleichzeitig der Hauptan-
wendungsbereich der Dialogsprachen im hier verstandenen Sinn charakterisiert.

Auf dem Gebiet des interaktiven Erlernens der Programmierung konkurrieren Dialogsprachen mit Programmiersprachen, die mittels Kommandosprachen manipulierbar
sind.

3. Dialog, Interaktion und Kommunikation

Im Gegensatz zu den Programmiersprachen allgemein spielt bei den Dialogsprachen
der zeitliche Ablauf eine wesentliche Rolle. Da hier deterministische Abläufe und
indeterministische Ereignisse, zum Beispiel Eingriffe (interrupts) vorkommen, ist es
notwendig, den logischen Ablauf von Dialogen exakt zu definieren.

Unter einem <u>Dialog</u> werde hier eine Sequenz von abwechselnd (zeitlich) aufeinander folgenden Äußerungen des Benutzers und des Rechnersystems verstanden. Gibt man
A und B als Benutzer- bzw. als Systemalphabet vor, so werden Dialoge <u>formal</u> darstellbar durch das Ein-/Ausgabeverhalten unendlicher initialer Mealy-Automaten mit

A^* als Eingabe- und B^* als Ausgabemenge. Eine ausführliche Darstellung ist bei Kupka, Wilsing (1972) angegeben. Ein Dialoge im obigen Sinn realisierendes System heiße Dialog-System, ein Automat der angegebenen Art ein <u>formales Dialog-System</u>. Eine <u>Dialogsprache</u> ist formal charakterisiert durch eine Äquivalenzklasse formaler Dialog-Systeme. In einem Dialog-System sind Eingriffe von außen nicht möglich, wohl aber vorprogrammierte Unterbrechungen und Unterbrechungen im Fehlerfall. Diese Möglichkeiten zusammen mit den zugehörigen Kontrollen werden <u>schwache Interaktivitäten</u> genannt. Sie sind also nur semantisch charakterisierbar.

Eingriffe des Benutzers in den Ablauf innerhalb des Systems, Unterdrückung von Ausgaben durch Eingriff und Beschränkungen, die das System dem Benutzer auferlegt, zum Beispiel durch zustandsabhängige Variation des Eingabealphabets wie in DIALOG, siehe Cameron et al. (1967), werden als <u>starke Interaktivitäten</u> bezeichnet. Sie sind äußerlich charakterisierbar. Systeme mit diesen Möglichkeiten seien <u>Interaktions-systeme</u> genannt. Ihre formale Beschreibung wird dadurch erschwert, daß man einen externen Zeichentakt, einen externen Worttakt und einen internen Takt ausführbarer Einheiten berücksichtigen muß. Dies ist jedoch kein grundsätzliches Problem sondern berührt die Transparenz der Darstellung.

Zu den sinnvollen Möglichkeiten an der Konsole gehört auch die Kommunikation verschiedener Benutzer miteinander über den Rechner. Dabei sollte man über das Senden und Empfangen von Botschaften, wie es zum Beispiel in APL\360 vorgesehen ist, hinaus allgemein Informationsaustausch mit Einwirkungen auf den Dialog mit in Betracht ziehen. Die entsprechenden Systeme seien <u>Kommunikationssysteme</u> genannt.

Für jede Dialogsprache gehört die Zuordnung zu den drei genannten Systemen nebst einer Spezifizierung möglicher Interaktionen und Kommunikationen zu dem formalen Rahmen, in den Syntax, Semantik und Pragmatik der Sprache einzubetten sind. Für viele Betrachtungen genügt es, Dialogsysteme zugrunde zu legen.

4. Forderungen der Pragmatik

Dialogsprachen für das oben geschilderte Einsatzgebiet sollten unter pragmatischer Sicht folgende Kriterien erfüllen (vgl. eine ähnliche Zusammenstellung bei Mitchell (1968)):

1. Zeilenorientierung mit der Möglichkeit direkt ausführbarer sowie vorprogrammierbarer Anweisungen,

2. Ausstattung mit Sprachelementen zur Unterbrechung und Ausführungskontrolle,

3. Möglichkeiten der Tischrechnerfunktion,

4. Bündige Notation (geringe Redundanz),

5. Konsistenz im Sinne eines einheitlich strukturierten Sprachkonzepts,

6. Flexibilität in der Benutzung,

7. Möglichkeit effizienter Interpretation,

8. Vorhandensein systemseitiger Hilfen für den Benutzer,

9. Leichte Erlernbarkeit.

Diese Kriterien sind eher als Leitkriterien zum Entwurf einer einzelnen Sprache denn
als allgemeine Beurteilungskriterien geeignet. Sie ermöglichen zwar Vergleiche, entziehen sich aber einer genaueren Nachprüfbarkeit. Der folgende Katalog von Bedingungen erfaßt nur einen Teil der obigen Kriterien, jedoch sind die Bedingungen nach-
prüfbar für prozedurale Sprachen, deren Semantik benennbare externe und zugeordnete
interne Objekte, zum Beispiel im Sinne des ALGOL 68 - Reports, Wijngaarden (1969),
S. 99, kennt.

I. **Zeichenbedingung**: Die Standardoperationen der Sprache sind als unmittelbare
Wirkung von Standardzeichenkombinationen erhältlich (z. B. '+' in der Ein-
gabezeile kann unmittelbar nach deren Eingabe zu einer Addition führen).

II. **Namensbedingung**: Die Verwendung von Namen ist ohne vorherige Deklaration
möglich.

III. **Wertebedingung**: Explizit zugewiesene Werte bleiben über beliebig viele Dia-
logschritte bis zu expliziter Aufgabe oder Überschreibung erhalten.

IV. **Anweisungsbedingung**: Anweisungen treten als Objekte des Dialogs auf.

V. **Interaktivitätsbedingung**: Es gibt Sprachelemente für die schwachen Interaktivitäten, so daß mehrstufige Unterbrechungen, Fortsetzung unterbrochener
Tasks und Aufgabe solcher möglich ist.

Diese pragmatisch begründete präzisere Charakterisierung von Dialogsprachen unter-
scheidet nun auch Dialogsprachen wie JOSS, LCC, APL\360 usw. von Kombinationen aus
Programmiersprachen und Kommandosprachen. Siehe hierzu die Beispiele bei Kupka (1972)
S. 167 f.

5. Semantische Charakterisierung von Dialogsprachen

Jeder Dialogsprache im Sinne von Abschnitt 4. läßt sich ein **programmiersprachlicher Kern** zuordnen bestehend aus einer Menge D von Zuständen, vergleichbar den
Zustandsvektoren nach McCarthy (1963), einer Menge F partieller Funktionen auf D
mit Werten in D und einer Menge P partieller Prädikate auf D . Die Zuordnung
erfolgt dabei so, daß bei Reduktion der Sprache auf direkt ausführbare Zeilen deren
Semantik durch partielle Funktionen auf D beschreibbar ist, die sich durch Hinter-
einanderausführungen und Alternativen bezogen auf Prädikate aus P aus den Elementen von F zusammensetzen lassen. Die Menge dieser über dem Kern definierten Funktionen heiße G .

Der Kern ist eingebettet in ein formales Dialogsystem mit einer Zustandsmenge S ,
so daß D als Bildmenge zu einer auf ganz S erklärten Abbildung d erhältlich
ist. Umgekehrt existiere eine Injektion s von D in S mit d∘s = id , wobei id
die Identität auf D bezeichnet und zu F gehören soll. Analog zu F bezeichnet
T eine Menge partieller Abbildungen auf S . Dabei besitzt jedes f ∈ F ein Bild
e(f) ∈ T, so daß gilt e(f)∘s = s∘f . Die Abbildung e heißt (direktes) Ausführungs-
kommando. Die allgemeine abstrakte Form für Anweisungszeilen ist (c,x) mit c aus
einer Menge C von Kommandos und einer passenden Spezifikation x , so daß c auf

x anwendbar ist und $c(x) \in T$ gilt. Jedem $c \in C$ ist eine Menge X_c als Menge der Spezifikationen zugeordnet. Es gilt $e \in C$ und $F \subset X_e$. Die Menge H der partiellen Funktionen auf D, die sich durch

$$d \circ c_k(x_k) \circ c_{k-1}(x_{k-1}) \circ \ldots \circ c_1(x_1) \circ s, \quad c_i \in C, \ x_i \in X_{c_i}, \ i=1,\ldots,k,$$

darstellen lassen, ist wegen

$$d \circ e(f) \circ s = d \circ s \circ f = id \circ f = f, \quad f \in F,$$

eine Obermenge von F. Die Elemente von H heißen <u>dialogberechenbare Funktionen</u> bezüglich des Kerns und der Kommandos. Von theoretischem und praktischem Interesse sind Zusammenstellungen von Kommandos, so daß $H \supset G$ gilt und H darüber hinaus rekursiv über dem Kern definierte Funktionen enthält.

Ein allgemeines Beispiel, welches in engem Zusammenhang mit der Struktur existenter Dialogsprachen steht, lautet:

Sei $\{e,a\} \subset C$, N eine Menge von sogenannten Namen, und die Spezifikationen seien durch das folgende System simultaner rekursiver Gleichungen erklärt:

$$X_e = F \oplus N \oplus Y$$

$$X_a = N \times Y$$

$$Y = \{e\} \times X_e \oplus \{a\} \times X_a \oplus Y \times Y \oplus P \times Y \times Y$$

Zur Problematik der rekursiven Mengendefinitionen siehe McCarthy (1963a), S. 49-52. Für die Wirkungen $c(x)$ der Kommandos (auch für sonstige außer e und a) gelte:

$$e(y) = (\ y = (c,x) \to c(x), \quad y = (y_1,y_2) \in Y \times Y \to e(y_2) \, e(y_1),$$

$$y = (p,y_1,y_2) \in P \times Y \times Y \to (p \to e(y_1), e(y_2)) \ ), \quad y \in Y,$$

$$e(n) \circ a(n,y) = e(y) \circ a(n,y), \quad n \in N, \ y \in Y,$$

$$d \circ a(n,y) = d, \quad n \in N, \ y \in Y,$$

$$e(f) \circ a(n,y) = a(n,y) \circ e(f), \quad f \in F, \ n \in N, \ y \in Y.$$

Die Schreibweise für bedingte Ausdrücke erfolgt hier wie bei McCarthy (1963a). Durch weitere Vertauschungs- und Verkürzungsregeln kann die Art der Verwendung von Namen genauer beschrieben werden. Die 'while-loop' <u>while</u> p <u>do</u> f mit $p \in P$, $f \in F$ läßt sich nun wie folgt als dialogberechenbare Funktion h darstellen:

$$h = d \circ e(n) \circ a(n, (p, ((e,f), (e,n)), (e,id))) \circ s, \quad n \in N.$$

Beweis: Man findet aufgrund der obigen Regeln $h = (p \to h \circ f, \ id)$. Detaillierte Aussagen über dialogberechenbare Funktionen für den Fall, daß D direkte Komponente von S ist, sind bei Kupka, Wilsing (1973a) angegeben.

Die Kommandos e und a in der obigen Bedeutung liefern auch die folgende Charakterisierung von Eingabezeilen entsprechend ihrer abstrakten Form nach den drei Modi (3. ist ein Spezialfall von 1.):

    1. direkter Modus: (e,h)

    2. indirekter Modus: (a, (n,h))

3. gemischter Modus: (e, ((a , (n,h)) , (e,h)))
    (h ∈ H, n ∈ N)

mit den Wirkungen e(h) im direkten, a(n,h) im indirekten und e(h)•a(n,h) im gemischten Modus. Beispiele:

zu 1.:   Set x=7.   (JOSS)

zu 2.:   1.2 Set x=7.   (JOSS)

zu 3.:   Der von den Autoren entwickelte dialogfähige APL-Dialekt HDL , siehe Kupka, Wilsing (1973), sieht für alle Zeilen im direkten Modus den gemischten Modus vor, so daß ein Rückgriff auf bereits direkt ausgeführte Zeilen möglich ist. Dem Speicherüberlauf wirkt ein Zeilenalterungsmechanismus entgegen.

Außer durch das Vorkommen und die Ausprägung der genannten Modi wird die Struktur von Dialogsprachen durch spezielle Kommandos zur gruppenweisen Ausführung gespeicherter ausführbarer Objekte bestimmt. Auf der Menge N ist dafür implizit eine partielle Nachfolgerfunktion zugrunde gelegt. Auf diese wird bei Kommandos der Art

     EXECUTE n THRU m ;

bzw.   EXECUTE n THRU ... ;

Bezug genommen. Diese Beispiele stammen aus der PL/I-ähnlichen Sprache CPS, siehe Sammet (1969), S. 232-240. In NAPSS und in CPS sind alle Elemente von N durch die Nachfolgerfunktion linear angeordnet. NAPSS kennt dabei übrigens nur die Möglichkeit, ab einer bestimmten Stelle durchgehend alle Zeilen auszuführen. Das Kommando hierzu lautet

     EDIT RESTART n   .

JOSS und LCC verwenden Dezimalzahlen i.k als Namen für Zeilen. Dabei verbindet die Nachfolgerfunktion nur Namen mit gleichen Ziffern vor dem Dezimalpunkt. Die dadurch ausgezeichneten Gruppen angeordneter Zeilen heißen 'parts'. Mit den 'parts' vergleichbar sind die 'functions' in APL\360. Jedoch kennt APL\360 keine Ausführung einzelner Zeilen aus Funktionen entsprechend dem

     Do step i.k .

in JOSS. In HDL sind die Möglichkeiten aus JOSS und APL\360 kombiniert.

Der Kern der Dialogsprache und die an Hand der Beispiele skizzierte Ebene der Kommandos bilden die zwei unteren Ebenen eines <u>Schichtenmodells</u> für die Semantik von Dialogsprachen. Der abstrakte Sprachumfang ist auf diesen Ebenen bereits festgelegt. Eine dritte Ebene enthält die in Abschnitt 2. aufgeführten Interaktivitäten. Sie bestimmt weitgehend die pragmatische Seite der Sprache. Beispiele für Anweisungen, die zu dieser Ebene gehören, sind (JOSS):

     Stop. , Demand x. , Quit. , Cancel.

Sie beziehen sich alle auf die Kontrolle von Tasks. In einer vierten Ebene werden übergeordnete Kontrollmöglichkeiten erfaßt, welche den Benutzer gleichsam in die Lage versetzen, den Gesamtdialogzustand zu konservieren und später zu restaurieren. Solche Möglichkeiten bieten die 'workspace control commands' und 'library control commands' in APL\360. Ein solches Schichtenmodell ermöglicht die Abtrennung der dialogspezifischen Probleme (Ebenen 2 bis 4) von solchen allgemeiner programmiersprachlicher Natur (Kern). Eine formale Darstellung eines solchen Modells enthält der Bericht Kupka, Wilsing (1973a).

6. Über die syntaktische Beschreibung von Dialogsprachen

Die äußerliche Charakterisierung von Dialogsprachen geschieht durch die Syntax. Zur syntaktischen Beschreibung eines Dialogs

$$A_1 \; B_1 \; A_2 \; B_2 \; \ldots \ldots \; A_n \; B_n \quad , \quad A_i \in A^*, \; B_i \in B^*, \quad i=1,2,\ldots,n,$$

benötigt man eine Syntax für die Eingaben (benutzerseitige lokale Syntax), eine entsprechende, wenn auch anders motivierte, für die Ausgaben (systemseitige lokale Syntax) und eine Syntax zur Beschreibung syntaktischer Kontextabhängigkeiten, die für aktuelle Ein- und Ausgaben aufgrund des voraufgehenden Dialogs bestehen (globale Syntax). Siehe hierzu die ausführliche Darstellung in Kupka, Wilsing (1972).

Die <u>benutzerseitige lokale Syntax</u> muß im Allgemeinen eine syntaktische Unterteilung der vollen Wortmenge A^* liefern, zum Beispiel durch Beschreibung einer Menge $1_1 = L(G_1)$ von 'regulären' Zeilen mittels einer Grammatik G_1, wodurch zugleich eine Menge $1_0 = A^* - 1_1$ von 'irregulären' Zeilen als Komplement beschrieben ist. Die konkrete Syntax der Eingaben beschreibt externe Abbilder einer internen abstrakten Syntax im Sinne von McCarthy (1963). Dies gilt jedoch auch für die konkrete Syntax der Ausgaben. Die <u>systemseitige lokale Syntax</u> braucht jedoch nur dann ganz B^* zu strukturieren, wenn alle Worte als Ausgaben vorkommen.

Aus der logischen Struktur von Dialogen folgt, daß im Allgemeinen die lokale Syntax vom Dialogzustand abhängt. Das folgende Beispiel einer einfachen <u>globalen Syntax</u> zeigt die syntaktische Beschreibung eines solchen Sachverhalts:

```
DIALOG := CLOSED-DIALOG | OPEN-DIALOG

CLOSED-DIALOG := EMPTY | CLOSED-DIALOG regular-input result |
                 CLOSED-DIALOG irregular-input error-message |
                 OPEN-DIALOG regular-answer result

OPEN-DIALOG := CLOSED-DIALOG regular-input question |
               OPEN-DIALOG irregular-answer error-message

EMPTY :=
```

Die benutzerseitige lokale Syntax enthält Beschreibungen für 'regular-input' nebst Komplement 'irregular-input' sowie für 'regular-answer' nebst Komplement 'irregular-answer'; hierfür sind also zwei Grammatiken erforderlich, von denen in jedem Dialogzustand jeweils eine aktuell ist. Die systemseitige lokale Syntax besteht aus Beschreibungen für 'result', 'error-message' und 'question'.

Bisherige Beschreibungen von Dialogsprachen enthalten verbale Formulierungen der globalen Syntax.

7. <u>Literatur</u>

Bell, C. G., and Gold, M. M. (1972)."An introduction to the structure of time-shared
    computers", <u>Advances in Information Systems Science</u> (Tou, J. T. ed.), 4, New
    York, 161-272

Bennett, J. L. (1972). "The user interface in interactive systems", <u>Annual Review of
    Information Science and Technology</u> (Cuadra, C. A. ed.), 7, 159-196

Cameron, S. H., Ewing, D., and Liveright, M. (1967). "DIALOG: A Conversational Pro-
    gramming System with a Graphical Orientation", <u>Comm. ACM</u>, 10, No. 6, 349-357

Falkoff, A. D., and Iverson, K. E. (1968). "APL\360: User's Manual", IBM

Floyd, R. W. (1972). "Toward Interactive Design of Correct Programs", <u>Proc. of the
    IFIP Congress 71</u> (Freiman, C. V. ed.), 1, North-Holland, Amsterdam, London,
    7-10

Fried, B. D. (1968). "On the User's Point of View", <u>Interactive Systems for Experi-
    mental Applied Mathematics</u> (Klerer, M., and Reinfelds, J. eds.), Academic Press,
    New York, London, 11-21

Kupka, I. (1972). "A Structural Model for Dialog Languages", <u>GI, 1. Fachtagung über
    Programmiersprachen</u> (Langmaack, H., und Paul, M. Hrsg.), Springer, Berlin, Hei-
    delberg, New York, 157-168

Kupka, I., and Wilsing, N. (1972). "A formal framework for dialog languages", <u>Ber.
    d. Inst. f. Informatik d. Univ. Hamburg</u>, 2

Kupka, I., und Wilsing, N. (1973). "Syntax und Semantik des Dialogsprachenkonzepts
    HDL", <u>Ber. d. Inst. f. Informatik d. Univ. Hamburg</u>, 3

Kupka, I., and Wilsing, N. (1973a). "An approach to formal semantics of dialog lan-
    guages", <u>Ber. d. Inst. f. Informatik d. Univ. Hamburg</u>, 4

McCarthy, J. (1963). "Towards a Mathematical Science of Computation", <u>Information
    Processing 1962, Proc. of the IFIP Congress 1962</u> (Popplewell ed.), North-Holland
    Amsterdam, 21-28

McCarthy, J. (1963a). "A Basis for a Mathematical Theory of Computation", <u>Computer
    Programming and Formal Systems</u> (Braffort, Hirschberg eds.), North-Holland,
    Amsterdam, 33-69

Mitchell, J. G., Perlis, A. J., and Van Zoeren, H. R. (1968). "LC^2: A Language for
    Conversational Computing", <u>Interactive Systems for Experimental Applied Mathe-
    matics</u> (Klerer, M., and Reinfelds, J. eds.), Academic Press, New York, London,
    203-214

Reinfelds, J. (1972). "AMTRAN 70", <u>Proc. of the IFIP Congress 71</u> (Freiman, C. V. ed.)
    1, North-Holland, Amsterdam, London, 370-375

Reinfelds, J., Flenker, L., Seitz, R., and Clem, P., Jr. (1966). "AMTRAN, a remote-
    terminal, conversational-mode computer system", <u>Proc. 21st Nat. Conf. ACM</u>,
    Thompson, Washington, D. C., London,

Sammet, J. E. (1969). "Programming Languages, History and Fundamentals", Prentice-
    Hall, Englewood Cliffs, N. J.

Smith, J. W. (1970). "JOSS-II: Design Philosophy", <u>Annual Review in Automatic Pro-
    gramming</u>, 6, 4, Pergamon Press, Oxford etc., 183-256

Symes, L. R., and Roman, R. V. (1969). "Syntactic and Semantic Description of the
     Numerical Analysis Programming Language (NAPSS)", Technical Report CSD TR 11,
     Purdue University, Lafayette, Indiana

Van Zoeren, H. R. (1969). "LCC Reference Manual", Carnegie-Mellon University, Depart-
     ment of Computer Science, Pittsburgh, Pennsylvania

Wijngaarden, A. van (ed.), Mailloux, B. J., Peck, J. E. L., and Koster, C. H. A.
     (1969). "Report on the Algorithmic Language ALGOL 68", _Num. Math._, 14, Springer,
     Berlin, Heidelberg, New York, 79-218

MODULARITÄT DURCH 'KONZEPTKLASSEN'

Walter Sonnenberg

1. Einführung

Bei größeren Programmierprojekten ist eine Aufgabenteilung nur mit Modultechniken möglich. Hier sollen Strukturprinzipien einer neuen Modularisierungsmethode erläutert werden.

Eine 'Konzeptklasse' soll verschiedene Implementierungsmöglichkeiten eines Schnittstellenkonzeptes zusammenfassend beschreiben. Ein Modul wird aus der Konzeptklasse nach Auswahl einer Implementierungsalternative durch Binden der Parameter ihrer Beschreibung gewonnen. Durch verallgemeinerte Formen der Parametrisierung ist eine Darstellung eines Programmsystems in Konzeptklassen weniger komplex als mit anderen Moduln. In der Konzeptklasse werden Implementierungsalternativen solange mitgeführt wie ihr Einsatz effektiv möglich wäre. So sind mit Konzeptklassen beschriebene Systementwürfe flexibler.

Durch generalisierende Beschreibung von Implementierungskonzepten in Konzeptklassen werden die erzeugbaren Moduln projektunabhängig wiederverwendbar oder als Standardmoduln einsetzbar. Das Denkmodell 'Konzeptklassen' ist ein Versuch, Softwarekomponenten im Sinne von McIlroy /7/ zu klassifizieren.

2. Komponenten von Konzeptklassen

Wir unterscheiden zunächst 'Gesicht' und 'Konzeptrumpf' einer Konzeptklasse. Das Gesicht ist eine für äußere Konzeptklassen sichtbare Beschreibung der Routinen, über die auf das Konzept zugegriffen werden kann. Der Rumpf beschreibt Implementierungsmöglichkeiten der im Gesicht spezifizierten Routinen.

2.1 Gesicht und Maske

Im <u>Gesicht</u> werden die Namen all der Routinen vereinbart, auf die in anderen Konzeptklassen Bezüge oder Referenzen vorkommen dürfen. Diese Routinen werden Zugriffsroutinen oder -funktionen genannt. Zum Schutz der konzeptklasseninternen Informationen muß jeder Zugriff über diese Wege führen.

Für den menschlichen Bearbeiter ist eine kurze, prägnante Beschreibung der beabsichtigten Wirkung der Routinen notwendig.

Die Zugriffsfunktionen können vielfältig parametrisiert werden. Zum Beispiel sind Zugriffe auf Plexe über Deskriptoren oder Zugriffe auf Felder über Indizes möglich.

Den Zugriffsroutinen wird im einfachsten Fall die <u>Einsatzform</u> 'Prozedur' zugeordnet. Für kompliziertere Operationen sind die Einsatzformen 'Koroutine' und 'paralleler Prozeß' vorgesehen. Erweiterungen sind beabsichtigt. Mögliche Modelle wurden auf einer ACM-Tagung /6/ erläutert.

Parameter und Resultate der Zugriffsroutinen müssen nach ihrer Art (syn. Typ) in ähnlicher Form wie in ALGOL 68 beschrieben werden /3,4,14/.

Im Gesicht kann auf andere Konzeptklassen Bezug genommen werden. Solche Bezüge werden wie Gesichter beschrieben und heißen <u>Masken</u>.

Masken und Gesichter sind die Schnittstellen, an denen erzeugte Moduln aneinander gefügt werden. Sie sind nach den Forderungen von Parnas /9,10/ über Spezifikationen und Annahmen über Moduln entworfen worden.

2.2 <u>Konzeptrumpf, Körper und Köpfe</u>

Der Konzeptrumpf beschreibt die Implementierungsalternativen eines Konzeptes. Jede Alternative wird in einem 'Körper' algorithmisch beschrieben und in einem 'Kopf' spezifiziert.

Der <u>Körper</u> ist ähnlich aufgebaut wie ein Klassenkörper in SIMULA 67 /2,11/ oder ein Block in ALGOL. Er enthält Vereinbarungen lokaler Datenstrukturen und Algorithmen zur Implementierung der im Gesicht beschriebenen Zugriffsroutinen. Zusätzlich ist es möglich, andere Konzepte in lokalen Konzeptklassen zu definieren oder externe Konzeptklassen über Masken zu referenzieren.

Im <u>Kopf</u> werden Entscheidungskriterien zur Auswahl der zugehörigen Implementierungsalternative gesammelt. Zum ersten werden Leistungskriterien für den Einsatz der Algorithmen beschrieben. Zum zweiten werden die im Gesicht der Konzeptklasse gegebenen Spezifikationen im allgemeinen eingeschränkt, sei es, daß durch Einschränkung der Wertebereiche von Parametern, oder daß durch Verzicht auf Zugriffsroutinen effizientere Implementierungen möglich wurden. Da Gesichter durch Konzeptverallgemeinerungen verändert werden können, werden die Spezifikationen hier als Positivkatalog unter Berücksichtigung der Einschränkungen aufgeführt, damit Inkonsistenzen ausgeschaltet werden können.

2.3 Modul, Auswahl und Bindung

Beim Entwurf und bei der Entwicklung eines Programmsystems aus Konzeptklassen werden Modulbeschreibungen manipuliert. Moduln werden aus den Konzeptklassen durch Auswahl von Implementierungsalternativen und Binden der Parameter erzeugt. Während der Programmentwicklung werden Auswahlen und Bindungen variiert; Moduln werden erst zum Verifizieren der Programme in Codeform generiert.

Die Auswahl einer Implementierungsalternative geschieht aufgrund der im zugehörigen Kopf gegebenen Kriterien. Insbesondere ist die Einhaltung der spezifizierten Einschränkungen durch die Bindungen zu überprüfen.

Eine Bindung wird durch Zuordnung von in Masken benutzten Zugriffsroutinen zu den im Gesicht spezifizierten Routinenamen beschrieben. Im später erzeugten Programmcode werden die Algorithmen der gewählten Implementierungsalternative eingesetzt. Dabei werden Makrotechniken für offene oder geschlossene Unterprogramme und andere Techniken der Codemanipulation benutzt.

3. Erstellen von Konzeptklassen

Eine Konzeptklasse faßt verschiedene Konzepte zur Realisierung einer Schnittstelle zusammen. Im Gesicht wird eine umfassende Aufzählung der verschiedenen möglichen Zugriffsroutinen gegeben. Eine Konzeptklasse wird entweder (a) aufgrund des Überblicks über die durch das Konzept gelösten Funktionen erstellt oder (b) aus funktionell gleichwertigen Alternativen zu bereits vorhandenen Algorithmen generalisiert.

(1) Es sind zunächst Spezifikationen bekannt, die in das Gesicht eingehen. Für spätere Konzeptverallgemeinerungen ist ein Ergänzen möglich.

(2) Es werden Algorithmen zur Bearbeitung der spezifizierten Zugriffsroutinen entworfen und in den Körper einer Implementierungsalternative eingebracht. Dem wird ein Kopf zugefügt, in dem die verfügbaren Zugriffsfunktionen und die Charakterisierungen ihrer Parameter aufgezählt werden.

(3) Die Leistung der Algorithmen wird mit mathematisch analytischen
oder mit Simulation ausgeführten Analysen bewertet oder abgeschätzt. Die Resultate werden als Entscheidungsgrundlagen in den
Köpfen der Implementierungsalternativen dokumentiert.

4. Programmsysteme aus Konzeptklassen

4.1 Zur Erstellung von Programmsystemen werden in der Projektierungs-
phase Modelle für die Moduln und die Querverbindungen des Systems
benötigt. Modelle für Moduln sind Spezifikationen. Modelle für
die Systemstruktur sind, vereinfachend besehen, Graphen der Mo-
dulbindungen wie z.B. Baumformen, Schichtenmodelle usw. /1,8/.
Die Konzeptklasse ist als Modell für die Moduln einsetzbar. Dasselbe Modell wird in die späteren Projektphasen übernommen. Ein
Umschreiben oder Übersetzen ist nicht erforderlich.

4.2 Es ist wünschenswert, ein projektiertes Softwaresystem zwecks Bestimmung seiner Leistungsdaten in kürzester Zeit vorzulegen; andererseits sollen aber beliebige Korrekturen möglich sein. Mit
Konzeptklassen wird versucht, einen Vorrat an Lösungen für den
schnellen Einsatz zur Verfügung zu stellen, andererseits Änderungen
auf eine kleine Zahl von Konzeptklassen zu beschränken,
idealerweise auf eine einzige. Daher ist die Konzeptklasse auf
Denkeinheiten, Konzepte, begründet.

4.3 Weiter soll während der Programmentwicklung eine freie Manipulation der Kommunikationsstruktur möglich bleiben. Daher ist jede
Konzeptklasse ein geschlossener Bereich, dessen Außenverbindungen
im Rahmen der Spezifikationen frei geknüpft werden können.

4.4 Programmsysteme sollten aus der Sicht ihrer Benutzer äußerst flexibel an spezielle Bedürfnisse anpaßbar sein. Durch Weitergabe
der Systeme in Konzeptklassenform mit voll ausprogrammierten Implementierungsalternativen könnten Änderungen der Systemstruktur
und an Algorithmen wesentlich erleichtert werden.

5. Beispiel: Skizze einer Konzeptklasse 'Tabellenorganisation'

5.1 Das Gesicht

Grundlagen
Eine Tabelle ist eine geordnete Liste von 'Tabelleneinträgen',

die durch einen 'Suchbegriff' identifiziert werden.

Maske 'Suchbegriff'

Zugriffsoperatoren '<' und '=' mit zwei Operanden der Maske 'Suchbegriff' und Resultat der Art <u>boolean</u>.

Maske'Tabelleneintrag'

Zugriffsfunktion 'Suchwert' ohne Parameter mit Resultat der Maske 'Suchbegriff'.

Zugriffsroutinen sind

die Prozedur 'Einfügen' mit einem Parameter der Maske 'Tabellen-eintrag' ohne Resultat,

die Prozedur 'Aufsuchen' mit einem Parameter der Maske 'Suchbe-griff' und Resultat der Maske 'Tabelleneintrag' und

die Koroutine 'Verfolgen' ohne Parameter mit Resultaten 'Ende-indikator' der Art <u>boolean</u> und 'Element' der Maske 'Tabellen-eintrag'.

Diese Koroutine liefert bei einer Aktivierung jeden Eintrag der Tabelle genau einmal an.

5.2 <u>Der Klassenrumpf</u>

Die alternativen Körper können das Gesicht (5.1) z.B. mit Hilfe

(a) linearer Listen,
(b) eines Plexes in der Form eines binären Baums oder
(c) einer Hashliste

implementieren. Passende Algorithmen werden von Knuth /5/ beschrieben.

In den Köpfen werden Informationen wie die folgenden möglichst in arithmetischen Formeln gegeben:

a) Der Suchaufwand ist proportional der Listenlänge.
b) Der Suchaufwand ist im Idealfall proportional dem Logarithmus der Listenlänge.
c) Ein gesuchtes Element wird im Idealfall beim ersten Suchzugriff gefunden.

5.3 <u>Anmerkungen</u>

Die Formulierung der Masken im Beispiel legt es nahe, sie mit der mode-Konstruktion in ALGOL 68 zu vergleichen:
Die beschriebenen Masken des Beispiels wären mit den Mitteln von

ALGOL 68 /14/ noch formulierbar. Für den allgemeinen Fall wären Konstruktionen wie

<u>mode</u> m (Modal)

notwendig, wobei m durch eine Reihe von Einschränkungen näher zu definieren wäre.

In SIMULA 67 /2,11/ ist das hier skizzierte Beispiel programmierbar; Masken werden durch Referenzen auf Verbunde implementiert; die Verbunde müssen global vereinbart und als Präfix zu den Klassen benutzt werden, deren Gesichter an die Masken angepaßt werden sollen. Die Klassen zur Implementierung der Koroutinen 'Verfolgen' müssen außerhalb der Tabellenklassen deklariert werden. So gehen fast alle Vorteile der Blockstruktur verloren.

6. Ausblick

Bei allen bisher durchgeführten Experimenten mit Konzeptklassen wurde versucht, Algorithmen an einer Stelle zu definieren und bei jeder Anwendung nur Namen zu benutzen. Dies Prinzip macht sich durch erhöhte Änderungsfreundlichkeit und -sicherheit bezahlt.

Schwierigkeiten bei der Eingliederung von Routinen in Konzepte treten zuerst bei Optimierungsversuchen über Konzeptabgrenzungen hinaus ein. Dazu wurden verschiedene Auflösungsregeln ausprobiert.

(a) Zuordnung von Algorithmenteilen zu den Einzelkonzepten unter intensiver Verwendung kommunizierender Ablaufformen (z.B. Koroutinen).

(b) Definition von Produktkonzepten aus Einzelkonzepten. Die Verallgemeinerung dieser Lösung führt zu einer Anwendung des Klassenkalküls auf Konzeptklassen.

Die Formulierung der Konzeptklassen ist soweit formalisiert, daß eine automatisierte Unterstützung der Programmentwicklung möglich ist. Die Arbeiten zur Modulgenerierung, Effizienzbeschreibung usw. sind im gewünschten Umfang ohne Automatisierung fast undurchführbar. Ein verwandtes Programmiersystem wird von Wegbreit /13/ beschrieben. Die hier erläuterten Konstruktionen werden am Institut für Datenverarbeitung in der Technik implementiert. Eine Vorstudie wurde in /12/ vorgestellt.

<u>7. Literaturverzeichnis</u>

/1/   Buxton J.N., Randell B. (eds)
      Software engineering techniques
      Nato Conf. Rep., Rome 1970

/2/   Dahl O.J., Myhrhaug B., Nygaard K.
      SIMULA 67 Common Base Language
      NCC Oslo 1970

/3/   Jorrand Ph.
      Data types and extensible languages
      SIGPLAN Notices, Vol.6, No.12, 1971, pp.75-83
      Proc. of International Symp. on extensible languages,
      Grenoble 1971

/4/   Jorrand Ph., Bert D.
      On some basic concepts for extensible programming languages
      Proc. International Comp. Symp., Venedig 1972

/5/   Knuth D.E.
      The Art of Computer Programming, Vol.1
      Stanford 1968

/6/   Leavenworth B.M. (ed)
      Control structures in programming languages
      SIGPLAN Notices, Vol.7, No.11 (special issue), Boston 1972

/7/   McIlroy H.D.
      'Mass produced' software components
      in /8/ pp.138-150

/8/   Naur P., Randell B. (eds)
      Software engineering
      Nato Conf. Rep., Garmisch 1968

/9/   Parnas D.L.
      A technique for software module specification
      CACM 15 (1972), pp. 330-336

/10/   Parnas D.L.
        On the criteria to be used in decomposing systems into
        modules
        CACM 15 (1972), pp. 1053-1058

/11/   Rohlfing H.
        Eine Einführung in die höhere Programmiersprache SIMULA 67
        Interner Bericht, Informatik Karlsruhe 1972

/12/   Sonnenberg W.
        Ein Programmiersystem zur problemnahen Erstellung adaptierter
        Software
        2. GI Jahrestagung Karlsruhe 1972, pp. 143-149

/13/   Wegbreit B.
        The ECL programming system
        AFIPS Fall Joint Comp. Conf. 1971, pp. 253-262

/14/   Wijngaarden A.v. (ed)
        Report on the algorithmic language ALGOL 68
        Num. Math. 14 (1969), pp. 79-218

PROGRAMMIERSPRACHEN
UND UEBERSETZER

L_o , THE BASIC LAYER OF THE WIDE SPECTRUM LANGUAGE L

F.GEISELBRECHTINGER, W.HESSE, B.KRIEG, H.SCHEIDIG

Abstract

The term "Wide Spectrum Language" (WSL in short) is defined and the introduction of WSL's is motivated. A WSL consists of n layers being programming languages themselves. The basic layer L_o of L, a special WSL, is presented. A survey of the language L_o is given mentioning the main aspects that influenced its development. Comparing L_o with assembly language and ALGOL 68, L_o is located in the hierarchy of known programming languages. The mode-model, a central feature of the language, is treated in more detail.

1   Introduction

1.1   Definition of the term <u>Wide Spectrum Language</u>:

1.1.1   A Wide Spectrum Language B consists of n layers $B_o, B_1, ..$
B_{n-1} (n>0).

1.1.2 $B_i \subset B_j$ holds for $0 \leq i < j \leq n$, i.e. B_i is a sublanguage
of B_j .

1.1.3   A B_j-program can make use of the language facilities of
B_i (i<j) in a simple way.

1.1.4 B_o is called the <u>basic layer</u> (basic language) of B.
Ranging at the low-level-language end of the spectrum,
B_o might even be an assembly language.

Remarks:

ad 1.1.1)

The main impulse to deal with WSL's has been the experience with
ALGOL 68. We consider ALGOL 68 a great step towards achieving generality
in the definition of general purpose languages. For systems programming
applications, however, it lacks reasonably efficient language constructs
- not talking about the well-known difficulties in understanding,
learning, teaching and implementing the language. We were thus induced
to look for other ways in defining programming languages comparable
to ALGOL 68.

In our opinion such a language should be decomposed into parts.
Because of the strong interdependence of the various concepts of a
programming language, it is hardly possible to separate single concepts
and define them irrespective of one another. Contrastingly, in a
language definition by means of layers, the relevant concepts of the
whole WSL are already present at the bottom layer B_o. Still being
relatively simple in B_o, they get increasingly structured,complex

and powerful at higher layers.

ad 1.1.2)

It will not generally be possible to maintain this relation strictly. All layers may contain "privileged" instructions not included in any higher layer. (Example: An unrestricted computed goto might be possible in B_o, but prohibited in B_1, B_2 etc.)

ad 1.1.3)

The transition from a B_i- construct x_i to an equivalent B_{i-1}-construct x_{i-1} is performed by so called "projections" (translations) p as illustrated below:

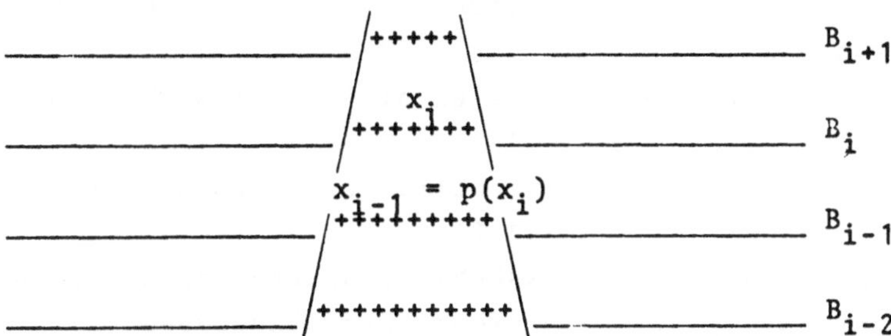

If the B_i-programmer wants to translate x_i differently from the compiler or generate more efficient code for x_i or use privileged B_j-instructions (j<i),then he is allowed to insert B_j-interludes in his B_i-program.

1.2   The Wide Spectrum Language L

At the Technical University of Munich a special WSL, called L, is being developed and implemented. L consists of the 3 layers L_0, L_1 and L_2, briefly characterized below:

1.2.1 L_o is the "static layer" of L. Storage allocation is completely performed at compile-time, the generated code is efficient and transparent. The fundamental concepts of L_1 and L_2 are already present but hardly structured and not interdependent. The underlying sementics are relatively simple. L_o will be used mainly as a systems programming language.

1.2.2 L_1 is the "dynamic layer" of L. Blocks and procedures, for example, are implemented in an ALGOL-like manner (runtime-stack, heap with garbage collection).

1.2.3 L_2 is the "meta layer" of L, where the manipulation of
programs as data is possible (heap implementation).

In the following sections we will present the basic layer L_o.

2   Brief survey of L_o

In this section, a brief survey of the properties of the language L_o
is given. Following the "historical" development of L_o we start with
the requirements imposed on L_o and then describe the concepts of L_o
which meet these requirements (section 2.1). Roughly they can be
classified in two groups:
   - requirements due to the definition of the terms "WSL" and "basic
     layer of a WSL" (section 2.1.1)
   - requirements due to the applicability of L_o as a systems pro-
     gramming language (section 2.1.2) .
In 2.2 L_o will be compared with assembly language and ALGOL 68 and thus
located in the hierarchy of known programming languages.

2.1   Properties of L_o

2.1.1 L_o as the basic layer of a WSL

In view of two contrasting aspects we had to make a compromise. Since
the fundamental concepts of all layers of L should already be present
in L_o and since the projections mentioned above should, of course,
be as simple as possible, L_o was to be defined as a rather "high"
language. On the other hand, the WSL L shall really cover a wide
spectrum of language facilities, therefore its bottommost layer L_o
should be rather "low".
Relatively "high" features of L_o are:
   - data types, called "modes" emphasizing their relationship to
     ALGOL 68 (cf.section 3)
   - mode-declarations and operator-declarations (making the language
     extensible)
   - procedures and functions
   - cooperations of coprocedures (coroutines)
   - convenient control constructs .
Among the "low" features there are :
   - static storage management (no runtime-stack,no block structure,
     no flexible bounds in arrays, no garbage collection)
   - no applied occurence of an object before its defining occurence
   - no precedence of binary operators, i.e. each formula contains

at most one binary operator. No bracketing of formulas.
- all changes of modes have to be explicitly stated by the
  programmer
- composed modes may only be formed from uncomposed modes .

2.1.2 L_o as a systems programming language

For this pupose L_o contains special features like
- the modes <u>table</u>, <u>stack</u>, <u>queue</u>, <u>collection</u> and <u>free</u> (described
  in section 3)
- address calculation and computed <u>gotos</u> (these constructs are
  "privileged", cf. remark to 1.1.2)
- declarations of read-only objects by means of <u>const</u>
- <u>overlap</u> - specifications which allow overlapping of storage areas
- generators providing dynamic storage allocation for objects of a
  particular mode (the amount of storage has to be declared in
  advance)
- a large supply of debugging facilities .

2.2   Comparison of L_o with other languages

Considering the properties of L_o described so far we find that L_o is
approximately located halfway on the scale of programming languages
ranging from assembly language up to ALGOL 68. Table 1 illustrates
how it is more closely connected to one or to the other.
Comparing example programs coded in assembly language, L_o
and ALGOL 68 we observe: In L_o - as in ALGOL 68 - declarations
unburden the programmer from typifying his data, which is necessary
in assembly language. Performing elementary operations in assembly
language costs more instructions than in L_o and ALGOL 68, but nested
expressions - common in ALGOL 68 - have to be split into a sequence of
extended 3-address-instructions in L_o.

3   The L_o - mode - model

The term "mode" is used the same way as in ALGOL 68 (cf. [A68],
rule 2.2.4.1) .
Now, let M be the set of all L_o-modes. M is the disjoint union of the
two subsets   EM (the set of elementary L_o-modes) and CM (the set of
composed L_o-modes). The elementary modes are described in 3.1-3.5, the
composed modes in 3.6 - 3.10. The components of composed modes have to
be elementary - this restriction being cancelled in higher layers.

	assembly language	L_o	ALGOL 68
block structure	none		present
mode changes	only explicite changes		many implicite changes
type-free data hand-ling	possible	available by means of the "mode" _free_	impossible
jumps	unrestricted, even jumps to label variables	only leave- and _return-jumps_ other _jumps_ are _privileged_	jumps to constant labels
nesting of formulas	not possible	hardly possible(no bracketing of formulas,no precedence of binary operators)	no restriction
data types	no types, or only rather pri-mitive types; no composed types, no type-declarations	variety of data-types("modes"), restricted composition spec.modes: _free_,_table_, _stack_,_queue_,_coll_	new modes are declarable unrestricted composition
subroutines	only closed subroutines without parameter passing mechanism	closed procedures with parameter passing mechanism procedures are modes spec.subroutines: _open proc_, _funct_,_open funct_,_coop_,_coproc_	
operations	only unary operators(general-ly) ; operands have prim. types or no types	unary and binary operations on data of all modes new operators are declarable spec.operations for spec. L_o-modes	
control constructs	only very primitive con-structs (conditioned jumps etc.)	if- and case-statements, do-loops, serial and collateral elaboration	

TABLE 1 : Language constructs available in ass.lang. - L_o - ALGOL 68

3.1   Primitive modes

are essentially analogous to ALGOL 68. L_o includes the primitive modes
int,real,bit ($\hat{}$bool),char,bits,chars ($\hat{}$bytes). We can do without compl
in L_o - and probably in L_1 and L_2, too.

3.2   long and short

Adding n longs or shorts (n≥1) to a primitive mode declarer you can

declare an object (of primitive mode) occupying more or less storage
than the corresponding standard object,respectively. If you want a
certain - possibly strange - realization on your machine, you can
specify your own long or short in a machine specification added to
your program as a description of the environment (for details cf.
[GHKS 1] , [GHKS 2]).

3.3   ref and const

In strict ALGOL 68, the n a m e of a variable is represented by an
additional reference to the mode of its values (cf. [A 68] , rule
6.0.1.e) . In L (not only in L_o), this reference is generally omitted.
thus the declarations of L-variables are similar to the extended
ALGOL 68 - declarations. Note that the L-notation is not due to an
extension but to the strict syntax. In this way, for example, the con-
fusion with ALGOL 68 - parameters is avoided (in extended ALGOL 68,
an object x declared as m x has the mode ref m, whereas a procedure
parameter x declared as m̲ x has the mode m̲).

The mentioned omission of one reference causes a new assignation rule:
In an assignation there must be as many references on the left hand
side as on the right hand side - not one more, as required in ALGOL 68.

Constants are denoted by an additional

const

in front of the mode declarer. Constants may only be initialized one
time during program execution and afterwards are read-only.

const may not only be added to complete declarers but also to declarers
occuring as components of composed declarers. E.g. the declarer

struct(const real s1,ref const int s2,const ref const int s3)

could be written.

Because the terms "variable" and "reference" are no longer mixed up,
L_o has enlarged declaration facilities by comparison to ALGOL 68.
Table 2 includes examples.

TABLE 2 : Examples of the use of ref and const

(strict) ALGOL 68	L_o
ref int x = loc int	int x
int pi = 3.14	const int pi is 3.14 (is denotes static initialization)
int x = y	const int x overlap y (overlap is not exactly the translation of the ALGOL 68 - equals-symbol. So in this L_o-declaration x and y need not have the same mode)

TABLE 2 (continued) :

(strict) ALGOL 68	L_o
ref ref int xx = loc ref int	ref int xx
-	ref const int x (the value of the reference may be changed, but not the referenced int-object(*))
-	const ref int x (unchangable reference to an int - variable)
-	const ref const int x (neither the reference nor the referenced object must be changed)

3.4   free

The L_o-mode free, which has no ALGOL 68 equivalent, is characterized by the following main properties :

3.4.1   By means of the declaration

free x[n]

storage of the length n is allocated (**). This can be used as an intermediate storage for any values irrespective of their a priori modes. Such values can be entered after application of "interpretations" (see below)

3.4.2   By "interpretation" we mean the transition from a mode m1 to a mode m2, where exactly one is the mode free. So there are the following two interpretations (let x be the object to be interpreted):

m1 = mode(x)	m2	name of the interpretation	notation	condition
$\neq$ free	free	strip	free << x	-
free [n]	$\neq$ free	dress	m2 << x	values of the mode m2 must have the length n

---

(*) Our const looks a little like M.RAIN's VAL (cf. [MARY]), but there are differences, e.g. in the assignation rule.
At about the same time, when MARY was developed, similar proposals were made by several people, e.g. by G.GOOS.

(**) That is, x consists of a sequence of n "units", where the length of one unit is the maximum of the lengths of all primitive objects.

Two examples are given and explained in the following table

interpretation	example	explanation
strip	int x; free y; y := free << x	The value of the int-object x is "strip"ped off its mode int and is given the mode free instead of int. After this it can be assigned to y.
dress	bits z;free y; z := bits << y	The value of the free-object y is "dress"ed with the mode bits i.e. given the mode bits instead of free.After this it can be assigned to z.

Note that interpretations are no coercions, interpretations do not imply any conversions. So the programmer himself is responsable for the consequences of possible "misinterpretations".

3.4.3   A certain analogy between free and ALGOL 68-union exists in so far as both concepts offer facilities to give up the strict connection of an object with its mode. In the following way,however, the union-concept is generalized by free :

- Whereas union is always a union of a certain, finite subset of the set of all ALGOL 68 - modes {e.g. union(int,real)} , free is the union of a l l L_o-modes .

- Dynamically, a union-value always keeps its mode; a free-value , however, loses its a priori mode by stripping it. So dynamic conformity relations are not available. Shortly: union only statically weakens the principle of modes, free does so statically a n d dynamically.

3.4.4   free-denotations are not available nor are arithmetic operations on free-objects .

3.4.5   free is an elementary mode, so it may be component of a composed mode. In L_o, this is the only way to declare two-dimensional objects directly, i.e. not using ref .

3.5   atom

atoms are mainly used as elements of collections (cf.3.8). There are no operations on atom-objects apart from = and $\neq$.

3.6   string

In a declaration

    string m s

the component mode m is restricted to bit and char.

3.7   struct

analogous to ALGOL 68. In a declaration

    struct(m1 s1,..   mn sn) s

mi ϵ EM must hold for i = 1,.. n.
PIexes are available,because references to composed modes are elementary themselves. Selection is performed like row-selection, so the ALGOL 68-selection s1 of s corresponds to the L_o-selection s[s1] .

3.8   <u>collection</u>

An object x of the mode <u>collection</u> may be declared by enumeration of its (elementary) elements ('explicite collection') or by definition of a decision algorithm ('implicite collection'). The decision algorithm has to be a function (cf.3.10) with <u>bit</u>-result. For a given element e, the function has to decide, whether or not e belongs to x.

Of particular interest are the explicite collections of <u>atoms</u>. Beside the common collection-operations ε and ¢ , for these special collections the usual set operations (like union, intersection,complement etc.) are available.

3.9   <u>row</u> , <u>table</u> , <u>stack</u> , <u>queue</u>

In this subsection rtsq ε{<u>row</u>,<u>table</u>,<u>stack</u>,<u>queue</u>} may hold. The declaration of a <u>rtsq</u> - object x looks as follows :

   <u>rtsq</u> <u>m</u> x[n]   (<u>m</u> ε EM)

If <u>m</u> is the mode <u>free</u>, you may write

   <u>rtsq</u> <u>free</u> x[n][m] .

The following properties are common to all 4 modes:

- the length specifications n,m do not belong to the declarer but to the declared object

- a <u>rtsq</u>-object consists of n "entries" of the fixed length m (where m = length of a particular <u>m</u>-object, if not stated)

- there are no flexible bounds

- internally an <u>rtsq</u>-object is represented by a linear storage section.

- all <u>rtsq</u>-objects are one-dimensional (but cf.3.4.5) .

The differences between the 4 modes arise mainly in the entering technique and the available operations:

- indexing may be performed on <u>rows</u>, <u>tables</u> and <u>stacks</u> as usual. The last entry of <u>tables</u>, <u>stacks</u> and <u>queues</u> can be reached by the operation <u>last</u> .

- to a <u>table</u> you can add a new entry by <u>enter</u>, the result of this operation will be the reference to the new entry.

- to a <u>stack</u> a new entry is added by <u>push</u>, it can be deleted by <u>pop</u>.

- at the end of a <u>queue</u> a new entry can be added by <u>put</u>, at the beginning be fetched and deleted by <u>get</u>. The operator <u>first</u>, applied to a <u>queue</u>, yields the reference to the entry which happens to be the first in the <u>queue</u>.

- using the operator <u>length</u> you will be told the actual length of a <u>table</u>, <u>stack</u> or <u>queue</u> .

- standard searching algorithms are available for <u>tables</u>,<u>stacks</u> and <u>queues</u>.

3.10   Routines

In L_0 there are four kinds of routines : <u>procs</u>,<u>functs</u>,<u>coops</u> and <u>coprocs</u>.

All routines may be declared with or without parameters. All parameters and the result - if any - have elementary modes. Additionally,they must be <u>const</u> (this restriction will be cancelled in higher layers).

Parameter passing is performed as in ALGOL 68, namely by identification of formal and actual parameters.

Routine variables are not available nor are recursive routines (in L_o).

Procedures (<u>proc</u>) may be declared <u>open</u> (i.e. as macros), otherwise they are <u>closed</u>.

Functions (<u>funct</u>) also may be open. They must have a result. If the programmer <u>tries</u> to generate a side-effect (e.g. by assignation to globals), an error message is given by the compiler.

A base for a general coroutine concept is atready present in L_o : A fixed set of <u>coprocedures</u> is framed by a <u>cooperation</u> which, in itself, acts <u>like</u> a subroutine (for details cf.[GHKS 1] , [GHKS 2]).

REFERENCES

[BG]   F.L.BAUER, G.GOOS : Informatik ,
           Springer-Verlag Berlin-Heidelberg-New York 1971

[GHKS 1]   F.GEISELBRECHTINGER, W.HESSE, B.KRIEG, H.SCHEIDIG :
           MAB1 - eine vorläufige und sehr informelle Beschreibung,
           Technische Universität München, SFB 49 Teilprojekt A2,
           interner Bericht Mai 1973

[GHKS 2]   F.GEISELBRECHTINGER, W.HESSE, B.KRIEG, H.SCHEIDIG :
           Language Layers, Portability and Program Structuring ,
           paper presented at the IFIP-TC 2 working conference on
           machine-oriented higher-level PL's, Trondheim Aug.1973

[MARY]   M.RAIN : Some formal language aspects of MARY,
           ALGOL Bulletin 34, p.45-81 , 1972

[A 68]   A.van WIJNGAARDEN (ed.), B.J.MAILLOUX, J.E.L. PECK,
           C.H.A. KOSTER: Report on the Algorithmic Language ALGOL 68,
           Num.Math.14,p.79 - 218, 1969

[PASCAL]   N.WIRTH: The Programming Language PASCAL (Revised Report)
           ETH Zürich, Bericht der Fachgruppe Computer-Wissenschaften,
           5, Nov. 1972

[BLISS]   W.A.WULF, D.B.RUSSELL, A.N.HABERMANN: BLISS, a Language
           for Systems Programming, CACM 14, p.780 ff, 1971

H. OVENHAUSEN
GEZIELTE PORTABILITÄT VON SOFTWARE

- Erfahrungen bei der gemeinsamen Implementierung eines Interpreters
  für die Steuersprache von POLYP auf den Systemen TR44o und IBM/36o.

Zusammenfassung: Portable Software, die auf bestimmte Rechner über-
tragbar sein soll, kann in einer höheren Programmiersprache programmiert werden. Datendeklarationen lassen sich mittels einiger system-
beschreibender Größen parametrisieren. Die Umwandlung von der allgemeinen, parametrisierten Darstellung einer Deklaration in die jeweilige maschinenabhängige kann ein geeigneter Pre-Prozessor durchführen.

Summary: Portable software which should be transferrable to a certain
group of machines may be coded in a high-level programming language.
Data declarations may be parametrized by some machine dependent values.
The transformation process from the portable representation of a data
declaration to its specific machine dependent representation will be
performed by a suitable .pre-processor.

I. Einleitende Betrachtungen über die Portabilität von Software

Die Notwendigkeit, komplexe Programmsysteme von einer Maschine
auf weitere zu übertragen, führte zur Entwicklung höherer Programmiersprachen. Doch die unterschiedlichsten Implementationen gleicher höherer Programmiersprachen haben das Erreichen dieses Zieles
beispielsweise für Realzeit-Anwendungen in Frage gestellt. Neue
Versuche u.a. im Bereich des Übersetzerbaus sind unternommen worden
(Poole, Waite, Brown).

Die folgenden drei Forderungen sind eine erste Antwort auf diese
Frage:

P1) Ausgehend von einer gleichen Zeichenfolge, die das portable
    Programm darstellt, muß auf allen in Frage kommenden Maschinen
    ein funktionsfähiges Objekt-Programm bereitgestellt werden kön-
    nen.

P2) Diese funktionsfähigen Objektprogramme müssen zu einer wohl-
    definierten Menge von Eingabe-Datensätzen auf allen Maschinen
    die gleichen Resultate liefern.

P3) Die Effizienz dieser Objektprogramme bezüglich Speicherbedarf
    und Laufzeitverhalten auf den unterschiedlichen Maschinen ist
    von vergleichbarer Qualität.

Wir stellen fest, daß auch Portabilität nur eine relative Größe
ist, denn ein Programm kann im Sinne von P1 und P2 durchaus portabel sein, die Übertragung auf einen bestimmten Rechner kann jedoch
zu nicht vertretbaren Ineffizienzen z.B. in der Ausnutzung des
Speichers oder in den resultierenden Ausführungszeiten führen.
Portabilität um jeden Preis ist manchmal möglich, erscheint jedoch
wenig sinnvoll.

Typische Portabilitätsfälle sind die beiden folgenden:

- ein Programm S soll zunächst nur auf einer bestimmten Maschine
  implementiert werden, es besteht jedoch die Möglichkeit, daß
  später auch weitere noch nicht genau festgelegte Maschinen
  als Zielmaschinen in Frage kommen können.

Hier wird ausgehend von einer Maschine die <u>freie Portabilität</u> auf
beliebige weitere Maschinen gefordert. Eher möglich als freie
Portabilität ist die Planung und Realisierung von <u>gezielter Porta-
bilität</u>:

- ein Programm S soll auf einer bereits festgelegten Menge von
  Zielmaschinen implementiert werden.

Eine spezielle Anwendung für gezielte Portabilität ist die Verla-
gerung von Entwicklungsarbeiten von Realzeitrechnern auf Großrechner. In diesem Fall kann die Forderung P3 in einer Richtung stark
aufgeweicht werden, auf dem Großrechner braucht das Laufzeitverhal-
ten von portabler Software bei weitem nicht so effizient zu sein
wie auf den Realzeitrechnern.

Beispiel:

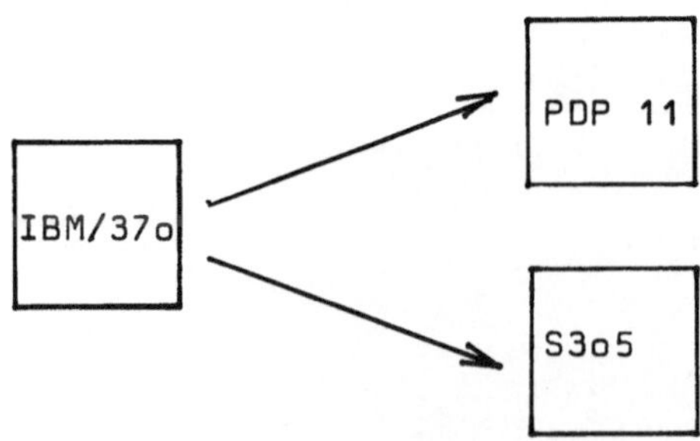

Im folgenden Text verstehen wir unter Portabilität immer gezielte
Portabilität.

Steht auf allen in Frage kommenden Zielmaschinen ein Übersetzer für
eine bestimmte höhere Programmiersprache zur Verfügung, so läßt
sich mittels eines geeigneten Pre-Prozessors (s. II.) gezielt portabel programmieren. Mehrfache Implementierung einer höheren Programmiersprache bedeutet in der Praxis, daß die jeweiligen Übersetzer unterschiedliche Sprachmengen der gleichen Programmiersprache
verarbeiten. Einzelne maschinen- und implementationsabhängige
Sprachelemente lassen sich nun mit Hilfe eines Pre-Prozessors ver-
allgemeinern, d.h. die portable Darstellung eines Programms (i.e.
Folge von verallgemeinerten Sprachelementen) wird mittels des Pre-
Prozessors auf die implementationsabhängige Darstellung der Zielmaschine abgebildet.

II. Maschinenunabhängigkeit von Datentypen

Eine Schlüsselfrage des Portabilitätsproblems ist die Maschinenunabhängigkeit von Datentypen. Anhand eines Beispiels ("Integer-Halb-
wort auf den Maschinen TR44o und IBM/36o") wird der Versuch zur Beantwortung der folgenden Frage unternommen: "Welche Größen charakterisieren einen bestimmten Datentyp auf einer bestimmten Maschine?"

Dazu betrachten wir kurz die Speicherstruktur der beiden Zielmaschinen.

TR44o: Ein Maschinenwort besteht aus zwei adressierbaren Halbwor-
          ten der Länge 24 Bits. Der Speicher ist linear angeordnet.

IBM/36o: Ein Maschinenwort besteht aus vier adressierbaren Einhei-
          ten der Länge 8 Bits (1 Byte). Zwei adressierbare Einhei-
          ten bilden ein Halbwort. Der Speicher ist linear angeord-
          net.

Die folgenden Fragen können für Zielmaschinen mit einer unterschiedlichen Speicherstruktur unterschiedliche Antworten haben. Sind sich
teilweise oder ganz überdeckende Hardware-Eigenschaften vorhanden,
so können die Antworten auf einzelne Fragen auch gleich sein.

a) Wie soll der Inhalt eines Teils des Speichers interpretiert
   werden?   Informationstyp

b) Welche Länge besitzt ein Datentyp in Bits oder in Zeichen?
                                              Informationslänge

c) Wo im Speicher (relativ zu adressierbaren Speichereinheiten) kann
   ein Datentyp gespeichert werden?   Informationspositionierung

d) Welche Werte kann ein Datentyp annehmen?
                                              Wertevorrat

In unserem Beispiel lauten die Antworten auf diese Fragen:

       TR44o   IBM/36o

a)   integer (= ganzzahlig)   integer
b)   24   16
c)   auf Halbwortgrenze   auf Halbwortgrenze
d) $-2^{22}-1$ bis $2^{22}-1$ -2^{15} bis $2^{15}-1$

Der obige Fragenkatalog enthält nur Fragen, die bei der Deklaration
von einfachen Variablen (im Sinne einer höheren Programmiersprache
wie ALGOL 6o) gestellt werden können. Bei komplizierteren Datenstrukturen wie Feldern, Tabellen und Bäumen muß die Menge der Fragen entsprechend erweitert werden.

In höheren Programmiersprachen wie ALGOL 6o, FORTRAN IV und PL/I
hat der Programmierer nur geringen Einfluß auf die explizite Festlegung von Informationslänge, -positionierung und Wertevorrat von
Datentypen.

In einer höheren Programmiersprache, in der diese Größen explizit
bei der Deklaration von Variablen gesetzt werden können, besteht
dann auch eher die Möglichkeit, gezielt portabel programmieren zu
können. Im Hinblick auf eine Gruppe von Zielmaschinen kann ein Datentyp parametrisiert werden, in unserem Beispiel durch

a) INTEGER
b) HALFWORD-LENGTH
c) RIGHTHALF, LEFTHALF
d) MIN-VALUE, MAX-VALUE

Die maschinenunabhängige Form der Deklaration von Integer-Halbwort-
Variablen könnte die folgende sein:

<u>variable</u> I,J,K (INTEGER,
                HALFWORD-LENGTH,
                RIGHTHALF,
                MIN-VALUE,
                MAX-VALUE),

Ein Pre-Prozessor hat nun die Aufgabe, diese portable Darstellung
auf die jeweilige "Zielmaschinen"-abhängige Darstellung abzubilden.
Diese Abbildung stellt eine statische Textersetzung dar, für alle
allgemeinen Größen (systembeschreibende Parameter) wie z.B. HALF-
WORD-LENGTH werden die maschinenabhängigen Werte eingesetzt (z.B.
TR44o: HALFWORD ⟶ 24).

III. <u>Gezielte Portabilität von Datentypen mit Hilfe des POLYP-Systems</u>
     Wie kann man nun mit Hilfe des POLYP-Systems gezielt portabel pro-
     grammieren?
     Zum besseren Verständnis wird nun kurz die Struktur des POLYP-Sy-
     stems erläutert.

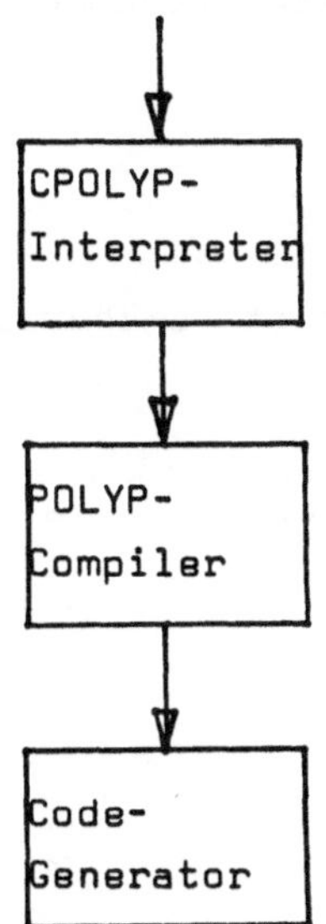

Der <u>CPOLYP-Interpreter</u> verarbeitet ein Gemisch
aus Steuersprache und POLYP-Problemsprache. Die
Elemente der Steuersprache werden interpretativ
abgearbeitet. Die Elemente der Problemsprache
werden kopiert und an den POLYP-Compiler als
Input weitergegeben. Der Interpreter dient (wie
im PL/I-System der PL/I-Preprocessor) zur Manipulation der Eingabe zum Hauptcompiler.

Der <u>POLYP-Compiler</u> übersetzt POLYP-Programme in
eine Zwischensprache und erzeugt eine Identi-
fierliste. Beides wird anschließend vom <u>Code-
Generator</u> verarbeitet, der ein Assembler-Pro-
gramm für die jeweilige Zielmaschine erzeugt.

Der CPOLYP-Interpreter kann u.a. die Funktion des im vorigen Abschnitt benötigten Pre-Prozessors übernehmen. Die POLYP-Problemsprache stellt die höhere Programmiersprache dar, für die es Übersetzer für verschiedene Zielmaschinen gibt.

Die Steuersprache CPOLYP ist eine Untermenge der Problemsprache
POLYP. Damit der CPOLYP-Interpreter die Elemente der Steuersprache von denen der Problemsprache unterscheiden kann, werden zwei
unterschiedliche Begrenzersätze definiert.

Beispiele:	Problemsprache	Steuersprache
	/	%/
	,	%, oder %
	begin	cbegin
	if	cif

In POLYP werden Variable deklariert, indem man ihren Typ und ihre
Länge und ihre Positionierung in Speicher angibt.

```
variable I,J,K(B(32,16),I16),
                      Typ und Länge
         Positionierung
```

Mit Hilfe der Boundary-Funktion B(b,d) wird die Information im
Speicher positioniert.

B(32,16) bedeutet: Informationsbeginn auf einer Bitadresse mo-
dulo 32+16.

Typ- und Längenbeschreibung geben

den Typ (I=integer, U=unsigned integer, R=real, T=target, C=character,
L=logical und A=address) und

die Länge der Information an, z.B. T32 bedeutet eine Label-Variable
der Länge 32 Bits.

Die Größen, die einen Datentyp auf einer bestimmten Maschine charakterisieren, können im POLYP-System durch Control-Variable[x] dargestellt werden.
Die Definition der Control-Variablen FW und HW reicht bereits aus,
um die im vorigen Abschnitt erwähnte portable Integer-Halbwort-
Deklaration zu realisieren.

Beispiel:
    cvariable FW,HW(I32), TR44o, S36o(L1), MACH(C5) %;
    MACH %:= 'S-36o' %;
   ccomment definition of the object machine %;
    cif MACH %= 'S-36o' ctrue S36o %:= BIN '1' %;
                        cfalse S36o %:= BIN 'o' %;
    cif MACH %= 'TR44o' ctrue TR44o %:= BIN '1' %;
                        cfalse TR44o %:= BIN 'o' %;
    ccomment definition of system parameters %;
    cif S36o ctrue FW %:= 32 %;
    cif TR44o ctrue FW %:= 48 %;
    HW %:= FW %/ 2 %;
    ccomment end of control part %

         .

         .

    comment problem part, portable declaration;
    variable I,J,K(B(FW,HW),I_HW);

In Abhängigkeit von den Control-Variablen TR44o und S36o, welche
die Zielmaschine identifizieren, werden die folgenden Texte erzeugt:
       im Fall TR44o: im Fall S36o:
    variable I,J,K(B(48,24),I24),   variable I,J,K(B(32,16),I16),

Der POLYP-Compiler verarbeitet diese Deklarationen und gibt das Ergebnis an den jeweiligen Code-Generator weiter. Hier zeigt sich,
daß im Fall der gezielten Portabilität im POLYP-System ein unmit-
telbarer Zusammenhang zwischen der interpretativen und der code-
erzeugenden Ebene besteht. Denn schon während der interpretativen

---

x) Control-Variable und Control-Prozeduren sind Elemente der
   Steuersprache CPOLYP.

Abarbeitung des portablen Programms werden die Weichen für die spätere Codeerzeugung gestellt, in unserem Beispiel werden allerdings nur Datendeklarationen behandelt.

Zur portablen Programmierung können in POLYP anstelle von Control-Variablen auch Control-Prozeduren benutzt werden, sie eignen sich u.a. zur Generierung von maschinenabhängigen Standard-Boundary-Funktionen und Typ- und Längenangaben.

Beispiel:
    <u>variable</u> ADDR1,ADDR2(ADDR),
                          ↑
                    Control-Prozedur-Aufruf

    wird zu:
    IBM/36o: <u>variable</u> ADDR1,ADDR2(B(32,8),A24),
    TR44o : <u>variable</u> ADDR1,ADDR2(B(24,o),A24),

Control-Prozeduren, die ein portables Sprachelement darstellen, können folgenden Aufbau haben:

a) Angenommen, alle Zielmaschinen lassen sich mit Hilfe einiger Systemparameter beschreiben, so werden diese Parameter (z.B. FW, HW usw.) zu Anfang der Interpretation eines portablen Programms mit den für die jeweilige Zielmaschine gültigen Werten vorbesetzt. Diese Parameter sind für alle verwendeten Control-Prozeduren global.

   Jedes portable Sprachelement kann nun durch eine Control-Prozedur dargestellt werden, die ihrerseits wieder portabel ist, denn sie benutzt zur Erzeugung von maschinenabhängigem POLYP-Problem-Text oben erwähnte System-Parameter.

   Beispiel:
            <u>cprocedure</u> ADDR%
            <u>cbegin</u>
              B(ADRL1,ADELTA),A_ADRL2
            <u>cend</u> %

Diese Control-Prozedur benutzt die System-Parameter
ADRL1, ADRL2 und ADELTA. Im Fall IBM/36o haben sie die
Werte 32,24,8 und im Fall TR44o die Werte 24,24,o.

b) Sie bestehen aus einer Reihe von Alternativen, wobei die i-te
Alternative jeweils den maschinenabhängigen POLYP-Text für die
Maschine M_i erzeugt.

Beispiel:

```
    cproc PORT §
    cbegin
        cif M1 ctrue cbegin ... cend§
          .

          .
        cif M11 ctrue cbegin ... cend§
    cend§
```

Die Größen M1,...,M1o sind globale Control-Flags, von denen jeweils genau eines gesetzt ist.
Der Vorteil dieser Lösung liegt in der leichten Anpaßbarkeit an
weitere Zielmaschinen, vielleicht M11 und M12.

Eine wünschenswerte Spracheigenschaft von POLYP oder anderen
höheren Programmiersprachen, in denen portabel programmiert werden soll, wäre die explizite Angabe von Wertebereichen für einzelne Variable.

Bei gezielter Portabilität hilft hier (bei genauer Kenntnis der
Hardware der Zielmaschinen und der zu programmierenden Anwender-
probleme) auch folgende Lösung weiter:
Problemstellung: Auf der Maschine X (Wortlänge = 32 Bits) wird
eine I16-Variable sowohl zur Aufnahme von Meßwertgrößen als auch
von Laufindizes benutzt. Beim Übergang auf eine Maschine Y (Wortlänge = 24 Bits) reicht für die Laufindizes eine I12-Variable
aus. Die Meßwertgrößen benötigen jedoch wegen einzuhaltender Ge-
nauigkeitsforderungen hier eine I24-Variable.

Die Abbildung

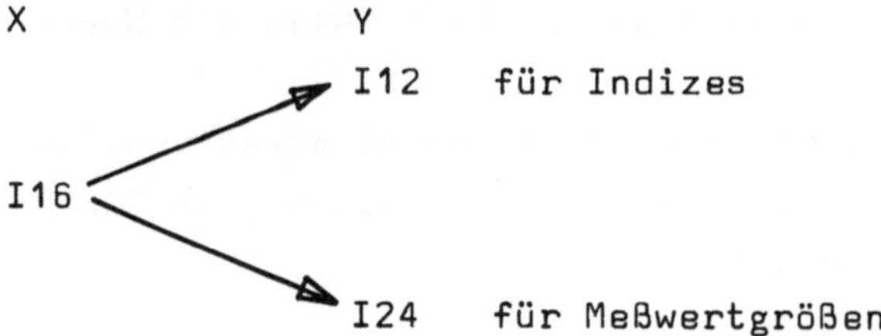

läßt sich mit dem CPOLYP-Interpreter leicht erledigen.

Zusammenfassend können wir sagen, daß das POLYP-System die Deklaration von portablen Datentypen ermöglicht. Die Maschinenunabhängigkeit wird durch ihre Parametrisierung erreicht. In der Praxis hat sich gezeigt, daß ca. 1o Systemparameter ausreichen, um z.B. bei einfachen Variablen- deklarationen die unterschiedlichen Speicherstrukturen von TR44o und IBM/36o zu beschreiben.

Die hier angedeuteten Methoden zur portablen Darstellung von Datenty- pen wurden erfolgreich bei der Entwicklung eines neuen, erweiterten CPOLYP-Interpreters angewandt. Dieser CPOLYP-Interpreter wurde gezielt portabel programmiert (Zielmaschinen sind TR44o und IBM/36o) und wird voraussichtlich Anfang Semptember 1973 auf IBM/36o und ca. zwei Monate später auf TR44o funktionsfähig sein.

Literaturverzeichnis

(1)   Brown, P.J. Using a Macro Processor to aid Software Implementa-
      tion, Comput. Joutnal 12, 327-331 (1969)

(2)   Brown, P.J. Levels of Language for Portable Software, CACM 15,
      1o59-1o61 (1972)

(3)   Mußtopf, G. Das Programmiersystem POLYP, Angewandte Informatik 1o,
      441-448 (1972)

(4)   Mußtopf, G. Sprachgesteuerte Modifikation von Quellprogrammen,
      2. Fachtagung Programmiersprachen GI, 1972

(5)   Poole, P.C., Waite, W.M. Portability and Adaptability, Advanced
      Course on Software Engineering, Springes-Verlag, 183-317 (1973)

(6)   Wilkes, M.V. Self-compiling Compiler, Annual Review in Automatic
      Programming, 31 ff. (1964)

ENTWURF UND REALISIERUNG DES
LEKTOR-SYSTEMS

A. Schmitt, K. Dürre, H. Hummel

1. ZIELSETZUNGEN

LEKTOR ist ein Programmiersystem, das speziell für die Bedürfnisse des rechnergestützten Unterrichts (RGU) entwickelt und implementiert wurde. Die Basis eines derartigen Systems ist eine Programmiersprache (Autorensprache), die es den "Lehrern" gestattet, sogenannte Lehrprogramme zu entwickeln und in die Systembibliothek einzubringen. Die im System vorrätigen Lehrprogramme können dann von "Schülern" abgerufen werden. Ein so aktiviertes Programm steuert z.B. über Sichtschirm-Terminal einen Dialog mit dem Schüler, durch den systematisch Lehrinhalte vermittelt werden sollen.

In den letzten Jahren hat sich im Bereich der RGU-Systeme ein tiefgreifender Wandel vollzogen. Während frühere Systeme in mehr oder weniger verallgemeinerter Form die Methode des programmierten Unterrichts unterstützten, wie sie z.B. bei Buchprogrammen gepflegt wird, hat sich das Spektrum der Anforderungen inzwischen deutlich ausgeweitet: Die Autorensprache muß möglichst weitgehend die simulative Modellierung von Lehrstoffen erlauben. An Beispielen konkretisiert bedeutet dies: Formales Differenzieren, Manipulation von Matrizen, Erzeugen graphischer Darstellungen, "Blättern" in umfangreichen Basis-Texten bzw. Nachschlagen in Wörterbüchern usw. muß durch die Autorensprache jeweils mit vernünftigem Programmieraufwand erledigt werden können. An diese Forderungen wird die Hoffnung geknüpft, daß algorithmisch ausgefeilte, also "intelligentere" Lehrprogramme beim Schüler auch größere Lernerfolge bewirken. Außerdem können derartige flexible Systeme allein durch entsprechende Programmierung an nahezu jede didaktische oder lerntheoretische Konzeption angepaßt werden. Daher können wir hier eine eingehendere Behandlung der Frage "Wie soll mit dem System gelernt werden?" zurückstellen.

Für das System LEKTOR wurde demgemäß der algorithmischen Flexibilität weitgehend Vorrang eingeräumt. Es wurde nach einer Lösung gesucht, die einerseits dem Lehrprogrammautor ein variables Programmier-Instrumentarium in die Hand gibt und andererseits mit erträglichem Aufwand zu implementieren ist. Dabei konnte auf Erfahrungen zurückgegriffen werden, die bei einer Testimplementierung der Autorensprache LIDIA [3] gemacht wurden.

2. DIE AUTORENSPRACHE LEKTOR

Die dem LEKTOR-System zugrunde liegende Programmiersprache wurde aus EULER [4] entwickelt. Die Anpassung an praktische Erfordernisse des RGU hat es aber mit sich gebracht, daß LEKTOR und EULER im Detail nur noch wenige Gemeinsamkeiten aufweisen. Auch der erste Bericht aus der Planungsphase des Systems [2] ist nicht mehr in allen Punkten zuverlässig.

2.1 Datenstrukturen

Variable müssen deklariert werden. Es gibt für sie die Deklaratoren

.NUM	(Aufnahme von Gleitkommazahlen mit Einschluß der ganzen Zahlen und der logischen Werte),
.LABEL	(Aufnahme von Sprungmarken-Werten),
.PROCVAR	(Aufnahme von Werten des Typs "Prozedur"),
.STRING	(Aufnahme von Zeichenketten variabler Länge),
.LIST	(Aufnahme von Listen beliebigen Umfangs),
.POINTER	(Aufnahme von Zeigern auf Variable und Listenelemente).

Eine Variable kann zur Lebenszeit ihren Typ nicht ändern, was im LEKTOR-Übersetzer zur Überprüfung der Typenkorrektheit, zur Codeoptimierung sowie zur Ausschaltung der z.B. in EULER wegen der Typenfreiheit ständig erforderlichen Typüberprüfung benutzt wird. Eine LEKTOR-Liste ist eine vollständig geordnete Menge $[D_1,D_2,...,D_n]$ von Datenobjekten D_i (i=1,2,...,n) mit evtl. n=0. Alle D_i müssen allerdings jeweils vom gleichen Typ sein, wobei sämtliche Typen (num, label, proc, string, list, pointer, undef) zulässig sind.

Die Wertzuweisung

    L = [['MATRIX A'],[[1,2,2],[-3,1,0],[2,1,0]]];

weist der .LIST-Variablen L einen Wert zu, so daß z.B. anschließend mit

    HD = [L[2,1,1],L[2,2,2],L[2,3,3]];

die Hauptdiagonale gebildet werden kann, d.h.

    HD ≡ [1,1,0].

Wird die Listenvariable ZEILE1 belegt durch

    ZEILE1 = [2,1];

so liefert   HD[ZEILE1] ≡ [1,2,2], d.h. auch num-Listen dürfen als Selektoren verwendet werden.

Da die Selektion eines Elementes auf einer Listenebene wegen konsekutiver Speicherung durch Einstich und nicht etwa durch Zeigerverfolgung erfolgt, ist die Indizierung auch bei hohen Indexwerten effektiv. Durch Benutzung von <u>num</u>-Listen als Selektoren ist ein recht befriedigender Umgang mit zusammengesetzten Informationseinheiten (Verbunden, Records) möglich. Variable des Typs <u>pointer</u> leisten sehr wertvolle Dienste beim Arbeiten innerhalb umfangreicher Listen, da so mit minimalem Selektionsaufwand Arbeitspositionen gekennzeichnet werden können. Allerdings wurde von der Retention-Mechanik Abstand genommen, weil durch dynamisches Löschen von Listen zusammen mit einem einfachen Schiebevorgang eine ziemlich effektive und weitgehend kontinuierliche Form der Speicherbereinigung realisiert werden konnte. Für die Manipulation von Listen und Zeichenketten (Strings) steht ein angemessener Satz von Operatoren zur Verfügung, so daß die beim RGU wünschenswerten Möglichkeiten zur strukturierten Speicherung, Verarbeitung und Umformung der verschiedenartigsten Informationen weitgehend bereitgestellt werden konnten.

2.2 Prozeduren und Programmaufbau

Beim Entwurf des Prozedurmechanismus von LEKTOR mußte sichergestellt werden, daß der Aufruf und das dynamische Anbinden externer Prozeduren (z.B. Systembibliothek) ebenso einfach erfolgen kann wie im Falle interner Prozeduren. Auf diesen Aspekt wurde daher beim Sprachentwurf besonders geachtet, so daß Programme hoher Komplexität und Modularität konstruiert werden können, obwohl LEKTOR keine Blockstruktur aufweist.

Alle Prozeduren sind sowohl funktional (mit evtl. undefiniertem Resultat) als auch prozedural (automatische Resultatvernichtung) aufrufbar. Bei der Parameterübergabe gibt es nur die beiden Möglichkeiten:

      a) Wertübergabe

      b) Übergabe durch Adresse

         (systemgenerierter Pointer, S-Pointer)

Nur die Form des aktuellen Parameters entscheidet, welche Übergabeart vorliegt: Bei

    MAXIMUM(+A, B, C[X[K[5]]], 3.0E-2+D)

werden der 1. und 4. aktuelle Parameter mit Wert, der 2. und 3. mit S-Pointer ("Adresse") übergeben, wenn B Variable (und nicht etwa Label- oder Prozedurkonstante) ist. Bemerkenswert ist noch, daß bei keinem Prozeduraufruf die Parameterklammern fehlen dürfen: Wenn FAK der Name einer Prozedur ist, so stellt

               FAK

die entsprechende Prozedurkonstante und

FAK()

einen Aufruf von FAK ohne aktuellen Parameter dar.

Ein Programm besteht aus einem Hauptprogramm und einigen angebundenen ("internen") Prozeduren, die am Schluß des Hauptprogrammes zu spezifizieren sind. Variable in internen Prozeduren können sein:

a) formale Parameter
b) lokale Variable
c) OWN-Variable
d) globale Variable (aus dem Hauptprogramm)
e) der Name der Prozedur als Variable für das explizite Resultat (vgl. ALGOL 60).

Neben den an Hauptprogrammen direkt angebundenen internen Prozeduren gibt es noch externe Prozeduren (z.B. Standard-Prozeduren in der Systembibliothek). Bei ihnen entfallen .OWN und .GLOBAL, da eine derartige Bindung weder zur Übersetzungszeit noch zur Laufzeit mit erträglichem Aufwand hergestellt werden kann. Es gibt folgende Arten externer Prozeduren:

a) im Interpreter aus Effektivitätsgründen fest eingebaute Prozeduren, die den Operatorenvorrat erweitern, z.B. aSIN, aTAKE, aISNUM ("a-Prozeduren"),

b) Bibliotheksprozeduren, die ohne besondere Bindevorkehrungen in jedem Programm verwendet werden können ("$-Prozeduren"),

c) aneinandergebundene Prozeduren (z.B. eines bestimmten Problembereiches wie formales Differenzieren), wobei ein Aufruf die Gestalt

<Name1>..<Name2>(<Parameter>)

hat und <Name1> der Familienname, <Name2> der Elementname des sogenannten Pools ist (Prozeduren-Pool),

d) eine Verwaltungsprozedur, die wesentliche Aufgaben bei der Systemverwaltung übernimmt ("$$-Prozedur"). Sie gibt u.a. Auskunft über Systeminhalte und führt den Dialog mit dem Benutzer, wenn er kein Lehrprogramm aktiviert hat. Dieses "Betriebssystem", das z.B. Lehrer und Schüler über die Möglichkeiten des Systems informiert, ist im Vergleich zu üblichen Betriebssystemen außerordentlich gesprächig, wenn entsprechende Fragen gestellt werden.

2.3 Anweisungen

Die Syntax der Sprache wurde bewußt auf ein für den Übersetzerbau günstiges"Schachtelprinzip" aufgebaut. Die wichtigsten Anweisungen haben folgende Struktur:

```
<Operand> = <Ausdruck>;
<Operand> .REF <Operand>;
<Operand>(<Liste akt.Parameter>);
.IF<Ausdruck> .THEN <Anweisungsfolge> .ELSE <Anweisungsfolge> .EIF
.GOTO <Operand>;
.GOSUB <SUB-Name>;
.FOR(<Laufvariable>,<Anfangswert>,<Schritt>,<Endwert>)
          <Anweisungsfolge> .EFOR
.REP(<Laufvariable>,<Endwert>) <Anweisungsfolge> .EREP
.SUB <Name> <Anweisungsfolge> .ESUB
```

Dabei ist bei <Anweisungsfolge> jede nichtleere Folge von Anweisungen zugelassen.

Besondere Vorkehrungen für die Lehrprogrammentwicklung wurden durch einige erfahrungsgemäß sehr brauchbare Anweisungstypen getroffen:

```
<Labelkonstante>;
```

ist äquivalent zu .GOTO <Labelkonstante>; ,

```
<Stringkonstante>;
```

bewirkt die Ausgabe der betreffenden Zeichenkette auf das Terminal (Ausgabepuffer).

Die .PRINT-Anweisung ist in der Konzeption dem PRINT von BASIC ähnlich und bietet sehr viel Flexibilität beim Ausdrucken von Informationen der verschiedensten Art. Unter anderem mußte hier das logisch nicht ganz einfache Problem gelöst werden, bei graphischen Terminals (z.B. Speicherröhren-Geräten) die Ausgabe von programmiererspezifizierten Nicht-Standard-Zeichen in einfacher Notation zu realisieren (z.B. Summenzeichen Σ , Sonderalphabete usw.).

Ganz eng auf die Bedürfnisse des RGU sind die TEST- und COND-Anweisungen (COND = Conditional) abgestimmt. Eine rekursive Prozedur zur Berechnung von $n! = 1 \times 2 \times 3 \times \ldots \times n$ würde unter Verwendung der COND-Anweisung folgende Gestalt annehmen:

```
        .PROC       FAK(X)
        .NUM        FAK, X;
        .COND
        :X>O:       FAK = X*FAK(X-1); M1;
        :X .EQ O:   FAK = 1; M1;
        :X<O:           'Negatives Argument in FAK'; FAK=O;
        .ECOND
  M1
        .EPROC
```

Erste Programmiererfahrungen zeigen, daß die COND-Anweisung eine syste-
matischere Behandlung komplexer Entscheidungen suggeriert und so zu einem deutlich verbesserten Programmierstil führt.

2.4. Leitlinien beim Sprachentwurf

Wie aus dieser bruchstückhaften Beschreibung der Autorensprache LEKTOR
entnommen werden kann, handelt es sich um eine Sprache, die sich nur
wenig von üblichen höheren Programmiersprachen absetzt. Datenstrukturen
und Ablaufsteuerung wurden so weit entwickelt, daß mit dem stark ausge-
bauten Prozedurenkonzept ein für die Programmierung von Dialogen brauchbares Hilfsmittel entstand. Durch Aufbau einer reichhaltigen Bibliothek
von Systemprozeduren werden die wichtigsten, von Lehrprogrammierern
immer wieder benötigten Operationen komplexen Charakters allgemein zugänglich gemacht. Dadurch ist eine laufende Neuanpassung an aktuelle
Autorenwünsche möglich. Gleichzeitig können umfangreiche Algorithmen
(Formelmanipulation, graphische Systeme, Numerik-Labor usw.) in Gestalt
von Prozeduren-Pools realisiert werden. Insbesondere die Behandlung von
Prozeduren als Datentyp wurde in LEKTOR (ähnlich wie in GEDANKEN [1])
sehr weitgehend zur Vereinfachung der Implementierung herangezogen. So
arbeitet das LEKTOR-interne File-System (zur Ablage permanenter Daten
auf Platte) nach folgendem Prinzip: Nur Listen (beliebig strukturiert!)
können als File abgelegt werden. Soll z.B. die Liste L permanent geret-
tet werden, so wird in der Systemdatei eine externe Prozedur aufgebaut,
die bei Aufruf die Liste L als Resultat liefert. Ein Programm besitzt
demgemäß Zugriff zu einer abgelegten Liste, wenn es über die entsprechende Prozedurkonstante verfügt.

Die Vorteile der Methode liegen klar auf der Hand: Das Lesen von Files
wird vollständig vom Prozeduraufrufmechanismus erledigt, wodurch sehr
viel Klarheit und auch Effektivität erreicht wird. Eine Systemverwaltung
für Files ist überflüssig, da es für externe Prozeduren natürlich entsprechende Vorkehrungen gibt. Da Files vollständig im Rahmen der gegebenen Datenstrukturen notiert und bezeichnet werden, sind im Großen ana-

loge Dateistrukturen möglich wie im Kleinen bei der Verbundbildung im
Arbeitsspeicher ("baumartige Dateistrukturen").

3. DIE LEKTOR IMPLEMENTIERUNG

Das LEKTOR-System besteht aus

    a) der Systemdatei (LSD = LEKTOR System Datei)
    b) dem Übersetzer
    c) dem Interpreter (LEKTOR-Prozessor).

Übersetzer und Interpreter sind in gereinigtem Fortran IV dokumentiert
und können nach geringfügigen Anpassungen auf Rechner übertragen werden, die mindestens 32 Bit Wortlänge aufweisen. Die zwei in bezug auf
Portabilität kritischen Anschlüsse
    Lesen und Schreiben von LSD-Blöcken (Seiten) sowie
    E/A-Anschluß an Terminals
sind logisch so vereinfacht, daß ihre Realisierung im FORTRAN des Gast-
rechners erfahrungsgemäß keine Schwierigkeiten macht. Die Wahl von
FORTRAN als Implementierungssprache erfolgte im wesentlichen wegen der
Maschinennähe und wegen der Verfügbarkeit auf nahezu allen Rechnern.
FORTRAN dient also als Ersatz für eine nicht vorhandene weit verbreite-
te niedere Programmiersprache.

Im Normalfall nimmt der Übersetzer LEKTOR-Programme im Stapelbetrieb
entgegen, übersetzt sie in den internen Zwischencode (im wesentlichen
Postfixcode für die abstrakte LEKTOR-Stackmaschine im Interpreter) und
trägt diesen Code in LSD ein. Der vom Übersetzer aus Effektivitätsgründen völlig getrennte Interpreter schließlich kann von einem Terminal
aus aufgerufen werden, aktiviert dann automatisch das Verwaltungspro-
gramm ($$-Prozedur) und eröffnet das Gespräch mit dem Dialogpartner.
Durch das $$-Programm, eine externe Prozedur mit Sonderstatus, konnte
der Interpreter weitgehend von Verwaltungsballast befreit werden. Wäh-
rend der Übersetzer aus einem Programm von ca. 3500 Zeilen FORTRAN besteht, hat der Prozessor nur ca. 2500 Zeilen.

Die Systemdatei hat eine sehr einfache Struktur: Bei maximalem Ausbau
besteht sie aus 4000 Blöcken zu je 200 Maschinenworten und wird wie ein
virtueller Speicherraum behandelt, d.h. der Interpreter greift blockweise zu und verwaltet im Kernspeicher einen bestimmten Vorrat an Code-
Blöcken. Bei Programmen mit geringem Speicherbedarf für Listen kann mit
ca. 1000 Worten Kernspeicherbedarf (ohne Interpretercode) gearbeitet
werden. Dieser Fall ist typisch für sogenannte tutoriale textorientierte
Lehrprogramme, bei denen im wesentlichen nur Text auf dem Bildschirm
ausgegeben wird und fällige Schülerantworten nach Standard-Verfahren

(z.B. Test-Anweisung) ausgewertet werden. Nennenswerte Datenbewegungen treten nicht auf bzw. sind mit geringem Speicherraum zu bewältigen. Im Falle simulativer Programme muß gelegentlich mit wesentlich mehr Kernspeicherbedarf gerechnet werden. Daher wurde der Interpreter so konstruiert, daß Arbeitsspeichergrößen bis zu 64 k Worten bewältigt werden können, wodurch dann Programme höchster Komplexität möglich werden.

Eine Grundkonzeption des LEKTOR-Systems besteht darin, daß jeder "Schüler" ein eigenes Exemplar des Interpreters betreibt. Die Einbettung in ein existierendes Teilnehmer-Rechensystem wird daher besonders ökonomisch, wenn das Betriebssystem jeweils maximal eine Kopie des Interpretercodes im Kernspeicher führt und jede Mehrfacheinlagerung automatisch verhindert.

Im Anhang wird ein kleines LEKTOR-Programm wiedergegeben, das die Verwendung von Listen, Printanweisungen und Splits (Einblendungen von Variablen und Ausdrücken in Ausgabetext), COND-Anweisungen, Label- und Stringanweisungen bei einem kleinen Testdialog demonstriert.

<u>Literaturangaben</u>

[1] Reynolds, J.C.: GEDANKEN - A Simple Typeless Language Based on the Principle of Completeness and the Reference Concept. Com. ACM 13 (1970) S. 308 - 319.

[2] Schmitt, A.: Zum Entwurf eines flexiblen und portablen Software-Systems für Rechnergestützten Unterricht. Interner Bericht Nr. 7 (1972) Fakultät für Informatik, Karlsruhe.

[3] Stobbe, P.: LIDIA Autorensprache für das Siemens-Lehrsystem 4004. Data Report 5 (1970) H.4, S. 14 - 19.

[4] Wirth, N., Weber, H.: EULER: A Generalization of ALGOL, and its Formal Definition, Part I, Part II. Com. ACM 9(1966) S. 11 - 23, S. 89 - 99.

ANHANG

```
        .PROGRAM LEKTORDEMONSTRATION
        ///Deklarationen:/// .NUM I,N,FEHLER; .STRING Y; .LIST X;
        ///Die Liste X erhält die entsprechenden Daten zugewiesen:///
        X = [['BERLIN', 'BREMEN', 'HAMBURG', 'SAARLAND',
             'SCHLESWIG-HOLSTEIN', 'NIEDERSACHSEN', 'NORDRHEIN-WESTFALEN',
             'HESSEN', 'RHEINLAND-PFALZ', 'BAYERN', 'BADEN-WÜRTTEMBERG']
            ,['BERLIN', 'BREMEN', 'HAMBURG', 'SAARBRÜCKEN','KIEL',
             'HANNOVER', 'DÜSSELDORF', 'WIESBADEN', 'MAINZ',
             'MÜNCHEN', 'STUTTGART']];
        .PRINT Ein kleiner Test soll zeigen, ob Du die Hauptstädte der
        deutschen Bundesländer kennst.
        .EPRINT  FEHLER=O;
        .FOR(I,1,1,11)  .PRINT Wie heißt die Hauptstadt von '(X[1,I])'?
        Wenn Du keine Lust mehr hast, schreibe einfach ENDE.
        .EPRINT  @INTO(Y);
        .COND(Y, @EQUAL)  N=O;
MAR     :?'ENDE':        ENDE;
        :?X[2,I] .AND  N .EQ O: 'Sehr gut!'; MNEU;
        :?X[2,I] .AND  N .EQ 1: 'Jetzt stimmts'; MNEU;
        :N .EQ O: 'Nicht richtig. Versuche es nochmal';
             'ganz in GROSSBUCHSTABEN'; N=N+1; @INTO(Y);MAR;
        : 1 : ///Entspricht 'IF' true 'THEN'...///
        .PRINT Leider wieder falsch.
        Die Hauptstadt von '(X[1,I])' ist '(X[2,I])'
        .EPRINT  FEHLER=FEHLER+1;
        .ECOND
MNEU .EFOR
ENDE .PRINT Du hast 'nur' '(FEHLER)' Fehler gemacht und
             '(I-1)' Fragen bearbeitet.
        .EPRINT
        ///keine internen Prozeduren in diesem Programm.///
        .EPROGRAM
```

ZUR MODELLIERUNG VON PROZESSYSTEMEN

A. JAMMEL

Vorstellungen, die mit dem Wort "Prozeß" verbunden werden, erweisen sich in zunehmendem Maße als geeignet und angemessen für Entwurf und Verständnis komplexer Rechensysteme. Bei der Gliederung dieser Systeme in Prozesse treten zwei Klassen von Problemen in den Vordergrund, die man mit den Worten "Kooperation" und "Koexistenz" von Prozessen charakterisieren kann. Eigentümlicherweise lassen sich die Phänomene der einen Klasse stets in solche der anderen transformieren bzw. in solchen der anderen ausdrücken. Die programmative (softwaremäßige) Durchführung einer solchen Transformation heißt Implementierung.

Als Beispiel für diese Bemerkungen betrachte man ein in Prozesse gegliedertes Rechensystem, in dem es Benutzerprozesse gibt und darüberhinaus einen Prozeß, der den Dateienkatalog verwaltet, sowie einen Prozeß, der die Transpoerte zwischen Dateispeicher (meistens auf Platten und Magnetbändern realisiert) und Hauptspeicher durchführt. Beim Betreiben von Dateien beauftragen die Benutzerprozesse den Transporteurprozeß, d.h. es liegt eine Kooperation zwischen den Benutzerprozessen und dem Transporteurprozeß vor. Die Anwesenheit des Transporteurprozesses ist Voraussetzung für den Betrieb von Dateien.

Bevor ein Benutzerprozeß eine Datei in Betrieb nehmen kann, muß er sie sich vom Katalogverwalter zuteilen lassen. Diese Zuteilung stellt sich als Kooperation zwischen den Benutzerprozessen und dem Katalogverwalter dar. Diese Kooperation dient jedoch dem Zweck, das Koexistenzproblem zwischen mehreren Benutzerprozessen zu lösen, das in der Koordination des Zugriffs auf Dateien besteht.

Eine gegensinnige Umdeutung erhält man bei Betrachtung der Technik der Prozeßkommunikation. Den Prozessen stehe ein Mechanismus zum Nachrichtenaustausch zur Verfügung. Dieser Mechanismus sei mit Hilfe eines von allen Prozessen gemeinsam benutzten Speicherbereichs realisiert, in dem die Nachrichten hinterlegt werden. Dabei entsteht das Koexistenzproblem der Zugriffskoordination auf diesen Speicherbereich. Läßt man die Bedeutung dieses Speicherbereichs als Übergabespeicher für Nachrichten außer Betracht, so sind in diesem Prozeßsystem lediglich Koexistenzfragen zu lösen.

Für Kooperation ist es charakteristisch, daß sich die Prozesse bei ihrer Arbeit unterstützen, bei Koexistenzfragen wird dagegen das Problem der gegenseitigen Behinderung behandelt.

Zur Darstellung der unterschiedlichen Interpretationen der Vorgänge
in einem Rechensystem kann man wie folgt vorgehen. Man definiert für
jede Interpretation einen für sie charakteristischen Satz von Elementaroperationen und beschreibt die Tätigkeit der Prozesse in diesen
Elementaroperationen. Zur Beschreibung von Kooperationsphänomenen bedient man sich beispielsweise der Elementaroperationen, die Nachrichtenaustausch bewirken - etwa "Sende Nachricht" und "Erwarte Nachricht".
Zur Beschreibung von Koexistenzphänomenen sind die P-Operation und
V-Operation für Mutexsemaphore geeignet. Wesentlich ist, daß die Pro-
zeßtätigkeiten im Sinne der vorliegenden Interpretation jeweils durch
geeignet zu wählende Elementaroperationen unmittelbar ausgedrückt werden. Die Definition eines Satzes von Elementaroperationen wird als Angabe einer Hardware- oder Softwareschnittstelle gedeutet. Man model-
liert dabei eine abstrakte Maschine (Firmware, Pseudohardware), indem man deren Befehlsvorrat festlegt. Der Begriff "Abstraktionsebene"
(level of abstraction) wird präzisiert durch Abstützung auf abstrakte
Maschinen, indem die Angabe einer Abstraktionsebene als Angabe einer
abstrakten Maschine definiert wird. Verschiedene Interpretationen derselben Vorgänge in Rechensystemen werden verglichen, indem man für
die zugeordneten abstrakten Maschinen erklärt, wie die Elementaroperationen der einen mit den Elementaroperationen der anderen implementiert werden.

Um die Vorgänge in einem Rechensystem in Prozesse zu gliedern, können
sich bei verschiedenen Interpretationen unterschiedliche Möglichkeiten anbieten. Etwa ist bei Betrachtung einer realen Multiprozessor-
Hardware die Zusammenfassung der auf einem Prozessor ablaufenden Befehle zu einem Prozeß denkbar. Faßt man dagegen den Ablauf eines Be-
nutzerprogramms als Prozeß auf, so wird dieser auf den prozessororien-
tierten Prozeßbegriff mit Hilfe des Prozessorzuweisungsmoduls(Schedu-
ler) abgebildet.
Geschieht die definierende Beschreibung der Prozesse abhängig von der
jeweiligen Interpretation, so kann man vorteilhafterweise die Bestim-
mungsstücke eines Prozesses mittels der der Interpretation zugrunde
liegenden abstrakten Maschine angeben. Häufig gestattet die Implementierung einer abstrakten Maschine durch eine andere die prozeßweise
Identifizierung der auf beiden Maschinen zu definierenden Prozeßsysteme.

Im folgenden soll eine Möglichkeit der formalen Beschreibung von abstrakten Maschinen und Prozessen umrissen werden.

Für die Angabe einer abstrakten Maschine verlangt man die Angabe eines Adressenvorrats und eines Wertevorrats. Als Zustände der abstrakten Maschine werden Abbildungen von dem Adressenvorrat in den Wertevorrat eingeführt. Diese Abbildungen werden so bestimmt, daß sie Auskunft geben, welche Adressen im betrachteten Zustand verfügbar sind und welche Werte ihnen zugeordnet sind. Darüberhinaus wird eine Relation in der Menge dieser Abbildungen verlangt, die die möglichen unmittelbaren Zustandsübergänge angibt. Diese Relation beschreibt die Elementaroperationen der abstrakten Maschine.

Die Hauptbestimmungsstücke eines Prozesses in (auf) einer abstrakten Maschine sind seine Zustände und der Algorithmus, nach dem diese fortgeschaltet werden. Ein Prozeßzustand ist eine Äquivalenzklasse von Zuständen der abstrakten Maschine. Die Bildung dieser Klassen erfolgt bezüglich einer für den jeweiligen Prozeßzustand charakteristischen Menge von Adressen, dem Adreßraum des Prozesses in diesem Zustand, und einer für den Prozeßzustand ebenfalls charakteristischen Wertezuordnung für diese Adressen. Für jeden Prozeßzustand und seinen Folgezustand gemäß dem Algorithmus des Prozesses wird verlangt, daß es repräsentierende Zustände der abstrakten Maschine gibt, die durch eine Elementaroperation verknüpft sind. Prozeßzustände, für die durch den Algorithmus kein Folgezustand definiert ist, sind Wartezustände oder Endzustände. Der Umstand, daß Prozeßzustände verschiedener Prozesse gemeinsame Repräsentanten haben können, ermöglicht die Definition des gleichzeitigen Vorhandenseins und gemeinsamen Ablaufs von Prozessen.

Die Abhängigkeiten von gemeinsam ablaufenden Prozessen untereinander, d.h. die Wartebeziehungen zwischen ihnen werden als zeitlich veränderliche Relation dargestellt. Diese Relation ist ein eigenständiges Strukturelement eines Prozeßsystems, das nicht in kanonischer Weise aus dem Auftreten von Wartezuständen der Prozesse hergeleitet werden kann. Der Zusammenhnag zwischen dieser Warterelation und Wartezuständen wird durch die Forderung hergestellt, daß sich ein Prozeß nur dann in einem Wartezustand befindet, wenn er zu wenigstens einem anderen Prozeß in Warterelation steht.

Eine Wartebeziehung zwischen Prozessen könnte etwa etabliert werden, wenn ein Prozeß einem anderen einen Auftrag erteilt. Mit der Erledigung des Auftrages wird die Wartebeziehung wieder aufgehoben. Die Auftragserteilung bedeutet nicht notwendigerweise, daß der Auftraggeber dabei auch sofort in einen Wartezustand eintritt, obwohl er mit der Auftragserteilung in gewissem Sinne auf die Erledigung des Auftrags "wartet". Schließlich kann der Fall eintreten, daß der Auftrag erledigt ist, bevor der Auftraggeber mit sonstigen Arbeiten zu Ende gekommen ist. D.h. die Wartebeziehung hat überhaupt keinen Wartezustand hervorgerufen. Der Verklemmungsfall liegt vor, wenn sich alle Prozesse eines Prozeßsystems in einem Wartezustand befinden. Die Gefahr solcher Verklemmungen ist dann nicht vorhanden, wenn die Warterelation zu jedem Zeitpunkt eine Halbordnung ist. Die obige Erörterung der Warterelation zeigt, daß diese Halbordnungsbedingung lediglich hinreichend für Verklemmungsfreiheit ist.

Betrachtet man mehrere Interpretationen der Vorgänge in einem Rechensystem, hat also mehrere Modelle von abstrakten Maschinen mit in ihnen vorhandenen Prozeßsystemen, so müssen die Wartehalbordnungen identifizierbarer Prozeßsysteme miteinander verträglich sein, um eine hinreichende Bedingung für die Verklemmungsfreiheit des Gesamtsystems zu erhalten.

Wie bereits ausgeführt verändern sich beim Wechsel der Interpretation auch die Kommunikationsphänomene. Dies kann dazu führen, daß bezüglich einer Interpretation eine Verklemmung vorhanden ist und bezüglich einer anderen nicht. Betrachten wir dazu ein Prozeßsystem mit einem Nachrichtenaustauschmechanismus. Die Prozesse mögen durch eine "Erwarte Nachricht" -Operation in einen Wartezustand eintreten, falls die gewünschte Nachricht nicht vorhanden ist. Außerdem werde der Nachrichtenaustausch mittels eines Übergabespeichers implementiert und dabei die "Erwarte Nachricht"-Operation durch eine Warteschleife realisiert. Sind alle Prozesse in die Ausführung einer "Erwarte Nachricht"-Operation eingetreten, so liegt im Sinne der Elementaroperationen des Nachrichtenaustausches eine Verklemmung vor, im Sinne der Implementierung dieses Mechanismus jedoch nicht. Diese Überlegung zeigt zusammen mit der Unmöglichkeit, "alle" Interpretationen der Vorgänge in einem Rechensystem aufzuzählen, eine Grenze für die vollständige Erfassung aller Verklemmungssituationen eines Rechensystems auf.

Literatur

[1] Dijkstra, E.W.   "The structure of the THE-multiprogramming system"
Comm. ACM 11, 5(1968), 341 - 346

[2] Brinch Hansen, P. "The nucleus of a multiprogramming system"
Comm. ACM 13, 4(197o), 238 - 241, 25o

[3] Horning, J.J. und "Process Structuring"
Randell, B.   Computing Surveys ACM 5,1(1973), 5 - 3o

[4] Jammel, A.   "Formale Behandlung des Verklemmungsproblems beim Mehrprogrammbetrieb"
Dissertation, München 1972

[5] Lampson, B.W.   "A scheduling philosophy for multiprocessing systems"
Comm. ACM 11, 5(1968), 347 - 36o

[6] Zurcher, F.W. und "Iterative multi-level modelling - a methodology
Randell, B.   for computer system design"
Proceedings of the IFIP Congress 68, vol 2,
867 - 871
NHPC, Amsterdam 1969

Dynamische Betriebsmittelverwaltung und Verklemmungsvermeidung in geschichteten Prozeßsystemen

H. Stiegler

1. Einleitung

1.1 Problemstellung

Verklemmungen (deadlocks) sind weit häufiger Thema theoretischer Untersuchungen, als sie in der Natur zu beobachten sind. Es handelt sich jedoch beim Verklemmungsproblem nicht um ein akademisches oder nur logisches Problem. Der Verklemmungsfall ist ein Fehlerfall, der nach Möglichkeit vermieden oder aber so rechtzeitig erkannt werden sollte, daß eine sinnvolle Fehlerbehandlung möglich ist. Strategien zur Vermeidung sind also Teil der Fehlererkennung des Systems. Die hierfür nötigen Vorkehrungen dürfen den Normalbetrieb nicht übermäßig belasten. Die Literatur über Verklemmungsvermeidung ist in zweierlei Hinsicht unvollständig:

- Die vorgeschlagenen Strategien werden zu aufwendig, sobald die dynamisch belegbaren Betriebsmittel zu zahlreich werden, da der Aufwand nichtlinear ansteigt.

- Einem in Schichten aufgebauten Betriebssystem entsprechen die Strategien nicht, da diese jeweils eine zentrale Verwaltung aller Betriebsmittel voraussetzen.

Im folgenden soll kein neuer Algorithmus zur Verklemmungsvermeidung dargestellt werden, sondern ein erweiterter Anwendungsrahmen für die bestehenden.

1.2 Erläuterung zum Modell

Unter Betriebsmitteln verstehen wir Objekte, die belegt und freigegeben werden können. Betriebsmittelverwaltung ist dann die Verwaltung der Belegungswünsche.
Dynamische Betriebsmittelverwaltung soll heißen, daß die Betriebsmittelbelegungen zur Laufzeit der anfordernden Prozesse zugeteilt werden, ohne daß eine Reservierung nach dem Maximalbedarf der Prozesse stattfindet.
Über das Prozeßsystem wird vorausgesetzt, daß es aus asynchron ablaufenden Prozessen besteht, die sich mit Hilfe eines Kommunikationssystems

Aufträge erteilen und deren Erledigung quittieren können.

Verklemmungsvermeidung als Teil der Fehlererkennung des Systems bedeutet dann, daß die Fehlermeldung "Verklemmungssituation" die verursachenden Prozesse zu von ihnen explizit zur Kenntnis genommenen Zeitpunkten erreicht. Das ist zum Beispiel der Fall, wenn sie die Quittung auf einen Betriebsmittelbelegungswunsch ist, durch den die Verklemmungssituation eintreten würde.

2. Die einfache Verklemmungssituation

2.1 Belegung von Betriebsmitteln

Die Belegung von Betriebsmitteln wird mit Hilfe eines Verwalterprozesses realisiert. Ein Prozeß P1 teilt den Wunsch, das Betriebsmittel B1 zu belegen, dem Verwalterprozeß V1 mit. Dieser ist allein berechtigt, die Belegung zuzuteilen oder - wenn eine ausschließende Belegung von B1 schon besteht - den Wunsch vorzumerken und zuzuteilen, sobald kein Hinderungsgrund mehr besteht.

Möglicherweise kann V1 den Belegungswunsch sofort nach Kenntnisnahme erfüllen. Aber auch eine Verzögerung der Belegungszuteilung durch V1 kann P1 nicht wahrnehmen, da P1 und V1 asynchron ablaufen. Von P1 aus gesehen, ist die Betriebsmittelbelegung in diesem Sinn ein ähnlicher Vorgang wie die P-Operation auf ein Semaphor.

2.2 Entstehen und Semantik einer Verklemmung

Verklemmungen können auf Grund von nachgeforderten Betriebsmittelbelegungen auftreten.
Der Prozeß P1 belegt das Betriebsmittel B1 und wünscht zusätzlich das Betriebsmittel B2. B2 ist von einem Prozeß P2 belegt, der seinerseits zusätzlich B1 belegen will. Sind die bestehenden Belegungen mit den Belegungswünschen unverträglich, so entsteht ein Zirkel von einander bedingenden unerfüllbaren Nachforderungen. Diese Situation kann einen Fehler in der Kooperation der beteiligten Prozesse bedeuten oder Ausdruck eines Koexistenzproblems sein, das zwischen ihnen besteht.
An einem solchen Zirkel, den wir als Verklemmung interpretieren, können natürlich beliebig viele Prozesse und Betriebsmittel beteiligt sein.

2.3 Erkennen einer Verklemmung

Ein erster Ansatz zur Vermeidung von Verklemmungen beruht darauf, den Graphen der bestehenden Auftragsbeziehungen zyklenfrei zu halten. Man

garantiert das durch eine strenge Schichtenstruktur des Systems. Das
skizzierte Beispiel zeigt, daß auf diesem Abstraktionsniveau nicht mehr
genügend Information vorhanden ist. Die Auftragssituation hat folgende
Gestalt:

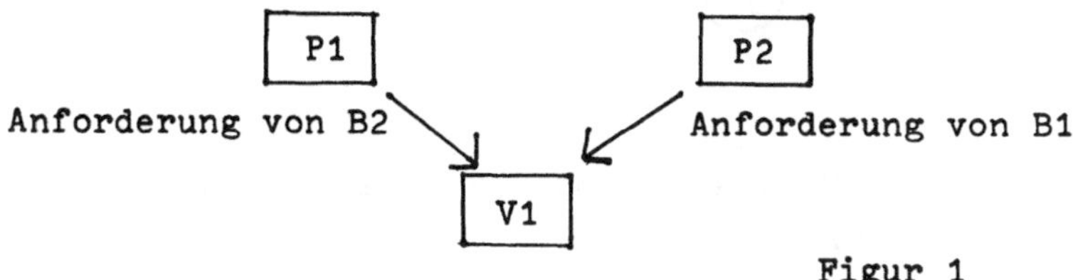

Figur 1

Es besteht kein Zyklus. Was man benötigt, um die Situation als Verklemmung interpretieren zu können, ist genau die Information, die V1 verwaltet:

"Ein P1-Belegungswunsch wartet auf die Freigabe von B2 durch P2"

"Ein P2-Belegungswunsch wartet auf die Freigabe von B1 durch P1"

Weder P1 noch P2 lassen erkennen, daß sie ihre Belegungen zurückgeben,
bevor ihre Wünsche erfüllt werden.

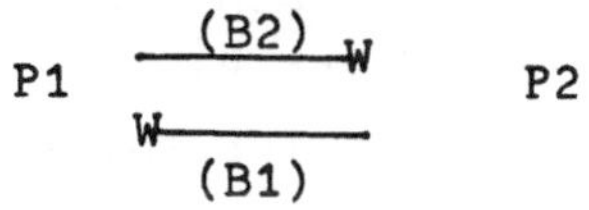

$$P1 \quad \xrightarrow{\quad (B2) \quad} W \qquad P2$$
$$W \xleftarrow{\quad (B1) \quad}$$

Figur 2

Ob sich ein Betriebsmittelwunsch mit bestehenden Belegungen und anderen Belegungswünschen verklemmt, kann also nur dort geprüft werden, wo
die Betriebsmittelwünsche in Warteschlangen eingereiht werden. Überdies
kann die Feststellung, ob in einer gewissen Situation eine Verklemmung
vorliegt, von der Warteschlangenstrategie abhängen.

2.4 Fehlermeldung

Sobald man feststellt, daß durch das Einreihen eines Betriebsmittel-
wunsches in eine Warteschlange eine Verklemmungssituation entsteht,
wird er abgelehnt. Dem Absender wird mit der Ablehnung mitgeteilt,wel-
che seiner Betriebsmittelbelegungen die Ablehnung bedingt haben.

In unserem Beispiel sei nun P1 ein Prozeß, der zwei logisch unabhängige Tätigkeiten parallel ausführt. Wir denken uns diese Tätigkeiten als
Teilprozesse P11 und P12 organisiert. Die von V1 als Verklemmung gemel-
dete Situation ist keine Verklemmung im herkömmlichen Sinn, wenn P11
B1 belegt, P12 B2 zu belegen wünscht.

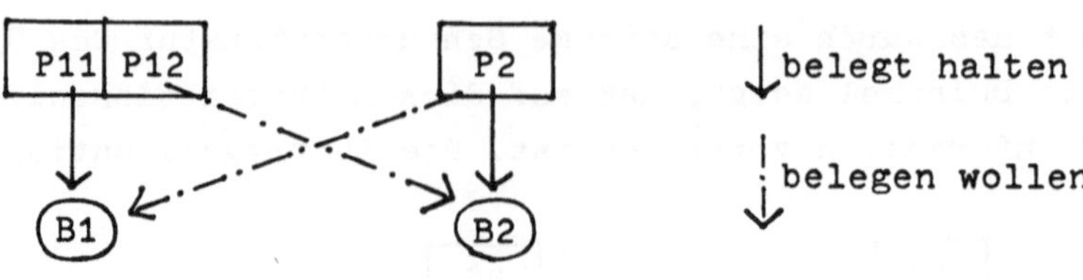

Figur 3

Sobald P11 B1 freigibt, kann P2 B1 belegen und P12 gefahrlos auf die
Freigabe von B2 seitens P2 warten.

V1 nimmt seinen Auftraggeber P1 als Einheit wahr, deren Teile er nicht
unterscheiden kann. Das Problem ist offensichtlich nur dadurch zu lösen, daß P1 selbst erkennt, welche Nachforderungen zu welchen bestehenden Belegungen gekoppelt sind. Die Teilprozesse P11 und P12 müssen
sich intern so synchronisieren, daß sie nach außen als ein Prozeß
-nämlich P1- in Erscheinung treten.

In der Situation von Figur 3 kann P12 - auf Grund der Fehlermeldung von
V1 und der globalen Listen von P1 - auf die Freigabe von B1 durch P11
warten, bis er B2 erneut zu belegen versucht. Aus einem externen Warten wird ein internes der Teiprozesse von P1. Die Fehlermeldung von V1
kann also sinnvoll von P1 interpretiert werden. Wesentlich ist, daß er
sie als Quittung auf die betreffende Betriebsmittelanforderung erhält.

Empfängt V1 die Belegungswünsche in anderer Reihenfolge, so wird die
Verklemmungssituation P2 gemeldet. P2 muß unabhängig von der inneren
Struktur seines Partners P1, die er nicht kennt, reagieren. Er muß vor-
zeitig B2 freigeben und von neuem B1 und B2 anfordern.

Daß dieses Vorgehen richtig ist, zeigt sich, wenn B2 nicht von P12 sondern von P11 nachgefordert wird.

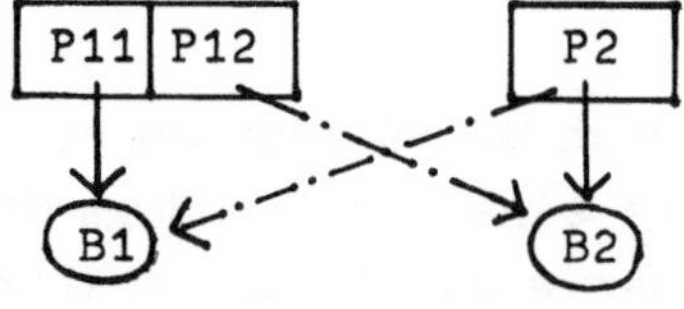

Figur 4

Dann ist im herkömmlichen Sinn noch keine Verklemmung eingetreten, solange P12 nicht erlischt oder seinerseits in eine Verklemmung gerät.
Aber im Sinne von 2.2 haben sich P11 und P2 verklemmt. Die Situation
ist von P12 nicht mehr beeinflußbar. V1 meldet die Fehlersituation also rechtzeitig.

2.5 Warten

Man kann nun das Verhalten von V1 verstehen als Interpretationsversuch
der Welt seiner Auftraggeber an Hand der Warteschlangen, die er verwaltet. Er nimmt an, daß ein Auftraggeber, dessen Betriebsmittelwunsch er verzögert, von diesem Zeitpunkt an auf das Betriebsmittel
wartet, unabhängig von sonstigen Tätigkeiten des Auftraggebers und deren Logik.

Dieser "Warte"-Begriff, der vom Begriff des Fortschreitens eines Prozesses unabhängig ist, ist offensichtlich an V1 und dessen Strategien,
und damit an die Betriebsmittel gebunden, die V1 verwaltet (das Warten
auf einen Rechnerkern ist dann eine spezielle Form des Wartens in diesem Sinn).

Nichtsdestoweniger kann man sich bzgl. dieses Wartens im herkömmlichen
Sinn mit Verklemmungsvermeidung beschäftigen und sich der bekannten
Strategien bedienen. Dabei hat man aber den Vorteil, daß man

- keine Annahme über die innere Struktur von Prozessen macht, ja sogar
  zulassen kann, daß ein Prozeß mehrere Rechnerkerne gleichzeitig benutzt.

- Verklemmungsvermeidung auf einem semantischen Niveau führen kann,das
  so nah wie möglich an der Semantik der Fehlerursachen liegt.

3. Die komplexe Verklemmungssituation

3.1 Betriebsmittelverwaltung durch mehrere asynchrone Prozesse

Wir haben bisher Betriebsmittelwünsche betrachtet, die sich an einen
einzigen Prozeß richten. Im allgemeinen werden aber in einem Betriebssystem von mehreren Prozessen Betriebsmittel verwaltet. Diese Prozesse
können auch untereinander in Auftragsbeziehungen stehen, derart daß
ein Prozeß ein Betriebsmittel bei einem anderen belegt, um ihm angetra-
gene Belegungswünsche zu realisieren.

Bei einer Beziehung wie in Figur 5 darf man nicht wie vorhin vorgehen.

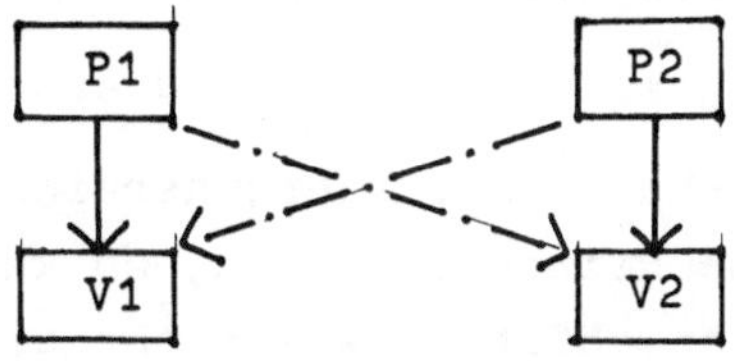

Figur 5

Um Verklemmungen von Belegungswünschen nach Betriebsmitteln, die in V1
und solchen, die in V2 verwaltet werden, zu erkennen, benötigt man

einen Prozeß, der die Warteschlangen in V1 und V2 gleichzeitig kontrolliert.

In einem geschichteten System, das aus mehreren übereinanderliegenden
Pseudohardwareschichten besteht,benötigt man dann in jeder Schicht, in
der ein asynchroner Prozeß ein weiteres Betriebsmittel verwaltet,
einen solchen Überwachungsprozeß. Dieser müßte alle Betriebsmittelwünsche, die sich an tieferliegende Prozesse richten, kontrollieren.
Das aber widerspricht gerade dem Modularisierungsgesichtspunkt,
dessentwegen man verschiedene Betriebsmittel von mehreren Prozessen
verwalten lassen will.

3.2 Mehrstufige Verklemmungsvermeidung

Betriebsmittel, die von einem Prozeß verwaltet werden, fassen wir zu
einer Qualität zusammen. Eine Betriebsmittelbelegung interpretieren
wir als zweistufige Belegung, nämlich als Belegung

- einer Qualität

und als Belegung

- eines Betriebsmittels innerhalb einer Qualität.

Die Belegung eines Betriebsmittels innerhalb einer Qualität wird
gemäß 2. behandelt. Die dort befolgte Strategie kann auf die Beson-
derheit der Qualität abgestimmt werden. Insbesondere werden innerhalb
einer Qualität nur wenige Betriebsmittel zur Konkurrenz stehen und
damit der Prüfaufwand klein bleiben.

Bei der Belegung von Qualitäten verhält man sich, als ob es sich um
einzelne Betriebsmittel handelt. Man verbindet die drei Prinzipien
der Verklemmungsvermeidung

- Verbot des Wartens

- vorzeitiger Entzug oder vorzeitige Rückgabe von Betriebsmitteln
  (preemption)

- ausgezeichnete Anforderungsreihenfolge

um in der Anwendung das allgemeine Spektrum zu erhalten:

Man definiert eine ausgezeichnete Anforderungsreihenfolge von Qualitäten. Hält ein Prozeß diese Reihenfolge ein, so kann er in keine
Verklemmungssituation geraten. Hält er sie nicht ein, wird der Wunsch
nach einer Betriebsmittelbelegung, die nicht unmittelbar erfüllt

werden kann, zurückgewiesen.

Auf Grund der dabei mitgelieferten Spezifikation erfährt der Prozeß,
welche Betriebsmittel in welcher Qualität er freigeben sollte, um
mit größerer Erfolgsaussicht den Betriebsmittelwunsch zu wiederholen.

4. Verklemmungen in geschichteten Systemen

4.1 Verträglichkeit mit Schichtenstrukturen

Die geschilderte zweite Stufe der Verklemmungsvermeidung erfordert
Kommunikation zwischen den beteiligten Prozessen, die Betriebsmittel
verwalten. Sie muß mit der Prozeßschichtung verträglich sein.
Es sind die beiden Fälle zu diskutieren:

Eine in einer höheren Schicht realisierte Qualität ist einer in einer
tieferen Schicht realisierten Qualität

- (a) übergeordnet
     ("wer unten warten will, darf oben nichts belegt haben")

- (b) untergeordnet
      ("wer oben warten will, darf unten nichts belegt haben")

Bei (a) wird jeder Betriebsmittelwunsch von der überliegenden Schicht
kontrolliert und mit dem Vermerk versehen, ob er vorgemerkt werden
darf oder nicht. Bei (b) wird bevor ein nicht sofort erfüllbarer
Betriebsmittelwunsch vorgemerkt wird, in der tieferen Schicht
nachgefragt, ob der zugehörige Prozeß dort etwas belegt, und eventuell
dann abgelehnt.

Beide Vorgänge sind bzgl. einer Schichtenstruktur erlaubt.
Schließlich besteht noch das nachgeordnete Problem Überholungen von
Kontrollfragen und Belegungswünschen zu vermeiden, was technisch vom
Kommunikationsmechanismus gelöst werden kann.

4.2 Zwei Beispiele

Daß es für die Fälle (a) und (b) von Rangordnungen zwischen Qualitäten
in einem geschichteten System sinnvolle Anwendungen gibt, zeigen die
nachfolgenden Beispiele.

Beispiele für (a) sind im Zugriff nachgeordnete Qualitäten.
Betrachten wir ein file-System, bei dem ein Satz erst dann bearbeitet
werden kann, wenn der ihn enthaltende file explizit an den Bearbeiter
gebunden worden ist. Gibt es nun noch die Möglichkeit, sich auf Sätzen

zu synchronisieren, indem man sie sperrt, so ist es sinnvoll, zu vereinbaren:

Wer einen Satz gesperrt hält, darf auf keine Dateibindung warten,
aber wer eine Datei gebunden hat, darf einen Satz sperren und
eventuell darauf warten.

Nimmt man an, daß Satzzugriffe oberhalb von Dateibindungen verwaltet
werden, so entspricht dies "(a)".

Beispiele für (b) liefern Qualitäten, die mit Hilfe anderer Qualitäten
realisiert sind.

Seien etwa Dateien auf Datenträgern realisiert, aber Dateien und
Datenträger unabhängig voneinander belegbar.

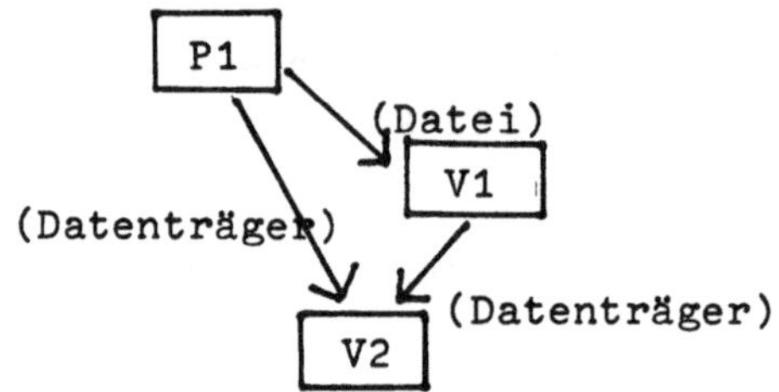

Figur 6

Belegungswünsche von V1 sollen dabei von V2 so interpretiert werden,
daß sie konkurrierende Belegungswünsche von P1 ausschließen.

Stellt nun P1 einen Belegungswunsch bzgl. des selben Datenträgers D
direkt bei V2 und indirekt über V1, so darf nur der indirekte bestehen
bleiben. Hält sich P1 nicht an die Anforderungsreihenfolge gemäß (b),
so wird V1 die Dateibelegung zurückweisen, mit der Bemerkung, daß die
direkte Belegung von D erst freigegeben werden muß. Andernfalls belegt
P1 zuerst D indirekt, so daß dann die direkte Belegung wegen der
Ausschließungsregel zurückgewiesen wird.

Wäre man nach (a) verfahren, hätte V2 dem Prozeß P1 die direkte Bele -
gung zwangsweise entziehen müssen, wobei inkonsistente Zustände der
Daten auftreten könnten.

Literatur

1   Coffman Jr.,E.G.,Elphick,M.J.,Shoshani,A.,
                "System Deadlocks"
                ACM Computing Surveys, vol.3,(June 1971),
                67-78

2   Coffman Jr.,E.G.,"Deadlocks in Computer Systems"
                Infotech State of the Art Report 14, (1972)
                353-374

3   Fontao,R.O.,   "A Concurrent Algorithm for Avoiding Deadlocks
                in Multiprocess Multiple Resource Systems"
                SIGOPS, vol.6, No. 1,2 (June 1971)
                72-79

4   Habermann,A.N.,   "Prevention of System Deadlocks"
                Comm. ACM 12, 7(1969)
                373-377

5   Holt, R.C.,   "Some Deadlock Properties of Computer Systems"
                SIGOPS, vol.6, No. 1,2 (June 1971)
                64-71

VARIABLE SEQUENTIALISIERUNGSSTRUKTUREN UND DEREN HARDWAREUNTERSTUETZTE REALISIERUNG

M. Fleck, P. Oliva

(Kurzfassung)[+]

Nehmen mehrere parallele Prozesse Manipulationen an ihren gemeinsamen Daten vor, so sind gewisse Zugriffe auf diese - oder ganze Gruppen derselben - zu sequentialisieren. Wir wollen folgende Anforderungen bezüglich der Sequentialisierung stellen: Erstens, sollte es ausgeschlossen sein, notwendige oder von Prozessen gewünschte Sequentialisierungen zu umgehen ("garantierte Sequentialisierung"). Zweitens, sollten Zugriffe auf beliebig zu definierende - jedoch disjunkte - Teile eines Datenobjektes voneinander unabhängig sequentialisierbar sein; etwa die Felder eines Satzes einer Datei ("Sequentialisierungsstruktur"), und schließlich, drittens, sollte die Sequentialisierungsstruktur variabel sein.

Diese Variabilität ist wünschenswert, wenn sich im Laufe der Zeit die (häufigst verwendete) logische Struktur des Datenobjektes ändert. Die Definition einer von vornherein "feinstmöglichen" Sequentialisierungsstruktur hätte den Vorteil ihrer Konstanz, jedoch den Nachteil der geringeren Effizienz. Die Sequentialisierungsstruktur soll also jeweils mit der (am häufigsten verwendeten) Datenstruktur des Datenobjektes übereinstimmen.

Die aus der Literatur bekannten Sequentialisierungsmethoden wie Semaphore, ENQUEUE und DEQUEUE Macros des Betriebssystems IBM/360, lesen und schreiben von Sätzen aus EXCLUSIVE Dateien von PL/1, etc., erfüllen nicht alle oben genannten Anforderungen.

Da im Vortrag von Unterschieden, die nur auf Grund verschiedener Speichermedien und deren Adressierung hinzukommen, abgesehen werden möchte, wird die Vereinbarung getroffen, daß alle betrachteten Datenobjekte auf höchstens je ein Segment eines virtuellen Speichers abgebildet sind. Jeder Zugriff auf ein Datenobjekt oder auf einen Teil eines solchen sei ein Zugriff auf einen zusammenhängenden Teil des entsprechenden Segmentes.

Die Realisierung einer solchen variablen Sequentialisierungsstruktur ist zwar theoretisch durch Programmierung unter der Zuhilfenahme eines primitiven Sequentialisierungsmittels - wie etwa der Semaphore - möglich, scheidet aber wegen zu

---

+) Manuskript nicht eingegangen

geringer Effizienz aus. Es kommen also nur intensiv hardwareunterstützte Lösungs-
wege in Betracht.

Es wird vorgeschlagen, jedem Segment ein sogenanntes Schattensegment zuzuordnen,
wobei ein Datenzugriff bloß das Segment adressiert, während die Adressierung des
Schattensegmentes über die Hardware erfolgt und somit für den Programmierer
unsichtbar bleibt. Dieses Schattensegment enthält die den Datenstrukturen zugeordneten momentanen Sequentialisierungsstrukturen, die ihrerseits den momentanen
Sequentialisierungszustand enthalten. Im Vortrag wird die Organisation des
Schattensegments und der enthaltenen Sequentialisierungsstrukturen im Zusammen-
spiel mit den verschiedenen Zugriffsarten und Sequentialisierungsbefehlen aus-
führlich behandelt.

Der durch das Schattensegment verursachte scheinbar hohe Speicherbedarf wird im
Vergleich zu anderen Lösungsversuchen diskutiert und es wird gezeigt, daß der
angegebene Vorschlag für feine Sequentialisierungsstrukturen optimal ist.

OPTIMALE ZERLEGUNG VON COMPUTERPROGRAMMEN DURCH ZERLEGUNG VON GRAPHEN

S. Schindler, J. Wagner

Zusammenfassung: Die Arbeit enthält einen Algorithmus, der zu einer beliebigen gegebenen Maschine $\mathfrak{M}$ und einem beliebigen gegebenen Fortran-ähnlichen Programm $\mathfrak{P}$ eine solche Ladestrategie $\mathfrak{L}(\mathfrak{P},\mathfrak{M})$ zu ermitteln versucht, daß - wird $\mathfrak{P}$ während seiner Ausführung entsprechend $\mathfrak{L}(\mathfrak{P},\mathfrak{M})$ in $\mathfrak{M}$ geladen - der Prozessor von $\mathfrak{M}$ vom Zeitpunkt des Startes der Ausführung von $\mathfrak{P}$ bis zu deren Ende nicht mehr wegen fehlender Programmteile unterbrochen zu werden braucht.
Summary: This paper contains an algorithm which tries to develop such a loading strategy $\mathfrak{L}(\mathfrak{P},\mathfrak{M})$ for an arbitrarily given Fortran-like program $\mathfrak{P}$ on an arbitrarily given computer $\mathfrak{M}$ that - after starting of execution of $\mathfrak{P}$ on $\mathfrak{M}$ - the processor of $\mathfrak{M}$ need not be interrupted (due to lacking parts of $\mathfrak{P}$) before completion of execution of $\mathfrak{P}$, if $\mathfrak{P}$ is loaded according $\mathfrak{L}(\mathfrak{P},\mathfrak{M})$.

1. Einleitung

Seit vielen Jahren bereits sind Techniken entwickelt, die es ermöglichen, von mehreren von dem (den) Prozessor(en) auszuführenden Programmen nur jeweils kleine Teile im schnellen Arbeitsspeicher zu halten. Die restlichen Teile dieser Programme können währenddessen im Hintergrundspeicher verbleiben und werden erst zu dem Zeitpunkt in den Arbeitsspeicher geladen, in dem sie der Prozessor benötigt, und zwar an die Stellen, die von nunmehr nicht mehr benötigten Programmteilen belegt sind. Die bekanntesten dieser Techniken sind die verschiedenen Overlay-, Segmentierungs- und Paging-Techniken (s. [1]). Für virtuelle Speicher wurden darüber hinausgehende Vorschläge vorgebracht (s. [5]).

Unabhängig von diesen Techniken wird in dieser Arbeit die naheliegende Frage untersucht, ob es überhaupt möglich ist - und gegebenenfalls wie - ein beliebiges vorgegebenes Programm auf einer beliebigen vorgegebenen Rechenanlage so zu laden, daß dessen Ausführung durch den (die) Prozessor(en) vom Zeitpunkt des Programmstarts an nicht mehr wegen fehlender (d.h. noch nicht nachgeladener) Programmteile (Code oder Daten) unterbrochen zu werden braucht. Untersucht wird also die Frage, ob eine vollständige Nutzung des (der) Prozessors (Prozessoren) durch vollständige Ausnutzung der Leistung der üblicherweise nur teilweise genutzten Kanäle und Speichersteuerung möglich ist.

Die Beantwortung dieser Frage gelingt dabei insofern, als ein Algorithmus angegeben wird, der (bei beliebigem gegebenem Programm mit Code- und Datenblöcken fester Größe und bei beliebig gegebenen Maschinenparametern) entscheidet, ob dies in 'einfacher Weise' möglich ist und gegebenenfalls angibt, wann welcher Programmteil zu laden ist. Aufgrund von Betrachtungen von Knuth (s. [2], Seite 128) und Denning (s. [1], S.177) ist der Algorithmus so konzipiert, daß er versucht, von vornherein bekannte Informationen über die Mindestlaufdauer von Programmabschnitten (z.B. subroutinen) zu berücksichtigen. Anders als in deren Arbeiten wird kein vorab zu sammelndes statistisches Material über das Verhalten des Programms benötigt, wie man es etwa mithilfe der 'frequency counts' oder 'histograms' erhält. Ausgenutzt werden vielmehr Kennt-

nisse über die Laufdauer von Programmabschnitten, die der Programmierer zum Zeitpunkt der Programmerstellung ohnehin hat und die er zusammen mit dem Programm dem
System übermittelt. Welchen zusätzlichen Aufwand diese Übermittlung verursacht, wird
in dieser Arbeit nicht diskutiert; der Aufwand, den der Algorithmus bei der Auswer-
tung dieser Kenntnisse verursacht, wird im vierten Abschnitt untersucht. Ob dieser
Gesamtaufwand gerechtfertigt ist bei sehr kurz laufenden Programmen, ist fraglich.
Dieser pro Programm einmalige Aufwand sollte sich jedoch bei länger laufenden Programmen auszahlen, insbesondere dann, wenn der Programmierer Angaben über die Mindestlaufdauer von möglichst vielen Teilen des Programms machen kann, weil dadurch
der Aufwand des Algorithmus erheblich reduziert wird. Dieser Fall liegt z.B. dann
vor, wenn das Programm fast vollständig aus Programmteilen aufgebaut ist, die einer
Bibliothek entnommen sind, in der es zu allen Routinen eine Funktion gibt, deren
Wert auf den aktuellen Parametern der Routine eine untere Schranke für die Laufdauer
der Routine bei diesen aktuellen Parametern liefert. Im wissenschaftlichen Bereich
scheinen diese für den folgenden Algorithmus günstigen Voraussetzungen weitgehend
vorzuliegen: Falls die Erhebungen in [4] und [1] allgemeingültig sind, verbrauchen
hier die verhältnismäßig wenigen lange laufenden Programme mehr als 90% der System-
zeit der Großrechenanlagen, wobei der Großteil dieser Anlagenbelastung wiederum nur
von Bruchteilen dieser Programme stammt und deshalb (s.[6]) besonderer Überprüfung
bedarf.

2. Problembeschreibung

In diesem Abschnitt wird zunächst ein graphentheoretisches Modell eines Programms $\mathfrak{P}$
entwickelt, die Allgemeinheit dieses Modells erörtert und seine Tauglichkeit zur Untersuchung unseres Problems erläutert. Danach wird ausgeführt, welche Parameter von
Rechenmaschinen $\mathfrak{M}$ bei der Untersuchung unseres Problems berücksichtigt werden. Am
Ende dieses Abschnittes wird eine mathematische Formulierung unseres Problems angegeben.

Unter einem __Programm__ $\mathfrak{P}$ verstehen wir ein Tripel $(\underline{V}, \underline{v}_o, \underline{E})$ [1]$, \mathfrak{P} := (\underline{V}, \underline{v}_o, \underline{E})$. Dabei ist
$\underline{V} = \underline{V}_C \cup \underline{V}_D$ mit $\underline{V}_C \cap \underline{V}_D = \Phi$, $\underline{v}_o \in \underline{V}_C$, und
$\underline{E} = \underline{E}_C \cup \underline{E}_D$ mit $\underline{E}_C \cap \underline{E}_D = \Phi$, wobei $\underline{E}_C \subset \underline{V}_C \times \underline{V}_C$, $\underline{E}_D \subset \underline{V}_C \times \underline{V}_D \cup \underline{V}_D \times \underline{V}_C$.
$\underline{v}_o$ heißt __Anfangsknoten__, die $\underline{v}_C \in \underline{V}_C$ heißen __Code-Knoten__, die $\underline{v}_D \in \underline{V}_D$ heißen __Daten-Knoten__.

Jeder Code-Knoten $\underline{v}_C \in \underline{V}_C$ enthält (s. [3]):
-   Daten, die außerhalb von $\underline{v}_C$ nicht benötigt werden;
-   sequentiell auszuführende Operationen auf solchen Daten, die in $\underline{v}_C$ enthalten
    sind oder in einem $\underline{v}_D' \in \{\underline{v}_D \in \underline{V}_D \mid (\underline{v}_D, \underline{v}_C) \in \underline{E}_D \vee (\underline{v}_C, \underline{v}_D) \in \underline{E}_D\}$; die letzte auszuführende
    Operation kann ein Prädikat sein, das die Verzweigung der Kontrolle bewirkt.

$\underline{v}_o$ ist der erste auszuführende Code-Knoten von $\mathfrak{P}$.

Jeder Daten-Knoten $\underline{v}_D \in \underline{V}_D$ enthält genau alle diejenigen Daten, die von mindestens
einer Operation in jedem Element aus $\{\underline{v}_C \in \underline{V}_C \mid (\underline{v}_C, \underline{v}_D) \in \underline{E}_D \vee (\underline{v}_D, \underline{v}_C) \in \underline{E}_D\}$ angesprochen
werden. Die Elemente $e_C \in \underline{E}_C$ kennzeichnen in leicht verständlicher Weise den möglichen

---

[1] Unterstrichene Buchstaben kennzeichnen stets Mengen.

238

Weg der Kontrolle durch $\underline{v}_C$ und die Elemente $e_D \in \underline{E}_D$ geben an,   welche (mehreren $\underline{v}_C \in \underline{v}_C$ gemeinsame) Daten von einem Code-Knoten aus gelesen bzw. geschrieben werden. $\mathfrak{P}$ betrachten wir als Graphen.

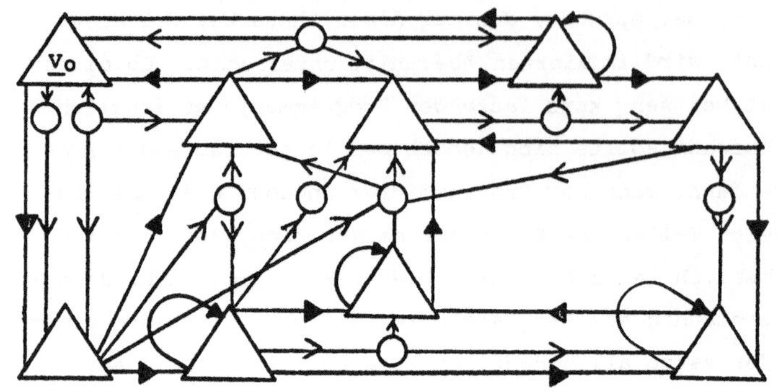

Dabei stellen dar:

Dreiecke die Code-Knoten,

Kreise die Daten-Knoten,

geschlossene Pfeile
Elemente aus E_C ,

offene Pfeile
Elemente aus E_D .

Bemerkungen:

- In Hinblick auf den folgenden Algorithmus beschränken wir uns auf Programme $\mathfrak{P}$, während deren gesamter Ausführungsdauer die Code- und Daten-Knoten ihren Knotenklassen $\underline{V}_C$ bzw. $\underline{V}_D$ zugeordnet bleiben und ihre 'Größe' nicht ändern. Wir beschränken uns damit im wesentlichen auf Fortran-ähnliche Programme.

- In Abhängigkeit von der zugrunde gelegten Maschine $\mathfrak{M}$ kann man für ein vorgegebenes Fortran-ähnliches Computerprogramm automatisch das zugehörige, eindeutig bestimmte Programm $\mathfrak{P}$ konstruieren lassen (s. [3], wo auch elementare strukturelle Eigenschaften von $\mathfrak{P}$ abgehandelt werden).

- Für $\underline{v}_C \in \underline{V}_C$ nennen wir die Menge $\{\underline{v}_C\} \cup \{\underline{v}_D \in \underline{V}_D \mid (\underline{v}_D, \underline{v}_C) \in \underline{E}_D \vee (\underline{v}_C, \underline{v}_D) \in \underline{E}_D\}$ die zu $\underline{v}_C$ gehörige <u>Arbeitseinheit</u> $\underline{WU}(\underline{v}_C)$. Man beachte, daß - wenn die Kontrolle die $\underline{WU}(\underline{v}_C)$ verläßt und nach $\underline{WU}(\underline{v}_C')$ geht - zwar $\underline{v}_C \cap \underline{v}_C' = \Phi$ ist, aber im allgemeinen $\underline{WU}(\underline{v}_C') \cap \underline{WU}(\underline{v}_C) \neq \Phi$.

Unter einer <u>Maschine</u> $\mathfrak{M}$ verstehen wir ein Quadrupel $((P,p),(C,c),(S,s,s_0),(H,h_0))$, also $\mathfrak{M} := ((P,p),(C,c),(S,s,s_0),(H,h_0))$. Dabei ist

- P die Anzahl der Prozessoren, die zur Ausführung eines Programms zur Verfügung stehen, p die Arbeitsgeschwindigkeit eines Prozessors;

- C die Anzahl der Kanäle, die zur Verfügung stehen, um Programmteile aus dem Hintergrund- in den Arbeitsspeicher zu kopieren (bzw. umgekehrt), c die Arbeitsgeschwindigkeit eines Kanals;

- S die Anzahl der Arbeitsspeichereinheiten, die zur Ausführung eines Programms zur Verfügung stehen, s die Größe einer Arbeitsspeichereinheit, s_0 die Arbeitsgeschwindigkeit der Speichersteuerung;

- H die Größe des Hintergrundspeichers, h_0 die maximale Zugriffszeit eines Kanals auf eine Information im Hintergrundspeicher.

Im folgenden setzen wir einen unendlich großen Hintergrundspeicher, vernachlässigbare Zugriffszeit und eine unendlich schnelle Arbeitsspeichersteuerung voraus, d.h. $H = \infty$, $h_0 = 0$, $s_0 = \infty$. Ist diese Idealisierung nicht haltbar, so läßt sich der nachfolgende Algorithmus problemlos an reale Werte dieser Maschinenparameter anpassen. Außerdem wird der Algorithmus o.B.d.A. für P = 1 entwickelt. Die hier angesprochenen Verallgemeinerungen werden an anderer Stelle im einzelnen ausgeführt werden.

Mittels der Arbeitsgeschwindigkeit p des Prozessors und der Größe einer Arbeitsspeichereinheit kann man nun Gewichte auf $\underline{\mathfrak{P}}$ definieren. Es sei

- $g(\underline{V}') :=$ Anzahl der Arbeitsspeichereinheiten, die von $\underline{\dot{V}}' \subset \underline{V}$ belegt werden,

- $t(\underline{v}_C) :=$ zur Ausführung aller Instruktionen in $\underline{v}_C$ benötigte Dauer, $\underline{v}_C \underline{\in} \underline{V}_C$

- $T(\underline{Y},\underline{y}) : =$ Mindestverweildauer der Kontrolle in $\underline{Y}$ nach ihrem Eintritt in $\underline{Y}$ an der Stelle $\underline{y}, \underline{Y} \subset \underline{V}_C$, $\underline{y} \underline{\in} \underline{Y}$.

Wir kommen nun zu der für unseren Zugang zu dem Problem wesentlichsten Voraussetzung. Nämlich: Von einigen $\underline{Y} \subset \underline{V}_C$ wissen wir, welche Dauer $T(\underline{Y}) \geq \sum_{\underline{v}\in\underline{Y}} t(\underline{v})$ die Kontrolle benötigt, um nach ihrem Eintritt in $\underline{Y}$ an irgendeiner Stelle $\underline{y}\in\underline{Y}$ diese Menge $\underline{Y}$ von Code-Knoten wieder zu verlassen. Solche $\underline{Y}$ entstehen durch Programmschleifen, wie sie etwa bei Matrix-Operationen, Integrations-Routinen oder Sortier-Algorithmen auftreten. $T(\underline{Y})$ ist hier bereits durch die Dimension der Matrizen, des Systems von Differentialgleichungen oder durch die Größe des Datenbestandes gegeben und vor der Programmausführung bekannt. Sei also mit einem Programm $\underline{\mathfrak{P}}$ auch $\underline{Z} := \{(\underline{Y}, T(\underline{Y}) \mid \underline{Y}\underline{\subset}\underline{V}_C \wedge T(\underline{Y}) > \sum_{\underline{y}\in\underline{Y}} t(\underline{y})\}$ gegeben mit $\underline{Y} \cap \underline{Y}' = \Phi \; \forall \; \underline{Y},\underline{Y}'\in\Pi\underline{Z}$, wobei $\Pi\{(a_i,b_i),i\underline{\in}\underline{I}\} := \{a_i,i\underline{\in}\underline{I}\}$.

Nach diesen Überlegungen können wir zu einer spezielleren Bezeichnungsweise übergehen: Ein Programm $\underline{\mathfrak{P}}$ sei nun ein Sextupel, $\underline{\mathfrak{P}} := (\underline{V},\underline{v}_o,\underline{E},g,t,\underline{Z})$, und die Maschine $\mathfrak{M}$ sei ein Paar, $\mathfrak{M} := ((C,c),(S,s))$, wobei die Bedeutung der einzelnen Komponenten im vorangehenden Text angegeben wurde.

Ziel der Arbeit ist nun, für vorgelegtes $\underline{\mathfrak{P}}$ und $\mathfrak{M}$ eine 'Ladestrategie' $\mathfrak{Q}(\underline{\mathfrak{P}},\mathfrak{M})$ zu entwickeln, so daß für die Verarbeitung von $\underline{\mathfrak{P}}$ auf $\mathfrak{M}$ entsprechend $\mathfrak{Q}(\underline{\mathfrak{P}},\mathfrak{M})$ gilt: Nach dem Start der Ausführung von $\underline{\mathfrak{P}}$ kann der Prozessor von $\mathfrak{M}$ bis zur vollständigen Ausführung von $\underline{\mathfrak{P}}$ ohne Unterbrechung weiterarbeiten. Um die Definition des Begriffes 'Ladestrategie' übersichtlich zu gestalten, werden zunächst noch **zwei** Abkürzungen eingeführt.

Für $\underline{Y} \subset \underline{V}_C$ bezeichnen wir die Menge $\underline{Q}(\underline{Y}) := \bigcup_{\underline{v}\in\underline{Y}} \underline{WU}(\underline{v})$ __als Arbeitssatz von $\underline{Y}$.__ (Eine Analogie zu Dennings 'working set', [1], wird später erst deutlich).

Sei $\underline{R}(\underline{Y}) := \{\underline{v}_C\underline{\in}\underline{V}_C\backslash\underline{Y} \mid \exists \underline{v}_C'\underline{\in}\underline{Y}: (\underline{v}_C',\underline{v}_C)\underline{\in}\underline{E}_C\}$.

Unter einer __Ladestrategie__ $\mathfrak{Q}(\underline{\mathfrak{P}},\mathfrak{M})$ verstehen wir ein Tripel $(\underline{WS},\underline{V}_U,a)$, also $\mathfrak{Q}(\underline{\mathfrak{P}},\mathfrak{M}) := (\underline{WS},\underline{V}_U,a)$, wobei

- $\underline{WS} := \{\underline{WS}_j, j\underline{\in}\underline{J}\}$, mit $\underline{WS}_j := (\underline{U}_j,\underline{R}(\underline{U}_j))$, so daß $\{\underline{U}_j, j\underline{\in}\underline{J}\}$ Überdeckung von $\underline{V}_C$ ist;

- $\underline{V}_U := \bigcup_{j\underline{\in}\underline{J}} \underline{R}(\underline{U}_j) \subset \underline{V}_C$, mit $\underline{v}_o\underline{\in}\underline{V}_U$;

- $a: \underline{V}_U \rightarrow \{\underline{U}_j, j\underline{\in}\underline{J}\}$ total und rechtseindeutig ist;

- $G_j := g(\underline{N}(\underline{U}_j)) \leq S\cdot s \; \forall \; j\underline{\in}\underline{J}$, wobei $\underline{N}(\underline{U}_j) := \underline{Q}(\underline{U}_j) \cup \bigcup_{\underline{U}\in a(\underline{R}(\underline{U}_j))} \underline{Q}(\underline{U})$;

- $T(\underline{U}_j,\underline{y}) \geq T_j^R + T_j^L$, $\underline{y}\in a^{-1}(\underline{U}_j)$, $\forall \; j\underline{\in}\underline{J}$, wobei

  $= T_j^R$ die Zeit angibt, die die $\underline{\mathfrak{P}}$ zur Verfügung stehenden Kanäle benötigen, um die Menge derjenigen Datenknoten $\underline{V}_D^j \subset \underline{V}_D$ aus dem Arbeitsspeicher auf den

Hintergrundspeicher zu kopieren,

a) von denen es noch keine Kopie auf dem Hintergrundspeicher gibt, aber zu einem späteren Zeitpunkt eine benötigt wird,

b) die in $\underline{N}(\underline{U}_j)$ nicht benötigt wird und

c) für die gilt $g(\underline{V}_D^j) + G_j \geq S \cdot s$;

$= T_j^L$ die Zeit angibt, die die $\mathfrak{P}$ zur Verfügung stehenden Kanäle benötigen, um $\underline{N}(\underline{U}_j) \setminus \underline{Q}(\underline{U}_j)$ zu laden (soweit deren Code- bzw. Daten-Knoten nicht bereits zum Zeitpunkt des Eintritts der Kontrolle in $\underline{U}_j$ über $\underline{y}$ im Arbeitsspeicher sind).

Die Verarbeitung von $\mathfrak{P}$ auf $\mathfrak{M}$ geschieht entsprechend $\mathfrak{L}(\mathfrak{P},\mathfrak{M})$, wenn wir in folgender Weise verfahren: Vor dem Start der Ausführung von $\mathfrak{P}$ wird $\underline{N}(a(\underline{v}_o))$ in den Arbeitsspeicher von $\mathfrak{M}$ geladen; sobald die Kontrolle während der Ausführung von $\mathfrak{P}$ ein $\underline{U}_i$ verläßt und über ein $\underline{v}_c \in \underline{R}(\underline{U}_i)$ in $\underline{U}_j := a(\underline{v}_c)$ eintritt, $i,j \in \underline{J}$, werden zunächst die Daten-Knoten aus $\underline{V}_D^j$ auf den Hintergrundspeicher kopiert und danach alle nicht im Arbeitsspeicher befindlichen Elemente von $\underline{N}(\underline{U}_j)$ in den Arbeitsspeicher geladen.

Man sieht, daß $\mathfrak{L}(\mathfrak{P},\mathfrak{M})$ trivial ausfällt, falls $g(\underline{V}) \leq S \cdot s$ (weil man dann einfach ganz $\mathfrak{P}$ in den Arbeitsspeicher von $\mathfrak{M}$ laden kann und deshalb nichts nachzuladen braucht) oder, falls die Kanäle schneller Code und Daten nachladen können, als der Prozessor von $\mathfrak{M}$ sie verarbeiten kann (in diesem Fall genügen einige wenige Arbeitsspeichereinheiten, man spricht dann von 'pipe-lining'). Für den allgemeinen Fall geben wir im folgenden Abschnitt einen Algorithmus an, der für beliebige vorgegebene $\mathfrak{M}$ und $\mathfrak{P}$ mit den oben beschriebenen Eigenschaften eine Ladestrategie $\mathfrak{L}(\mathfrak{P},\mathfrak{M})$ zu konstruieren versucht. Um diesen Algorithmus effektiv zu gestalten, wird darin mit zwei erheblichen Vereinfachungen gearbeitet: Zum einen fordern wir

$$\overline{T} := \frac{2 \cdot S \cdot s}{\overline{C} \cdot c} \leq T(\underline{U}_j,\underline{y}),\ \underline{y} \in a^{-1}(\underline{U}_j),\ \forall\ j \in \underline{J},\ 1 < \overline{C} \leq C,$$

wobei $\overline{C}$ angibt, wieviele Kanäle wir anfangs dem Programm $\mathfrak{P}$ zur Verfügung stellen ($\overline{C}$ wird bis auf C vergrössert, falls der Algorithmus dies erfordert); offenbar gilt dann

$$T(\underline{U}_j,\underline{y}) > T_j^R + T_j^L,\ \underline{y} \in a^{-1}(\underline{U}_j),\ \forall j \in \underline{J}.$$

Zum anderen fordern wir

$$g(\underline{Q}(\underline{U}_j)) \leq \overline{S} \cdot s,\ 1 < \overline{S} \leq S,\ \forall\ j \in \underline{J}.$$

Die Diskussion dieser beiden Parameter $\overline{T}$ und $\overline{S}$ ist erst nach der Darstellung des Algorithmus möglich und wird deshalb bis zum 4. Abschnitt zurückgestellt. Der Preis für diese Vereinfachung besteht jedenfalls darin, daß der Algorithmus eine Anzahl von $\mathfrak{P}$ zur Verfügung zu stellenden Kanäle bzw. Arbeitsspeichereinheiten berechnet, die im allgemeinen größer ist als die zur Lösung des Problems erforderliche Minimalzahl.

3. Der Algorithmus

Für beliebig gegebenes $\mathfrak{P}$ und $\mathfrak{M}$ versucht der folgende Algorithmus LPM($\mathfrak{P}$, $\mathfrak{M}$,$\underline{Z}$,$\overline{C}$,$\overline{S}$) in 'einfacher Weise' eine Ladestrategie $\mathfrak{L}(\mathfrak{P},\mathfrak{M})$ zu ermitteln, die die eingangs beschriebenen gewünschten Eigenschaften hat. Seine Formulierung soll seine strukturellen Aspekte hervorheben und vernachlässigt demgegenüber Effektivitätsgesichtspunkte (auf die im nächsten Abschnitt eingegangen wird). Wir beschreiben ihn auf zwei verschiedene Weisen, nämlich erst in einer Algol-ähnlichen Notation (abweichend von

Algol 60 benutzen wir keine Deklarationen und erlauben den Typ 'Menge') und danach durch ein Strukturdiagramm. Die Bedeutung der verwandten Symbole – soweit sie nicht in der folgenden Beschreibung des Algorithmus definiert wird – wurde im vorigen Abschnitt bereits festgelegt, mit Ausnahme von h und $\underline{S}$, die für folgende Abbildungen stehen

$$h:\ \underline{W}_{\underline{v}'} \to (0,\infty),\qquad\text{definiert durch } h(\underline{v}'')=b,\text{ wobei } (\underline{v}'',b)\in\underline{W}_{\underline{v}'};$$

$$\underline{S}:\ \underline{V}_C \to \text{Potenzmenge von } \underline{V}_C,\text{ definiert durch } \underline{S}(\underline{v}) = \{\hat{\underline{v}}\in\underline{V}_C \mid (\underline{v},\hat{\underline{v}})\in\underline{E}_C\}.$$

Außerdem haben wir die Kontrollstruktur von Algol 60 um das Element

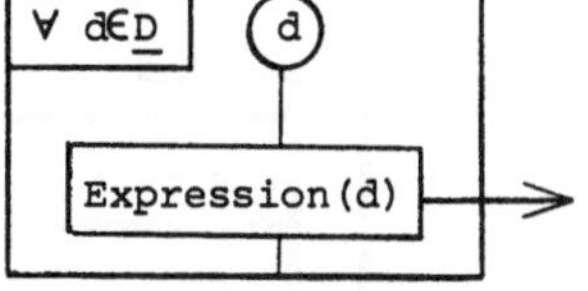

$$\text{for } d\in\underline{D} \text{ pardo Expression (d)}$$

erweitert (rechts daneben ist das im Strukturdiagramm dafür verwandte Symbol abgebildet), das besagt, daß für jedes $d\in\underline{D}$ Expression (d) einmal berechnet werden muß, wobei mehrere solcher Berechnungen gleichzeitig ('parallel') erfolgen können, und wobei $\underline{D}$ selbst in Expression (d) vergrößert werden kann; erfolgt für ein $d\in\underline{D}$ bei der Berechnung von Expression (d) ein Sprung auf eine Marke außerhalb von Expression (d), so wird die Berechnung von Expression (d) $\forall d\in\underline{D}$ eingestellt.

Schließlich stehen exit 1 und exit 2 für Expressions, in denen unterschiedliche Ziele des Algorithmus implementiert werden können; sie werden später diskutiert.

procedure LPM $(\Phi,\mathfrak{M},\underline{z},\overline{C},\overline{S})$ begin

L1: if $\overline{C}>C$ then exit 1;

$\overline{T}:=2*S*s/(\overline{C}*c)$; $\underline{V}_U:=\{\underline{v}_0\}$; UMGEBUNG$(\underline{v}_0)$; $a(\underline{v}_0):=\underline{U}_{\underline{v}0}$;

for $\underline{v}\in\underline{V}_U$ pardo   begin

for $\underline{v}'\in\underline{R}(a(\underline{v}))$ pardo begin UMGEBUNG$(\underline{v}')$; $a(\underline{v}'):=\underline{U}_{\underline{v}'}$; $\underline{V}_U:=\underline{V}_U\cup\underline{R}(a(\underline{v}'))$; end;

if $G_{\underline{v}}>S*s$ then begin $\overline{C}:=\overline{C}+1$; goto L1; end;   end;   end

procedure UMGEBUNG$(\underline{v}')$ begin

if $\exists\ \underline{Y}\in\Pi\underline{Z} : \underline{v}'\in\underline{Y}$ and $\sum_{\underline{y}\in\underline{Y}} t(\underline{y})\leq\overline{T}$ then $\underline{W}_{\underline{v}'}:=\{(\underline{y},T(\underline{Y}))\mid\underline{y}\in\underline{Y}\}$ else $\underline{W}_{\underline{v}'}:=\{(\underline{v}',t(\underline{v}'))\}$;

while $\underline{U}'_{\underline{v}'}:=\{\underline{u}\in\Pi\underline{W}_{\underline{v}'}\mid h(\underline{u})<\overline{T}\wedge\underline{S}(\underline{u})\setminus\Pi\underline{W}_{\underline{v}'}\neq\Phi\}\neq\Phi$ do   begin

$\underline{U}''_{\underline{v}'}:=\{\underline{u}\in\underline{U}'_{\underline{v}'}\mid h(\underline{u})\leq h(\underline{u}')\ \forall\underline{u}'\in\underline{U}'_{\underline{v}'}\}$;

for $\underline{v}''\in\underline{U}''_{\underline{v}'}$ pardo

for $\underline{x}\in\underline{S}(\underline{v}'')\setminus\Pi\underline{W}_{\underline{v}'}$ pardo

if $\exists\ \underline{Y}\in\Pi\underline{Z} : \underline{x}\in\underline{Y}$ and $h(\underline{v}'')+\sum_{\underline{y}\in\underline{Y}}t(\underline{y})<\overline{T}$ then $\underline{W}_{\underline{v}'}:=\underline{W}_{\underline{v}'}\cup\{(\underline{y},h(\underline{v}'')+T(\underline{Y}))\mid\underline{y}\in\underline{Y}\}$

else $\underline{W}_{\underline{v}'}:=\underline{W}_{\underline{v}'}\cup\{(\underline{x},h(\underline{v}'')+t(\underline{x}))\}$;

$\underline{U}_{\underline{v}'}:=\Pi\underline{W}_{\underline{v}'}$; if $g(\underline{Q}(\underline{U}_{\underline{v}'}))>\overline{S}*s$ then exit 2;   end;   end

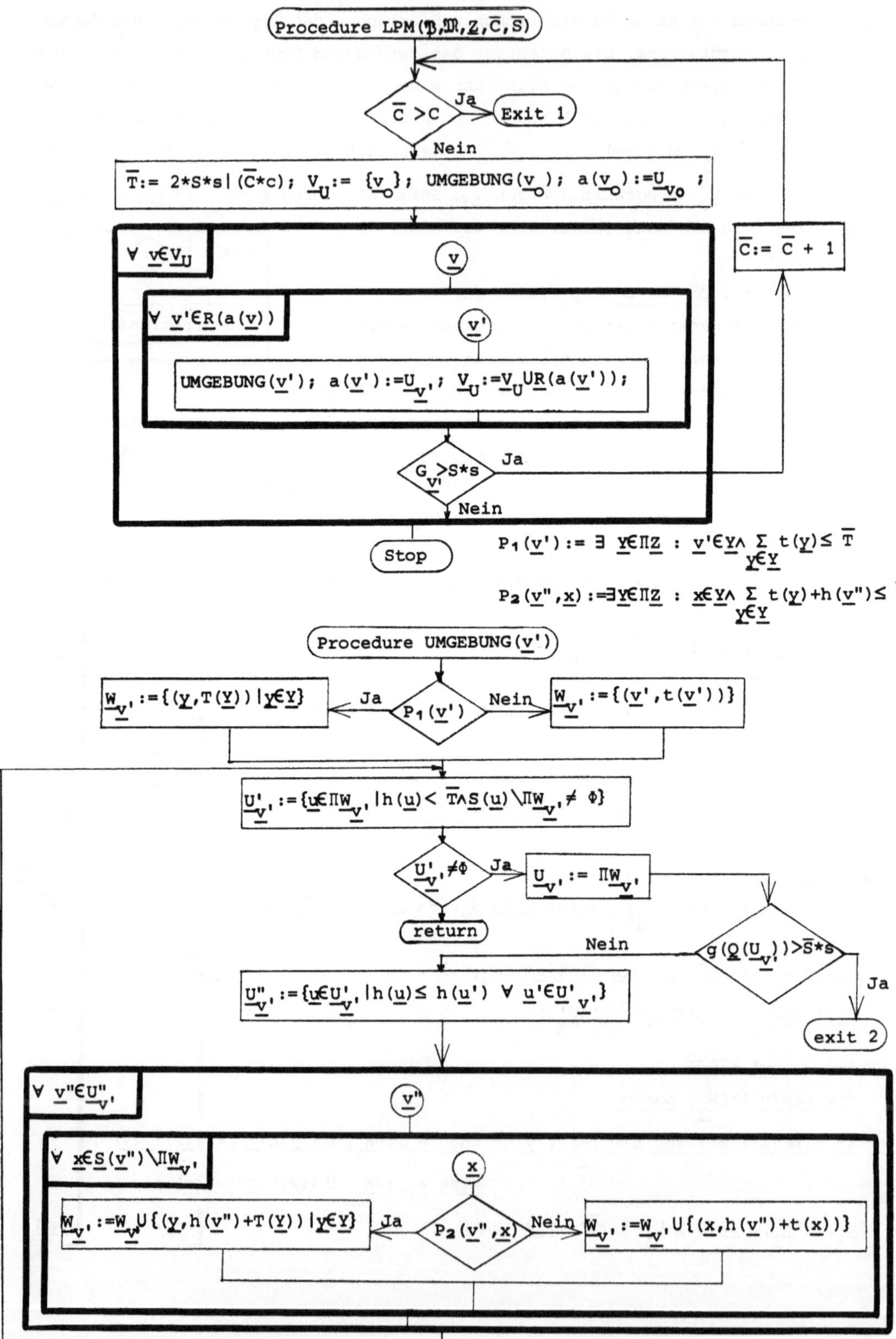

Procedure LPM($\underline{\mathfrak{B}},\underline{\mathfrak{M}},\underline{Z},\overline{C},\overline{S}$)
$\overline{C} > C$
Ja
Exit 1
Nein
$\overline{T}:= 2*S*s \mid (\overline{C}*c);$ $\underline{V}_U := \{\underline{v}_o\};$ UMGEBUNG$(\underline{v}_o);$ $a(\underline{v}_o):=U_{\underline{v}_o}$;
$\forall\ \underline{v}\in\underline{V}_U$
$\underline{v}$
$\forall\ \underline{v}'\in\underline{R}(a(\underline{v}))$
$\underline{v}'$
UMGEBUNG$(\underline{v}');$ $a(\underline{v}'):=U_{\underline{v}'};$ $\underline{V}_U:=\underline{V}_U\cup\underline{R}(a(\underline{v}'));$
$G_{\underline{v}'} > S*s$
Ja
Nein
$\overline{C}:= \overline{C} + 1$
Stop
$P_1(\underline{v}') := \exists\ \underline{Y}\in\Pi\underline{Z}\ :\ \underline{v}'\in\underline{Y}\wedge \sum_{\underline{y}\in\underline{Y}} t(\underline{y})\leq \overline{T}$
$P_2(\underline{v}'',\underline{x}) := \exists\underline{Y}\in\Pi\underline{Z}\ :\ \underline{x}\in\underline{Y}\wedge \sum_{\underline{y}\in\underline{Y}} t(\underline{y})+h(\underline{v}'')\leq \overline{T}$
Procedure UMGEBUNG$(\underline{v}')$
$\underline{W}_{\underline{v}'}:=\{(\underline{y},T(\underline{y}))\mid\underline{y}\in\underline{Y}\}$
Ja
$P_1(\underline{v}')$
Nein
$\underline{W}_{\underline{v}'}:=\{(\underline{v}',t(\underline{v}'))\}$
$\underline{U}'_{\underline{v}'}:=\{\underline{u}\in\Pi\underline{W}_{\underline{v}'}\mid h(\underline{u})<\overline{T}\wedge\underline{S}(\underline{u})\setminus\Pi\underline{W}_{\underline{v}'}\neq\Phi\}$
$\underline{U}'_{\underline{v}'}\neq\Phi$
Ja
$\underline{U}_{\underline{v}'}:=\Pi\underline{W}_{\underline{v}'}$
return
$g(\underline{Q}(\underline{U}_{\underline{v}'}))>\overline{S}*s$
Nein
Ja
$\underline{U}''_{\underline{v}'}:=\{\underline{u}\in\underline{U}'_{\underline{v}'}\mid h(\underline{u})\leq h(\underline{u}')\ \forall\ \underline{u}'\in\underline{U}'_{\underline{v}'}\}$
exit 2
$\forall\ \underline{v}''\in\underline{U}''_{\underline{v}'}$
$\underline{v}''$
$\forall\ \underline{x}\in\underline{S}(\underline{v}'')\setminus\Pi\underline{W}_{\underline{v}'}$
$\underline{x}$
$\underline{W}_{\underline{v}'}:=\underline{W}_{\underline{v}'}\cup\{(\underline{y},h(\underline{v}'')+T(\underline{y}))\mid\underline{y}\in\underline{Y}\}$
Ja
$P_2(\underline{v}'',\underline{x})$
Nein
$\underline{W}_{\underline{v}'}:=\underline{W}_{\underline{v}'}\cup\{(\underline{x},h(\underline{v}'')+t(\underline{x}))\}$

Die beiden vorangehenden Darstellungen des Algorithmus zur Ermittlung einer $\Omega(\mathfrak{P},\mathfrak{M})$ geben dessen grundsätzliche Aufgaben wieder. In LPM wird - ausgehend von vorgegebenen $\mathfrak{P}$, $\mathfrak{M}$ und $\overline{C}$ - zunächst ein solches $\overline{T}$ berechnet, daß in der Zeit $\overline{T}$ der gesamte Arbeitsspeicher von $\mathfrak{M}$ über die $\overline{C}$ Kanäle auf den Hintergrundspeicher kopiert werden kann und von dort neu beschrieben werden kann. Sodann wird für den Anfangsknoten $\underline{v}_0$ eine $\overline{T}$-Umgebung $\underline{U}_{v_0}$ berechnet (durch Aufruf der Prozedur UMGEBUNG $(\underline{v}_0)$), d.h. ein solches $\underline{Y} \subset \underline{V}_C$, daß $T(\underline{Y},\underline{v}_0) \geq \overline{T}$. Für jedes $\underline{v}' \in R(\underline{U}_{v_0})$ wird wieder eine $\overline{T}$-Umgebung $\underline{U}_{v'}$ berechnet, usw. $\underline{V}_U$ enthält anfangs nur $\underline{v}_0$, wird sobald $\underline{U}_{v_0}$ berechnet wurde um $\underline{R}(\underline{U}_{v_0})$ vergrößert, usw.; $\underline{V}_U$ besteht also stets aus der Menge aller Randpunkte aller bereits berechneter $\overline{T}$-Umgebungen. Grundsätzlich ist es möglich, daß schließlich $\underline{V}_U = \underline{V}_C$. (Falls $\overline{T}$ sehr klein ist, ist dies vernünftig; andernfalls kann man sich überlegen, wie man diesen Fall durch geeignete Maßnahmen im allgemeinen ausschließen kann (s.[3]), so daß dann LPM mit $|\underline{V}_U| \ll |\underline{V}_C|$ zu seinem Ende kommt.)

Wenn für ein $\underline{v} \in V_U$ nicht nur $\underline{U}_v$ sondern auch $\underline{U}_{v'}$ $\forall$ $\underline{v}' \in R(\underline{U}_v)$ berechnet wurde, wird in LPM geprüft, ob $g(\underline{N}(\underline{U}_v)) \leq \overline{S} * s$, d.h. ob $\underline{N}(\underline{U}_v)$ überhaupt in den verfügbaren Speicher paßt. Falls dies nicht der Fall ist, wird die Anzahl der $\mathfrak{P}$ zur Verfügung stehenden Kanäle um 1 erhöht, wodurch $\overline{T}$ kleiner wird. Für dieses kleinere $\overline{T}$ wird LPM von neuem begonnen, wobei nun kleinere $\overline{T}$-Umgebungen der Elemente der neuen $\underline{V}_U$ berechnet werden, so daß damit u.U. $g(\underline{N}(\underline{U}_v)) \leq \overline{S} * s$ $\forall$ $\underline{v} \in V_U$. Man beachte, daß also $\underline{V}_U = \underline{V}_U(\overline{T})$. Falls auch für $\overline{C} = C$ für ein $\underline{v} \in V_U$ gilt $g(\underline{N}(\underline{U}_v)) > \overline{S} * s$, so betrachten wir $\mathfrak{P}$ auf $\mathfrak{M}$ nicht in der beabsichtigten 'einfachen Weise' verarbeitbar (exit 1). In der vorliegenden Fassung von LPM gehen wir also von einer festen Größe S * s des Arbeitsspeichers von $\mathfrak{M}$ aus und versuchen eine $\Omega(\mathfrak{P},\mathfrak{M})$ für eine möglichst kleine Anzahl $\geq \overline{C}$ von Kanälen zu gewinnen.

In der Prozedur UMGEBUNG (v'), $\underline{v}' \in V_U$, wird bei der Berechnung der $\overline{T}$-Umgebung von $\underline{v}'$ Gebrauch gemacht von $\underline{Z}$, d.h. von der a priori bekannten Information über die Mindestverweildauer der Kontrolle in gewissen $\underline{Y} \subset \underline{V}_C$. Zunächst wird dabei geprüft, ob für $\underline{v}'$ selbst gilt $\exists \underline{Y} \in \Pi \underline{Z} : \underline{v}' \in \underline{Y} \wedge \sum_{\underline{y} \in \underline{Y}} t(\underline{y}) \leq \overline{T}$. In diesem Fall wird $\underline{Y}$ in $\underline{U}_{v'}$ aufgenommen (dies muß geschehen, da selbst ein 'längster einfacher Weg' in $\underline{Y}$ kürzer ist als $\overline{T}$), genauer: die Menge von Paaren $\underline{W}_{v'}$ wird definiert als $\underline{W}_{v'} := \{(\underline{y},T(\underline{y})) \mid \underline{y} \in \underline{Y}\}$; andernfalls wird $\underline{W}_{v'} := \{(\underline{v}',t(\underline{v}'))\}$. $\underline{W}_{v'}$ stellt so eine Gewichtung der Knoten $\underline{v}''$ von $\underline{U}_{v'}$ dar, wobei das Gewicht $h(\underline{v}'')$ von $\underline{v}''$ angibt, welche Zeit nach dem Eintritt der Kontrolle in $\underline{v}'$ mindestens verstreicht, bevor die Kontrolle $\underline{v}''$ verlassen kann. Man sieht hier exemplarisch, wie die in $\underline{Z}$ angegebenen Informationen beim Aufbau von $\overline{T}$-Umgebungen ausgenutzt werden, um diese möglichst klein zu halten. Anschließend wird $\underline{W}_{v'}$ solange vergrößert, bis $\underline{U}'_{v'} = \Phi$ (d.h. die $\overline{T}$-Umgebung $\underline{U}_{v'}$ von $\underline{v}'$ vollständig berechnet wurde) oder $g(\underline{Q}(\underline{U}_{v'})) > \overline{S} * s$ (d.h. exit 2 und wird im folgenden Abschnitt diskutiert). Beim Vergrößern der $\underline{W}_{v'}$ wird dabei nach folgendem Prinzip verfahren: Beim einmaligen Ausführen der while-Expression wird $\underline{W}_{v'}$ erweitert um die Paare $(\underline{u},h(\underline{u}))$ mit $\underline{u} \in U''_{v'}$, wobei $h(\underline{u})$ in der aus UMGEBUNG(v') ersichtlichen Weise festgelegt wird (in unterschiedlicher Weise für $\underline{u} \in \underline{Y} \in \Pi \underline{Z}$ und $\underline{u} \notin \underline{Y}$ $\forall$ $\underline{Y} \in \Pi \underline{Z}$). In [3] wird

bewiesen, daß damit die $\overline{T}$-Umgebung von $\underline{v}'$ tatsächlich berechnet wird. Durch die letzte Abfrage $g(\underline{Q}(U_{\underline{v}'})) > \overline{S} * s$ wird sichergestellt, daß die einzelnen $\overline{T}$-Umgebungen eine willkürlich vorgegebene Maximalgröße $\overline{S} * s$ nicht überschreiten; falls dies doch der Fall ist (exit 2) kann wiederum $\overline{C}$ erhöht werden oder $\overline{S}$ erhöht werden.
Läuft LPM schließlich auf STOP, so hat man offenbar eine $\mathfrak{Q}(\mathfrak{P}, \mathfrak{M})$ berechnet. In dem vorliegenden sehr einfachen Algorithmus ist dann $\underline{J} := \underline{V}_U$; durch leichte Modifikationen (s.[3]) kommt man jedoch zu wesentlich effektiveren Formulierungen, in denen im allgemeinen $|\underline{J}| < |\underline{V}_U|$.

4. Diskussion der Komplexität des Algorithmus

Untersucht man die vorangehenden Darstellungen des Algorithmus in Hinblick auf seine Komplexität, so sieht man sofort, daß die Anzahl von Operationen zur Ausführung von LPM nach oben beschränkt ist durch Konstante $* C * |\underline{V}_C| *$ Komplexität von UMGEBUNG. Die Anzahl der Operationen zur Ausführung von UMGEBUNG ist zunächst sehr stark abhängig von dem Verhältnis der Arbeitsgeschwindigkeit des Prozessors zu der der Kanäle. Während UMGEBUNG nur wenige Operationen benötigt, wenn dieses Verhältnis klein ist, wächst die Anzahl der benötigten Operationen (d.h. die $\overline{T}$-Umgebungen werden grösser) mit wachsendem Verhältnis stark an. Um der Komplexität von UMGEBUNG für jedes $\overline{C}$ eine von $|\underline{V}_C|$ unabhängige Schranke aufzuerlegen, wurde deshalb der Parameter $\overline{S}$ und die Abfrage $g(\underline{Q}(U_{\underline{v}'})) > \overline{S} * s$ eingeführt. Auf diese Weise wird ein zu starkes Anwachsen der Komplexität des Algorithmus, das entstehen könnte durch zu große $\underline{U}_{\underline{v}'}$, verhindert. Weitere Verbesserung der Effektivität erhält man durch die Nutzung geeigneter, bereits berechneter $\overline{T}$-Umgebungen bei der Initialisierung von UMGEBUNG und bei der Vergrößerung von $\overline{C}$ sowie durch die Berechnung der T_j^R und $T_j^L \ \forall \ j \in \underline{J}$ (s.[3]). Insgesamt sieht man, daß der Algorithmus jedenfalls eine $\mathfrak{Q}(\mathfrak{P}, \mathfrak{M})$ ökonomisch ermittelt, wenn die Arbeitsgeschwindigkeit der Kanäle viel größer ist als die des Prozessors, weil dann die $\overline{T}$-Umgebungen klein sind; in diesem Fall wird von den in $\underline{Z}$ enthaltenen Informationen weniger Gebrauch gemacht (für beliebiges $\overline{T}$ können nur jeweils solche $\underline{y} \in \Pi \underline{Z}$ ausgenutzt werden, für die $\sum\limits_{\underline{y} \in \underline{Y}} t(\underline{y}) \leq \overline{T}$). Ist dagegen die Arbeitsgeschwindigkeit des Prozessors größer als die der $\mathfrak{P}$ zugewiesenen Kanäle, so kommt der Menge $\underline{Z}$ viel größere Bedeutung zu. Sollen trotz des in diesem Fall großen $\overline{T}$ die $\overline{T}$-Umgebungen hinreichend klein ausfallen, so müssen möglichst viele Wege der Kontrolle in jeder $\overline{T}$-Umgebung durch irgendwelche $\underline{y} \in \Pi \underline{Z}$ verlaufen. Man sieht hier, wieso die Effektivität des Algorithmus durch die Angabe möglichst vieler solcher $\underline{Y}$ verbessert wird.

5. Ausblick

Die vorangehenden Untersuchungen wurden für den Fall $h_o = 0$, d.h. vernachlässigbare Zugriffszeit, durchgeführt. Erweitert man die Betrachtungen auf den Fall $h_o \geq 0$ - dies bedeutet eine triviale Modifikation von UMGEBUNG - so hat man mit der Speichergröße, der Übertragungsrate und der Zugriffszeit die für das Speicherverwaltungsproblem wohl signifikantesten Parameter erfaßt. Für beliebige Werte dieser Parameter

möchte man für ein beliebiges vorgegebenes Programm der betrachteten Art eine Ladestrategie ermitteln, die eine gute Ausnutzung der Anlage gewährleistet, d.h. irgendeine gegebene Kostenfunktion von S',C' und T' klein hält, wobei S' bzw. C' für die
Anzahl der dem Programm zugewiesenen Speichereinheiten bzw. Kanäle steht und T' für
die Verarbeitungsdauer des Programms. Ohne hier zu versuchen, zu genauen Angaben zu
kommen, kann man folgende Struktur des Problems angeben.

Für sehr kleine Zugriffszeiten und sehr großes C' kann man (unabhängig von den in $\underline{Z}$
enthaltenen Angaben) mit kleinem S' minimales T' erreichen. Werden die Zugriffszei-
ten größer und|oder C' kleiner, so ist minimales T' noch immer zu erreichen, wenn S'
vergrößert wird und|oder $\underline{Z}$ ausgenutzt wird. Wird die Zugriffszeit weiter vergrößert
und|oder ist die Kanalleistung so 'teuer', daß C' weiter verkleinert werden muß,
dürfen nur noch solche Programmteile übertragen werden, bei denen die Wahrscheinlichkeit ihrer unmittelbar bevorstehenden Nutzung groß ist. Läuft die Kontrolle also in
ein im Arbeitsspeicher befindliches $\underline{U}_j$, darf dann demnach nicht mehr ganz $\underline{N}(\underline{U}_j)$
nachgeladen werden, wodurch sich der Vorteil eines geringeren Kernspeicherbedarfs
ergibt. Allerdings wird in diesem Fall T' im allgemeinen nicht mehr minimal, so daß
der Arbeitsspeicher des Programms für einige Zeit zwar belegt, aber völlig ungenutzt
bleibt. Da die Kontrolle beim Verlassen von $\underline{U}_j$ mit großer Wahrscheinlichkeit in eine
der zu diesem Zeitpunkt bereits nachgeladenen Nachbar-Umgebungen von $\underline{U}_j$ läuft, kann
der Zuwachs von T' gegenüber den vorigen Fällen noch recht klein sein. Werden bei
gegebenem S' übertragungsseitig weitere Einschränkungen vorgenommen - etwa durch Minimierung der gesamten Übertragungsarbeit oder durch die Voraussetzung, daß die Zugriffszeit größer ist als die Verweildauer der Kontrolle in den in die S' Arbeitsspeichereinheiten geladenen Programmteilen - so wächst T' und damit der Verlust
durch belegten aber ungenutzten Arbeitsspeicher weiter an; die nachzuladenden Teile
werden in diesem Fall erst zu dem Zeitpunkt bestimmt, in dem die Kontrolle die geladenen Programmteile verlassen will.

Die qualitative und quantitative Präzisierung der eben ausgeführten Überlegungen in
Hinblick auf das Problem der Organisation einer Speicherhierarchie und die Erweite-
rung des angegebenen Algorithmus dafür sollen an anderer Stelle geschehen, ebenso die
Erweiterung auf den probabilistischen Fall.

Literatur

[1] Denning, P. J.: Virtual Memory, Computing Surveys, Vol. 2, No. 3 (70)
[2] Knuth, D. E.: An Empirical Study of Fortran Programs, Software-Practice and
     Experience, Vol. 1, 1971
[3] Wagner, J.: Untersuchungen von Computer-Programmen mit graphentheoretischen
     Hilfsmitteln, Diplomarbeit an der TU Berlin, 1973
[4] EDV-Gesamtplan für die Wissenschaft im Land Berlin, 1972-1976
[5] Hatfield, D. J., Gerald, J.: Program Restructuring for Virtual Memory,
     IBM System Journal, No. 3, 1971
[6] Gentleman, W. M.: On the Relevance of Various Cost Models of Complexity,
     7. Annual Princeton Conference on Information Sciences and Systems,
     March 22-23, 1973

<u>SYSTEMIC ASPECTS OF MUSICAL ACTIVITY</u>
Stephen W. Smoliar

THE PROBLEM: THE MODELING OF MUSICAL ACTIVITY

In 1971 we presented a programming language, EUTERPE, as a tool for modeling musical
structures ([Smoliar, 1971]). We demonstrated that this language provided a formalism
wherein familiar concepts of musical analysis could be readily expressed. We also
discovered that the language could be used to produce intriguing specimens of original
composition ([Smoliar, 1972]). In this paper we wish to consider extending the
analytical and compositional potential of EUTERPE.

EUTERPE's modeling capabilities were founded on four basic concepts. First, the
language was an extension of assembly language (in this particular case, the MIDAS
assembler for a PDP-10 ([Samson])). Individual notes were represented by individual
words in memory; and sequences of these notes were represented by successive words -
as is the case with machine instructions. Second, repeated musical ideas could be
represented by subroutines. Third, pitch and duration were regarded as parameters,
external to the specification of a note, which could be altered by program control.
Finally, polyphony was represented by several programs running in parallel.

The design of EUTERPE was strongly influenced by conventions of music notation and
traditional style analysis ([Apel]). As the note is the basic unit of notation, so
the "note word" was the basic unit of execution ([Smoliar, 1972]). Within this framework, polyphony could be regarded as several of these note words being executed in
parallel. The individual programs which were simultaneously processed are closely
akin to the partbooks of the 15th and 16th centuries ([Apel]). The representation
of pitch and duration as independent external parameters also has its origins in
conventional clef signs, metronome markings, key signatures, etc. However, the
ability of subroutine calls to represent redundant musical elements, which, in more
traditional terms might be called themes, phrases, periods, and so forth ([Berry]),
was the major facility of the EUTERPE model.

Nevertheless, there are many aspects of musical compostion for which this model can
not adquately account. In order to cope with these aspects, we need the power of a
<u>system</u> capable of manipulating a hierarchy of programs of different faculties. If
we regard a musical composition as a EUTERPE program which, when it is executed by a
EUTERPE processor, produces a sequence of sounds which is recognizable as that particular composition, then we may consider to what extent the program is a reliable
model of the composition. For example, we can divide the program into those instructions which are note words and those which exercise control over note words - para-

meter alterations, sequencing, etc. - and form a program <u>schema</u> by abstracting all or
some of the information contained in each of the note words. We may now ask if it is
possible to obtain a schema which may then be said to represent the general <u>style</u> of
the composition.

On the surface this is similar to taking a strictly composed piece of twelve-tone
music, changing the permutation of the prime row, and "cranking out" a new piece.
However, suppose we are dealing with a more traditional form. [Smoliar, 1971] gives
a EUTERPE representation of Bach's two-part invention in D minor. Consider what
happens if we decide to alter the pitches of the principal theme. (To make matters
simpler, we shall leave the rhythm intact.) Our first observation is that if the
notes we choose are incompatible with the D minor tonality, the results will hardly
pass as fake Bach or, for that matter, as any representative of baroque invention.
However, even if we pay the tonality its proper respect, we still run the risk that
our program might produce parallel fifths or improper progressions involving the
tritone. These are, from the baroque point of view, "bugs" which the schema fails to
take into proper account. Furthermore, these bugs cannot be expressed in terms of
program flow or parameter manipulation and, as such, cannot be properly modeled within the EUTERPE formalism.   Therefore, we need a higher-level program capable of
supervising each realization of this schema with the intention of detecting and
resolving such bugs.

THE PROPOSAL: SOLUTION THROUGH SYSTEMS

As soon as we consider such a supervisor, we are talking in systemic terms. In fact,
many of our desiderata may be formulated in terms of computer operating systems.
What we called bugs in the preceding section may now be called "exceptions," inter-
ruptions which transfer control to the supervisor wherein the proper remedial action
is taken.   Notice that since "the proper remedial action" (if it exists at all) may
involve reworking a passage which, up to the point of interruption, had been satis-
factory, such actions cannot take place during "on-line performance." This dialogue
between schema and supervisor is essentially a compilation process the result of
which should be suitable for performance.

The introduction of a supervisor does not, in any way, detract from the activity at
the "voice program" level. Individual voice programs will still maintain control of
their subroutine calling sequences, pass parameters to each other, cue each other's
entries, etc. However, while in [Smoliar, 1971] the only supervisory function of the
EUTERPE interpreter was the synchronization of the voices' "performance" (i.e. the
realization of the note words as sound), we now stipulate a supervisor which may
observe events of which individual voice programs are implicitly "unaware" (such as
harmonic progressions) and, on the basis of these observations, influence and alter

the behavior of the voice programs.

Hence, the key role of the supervisor amounts to a debugging of an attempted execution of a given schema. The tools for this debugging process will consist of the specification of some basic set of exceptions accompanied by an appropriate library of "service routines" for coping with them. We claim that these tools embody the basic functions of what we conventionally call "music theory" and the "style" is simply a matter of the manner in which these facilities are employed.

To reiterate, we would like to model the _process_ of composition with respect to some particular style. (This latter qualification, we claim, is necessary. It is tantamount to the fact that we can only formulate a program with respect to some set of syntactic and semantic conventions - even if they are only implicit within the compiler.) This model is achieved through a four-stage process. First, we have a program schema, derived from some corpus of EUTERPE models of known compositions. Second, we have a proposed assignment of variables which will determine a specific realization of the schema. Third, we have the set of exceptions which determine the conditions for interrupting the attempted realization. Finally, we have the service routines which determine the course of action when an exception arises. Furthermore, these four stages constitute four independent variable levels of a system which, as a whole, is modeling the compositional process. If the user does not explicitly specify all four stages, then the system will have to fill in any existing gaps by drawing upon the available resources of a data library; but only after all four stages are set up can the attempted realization begin.

Thus, we may also encounter the problem of deciding _which_ procedures are to be fetched from the library and defining _what_ constitutes an exception. In a sense, the supervisor may need a supervisory state of its own, capable of manipulating catalogued procedures and possibly experimenting with more than one technique in search of a "best fit." Indeed, the more the system has to figure out "on its own," the more dependent it becomes on a firm basis for task creation and management, both on the voice program level and on the supervisory level.

Notice that we are, as in [Smoliar, 1971], considering a system which may be applied in matters of both analysis and composition. In this respect, we advocate [Laske]'s use of the word "performance" to designate "the different kinds of activity in which musical competence is manifested." There is no reason why a system capable of composition should not also be capable of analysis. On the one hand, we consider the realization of a schema as a compilation process which results in a data set which may be "played" (i.e. performed). Alternatively, we may consider such a data set as _input_ to an analysis program. Such a program may then hypothesize a schema (perhaps relying on "traditional" model-building techniques stored in a library) to which a particular realization is applied. The result of this realization may then be compared with the original input. Once the schema and realization procedure are suitably altered to match the input, we may claim to have an anlysis of the input.

THE CONSEQUENCES

One of the original intentions of EUTERPE was to provide a more formal approach to musical analysis ([Smoliar, 1971]). We claim that the approach taken in this paper is a further step in this direction. We have now broadened our domain from that of musical structures to the general process of composition. Musical structures are a significant element of this process, but they are just one component of a more complex system.

In certain respects, we may try to consider the natural language concepts of syntax and semantics in terms of how they would relate to our proposed system. Syntax, being a matter of well-formedness, may be regarded in terms of the representation of a musical activity as a EUTERPE program. Thus, with respect to the problem posed in the previous section, we may regard the parsing of our input data set as the composition of the EUTERPE program whose compilation will yield that same data set. Semantics, on the other hand, is the relationship between syntactic parsings and stylistic ideas, which is to say, musical forms. Thus, the semantic aspect of an analysis involves the search for the appropriate program schema and the proper supervisory environment for its realization.

In addition, we cannot afford to overlook the possible educational applications of such an approach. First of all, the student (and teacher) may consider music theory and composition in terms which, in [Laske]'s words, are "explicit and formal." Secondly, the attitude is constructive; one may approach the study of a given style as a problem in formulating procedures for the system to compose in that style. Finally, the student may use the system to analyse his own work, thus gaining deeper insight into its structural characteristics.

Finally, there are the creative implications of such a system. Thus far, we have only considered exercises of style as realizations of known schemata. On the other hand, if we can program the supervisor to monitor output with respect to a traditional theory, why not formulate an <u>original</u> theory for it to enforce? In fact, such a theory need not even have foundations which we would be inclined to call "musical." "Variations on a Theme of Steve Reich," discussed in [Smoliar, 1972], arose from experiments with pushdown stacks and interruption during an overflow. Nevertheless, the results are undisputedly musical. Composers would do well to consider [Dijkstra]'s description of LISP as a programming language which "has assisted a number of our

most gifted fellow humans in thinking previously impossible thoughts," for is this
not the ultimate goal of any creative artist? By influencing the way he thinks about
music, such a system can only extend the creative intellect of the composer.

R E F E R E N C E S

[Apel]   Apel, W. _Harvard Dictionary of Music_, The Belknap Press of
                 Harvard University Press, 1969.

[Berry]   Berry, W. _Form in Music_, Prentice-Hall, Inc., 1966.

[Dijkstra]   Dijkstra, E.W. The humble programmer. _Comm. ACM 15_, 10
                 (October 1972), 859–866.

[Laske]   Laske, O.E. Introduction to a generative theory of music.
                 Sonological Report No. 1, Institute of Sonology, Utrecht
                 State University, 1973.

[Samson]   Samson, P. MIDAS. Artificial Intelligence Project Memo 90,
                 Massachusetts Institute of Technology Project MAC, October,
                 1965.

[Smoliar, 1971] Smoliar, S.W. A parallel processing model of musical
                 structures. AI TR-242, Massachusetts Institute of Technology
                 Artificial Intelligence Laboratory, September, 1971.

[Smoliar, 1972] Smoliar S.W. Music theory – a programming linguistic
                 approach. _Proceedings of the ACM Annual Conference_, 1972,
                 1001–1014.

RECHNERORGANISATION
UND SCHALTWERKE

Ein Rechner mit der höheren Maschinensprache BASIC

A. Frick, H.J. Bürkle, Ch. Schlier

1.Einführung

Die natürliche Arbeitsweise eines Interpreters und die damit verbundenen Vorteile haben verschiedene Arbeiten zur Entwicklung von Rechnern mit höheren Maschinensprachen (high level language maschines) angeregt. Baskow, Sasson, Kronfeld (1) entwerfen eine FORTRAN- Maschine, Melbourne und Pugmuire (5) diskutieren eine mikroprogrammierte Maschine zu derselben Sprache. Weber (7) implementiert einen Interpreter zur Sprache EULER durch einen der Sprache angepaßten Maschinenbefehlsvorrat, dasselbe geschieht bei Hassitt, Lageschulte und Lyon (3) für APL. Vor allem aber ist die von Smith ,Rice, Chesley und anderen (6) entwickelte Timesharingmaschine mit der Sprache SYMBOL zu erwähnen.

In der hier vorgestellten Arbeit wird über einen Rechner berichtet, der als Maschinensprache die von Kemeny und Kurtz (4) entwickelte Dialogsprache BASIC hat, wobei im wirtschaftlichen Rahmen eines kleineren Rechners eine Anpassung der Register- und Zuordnerstruktur und des Steuerwerkes an die Aufgabe "Interpretation der Sprache BASIC durch Hardware" vorgenommen wurde. Der Hauptnachteil eines Softwareinterpreters, ineffiziente Durchführung, wird auf diese Weise beseitigt.

Im folgenden wird zunächst die Register- und Zuordnerstruktur erläutert, dann die Arbeitsweise des Steuerwerkes am Beispiel der Statement- und Ausdrucksverarbeitung demonstriert.

2.Rechnerstruktur

Das Steuerwerk des Rechners ist ein endlicher Automat. Zunächst wird seine Ein/Ausgabemenge behandelt, die alle Kombinationen von Steuer- und Abfragesignalen umfaßt, die an den verschiedenen Registern und Zuordnern zur Interpretation der Maschinensprache zur Verfügung stehen. Danach wird die Zustandsübergangs- und Ausgabefunktion dargestellt, die aus der Analyse der Syntax und Durchführung der Semantik der Sprache BASIC bestimmt sind.

2.1 Registertransferstruktur

Bild 1 zeigt die wichtigsten daten- und infomationsspeichernden Komponenten, ihre Zusammenschaltung und die in den folgenden Beispielen gebrauchten Steuer- und

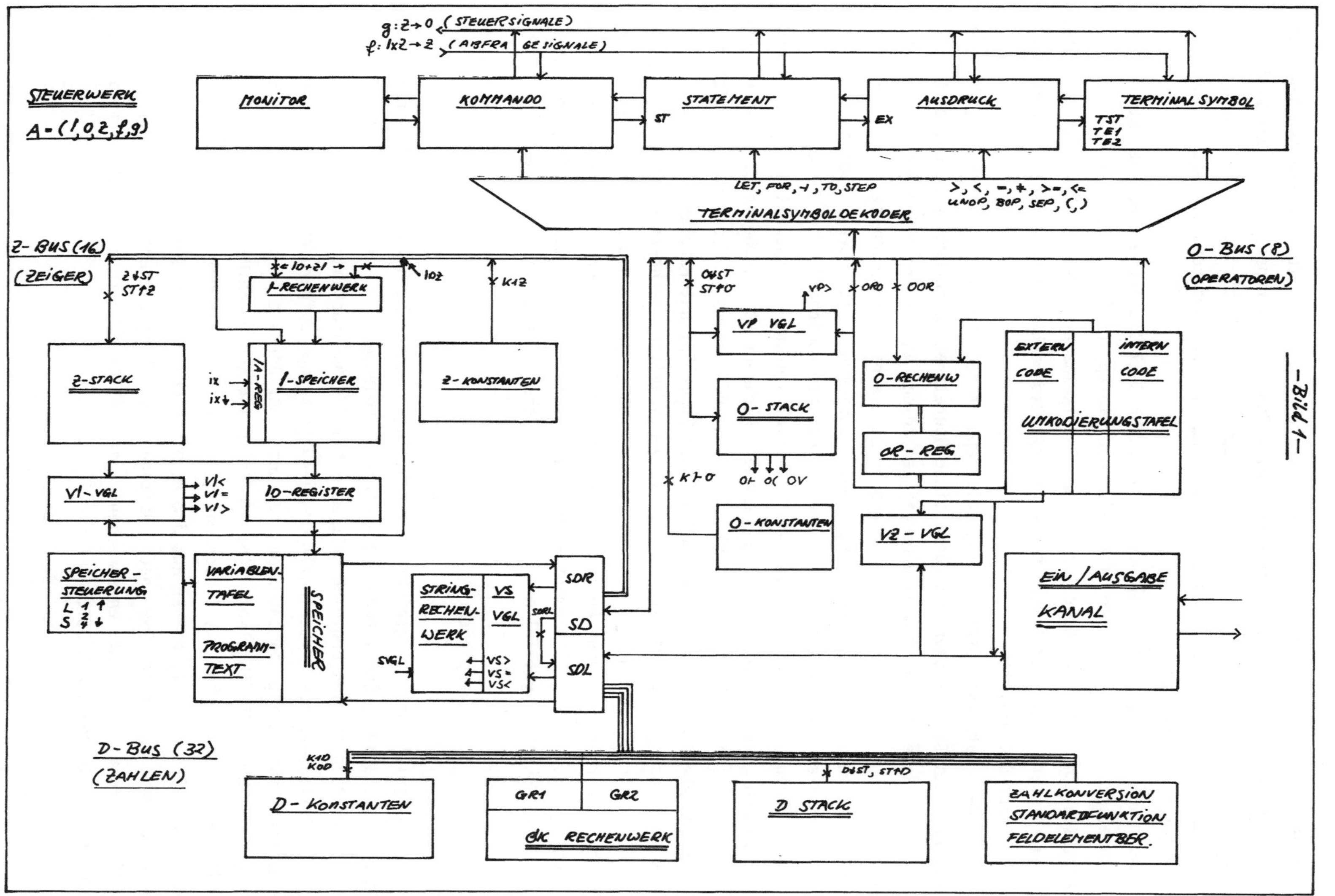

g: z → 0 (STEUERSIGNALE)
l: |x2 → 2 (ABFRAGE SIGNALE)
STEUERWERK
A = (l, o₂, l, g)
MONITOR
KOMMANDO
ST
STATEMENT
EX
AUSDRUCK
TERMINAL SYMBOL
TST TE1 TE2
TERMINALSYMBOLDEKODER
LET, FOR, →, TO, STEP
>, <, =, +, >=, <=
UNOP, BOP, SEP, (,)
Z-BUS (16) (ZEIGER)
O-BUS (8) (OPERATOREN)
ZVST STIZ
< IO+ZI >
IOZ
I-RECHENWERK
K1Z
OUST STPO
VP>
ORO OOR
VP VGL
Z-STACK
ix< ix+
IA-REG
I-SPEICHER
Z-KONSTANTEN
O-STACK
O-RECHENW
EXTERN CODE
INTERN CODE
UMKODIERUNGSTAFEL
OR-REG
K → O
O+ O- OV
V1-VGL
V1< V1= V1>
IO-REGISTER
O-KONSTANTEN
V2-VGL
SPEICHER-STEUERUNG
L 1 ↑ 2 S 4 ↓
VARIABLEN-TAFEL
PROGRAMM-TEXT
SPEICHER
STRING-RECHEN-WERK
VS-VGL
SVGL
VS> VS= VS<
SDR SD SDL
SDRL
EIN / AUSGABE KANAL
—Bild 1—
D-BUS (32) (ZAHLEN)
KID KOD
DST, STD
D-KONSTANTEN
GR1 GR2
DK-RECHENWERK
D-STACK
ZAHLKONVERSION
STANDARDFUNKTION
FELDELEMENTBER.

Abfragesignale. Entsprechend den verschiedenenen zu verarbeitenden Informationselemenenten besitzt der Rechner eine Komponentengruppe für Zahlen(Wortlänge 4 byte), für Zeiger(2 byte) und für Operatoren und Stringzeichen(1 byte). Alle Komponenten einer Gruppe sind unter sich und mit dem Speicherdatenregister durch je eine Sammelleitung verbunden.

Auf dem Datentyp Zahl, welcher in BASIC für Real,Integer und Boolean steht, sind arithmetische, logische und Vergleichsoperatoren erklärt. Ihre Durchführung wird hauptsächlich auf die Operationen am Gleitkommarechenwerk zurückgeführt. Dessen Datenregister (GR1, GR2) werden zur prioritätsgerechten Ausdrucksbearbeitung durch einen Stack DST erweitert.

Auf dem Datentyp String sind die Operatoren Vergleich, Verketten, Zerlegen erklärt. Das Stringrechenwerk führt diese Operatoren zeichenweise durch, da Strings variable Länge haben. Die dazu benötigten Zeiger auf Stringanfang und -ende stehen wie alle zur Interpretation gebrauchten Zeiger nicht im Hauptspeicher, sondern in einem besonderen Indexspeicher, der zusammen mit den Komponenten IA, ID,I-Rechenwerk,Vergleicher VI und Konstantenspeicher die Durchführung der verschiedenen Adreßoperationen wie "Initialisieren, Fortschalten, Umspeichern, Vergleichen von Zeigern" in einem Rechnertakt ermöglicht. Wegen der Schachtelungsmöglichkeit von Schleifen, Unterprogrammen, Funktionen, indizierten Variablen wird der Indexspeicher durch einen Stack ZST unterstützt.

Dem Instruktionsregister eines konventionellen Rechners entspricht hier das Operatorregister OR und der Operatorenstack OST, der mit dem Prioritätsvergleicher VP zur Abarbeitung von Ausdrücken notwendig ist. Zur Erkennung von Oper toren, Funktions-,Kommando-, Statementnamen und reservierten Worten bei Programmeingabe dient die Umkodierungstafel mit Zeichenvergleicher VZ und das O-Rechenwerk.

2.2 Operator Stringvergleich

Am Beispiel des Vergleichs zweier Strings beschreibt Bild 2 in ISP-Notation(2) Struktur, Steuerung und Verwendung einiger Komponenten.
Die Operation Stringvergleich SVGL wird bei der Ausdrucksbearbeitung nach Erkennen eines Teilausdruckes <String>{=|≠|>|<|>=|<=}<String> aufgerufen, wobei Anfangs- und Endzeiger für String1 im Indexspeicher unter der Adresse i1 bzw. i2 und für String2 unter i3 bzw. i4 abgelegt sind. In Zeile 1-4 der Durchführung wird zunächst mit Hilfe des Vergleichers VI abgefragt, ob ein String bereits abgearbeitet ist, in Zeile 5-6 wird ein Zeichenpaar aus dem Hauptspeicher in das Speicherdatenregister SD gelesen und in Zeile 7-9 nach Abfragen des Vergleichers VS verzweigt. Als Vergleichsresultat kommt entsprechend der BASIC-Semantik eine 1 (Vergleich wahr) oder eine o in den Stack DST.

$Bild 2$

1. KOMPONENTEN

$$S[0:16191]<8:1>, \quad SD<32:1>, \quad SDR = SD<16:1>, \quad SOL = SD<32:17>$$

$$I[0:15]<16:1>, \quad IA<4:1>, \quad ID<16:1>$$

$$DST[0:15]<32:1>, \quad OST[0:15]<8:1>$$

2. STEUER / ABFRAGE SIGNALE

$$VS \gtreqless := SOL \gtreqless SDR, \quad VI \gtreqless := ID \gtreqless I[IA]$$

$$SDRL \Rightarrow SOL \leftarrow SDR$$

$$ix \Rightarrow IA \leftarrow x \quad \{x := 1....16\}; \; \not{v} \Rightarrow ID \leftarrow I[IA]$$

$$L \Rightarrow SDR \leftarrow S[ID]; \; I[IA] \leftarrow I[IA] + 1$$

$$D\not{v}ST \Rightarrow DST[x] \leftarrow DST[x-1] \quad \{x := 1....16\}; \; DST[0] \leftarrow D\text{-}BUS$$

$$K1D \Rightarrow D\text{-}BUS \leftarrow 1, \quad K0D \Rightarrow D\text{-}BUS \leftarrow 0$$

$$ST\not{v}O \Rightarrow O\text{-}BUS \leftarrow OST[0]; \; OST[x-1] \leftarrow OST[x] \quad \{x := 1....16\}$$

3. STRINGVERGLEICH

$$SVGL \Rightarrow i1\not{v}; \; i2; \; (\neg VI< \Rightarrow; \; next \; i3\not{v}; \; i4; \; (\neg VI< \Rightarrow; \; next \; GL) \qquad 21$$

$$(VI< \Rightarrow; \; next \; KL) \qquad 22$$

$$(VI< \Rightarrow; \; next \; i3\not{v}; \; i4; \; (\neg VI< \Rightarrow; \; next \; GR) \qquad 23$$

$$(VI< \Rightarrow; \; next \qquad 24$$

$$i1\not{v}; \; L; \; SDRL; \; next \qquad 25$$

$$i3\not{v}; \; L; \qquad 26$$

$$(VS = \Rightarrow; \; next \; SVGL) \qquad 27$$

$$(VS > \Rightarrow; \; next \; GR) \qquad 28$$

$$(VS < \Rightarrow; \; next \; KL\;))) \qquad 29$$

$$KL := ST\not{v}O; \; (<_v <= \Rightarrow K1D; \; D\not{v}ST)$$

$$(\neg< \wedge \neg<= \Rightarrow K0D; \; D\not{v}ST)$$

$$GL := ST\not{v}O; \; (=_v <=_v >= \Rightarrow K1D; \; D\not{v}ST)$$

$$(\neq_v <_v > \Rightarrow K0D; \; D\not{v}ST)$$

$$GR := ST\not{v}O; \; (>_v >= \Rightarrow K1D; \; D\not{v}ST)$$

$$(\neg> \wedge \neg>= \Rightarrow K0D; \; D\not{v}ST)$$

2.3 Struktur des Steuerwerkes

Der Befehlshol- und Durchführungsphase eines konventionellen Rechners entspricht hier die Analyse der Syntax und die Durchführung der BASIC-Semantik. Die Struktur des Steuerwerkes ist deshalb durch die Syntax vorgegeben, die "Top-down" analysiert wird, semantische Teile fügen sich ein. Entsprechend der Aufteilung der BASIC-Grammatik in Feingrammatiken besteht das Steuerwerk aus den Unterwerken Kommando-, Statement-, Ausdruck- und BASIC-Endsymbolverarbeitung (Bild 1). Die dem letzten Werk zugrundeliegende Grammatik beschreibt die Zusammensetzung von Sprachelementen wie Statementcodes, Operatorcodes, Zahlen, Variablen in der mnemotechnisch redundanten externen und in der transliterierten internen Darstellung. Dagegen sind die übrigen Grammatiken intern und extern von derselben Struktur und stützen sich nur auf eine interne Darstellung der Terminalsymbole. Im übrigen muß die Formulierung der Grammatik der Realität der Implementierung angepaßt sein und folgende Forderung erfüllen:

1. Sie sollte eine minimale Zahl von Nichtterminalsymbolen enthalten, da jedem von ihnen ein innerer Zustand des Steuerautomaten entspricht.

2. Sie muß sackgassenfrei sein, damit das Zerteilungsverfahren effektiv ("non back up ") arbeitet.

3. Es dürfen keine Produktionen vorkommen, die ein endlicher Automat nicht verarbeiten kann wie beispielsweise <exp> →(<exp>).

Die übliche BNF (Chomsky 2)- Formulierung erfüllt diese Forderungen nicht. Eine Chomsky 3- Formulierung andererseits verlangt die Einführung sehr vieler Nichtterminalsymbole. Dagegen wird in der in den folgenden Beispielen verwendeten kontextsensitiven Formulierung die Äquivalenz mit der tatsächlichen Arbeitsweise der Maschine deutlich. Sie kommt bei der Syntaxanalyse von BASIC mit 1oo inneren Zuständen aus.

2.4 Statementautomat

Bild 3 zeigt am Beispiel des Statement für Zuordnung LET und für Schleifeneröffnung FOR, wie das grammatikalische Symbol < Statement> durch das Statementwerk bearbeitet wird.

Die erste Produktion bewirkt zunächst den Aufruf des Unterautomaten TST (Terminalsymbol Statement), der den nächsten Statementcode beschafft und dessen internen Code (LET, FOR,..) im Operatorenregister OR ablegt. Durch Abfrage dieses Codes (ORO ⇒ OBus← OR) ist eine sackgassenfreie Entscheidung darüber möglich, wodurch danach <St-body> zu ersetzten bzw. wohin im Automatengraphen zu verzweigen ist. Beim Statement LET erfordert Produktion P3L den Aufruf des Ausdrucksautomaten EX, wobei durch den Merker A (Assignement) diesem mitgeteilt wird, daß der Ausdruck

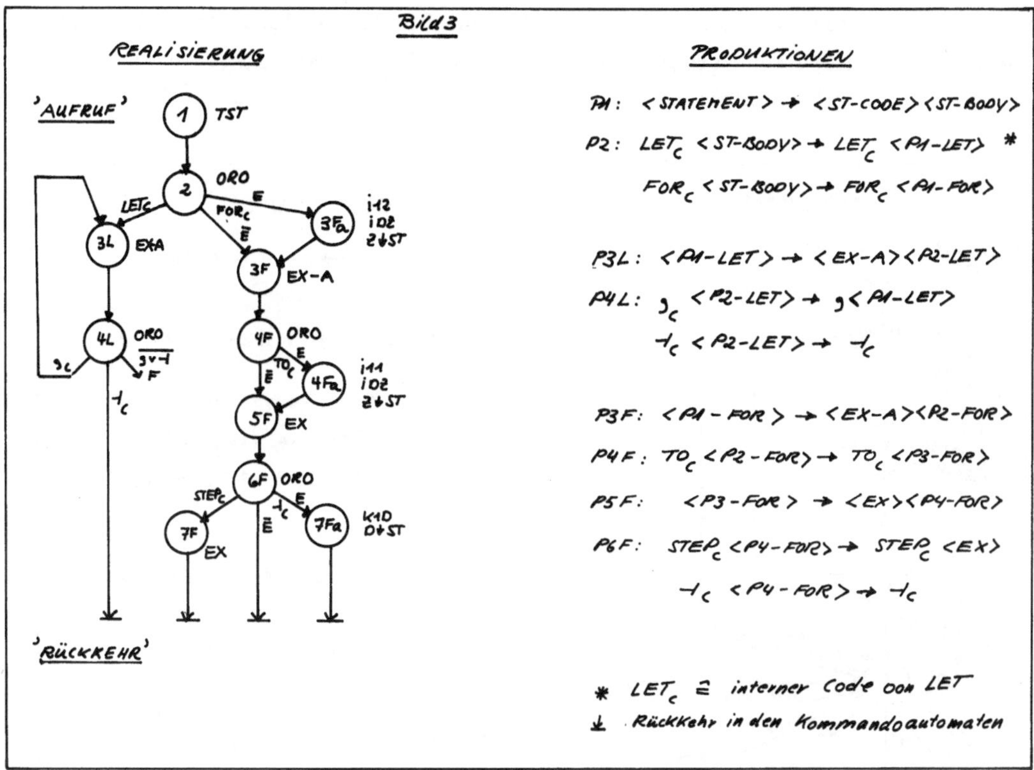

als erstes Symbol eine Variable, als ersten Operator einen Zuordnungsoperator enthalten muß. Der Ausdrucksautomat meldet sich mit einem Endzeichen zurück, das als Kontext für die Produktion P4L abgefragt wird. Beim Statement FOR wird in P3F ebenfalls ein Zuordnungsausdruck erwartet, der mit dem Endsymbol TO abschließen muß. Die Produktionen P4F-P6F beschreiben die restliche Syntax.

Der Graph zur Syntaxanalyse wird sowohl bei Programmeingabe zur Fehlererkennung als auch bei Durchführung (Merker E=Execution gesetzt) zur Anwendung der Semantik durchlaufen. Während bei LET die gesamte Durchführung bei EX liegt, sind bei FOR weitere Zustände nötig, wo die Schleifenanfangsadresse in Register i12(Zustand 3a) und der Name der Schleifenvariablen in Register i11(4a) auf dem Z-Stack gestapelt (IDZ;Z↓ST) und bei Fehlen von STEP(7a) als Defektschrittweite eine 1 auf dem D-Stack abgelegt wird (K1D;D↓ST).

2.5 Ausdrucksautomat

Die Grammatik der Statements ruft an mehreren Stellen die der Ausdrücke auf. Bild 4 zeigt die der Arbeitsweise des Rechners entsprechende Syntax und ihre Realisierung durch einen Automatengraphen, wobei die Behandlung der Felder, Funktionen und

Strings der Übersicht halber weggelassen sind. Die Abarbeitung der hierarchischen Struktur von Ausdrücken stützt sich auf den Operatorenstack, wobei dessen Belegungshöhe durch Indizierung der Produktionen der Ausdrucksgrammatik ausgedrückt werden kann.

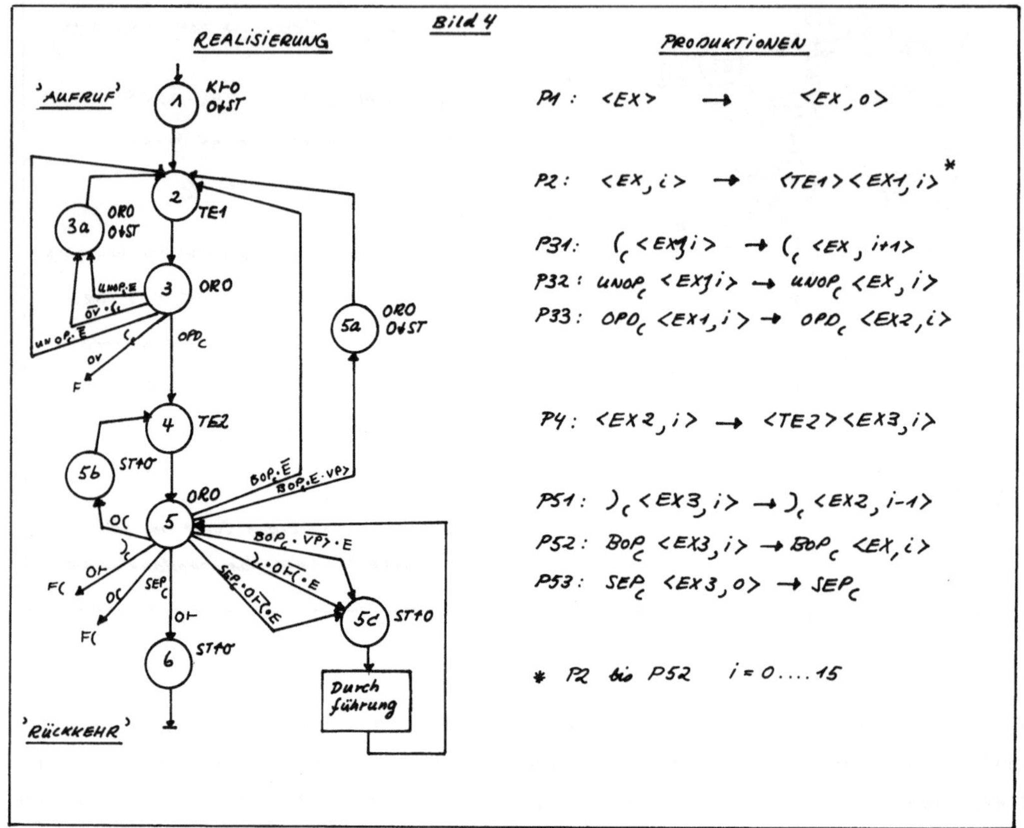

Bei der Produktion P1 wird der Index auf o gesetzt, was dem Ablegen des Stackbodenzeichens (K⊢O;O↓ST) entspricht. Produktion P2 bis P52 gilt für die Indizes i=o bis 15 entsprechend der Stackhöhe, Produktion P53 nur für i=o.
P2 verlangt das Aufrufen des Unterautomaten TE1, der das nächste anstehende Terminalsymbol, welches eine Klammer, ein unitärer Operator(UNOP) oder ein Operand (OPD) sein kann, beschafft und seinen internen Code in OR ablegt. Im Zustand 3 wird gemäß den Produktionen P3 verzweigt. Bei einer Klammer wird der Index erhöht. Dem entspricht das Ablegen der Klammer auf dem Stack im Zustand 3a. Entsprechend Produktion P4 wird im Zustand 4 der Unterautomat TE2 aufgerufen, der als nächstes Terminalsymbol eine Klammer, einen binären Operator (BOP) oder einen Seperator (SEP:= ⊢ v,vTOvSTEP usw)in OR ablegt. Bei der Klammer wird der Index erniedrigt, was dem Entfernen der entsprechenden öffnenden Klammer vom Stack im Zustand 5b

entspricht.

Der Fehler "Stacküberlauf" wird in Produktion P31 (i=15), "Linke Klammer fehlt " in Produktion P51 (i=o), "rechte Klammer fehlt" in P53 (i≠o) und in den entsprechenden Zuständen 3 (Ov:= OST voll) bzw. 5 (O⊢ und O(:= Zeichen auf OST ist⊢ oder Klammer) erkannt.

Die Einschränkung, die von dem Merker A verlangt wird, erfordert weitere Fehlerabfragen in Zustand 3 und 5, die durch Einführung eines Kontext in der Grammatik ausgedrückt werden können, was im Bild aber nicht geschehen ist.

Zur Durchführung der Semantik sind zusätzlich 2 Zustände nötig, wo nach dem bekannten Stackverfahren mithilfe des Prioritätsvergleichers VP(VP>:= Priorität(OR) Priorität(OST[o])) die Operatoren auf dem Stack abgelegt (5a) bzw. gelesen (5c) und durchgeführt werden. Die Aufbereitung der Operanden, d.h. Lesen und Ablegen ihrer Werte bzw. Zeiger in den D bzw. Z-Stack leistet der Unterautomat TE1. Ein Durchführungsbeispiel für einen Operator ist der in 2.2 behandelte Stringvergleich.

Wie man am Graphen sieht, liegt sowohl bei Programmeingabe als auch bei Durchführung seiner Arbeitsweise die Infixnotation von Ausdrücken zugrunde. Die Postfixnotation (UPN) würde zwar die Einsparung von Zustand 5a und 5c ermöglichen, wo ein Operator auf dem O-Stack abgelegt und wieder gelesen wird, was gegenüber dem Lesen der Operanden und Operatoren aus dem Speicher, dem Abfragen und Durchführen etwa 1o% Zeitgewinn bringen würde, jedoch 3 verschiedene Algorithmen erfordern, "Infix-Postfix-Übersetzung","Durchführung von Postfix" und "Postfix- Infix-Übersetzung" für die Programmauflistung, was etwa den doppelten Implementierungsaufwand bedeuten würde. In einer Softwareimplementierung dagegen fällt der Zeitbedarf viel stärker ins Gewicht, da Zugriffe auf die im Speicher liegenden Stacks und Abfragen von Stackzeichen, Priorität, Operatortyp verglichen mit dieser Maschine unverhältnismäßig viel Zeit brauchen.

3. Schlußbemerkungen

Vergleicht man die Arbeitsweise des BASIC-Rechners bei der Behandlung der geschilderten Beispiele mit einem Interpreter, der eine konventionelle Rechnerstruktur verwendet, so wird deutlich, wie durch relativ einfachen Ausbau der Steuer- und Abfragemöglichkeiten die Zahl der zur Durchführung benötigten Zustände verringert wurde. Während bei ca. 3oo Steuer- und Abfragesignalen hier etwa 55o Zustände für Analyse und Durchführung der Gesamtsprache benötigt wurden, sind dies bei einem Softwareinterpreter für die Implementierung derselben Sprache bei etwa 5o Steuer- und Abfragesignalen 1oKbyte Befehle, was mindestens 2o K Zuständen entspricht. Wie verschiedene GAMM-Mix-Vergleiche zeigen, ist die Laufzeit eines Programmes auf diesem BASIC-Rechner deshalb 25-5o mal kürzer als bei Softwareinterpretern und auch kürzer als bei Assemblercodierung desselben Problems (bei gleichem Grundtakt, Speicherzugriff und gleicher Rechengeschwindigkeit).

Der Aufwand für die Realisierung der Automatengraphen, die in Schrittsteuerung abgebildet wurden, beträgt etwa 6oo SSI-TTL- und für die Registerstruktur 4oo MSI-TTL Schaltkreise.

Aus der Implementierung ergeben sich viele Hinweise darauf, welcher Art ein zweckmäßiger höherintegrierter Bausatz zur Realisierung eines sprachorientierten Rechners sein sollte.

Die Arbeit wurde mit einer Entwicklungs- und Bauzeit von 3 Mannjahren unter finanzieller Unterstützung der Deutschen Forschungsgemeinschaft durchgeführt.

Literatur

(1) Bashkow,T.R.,Sasson,A., and Kronfeld, A. System design of a Fortran machine. IEEE Trans. Electronic Computers,EC-16(1967) 485-499.

(2) Bell,C.G., Newell,A, Computer Structures: Readings and Examples Mc Graw-Hill,Inc. 1971.

(3) Hassitt,A.,Lageschulte,J.W., and Lyon,L.E., Implementation of a High Level Language Machine. Comm. ACM 16,4 (April 9. 1973) 199-212.

(4) Kemeny,J.K. and Kurtz,T.E., BASIC Programming, John Wiley&Sons, Inc., New. York, 1972.

(5) Melbourne,A.J. and Pugmire,J.M., A small computer for the direct processing of Fortran statements. Comput. J. 8 (1965), 24 -27.

(6) Smith, W.R., Rice,R., Chesley,G.D., Laliotis,T.A., Lundstrom,S.F., Calhoun,M.A., Gerould,L.D and Cook,T.G., SYMBOL: A large experimental system exploring major replacement of software. PROC.AFIPS 1971 SJCC, Vol 39, AFIPS Press, Montvale,N.J. pp 6o1-616.

(7) Weber,H., A microprogrammed implementation of Euler on IBM 36o/3o. Comm ACM 1o,9 (Sept. 1967),549-558.

HIERARCHY OF INTERPRETERS FOR MODELLING COMPLEX DIGITAL SYSTEMS

R. Hartenstein

Summary

The purpose of this paper is to present the proposal of a partitioning scheme as a method for modelling complex digital hardware systems. This proposal is aiming at the use of uniform descriptional tools for as many levels as possible within the hierarchy of languages in an implementation of a hardware/software system. And it is aiming at the use of a uniform functional partitioning scheme in modelling each of the implementation layers. This paper is an attempt of a contribution for bridging the educational gap between the fields of software engineering and hardware engineering. The first part of this paper deals with the description of the model and its application to modelling existing systems for pedagogic purposes. In the final part of this paper a guideline for architectural designs derived from the model, is discussed.

Introduction

The advent of LSI technology and the rapidly decreasing hardware cost more and more gives reason for a discussion on the replacement of pieces of software by additional hardware. (The consequences of this development are discussed elsewhere, e.g. $|1|$.) But one severe difficulty in making use of the increased freedom in design decisions is (1.) the mutual lack of understanding between the fields of hardware engineering and software engineering. Another obstackle is (2.) the common complexity problem, causing lack of transparency in a pedagogical sense. Complexity problems, being one reason of the "software crisis", are growing more and more important on the side of the hardware, due to growing complexity of hardware by using _more_ hardware than before.

To meet those 2 types of problems mentioned above, a method for an integral modelling of all implementational levels is needed, that (1.) reveals the underlying common principles of hardware and software more clearly, and (2.) gives structuring rules for meeting complexity in (a.) modelling existing systems and in (b.) designing new systems and (3.) delivers implementation-independant notional and notational tools. Known semantic models of programming languages are not very helpful for the hardware man, as they deal with abstract data structures, but not with the physical carriers of semantic processes on data. What is needed, is the establishment of a low level semantics, which may appear as some kind of pragmatics with respect to traditional semantic modelling. An approach into this direction will be sketched below.

On modelling digital processors

The subject of this paper is based on the sequential version of the information structure model on the execution of programs, described elsewhere (e.g. in chapter 4 of $|2|$), where an information structure model is a tripel $M = (J,J^o,F)$, with the set J of information configurations (snapshots), the subset $J^o \subset J$ of initial information configurations, and the set F of transformation operators on J. The set J is subdivided by $J = (C,P,D)$ into a control component C, a program component P, and a data component D, according to fig. 1 (instruction pointer ip and data pointer dp are used for scanning P and D under control of C). Fig. 1, not being delivered from hardware men, is uncomplete for architectural use, as it is not showing the embedding of F into the model. This embedding of F is performed by another model, not delivered by software men, and showed by the block diagram in fig. 2, and described elsewhere (e.g. $|3|$ and $|4|$). The "controller" K combines P and C from fig. 1, and F containes the "resources" for the implementation of the set F of transformations. F and D are connected by data paths for the transfer of arguments and results. The "order vector" Y is a selector word for selecting and activating the subset of F, required for the actual step in the sequence of transformations on D. Status vector X denotes feedback from F to C for decision purposes.

Supplement to this paper: see page 508 of this volume.

Automata-oriented Modelling

Some authors model K separately (e.g. $|5|$ and $|6|$) and one models the combination of K and C (see $|3|$ and $|4|$) by finite state machines. It has been demonstrated $|7|$, that these models may be extended into a hierarchy by replacing the model of K by a finite state transducer (see fig. 3). Thus we get a hierarchical model, according to fig. 4, where each F_i of a level i appears being implemented by use of K_{i-1} and F_{i-1} of the next lower level i-1. By using this hierarchical model we have the free choice to look at a specific arbitrary level i out of this hierarchy by modelling it according to fig. 2.

Programming-Language-oriented Modelling

The hierarchy of processes in a program-controlled digital processor implements a hierarchy of languages (demonstrated e.g. in $|8|$), and does not primarily appear as a hierarchy of automata. Fig. 5 shows an example for the levels of languages, according to $|8|$, in a microprogrammed DHLLP (direct high level language processor, for a survey see $|9|$) as an example with L for 'language', h for 'hi level', j for 'intermediate', m for 'machine' μ for 'micro', and r for 'submicro structures', and M for 'execution means'. This is an arbitrary example with respect to number, sequence, and types of the used language layers. In terms of language hierarchy the program P_{i-1} is an interpreter for program P_i, as for instance P_μ for P_m, as showed by fig. 5. It would be very useful to have a model, which is more language-oriented, than the more automata-oriented models mentioned above, and which should have the following characteristics:

1. applicability to modelling hardware and software, and both integratedly,

2. capability to form hierarchies,

3. independancy from the means of implementation.

The characteristic Nr. 1 is gained by utilizing proximities between programming languages and register transfer languages. This leads to modelling in terms of interpretations, and not in terms of state transitions. Such a model should be more detailed and less abstract than automata models.

Interpreter scheme used as a model

A model, which may be regarded as an implementation or a refinement of the automata-oriented models, can be derived from the fact, that each program execution can be subdivided into cycles with the following 3 subcycles, showed by flow diagram in fig. 6:

1. <u>the fetch subcycle</u> for the selection of the next element $l_k \in L$ from the program store, where L is the language $L = \{l_1, l_2,...,l_k,...,l_n\}$. This selection is performed via adjustment of the instruction pointer ip (see fig. 1);

2. <u>the recognition subcycle</u>, which performes a test, whether the selected element $P|p_i|$ is a legal element with $P|p_i|\in L$, and which performs the recognition of the specific $l_k \in L$, being represented by $P|p_i|$, if legal;

3. <u>the execution subcycle</u>, which performs the proper semantic operations on the data structure D, as resulting from the recognition subcycle.

The hardware carrier media, implementing this interpretation process, may be subdivided into modules by establishing interfaces according to these subcycles. Such a functional partitioning of carrier media results in a hardware block structure, as showed by fig. 7, which is yielded by imbedding into the structure in fig. 1. In fig. 7 P denotes the programm store, C the control module, responsible for proper sequencing of the stream of language objects from P, entering C via instruction buffer IB, R denotes the recognition device, having the two submodules (not showed here) CL (classifier) and AL (action lexicon), the output of R (which is produced by AL) is the order vector Y, evoking semantic actions to be performed by the semantic module F, and the control vector Y', evoking control actions to be performed

by control module C. F is the implementation of the available set of transformations
F on the data structure D, represented by the register set in Block D of Fig. 7.

Linking Interpreters together to form a Hierarchy

Before the description of signal transfers between the modules in fig. 7 is completed, the synthesis of a hierarchy of such structures is demonstrated (see fig. 8):
the programs in P_{i-1} and the resources C_{i-1}, P_{i-1}, F_{i-1} are tools for implementing
the interpreter I_i for the interpretation of programs stored in P_i. F_i formes a conceptual machine (or real machine), which receives orders via the transfer path A
(see fig. 7) from the R-module R_i of the next higher level carriers. After having
transmitted an order word via A to F_i, the module C_i, together with P_i and R_i and
all modules of higher levels, remain in an inactive "waiting state", until via path
S (see fig. 7) and "end-of-exection" message "end" is fed back from F_i. Thus the
two paths A and S (see also fig. 3) are links to the next higher level of carrier
hardware modules. On the other side the two paths Y and X (see fig. 7) are links to
the next lower level of modules, formed inside F (see also fig. 3). Thus a hardware
- supported block structure of nested interpreters is formed, called HIM, as an
acronym for "Hierarchy of Interpreter Models".

Connections inside one level

Inside one level of HIM, there are the following transfer paths for interconnecting
the modules (see fig. 7). Calling a program via path A causes the transition of the
interpreter I into an initial state via adjustment of IP to the appropriate program
entry point in P. Such a call is evoked by the end message of the forerunner pro-
gram in P, recognized by R as described above. The fetched instruction P |IP|
buffered into IB, is analyzed by R. The resulting order Vector Y is looked up from
AL in R and fed to F, evoking the activation of the required subset of data paths
in F for the appropriate register transfers between registers in D, from E (emit
field in IB), E^+ (emit fields from higher levels, if implemented), to D, or for performing I/O.

I/O to or from D is activated in an indirect manner by placing I/O control messages
into special interface registers in D, as for instance a "read"-bit or a "write"-bit,
when core storage is external as in the microprogram level. The control vector Y',
derived by R from the contents of IB controls via decision logic DL(see fig. 9) inside C the adjustment of IP for the next fetch cycle. By path X the following in-
fluences on the operation of C are implemented: the cycle time of C via a clock bit
or a synchronization bit in X, the decision for the adjustment of IP by status bits
in X, and the request of a call from the next higher level by an end-bit in Y', as
described above. The combination of modules C, R and F is the interpreter I, inter-
preting the program(s) in P.

Functional partitioning of resources may be modelled by splitting Y into subvectors
$Y^{(1)}$, $Y^{(2)}$ and transmitting them to separate submodules $F^{(1)}$, $F^{(2)}$,... of module F.
Such a partitioning may be modelled in any level.

The use of the HIM scheme

In a course on computer architecture fundamentals this conceptual framework of HIM
is used for imbedding various register transfer structures and microprogrammed control structures, as well as hardware carriers for higher level language processes
into the complex hardware/software structure of a system. In this course the HIM
concept was used for a implementation-invariant modelling of different levels in a
uniform manner (see |9|), and with approaches for revealing analogies in different
leyers of implementation. The following section shows some examples for modifications of the HIM-modules for adapting them to different levels of language and different degrees of complexity.

The modules in one level of a HIM scheme

The C-module may be a relatively simple structure, if no subprogram techniques are
used, and all programs are always resident in P. For the modelling of subprogram
techniques the instruction pointer IP is extended to a pointer stack IPS, and in the

case of an internal subroutine call the request of an order via path A is replaced
by a stack operation on IPS. C is extended by a paging mechanism, when P is a multi-
level storage.

The R-module may be a decoder network, when used for modelling the decoding of a
machine instruction or a microinstruction. R may be implemented in a more sophisticated manner and sequentially, when constructs of a higher level language with a
wide variety of sentence formats have to be analyzed. The decoding of instructions
of byte-oriented machines is an example of decoding variable length objects parallely.
In |14| is demonstrated, how the equivalence of sequential networks and combinational
networks can be used for a uniform modelling of decoder networks and a class of parsing algorithms in terms of a set of register transfer primitives. This idea allows
a uniform modelling of a wide variety of R-modules from different levels of a complex
digital systems. So the AL-submodule of R may be a table (in higher levels), a wiring
scheme (in lower levels) or even a model for the pulse phase level below the register
transfer level, which is useful for pedagogic purposes and for the analysis of the
behavior of certain register transfer structures without using formal tools of the
level of logic design (see |14|).

The F-module is a combination of all transfer carriers, used for semantic purposes,
such as gated transfer paths, paths from and to registers for the implementation of
register assignment operations, and transformational transfer paths, such as arithmetic and logic nets, when it is used for modelling F in the microprogram level. In
higher levels the F-module appears as a combination of abstract transfer carriers,
yielded by omittion of intermediate transfer steps implemented in lower levels.

The D-module is the set of all data containers, such as read/write registers and
read-only registers (constants or emit field inputs), which are directly or implicitly adressable by constructs of the language L, used for P. Those data containers,
which are adressable by language L only indirectly, are parts of the external data
structures, called I/O in fig. 7. Those data containers are directly or implicitly
addressable only within one of the higher levels of the hierarchy. Those registers,
which are not at all addressable by language L, may be addressable within lower levels
of the hierarchy, not modelled in the present level. Sometimes there are registers,
which belong to 2 (or more?) levels D-modules simultaneously, as for instance the
accumulator register or sometimes other general registers, addressable by L_m and by
L_μ and thus belonging to D_m and D_μ simultaneously (see fig. 9). In such a case D_m and
D_μ are overlapping, as e.g. shown in fig. 9.

Problems of using the HIM scheme for modelling existing systems

Fig. 9 demonstrates the pedagogic use for structuring the register transfer carriers
of a microprogrammed instruction set processor by modelling it into a 2 - levels'
scheme. The HIM scheme is also useful for modelling more than 2 levels and also for
modelling higher language levels. It is difficult, to embed compiler software and
assemblers into the HIM scheme, but the HIM scheme is especially appropriate and useful for modelling a particular class of architectures, getting more and more into
focus of common interest: the DHLLP-architecture. Before giving more explanation to
the problem of the applicability of the HIM, let me define 2 types of architectural
implementations:

        1. structured hardware, and

        2. tricky hardware.

"Structured hardware" is easily modelled by HIM scheme in a straight-forward manner,
whereas "tricky hardware" is a very bad object for being modelled by a HIM. The reason
for the difficulties in modelling is the use of functional time-sharing in hardware
modules of a "tricky hardware". This functional time-sharing requires different HIM
schemes for different snapshots of the system at different subcycles of operation.
A complete modelling would require a separate sampling time pattern for each particular level of the model, in order to get separate snapshot sequences for each particular level. May be, that some cases of tricky hardware, such a set of snapshot
sequences would be a better description, than an informal description would be. But
at least it is true, that "structured hardware" is easily modelled by a HIM scheme,

whereas "tricky hardware" is not.

Tricky hardware

Typical examples of tricky hardware are the von NEUMANN - machine and the "stored-logic machine" (see e.g. in $|10|$), where we find a timeshared use of one storage device with its accessing organs for P_m and D_m (von NEUMANN machine) or for P_m and P_μ and D_m (stored-logic machine). But the working storage is not the only hardware module used in a time-shared manner. Parts of the F_m-module are often used for implementing parts of the C_m and R_m modules. It may be summarized, that the design of tricky hardware is a typical phenomenon of the pioneers times in the design of computers. The motivation for tricky design efforts came from the very high hardware cost, from the volume of hardware, and from problems of heat dissipation in early times, and it came from tradition in later times. May be, that in some cases the wish for demonstrating skill was a motivation, caused by an inferiority complex, rooted in the educational situation of the young discipline of computer architecture (which was poor, compared to the well-established glamorous formalisms of neighbour disciplines).

Towards structured hardware

In the 70ies there is a tendency for transfering more and more complexity from the software part to the hardware part of a system. This is demonstrated by the successive advent of the following classes of architectures, as classified by CHU $|9|$:

1. von NEUMANN-type architectures (classical instruction set proc.)

2. syntax-oriented architecture (one example is the B 5500)

3. IHLL-architecture (indirect-HLL, survey: see $|9|$, see also $|11|$)

4. DHLL-architecture (survey: see $|9|$, see also $|12,13|$).

This sequence of architecture types demonstrates the following developmental trends in system concepts:

a) the upper boundary language level for easy application of the HIM scheme is raized from class to class. The HIM scheme easily includes the hardware support of problem-oriented high level languages, when a DHLLP is modelled;

b) the increasing complexity of hardware carriers makes it more and more advisable not to produce tricky hardware, but to produce structured hardware instead;

c) because of low hardware cost, the extremely efficient utilization of particular hardware submodules is no more a relevant design objective. This leads to using more hardware instead of trickiness;

d) a growing tendency to functional partitioning of hardware (e.g. see $|1|$) yields a tendency to more structured hardware.

These developments make systems more and more appropriate for presentation within the conceptual framework of the HIM scheme. One effect of using the HIM scheme is an increase of transparency in presentation, and, as increasing complexity of hardware requires more transparency, so the HIM scheme is a method for designing "structured hardware" to meet complexity problems. So let me list some guidelines for the design of structured hardware, guidelines, derived from the HIM scheme. One suggestion in this direction is: separate storage media for program information from those for data information, or at least provide separate accessing interfaces for emulating the separation of P from D. In a similar manner there should be a strict separation between different levels within the hierarchy, and between the storage of definitional information (tables e.t.c.) and value information (D modules). By following this suggestion it would be possible to realize another suggestion: the design should utilize a functional partitioning of hardware modules, fitting into the framework of the HIM scheme. The hardware modules should not form overlaps between HIM modules. A deviation from HIM scheme should only form submodules of HIM modules.

Final remarks

One important application for structured hardware (and structured representation of hardware) would be the field of education in computer science. Besides another important application seems to be in the commercial field. The "software crisis" demonstrated the usefulness of pedagogic structuring concepts as parts of designing guidelines to meet complexity problems of practitioners. The HIM scheme of block-structured hardware is an attempt of contributing such a structuring concept. The author is aware of the fact, that the limited space of this paper does not allow to demonstrate the versatility and the usefulness of this interpretation-oriented framework.

References:

1 Foster, C.C.: "A view of Computer Architecture", CACM 15 (1972), 7 (July).

2 Wegner, P.: "Data Structure Models for Programming Languages", SIGPLAN-NOTICES.

3 Wendt, S.: "Eine Methode zum Entwurf komplexer Schaltwerke unter Verwendung spezieller Ablaufdiagramme", Elektron. Rechenanl. (eR), 12 (1970), 6 (Dec.)

4 Wendt, S.: "Zur Systematik von Mikroprogramm-Strukturen", Elektron. Rechenanl. (eR), 13 (1971), 1 (Febr.)

5 Ghushkov, V.: "Automata theory and formal microprogram transformations" KIBERNETIKA, vol. 1, no. 5 (1965)

6 Cascaglia, G.F., Gerace, G.B., Vanneschi, M.: "Equivalent models and comparison of microprogrammed Systems", Internal report no. 3, Spec. Ser. Conv. CNR-ENI, CNR Pisa 1971

7 Hartenstein, R.: "Über die Schnittstelle zwischen Hardware und Software", Informatik Colloquium der Universität Hamburg, 19. Mai 1971

8 Lawson jr., H.W.: "The Changing Role of Microprogramming", ACM, Seminar Course, Readings, 1972

9 Chu, Y.: "Introducing to High-level-language Computer Architecture", TR-227, Univ. of Maryld., Comp. Sc. Center, Febr. 1973

10 Chu, Y.: "Computer Organization and Microprogramming", Prentice Hall, Englewood Cliffs 1972

11 Hassitt, A., Lageschulte, J.W., Lyon, L.E.: "Implementation of a High Level Language Machine", CACM 16 (1973), 4 (April)

12 Bjørner, D.: "On the Definition of Higher-Level-Language Machines", Proc. Symp. on Computers and Automata, New York 1971, Polytechnic Press, Brocklyn, N.Y. 1971.

13 Frick, A.: "Ein Rechner mit problem-orientierter Maschinensprache BASIC", Informatik-Kolloquium, Univ. Karlsruhe, 9. Juli 1973.

14 Hartenstein, R.: "On a Set of Register Transfer Primitives", SIGMICRO Newsletter, to appear in vol. 4 (1973).

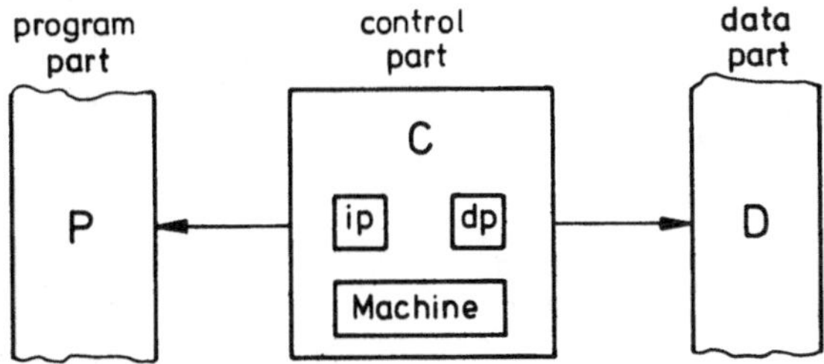

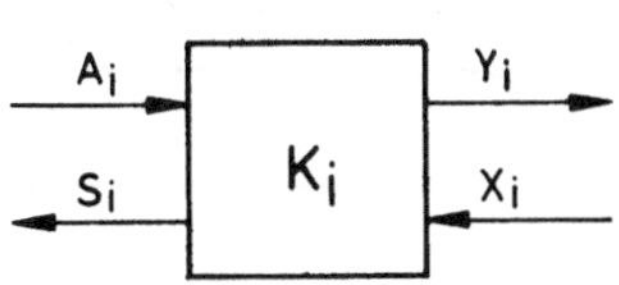

Y_i order alphabet

X_i feedback alphabet

A_i start alphabet
(transitions to an initial
state)

S_i status alphabet
(labels of final states)

fig. 3

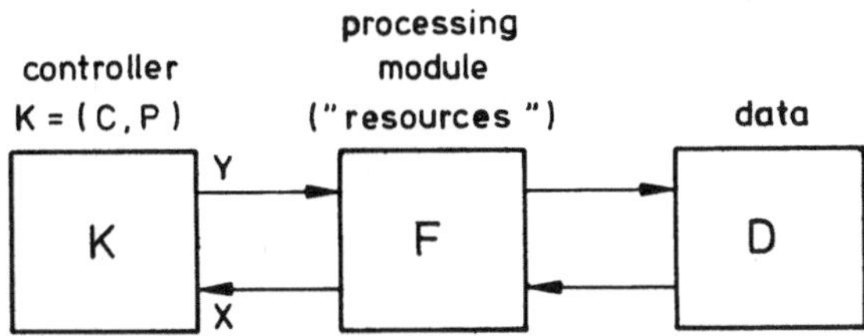

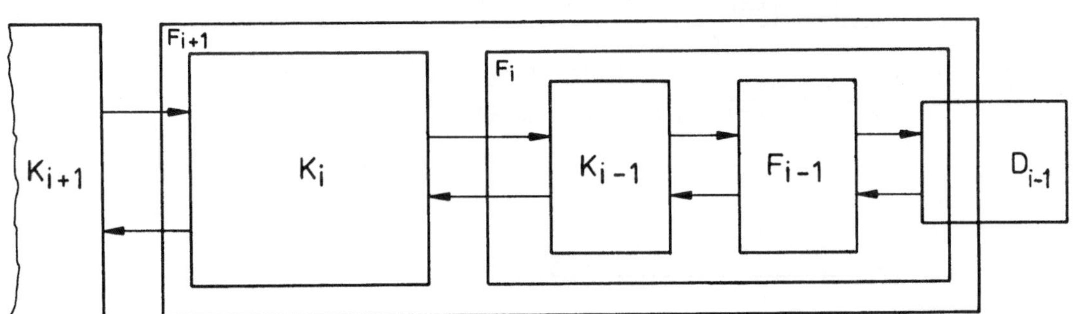

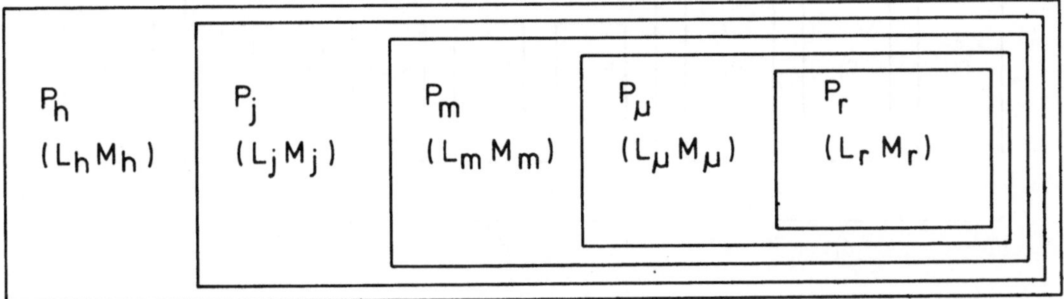

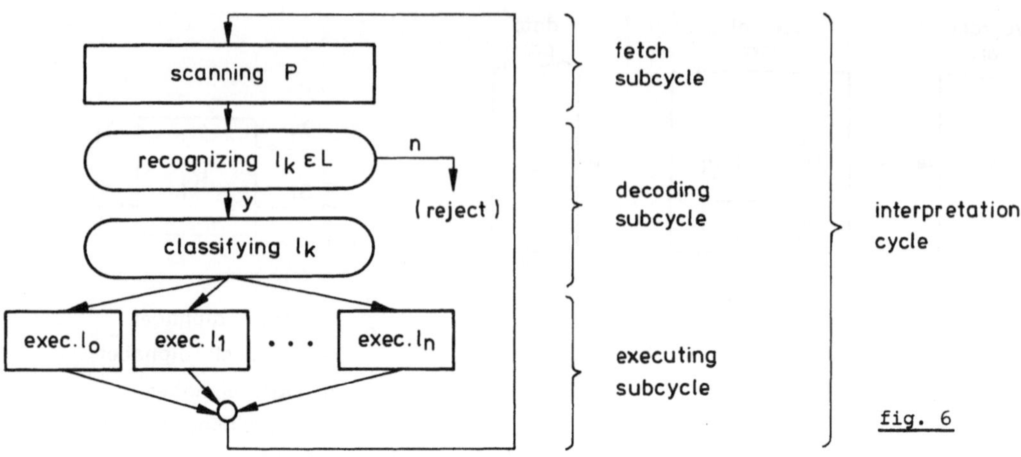

fig. 6

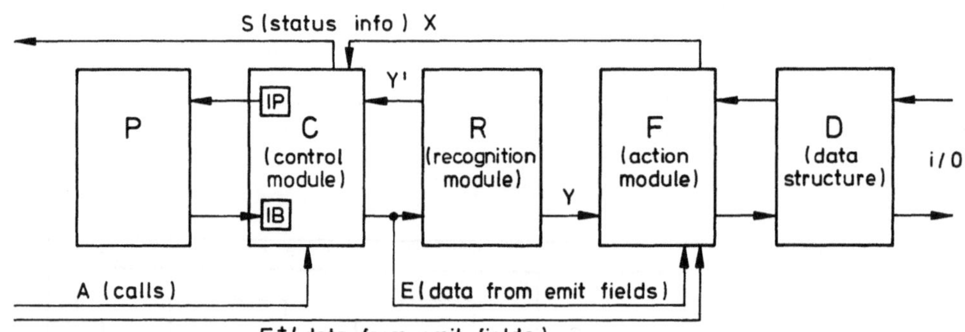

fig. 7

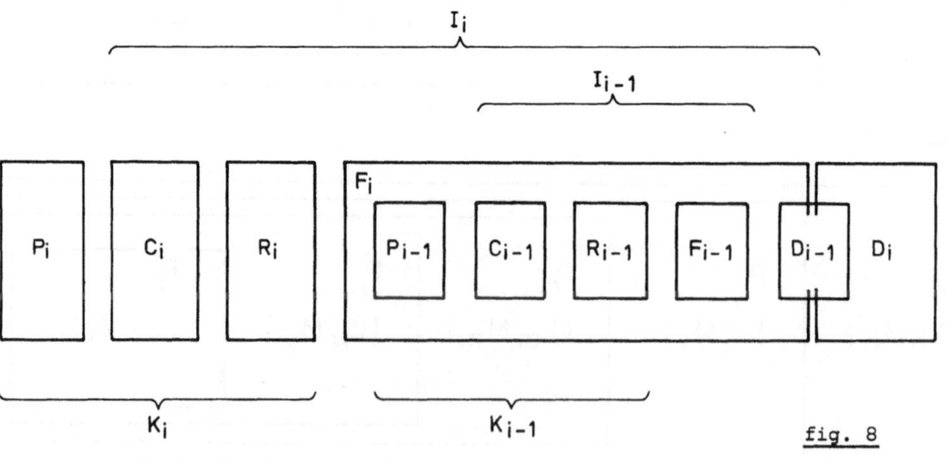

fig. 8

Core Stor.
XR
MQ
ACC
Dm
Dμ
AR
K
Fμ (ALU, Gates, etc.)
Rμ
DL
Cμ
μP
+1
μB
Pμ (Lμ)
emit field of mB
Fm
Rm
DL
Cm
mP
+1
mB
Pm (Lm)
Am

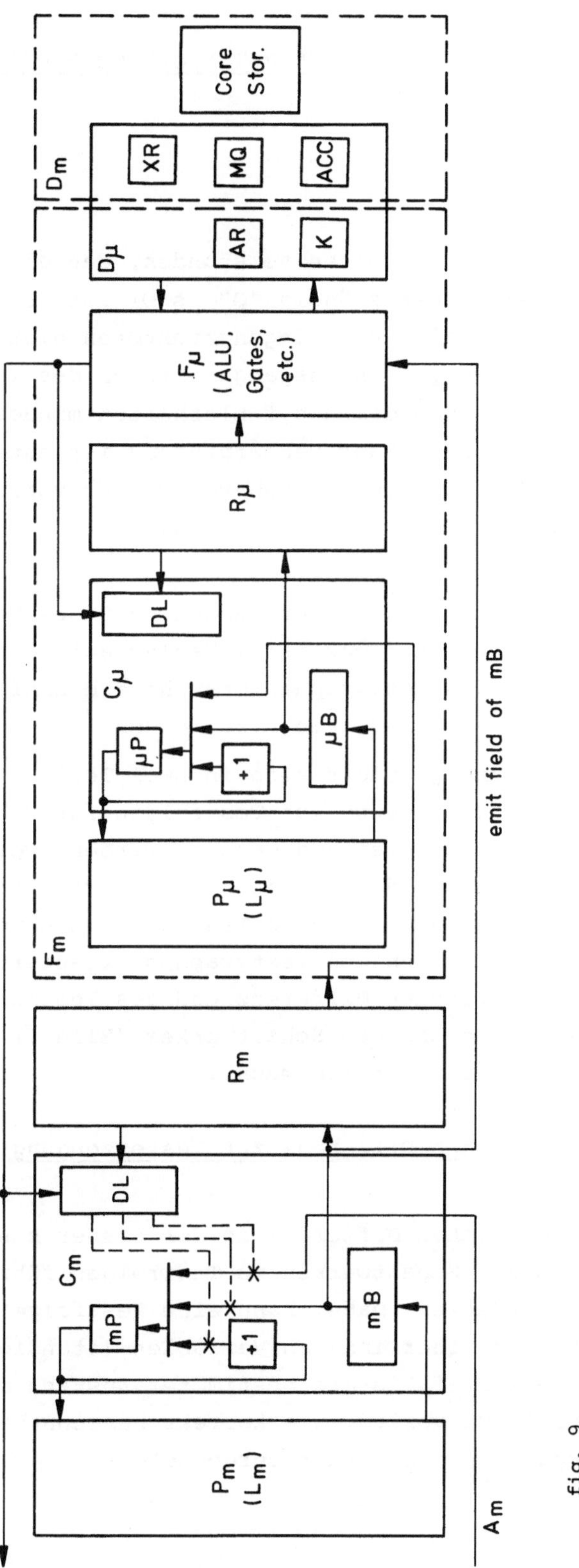

fig. 9

Wolfgang Escher

ERZEUGUNG VON BRAUCHBAREN TESTFOLGEN MIT BOOLESCHER DIFFERENZ UND TESTGRAPHEN

1. Einleitung

Definitionen:

Unter einem Fehler sei im folgenden verstanden, daß eine logische Variable ständig "1" (s 1) oder ständig "O" (s O) ist. Ein Fehler ist erkennbar, wenn es eine Folge von Eingangsvektoren gibt (eine Testfolge) derart, daß die Folge von Ausgangsvektoren des intakten Schaltnetzes bzw. -werkes sich von der des fehlerhaften mindestens einmal unterscheidet. Das Ergebnis einer Fehlerprüfung ist entsprechend die Feststellung, ob mindestens ein erkennbarer Fehler vorliegt oder nicht. Die Fehlerlokalisierung stellt darüber hinaus fest, in welchem Teil des Schaltwerkes ein Fehler vorliegt.

Unter der "Einfehlerannahme" wird verstanden, daß das betrachtete Schaltnetz bzw. Schaltwerk nur maximal 1 Fehler aufweist. Bei dem vorgeschlagenen Verfahren des Testgraphen braucht die Einfehlerannahme nicht notwendigerweise zugrunde gelegt zu werden.

Die folgende Beschreibung gliedert sich in zwei Teile:
Zum einen soll auf die Berechnung von Testfolgen für Schaltwerke mit Boolescher Differenz eingegangen und gezeigt werden, welche inkorrekten Tests sich bei Anwendung der Booleschen Differenz ergeben können und wie die genaue Berechnung korrekte Testfolgen nachweist.
Zum anderen soll das Verfahren des Testgraphen erläutert werden.
Beide Verfahren der Booleschen Differenz und des Testgraphen werden an dem Beispiel eines sehr einfachen Schaltwerkes (Bild 1) demonstriert, das jedoch die Problematik deutlich macht.

2. Anwendung der Booleschen Differenz zur Testerzeugung bei Schaltwerken

Die Anwendung der Booleschen Differenz in der bisher beschriebenen Form ($|3|,|8|$) kann bei Schaltwerken zu Testfolgen führen, die gewisse Fehler nicht entdecken. Dabei kann eine Testfolge bei einem Schaltwerk einen Fehler einer inneren Variablen (ständig 1 oder ständig O) nur entdecken, falls ein bestimmter Zustand des Schaltwerks vor Anlegen der Testfolge vorlag. Die korrekt berechnete Testfolge ist im allgemeinen länger als die vorher berechnete.

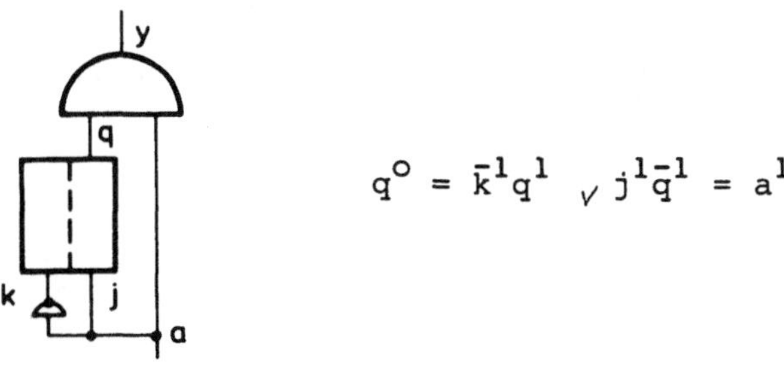

$$q^O = \bar{k}^1 q^1 \; _V \; j^1 \bar{q}^1 = a^1$$

<u>Bild 1:</u> Schaltwerk: $q^O = \bar{k}^1 q^1 \; _V \; j^1 \bar{q}^1 = a^1$ *)

Für die folgende Berechnung wird die Einfehlerannahme zugrunde gelegt.
Bei dem in Bild 1 gezeigten Beispiel eines Schaltwerkes ergibt sich
bei der üblichen Berechnung der Booleschen Differenz für den Fehler
jsl die Testfolge:

$$TF \; (aa^1 a^2) = 100 \tag{1}$$

mit

$$y = 1 \text{ für } j \text{ s } 1$$

Diese Folge erkennt den Fehler j s 1 nicht , falls $q^2 = O$ ist, wie
man sich leicht herleiten kann. Zu beachten ist, daß die Testfolge
die Zeiten 1,2 umfaßt, die Beobachtung aber zur Zeit O stattfinden
muß.

Bei Schaltnetzen, bei denen die Einfehlerannahme sicherstellt, daß
keine weiteren fehlerbehafteten Variablen in die betrachteten Funktionen eingehen, wird die fehlerbehaftete Variable nach Bildung der Booleschen Differenz eliminiert. Alle restlichen Variablen, die zur Rechnung
herangezogen werden, sind als fehlerfrei angenommen.

Bei Schaltwerken tritt die fehlerbehaftete Variable in den zur Berechnung weiterhin herangezogenen Zeitabschnitten (vorher oder nachher)
noch auf.

Der Rechnungsgang zur Erzeugung der Testfolge ist:

$$y = aq = a(j\bar{q} \; v \; \bar{k}q)^1 = a(j\bar{q} \; \ddagger \; \bar{k}q)^1 \tag{2}$$

$$y_{j1} = a\bar{q}^{-1} \tag{3}$$

außerdem muß gelten:

$$j^1 = O \text{ d.h.: } a^1 = O \tag{4}$$

Daher folgt die "Testbedingungsfolge":

---

*) Schreibweise: Der hochgestellte Index gibt den (negativen) Zeitindex
   an: a zur Zeit t= -2: a^2 , der Zeitindex O wird ggf. weggelassen.

$$\text{TF } (aa^1 q^1) = (100) \tag{5}$$

Bis hierher ist der Rechnungsgang korrekt, da keine zeitverschiedenen Funktionen verwendet wurden.

$$q^1 = (j\bar{q} \vee \bar{k}q)^2 \tag{6}$$

Im fehlerfreien Fall gilt:

$$\bar{q}^1 = \bar{a}^2 \tag{7}$$

Für die Berechnung der Testfolge aus der Testbedingungsfolge (5) darf man nicht die Fehlerfreiheit von (6) annehmen und Gleichung (7) in (5) substituieren. Statt dessen muß $\bar{q}^1$ berechnet werden:

$$\bar{q}^1 = (\overline{j\bar{q} \vee \bar{k}q})^2 = (\bar{j}k \vee \bar{j}\bar{q} \vee kq)^2 \tag{8}$$

Da: $\bar{q}^1 = 1$ sein soll, wird probeweise gesetzt:

$$\bar{j}^2 k^2 = 1 \tag{9}$$

es folgt daher $j^2 = 0$ und $k^2 = 1$.

Dies ist aber ein Widerspruch zur Fehlerannahme (j ständig 1)!

Zwanglos resultiert, daß der Term $k^2 q^2$ hier die Bedingung $\bar{q}^1 = 1$ ergibt, jedoch nur dann, wenn $q^2 = 1$ ist. Das ist genau der Fall, an dem die oben angeführte Testfolge (1) zu korrektem Ergebnis führt. Zur genauen Berechnung ist also die Betrachtung von:

$$k^2 j^3 \bar{q}^3 \vee k^2 \bar{k}^3 q^3 = 1 \tag{10}$$

nötig. Hier gilt die Fallunterscheidung:

α) für $\bar{q}^3 = 1$ muß $k^2 j^3 = 1$ und $\tag{11}$

β) für $q^3 = 1$ muß $k^2 \bar{k}^3 = 1$ sichergestellt werden. $\tag{12}$

Da

$$k^i = \bar{a}^i \tag{13}$$

ist, folgt, daß nur Bedingung β erfüllt werden muß, wenn man den Fehler js1 nachweisen will. Daher ergibt sich als korrekte Testfolge:

$$\text{TF } (aa^1 a^2 a^3) = (1001) \tag{14}$$

Tabelle 1 zeigt das Verhalten des fehlerfreien und des fehlerbehafteten Schaltwerks bei Anlegen dieser Testfolge.

Bei entsprechender genauer Berechnung der Booleschen Differenz kann diese also ein geeignetes Mittel sein, um Testfolgen auch bei Schaltwerken aufzufinden. Ein Vorteil ist die konsequente Berechenbarkeit aus dem in (3) angegebenen Ansatz. Als Nachteil ist zu werten, daß die schon in diesem Beispiel auftretende Fallunterscheidung in kombinatorische Probleme münden kann, die den Rechengang ausweiten.

-t	3	2	1	0
a	1	0	0	1
q	x	1	0	0
y	x	0	0	0
q	x	1	0	1
y	x	0	0	1

bei jsl { (Zeilen q, y)

Tabelle 1: Verhalten des fehlerfreien und fehlerbehafteten
Schaltwerkes.

3. Testfindung mit dem Testgraphen TG:

Das Originalschaltnetz bzw. -schaltwerk wird durch eine bzw. mehrere
Transformationen in den sogenannten Testgraphen für den Ausgang 0
(TG^O) und den Testgraphen für den Ausgang 1 (TG^1) überführt. Es wird
die folgende Schreibweise der Variablen bzw. der die Variablen reprä-
sentierenden Knoten des Graphen vereinbart:

Knoten
bzw. : a_b , a_b^d Wert einer Variablen a_b^{dc} a_b^c
Variable   zur Zeit c

Indices: b: Zählindex b = 1, 2, 3, ..., R

             c: Zeitvariable c = 0, 1, 2, ..., P, c = 1 entspr. t = -1
                für getaktete Variablen, c = 0 aktuelle Zeit. (Der In-
                dex c = 0 kann entfallen.)

             d: Wertangabe: d = 0, 1

             Nicht benötigte Indices werden gegebenenfalls weggelassen.

Eine Variable im Schaltnetz bzw. Schaltwerk beschreibt einen Anschluß
(Eingang oder Ausgang eines Schaltgliedes). Im Graphenbild wird eine
Variable durch einen oder zwei Knoten repräsentiert. Für den Fall, daß
eine Variable durch einen Knoten repräsentiert wird, kann diesem Knoten ein Wert zugeordnet werden, der aussagt, ob die diesem Knoten entsprechende Variable den Wert 0 oder 1 annimmt.

Für den Fall, daß eine Variable durch zwei Knoten repräsentiert wird,
bedeutet es, daß ein Knoten für den Wert 0 und ein Knoten für den Wert
1 der Variablen auftritt. Der Wert dieses Knotens ist dann folgendermaßen definiert: der Wert des Knotens ist 1, wenn der Wert der zugehörigen Variablen dem Knoten entspricht und umgekehrt.

Die zwei Knoten verbindende Kante kann den Wert L annehmen, dabei ist
L eine positive ganze Zahl: L = O, 1, 2, ..., n. Die Bedeutung dabei
ist, daß L der Zeitverzögerung entspricht. Wenn Laufzeiten nicht betrachtet werden , besitzen bei Schaltnetzen alle Kanten die Länge L = O.
In diesem Fall kann die Länge weggelassen werden. Zwischen dem Knoten
a_i^d und dem Paar a_{Ni}^1 , d_{Ni}^O (a_{Ni}: Nachfolger des Knoten a_i) können keine,
eine oder zwei Kanten angeordnet sein:

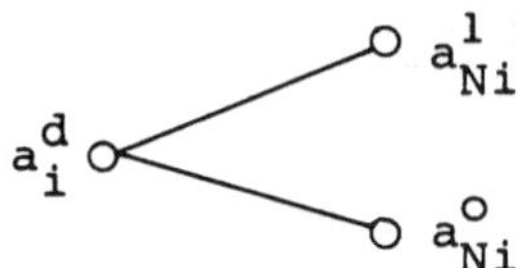

F entspricht einem Fehler in der Weise, daß der Wert einer Variablen
ständig O oder ständig 1 ist.

F_i^d: Fehler an a_i^d liegt vor, in der Form, daß a_i ständig d ist.

$\overline{F}_i^d$:   Fehler a_i ständig d liegt nicht vor.

In Bild 2 sind die während des Verfahrens erzeugten Graphen und die
notwendigen Transformationen dargestellt. Die Transformation TT ist
eine topologische Transformation.

Sie muß feststellen, ob ein Schaltnetz bzw. Schaltwerk vorliegt und
gegebenenfalls Rückkopplungen auftrennen bzw. bei Speichergliedern
entsprechende Rückführungsknoten einfügen. Weiterhin sind Verzwei-
gungspunkte einzuführen. Der sich ergebende Graph MSG wird danach
auf Fehlerklassen-Strukturen untersucht. Eine Fehlerklassen-Struktur
entspricht dabei einer Fehlerfortpflanzung in der Weise, wie sie in
Bild 3 für ein UND-Glied dargestellt ist.

Bei einem UND-Glied wird ein Fehler am Eingang (a_1 ständig O oder a_2
ständig O) am Ausgang erkannt, da sich der Ausgang dann verhält, als
wenn ein Fehler a_3 ständig O vorliegt. Dieses wird in dem Fehler-
klassen-Strukturgraphen FCSG dargestellt. Dieser Graph enthält dementsprechend sämtliche Fehlerfortpflanzungen (Klassen nicht unter-
scheidbarer Fehler). Er enthält doppelt so viel Knoten, wie der Graph
MSG wegen der Aufspaltung der Variablen. Aus diesem Graphen erhält man
durch Zusammenziehen je zweier Knoten zu einem den Fehlergraphen FG.
Dabei muß das Knotenargument KA 1 festgestellt werden. Es gibt an, ob
der Fehler ständig O oder der ständig 1, beide oder gar kein Fehler
fortgepflanzt werden. Gleichzeitig muß die Länge der Kante bei Schaltwerken eingeführt werden.

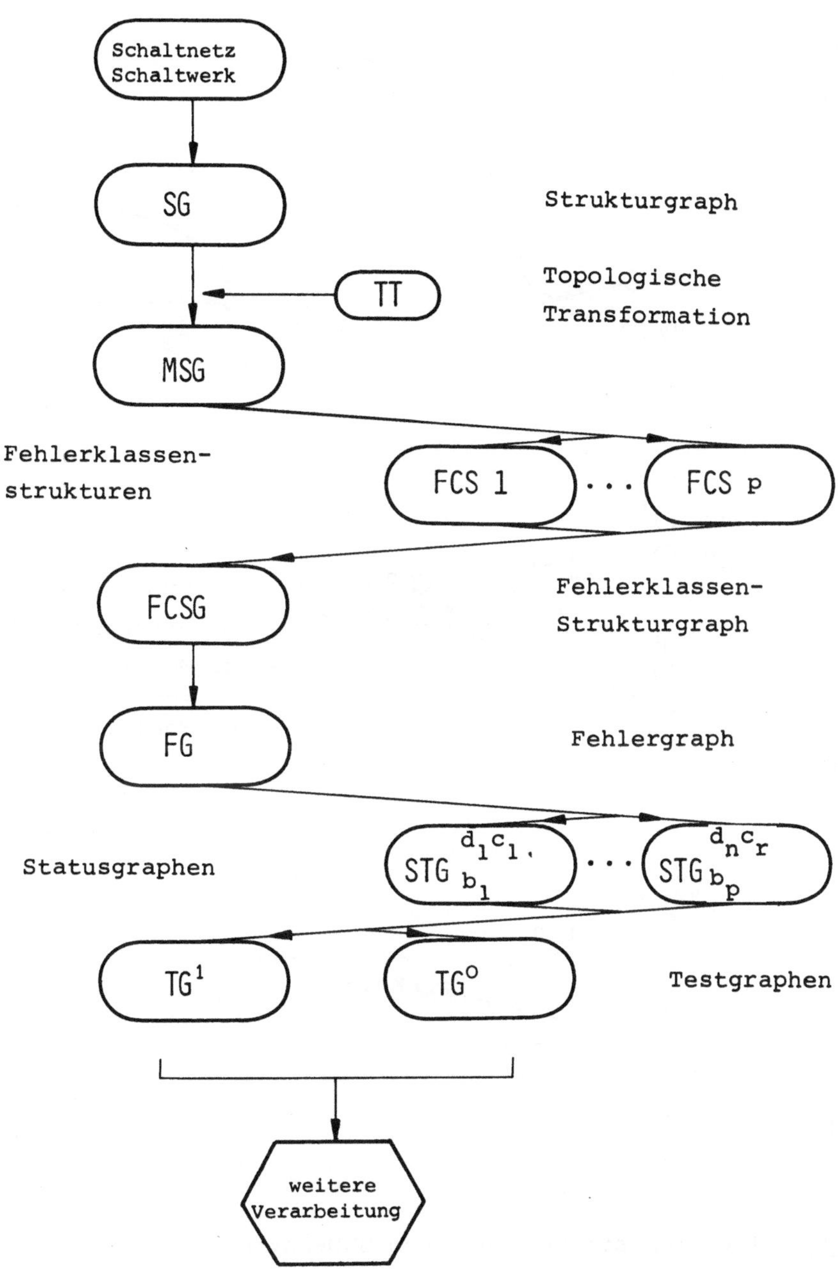

Bild 2: Reihenfolge des Vorgehens zur Erzeugung des Testgraphen.

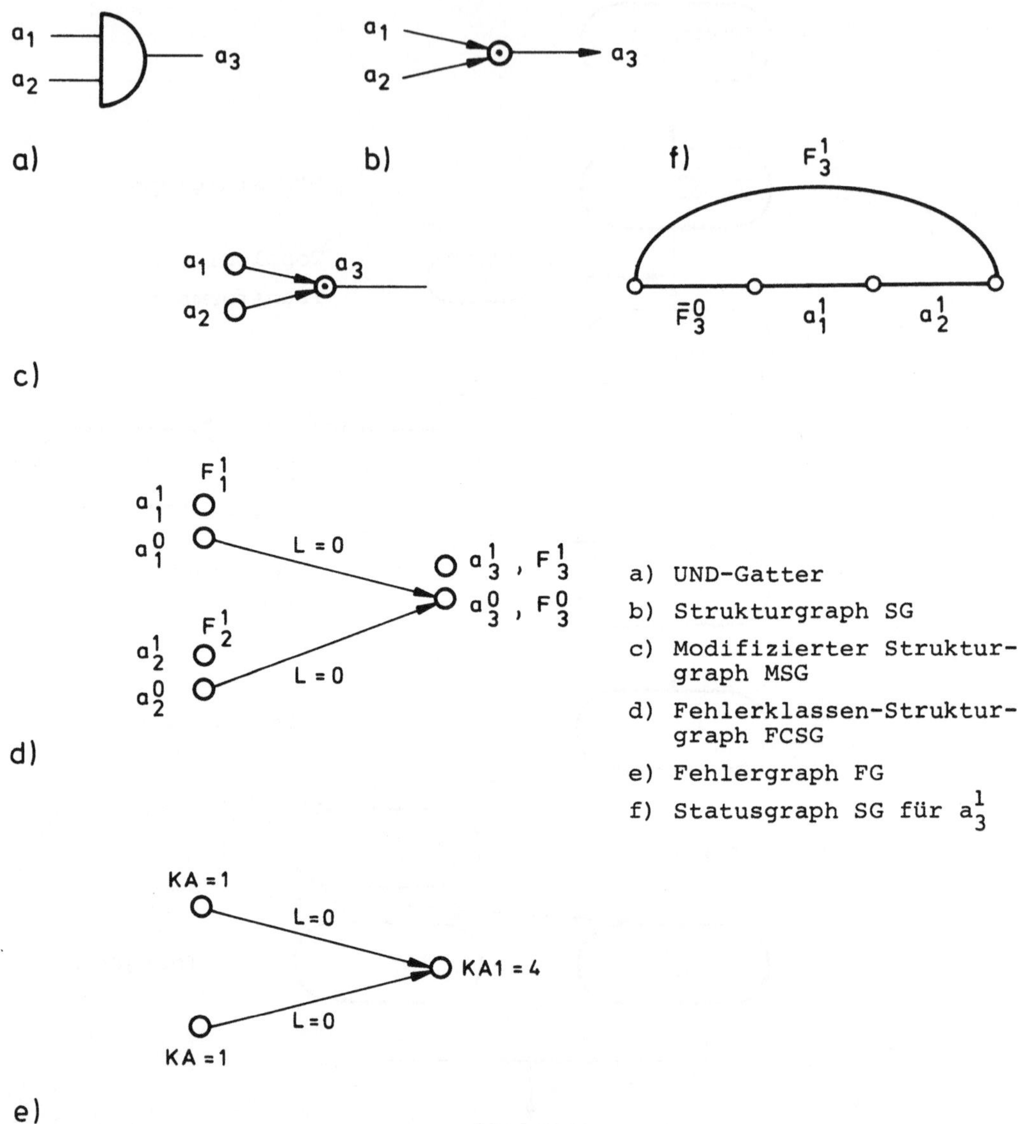

Bild 3: Transformationen an einem UND-Gatter.

Tabelle 2 gibt die Werte des Knotenargumentes für die verschiedenen
Fälle an.

KA l	Fehler-fortpfl.	Vorhandene Kanten	Variable	
			$a_i^{1j} =$	$a_i^{0j} =$
1	ständig 0	$\lvert a_i^0 , a_{Ni}^{0,1} \rvert$ *)	$F_i^1 + G(a_{Vi}^{dj}...)$	$\bar{F}_i^1 \cdot G(a_{Vi}^{dj}...)$
2	ständig 1	$\lvert a_i^1 , a_{Ni}^{0,1} \rvert$	$G(a_{Vi}^{di}...)\bar{F}_i^0$	$F_i^0 + \bar{G}(a_{Vi}^{dj}...)$
3	ständig 1 ständig 0	$\lvert a_i^0 , a_{Ni}^{0,1} \rvert$ $\lvert a_i^1 , a_{Ni}^{0,1} \rvert$	$G(a_{Vi}^{dj}...)$	$\bar{G}(a_{Vij}^{d}...)$
4	−	keine Kante	$F_i^1 + G(a_{Vi}^{dj}...)\bar{F}_i^0$	$F_i^0 + \bar{G}(a_{Vi}^{dj}...)\bar{F}_i^1$

*) Bedeutung: $\lvert a_i^0 , a_{Ni}^{0,1} \rvert$ Es existiert eine Kante von a_i^0 nach a_{Ni}^0
oder von a_i^0 nach a_{Ni}^1.

<u>Tabelle 2:</u> Knotenargumente

Die Funktion $G(a_{Vij}^{d}...)$ gibt an, wie die Variable a_i von den Vorgängern von a_i (a_{Vij}) abhängt (logische Funktion des Gatters).

Der Fehlergraph FG ist offensichtlich dem modifizierten Graph MSG
isomorph. Aus dem Fehlergraphen werden Statusfunktionen und entsprechend Statusgraphen STG erzeugt. Dabei wird die ursprüngliche Funktion des Schaltgliedes verwendet und gleichzeitig eine Fehlersubsti-
tution nach Tabelle 2 durchgeführt. Man erhält so für jeden Knoten
einen Statusgraphen. Zu berücksichtigen ist dabei die Indextransfor-
mation des Index G für den Fall, daß es sich um ein Schaltwerk handelt.
Die Statusgraphen werden ineinander geschachtelt, in der Weise, daß
von dem dem Ausgang entsprechenden Statusgraphen ausgegangen wird und
solange geschachtelt wird, bis nur noch Eingangsvariablen, Zustands-
variablen und Fehler auftreten. Das Ergebnis ist der Testgraph TG, und
zwar der Testgraph TG^1 für den Ausgang 1 und der Testgraph TG^0 für den
Ausgang O. Für den Fall, daß für eine Fehlerprüfung die Zustandsvari-
ablen, die auftreten, einen bestimmten Wert annehmen müssen, muß gegebenenfalls der Zustandsgraph durch einen entsprechenden Testgraphen
für diesen Zustand substituiert werden. Dabei wird offensichtlich der

Zeitindex c um 1 erhöht. Ein Test entspricht dann einem Einfach- oder
Mehrfachweg durch diesen Testgraphen vom Anfang bis zum Ausgang. Dabei
werden jeweils eine Reihe von Fehlern "durchlaufen". Man kann entweder
von einer Simulation der Fehler ausgehen oder von einer geeigneten Op-
timierung der Wege. Es besteht die Möglichkeit der Untersuchung von
Mehrfach-Fehlern sowie der Fehlerlokalisierung.

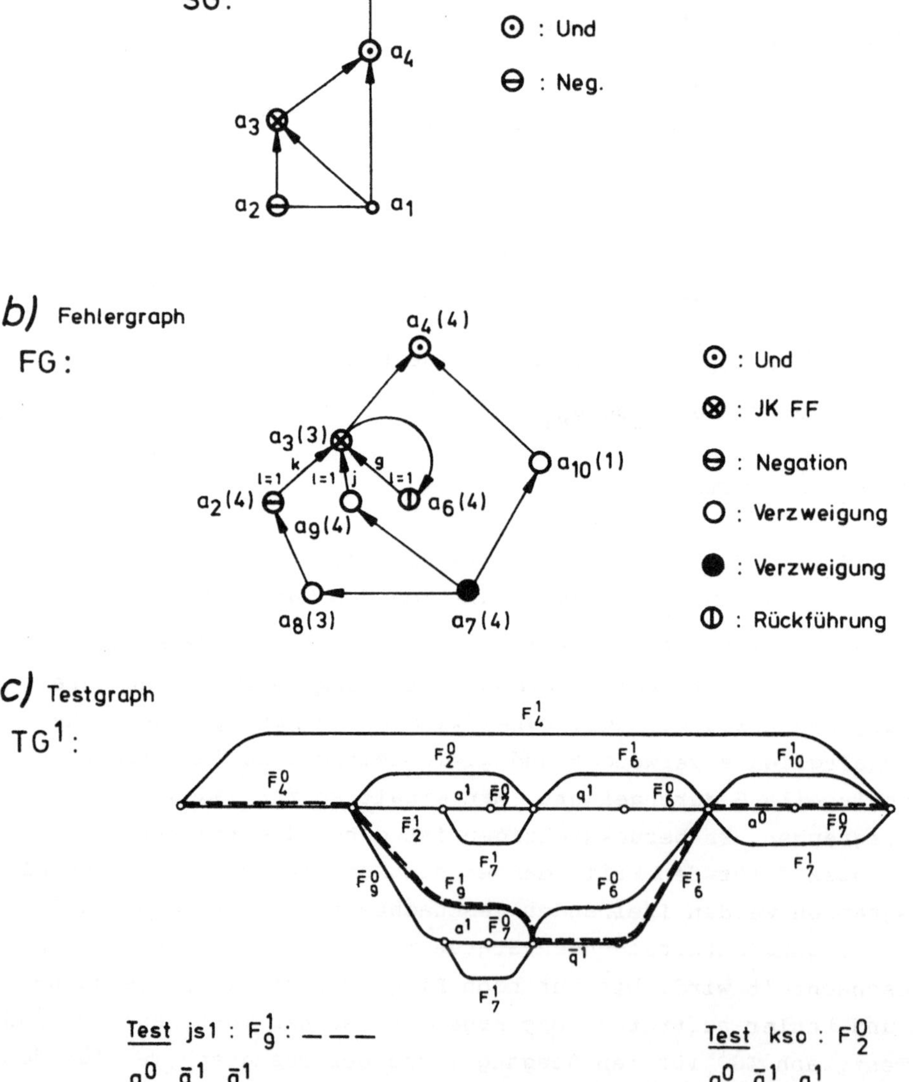

<u>Test</u> js1 : F_9^1 : — — —
$a^0 \; \bar{a}^1 \; \bar{q}^1$

<u>Test</u> kso : F_2^0
$a^0 \; \bar{a}^1 \; q^1$

<u>Bild 4:</u> Strukturgraph, Fehlergraph und Testgraph für das in Bild 1
gezeigte Schaltwerk.

Bilder 4 a - c zeigen eine Durchrechnung des in Abbildung 1 dargestellten Beispiels. Die Abbildungen 4 a und 4 b zeigen den Struktur-
graphen und den Fehlergraphen. Die Abbildung 4 c zeigt dabei den Testgraphen für den Ausgang 1. Der Fehlerprüfung auf js1 ist die gestri-
chelte Linie zugeordnet. Der sich ergebende Testgraph TG^1 ist relativ
anschaulich und zeigt, daß der Fehler js1 mit einer Folge von zwei Ein-
gangssignalen nicht aufdeckbar ist, falls man den Wert der Zustands-
variablen q^1 nicht kennt. Analoges gilt für den Fehler ks0. Der genaue
Test wird durch Substitution der Variablen $\bar{q}^1$ in den Testgraphen erzeugt; es ergibt sich der in Gleichung (14) angegebene Test.

<u>Literaturangaben:</u>

|1| Bouricius, Hsieh,   Algorithms for detection of faults
      Putzolu, Roth,   in logic circuits,
      Schneider, Chung-Jentan: IEEE Trans. on Comp. Vol. C-20, No. 11
                                 Nov. 1971.

|2| Chang, Reed, Banes: Path sensitization, partial Boolean
                                 Difference, and automated fault diag-
                                 nosis,
                                 IEEE Trans. on Comp. Vol C-21, No. 2
                                 Febr. 1972.

|3| Görke, W.:   Zur Fehlerdiagnose von logischen
                                 Schaltwerken mit Hilfe der Booleschen
                                 Differenzen,
                                 Elektron. Rechenanl. 2/72.

|4| Marinos, P.N.:   Derivation of minimal complete sets of
                                 test-input sequences using Boolean
                                 Differences,
                                 IEEE Trans. on Comp. Vol. C-20, No. 1
                                 Jan. 1971.

|5| Putzolu, G.R.   A heuristic algorithm for the testing
      Roth, J.P.:   of asynchronous circuits,
                                 IEEE Trans. on Comp. Vol. C-20, No. 6
                                 June 1971.

|6| Ramamoorthy, C.V.:   A structural theory of machine diag-
                                 nosis,
                                 AFIPS 1967, SJCC 30.

|7| Schertz, D.R.   The use of connection graphs for the
      Metze, G.A.:   detection of digital faults,
                                 7. Annual Allerton Conf. on circuits
                                 and systems theory Oct. 1969,
                                 Monticello, Ill.

|8| Thayse, A.:   Boolean Differential Calculus,
                                 MBLE Research Laboratory Bunds,
                                 Febr. 1971.

DIE METHODE DER AUSGEWOGENEN ABWEICHUNG;
EIN HILFSMITTEL ZUR
ZIELSTREBIGEN LEISTUNGSVERBESSERUNG VON RECHENSYSTEMEN

Heinz Beilner

Abstract: Die Methode der ausgewogenen Abweichung wurde entwickelt mit dem Ziel, dem Konstrukteur eines geplanten oder zu verbessernden Rechensystems (bzw. dem Manager eines im Einsatz befindlichen Rechensystems) ein Hilfsmittel an die Hand zu geben, das ihm erlaubt, das Leistungsverhalten seines Systems in gezielter Weise an ein gewünschtes oder angestrebtes Leistungsverhalten heranzuführen. Die Methode erreicht dies, indem sie unter Einsatz statistischer Verfahren Aussagen darüber liefert, welche Betriebsmittelanforderungen die krassesten Unterschiede zwischen tatsächlicher und gewünschter Leistung hervorrufen; in gewissen Fällen ermöglicht sie eine zusätzliche Lokalisierung durch Angabe des für die Abweichung verantwortlichen Teilsystems. Die Methode arbeitet automatisch und ist damit als geeignetes Werkzeug anzusehen, etwaige Maßnahmen zur Systemverbesserung auf die jeweils wesentlichsten Punkte zu konzentrieren.

1. Ü b e r s i c h t

Grossrechensysteme haben innerhalb des letzten Jahrzehnts einen Komplexitätsgrad erreicht, der herkömmliche - auf Intuition und Erfahrung ba-
sierende - Wege zur Steigerung ihrer Leistungsfähigkeit fragwürdig macht.
Folgerichtig ist in jüngster Zeit ein starkes Interesse an systematischen und zielstrebigen Methoden zur Erhöhung der Leistungsfähigkeit
von Rechensystemen wachgeworden.

Analytische Modelle gesamter Rechensysteme samt ihrer Last böten sicher
eine ideale Möglichkeit zur Bewältigung der anstehenden Probleme; leider sind derartige Modelle derzeit nicht greifbar und wohl auch für die
nächste Zukunft nicht zu erwarten - sowohl wegen der Komplexität der
Struktur von Großrechensystemen als auch wegen der statistischen Besonderheiten ihrer Auftragslasten. Dementsprechend ist man heute darauf
angewiesen, Methoden zur Steigerung der Leistungsfähigkeit von Rechensystemen auf Stichproben ihres input-output-Verhaltens abzustützen; solche Stichproben werden aus Experimenten gewonnen, die entweder am realen
System selbst oder aber an einem Simulationsmodell des Systems durchgeführt werden.

Die möglichen Maßnahmen der Veränderung eines Rechensystems zur Erhöhung
seiner Leistungsfähigkeit entstammen zwei unterschiedlichen Bereichen:
Zum einen bieten sich numerische Systemparameter zur Veränderung an (Anzahl und Kapazität von Maschinenorten, Puffergrößen, Warteschlangenlän-
gen, etc.) - zum anderen eröffnen strukturelle Eigenschaften (schedu-
ling- und dispatching-Strategien, Taktiken der Speicherbelegung, Resi-
denz von Betriebssystemmoduln, etc.) Möglichkeiten der Variation.

Das Problem der systematischen Leistungsverbesserung durch Veränderung
der Werte numerischer Systemparameter ist in verschiedenen Ansätzen an-
gegangen worden mittels stochastischer Optimierungsverfahren zum Experi-
mentieren sowohl mit realen Systemen als auch mit den entsprechenden
Simulationsmodellen (vgl. z.B. Blatny [2], Schmidt [5]). Dagegen sind
hinsichtlich des Problems der zielstrebigen Variation struktureller Sy-
stemeigenschaften derzeit keine systematischen Methoden bekannt (vgl.
auch Graham [4]).

Die hier vorzustellende "Methode der ausgewogenen Abweichung" liefert
eine automatische Anzeige von Unzulänglichkeiten des Systems (in bezug
auf vorgegebene Leistungsziele) und erlaubt in gewissen Fällen eine Lokalisierung solcher Unzulänglichkeiten. Die Methode ist damit ein erster
Schritt in Richtung auf systematische Wege der Leistungsverbesserung
ohne die übliche Beschränkung auf numerische Systemparameter.

2. D i e   M e t h o d e

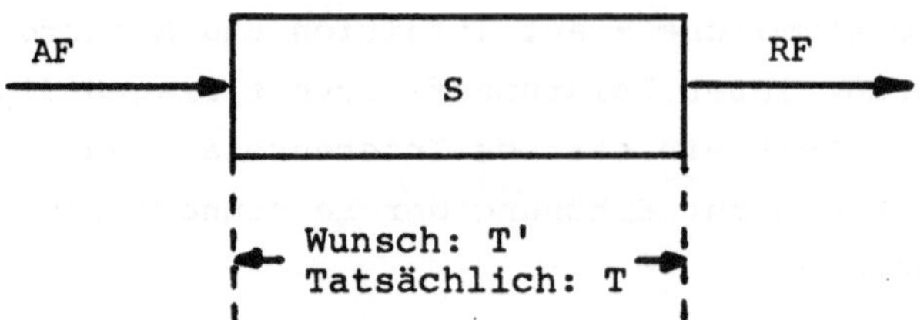

Sei S ein System zur Bearbeitung einer Aufgabenfolge

$$AF = (A_1, A_2, \ldots A_n) \ ,$$

dessen Antwort auf AF aus der Erzeugung einer Resultatfolge

$$RF = (R_1, R_2, \ldots, R_n)$$

besteht, wo ein Resultat R_i der entsprechenden Aufgabe A_i eindeutig zugeordnet sei. Werde die Leistung des Systems S bestimmt auf der Basis
der Zeitspannenfolge

$$TF = (T_1, T_2, \ldots T_n) \ ,$$

wo T_i die Bearbeitungszeit bezeichne, die vom Zeitpunkt des Vorliegens
einer Aufgabe A_i bis zum Zeitpunkt der Bereitstellung des zugehörigen
Resultats R_i verstreicht. Verwalte das System insgesamt m verschiedene
Betriebsmittel, so dass eine Aufgabe A_i sich charakterisieren lässt
durch das Ausmaß der jeweiligen Inanspruchnahme dieser m verschiedenen
Betriebsmittel, etwa in Form eines Anforderungsvektors

$$A_i = (a_{i1}, a_{i2}, \ldots, a_{im}) \ ,$$

wo a_{ij} die Anforderung der Aufgabe A_i hinsichtlich des Betriebsmittels
j bezeichne.

Seien weiterhin genaue Vorstellungen bezüglich der gewünschten Leistung
des Systems definiert in Form einer Zeitspannenfolge

$$TF' = (T_1', T_2', \ldots, T_n') \ ,$$

die für jede Aufgabe A_i die jeweilige Wunschbearbeitungszeit T_i' angibt.

Ein von der Wunschvorstellung abweichendes Leistungsverhalten des Systems
bei Bearbeitung einer bestimmten Aufgabe A läßt sich messen mithilfe einer Abweichungsfunktion

$$D = D(T, T')$$

von der im Hinblick auf die folgenden Überlegungen gefordert wird, daß sie im interessierenden Bereich T $\gtrless$ O, T' $\gtrless$ O den Bedingungen genügt:

$$D = O \text{ für } T' = T$$
$$D > O \text{ für } T' > T$$
$$D < O \text{ für } T' < T$$
$$D \quad \text{monoton nichtfallend in } T'$$
$$D \quad \text{monoton nichtsteigend in } T$$

Um konkreter zu werden: Als Abweichungsfunktion im obigen Sinne geeignet ist beispielsweise die normale Differenz $D_1 = T' - T$ oder die relative Differenz $D_2 = (T' - T)/T'$, aber auch nach sonstigen Gesichtspunkten gewogene Differenzen. Die gesamte Abweichung des Systems von seinem Wunschverhalten ist somit beschrieben durch die Abweichungsfolge

$$DF = (D_1, D_2, \ldots, D_n) \; ,$$

wo $\qquad D_i = D(T_i, T_i') \quad i = 1(1)n$

Die grundlegende Idee der hier zu schildernden Methode der ausgewogenen Abweichung besteht nun darin, eine statistische Analyse der Folge von Abweichungs-Aufgabenpaaren durchzuführen, bzw. eine statistische Analyse der Folge von $(m + 1)$-tupeln

$$((D_i, a_{i1}, a_{i2}, \ldots a_{im}); \quad i = 1(1)n)$$

mit dem Ziel

* etwa vorliegende statistische Abhängigkeiten der Abweichungen D vom Ausmaß a_j an Betriebsmittelanforderungen einer oder mehrerer Arten aufzudecken,

* derartige Abhängigkeiten als Indikatoren für Unzulänglichkeiten des Systems zu interpretieren, die im Zusammenhang mit der Anforderung der betreffenden Betriebsmittel zu besonders starken Abweichungen des Systemverhaltens vom Wunschverhalten führen,

* diese Indikationen als Basis für zielstrebige Maßnahmen zur Angleichung des Systemverhaltens an die Wunschvorstellungen zu verwenden.

Die gefragte statistische Untersuchung kann durchgeführt werden mithilfe einer normalen Regressionsanalyse (vgl.z.B. Draper [3]); bekanntlich besteht eine solche aus der (versuchsweisen) Einführung eines Modells, hier etwa der Form

$$D_i = F(A_i) + \hat{h}_i \; ; \qquad i = 1(1)n$$

das die Werte D_i zu erklären versucht als Überlagerung einer deterministische Funktion $F(A)$ mit gewissen Zufallsvariablen $\hat{h}_i$ (man beachte, daß A einen Vektor bezeichnet); die Parameter von F werden aus den Paaren (D_i, A_i) geschätzt im Hinblick auf minimale mittlere quadratische

Abweichung der (D_i, A_i) und das Modell abschliessend auf seine statistische Signifikanz getestet.

Beim Einsatz von Regressionsanalysen ist man normalerweise an den numerischen Werten der Regressionskoeffizienten interessiert. Im Gegensatz dazu ist für die Methode der abgewogenen Abweichung lediglich die Tatsache signifikanter Abhängigkeit wesentlich. Im Rahmen dieser qualitativen Untersuchung spielt die Wahl einer spezifischen Funktion F keine so wesentliche Rolle wie bei einem quantitativ orientierten Einsatz der Regressionsanalyse und die Verwendung einer linearen Regressionsanalyse 1. Ordnung dürfte in der Mehrzahl der Fälle ausreichende Ergebnisse liefern. Man gelangt damit zu

$$F(A) = b_o + \sum_{j=1}^{m} b_j \, a_j \quad ,$$

einer linearen Funktion in den Betriebsmittelanforderungen a_j, deren Parameter b_j $(j=O(1)m)$ sich in üblicher Weise als Regressionskoeffizienten auf der Grundlage der vorliegenden Paare (D_i, A_i) errechnen lassen.

Wie schon angedeutet, muß die statistische Signifikanz der gewonnenen Funktion F untersucht werden. Das übliche Vorgehen besteht aus der Durchführung einer Varianzanalyse mit nachfolgendem F-Test auf Signifikanz der Regressionsfunktion sowie einer Reihe von t-Tests, die über die Signifikanz der einzelnen Regressionskoeffizienten Aufschluss geben. Allerdings beruhen diese Tests auf gewissen Voraussetzungen hinsichtlich der Zufallsvariablen $\hat{h}_i$:

$$\hat{h}_i \, , \quad i = 1(1)n \quad \text{sind paarweise unkorrellierte} \quad N(O, \sigma^2)\text{-Variable}$$

Die Voraussetzungen sind sicher nicht in allgemein gültiger Weise erfüllt und die Tests daher nur mit der gebotenen Konservativität (also unter Wahl äußerst geringer Fehlerwahrscheinlichkeiten) durchzuführen. Ein Einsatz entsprechender nichtparametrischer Tests bzw. die Verwendung einer der Regressionsanalyse analogen, verteilungsfreien Methode wäre selbstredend befriedigender; leider ist mir über die Existenz solcher Tests bzw. Methoden derzeit nichts bekannt.

Das Ergebnis der durchgeführten Regressionsanalyse läßt sich nun wie folgt interpretieren:

* Bei signifikanter Regressionsfunktion bildet jede Signifikanz eines Regressionskoeffizienten b_j $(j = 1(1)m)$ einen Hinweis darauf, daß die zugehörige Betriebsmittelanforderung a_j als "Ursache" für eine aus dem Rahmen fallende Abweichung der tatsächlichen Bearbeitungszeiten von den Wunschbearbeitungszeiten anzusehen ist.

- $b_j < 0$ deutet auf eine Benachteiligung bei der Abfertigung. Je mehr des Betriebsmittels a_j angefordert wird, desto langsamer ist die Bearbeitung - langsamer nicht absolut gesehen, sondern in bezug auf das insgesamt (für alle Aufgaben) bestehende Niveau der Abweichung von der Wunschbearbeitungszeit. Eine gezielte Annäherung des Systemverhaltens an das Wunschverhalten (genauer: eine Annäherung an einen Zustand der - hinsichtlich der Anforderungen - ausgewogenen Abweichung des Systemverhaltens vom Wunschverhalten) kann demnach erreicht werden durch Verbesserung der Vergabe dieses Betriebsmittels.

- $b_j > 0$ deutet auf eine Bevorzugung bei der Abfertigung. Je mehr des Betriebsmittels a_j angefordert wird, desto schneller ist die Bearbeitung - schneller wieder nicht absolut gesehen, sondern in bezug auf das Normalniveau der Abweichung von der Wunschbearbeitungszeit. In diesem Falle ist also die Vergabe des Betriebsmittels a_j zu verschlechtern, um zu einem Zustand ausgewogener Abweichung zu gelangen.

* Eine nicht signifikante Regressionsfunktion ist ein Indiz dafür, daß das Ziel der Methode erreicht ist: Ein Zustand, in dem nicht etwa das System keine Abweichung von seinem Wunschverhalten zeigt, sondern ein Zustand, in dem existierende Abweichungen vom Wunschverhalten keinen bestimmten Betriebsmittelanforderungen zugeschrieben werden können, demnach in zufälliger Weise auf Aufgaben aller vorkommenden Arten verteilt sind; ein Zustand also der - in bezug auf die verschiedenen Anforderungen - ausgewogenen Abweichung.

Die Methode kann verfeinert werden, wenn das System aus verschiedenen Teilsystemen besteht und sowohl das Verhalten dieser Teilsysteme (also die Abwicklungsdauer dort bearbeiteter Teilaufgaben) meßbar ist als auch genaue Vorstellungen über das gewünschte Verhalten der Teilsysteme bestehen. In diesem Fall kann man (analog zu dem oben geschilderten Vorgehen bezüglich des Gesamtsystems) statistische Analysen durchführen mit dem Ziel, etwaige Abhängigkeiten zwischen den auftretenden Abweichungen der Teilsysteme von ihrem Wunschverhalten und den bezüglich der Teilsysteme bestehenden Betriebsmittelforderungen aufzudecken. Diese Verfeinerung ermöglicht zusätzlich zu globalen Aussagen der Form "Anforderungen des Betriebsmittels a_j erzeugen starke positive (bzw. negative) Abweichungen des Systems von seinem Wunschverhalten" eine Lokalisierung der Systemunzulänglichkeiten dadurch, dass die Teilsysteme angebbar sind, welche die Unzulänglichkeiten beinhalten.

3. Einsatz der Methode beim Calibrieren von Simulationsmodellen

Die Calibrierung eines Simulators hat zur Aufgabe, das Verhalten des Simulationsmodells dem Verhalten des entsprechenden realen Systems so weit wie möglich zu nähern. Die Methode der ausgewogenen Abweichung bietet ein geeignetes Hilfsmittel zur Durchführung eines zielstrebigen derartigen Calibrierungsprozesses. Das zu verändernde System S ist hier dargestellt durch das Simulationsmodell eines Rechensystems. Verwendet man als Last des Systems die Aufzeichnung realer Aufgabenströme ("Traces"), dann übernehmen die im realen Rechensystem aufgetretenen Bearbeitungszeiten die Rolle der Wunschbearbeitungszeiten T_i', die im Modell auftretenden Simulationsbearbeitungszeiten die Rolle der T_i. Die im Verlauf der Regressionsanalyse ermittelten signifikanten Regressionskoeffizienten b_j berechtigen zur folgenden Interpretation:

$b_j > 0$ (< 0) ist ein Hinweis darauf, dass die Vergabe des Betriebsmittels a_j im Simulator unter Umständen stattfindet, die so zeitgünstig (zeitungünstig) sind, daß sie signifikant aus dem Rahmen der normalen - selbstverständlich vorhandenen! - Verhaltensunterschiede Realität/Modell fallen. Um eine gleich gute Simulation von Aufgaben aller vorkommenden Arten - d.h. aller vorkommenden Kombinationen von Betriebsmittelanforderungen - zu erreichen, muß im Simulator die Ursache dieser zu "guten" ("schlechten") Vergabe beseitigt werden. Die Methode liefert also Hinweise auf die Ursachen der krassesten Verhaltensunterschiede Realtität/ Modell und bei Anwendung der Verfeinerung auf Teilsysteme eine Lokalisierung der Unzulänglichkeiten im Simulator. Um Mißverständnisse auszuschließen: Die Methode erlaubt nicht etwa, solche Unzulänglichkeiten automatisch zu beseitigen - Behebung der Fehler bleibt Aufgabe des Modellkonstrukteurs, der allerdings durch den automatischen Hinweis auf die Fehlerorte stark unterstützt wird.

Die Methode wurde bei der Calibrierung eines Simulationsmodells für ein großes batch-Rechensystems (Beilner/Waldbaum [1] , [6]) erfolgreich eingesetzt. Ein einfaches Beispiel aus diesem Projekt sei zur Illustration hier angeführt.

Untersuchtes Teilsystem:

        Wartephase (von vollendeter Eingabe der Jobs
        bis zur Kernspeicherzuteilung)

Interessierende Betriebsmittel:

        TSUPS7 : Zahl der angeforderten 7-Spur-Bänder

        TSUPS9 : Zahl der angeforderten 9-Spur-Bänder

        DSUPS   : Zahl der angeforderten Plattenstapel

Interessierende Modellparameter:

      TIMNTOT : Basiszeit für Bandmontage durch Operateur
      TIMNTOD : Basiszeit für Plattenmontage durch Operateur
      TIMSLOS : Bedeutung hier nebensächlich

Abweichungsfunktion:

      $D(T,T') = T' - T$

Ergebnis der Regressionsanalyse an einem Punkt $\overline{P}_1$

		Wert bei $\overline{P}_1$	
	TIMNTOT	500 sec	
Parameter	TIMNTOD	100 sec	
	TIMSLOS	1.5 sec	
Regressions-	TSUPS7	*	* nicht signifikant
koeffizien-	TSUPS9	31	
ten	DSUPS	15	

Interpretation und Empfehlung:

      Montage von 9-Spur-Bändern zu schnell simuliert (b $>$ 0),
      ohne Messungen geschätzte Montagezeit TIMNTOT erhöhen

Ausführung der Empfehlung:

		Wert $(\overline{P}_1)$	Wert $(\overline{P}_2)$	Wert $(\overline{P}_3)$
	TIMNTOT	500	800	1000 ⟵
Parameter	TIMNTOD	100	100	100
	TIMSLOS	1.5	1.5	1.5
Regressions-	TSUPS7	*	*	*
koeffizien-	TSUPS9	31	21	*
ten	DSUPS	15	11	*

Resultat:

      Zustand ausgewogener Abweichung in 2 Schritten erreicht.

4. Einsatz der Methode beim Experimentieren mit realen Systemen oder deren Simulationsmodellen

Eine Grundvoraussetzung für die Anwendbarkeit der Methode der ausgewogenen Abweichung war die Existenz von genauen Vorstellungen bezüglich der gewünschten Leistung des zu untersuchenden Systems. Sei also für ein bestimmtes Rechensystem $T' = T'(A)$ eine vorgegebene Funktion, die für beliebigen Vektor A an Betriebsmittelanforderungen die Wunschbearbeitungszeit $T'(A)$ festgelegt. Es spielt dabei keine Rolle, ob etwa $T'(A)$ in Form einer mehrdimensionalen stetigen Funktion in den Betriebsmitteln a_j vorliegt oder z.B. $T'(A)$ nur diskreter Werte fähig ist, die aus einer mehrdimensionalen (auf disjunkten Intervallen für die Betriebsmittel a_j basierenden) Tabelle entnehmbar sind; der letzte Fall dürfte sogar der häufigere sein - liegen doch allen Prioritätsschemata, die von Auftragscharakteristiken angeben, zumindest implizit derartige Leistungsziele zugrunde.

Interessant wird dieser Fall durch die Möglichkeit, in gezielter
Weise Systemveränderungen zu planen, die zu einem eventuellen Kom-
pensationsvorgang führen - zuungunsten der Abfertigung hinsichtlich
des als bevorzugt erkannten Betriebsmittels a_j, zugunsten der Abfertigung eines anderen (z.B. eines als benachteiligt erkannten) Betriebsmittels. Voraussetzung für eine solche Kompensation ist natürlich das Vorliegen einer geeigneten trade-off-Situation.

Die Methode liefert also Hinweise auf die Ursachen der krassesten Unterschiede zwischen Systemverhalten und erwünschtem Systemverhalten
und bei Anwendung der Verfeinerung auf Teilsysteme eine Lokalisierung
der Systemunzulänglichkeiten. Wieder ist anzumerken, daß die Methode
nicht erlaubt, diese Unzulänglichkeiten etwa automatisch zu beseitigen
- Behebung der Fehler bleibt Aufgabe des Systemkonstrukteurs bzw. des
Systemmanagements, die allerdings durch den automatischen Hinweis auf
die Fehlerorte stark unterstützt werden.

Der Einsatz der Methode zur Verbesserung eines Grossrechnersystems ist
in Vorbereitung. Diesbezügliche Ergebnisse bleiben aus Zeitgründen
einer späteren Veröffentlichung vorbehalten.

Literaturverzeichnis

[1]   Beilner, H. und Waldbaum, G.
      "Statistical Methodology for Calibrating a Trace-Driven
      Simulator of a Batch Computer System"

      in Freiberger, W. (ed.):
      Statistical Computer Performance Evaluation
      Academic Press, 1972

[2]   Blatny, J., Clark, S.R. und Rourke, T.A.
      "On the Optimization of Performance of Time-Sharing Systems
      by Simulation"
      CACM vol 15 (1972) nr. 6, pp 411-420

[3]   Draper, N.R. und Smith, H.
      "Applied Repression Analysis"
      J. Wiley, 1966

[4]   Graham, R.M.
      "Performance Prediction"

      in Bauer, F.L. (ed.):
      Advanced Course in Software Engineering
      Springer, Lecture Notes vol. 81

[5]   Schmidt, J.W. und Taylor, R.E.
      "System Optimization through Simulation"
      Simulation, Febr. 1972, pp. 41-46

[6]   Waldbaum, G. und Beilner, H.
      "SOUL: A Simulation of OS under LASP"
      Proc. of the 1972 Summer Computer Simulation Conference,
      San Diego

AN INTERPRETATIVE PERFORMANCE MONITOR FOR

TIME SHARING SYSTEM EVALUATION

G. Gschwind und J. Pachaly
(Kurzfassung)[+]

In this paper, we describe a new kind of software monitor for the performance
analysis of CP67/CMS,-a time sharing system running on the IBM 360/67, and a
method for designing representative workloads to simulate time-sharing loads.

Monitor design:

SPAS (for System Performance Analysis and Statistics) is a software monitor
developed for CP67/CMS.

It runs in a dormant virtual machine activated by timer interrupts at specified
intervals of time and collects internal information on the dynamic behavior of the
system.

SPAS has been designed to be independent of system modifications and releases and
will run with minor modifications under VM/370.

In comparison to other monitors, SPAS has an interesting new feature, which makes
its use very flexible. It works interpretatively and accepts as input a "measurement
program". This concept is illustrated on the following Figure:

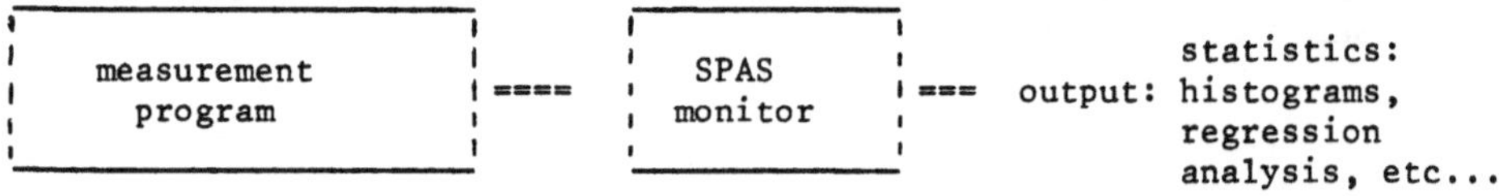

The input program describes the performance measurements and statistical analysis
to be performed by a sequence of easily coded instructions.

At the start of a measurement run, the program is read into core and the instructions will be interpreted and executed by SPAS.

Instructions are provided, for instance, to:
- fetch data from specified CP67 core locations,
- perform arithmetic operations,
- provide sequence and timing control: loops,
  conditional jumps, pauses, and the setting of
  duration and interval of measurement,
- scan lists,

+ Manuskript nicht eingegangen

- reduce and analyse data
- switch on and off hooks in cp67 code.

Groups of instructions can be invoked as macro-instructions.

An example of such a measurement program will be shown.

Characterization of real workload and design of drive workloads:
In order to quantify system performance and workload characteristics, we have
selected a set of system variables.
At sampling time, the software monitor collects the instantaneous, cumulative or
time integrated values of these variables.
Their statistical analysis yields quantitative information about system performance
and load characteristics of the user environment.

Real workloads, however, fluctuate strongly.
This would require measurements over extended periods of time for performance evalu-
ations, in order to obtain reproducible results.
Two main difficulties arise:
  - measurement duration is limited by system changes
  - trends in load characteristics may falsify the results.

In order to obtain reproducible results under reproducible load conditions within
reasonably short measurement periods, it is necessary to simulate the real workload
by well defined drive loads.
For this purpose, we use the information gained by extended measurements and analysis of real user load profiles to build mixes representing typical terminal or
background users.
We combine and weight these mixes to time sharing mixes representing stationary
states of real workload, adjusting the statistical distributions of system variables to these of real workload.

<u>Applications</u>:
Some examples of application of SPAS will be presented in this paper, for instance:
  - influence of different parameters on system response
    and throughput
  - improvements of system performance by dynamic
    adaptation of scheduling parameters to changing load.

MESSUNG, SIMULATION UND BERECHNUNG DER ABHÄNGIGKEITEN DES AUFTRAGSDURCHSATZES

G. Mersmann
TELEFUNKEN COMPUTER GMBH

Inhalt

1. Beschreibung des Rechensystems
   - Konfiguration
   - Aufträge

2. Der Auftragsdurchsatz
   - Definitionen
   - Abhängigkeiten

3. Die Untersuchungen
   - Theoretische Lösung
   - Simulationen
   - Messungen

4. Diskussion der Resultate

Zusammenfassung

Die wichtigsten Abhängigkeiten des Auftragsdurchsatzes in Rechensystemen sind gegeben durch die Anzahl der Rechnerkerne und Transportkanäle, die Rechenintensität des Auftragsmixes und den Speicherausbau, der über die Zahl der nutzbaren Programmplätze das Multiprogramming beeinflußt. Drei Untersuchungsmethoden - Berechnungen, Simulationen und Messungen - werden einander gegenübergestellt. Einige ausgewählte Ergebnisse werden dargestellt und diskutiert.

Die Eigenschaften eines Rechensystems werden bestimmt durch die Konfiguration, die Beschaffenheit der Aufträge und die Antwort des Systems auf eine Belastung.

1. Beschreibung des Rechensystems

Eine Konfiguration wird beschrieben durch Anzahl und Operationsgeschwindigkeit der Rechnerkerne, Anzahl und Leistungsdaten der Transportkanäle, durch den Ausbau von Hintergrundspeicher und Arbeitsspeicher.

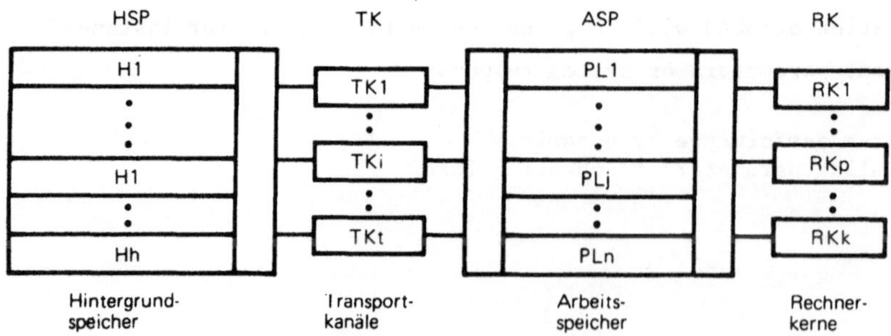

Bild 1: Struktur des Rechensystems

Die Zuordnung von Kanälen zu Geräten ist fest. Es ist möglich, mehrere unabhängige Kanäle pro Gerät anzuschließen. Die Anzahl der Geräte ist variabel, pro Gerät können mehrere, nahezu unabhängige Moduln vorhanden sein. **Mehrprozessorsysteme werden untersucht. Die einzelnen Rechnerkerne arbeiten autonom und können auf den gesamten Arbeitsspeicher zugreifen. In der Praxis behindern mehrere Rechnerkerne einander.** Dies wird bei den Messungen erfaßt und bei den Simulationen berücksichtigt. Die Transportkanäle bilden das Verhalten der angeschlossenen Trommeln und Platten nach, die durch Positionierzeit, Latenzzeit und Übertragungsrate beschrieben werden. Transportaufträge werden in der Reihenfolge ihres Eintreffens bearbeitet. Transporte sind nicht unterbrechbar. Im Arbeitsspeicher ermöglicht Paging eine verschnittfreie Ausnutzung. Die Abbildung von virtuellem auf physikalischen Speicher ist freizügig. Im realen Rechensystem gibt es eine vorgebbare Anzahl gleichzeitig bearbeitbarer Programme. Die aktuelle Anzahl der zu einem Zeitpunkt geladenen Programme ergibt sich aus der Bedingung, daß der momentane Arbeitsspeicherbedarf aller Programme zuzüglich einer Stabilisierungszwecken dienenden Reserve kleiner als der verfügbare Speicher ist. Während sich bei den Messungen während der Auftragsbearbeitung der Speicherbedarf der Aufträge ändert, wird bei den Simulationen der Mittelwert des Speicherbedarfs eingesetzt. Dies bedeutet, daß sich die Zahl der belegten Programmplätze nicht ändert, bis ein Auftrag fertiggestellt oder unterbrochen wird. Bei den Berechnungen wird eine feste Anzahl von Programmplätzen angenommen.

Ein Auftrag wird beschrieben durch seinen Arbeitsspeicherbedarf und die Zahl der Transporte bei der Bearbeitung. Während der Bearbeitung wechseln Rechenphasen und Transporte einander ab. Jeder Auftrag kann von jedem der Rechnerkerne bearbeitet werden. Dagegen erfolgen die Zugriffe zu den einzelnen Hintergrundspeichern mit Häufigkeiten, die gemessen sind. Aufträge können zu jedem Zeitpunkt auf den Hintergrundspeicher verdrängt werden. Dies ist für die Messungen von Bedeutung und kommt vor, wenn die Bearbeitung strategiebedingt zurückgestellt wird, ein Arbeitsspeicherengpaß eintritt oder ein langfristiger Wartezustand beginnt. Die Dauer der Rechenphasen und Transporte sind Zufallsvariable mit gemessenen Verteilungen, die allerdings wiederum von der Konfiguration und der Software des Systems abhängen.

Wichtige Eigenschaften eines Auftragsmixes sind gegeben durch die Zahl der zu bearbeitenden Aufträge und die Rechenintensität. Sie wird definiert als Verhältnis von Rechenzeiten zu Transportzeiten, die zur Bearbeitung notwendig sind. Ferner ist die effektive Anzahl der belegten Programmplätze von Bedeutung. Sie kann bestimmt werden, wenn man die Summe aller Zeitintervalle kennt, während derer $1, 2 \ldots N$ Plätze im Arbeitsspeicher belegt werden konnten.

Das Systemverhalten auf einen angebotenen Auftragsmix wird bestimmt durch die Strategien, die im Multiprogramming und Multiprozessing angewendet werden. Maßzahlen zur Beurteilung sind die Verweilzeiten der Aufträge und der Auftragsdurchsatz. Im folgenden werden Verweilzeiten, die im Dialogbetrieb besonders wichtig sind, nicht weiter behandelt.

2.   Der Auftragsdurchsatz

Im batch-Betrieb, für den die Untersuchungen hauptsächlich bedeutsam sind, ist der Durchsatz die wichtigste, zur Beurteilung der Leistung herangezogene Größe. Er wird definiert als die pro Zeiteinheit fertiggestellte Anzahl von Aufträgen.

$$D = \frac{z_A}{T_A} \quad \left[\frac{\text{Aufträge}}{\text{Zeiteinheit}} \right] \tag{1}$$

D = Durchsatz
z_A = Zahl der bearbeiteten Aufträge; $z_A \gg 1$
T_A = zur Bearbeitung erforderliche Zeit

Der Auftragsdurchsatz hängt ab von der Anzahl der Rechnerkerne und Transportkanäle, der Rechenintensität des Auftragsmixes und der Anzahl der Programmplätze.

$$D = D (RK, TK, RI, N) \tag{2}$$

RK = Anzahl der Rechnerkerne
TK = Anzahl der Transportkanäle
RI = Rechenintensität des Auftragsmixes
N = Anzahl der Programmplätze

$$RI = T_{RK}/T_{EA} \tag{3}$$

T_{RK} = Rechenzeiten der Aufträge des Mixes
T_{TK} = Transportzeiten der Aufträge des Mixes

Es ist zweckmäßig, den erzielten Durchsatz zu beziehen auf den Durchsatz ohne Multiprogramming

$$D_0 = D(N = 1) = z_A/(T_{RK} + T_{EA}) \tag{4}$$

Der Durchsatz kann aus den Betriebsmittelbelegungen berechnet werden

$$D = BRK/(T_{RK}/z_A) = BTK/(T_{TK}/z_A) \tag{5}$$

BRK = relative Belegung der Rechnerkerne
BTK = relative Belegung der Transportkanäle

Der bezogene Durchsatz D/D_0 ist gleich der Summe der Belegungen aller aktiver Betriebsmittel. Dies wird folgendermaßen hergeleitet:

$$D/D_0 = BRK/BRK_0 = BTK/BTK_0 \tag{6}$$

Unter der Voraussetzung, daß sich das Auftragsprofil bei Übergang auf Multiprogramming nicht ändert, gilt

$$BRK_0/(BRK_0 + BTK_0) = BRK/(BRK + BTK) \tag{7}$$

Außerdem ist $\qquad BRK_0 + BTK_0 = 1 \tag{8}$

Damit wird $\qquad D/D_0 = BRK/(BRK_0/(BRK_0 + BTK_0)) = BRK/(BRK/(BRK + BTK)) = BRK + BTK \tag{9}$

Ändert sich das Profil bei Multiprogramming, so kann D_0 interpretiert werden als der Durchsatz im Single-Programming, der sich bei gleichem Profil ergeben würde. Die Werte (9) sind also konsistent.

Ist die Anzahl besetzter Programmplätze während der Bearbeitung auf Grund des verschiedenen und sich zeitlich ändernden Arbeitsspeicherbedarfs der Aufträge nicht konstant, so errechnet sich der Durchsatz zu

$$D/D_0 = \sum_{P=1}^{N} D_P/D_0 \cdot T_P/T_A \tag{10}$$

D_P = Durchsatz bei genau P Programmplätzen
T_P = Summe aller Zeitintervalle, während derer P Programmplätze besetzt sind

Die Zeiten T_P hängen von den Eigenschaften der Aufträge und vom Arbeitsspeicherausbau ab und sind einer quantitativen Untersuchung leicht zugänglich.

3. Die Untersuchungen

Theoretische Lösung

Es wird angenommen, daß eine feste Anzahl von Programmplätzen zur Verfügung steht, die zu jedem Zeitpunkt besetzt werden kann, ferner, daß mehrere Rechnerkerne einander nicht behindern und mehrere Transportkanäle gleichzeitigen und unabhängigen Zugriff auf den Hintergrundspeicher ermöglichen. Der Auftragsmix wird vollständig beschrieben durch seine Rechenintensität und die Voraussetzung, daß alle Zeitabstände zwischen auftragsspezifischen Ereignissen exponentiell verteilt sind. Außerdem wird unterstellt, daß die Organisation des Multiprogramming verlustfrei erfolgt und Auftragsverdrängungen während der Bearbeitung nicht vorkommen. Da das Rechensystem eine endliche Anzahl von Zuständen besitzt und die Ereignisfolgen bei der Bearbeitung festliegen, ist es möglich, die Zustandswahrscheinlichkeiten zu berechnen. Sei

$$\mu_j^{-1} = f\,(RK) = \text{mittlere Fertigstellungszeit von Rechenphasen im Zustand } j$$

$$\lambda_j^{-1} = f\,(TK) = \text{mittlere Fertigstellungszeit von Transporten im Zustand } j$$

$$p_j = \text{Wahrscheinlichkeit, daß } j \text{ Aufträge auf Zuteilung eines Rechnerkerns warten oder rechnen } (j = 0, 1 \ldots N).$$

Dann gilt

$$\frac{dp_0}{dt} = -\lambda_0\,(TK)\cdot p_0\,(t) + \mu_1\,(RK)\cdot p_1\,(t) \tag{11A}$$

$$\frac{dp_j}{dt} = -(\mu_j\,(RK) + \lambda_j\,(TK))\cdot p_j\,(t) + \lambda_{j-1}\,(TK)\cdot p_{j-1}\,(t) + \mu_{j+1}\,(RK)\cdot p_{j+1}\,(t) \tag{11B}$$
$$\text{für } j=1 \ldots (N-1)$$

$$\frac{dp_N}{dt} = \mu_N\,(RK)\cdot p_N\,(t) + \lambda_{N-1}\,(TK)\cdot p_{N-1}\,(t) \tag{11C}$$

ferner

$$\sum_{j=0}^{N} p_j = 1 \tag{11D}$$

Im stationären Zustand, d. h. für $d/dt=0$, ergibt sich als Lösung

$$\frac{1}{p_0} = 1 + \sum_{j=1}^{N} \prod_{k=1}^{j} \frac{\lambda_{k-1}\,(TK)}{u_k\,(RK)} \tag{12A}$$

$$p_k = \frac{\lambda_{k-1}\,(TK)}{\mu_k\,(RK)} \cdot p_{k-1} \tag{12B}$$

In den einzelnen Summanden läßt sich die Rechenintensität als Eigenschaft der Aufträge abspalten. Damit wird

$$\frac{1}{p_0} = 1 + \sum_{j=1}^{N} RI^j \prod_{k=1}^{j} \frac{t_{k-1}}{r_k} \tag{13A}$$

$$p_k = RI \cdot \frac{t_{k-1}}{r_k} \cdot p_{k-1} \tag{13B}$$

mit

$$t_k = \begin{Bmatrix} k \\ TK \end{Bmatrix} \text{ für } \begin{Bmatrix} (N-TK)\le k \le (N-1) \\ 0 \le k \le (N-TK) \end{Bmatrix} \quad \text{und} \quad r_k = \begin{Bmatrix} k \\ RK \end{Bmatrix} \text{ für } \begin{Bmatrix} 1 \le k \le RK \\ RK \le k \le N \end{Bmatrix} \tag{13C, 13D}$$

Aus den Werten p_j lassen sich die Betriebsmittelbelegungen und damit der Durchsatz berechnen

$$\frac{D}{D_0} = BRK + BTK = \sum_{j=1}^{N} (r_j \cdot p_j + t_{N-j} \cdot p_{N-j}) = f\,(RK,\ TK,\ RI,\ N) \tag{14}$$

Ergebnisse sind in den Bildern 4, 6 und 7 dargestellt.

Simulationen

Im folgenden werden die zur Bestimmung des Auftragsdurchsatzes wichtigen Betriebsmittel, Warteschlangen, Strategien und Zufallsvariablen des Simulators erläutert.

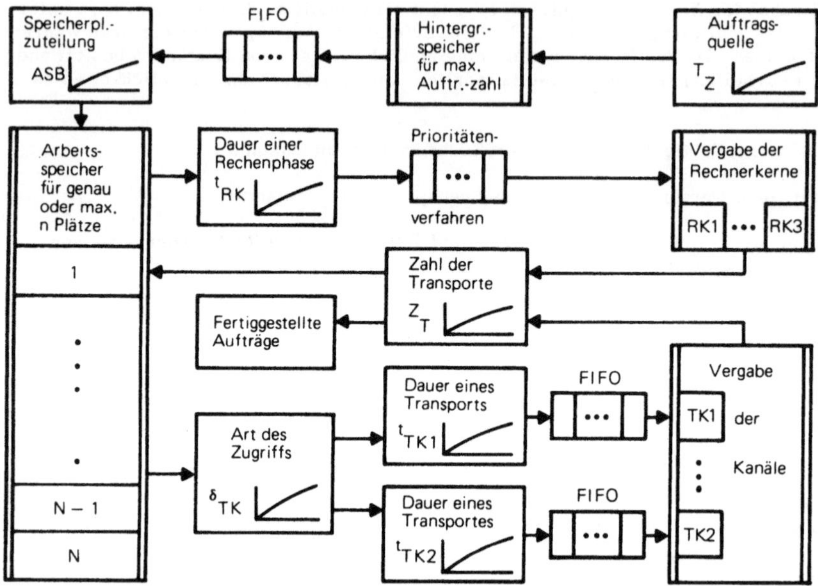

Bild 2: Betriebsmittel, Warteschlangen und Zufallsvariablen des Simulationsmodells

Für eine maximal vorgebbare Anzahl von Aufträgen ist Hintergrundspeicher und Arbeitsspeicher vorgesehen. Es können mehrere Rechnerkerne vorhanden sein, die einander bei Zugriffen auf den Arbeitsspeicher behindern. Das Modell enthält zwei voneinander unabhängige Warteschlangen vor den beiden Hintergrundspeichertypen Trommel und Platte. Die Leistung der Kanäle kann durch parallele Wege zu den einzelnen Moduln der Hintergrundspeicher erhöht werden. Auf dem Hintergrundspeicher liegende Aufträge werden in einer Warteschlange gesammelt. Die Platzzuteilung erfolgt, wenn genügend Arbeitsspeicher vorhanden ist, in der Reihenfolge des Eintreffens der Aufträge. Geladene Aufträge bewerben sich entweder um einen Rechnerkern oder einen der Transportkanäle. Für alle geladenen Aufträge wird eine Prioritätskennzahl errechnet. Ein Auftrag erhält einen Rechnerkern dann, wenn er die höchste Prioritätszahl unter allen konkurrierenden Aufträgen besitzt. Während der Bearbeitung kann zu beliebigen Zeitpunkten die Prioritätszahl umdefiniert werden und den Entzug des Rechnerkerns zur Folge haben. Aufträge, die transportieren wollen, werden entsprechend dem Transportwunsch in eine der beiden Warteschlangen eingereiht, aus der die Aufträge dann in der Reihenfolge ihres Eintreffens bearbeitet werden. Transporte sind im Gegensatz zu Rechenphasen nicht unterbrechbar. Die wichtigsten Zufallsvariablen erläutert die folgende Tabelle:

Name	Verteilung	Bedeutung
T_Z	Poisson-verteilt	Zeitabstand zwischen dem Eintreffen zweier Aufträge; auch saturated-mode möglich
ASB	gemessen	Arbeitsspeicherbedarf eines Auftrags
t_{RK}	gemessen	Dauer der Rechenphase eines Auftrags (ohne Unterbrechungen)
t_{TK}	gemessen	Dauer eines Transportes; die für die beiden Warteschlangen generierten Variablen t_{TK1} und t_{TK2} sind unabhängig voneinander
δ_{TK}	gleichverteilt	Art des Zugriffs; die Zugriffshäufigkeiten zu den Hintergrundspeichern sind gemessen
z_T	gemessen	Zahl der Transporte pro Auftrag

Tabelle 1: Zufallsvariable des Simulationsmodells

Die systemglobalen Ergebnisgrößen sind die

> Belegung der einzelnen Rechnerkerne (BRK_i)
> Belegung der einzelnen Transportkanäle (BTK_i)
> Zahl der bearbeiteten Aufträge (z_A)
> Simulationszeit und verbrauchte Rechenzeit

Die auftragsspezifischen Ergebnisgrößen sind die

> Klasse eines Auftrags (TYP)
> verbrauchte Rechenzeit (T_R)
> verbrauchte Transportzeit (T_T)
> Verweilzeit in der Anlage und die Wartezeiten auf
> Zuteilung von Arbeitsspeicher, eines der Rechnerkerne
> und der verschiedenen Transportkanäle

Ergebnisse sind in den Bildern 4 und 5 dargestellt.

Messungen

Der verwendete Auftragsmix muß verschiedenen Anforderungen genügen. Die Auftragsstichprobe soll so umfangreich sein, daß der stationäre Zustand erreicht und genügend lange gehalten wird. Die verschiedenen Auftragstypen mit den Klassenmerkmalen Rechenintensität, Problemsprache, Speicherbedarf und Laufzeit sollen gemessenen Häufigkeiten entsprechen.

Gemessen wird die zur Bearbeitung des Mixes notwendige Absolutzeit sowie die Aktivität der Komponenten des Systems und der Aufträge. Aus ihnen ergeben sich die Betriebsmittelbelegungen. Ein Meßexperiment läuft folgendermaßen ab: zunächst werden alle Aufträge des Mixes in natürlicher Reihenfolge eingelesen, während die Bearbeitung durch das System noch gesperrt ist. Ein Meßprogramm, das sowohl statisch, d.h. speicherbedarfsmäßig, als auch dynamisch, d.h. laufzeitmäßig, so beschaffen ist, daß es keine merkliche Veränderung des Systemverhaltens hervorruft, registriert den Beginn der Bearbeitung, mit der nach einem Freigabekommando begonnen wird. Das Ende des Experiments wird erreicht, wenn der letzte Auftrag fertig bearbeitet ist. Die von der eigentlichen Bearbeitung getrennt ablaufenden Ausgabevorgänge werden hierbei nicht berücksichtigt. Diese Vorgehensweise bedeutet, daß bei Beginn des Experiments ein Stoßzugang und gegen Ende eine Auslaufphase enthalten ist, hat aber den Vorteil, daß bei verschiedenen Versuchen jeweils die gleiche Arbeit geleistet wird. Durch genügend lange Laufzeiten ist sicherzustellen, daß der gemessene Durchsatz sich entsprechend der geforderten Genauigkeit nur wenig von den stationären Werten unterscheidet.

Ergebnisse sind im Bild 3 dargestellt.

4. Diskussion der Resultate

In Bild 3 und 4 sind Durchsatzabhängigkeiten von der Zahl der Programmplätze dargestellt. Simulations- und Berechnungsergebnisse stimmen mit guter Genauigkeit überein. Die Meßergebnisse gelten für Konfigurationen mit zwei unabhängigen Hintergrundspeichern. Man erkennt, daß ab einer bestimmten Anzahl maximal verfügbarer Programmplätze keine merkliche Durchsatzsteigerung mehr erzielt wird. Der Grund dafür ist unter anderem, daß für den untersuchten Mix der verfügbare Arbeitsspeicher nicht mehr ausreicht und es zu Speicherengpässen kommt, die erst durch Verwaltungsmaßnahmen des Systems wieder aufgelöst werden können. Bei einer größeren Anzahl aktiver Betriebsmittel, besonders bei starkem Magnetbandbetrieb, kann der Durchsatz durch größeren Speicherausbau und mehr Programmplätze weiter gesteigert werden.

In Bild 5 und 6 sind für eine (2, 2)-Konfiguration Berechnungs- und Simulationsergebnisse gegenübergestellt. Es fällt auf, daß die Simulation bei Auftragsmixen geringer Rechenintensität die Wirklichkeit besser wiedergibt. Dies liegt daran, daß bei der Rechnung Zugriffe über die parallel arbeitenden Kanäle auf den gleichen Hintergrundspeicher erfolgen, während bei den Simulationen auf verschiedenen Hintergrundspeicher mit gemessenen Häufigkeiten zugegriffen wird.

Bild 7 stellt für eine feste Anzahl von Programmplätzen sehr anschaulich die Lage und Verschiebung der Durchsatzmaxima dar. In der Praxis werden jedoch die berechneten Durchsatzwerte kaum erreicht, da mehrere Rechnerkerne einander behindern, die Transportkanäle auch bei transportintensivem Mix oft nicht vollständig genutzt werden können und die notwendige Verwaltungsarbeit die verfügbare Rechenleistung mindert.

Literaturhinweis:

Den Berechnungen wurden Betrachtungen aus dem Buch

 Theory of scheduling
 R. W. Conway, W. L. Maxwell, L. W. Miller
 Addison-Wesley Publishing Company
 Reading, Massachusetts

auf den Seiten 147 und 209 zugrunde gelegt.

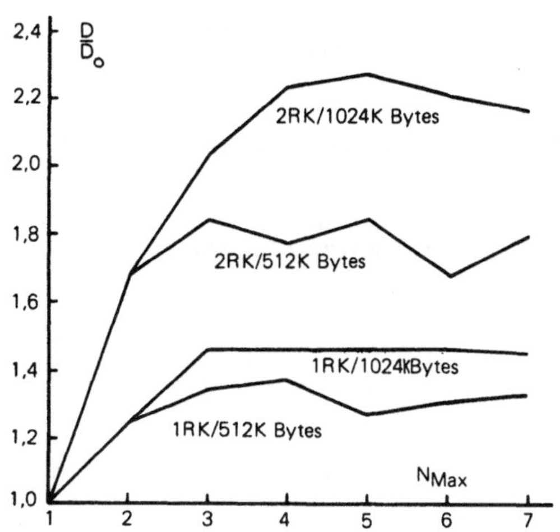

Bild 3: Durchsatz und Zahl der maximal verfügbaren Programmplätze -Meßergebnisse

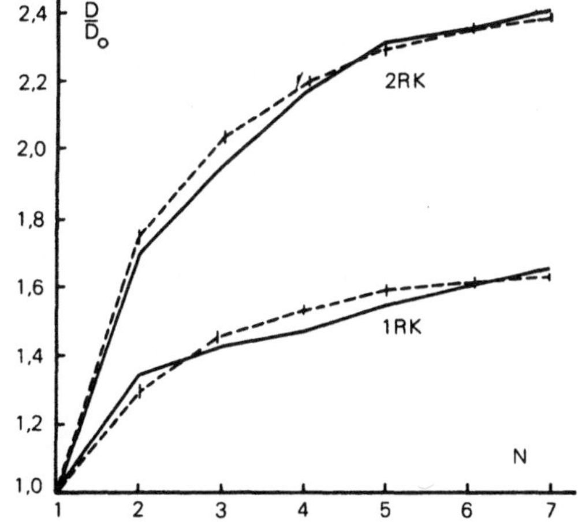

Bild 4: Durchsatz und Zahl der besetzten Programmplätze
-Simulations- und Berechnungsergebnisse

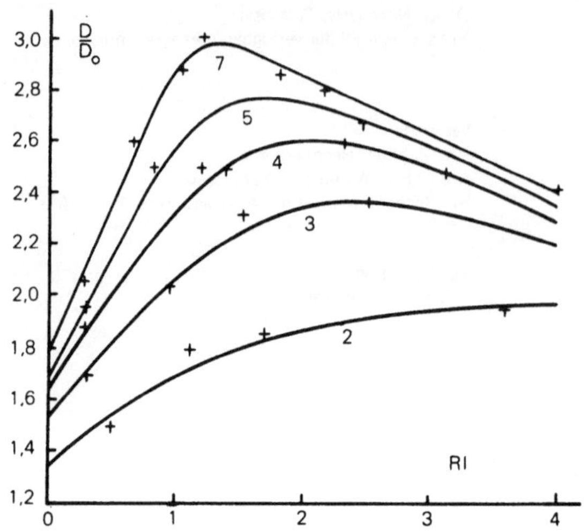

Bild 5: Durchsatz und Rechenintensität der Aufträge -Simulationsergebnisse

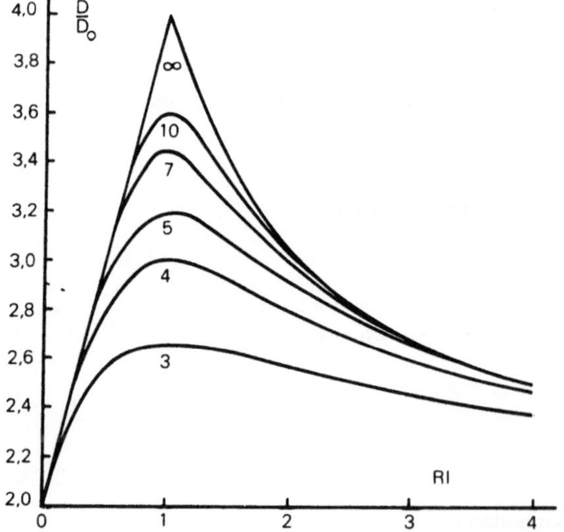

Bild 6: Durchsatz und Rechenintensität der Aufträge -Berechnungsergebnisse

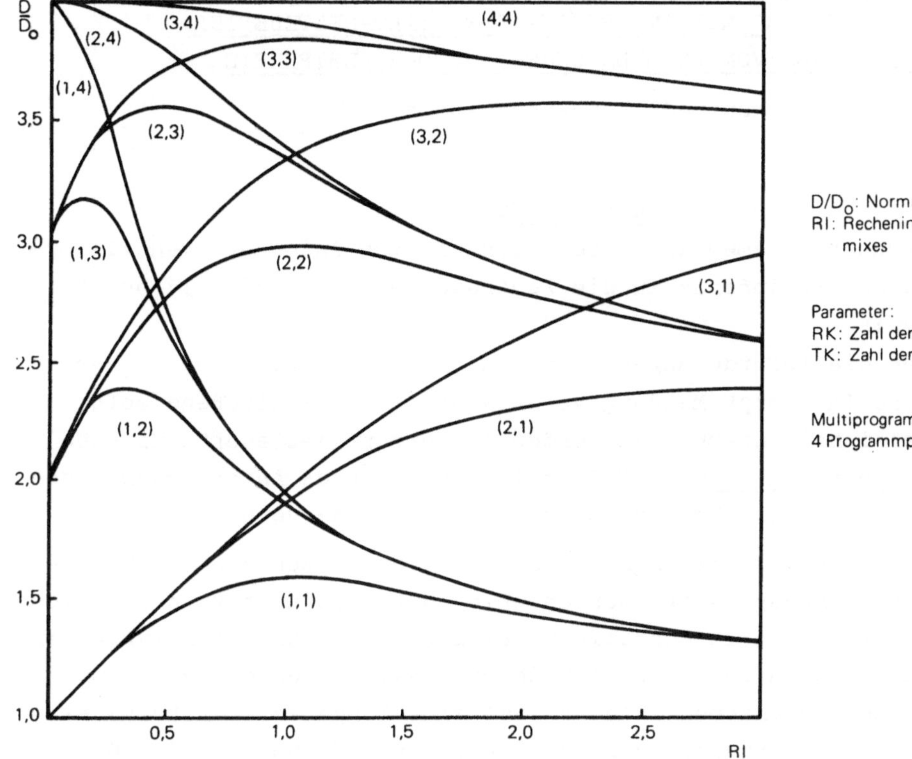

Bild 7: Durchsatz und Konfigurationsabhängigkeiten - Berechnungsergebnisse

VERGLEICH ZWEIER WARTESCHLANGENMODELLE FÜR REALZEIT-RECHNERSYSTEME MIT INTERRUPT- BZW. TAKT-GESTEUERTER ÜBERNAHME VON ANFORDERUNGEN AUS DER PERIPHERIE

Manfred Langenbach-Belz

1. EINLEITUNG

In Realzeitrechnersystemen kann die Übernahme von Anforderungen (Informationen) aus der Peripherie in die Zentraleinheit prinzipiell auf 2 Arten erfolgen:

Erstens können die Anforderungen direkt nach ihrer Entstehung in der Peripherie eine Interrupt-Meldung verursachen und anschließend sofort in die Zentraleinheit übernommen werden (interrupt-gesteuerte Eingabe). Somit ist für <u>jede einzelne</u>, zufallsmäßig entstehende Anforderung eine gewisse Verwaltungszeit für ihre Eingabe nötig (E/A-overhead).

Zweitens können die Anforderungen in der Peripherie zunächst nach ihrer Entstehung zwischengespeichert werden. Die Zentraleinheit kann dann von sich aus die Peripherie in bestimmtem zeitlichen Abstand nach wartenden Anforderungen abfragen und in diesen Abfragezeitpunkten ganze Gruppen von Anforderungen übernehmen. Dadurch ist eine Eingabe-Verwaltungszeit <u>nur in den Abfragezeitpunkten</u> erforderlich. Diese Methode wird z.B. bei modernen rechnergesteuerten Fernsprech- oder Datenvermittlungssystemen angewendet, wobei der zeitliche Abstand zwischen 2 Abfragezeitpunkten konstant ist (takt-gesteuerte Eingabe).

Die Arbeit befaßt sich mit der Frage, wie sich die obigen prinzipiellen Betriebsweisen insbesondere auf die <u>mittleren Wartezeiten</u> der Anforderungen auswirken. Zu diesem Zweck werden 2 Warteschlangenmodelle analytisch behandelt und deren numerische Ergebnisse einander gegenübergestellt.

2. BESCHREIBUNG DER BEIDEN WARTESCHLANGENMODELLE

2.1 Modell mit interrupt-gesteuerter Eingabe (Modell 1)

Die Anforderungen entstehen in g peripheren Geräten mit der Ankunftsrate λ_i (i=1,2,...,g) in negativ-exponentiell verteilten zeitlichen Abständen. Jede in der Peripherie entstehende Anforderung hat <u>unmittelbar</u> eine Interrupt-Meldung an die Zentraleinheit zur Folge, welche in eine Warteschlange für Interrupt-Meldungen eingeordnet wird (vgl. Bild 1a). Die Bedienungseinheit der Zentraleinheit benötigt zur Behandlung einer Interrupt-Meldung die konstante Zeit v (Verwaltungszeit für Eingabe). Während dieser Zeit v soll auch die zugehörige Anforderung, welche seit-

her in der Peripherie gewartet hatte, in den Speicher der Zentraleinheit
geholt werden. Zur Bearbeitung einer Anforderung benötige die Bedienungseinheit die konstante Bedienungsdauer h. Die Interrupt-Meldungen haben
<u>unterbrechende Priorität</u> gegenüber der Verarbeitung von Anforderungen.
Unterbrochene Anforderungen werden später in ihrer Verarbeitung fortgesetzt. Die Warteschlangendisziplin innerhalb wartender Anforderungen
bzw. Interrupt-Meldungen sei "first-in, first-out" (FIFO).

Aufgrund der oben beschriebenen Betriebsweise kann das in Bild 1a aus-
führlich gezeichnete Modell wie in Bild 1b vereinfacht dargestellt werden. Dabei wird angenommen, daß die Wartespeicher für Anforderungen und
Interrupt-Meldungen unbegrenzt groß seien.

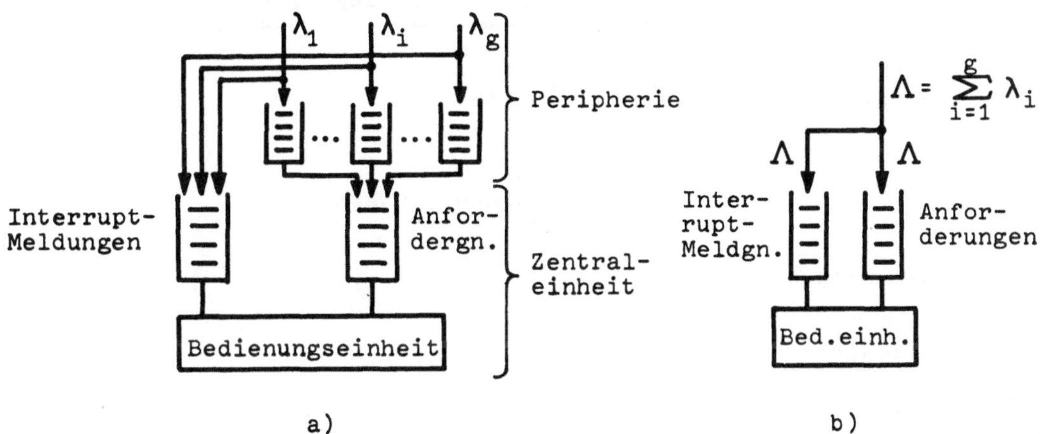

<u>Bild 1:</u> Warteschlangenmodell für interrupt-gesteuerte Eingabe (Modell 1)
a) ausführliches Modell b) vereinfachte Darstellung

2.2 Modell mit takt-gesteuerter Eingabe (Modell 2)

Die Anforderungen entstehen auch hier in negativ-exponentiell verteilten zeitlichen Abständen. Sie werden zunächst in g parallelen Primärspeichern (PS) in der Peripherie zwischengespeichert (vgl. Bild 2).
Jeweils in <u>konstanten Taktabständen T</u> werden die Anforderungen aus den
Primärspeichern in einem Pufferspeicher (Sekundärspeicher SS) der Zentraleinheit übernommen. Dabei wird allerdings pro Taktzeitpunkt aus
einem Primärspeicher i eine Gruppe von max. n_i Anforderungen entnommen.
Befinden sich zu diesem Zeitpunkt mehr als n_i Anforderungen in diesem
PS_i, so müssen die restlichen Anforderungen weiterhin warten. Die im SS
wartenden Anforderungen werden von der zentralen Bedienungseinheit nach
der Disziplin FIFO einzeln abgearbeitet. Zur Bearbeitung einer Anforderung wird die konstante Bedienungsdauer h benötigt. In den Taktzeitpunkten wird die zentrale Bedienungseinheit zur Durchführung der Abfrage
und Eingabe für die konstante Zeitdauer v belegt. Es wird angenommen,

daß T=v+c·h sei, wobei c eine feste ganze Zahl ist. Alle Wartespeicher
seien unbegrenzt groß. Weitere Voraussetzung sei, daß $\text{Min}[n_i] \geq c$ ist, da
sonst der Fall auftreten könnte, daß in einem Taktzeitpunkt noch Anforderungen in einem Primärspeicher zurückgelassen würden, andererseits
die Bedienungseinheit aber bis zum nächsten Taktzeitpunkt nicht voll
beschäftigt wäre.

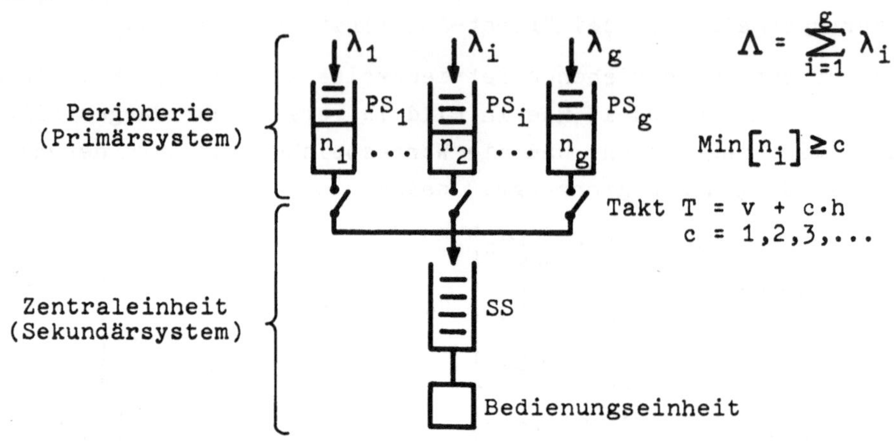

Bild 2: Warteschlangenmodell mit takt-gesteuerter Eingabe (Modell 2)

3. ANALYTISCHE BEHANDLUNG BEIDER MODELLE

3.1 Modell mit interrupt-gesteuerter Eingabe (Modell 1)

Bei Modell 1 (vgl. Bild 1) handelt es sich im Prinzip um ein Wartesystem mit 2 Prioritätsklassen. Die Prioritätsklasse p=1 enthält die
Interrupt-Meldungen, welche unterbrechende Priorität gegenüber den Anforderungen in der Prioritätsklasse p=2 besitzen. Im folgenden werden
die Interrupt-Meldungen deshalb allgemein als 1-Anforderungen bezeichnet
und die eigentlichen Anforderungen als 2-Anforderungen.

Wegen der unterbrechenden Priorität der 1-Anforderungen gegenüber den
2-Anforderungen können sämtliche charakteristischen Verkehrsgrößen der
1-Anforderungen so bestimmt werden, als ob die 2-Anforderungen nicht
vorhanden wären (Wartesystem M/D/1). Die mittlere Wartezeit aller 1-An-
forderungen ist deshalb

$$w(1) = \frac{\Lambda v}{2(1-\Lambda v)} \cdot v = \frac{A(1)}{2(1-A(1))} \cdot v \qquad (1)$$

mit $\quad A(1)=\Lambda v=$Angebot der Klasse p=1.

w(1) ist gleichzeitig diejenige Wartezeit, welche eine 2-Anforderung bis
zu ihrer Übernahme in die Zentraleinheit im Mittel in der Peripherie
warten muß (vgl. Bild 1a).

Die mittlere Wartezeit der 2-Anforderungen wird mittels der Momenten-Methode bestimmt (vgl./1,2,3/). Dazu wird eine beliebige ankommende 2-Anforderung betrachtet und zunächst der Erwartungswert für ihre Durchlaufzeit $f(2)$ (Wartezeit + Bedienungszeit) ermittelt. Der Erwartungswert der Durchlaufzeit $f(2)$ setzt sich aus folgenden 5 Anteilen zusammen:

a) Mittlere Durchlaufzeit $f(1)$ der gleichzeitig mit der 2-Anforderung eintreffenden 1-Anforderung

$$f(1) = w(1) + v \qquad (2)$$

b) Mittlere Restbedienungszeit h_R einer 2-Anforderung, welche evtl. gerade die Bedienungseinheit belegt.

c) Mittlere Bedienungszeit $w_2(2)$ aller 2-Anforderungen, welche bei der Ankunft der 2-Anforderung bereits im System <u>warten</u>.

d) Bedienungszeit h der betrachteten 2-Anforderung.

e) Bedienungszeit $w_1(2)$ aller während der mittleren Durchlaufzeit $f(2)$ der betrachteten 2-Anforderung im Mittel eintreffenden 1-Anforderungen.

Damit ist der Erwartungswert der Durchlaufzeit $f(2)$ von 2-Anforderungen:

$$f(2) = f(1) + h_R + w_2(2) + h + w_1(2) \qquad (3)$$

In (3) müssen noch h_R, $w_2(2)$ und $w_1(2)$ berechnet werden.
Befindet sich bei der Ankunft einer 2-Anforderung eine 2-Anforderung in der Bedienungseinheit, so beträgt deren mittlere Restbedienungszeit $h/2$ (wegen Poisson-Ankunftsprozeß). Die Wahrscheinlichkeit, daß sich aber überhaupt eine 2-Anforderung in der Bedienungseinheit befindet, ist $A(2) = \Lambda h$. Damit ist

$$h_R = \frac{h}{2} \cdot A(2) \qquad (4)$$

Zur Bestimmung von $w_2(2)$ muß man bei den <u>wartenden</u> 2-Anforderungen unterscheiden zwischen jenen, welche noch nicht unterbrochen wurden und jenen, die bereits einmal unterbrochen wurden. Die noch nicht unterbrochenen müssen jeweils noch ihre volle Bedienungsdauer h absolvieren, während die bereits unterbrochenen im Mittel nur noch $h/2$ zur Bedienung benötigen. Der Anteil der unterbrochenen bzw. nicht unterbrochenen wartenden 2-Anforderungen kann wieder mit Hilfe der Momenten-Methode bestimmt werden, worauf hier allerdings nicht genauer eingegangen werden soll (vgl. /2/).Als Ergebnis erhält man:

$$w_2(2) = \left[f(2)-h\right]A(2) - \frac{1}{2}\frac{A(1)A(2)}{1-A(1)}\,h \qquad (5)$$

Schließlich kommen während der mittleren Durchlaufzeit $f(2)$ einer 2-Anforderung im Mittel noch $\Lambda f(2)$ neue 1-Anforderungen an, d.h. es gilt

$$w_1(2) = \Lambda f(2)\cdot v \qquad (6)$$

Setzt man (1), (2), (4), (5) und (6) in (3) ein, so kann die entstehende Gleichung nach f(2) aufgelöst werden. Daraus folgt dann für die mittlere Wartezeit w(2)=f(2)-h der 2-Anforderungen:

$$w(2) = \frac{h}{1-A(1)-A(2)}\left[\frac{A(1)}{2(1-A(1))}\left(\frac{v}{h} - A(2)\right) + A(1) + \frac{A(2)}{2} + \frac{v}{h}\right] \tag{7}$$

3.2 Modell mit takt-gesteuerter Eingabe (Modell 2)

Modell 2 (vgl. Bild 2) wurde ohne Verwaltungszeit, d.h. v=0, bereits in / 4/ und / 5/ analytisch behandelt. Deshalb soll hier nur der prinzipielle Lösungsweg angedeutet und die für den vorliegenden Bericht relevanten Ergebnisse eines Systems mit v=0 dargelegt werden. Darauf aufbauend werden die Ergebnisse für Systeme mit einer Verwaltungszeit v>0 abgeleitet.

Zur Lösung der charakteristischen Verkehrsgrößen dieses Systems wird die Methode der eingebetteten Markoff-Kette verwendet. Dabei wird der Zustand des Systems jeweils nur zu bestimmten Zeitpunkten betrachtet, im vorliegenden Fall z.B. jeweils kurz nach den Taktzeitpunkten. Mit Hilfe der Übergangswahrscheinlichkeiten von einem Zustand x_i nach dem Taktzeitpunkt i in einen Zustand x_{i+1} nach dem Taktzeitpunkt i+1 wird ein Gleichungssystem für die Zustandswahrscheinlichkeiten p(x) aufgestellt, mit welchem die erzeugende Funktion

$$G(z) = \sum_{x=0}^{\infty} p(x) z^x$$

der Zustandswahrscheinlichkeiten ermittelt wird. Aus der erzeugenden Funktion G(z) erhält man die mittlere Anzahl von Anforderungen im System als dG(z)/dz an der Stelle z=1. Durch eine Rücktransformation der erzeugenden Funktion lassen sich explizite Formeln für die Zustandswahrscheinlichkeiten p(x) angeben.

Die charakteristischen Verkehrsgrößen eines einzelnen Primärspeichers i hängen nur von der Ankunftsrate λ_i, der Abfrageplatzzahl n_i und der Taktzeit T ab. Somit können die entsprechenden Größen direkt von dem System ohne Verwaltungszeiten übernommen werden (vgl. /4/,/5/). Insbesondere sind hier die folgenden beiden Verkehrsgrößen für einen Primärspeicher i von Interesse:

- Mittlere Anzahl von Informationen $E_{Pi}[x,T]$ in Primärspeicher i kurz nach dem Takt:

$$E_{Pi}[x,T] = \sum_{v=1}^{n_i-1} \frac{1}{1-z_v} + \frac{(n_i-\lambda_i T)^2 - n_i}{2(\lambda_i T - n_i)} - \lambda_i T \tag{8}$$

wobei z_v die n Nullstellen mit $|z_v| \leq 1$ der Bestimmungsgleichung $z^{n_i} e^{\lambda_i T(1-z)} - 1 = 0$ sind. ($z_0=1$ ist immer Nullstelle).

- Mittlere Wartezeit w_{Pi} aller Anforderungen im Primärspeicher i:

$$w_{Pi} = \frac{1}{\lambda_i}\left[\sum_{v=1}^{n_i-1}\frac{1}{1-z_v} + \frac{n_i}{2}\left(\frac{1}{n_i-\lambda_i T} - 1\right)\right] \tag{9}$$

Über das Sekundärsystem bzw. Gesamtsystem (Sekundärsystem+Primärsystem) kann folgende Aussage gemacht werden:

In einem System **mit** Verwaltungszeiten (v>0) können wie in einem System **ohne** Verwaltungszeiten (v=0) zwischen 2 Taktzeitpunkten max. c Anforderungen bedient werden. Deshalb gelten im System mit v>0 für die Zustandswahrscheinlichkeiten und die direkt damit zusammenhängende mittlere Anzahl von Anforderungen **kurz nach dem Takt** dieselben Formeln wie im System mit v=0. Die mittlere Anzahl $E_G\left[x,T\right]$ von Anforderungen im Gesamtsystem kurz nach dem Takt ist dann nach /4/ bzw. /5/:

$$E_G\left[x,T\right] = \sum_{v=1}^{c-1}\frac{1}{1-z_v} + \frac{(c-\Lambda T)^2-c}{2(\Lambda T-c)} \tag{10}$$

wobei hier z_v die c Nullstellen mit $|z_v| \leq 1$ der Bestimmungsgleichung $z^c \cdot e^{\Lambda T(1-z)} - 1 = 0$ sind ($z_0=1$ ist immer Nullstelle).

Die mittlere Anzahl von Anforderungen $E_S\left[x,T\right]$ im Sekundärsystem kurz nach dem Takt ist somit

$$E_S\left[x,T\right] = E_G\left[x,T\right] - \sum_{i=1}^{g} E_{Pi}\left[x,T\right] \tag{11}$$

Weiterhin erhält man nach /4/ bzw. /5/ für die Zustandswahrscheinlichkeiten $p_S(x,T)$ des Sekundärsystems kurz nach dem Takt

$$p_S(x,T) = \frac{\Lambda T - c}{\prod\limits_{v=1}^{c-1}(1-z_v)}(-1)^{c-x}S_{c-x} \qquad \underline{\text{für } x<c} \tag{12}$$

wobei z_v wie bei Gl. (10)

$$\text{und} \quad S_1 = z_0+z_1+z_2+\ldots+z_{c-1} = \sum_{i=0}^{c-1} z_i$$

$$S_2 = z_0 z_1+z_0 z_2+\ldots+z_{c-2}z_{c-1} = \sum_{\substack{i1,i2=0 \\ (i1<i2)}}^{c-1} z_{i1}z_{i2}$$

$$\vdots$$

$$S_c = z_0 z_1 z_2 \ldots z_{c-1}$$

Zur Bestimmung der mittleren Speicherbelastung Ω_S des Sekundärspeichers dient nun folgende Überlegung:

Kurz nach dem Takt kann wegen der Verwaltungszeit keine Anforderung die Bedienungseinheit belegen, d.h. alle im Sekundärsystem enthaltenen Anforderungen befinden sich im Sekundärspeicher. Nach der Verwaltungszeit v kann eine Anforderung aus dem Sekundärspeicher in die Bedienungseinheit übernommen werden (falls vorhanden), nach einer Bedienungsdauer h die nächste usw. Die mittlere Schlangenlänge im Sekundärspeicher ist also eine Treppenfunktion in Abhängigkeit von der Zeit (vgl. Bild 3).

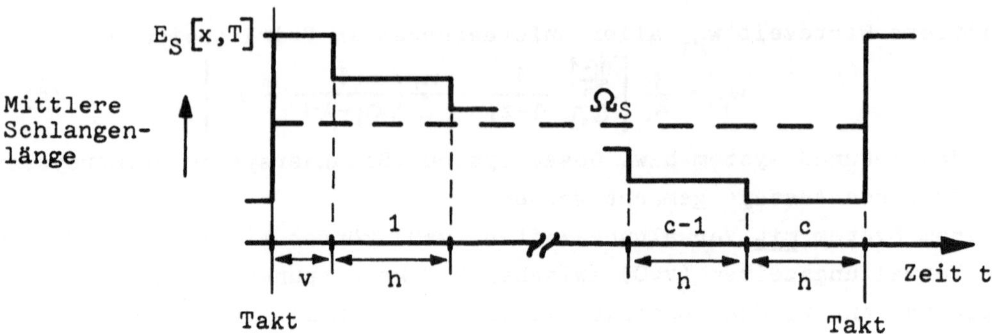

__Bild 3:__ Mittlere Schlangenlänge im Sekundärspeicher über der Zeit

Die einzelnen Stufenhöhen der Treppenfunktion in Bild 3 werden durch die Zustandswahrscheinlichkeiten $p_S(x,T)$ kurz nach dem Takt bestimmt. Die mittlere Speicherbelastung Ω_S des Sekundärspeichers ist die über die Taktzeit T gemittelte mittlere Schlangenlänge:

$$\Omega_S = E_S[x,T] - \frac{h}{T} \sum_{j=1}^{c} \left[j - \sum_{x=0}^{j-1} (j-x)\, p_S(x,T) \right] \tag{13}$$

$E_S[x,T]$ bzw. $p_S(x,T)$ sind aus (11) bzw. (12) bekannt.
Für die mittlere Wartezeit w_S im Sekundärspeicher gilt allgemein:

$$w_S = \frac{\Omega_S}{\Lambda} \tag{14}$$

Die mittlere Gesamtwartezeit w_G bezüglich aller Anforderungen im Gesamtsystem setzt sich zusammen aus der mittleren Wartezeit der Anforderungen im Primärsystem und der mittleren Wartezeit der Anforderungen im Sekundärsystem:

$$w_G = \sum_{i=1}^{g} \frac{\lambda_i}{\Lambda}\, w_{Pi} + w_S \tag{15}$$

Solange die Voraussetzung $\mathrm{Min}[n_i] \geq c$ erfüllt ist, ergibt sich für gleiche Gesamtankunftsrate Λ immer die gleiche Gesamtwartezeit w_G, unabhängig von der Anzahl g der Primärspeicher sowie den Einzelwerten n_i. Die Paramter g und n_i beeinflussen lediglich die Aufteilung der Gesamtwartezeit w_G auf das Primär- und Sekundärsystem.

Von besonderem Interesse ist nun ein Vergleich der mittleren Wartezeit w(2) (vgl. Gl.(7)) des Modells 1 und der mittleren Wartezeit w_G (vgl. Gl.(15)) des Modells 2. Dieser Vergleich wird in Abschnitt 4.1 durchführt. Ein Vergleich der Bedienungseinheitbelastung folgt in Abschn.4.2.

4. NUMERISCHE ERGEBNISSE UND VERGLEICH

4.1 Mittlere Wartezeit der Anforderungen

Im folgenden Vergleich numerischer Ergebnisse wurde davon ausgegangen, daß die Verwaltungszeiten v bei beiden Modellen gleich groß sind.

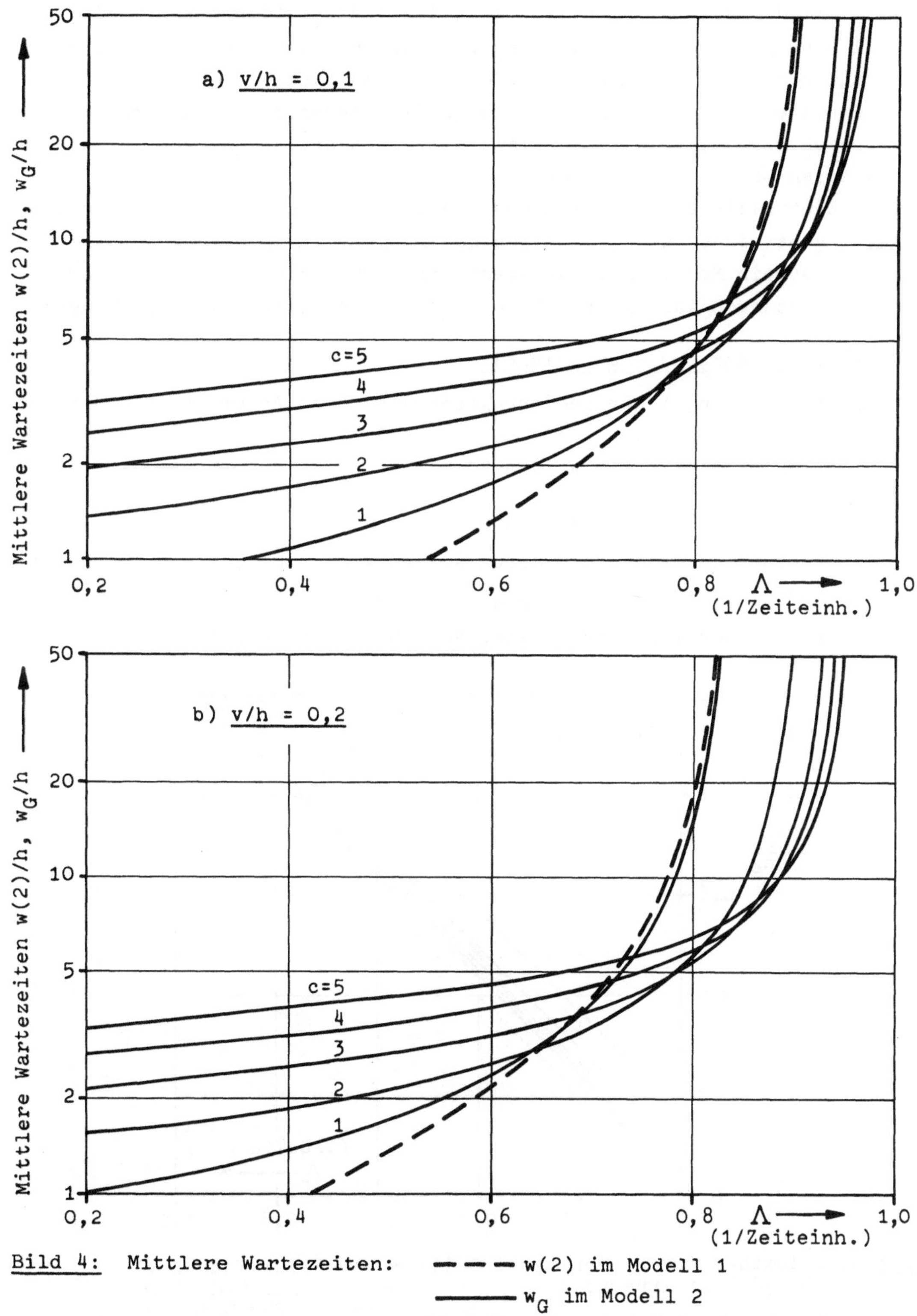

Bild 4: Mittlere Wartezeiten: $- - -$ w(2) im Modell 1
$\quad\quad\quad\quad\quad\quad\quad\quad\quad\quad\quad$ —— w_G im Modell 2
(jeweils h = 1,0 Zeiteinheiten)

Wie aus Bild 4 a),b) ersichtlich ist, liegt die mittlere Wartezeit im
Modell 2 bei kleinen Ankunftsraten wesentlich höher als im Modell 1.
Dies rührt daher, daß bereits die mittlere Wartezeit in der Peripherie
(Primärsystem) schon $\geq$ T/2 ist. Bei großen Ankunftsraten allerdings
wirkt sich zu Gunsten des Modells 2 die geringere Anzahl von Verwal-
tungszeiten pro Zeiteinheit aus.

Da die Zentraleinheit von rechnergesteuerten Systemen meist mit hoher
Belastung betrieben wird, kann aus den Diagrammen in Bild 4 gefolgert
werden, daß ein Modell mit takt-gesteuerter Eingabe unempfindlicher gegen Überlastungen ist als ein Modell mit interrupt-gesteuerter Eingabe.

4.2 Belastung der Bedienungseinheit

Die Gesamtbelastung Y der Bedienungseinheit durch Anforderungen und
Verwaltungszeiten ist

- bei Modell 1: $Y = A(1)+A(2) = \Lambda(v+h)$

- bei Modell 2: $Y = \frac{1}{T} v + \Lambda h$.

Für beide Modelle ist die nur durch Anforderungen bedingte Belastung Y_A
der Bedienungseinheit: $Y_A = \Lambda h$

Bild 5 zeigt einen Vergleich dieser verschiedenen Belastungen.

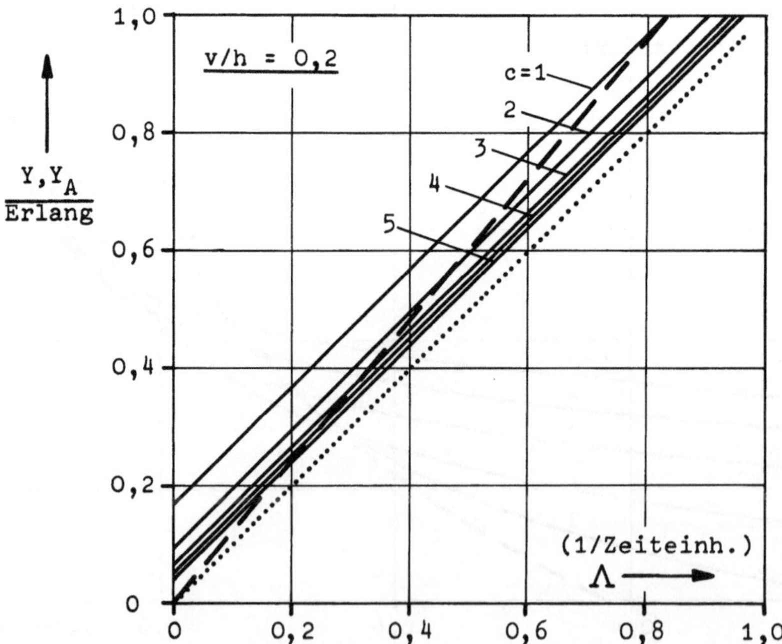

Bild 5: Belastung der Bedienungseinheit: — — —Y für Modell 1
        (h=1,0 Zeiteinheiten)   ——————Y für Modell 2
                                           ···········Y_A für beide Modelle

Aus Bild 5 ist ersichtlich, daß im interessierenden Bereich der Ankunftsrate $\Lambda \geq 0,5$ die Belastung der Bedienungseinheit im Modell 2 für $c > 1$
geringer ist als im Modell 1. Das bedeutet, daß im Modell mit takt-gesteuerter Eingabe mehr Kapazitätsreserve der Bedienungseinheit z.B. für
Hintergrundprogramme zur Verfügung steht.

5. ZUSAMMENFASSUNG

Es wurden 2 Warteschlangenmodelle für ein Realzeitrechnersystem vorgestellt, eines mit interrupt-gesteuerter und eines mit takt-gesteuerter
Übernahme der Anforderungen aus der Peripherie. Bei beiden Modellen
wurde eine konstante Verwaltungszeit für die Eingabeoperation vorgesehen. Nach einer Beschreibung der analytischen Behandlung beider Modelle folgte ein Vergleich der mittleren Gesamtwartezeiten von Anforderungen sowie der Belastung der Bedienungseinheit in beiden Modellen.
Dabei zeigte sich, daß bei hohen Belastungen das Modell mit takt-gesteuerter Eingabe etwas günstigere Resultate aufwies als das Modell mit
interrupt-gesteuerter Eingabe.

Der Autor dankt Herrn Prof. Dr.-Ing. A. Lotze sowie den Herren
Dr.-Ing. U. Herzog, Dr.-Ing. P. Kühn und Dipl.-Ing. H. Weisschuh für
viele anregende und wertvolle Diskussionen bezüglich des behandelten
Problemkreises.

LITERATUR

/1/ Herzog,U.: Preemption-Distance Priorities in Real-Time Computer
    Systems. NTZ 25(1972)4, 201-203.

/2/ Herzog,U.: Verkehrsfluß in Datennetzen.
    Habilitationsschrift, Universität Stuttgart, 1973.

/3/ Herzog,U., Kühn,P., Zeh,A.: Klassifizierung und Analyse von Ver-
    kehrsmodellen für das Ablaufgeschehen in Rechnersystemen.
    Nachrichtentechnische Fachberichte, Band 44 (1972), 181-198.

/4/ Langenbach-Belz,M.: Two-Stage Queuing System with Sampled Parallel
    Input Queues. Congressbook "7th International Teletraffic Congress
    (ITC)", Stockholm, 1973, Paper 434.

/5/ Langenbach-Belz,M.: Getaktete Wartesysteme bei Rechnern und zen-
    tralgesteuerten Nachrichtenvermittlungsanlagen.
    Dissertationsschrift, Universität Stuttgart, 1973.

MODELL FÜR DEN BEFEHLSABLAUF IN EINER RECHENANLAGE:

EINE SERVERKETTE MIT VORGEBBARER VARIANZ DER BELEGUNGSDAUERN

JOACHIM SWOBODA   und   WILHELM ROSENBOHM

Zusammenfassung

Für die Berechnung des Durchsatzes an Befehlen je Zeiteinheit durch einen Prozessor wird ein Näherungsverfahren angegeben. Der Prozessor bestehe aus einer
Kette von Bearbeitungsstationen bzw. Servern. Für das Berechnungsverfahren
werden die beiden ersten Server zu einem Ersatzserver zusammengefaßt, der wiederum mit dem nächsten Server zu einem Ersatzserver für die drei ersten Server
zusammengefaßt werden kann, usw. Die Server und Ersatzserver werden durch Erwartungswert und Streuung ihrer Belegungsdauer gekennzeichnet. Im Gegensatz
zur exakten Rechnung, die bereits bei wenigen Servern in einer Kette praktisch
nicht mehr durchzuführen ist, erfordert die Näherungsrechnung geringen Aufwand.

Die Durchsatzberechnung wird auf die Befehlsabläufe realer Rechenanlagen angewandt, für die eine Verteilung der Belegungsdauer in den einzelnen Unterwerken
bekannt ist. Die berechneten Durchsätze stimmen mit den durch Verkehrssimula-
tion ermittelten Durchsätzen sehr gut überein. Das behandelte Verfahren soll
ein Beitrag sein, die Betriebsabläufe in einer Rechenanlage analytisch zu erfassen.

1. EINFÜHRUNG

Die Bearbeitung von Befehlen in einem Prozessor läßt sich beschleunigen, wenn
dazu einzelne autonome Unterwerke als Fließband organisiert sind. Solche Unterwerke sind z.B. ein Befehlswerk für die Aufbereitung der Befehle und ein
anschließendes Rechenwerk für die Ausführung der Befehle. Eine noch differen-
ziertere Arbeitsteilung findet sich in einer sog. Befehls-Pipeline zur Aufbereitung der Befehle mit den autonomen Unterwerken für das Holen der Befehle,
für Decodieren und Adreßrechnung und für das Holen von Operanden.

Die einzelnen Unterwerke bilden eine Kette von Bedienungsstationen bzw. Servern, und die zu bearbeitenden Befehle sind Aufträge, welche die einzelnen
Stationen nacheinander belegen. Unterschiedliche Befehle belegen die Unterwerke unterschiedlich lang. Aus der Sicht eines Unterwerkes kann die Folge der
Befehle nicht vorausgesagt werden. Deshalb erscheint für ein Unterwerk die
Folge der zu bearbeitenden Befehle als eine Folge von Aufträgen mit zufällig
schwankender Bedienungsdauer. Der Durchsatz von Aufträgen durch die Serverkette hängt von der Bedienungsdauer in den einzelnen Servern ab. Neben dem Erwartungswert der Bedienungs- bzw. Belegungsdauer wirkt insbesondere eine große
Streuung der zufällig schwankenden Belegungsdauer sich durchsatzmindernd aus.
Für die Berechnung des Durchsatzes sollte deshalb sowohl der Erwartungswert
als auch die Streuung bzw. Varianz der einzelnen Belegungsdauerverteilungen
berücksichtigt werden.

Um einen anschaulichen Eindruck solcher Verteilungen zu geben, werden folgende
zwei Beispiele angeführt:

Für einen realen Prozessor (TR 440), der aus Befehlswerk (1. Stufe) und Rechenwerk (2. Stufe) besteht, sind in Bild 1 die einzelnen Belegungsdauerverteilungen aufgetragen. Es ist $w(\leq t)$ die relative Häufigkeit, daß ein Befehl
die 1. bzw. 2. Stufe für die Dauer von höchstens t Takten belegt unter der Bedingung, daß er diese Stufe überhaupt belegt. Der Anteil v_1 aller Befehle kann
in der 1. Stufe beendet werden und verläßt die Serverkette. Befehle, die nach
der 1. Stufe in der 2. Stufe weiterbearbeitet werden, müssen gegebenenfalls
warten, bis die 2. Stufe frei wird; zwischen den Stufen sind keine Warteplätze
vorgesehen. Die Belegungsdauerverteilungen hängen davon ab, mit welcher Häufigkeit unterschiedliche Befehle auftreten. Dem Bild 1 liegt ein Befehlsmix
aus FORTRAN-Objekten zugrunde.

Für ein weiteres Beispiel sind in Bild 2 die Belegungsdauerverteilungen bei
4-stufiger Befehlsbearbeitung dargestellt (Modellprozessor für TR 440-Befehle,
technisch-wissenschaftlicher Befehlsmix). Bei diesem Modellprozessor wurde u.a.

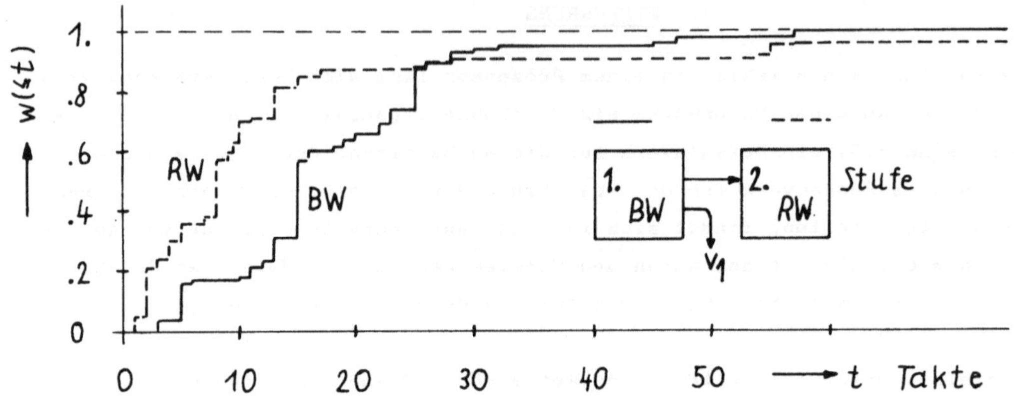

Bild 1 Belegungsdauerverteilung w($\leq$t) für das Befehlswerk (BW) und Rechenwerk (RW) eines realen Prozessors (TR 440, FORTRAN-Befehlsmix).
1. Stufe: BW E_1 = 17.9 S_1 = 10.4
2. Stufe: RW E_2 = 17.7 S_2 = 39.4 .
Es ist E_i der Erwartungswert bzw. S_i die Streuung der Belegungsdauer
in der Stufe i. Der Anteil v_1 = 0.28 aller Befehle kann in der 1. Stufe beendet werden und verläßt die Serverkette.

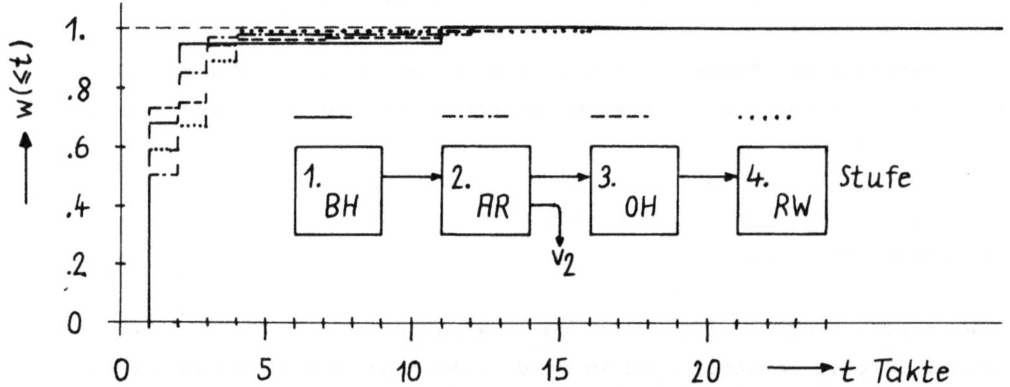

<u>**Bild 2**</u> Belegungsdauerverteilung w($\leq$t) bei einer 4-stufigen Befehlsbearbei-
tung (Modellprozessor für TR 440-Befehle).
1. Stufe: Befehl Holen   E = 1.78   S = 2.22
2. Stufe: Adreß-Rechnung   E = 1.75   S = 1.31
3. Stufe: Operand Holen   E = 1.81   S = 2.02
4. Stufe: Rechenwerk   E = 2.00   S = 1.93
Es ist E_i der Erwartungswert bzw. S_i die Streuung der Belegungsdauer
in der Stufe i. Mit dem Anteil v_2 = 0.50 wird ein Befehl in der
2. Stufe völlig beendet.

unterstellt, daß die Stufen 1 bis 3 schnelle lokale Speicher für Befehle bzw.
Adreß-Operanden bzw. für gewöhnliche Operanden enthalten, die 95 % aller Zugriffswünsche erfüllen können. Die restlichen 5 % der Zugriffswünsche werden
von dem langsameren Zentralspeicher erfüllt.

Die Verteilungskurven von Bild 2 und Bild 1 (für RW) zeigen einen anfänglich schnellen Anstieg und einen langen 'Verteilungsschwanz". Das bedeutet, daß eine Belegungsdauer mit großer Wahrscheinlichkeit kurz ist, und wenn sie nicht kurz ist, dann ist sie vergleichsweise sehr lang. Für die Belegungsdauer der einzelnen Stufen sind die Erwartung E_i und die Streuung S_i angegeben. (Zum Vergleich sind bei einer negativ exponentiellen Verteilungsfunktion, mit der häufig / 4 / gerechnet wird, Erwartungswert und Streuung gleich groß.) In dem folgenden verkehrstheoretischen Modell kann die Streuung der Belegungsdauerverteilungen vorgegeben werden.

2. DAS VERKEHRSTHEORETISCHE MODELL

Die in der Literatur behandelten Serverketten beschränken sich auf negativ exponentielle Verteilung der Belegungsdauern / 1 /, / 2 / oder sie beschränken sich auf eine geringe Stufenzahl (z.B. 2) für die Serverkette / 3 /. Diese Modelle können den Ablauf der Befehlsbearbeitung in einer Rechenanlage nur sehr ungenau erfassen. Die im folgenden behandelte Serverkette ist in ihrer Stufenzahl nicht eingeschränkt, dagegen wird eine spezielle Belegungsdauerverteilung angenommen, die dem vorliegenden Problem angepaßt ist.

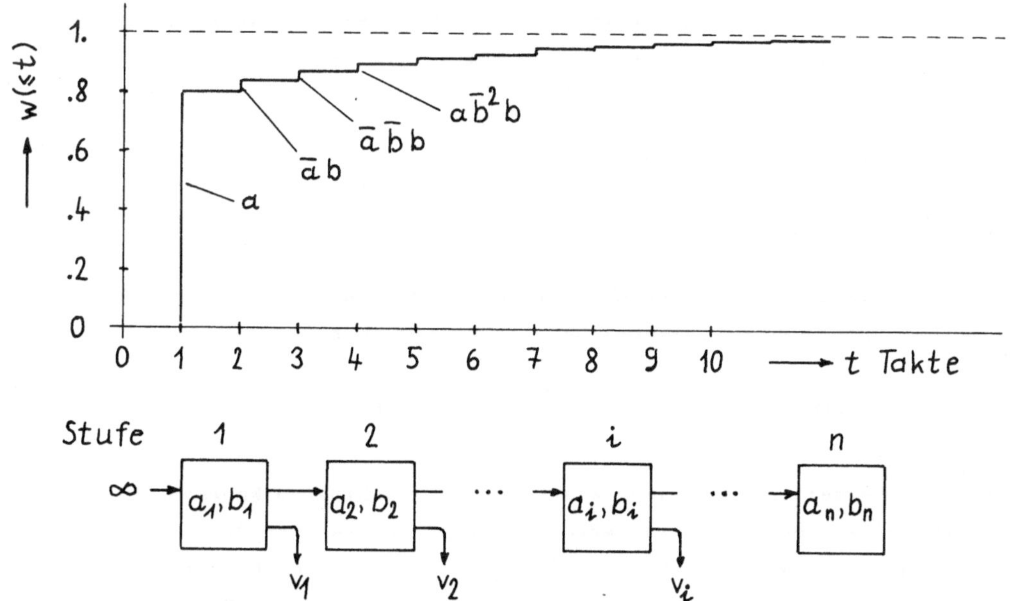

__Bild 3__   Belegungsdauerverteilung für eine Stufe und n-stufige Serverkette.
a_i Wahrscheinlichkeit für Beenden der Belegung mit dem ersten Takt,
b_i Wahrscheinlichkeit für Beenden der Belegung mit jedem späteren Takt,
v_i Wahrscheinlichkeit für das Verlassen der Serverkette.

In Bild 3 sind Serverkette und Belegungsdauerverteilung dargestellt. Im einzelnen werden folgende Annahmen gemacht:

a) Die Kette besteht aus n Stufen ohne Wartepuffer dazwischen.

b) Die Serverkette arbeitet taktweise. Jede Stufe kann mit Ende eines jeden Taktes einen Auftrag an den Nachfolger weitergeben, falls dieser frei war oder frei wird.

c) Vor der 1. Stufe wartet ein unbegrenzter Vorrat von Aufträgen; die letzte Stufe (n) kann bearbeitete Aufträge ohne Hemmung abgeben.

d) Ein Auftrag belegt die Stufe i genau einen Takt lang mit der Wahrscheinlichkeit a_i, und falls die Belegung noch andauert, endet sie mit dem Ende des laufenden Taktes mit der Wahrscheinlichkeit b_i.

e) Ein Auftrag, dessen Bearbeitung in Stufe i beendet wird, verläßt die Serverkette mit der Wahrscheinlichkeit v_i.

Entsprechend der Annahme d) tritt die Belegungsdauer t=1 mit der Wahrscheinlichkeit a auf. (Der Stufenindex i wird hier und im folgenden der besseren Übersicht wegen weggelassen, soweit die einzelnen Stufen nicht unterschieden werden müssen.) Die Belegungsdauer t für t > 1 kommt zustande, wenn die Belegung nicht nach dem 1. Takt endet (Wahrscheinlichkeit $\bar{a}$ = 1-a) und nicht nach einem der t-2 folgenden Takte endet (Wahrscheinlichkeit $(1-b)^{t-2} = \bar{b}^{t-2}$) und dann aber mit dem Takt t endet (Wahrscheinlichkeit b). Die Wahrscheinlichkeit p(t) für eine Belegungsdauer von genau t Takten ist somit

$$p(t) = \left|\begin{array}{ll} a & \text{für } t = 1 \\[2mm] \bar{a} \cdot \bar{b}^{t-2} \cdot b & \text{für } t > 1 \end{array}\right. \tag{1}$$

mit

$$\bar{a} = 1-a, \quad \bar{b} = 1-b \quad . \tag{2}$$

Die in Bild 3 dargestellte Wahrscheinlichkeit für höchstens t Takte ergibt sich aus der Summe der Einzelwahrscheinlichkeiten nach (1)

$$w(\leq t) = \sum_{\tau=1}^{t} p(\tau) = \ldots = 1 - \bar{a} \cdot \bar{b}^{t-1} \qquad \text{für } t \geq 1 \quad . \tag{3}$$

Das ist eine Verteilung bestehend aus einer frei wählbaren Wahrscheinlichkeit für t=1 und einer geometrischen Verteilung für den Rest der Belegungsdauer ab $t \geq 2$. Durch die Wahl der Parameter a und b lassen sich Erwartungswert und Streuung dieser Verteilung in weiten Grenzen einstellen. Der Erwartungswert E und die Varianz V bzw. die Streuung S für die Belegungsdauer in einer Stufe ergeben sich in üblicher Weise / 4 /.

$$E = \sum_{t=1}^{\infty} t \cdot p(t) = \ldots = 1 + \frac{\bar{a}}{b} \tag{4}$$

$$V = S^2 = \sum_{t=1}^{\infty} (t-E)^2 \cdot p(t) = \ldots = \frac{\bar{a}}{b^2} (\bar{b}+a) \tag{5}$$

Diese beiden Gleichungen lassen sich umformen, so daß aus gegebener Erwartung E und Varianz V die Parameter a und b ermittelt werden können:

$$a = \frac{V - (E-1)\cdot(E-2)}{V + E(E-1)} \tag{6}$$

$$b = \frac{2(E-1)}{V + E(E-1)} \tag{7}$$

Die Wahl von E und V unterliegt der Einschränkung, daß a und b Wahrscheinlichkeiten sind:

$$0 \leq a \leq 1, \qquad 0 \leq b \leq 1 \ . \tag{8}$$

Die Einschränkung (8), beachtet in (6) und (7), führt auf die folgende Einschränkung für E und V:

$$E \geq 1, \qquad V \geq \big| (E-1)\cdot(E-2) \big| . \tag{9}$$

Der sich aus (9) ergebende Bereich, der für die Paare (E, V) zugelassen werden kann, ist in Bild 4 dargestellt. Es zeigt sich, daß der Erwartungswert der Belegungsdauer E nicht kleiner als t=1 Takt sein darf. Für E=1+ε $\big($mit $\ \varepsilon \to 0\big)$ und für E=2 unterliegt die Varianz V keiner Einschränkung, und sonst kann sie beliebig groß, aber nicht beliebig klein vorgegeben werden.

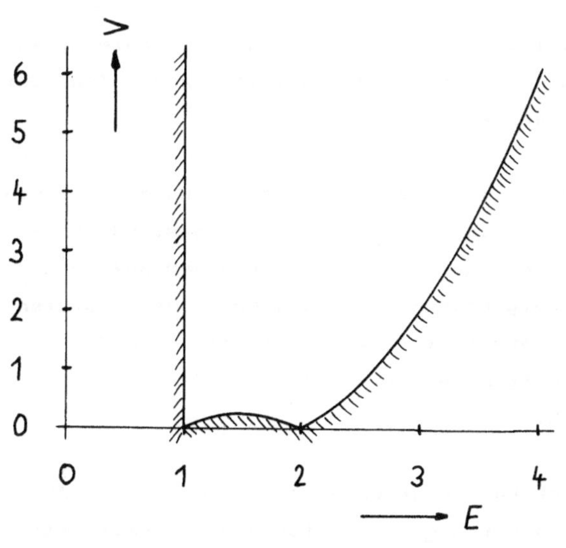

Bild 4

Zulässiger Raum für die Wahl von Erwartung E und Varianz V der Belegungsdauer einer Stufe.

2.1 Motivation des Modells

Mit dem vorgestellten verkehrstheoretischen Modell läßt sich die fließbandartige Bearbeitung der Befehle erfassen. Bei dieser gibt jede Station den bearbeiteten Befehl im Regelfall nach einem Takt weiter. Dieser Regelfall wird im Modell durch eine (große) Endewahrscheinlichkeit a berücksichtigt. Im nicht-Regelfall - etwa, weil die Bearbeitung komplizierter ist oder weil ein Zugriff zu einem lokalen Schnellspeicher oder gar zu dem langsameren Zentralspeicher nötig ist - dauert die Bearbeitung zufällig mehrere Takte. Dieser Fall wird im Modell durch eine (kleine) Endewahrscheinlichkeit b erfaßt.

Das im Modell vorgesehene vorzeitige Verlassen der Serverkette tritt real z.B. bei der Bearbeitung von Sprungbefehlen auf, die keinen Operanden oder das Rechenwerk erfordern (vgl. Bild 2).

Ferner gibt es real Befehle, die mehrere Bearbeitungsstufen gleichzeitig belegen. Das sind. z.B. bedingte Sprungbefehle, die von Ergebnissen des Rechenwerkes abhängen, oder auch Zeichen- und Wortgruppenbefehle. Für diese Befehle wird deutlich, daß das Modell eine Näherung an die Realität darstellt: Im Modell hängt die Belegungsdauer nur von der Bedienungsstufe ab und real auch von dem durchlaufenden Befehl.

In dem Modell sind keine Warteplätze vor den einzelnen Bedienungsstufen vorgesehen, sondern nur ein Warteplatz implizit in den Stufen.

3. BERECHNUNG DES DURCHSATZES FÜR DIE SERVERKETTE

Als Durchsatz D wird definiert die mittlere Zahl von Aufträgen (Befehlen), welche die 1. Stufe der n-stufigen Serverkette (Bild 3) pro Takt durchlaufen. Der Durchsatz kann maximal den Wert D=1 annehmen.

Für eine exakte Berechnung müssen die Zustände der Serverkette und deren Übergänge betrachtet werden. Jede Stufe für sich kann im Prinzip 4 Zustände annehmen (frei; Auftragsbearbeitung im 1. Takt; Auftragsbearb. in einem späteren Takt; Auftrag bearbeitet und von nachfolgender Stufe blockiert). Bei 5 Stufen ergibt das 4^5 = 1024 Zustände für die Serverkette. Wegen der Zahl der Zustände und der vielfältigen Übergangsmöglichkeiten verbietet sich die Berechnung der Zustandswahrscheinlichkeiten praktisch.

Es wird deshalb hier eine Näherungsrechnung vorgeschlagen. Bei dieser werden die anfänglichen Stufen der Serverkette durch _eine_ Ersatzstufe ebenfalls mit einem unbegrenzten Auftragsvorrat davor ersetzt. Diese Ersatzstufe wird so gewählt, daß bei ungehemmter Auftragsweitergabe die Erwartung und die Varianz

der Zeit von Weitergabe zu Weitergabe ebenso groß sind wie bei den Stufen, die
ersetzt werden sollen. Erwartung und Varianz für die Auftragsabgabeabstände
lassen sich ebenso wie in dem Modell durch Verteilungsparameter a und b ausdrücken. Die Ersatzstufe und die Folgestufe können dann zu einer neuen Ersatzstufe zusammengefaßt werden, bis durch iterative Anwendung des Verfahrens die
ganze Serverkette durch eine Ersatzstufe ersetzt ist. Von deren Erwartung der
Auftragsabgabeabstände kann dann auf den Durchsatz der 1. Stufe zurückgerech-
net werden.

Beim iterativen Ersetzen der Serverkette bildet nicht nur die Hinzunahme der
nächsten Bearbeitungsstufe einen Iterationsschnitt; auch die Möglichkeit, die
Serverkette nach einer Bearbeitungsstufe zu verlassen, wird zweckmäßigerweise
als eine Verzweigungsstufe interpretiert. In den folgenden beiden Abschnitten
werden Formeln für die Ersatzstufe hergeleitet, wenn in diese eine Verzweigungsstufe einbezogen werden soll (Abschn. 3.1), bzw. wenn in diese eine Bearbeitungsstufe einbezogen werden soll (Abschn. 3.2).

3.1 Ersatzstufe bei Hinzunahme einer Verzweigung

Eine Bearbeitungsstufe mit den Belegungsdauerparametern (a,b), mit einem unbeschränkten Auftragsvorrat davor und einer Verzweigungsstufe danach gibt ohne
weitere hemmende Stufen die Aufträge in Zeitabständen mit dem Erwartungswert E
und der Varianz V entsprechend (4) und (5) ab. Diese Stufe ist die 1. Bearbeitungsstufe der Kette oder bereits eine Ersatzstufe.

$$\infty \rightarrow \boxed{a,b} \xrightarrow{E,V} \dashedbox \rightarrow E_e,V_e \quad \Longrightarrow \quad \infty \rightarrow \boxed{a_e,b_e} \rightarrow E_e,V_e$$

In der Verzweigungsstufe \verlassen Aufträge mit Wahrscheinlichkeit v den geraden Weg, so daß dort größere Zeitabstände zwischen den Aufträgen mit Erwartung E_e und Varianz V_e entstehen. Diese Anordnung soll durch <u>eine</u> Stufe, deren Auftragsabgabeabstände die Erwartung E_e und Varianz V_e aufweisen, ersetzt
werden. Aus (E_e, V_e) erhält man mit Hilfe von (6) mit (7) die Parameter a_e
und b_e. Im folgenden muß noch (E_e, V_e) aus E, V und v berechnet werden:

Aus der abgegebenen Folge werden Aufträge mit Wahrscheinlichkeit v gestrichen.
Wenn j-1 aufeinanderfolgende Aufträge gestrichen werden und der j-te Auftrag
erhalten bleibt, dann entsteht ein neuer Abstand aus j alten Abständen. Die
Wahrscheinlichkeit dafür ist

$$p_j = v^{j-1} \cdot \bar{v} \qquad \text{für} \quad j = 1, 2, \ldots \qquad \text{mit } \bar{v} = 1-v \quad . \qquad (10)$$

Die Erwartung der Summe j alter Abstände ist

$$E_j = j \cdot E \ . \tag{11}$$

Der Erwartungswert E_e für die Abstände nach Herausstreichen von Aufträgen ergibt sich aus (10) und (11) als gewichtete Summe

$$E_e = \sum_{j=1}^{\infty} p_j \cdot E_j = \bar{v} \cdot E \cdot \sum_{j=1}^{\infty} j \cdot v^{j-1} = \ldots = E/\bar{v} \ . \tag{12}$$

Für die Varianz der Summe von j alten Abständen dürfen bei unabhängigen Zufallsgrößen die einzelnen Varianzen addiert werden:

$$V_j = j \cdot V \ . \tag{13}$$

Die Varianz V_j für die Summe von j alten Abständen ist das 2. Moment zentriert auf den Erwartungswert E_j. Bezüglich des gemeinsamen Erwartungswertes E_e ist die Varianz V_j nach dem Steiner'schen Satz / 4 / zu transformieren:

$$V_j^* = V_j + (E_e - E_j)^2 \ . \tag{14}$$

Die Varianz V_e für die Abstände nach Herausstreichen von Aufträgen ergibt sich dann als gewichtete Summe der zweiten Momente bezüglich E_e mit (10) und (14)

$$V_e = \sum_{j=1}^{\infty} p_j \cdot V_j^* = \ldots = V/\bar{v} + v \cdot E_e^2 \ . \tag{15}$$

Mit Hilfe der Ergebnisse (12) und (15) ist die Ersatzquelle, die durch Hinzunahme einer Verzweigungsstufe entstand, definiert. Es ist sichergestellt, daß die Parameter (a_e, b_e) der Ersatzstufe im Intervall $[0,1]$ liegen, wenn auch (a, b) in diesem Intervall liegen (hier nicht bewiesen).

3.2 Ersatzstufe bei Hinzunahme einer Bearbeitungsstufe

Es wird eine Ersatzstufe i-1 mit den Parametern (α, β), mit einem unbeschränkten Auftragsvorrat davor und einer anschließenden Bearbeitungsstufe i mit den Parametern (a,b) bzw. (E,V) betrachtet. Die Ersatzstufe kann auch die erste Stufe der Serverkette sein.

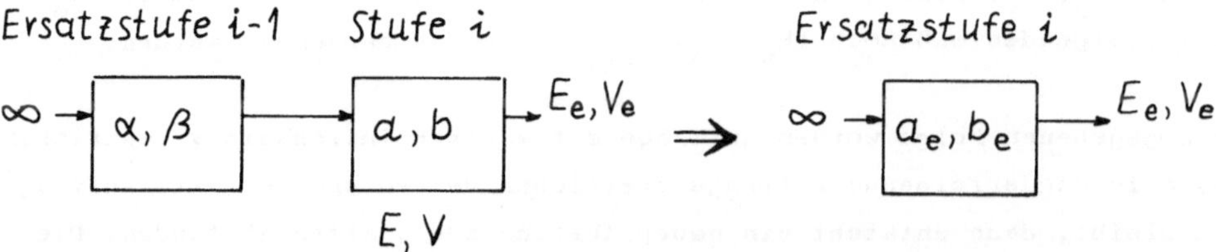

Diese Anordnung soll ersetzt werden durch _eine_ Ersatzstufe i, deren Auftragsabgabeabstände die Erwartung E_e und Varianz V_e aufweisen. Aus (E_e, V_e) erhält man mit Hilfe von (6) und (7) die Parameter (a_e, b_e). Im folgenden muß noch

(E_e, V_e) aus den gegebenen Parametern berechnet werden.

Wir gehen davon aus, daß die Stufe i gerade einen bearbeiteten Auftrag abgibt. Der Zeitabstand bis zur Abgabe des nächsten Auftrags ist

- die Bearbeitungsdauer in der Stufe i allein, wenn die Bearbeitungsdauer des nachfolgenden Auftrags in der davorliegenden Ersatzstufe i-1 nicht länger war als die Bearbeitungsdauer des fertiggestellten Auftrages in der Stufe i;

- die Bearbeitungsdauer in der Stufe i plus die restliche Bearbeitungsdauer des nachfolgenden Auftrages in der Ersatzstufe i-1, wenn letztgenannter Auftrag dort noch nicht fertiggestellt ist.

Wenn ein Auftrag von der Ersatzstufe i-1 in die Stufe i weiterrückt, dann rückt gleichzeitig ein nachfolgender Auftrag von dem unbegrenzten Vorrat in die Ersatzstufe i-1 nach. Die Wahrscheinlichkeit q , daß der Auftrag in der Ersatzstufe i-1 <u>nach</u> dem Auftrag in der Stufe i beendet wird, ergibt sich als Summe der Wahrscheinlichkeiten für das Enden der Belegung in der Stufe i nach genau t Takten und das Enden der Belegung in der Ersatzstufe i-1 nach mehr als t Takten (1), (3):

$$q = a \cdot \bar{\alpha} + \sum_{t=2}^{\infty} \bar{a} \cdot \bar{b}^{\,t-2} \cdot b \cdot \bar{\alpha} \cdot \bar{\beta}^{\,t-1} = \ldots \qquad (\text{mit } \bar{\alpha} = 1-\alpha,\ \bar{\beta} = 1-\beta)$$

$$= \bar{\alpha} \cdot \left(1 - \frac{\beta \bar{a}}{1 - \bar{b}\bar{\beta}} \right) \; . \tag{16}$$

Die Erwartung und Varianz der Belegungsdauer in der Stufe i ergeben sich nach (4) und (5)

$$E = 1 + \frac{\bar{a}}{b} \qquad\qquad V = \frac{\bar{a}}{b^2} \, (\bar{b} + a) \tag{17},(18)$$

Die Erwartung E_r und Varianz V_r im Falle einer Restbelegungsdauer in der Ersatzstufe i-1 ergeben sich, indem in (4) und (5) für a und für b die Endewahrscheinlichkeit ß der geometrischen Restverteilung eingesetzt wird.

$$E_r = 1 + \frac{\bar{\beta}}{\beta} = \frac{1}{\beta} \qquad\qquad V_r = \frac{\bar{\beta}}{\beta^2} \; . \tag{19},(20)$$

Entsprechend der obengenannten Fallunterscheidung

- Belegungsdauer in Stufe i allein mit der Wahrscheinlichkeit $\bar{q} = 1-q$,

- Belegungsdauer in Stufe i plus Restbelegungsdauer in Stufe i-1 mit der Wahrscheinlichkeit q

ergibt sich der Erwartungswert E_e für den Auftragsabgabeabstand nach der Stufe i:

$$E_e = \bar{q} \cdot E + q \cdot (E + E_r) = \ldots$$

$$= E + q/\beta \; . \tag{21}$$

In ähnlicher Weise ergibt sich die Varianz V_e, wobei jedoch entsprechend (14) die Varianz V bzw. $V+V_r$ mit dem zugehörigen Erwartungswert E bzw. $E+E_r$ auf den gemeinsamen Erwartungswert E_e nach dem Steiner'schen Satz zu transformieren ist:

$$V_e = \bar{q} \cdot \left[V + (E_e-E)^2 \right] + q \cdot \left[V + V_r + (E_e-E-E_r)^2 \right] = \ldots$$

$$= V + \frac{q}{\beta^2} \cdot (\bar{\beta}+\bar{q}) \quad . \tag{22}$$

Die Erwartung E_e (21) bzw. die Varianz V_e (22) der Ersatzstufe i enthält die Erwartung E bzw. Varianz V der ursprünglichen Stufe i als Grundanteil. Mit Hilfe der Ergebnisse (21) und (22) mit (16), (17) und (18) ist die Ersatzquelle i, die durch Hinzunahme der Bearbeitungsstufe i entstand, festgelegt. Die Parameter (a_e, b_e) der Ersatzstufe i ergeben sich mittels (6), (7) aus E_e und V_e.

3.3 Anwendung der einzelnen Formeln und Durchsatz

Für ein Beispiel einer dreistufigen Serverkette mit Ausscheidemöglichkeit nach der 2. Bearbeitungsstufe ist im folgenden gezeigt, wie die Stufen iterativ durch eine Ersatzstufe abgebaut werden, und welche Gleichungen dazu herangezogen werden.

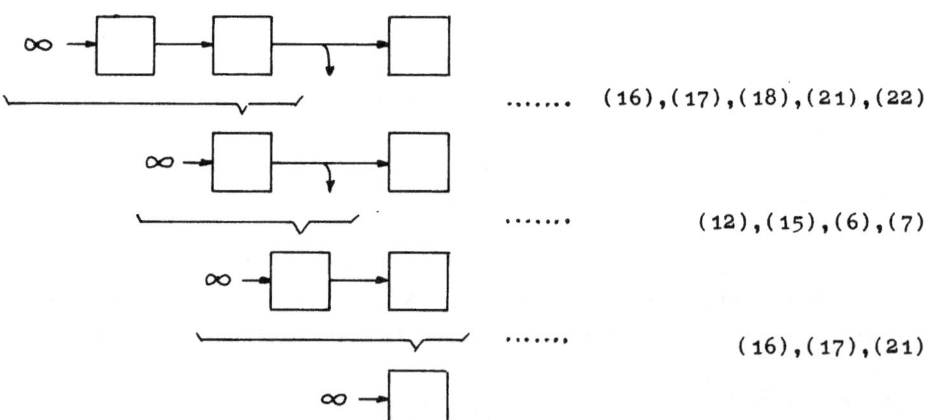

Bei der letzten Ersatzstufe interessiert nur noch der Erwartungswert E_e für den Abstand zwischen der Beendung aufeinanderfolgender Aufträge. Wir wollen ihn mit E_{en} bezeichnen

$$E_{en} = E_e \quad \text{(für die letzte Ersatzstufe n)} \quad . \tag{23}$$

Bei den Ersatzstufen wurde ja angestrebt, daß die Abstände zwischen zwei beendeten Aufträgen bei ungehemmter Weitergabemöglichkeit gleiche Erwartung (und Varianz) aufweisen wie bei der Serverteilkette, die eine Ersatzstufe ersetzen soll.

Der Durchsatz durch die Stufe n ist damit der Kehrwert von E_{en}. Nach einer Stufe i wird nur der Anteil $\bar{v}_i = 1 - v_i$ zur Stufe i+1 weitergeleitet. Somit folgt für den Durchsatz durch die 1. Stufe, der anfangs als Durchsatz D definiert wurde:

$$D = \frac{1}{E_{en}} \cdot \prod_{i=1}^{n-1} \frac{1}{\bar{v}_i} \quad . \tag{24}$$

Das angegebene Berechnungsverfahren für den Durchsatz enthält Näherungen. Der Rechenaufwand ist gering, wogegen eine exakte Bedeutung bei längeren Ketten praktisch undurchführbar ist. Näherungsverfahren ohne Fehlerabschätzung bringen eine Unsicherheit über die Genauigkeit mit sich. Die folgenden numerischen Auswertungen sollen dazu beitragen, diese Unsicherheit abzubauen und zeigen, wie genau das Verfahren arbeitet.

4. NUMERISCHE ERGEBNISSE UND VERGLEICH MIT SIMULATION

Für einige praktische Anwendungsfälle, unter anderem für die Beispiele von Bild 1 und Bild 2, sind in der folgenden Tabelle numerische Ergebnisse zusammengestellt. Der Kehrwert 1/D des Durchsatzes gibt die mittlere Zahl der benötigten Takte je Befehl an.

1/D, mittlere Zahl v. Takten je Befehl	Simulation		Rechnung
	reale Befehle	Modell	Modell
TR 440, FORTRAN-Obj. (vgl.Bild 1)	24,85	24.4...25.3	24.91
TR 440, FORTRAN-Übers.	15.50	15.8...16.2	15.46
Modellproz.,Zugr.100% aus Lokalspeicher	1.84	1.96...2.05	2.11
Modellproz.,Zugr. 95%......(vgl. Bild 2)	2.47	2.70...2.90	2.85
Modellproz.,Zugr. 70%	5.61	5.03...5.72	5.65

Die Zahlenwerte in der linken Spalte wurden durch Simulation mit realen Befehlen und der echten Belegungsdauer in den einzelnen Stufen ermittelt. Die Zahlenwerte in der rechten Spalte wurden nach dem in Abschnitt 3 vorgestellten Verfahren berechnet. Die Zahlenpaare in der mittleren Spalte geben die Vertrauensintervalle einer Simulation des der Rechnung zugrundeliegenden verkehrstheoretischen Modells (Abschn. 2) an. Die Genauigkeit des angegebenen Rechenverfahrens erweist sich als gut. (In den ersten beiden Rechenbeispielen in obiger Tabelle ist noch anzumerken, daß fünf Takte des realen Prozessors im Interesse einer geeigneten Approximation zu einem Modelltakt zusammengefaßt wurden.)

Für eine weitere Beurteilung der Genauigkeit des Rechenverfahrens können in Bild 5 Rechenwerte und durch Simulation ermittelte Werte des Durchsatzes D

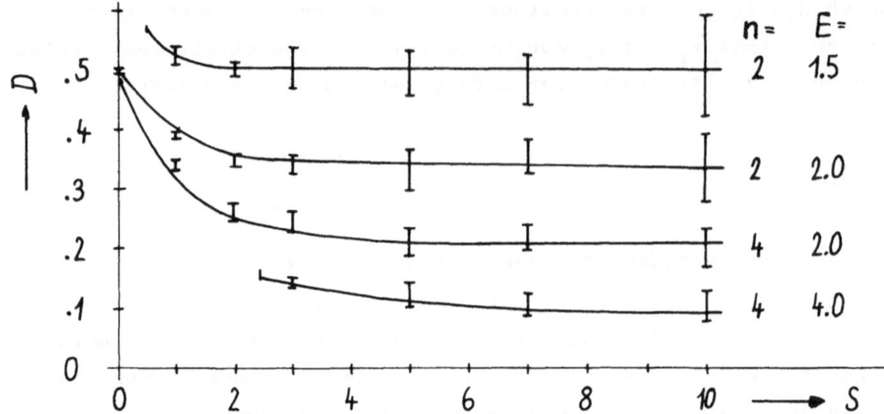

Bild 5   Berechnete Kurven und durch Simulation gewonnene Vertrauensintervalle des Durchsatzes D. Die Erwartung E mit der Streuung S aller n Serverstufen wurde als gleich angenommen.

verglichen werden. Um die Zahl der Parameter einzuschränken, wurde angenommen, daß die n Stufen der Serverkette die gleiche Belegungsdauerverteilung haben. In Bild 5 ist der Durchsatz D über der Streuung S der Belegungsdauerverteilung aufgetragen. Die Erwartung E der Belegungsdauer und die Stufenzahl n sind Parameter. Die senkrechten Strecken geben die 95%-Vertrauensintervalle der Simulation an.

Für ein einschlägiges Fachgespräch wird Herrn W. Krämer, Inst. f. Nachrichtenvermittlung und Datenverarbeitung, Stuttgart, an dieser Stelle gedankt.

/ 1 /   Hunt, G.C., Sequential arrays of waiting lines, Opns. Res., 4 (1956), 674-683.

/ 2 /   Hillier, F.S., Boling,R.W., Finite queues in series with exponential and Erlang service times, Opns. Res., 15 (1967), 286-303.

/ 3 /   Makino, T., On the mean passage time concerning some queueing problems of the tandem type, J. Opns. Res. Soc. Japan, 7 (1964), 17-47.

/ 4 /   Feller, W., An introduction to probability theory and its application, John Wiley, New York, 1957.

OPTIMALE NACHLADESTRATEGIEN UNTER BERÜCKSICHTIGUNG DER PROGRAMMSTRUKTUR

Otto SPANIOL

1. Überblick

Aus Kostengründen ist es bei digitalen Rechenanlagen notwendig, die Kapazität des relativ teuren Kernspeichers klein gegenüber dem praktisch unbegrenzten Fassungsvermögen der billigeren Hintergrundspeichermedien (Platte, Band, Trommel) zu halten.

Die Motivation dafür ist neben technischen Restriktionen die Tatsache, daß Hintergrunddaten im Vergleich zur Gesamtzahl der während des Programmlaufs angeforderten Daten relativ selten benötigt werden, weshalb man bei geeigneter Programmierung den Zeitverlust durch die längere Zugriffszeit zum Hintergrund in Kauf nehmen kann.

Eine Erweiterung dieses Prinzips bietet sich durch Ausdehnen dieser Speicherhierarchie mittels Einfügen von weiteren Speicherstufen an; die neu hinzukommenden inneren Stufen der Hierarchie werden als Pufferspeicher (PSP) bezeichnet. Je weiter eine Stufe vom Rechenwerk entfernt steht, desto größer muß ihr Fassungsvermögen sein, wenn das Prinzip sinnvoll angewandt werden soll; gleichzeitig wird die Zugriffszeit mit dem Abstand vom Rechenwerk anwachsen.

Das Prinzip arbeitet in der Weise, daß die als nächste benötigte Information (d.h. die Adresse eines Befehls oder eines Rechendatums) in der höheren Speicherstufe gesucht wird, sofern sie in der niedrigeren nicht vorhanden ist. Die gefundene Information wird in die rechenwerksnäheren Pufferspeicherstufen und ins Rechenwerk transportiert; dieses Nachladen erfolgt aufgrund einer Strategie, die festlegt, welche Daten des kleineren Speichers durch die neuen Daten zu ersetzen sind. Die Art der Nachladestrategie spielt solange keine große Rolle, wie der kleinere Pufferspeicher noch nicht mit relevanten Daten gefüllt ist, also beispielsweise zu Beginn eines neuen Programms oder bei einem anderen Kontextwechsel. In diesem Fall enthalten die PSP-Stufen wertlose Informationen, die zunächst möglichst rasch durch aktuelle Daten zu ersetzen sind. Dieser "Einschwingvorgang" wird in der vorliegenden Arbeit nicht betrachtet.

Der Grund für die Einführung einer Pufferspeicherhierarchie ist in erster Linie darin zu sehen, daß die meisten Programme aktive und weniger aktive Bereiche ("working set" |1|, |2|) haben. Die Aktivität eines Programmbereichs ändert sich während des Programmlaufs, ein Effekt, der nicht zuletzt auf die Schleifenstruktur der meisten Programme sowie auf andere Programmiergewohnheiten zurückzuführen ist.

Entscheidend für den Zeitgewinn, der sich durch Verwendung einer oder mehrerer Pufferspeicherstufen erzielen läßt, sind zwei Punkte:

a. das Verhältnis der Zugriffszeiten zwischen zwei benachbarten Stufen der Speicherhierarchie; dieser Punkt ist - abgesehen von technischen Restriktionen - im wesentlichen eine Kostenfrage. Er wird in diesem Vortrag nicht berücksichtigt, da sein Einfluß leicht zu überschauen ist.

b. die Fehlraten zwischen benachbaren Pufferspeicherstufen (hiermit bezeichnen wir die Wahrscheinlichkeit dafür, daß die gewünschte Information in der äußeren, aber nicht in der inneren der beiden Stufen steht). Wir untersuchen in diesem Vortrag das Problem der Minimisierung der Fehlrate bei Verwendung eines einzigen Pufferspeichers zwischen Rechenwerk und Kernspeicher.

Die Fehlrate ist abhängig von der Größe des Pufferspeichers, der Größe der Nachladeeeinheit, der Nachladestrategie und der Struktur des "durchschnittlichen" Programms, d.h. von den Eigenschaften der zeitlichen Folge der Zugriffe zu den Adressen von Rechendaten bzw. von Befehlen.

Der letzte Punkt, der alle anderen (und ganz besonders die Güte der Nachladestrategie) entscheidend beeinflußt, ist bei den meisten bisher über diesen Themenkreis veröffentlichten Arbeiten nicht oder nur ungenügend berücksichtigt worden. Meist wird sogar vorausgesetzt, daß die der Blöcke des für das Programm reservierten Speicherbereichs sich während des gesamten Ablauf des Programms nicht ändert. Unter diesen starken Voraussetzungen kann man eine Reihe von mehr oder weniger einleuchtenden Strategien herleiten bzw. nachträglich rechtfertigen.

Im Gegensatz dazu basiert die diesem Vortrag zugrundeliegende Arbeit auf einem Modell für die Struktur der Folge der Adressen von Rechendaten bzw. Befehlen, die während des Programmlaufs nacheinander benötigt werden. Die natürlich auch hier notwendigen einschränkenden Voraussetzungen sind nach unserer Ansicht zumindest nicht weniger realisisch als die in anderen Arbeiten zugrundegelegten Annahmen. Unter Verwendung dieses Modells für die Programmstruktur wird eine Nachladestrategie hergeleitet, welche zu einer minimalen mittleren Fehlrate führt.

2. Die Verteilung der Datensprünge in Programm. und Rechenspeicher

Wegen der völlig unterschiedlichen Struktur der Folge von Adressen von Befehlen bzw. Rechendaten ist es sinnvoll, getrennte Pufferspeicher für Programmspeicher und Rechenspeicher vorzusehen.

Da die meisten Untersuchungen für beide Speichertypen gelten, wird allgemein vorausgesetzt, daß jeder der beiden Pufferspeicher aus n Blöcken der Größe k besteht und daß ein Programm a > n Blöcke (von Π bzw. R) für Befehle bzw. Rechendaten benötigt.

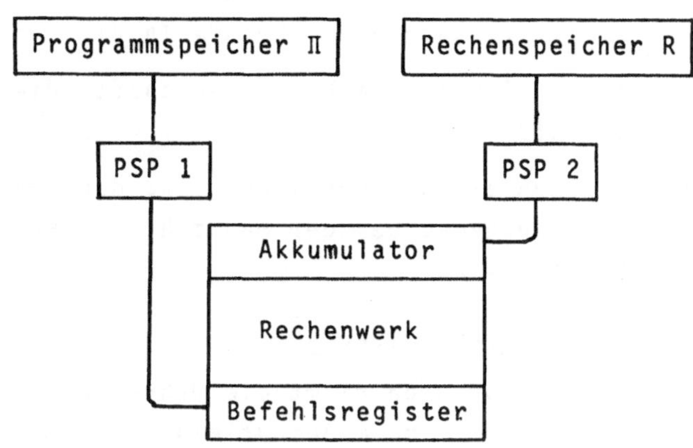

Wir vereinbaren zunächst einige Bezeichnungen:

$x_{-r},\ldots,x_{-1},x,\ldots$ sei die Folge der Adressen von Daten bzw. Befehlen, die ein Programm nacheinander benötigt. $B_{-r},\ldots,B_{-1},B,\ldots$ seien die zugehörigen Kernspeicherblöcke.

Die Adresse x des Datums, auf das als nächstes zugegriffen werden soll, heißt *aktuelles Datum*.

$X \subset \bigcup_{i=1}^{r} B_{-i}$ sei der Inhalt des PSP beim Aufruf des aktuellen Datums x; hier wie im folgenden ist vorausgesetzt, daß der Pufferspeicher mit Daten des gerade laufenden Programms gefüllt ist.

$z = z(x) \in X$ heißt *zugehöriges Vorgängerdatum* von x, wenn gilt:
$|z - x| \leq |u - x|$ für alle $u \in X$,

Gibt es mehrere Elemente mit dieser Eigenschaft, wird eines davon durch einen Zufallszahlengenerator ausgewählt.

$P := P(x \notin X)$ heißt *Fehlrate*. $Q := 1 - P$ heißt *Vorhandenrate*.

Die Differenz x - z der Adressen des aktuellen Datums und des zugehörigen Vorgängerdatums heißt *Datensprung* (der Länge x - z).

Wir kommen nun zu den entscheidenden Voraussetzungen unseres Modells für die Programmstruktur:

1. Die Datensprünge werden als unabhängige Zufallsvariable interpretiert, die aus diskreten Verteilungen y^{Π} bzw. y^{R} stammen, welche die auf der nächsten Seite angegebenen charakteristischen Eigen-

schaften während des Programmlaufs nahezu unverändert beibehalten. Aus diesem Grund und da wir außerdem die Fehlrate zu jedem Zeitpunkt für das gerade aktuelle Datum berechnen, verzichten wir bei den Datensprungverteilungen auf einen Zeitindex.

2. Für die Fehlraten P_Π bzw. P_R in Programm- bzw. Rechenspeicher gelte:

$$P_S = P_S(k,z,x,a,n,y^S) \quad \text{für } S \in \{\Pi,R\}$$

Dies ist eine Art Markow-Eigenschaft, die streggenommen nicht erfüllt ist.

Wir geben nun einige Charakteristika der Verteilungen y^Π und y^R an, die erfahrungsgemäß bei der Mehrzahl der Programme in ähnlicher Form zu beobachten sind:

<u>Rechenspeicherverteilung y^R</u>:

Bei vielen Programmen nimmt die Wahrscheinlichkeit für einen Datensprung der Größe i beim Aufruf eines Datums mit wachsender Sprunggröße ab, da große Sprünge hauptsächlich durch die Schleifenstruktur der Programme und die Indexänderungen der darin vorkommenden Felder verursacht werden und Schleifen mit wachsender Größe immer seltener werden (abgesehen von den Unregelmäßigkeiten, die dadurch verursacht werden, daß als Laufgrenzen von Schleifen runde Zahlen bevorzugt werden). Für kleine Werte der Sprunggröße kann man diese Argumentation zwar nicht mehr verwenden, da zu kleine Schleifen nicht sinnvoll sind, doch wird diese Lücke durch die häufige Verwendung von einfachen Variablen, die meist zusammenhängend abgespeichert sind, geschlossen.

Mit Abstand am häufigsten sind die Sprünge der Länge ± 1 und 0; erstere entstehen zum Beispiel als Folge der linearen Fortschaltung in Aufwärts- bzw. Abwärtsschleifen; letztere treten immer dann auf, wenn eine Adresse mehrfach benutzt wird und der diese Adresse enthaltende Pufferspeicherblock nicht zwischen zwei aufeinanderfolgenden Aufrufen der betreffenden Adresse aufgrund der Kriterien der Nachladestrategie ausgetauscht wurde.

Für viele Programme darf weiter angenommen werden, daß Vorwärtssprünge im Mittel etwa ebenso wahrscheinlich sind wie gleichgroße Rücksprünge. Diese Beziehung ist mehr oder weniger stark verletzt, wenn das zugehörige Vorgängerdatum des aktuellen Datums in der Nähe des Randes des für das Programm reservierten Speicherbereichs steht.

Für die Werte $y_i^R = P(x^R - z^R = i)$ setzen wir daher die Gültigkeit von $y_i^R \geq y_{i+1}^R$ sowie der Relationen $y_{-i}^R \geq y_{-i-1}^R$ für $i \geq 1$ voraus. Wenn das Vorgängerdatum des aktuellen Datums nicht zu nahe am Rand

des für die Rechendaten des Programms reservierten Speicherbereichs
steht, ist die Verteilung y^R im wesentlichen symmetrisch ($y_i \simeq y_{-i}$
bis zum Rande des Speicherbereichs).

Programmspeicherverteilung y^{Π}:

Unabhängig davon, ob es sich um ein compiliertes oder um ein handge-
schneidertes Maschinenprogramm handelt, sind hier im Gegensatz zur
Rechenspeicherverteilung die Sprünge der Länge +1 dominierend
($y_1^{\Pi} \gg y_j^{\Pi}$ für $j \neq 1$).

Alle anderen Werte der Programmspeicherverteilung sind demgegenüber
praktisch vernachlässigbar. Vorwärtssprünge der Länge > 1 und Rücksprünge unter einer programmabhängigen Grenze sind nahezu ausgeschlossen; auch Sprünge der Länge 0 sowie große Rücksprünge (nach Beendigung
eines Schleifendurchlaufs oder als Folge eines goto-Befehls) sind
vergleichsweise selten. Der einzige Ausnahmefall (zugehöriges Vorgängerdatum am rechten Rand des für die Befehlsliste reservierten Speicherbereichs, nur Rücksprünge möglich) wird vernachlässigt.

3. Berechnung von optimalen Nachladestrategien

Wir berechnen zunächst die Vorhandenrate, d.h. die Wahrscheinlichkeit
dafür, daß sich das aktuelle Datum im Pufferspeicher befindet; hierbei
können wir davon ausgehen, daß das zugehörige Vorgängerdatum z des
aktuellen Datums x noch im Pufferspeicher steht. Durch Maximieren des
Ausdrucks für Q = Q(k,z,x,a,n,y) erhalten wir optimale Nachladestra-
tegien.

Die Urbilder von x und z im Kernspeicher seien $f^{-1}(x)$ bzw. $f^{-1}(z)$.
Bezeichnen wir die Blöcke des Kernspeichers der Reihe nach mit
$B_1,\ldots,B_a$ sowie den Inhalt des Pufferspeichers beim Aufruf von x mit
$X = \{X_1,\ldots,X_n\}$ (hierbei gilt $X_i = B_{j(i)}$ mit $j(i) \in \{1,\ldots,a\}$ für
$i = 1,\ldots,n$, da wir den Einschwingvorgang als beendet vorausgesetzt
haben), so erhält man:

$$Q = P(x \in X) = \sum_{i=1}^{a} P(f^{-1}(x) \in B_i \wedge B_i \in X)$$

$$= \sum_{i=1}^{a} \sum_{m=1}^{a} P(f^{-1}(x) \in B_i \wedge B_i \in X \wedge f^{-1}(z) \in B_m)$$

$$= \sum_{i=1}^{a} \sum_{m=1}^{a} w_{m,i} \cdot Q_{i-m,m} \cdot r_m \tag{1}$$

Hierbei wurden die folgenden Abkürzungen verwandt:

$$w_{m,i} := P(\ B_i \in X \ | \ f^{-1}(z) \in B_m \ )$$

$$Q_{i,j} := P(\ f^{-1}(x) \in B_{j+i} \ | \ f^{-1}(z) \in B_j \wedge B_{j+i} \in X \ )$$

$$r_m \quad := P(\ f^{-1}(z) \in B_m \ )$$

Die Größen $w_{m,i}$ geben die Wahrscheinlichkeit an, mit der ein $i - m$ Blöcke vom Block des zugehörigen Vorgängerdatums entfernt stehender Block im Pufferspeicher steht. Diese Wahrscheinlichkeiten charakterisieren die Nachladestrategie entscheidend, da man versuchen wird, diese Koeffizienten durch geschicktes Nachladen so zu wählen, daß die Vorhandenrate maximal wird.

Erwünscht sind natürlich möglichst "einfache" Werte für die $w_{m,i}$, ohne die auch eine Nachladestrategie mit noch so geringer Fehlrate unbrauchbar ist. Wir werden zeigen, daß sich unter den in Abschnitt 2 getroffenen Voraussetzungen über die Gestalt der Datensprungverteilungen in Programm- und Rechenspeicher eine Nachladestrategie als optimal herausstellt, bei der alle Elemente der Matrix $W = (w_{m,i})$ entweder Null oder Eins sind. Die Blöcke, die nachzuladen sind, um eine optimale Vorhandenrate zu erzielen, sind damit eindeutig festgelegt.

Die Werte r_m geben den Belegungsgrad der einzelnen Kernspeicherblöcke an; wir setzen $r_m > 0$ (das Programm soll also keine überflüssigen Speicherblöcke reservieren), doch sind die von uns angegebenen Strategien auch dann optimal, wenn $r_m = 0$ für einzelne Werte von m gilt.

Aus der Formel (1) für die Vorhandenrate Q wird ersichtlich, daß die Teilsummen

$$\sum_{i=1}^{a} w_{m,i} \cdot Q_{i-m,m} \cdot r_m \qquad \text{für } m = 1,\ldots,a$$

unabhängig voneinander maximiert werden können. Hieraus ergibt sich, daß die Größe der Koeffizienten $r_m \neq 0$ keinen Einfluß auf die optimale Strategie hat.

Um eine maximale Vorhandenrate zu erhalten, sind größeren Werten $Q_{i-m,m}$ auch größere Wahrscheinlichkeiten $w_{m,i}$ zuzuordnen; dabei ist die Wahl der $w_{m,i}$ durch die Restriktion $0 \leq w_{m,i} \leq 1$ und die folgende Summenbedingung eingeschränkt:

<u>Lemma 1:</u>

$$\sum_{i=1}^{a} w_{m,i} = n \qquad \text{für } m = 1,\ldots,a$$

Beweis:

$$\sum_{i=1}^{a} w_{m,i} = \sum_{i=1}^{a} P(B_i \in X \mid f^{-1}(z) \in B_m)$$

$$= \sum_{i=1}^{a} \sum_{j=1}^{n} P(B_i = X_j \mid f^{-1}(z) \in B_m)$$

$$= \sum_{j=1}^{n} \sum_{i=1}^{a} P(X_j = B_i \mid f^{-1}(z) \in B_m)$$

$$= \sum_{j=1}^{n} 1 = n$$

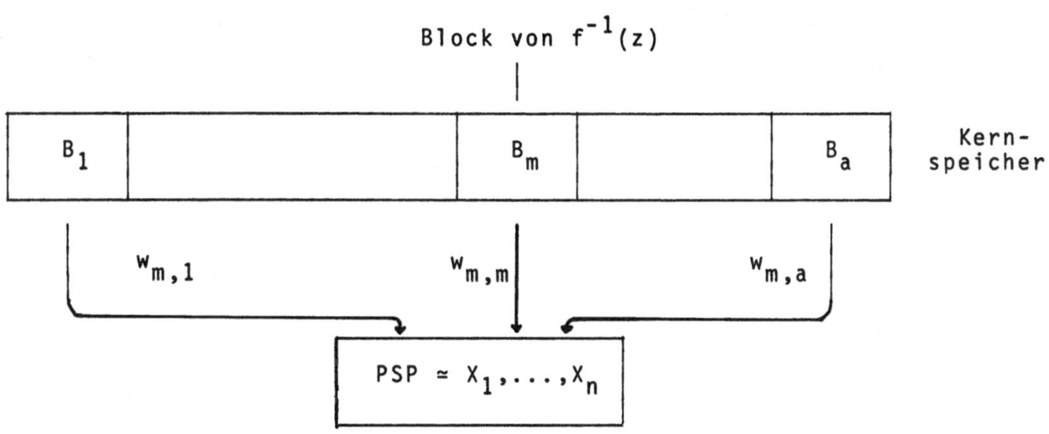

Unter Berücksichtigung aller Restriktionen erhält man zunächst das folgende Ergebnis für die optimale Wahl der Koeffizienten $w_{m,i}$:

Lemma 2:

Ist $(\hat{Q}_{1,m};\hat{w}_{m,k_1}),\ldots,(\hat{Q}_{a,m};\hat{w}_{m,k_a})$ eine Umordnung der Folge

$(Q_{1-m,m};w_{m,1}),\ldots\ldots,(Q_{a-m,m};w_{m,a})$ mit der Eigenschaft

$\hat{Q}_{i,m} \geq \hat{Q}_{i+1,m}$ für $i = 1,\ldots,a-1$,

dann erhält man eine maximale Vorhandenrate $Q_{max} = Q(w_{m,i},Q_{i,m},r_m)$

durch folgende Wahl der Elemente der Matrix W:

$$\hat{w}_{m,k_i} = \begin{cases} 1 & \text{für } i = 1,\ldots,n \\ 0 & \text{für } i = n+1,\ldots,a \end{cases}$$

Ist $\hat{Q}_{n,m} > \hat{Q}_{n+1,m}$ für $m = 1,\ldots,a$, so ist die Matrix W bei optimaler Nachladestrategie eindeutig festgelegt.

Im Falle $\hat{Q}_{n,m} = \hat{Q}_{n+1,m}$ für mindestens ein m gibt es mehrere Strategien, die zur gleichen maximalen Vorhandenrate Q_{max} führen.

Unter etwas stärkeren Voraussetzungen erhält man die schärferen Aussagen von Lemma 3 und Lemma 4.

Daß auch die dort zugrundegelegten Voraussetzungen noch sinnvoll sind, läßt sich anhand der von uns angenommenen Gestalt der Datensprungverteilungen verifizieren; wir können jedoch in diesem Vortrag nicht näher darauf eingehen. Einzelheiten sind in der Originalarbeit |6| nachzulesen.

<u>Lemma 3</u>:

<u>Vor</u>: $Q_{i,r} \geq Q_{j,r}$ und $Q_{-i,r} \geq Q_{-j,r}$ für $0 \leq i < j \leq a$ $\Big\}$ $\quad r = 1,..,a$

$\qquad Q_{n-1,r} > Q_{n,r}$ und $Q_{-n+1,r} > Q_{-n,r}$

$\qquad r_m > 0$ für $m = 1,...,a$

<u>Beh</u>:

Die Matrix W hat bei optimaler Nachladestrategie folgende Gestalt:

$$
W =
\begin{array}{c}
\overset{\longleftarrow n \longrightarrow}{}
\end{array}
$$

Die Koeffizienten $w_{m,i}$ in den Bereichen (†) lassen sich erst dann festlegen, wenn die Größe der Werte $Q_{i,r}$ im Vergleich zu den Werten $Q_{-j,r}$ $(i,j \geq 0)$ genauer bekannt ist. Lemma 4 basiert auf einer solchen Größenordnungsrelation, die sich wiederum aus der Gestalt der

Datensprungverteilungen motivieren läßt.

<u>Lemma 4:</u>

<u>Vor:</u> $Q_{i,s} \geq Q_{j,s}$ für $0 \leq |i| < |j| \leq \min (s-1 , a-s+1)$

$$s \in \{1,\ldots,a\}$$

<u>Beh:</u> Die durch folgende Matrix W beschriebene Strategie ist optimal:

a. $n = 2t+1$ für $t \in \mathbb{N}_0$ (n = Blockzahl des Pufferspeichers):

$$w_{i,j} = \begin{cases} 1 & \text{für } j = i , i \otimes 1, \ldots , i \otimes t \qquad \otimes \in \{\oplus , \ominus\} \\ 0 & \text{sonst} \end{cases}$$

Dabei sind die Operationen $\oplus$ und $\ominus$ wie folgt definert:

$$w_{i,i \oplus m} = \begin{cases} w_{i,i+m} & \text{falls } i+m \leq a \\ w_{i,i+m-n} & \text{"} \quad i+m > a \end{cases}$$

$$w_{i,i \ominus m} = \begin{cases} w_{i,i-m} & \text{falls } i-m \geq 1 \\ w_{i,i-m+n} & \text{"} \quad i-m < 1 \end{cases}$$

b. $n = 2t+2$ für $t \in \mathbb{N}_0$:

$$w_{i,j} = \begin{cases} 1 & \text{falls } j = i,i \otimes 1, \ldots , i \otimes t \qquad \otimes \in \{\oplus , \ominus\} \\ 1 & \text{"} \quad j = i+t+1 \text{ und } i-t-1 < 1 \\ 1 & \text{"} \quad j = i-t-1 \text{ und } i+t+1 > a \\ u_{i+t+1} & \text{falls } j = i+t+1 \text{ und } 1 \leq i-t-1 < i+t+1 \leq a \\ v_{i-t-1} & \text{"} \quad j = i-t-1 \text{ und } 1 \leq i-t-1 < i+t+1 \leq a \\ 0 & \text{sonst} \end{cases}$$

Die Zahlen u_{i+t+1} und v_{i-t-1} sind dabei durch folgende Bedingung aneinander gekoppelt:

$$u_{i+t+1} = 0 \qquad v_{i-t-1} = 1 \qquad \text{falls } Q_{-t-1,i} > Q_{t+1,i}$$

$$u_{i+t+1} = 1 \qquad v_{i-t-1} = 0 \qquad \text{"} \quad Q_{-t-1,i} < Q_{t+1,i}$$

$$u_{i+t+1} + v_{i-t-1} = 1 \qquad \text{"} \quad Q_{-t-1,i} = Q_{t+1,i}$$

Es gibt also eine optimale Nachladestrategie mit der Eigenschaft $w_{i,j} \in \{ 0 , 1 \}$ für $i,j = 1,\ldots,a$.

Die Beweise von Lemma 2, Lemma 3 und Lemma 4 sind in der dem Vortrag zugrundeliegenden Arbeit nachzulesen.

__Beispiel:__   a = 16 , n = 8

<table>
<tr>
<td>

```
        ┌                                        ┐
        │ 1 1 1 1 1 1 1 1                         │
        │ 1 1 1 1 1 1 1 1                         │
        │ 1 1 1 1 1 1 1 1                         │
        │ 1 1 1 1 1 1 1 1                         │
        │ † 1 1 1 1 1 1 1 †           0           │
        │   † 1 1 1 1 1 1 1 †                     │
        │     † 1 1 1 1 1 1 1 †                   │
W   =   │       † 1 1 1 1 1 1 1 †                 │
        │         † 1 1 1 1 1 1 1 †               │
        │           † 1 1 1 1 1 1 1 †             │
        │             † 1 1 1 1 1 1 1 †           │
        │     0         † 1 1 1 1 1 1 1 †         │
        │                 1 1 1 1 1 1 1 1         │
        │                 1 1 1 1 1 1 1 1         │
        │                 1 1 1 1 1 1 1 1         │
        │                 1 1 1 1 1 1 1 1         │
        └                                        ┘
```

</td>
<td>

Die durch † gekenn-
zeichneten Matrix-
elemente sind nach
Lemma 4.b. in Abhän-
gigkeit von den ent-
sprechenden Wahr-
scheinlichkeiten
$Q_{i,j}$ mit 0 oder 1
zu besetzen.

</td>
</tr>
</table>

4. Literatur

|1| Denning, P. J.:
      Virtual Memory
      Computer Surveys, Vol. _2_ (1970), S. 153 - 189

|2| Denning, P. J.:
      The Working Set Model for Program Behaviour
      Communications of the ACM _11_ (1968), S. 323 - 333

|3| Aho, A. V., Denning, P. J. und Ullman, J. D.:
      Principles of Optimal Page Replacement Algorithms
      Journal of the ACM _18_ (1971), S. 80 - 93

|4| Gelenbe, E.:
      A unified Approach to the Evaluation of a Class of
      Replacement Algorithms
      1972. Erscheint in IEEE Transactions of Computers

|5| Lee, F. F.:
      Study of "Look - aside" - Memory
      IEEE - EC _18_ (1969), S. 1062 - 1064

|6| Spaniol, O.:
      Optimale Nachladestrategien für Pufferspeicher unter Berück-
      sichtigung der Programmstruktur
      Universität des Saarlandes, Fachbereich 10, Bericht A 73 - 02
      (Eingereicht bei Acta Informatica)

In |1|, |3| und |4| sind mehr als 80 weitere Literaturstellen über
diesen Themenkreis angegeben.

I N F O R M A T I O N S S Y S T E M E

RESULTATSPEZIFIZIERENDE HANDHABUNG VON DATENSYSTEMEN

E. FALKENBERG ET AL.

1. E i n f ü h r u n g

Weitaus die meisten Datenbankbenutzer werden in Zukunft Nichtprogrammierer sein, welche die Datenbank als Instrument für die Bewältigung ihrer fachbezogenen Aufgaben heranziehen. Ein generalisiertes Datenbank-Management-System (GDBMS) sollte deshalb so konstruiert sein, daß ein solcher Benutzer möglichst leicht mit der Datenbank umgehen kann. Mit dieser Problematik sowie mit der Konzeption einer entsprechenden Datenhandhabungssprache beschäftigt sich die vorliegende Arbeit.

1.1 Einige Beurteilungskriterien für Datenhandhabungssprachen

Viele der üblichen Datenhandhabungssprachen sind so konzipiert, daß der Benutzer die einzelnen Schritte, das "Procedere" bzw. die Prozedur, angeben muß, welche das GDBMS auszuführen hat, um das gewünschte Resultat zu erzielen. Pro Schritt wird dabei ein Teilresultat spezifiziert, welches i.a. die Voraussetzung für den nächsten Schritt ist. Die Prozedur fügt die verschiedenen Teilresultate successive zum Gesamtresultat zusammen. Der reziproke Wert der durchschnittlichen Anzahl der pro Gesamtresultat nötigen Schritte heißt Resultatorientierung. Geringe Resultatorientierung bedeutet, daß der Benutzer eine langwierige Prozedur formulieren muß, welche viele kleine Teilresultate zum gewünschten Gesamtresultat vereinigt. Maximale Resultatorientierung liegt vor, wenn sich das Gesamtresultat stets mit Hilfe eines einzigen Ausdrucks bzw. Satzes spezifizieren läßt, ohne daß die Angabe einer Prozedur nötig ist. Dies erleichtert insbesondere dem Nichtprogrammierer, welcher keinerlei Übung im Formulieren von Prozeduren hat, den Umgang mit der Datenbank sehr.

Die Universalität einer Datenhandhabungssprache ist ein Maß dafür, welcher Anteil aller denkbaren Zugriffswünsche zur Datenbank direkt formulierbar sind, ohne daß man diese Zugriffswünsche durch Programmierungstricks den Möglichkeiten der Datenhandhabungssprache anpassen muß. Es gibt dabei zwei Standpunkte zu unterscheiden. Betrachtet man das gesamte Anwendungsspektrum eines GDBMS, also die verschiedensten Datenbankimplementierungen, so sind die denkbaren Zugriffswünsche i.a. wesentlich vielfältiger als wenn man nur eine bestimmte Anwendung herausgreift. Im ersteren Fall spricht man von absoluter Universalität, im letzteren von relativer Universalität einer Datenhandhabungssprache. Da ein Benutzer

i.a. nur eine bestimmte Anwendung bzw. einen kleinen Teil davon im Auge
hat, kann für ihn nur die relative Universalität maßgebend sein.

Viele der existierenden Datenhandhabungssprachen sind Gastsprachen, welche an zumeist prozedurorientierte Wirtssprachen angeschlossen werden
müssen, um eine ausreichende Universalität zu erlangen. Eine selbständi-
ge Datenhandhabungssprache sollte universell sein, was jedoch bei den
existierenden selbständigen Sprachen häufig nicht der Fall ist. Die übliche Unterscheidung zwischen selbständigen Sprachen und Gastsprachen
ist ungenau, da es bei den Gastsprachen darauf ankommt, wie oft ein Anschluß an die Wirtssprache erforderlich ist. So gibt es Gastsprachen,
bei denen dieser Anschluß nur in wenigen, bestimmten Fällen durchgeführt
werden muß. Um derartige Verhältnisse genauer erfassen zu können, wird
der Begriff der <u>Selbständigkeit</u> eingeführt. Sie ist ein Maß dafür, welcher Anteil aller denkbaren Zugriffswünsche ohne den Anschluß an eine
Wirtssprache formulierbar sind. Datenhandhabungssprachen sollten eine
hohe Selbständigkeit aufweisen, da der ständige Wechsel zwischen Gast-
und Wirtssprache besonders dem Nichtprogrammierer den Umgang mit der Datenbank erheblich erschwert.

Die <u>Implementierungsunabhängigkeit</u> einer Datenhandhabungssprache ist ein
Maß dafür, inwieweit sie unabhängig von implementierungsspezifischen
Problemen ist. Hierzu gehören Fragen der Effizienz und Redundanz, der
Speicherplatzbelegung, der Datenorganisation, hierzu gehören Begriffe
wie Block, Arbeitsbereich, Kette oder Pointer, um nur einige zu nennen.
Insbesondere sollte der Nichtprogrammierer von diesen Problemen entlas-
tet sein, da für ihn ausschließlich die <u>problemspezifischen</u> Aspekte von
Interesse sind. Die Kontrolle über die Implementierung sollte, soweit
dies überhaupt erforderlich ist, dem <u>Datenbankadministrator</u> vorbehalten
sein.

Das am schwersten quantifizierbare Beurteilungskriterium, bei dem alle
vorgenannten Kriterien eine Rolle spielen, ist die <u>Benutzerorientierung</u>
einer Datenhandhabungssprache. Je größer die Benutzerorientierung ist,
desto leichter ist ein Benutzer in der Lage, seine Zugriffswünsche zu
formulieren; desto geringer ist der <u>konzeptionelle Abstand</u> zwischen dem
Zugriffswunsch an sich und seiner Formulierung mit Hilfe der Datenhandhabungssprache. Hohe Benutzerorientierung setzt hohe Resultatorientierung, Selbständigkeit sowie Implementierungsunabhängigkeit voraus. Dazu
gehören auch eine der <u>natürlichen Sprache</u> angepaßte Notation und eine
semantische Konzeption der Datenhandhabungssprache, welche der Denkweise
des Benutzers adäquat ist. Auch muß das handzuhabende <u>Datensystem</u> selbst
benutzerorientiert, d.h. leicht erfaßbar und überschaubar sein.

1.2 Stand der Technik

Legt man die oben genannten Beurteilungskriterien zugrunde, so kann man
grob drei Klassen von Datenhandhabungssprachen unterscheiden.

Die erste Klasse besitzt zwar i.a. hohe absolute Universalität, dafür
aber nur geringe Resultatorientierung und Selbständigkeit. Implementierungsunabhängigkeit und Benutzerorientierung sind äußerst mangelhaft.
Zu dieser Klasse gehören z.B. die Datenhandhabungssprachen von DBTG [2]
und IMS [10].

Demgegenüber finden sich bei der zweiten Klasse hohe Selbständigkeit
und etwas bessere Resultatorientierung, Implementierungsunabhängigkeit
und Benutzerorientierung. Dagegen ist die absolute Universalität geringer und in vielen Anwendungsfällen unzureichend. Typische Vertreter dieser Klasse sind z.B. die Datenhandhabungssprachen von GIS [11] und UL/1
[13].

Die Datenhandhabungssprachen der dritten Klasse basieren durchweg auf
einem Relationenmodell von Daten [5]. Das Modell sowohl als auch die
Sprachen sind weitgehend implementierungsunabhängig. Jedoch lassen vor
allem Resultatorientierung, Selbständigkeit und Benutzerorientierung
noch etliche Wünsche offen. Zu dieser Klasse gehören z.B. die Datenhandhabungssprachen ALPHA [4], COLARD [1] und IS/1 [12].

Die folgende graphische Darstellung zeigt die ungefähre Positionierung
der genannten Datenhandhabungssprachen bezüglich der fünf Beurteilungskriterien. Da diese Kriterien nur schwer exakt quantifizierbar sind,
gibt diese Darstellung nur einen subjektiven Eindruck wieder. Dies ist
auch der Grund für das Fehlen eines Maßstabs. Um einen Bezug zu den üblichen Programmiersprachen herzustellen, ist zusätzlich die ungefähre
Position der Sprache COBOL eingezeichnet.

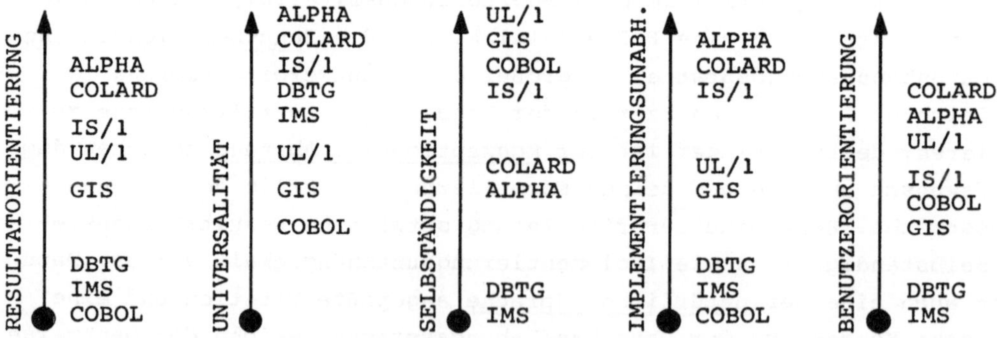

Die vorliegende Arbeit ist als ein Versuch zu verstehen, einer Idealvor-
stellung von einer Datenhandhabungssprache ein wenig näher zu kommen.

2. K o n z e p t i o n e l l e   F r a g e n

Aus der Vielzahl der konzeptionellen Probleme werden zwei markante herausgegriffen. Das eine ist die Widersprüchlichkeit zwischen Resultatorientierung und Universalität, das andere betrifft den Einfluß des Datenmodells auf die Benutzerorientierung der Datenhandhabungssprache.

2.1 Problematik der Resultatorientierung

Ein wichtiger Gesichtspunkt bei der Diskussion über Resultatorientierung
ist, ob die Daten nur transferiert, oder ob sie darüber hinaus auch
transformiert werden sollen. Im Gegensatz zum reinen <u>Datentransfer</u> treten bei der <u>Datentransformation</u> z.B. infolge von Berechnungen neue Datenwerte in Erscheinung, welche vorher weder beim Benutzer noch in der
Datenbank explizit vorhanden waren.

Hohe Resultatorientierung zu erreichen ist bei reinen Datentransfers
relativ unproblematisch, nicht aber bei Datentransformationen. Dies
rührt daher, daß bei Datentransformationen die Anzahl der möglichen Arten von Resultaten wesentlich größer ist als bei Datentransfers. Es ist
leichter, diese größere Vielfalt mit Hilfe von Prozeduren zu meistern,
als für jede Art von Datentransformation eine eigene Resultatspezifikation vorzusehen. Dies ist einer der Hauptgründe für das Gastsprachenkonzept, an dem vielerorts so hartnäckig festgehalten wird.

Obige Argumentation, welche für das Gastsprachenkonzept spricht, ist allerdings nur dann richtig, wenn man hohe <u>absolute</u> Universalität fordert.
Es wurde bereits erwähnt, daß der Benutzer aber nur an einer ausreichenden <u>relativen</u> Universalität interessiert ist, daß er im Gegenteil ein
Zuviel u.U. sogar als Ballast empfindet. Dieser Tatsache wird das Gastsprachenkonzept in keiner Weise gerecht.

Das folgende Konzept ist wesentlich besser geeignet, die Problematik der
Resultatorientierung zu meistern. Und zwar muß der Datenbankadministrator in die Lage versetzt werden, nicht nur wie üblich Datenstrukturen,
sondern auch beliebige Arten von <u>Resultatspezifikationen</u> in Anpassung
an die jeweilige Anwendung zu <u>definieren</u>, insbesondere für Datentransformationen. Die Definition einer bestimmten Art von Resultatspezifikation erfolgt dabei durch Formulierung einer Prozedur. Der Benutzer tätigt den Aufruf dieser Prozedur i.a. nicht bewußt, da der Prozedurname
voll in die Konzeption der Datenhandhabungssprache integriert wird. Auf
diese Weise ist die Sprache beliebig <u>erweiterbar</u>, ohne daß man auf das
Gastsprachenkonzept zurückgreifen muß. Dem Benutzer steht somit eine
Datenhandhabungssprache von ausreichender relativer Universalität sowie
maximaler Resultatorientierung und Selbständigkeit zur Verfügung.

2.2 Benutzerorientierte Datensysteme

Universalität und Implementierungsunabhängigkeit einer Datenhandhabungssprache stehen und fallen mit der Universalität bzw. Implementierungsunabhängigkeit des zugrundeliegenden Datenmodells. Für die Benutzerorientierung ist es hingegen weniger von Bedeutung, ob das Datenmodell _an
und für sich_ besonders einfach ist. Die Einfachheit von Datenmodellen
hat keineswegs eine hohe Benutzerorientierung der darauf bauenden _Daten-
systeme_ notwendig zur Folge und darf damit nicht verwechselt werden.
Einfache Datenmodelle interessieren wohl den Theoretiker und ggf. den
Implementierer eines GDBMS, dem Benutzer kann jedoch nur die Einfachheit
und Überschaubarkeit des handzuhabenden Datensystems von Bedeutung sein.

Wohin eine derartige Verwechslung führen kann, läßt sich am Beispiel des
Relationenmodells von Daten [5] bzw. der Sprache ALPHA [4] demonstrie-
ren. Nach dem Relationenmodell, welches der Sprache ALPHA zugrundeliegt,
sind _Relationen auf Relationen_ nur mit Hilfe von Schlüsseln realisierbar, welche mit dem Problem a priori gar nichts zu tun haben, sondern
nur datenmodellspezifisches Beiwerk darstellen [7]. Auf diese Schlüssel
muß man bei der Handhabung immer dann Bezug nehmen, wenn auf solche Relationen auf Relationen zugegriffen werden soll, auch wenn die Schlüssel
vom Problem her gar nicht gefragt sind. Diese und ähnliche Umständlich-
keiten sind eine unmittelbare Folge des allzu einfachen Relationenmodells und sie lassen sich deshalb auch nicht etwa durch eine Verbesserung der Datenhandhabungssprache ausräumen.

Ein Datenmodell, welches zwar etwas komplizierter als das Relationenmodell ist, die genannten Nachteile aber vermeidet und wesentlich benut-
zerorientiertere Datensysteme liefert, liegt im _Gegenstandsmodell_ [8]
vor. Dieses Modell verwendet den an und für sich klassischen _Gegen-
standsbegriff_ und untermauert ihn, indem es unmittelbar vom Anwendungs-
problem abgeleitete Kriterien für eine standardisierte Gliederung von
Datensystemen in Gegenstände liefert. Eine solche Gliederung verbessert
die Überschaubarkeit des Datensystems für den Benutzer erheblich, da
dieser gewohnt ist, seine Umwelt in ähnlicher Weise und nach ähnlichen
Gesichtspunkten zu gliedern. Da verschiedene Benutzer durchaus unterschiedliche Ansichten über diese Gliederung haben können, besteht die
Möglichkeit, auch andere, vom Standard abweichende Gliederungen zu definieren. Ein Gegenstand wird i.a. durch eine Reihe von _Attributen_ charakterisiert. _Relationen_ zwischen Gegenständen werden beim Gegenstandsmodell _explizit_ definiert und benannt, sie entsprechen in etwa den oben
genannten Relationen auf Relationen.

3. Anmerkungen zur Realisierung

Zunächst wird ein grober Überblick über den Entwurf einer resultatorientierten Datenhandhabungssprache gegeben, welche auf dem Gegenstandsmodell basiert. Einige Anwendungsbeispiele sollen die wesentlichsten semantischen Merkmale dieser Sprache erläutern. Schließlich werden noch einige Probleme, welche bei der Implementierung eines Sprachübersetzers auftreten, andiskutiert.

3.1 Elemente einer resultatorientierten Datenhandhabungssprache

Entsprechend der Forderung nach Anpaßbarkeit der Sprache an die jeweilige Anwendung sind die Sprachelemente nur bis zu einem gewissen Grad fest vorgegeben. Umfang und Notation der Sprachelemente sind vom Datenbankadministrator frei zu wählen. Dieser kann darüber hinaus mit Hilfe einer üblichen Programmiersprache Prozeduren formulieren, deren Namen für den Benutzer der Datenhandhabungssprache als Funktionsoperatoren zur Spezifikation von Datentransformationen in Erscheinung treten. Eine andere Möglichkeit, die Sprache an die Anwendung anzupassen, besteht durch Vorformulierung von Standard-Spezifikationen bzw. Standard-Prozessen durch den Datenbankadministrator.

Eine weitere vorteilhafte Eigenschaft der Sprache ist, daß die verschiedenen Teilspezifikationen innerhalb einer Resultatspezifikation gemischt bzw. in beliebiger Reihenfolge verwendet werden können, soweit dies die Klarheit der Formulierung nicht beeinträchtigt. Für die verschiedenen Arten der Handhabung wird, von gewissen Ausnahmen abgesehen, jeweils dieselbe Notation eingesetzt, was der Übersichtlichkeit der Sprache sehr dienlich ist.

Eine Resultatspezifikation besteht i.a. aus drei Teilen, der Artspezifikation, der Quantitätsspezifikation und der Ausgabespezifikation.

Die Artspezifikation bezeichnet die Art der Handhabung. Es gibt die folgenden vier Artspezifikationen;
- Abfragen   - Datensystem bleibt unverändert
- Einfügen   - neue Behälter nebst Inhalt werden erzeugt
- Löschen   - vorhandene Behälter nebst Inhalt werden vernichtet
- Ersetzen   - vorhandener Inhalt wird vernichtet,
                      dafür wird neuer Inhalt erzeugt

Die Quantitätsspezifikation definiert denjenigen Ausschnitt aus dem Datensystem, welcher gehandhabt werden soll. Die hierfür wichtigsten Sprachelemente sind die folgenden:

- Attributnamen   - Namen von Attributen von Gegenständen
- Gegenstandsnamen   - Namen von Gegenständen
- Relationennamen   - Namen von Relationen zwischen Gegenständen
- Datenwerte   - z.B. Vergleichswerte
- Operatoren   - Vergleichsoperatoren,
                         aussagen- und prädikatenlogische Operatoren,
                         Funktionsoperatoren für die Datentransformation

Die <u>Ausgabespezifikation</u> gibt bei der Abfrage bzw. beim Einfügen, Löschen oder Ersetzen mit Protokoll an, wie die Ausgabedaten dargestellt
werden sollen. Sie kann auch entfallen, wenn eine Standard-Ausgabespezifikation ausreicht, welche der Datenbankadministrator vorformuliert hat.
Bei der Ausgabespezifikation lassen sich die folgenden drei Teile unterscheiden:

- Darstellungsart   - Tabellen-, Relationen- oder Graphendarstellung
- Ordnung   - Angabe einer Hierarchie von Ordnungskriterien
- Positionierung   - Anordnung der Ausgabedaten auf dem Ausgabemedium

Zur Charakterisierung und Trennung der verschiedenen Sprachelemente werden <u>Delimiter</u> bzw. <u>Schlüsselwörter</u> verwendet, welche der Datenbankadministrator vordefiniert hat.

3.2 Anwendungsbeispiele

Der Datenbankadministrator habe folgende Artspezifikationsnamen, Delimiter, Schlüsselwörter und Operatorennamen bzw. Operatoren definiert:

- <u>FINDE</u>   - Artspezifikation "Abfragen"
- <u>ERGÄNZE</u>   - Artspezifikation "Einfügen"
- <u>LÖSCHE</u>   - Artspezifikation "Löschen"
- <u>ERSETZE</u>   - Artspezifikation "Ersetzen"
- ( )   - logische Klammern
- -   - Delimiter für die Trennung von Gegenstandsnamen und
                      Attributnamen: <Gegenstandsname> - <Attributname>
- <u>VON</u>   - Schlüsselwort für die Trennung von Gegenstands-At-
                      tribut-Ausdrücken und Relationennamen:
                      <Gegenstandsn.> - <Attributn.> <u>VON</u> <Relationenname>
- <u>MIT</u>   - Schlüsselwort für die Kennzeichnung einer Bedingung
- <u>DURCH</u>   - Schlüsselwort für die Kennzeichnung neuen Inhalts
- <u>GLEICH</u>   - Vergleichsoperator " = "
- <u>GRÖSSER</u>   - Vergleichsoperator " > "
- <u>UND</u>   - aussagenlogischer Operator "und"
- <u>OB EXISTIERT</u>   - Funktionsoperator; ist die spezifizierte Datenmenge
                      leer, wird "NEIN", andernfalls "JA" ausgegeben

Weiterhin habe der Datenbankadministrator ein Schema eines Datensystems
definiert. Dieses ist in zwei Gegenstände gegliedert, in den Gegenstand
PERSON mit den Attributen NAME, ADRESSE und GEHALT sowie in den Gegenstand PROJEKT mit dem Attribut NAME. Zwischen PERSON und PROJEKT gibt
es die Relationen MITARBEITER und PROJEKTLEITER, jeweils mit PERSON im
Vorbereich, PROJEKT im Nachbereich der Relation. Zwischen PERSON allein
sind die Relationen VORGESETZTER und UNTERGEBENER definiert, wobei im
Vorbereich der ersteren Relation die vorgesetzte Person, im Vorbereich
der letzteren die untergebene Person steht.

Gegenstände:

- PERSON   = (NAME, ADRESSE, GEHALT)
- PROJEKT   = (NAME)

Relationen:

- MITARBEITER   = (PERSON, PROJEKT)
- PROJEKTLEITER   = (PERSON, PROJEKT)
- VORGESETZTER   = (PERSON, PERSON)
- UNTERGEBENER   = (PERSON, PERSON)

Die nebenstehende graphische Darstellung
dient zur Veranschaulichung des Datensystems:

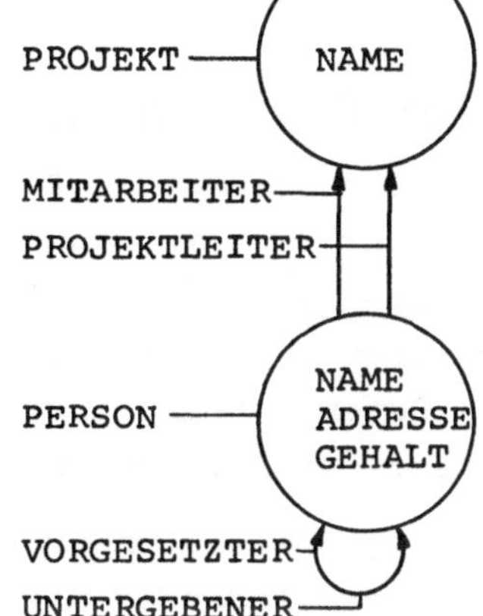

Bei den folgenden Beispielen wird der betreffende Zugriffswunsch zunächst verbal erläutert, anschließend in der Datenhandhabungssprache
formuliert. Es wird eine Standard-Ausgabespezifikation vorausgesetzt.

Beispiel 1: Alle Daten aller Projekte sollen aufgelistet werden.

FINDE PROJEKT

Beispiel 2: Die Person namens P scheidet aus (P ist dem System bekannt).

LÖSCHE PERSON MIT PERSON-NAME GLEICH P

Beispiel 3: Die neue Adresse der Person namens P ist A (P ist dem System bekannt; die alte Adresse wird überspeichert).

ERSETZE PERSON-ADRESSE (MIT PERSON-NAME GLEICH P) DURCH A

Beispiel 4: Die Person namens P tritt dem Projekt namens X als neuer
Mitarbeiter bei (P und X sind dem System bekannt und werden
nicht verändert; es wird nur die neue Relation eingefügt).

ERGÄNZE MITARBEITER (MIT PERSON-NAME GLEICH P UND
PROJEKT-NAME GLEICH X)

Beispiel 5: Wer verdient mehr als sein Vorgesetzter? Die Problematik
dieser Anfrage liegt in der Zuordnung des Attributs GEHALT
zu den Bereichen der Relation VORGESETZTER bzw. UNTERGEBENER.

Der hier beschrittene Lösungsweg ist, das Attribut (GEHALT)
stets auf den <u>Vorbereich</u> der nachfolgenden Relation (<u>VON</u>
VORGESETZTER bzw. <u>VON</u> UNTERGEBENER) zu beziehen.
<u>FINDE</u> PERSON-NAME <u>VON</u> UNTERGEBENER <u>MIT</u> PERSON-GEHALT <u>VON</u>
UNTERGEBENER <u>GRÖSSER</u> PERSON-GEHALT <u>VON</u> VORGESETZTER

<u>Beispiel 6</u>: Verdient der Leiter des Projekts namens X mehr als G(DM)?
Als Antwort wird "JA" oder "NEIN" erwartet, welche der Funktionsoperator <u>OB EXISTIERT</u> liefert.
<u>FINDE</u> <u>OB EXISTIERT</u> PROJEKTLEITER (<u>MIT</u> PROJEKT-NAME <u>GLEICH</u> X
<u>UND</u> PERSON-GEHALT <u>GRÖSSER</u> G)

3.3 Übersetzung von Resultatspezifikationen

Die Übersetzung von Resultatspezifikationen erfolgt in drei Stufen.
Nach der Syntaxprüfung wird die Resultatspezifikation in einer <u>maschi-
nenorientierten</u> Form dargestellt. Anschließend folgt die Umsetzung der
Resultatspezifikation in eine <u>Prozedur</u>, welche mit dem <u>logischen</u> Aspekt
des Datensystems korrespondiert. In der dritten Stufe wird der <u>physische</u>
Aspekt des Datensystems behandelt.

Die Implementierung von <u>Gegenstandsexemplaren</u> erfolgt nach Maßgabe einer
Standardgliederung mit Hilfe des <u>Bausteinkonzepts</u> [9]. Gegenstände, die
sich aufgrund anderer Gliederungen des Datensystems ergeben, werden
nicht als Exemplare, sondern nur als <u>Schemata</u> implementiert. Die Nicht-
Standard-Gegenstandsexemplare werden zur Laufzeit aus diesen Schemata
und den Standard-Gegenstandsexemplaren gewonnen. Da auf diese Nicht-
Standard-Gegenstände selten zugegriffen wird, ergibt sich nur ein geringer Verlust an Zeiteffizienz bei der Abfrage, dem ein erheblicher Gewinn
an Zeiteffizienz beim Einfügen, Löschen bzw. Ersetzen gegenübersteht,
vom Vorteil der geringeren Redundanz ganz zu schweigen.

Wegen der weitgehend redundanzfreien Implementierung des Datensystems
sind Relationen zwischen Gegenständen i.a. nur mit Hilfe mehrerer physi-
scher Zugriffe erreichbar. Dies führt zum Problem des Auffindens von
<u>Pfaden</u>. Diese werden von der Quantitätsspezifikation abgeleitet und mit-
tels einer Zwischensprache, dem <u>Prämissenschema</u> [9], dargestellt.

Effizienzerwägungen, sofern sie nicht automatisch vom Übersetzer ange-
stellt werden können, sind Sache des Datenbankadministrators. Dieser
trifft z.B. die Entscheidung, welche Arten von Operationen effizienter
sein sollen als andere. Eines der Instrumente, welche ihm hierfür zur
Verfügung stehen, ist z.B. die Möglichkeit, beliebige <u>Indexsysteme</u> zu
erzeugen bzw. zu vernichten.

4. Literaturverzeichnis

[1] Bracchi, G. et al: A Language for a Relational Data Base Management System, 6. Annual Princeton Conference on Information Sciences and Systems, 1972

[2] CODASYL-DBTG: Data Base Task Group Report,,April 1971

[3] CODASYL-Systems Committee: Feature Analysis of GDBMS, Mai 1971

[4] Codd, E.F.: A Data Base Sublanguage Founded on the Relational Calculus, ACM SIGFIDET Workshop on Data Description, Access and Control, 1971

[5] Codd, E.F.: A Relational Model of Data for Large Shared Data Banks, Communications of the ACM, Nr. 6, 1970

[6] Codd, E.F.: Relational Completeness of Data Base Sublanguages, Courant Computer Science Symposia 6 Data Base Systems, Mai 1971

[7] Durchholz, R.: Das Datenmodell bei Codd, GMD, Interner Bericht Nr. 60, Juli 1972

[8] Falkenberg, E. et al.: Datenstrukturen eines Instituts-Verwaltungs- und Auskunftssystems, GI-Fachgespräch "Problemgegebene Datenstrukturen", St. Augustin, Februar 1973

[9] Falkenberg, E. et al.: NEOS - Ein Ansatz zur Lösung einiger offener Probleme bei der Konzeption von Datenbanksystemen, 2. GI-Jahrestagung, Lecture Notes in Economics and Mathematical Systems 78, 1973

[10] Klimesch, H.: Information Management System, IBM-Nachrichten, August 1969

[11] Lutz, T.: Generalized Information System - Ein Exekutivsystem für Datenbankprobleme, IBM-Nachrichten, Juni und August 1969

[12] Notley, M.G.: The Peterlee IS/1 System, IBM UKSC-0018, März 1972

[13] Olle, T.W.: A Non-Procedural Language for Retrieving Information from Data Bases, Proceedings of the IFIP Congress 68, Vol. 1, 1969

[14] Reiter, A. et al.: Representation and Execution of Searches over Large Tree-Structured Data Bases, Proceedings of the IFIP Congress 71, TA-3, 1972

[15] Schneider, H.-J.:et al.: Die Strukturiertheitshierarchie bei den verschiedenen Modellen einer Problemlösung, GI-Fachgespräch "Problemgegebene Datenstrukturen", St. Augustin, Februar 1973

[16] Senko, M.E. et al.: Data Structures and Accessing in Data-Base Systems, IBM-Systems Journal, Nr. 1, 1973

Gibt es ein Alternativkonzept zu den Datenbanktechniken der Data Base Task Group (CODASYL) ?

H.J. Skronn

Das CODASYL-Committee hat in den letzten Jahren die meisten größeren Datenbanksysteme untersucht [2] und schließlich einen eigenen Vorschlag zur Erweiterung von Cobol zu einer Datenbanksprache gemacht [3]. Mindestens ein Hersteller ist dabei, diesen Vorschlag durchzuführen.

Ebenso wie andere [5] bin ich der Meinung, daß man sich noch einmal - bevor man weitere Millionen investiert - überlegt, ob nicht das Grundkonzept für viele Anwendungen unzureichend ist.

Die Datenstrukturen bei CODASYL

Zunächst möchte ich kurz andeuten, wie die Datenstrukturen und Zugriffsmethoden beim CODASYL-Vorschlag [3] aussehen.

1. Es gibt *Files (record occurences)*. Das sind Ansammlungen von Records mit gleichartigem Aufbau und Inhalt. Den einzelnen Record kann man meist aufgrund eines eindeutigen *keys (identifier)* wiederfinden.

2. Mit Hilfe von *pointern* lassen sich Beziehungen zwischen einzelnen Records einer oder verschiedener Files konstruieren. Graphisch lassen sich diese Beziehungen wie folgt darstellen:

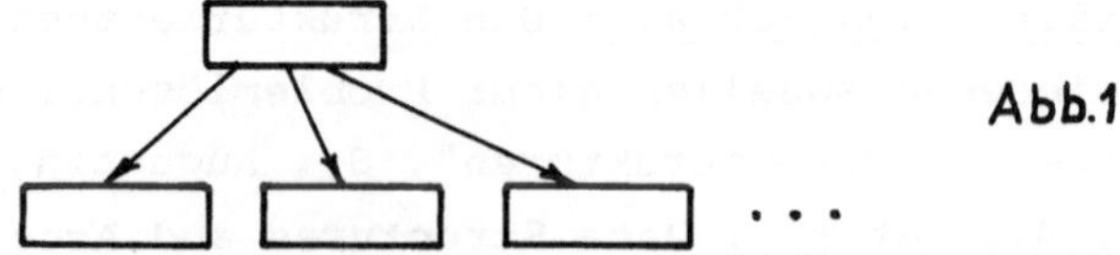

Abb.1

Also einem Record *(owner record)* sind n Records *(member records)* untergeordnet (n=0,1,2,...). Das ganze Gebilde wird *set* genannt. Abb.1 ist nur eine schematisierte Darstellung. Meist sieht die tatsächliche Darstellung wie folgt aus:

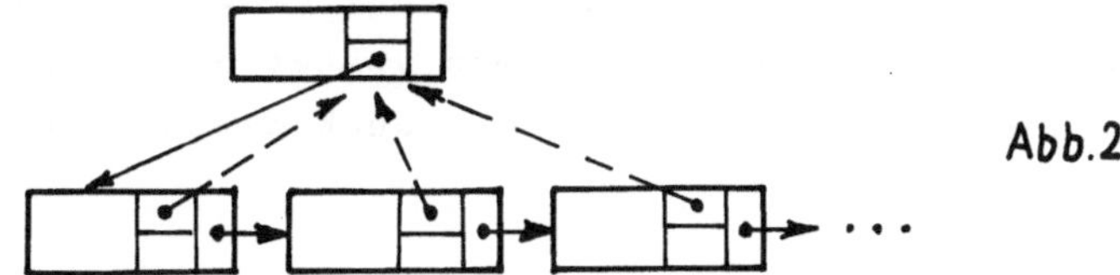

Abb.2

Da jeder Record gleichzeitig *owner record* in verschiedenen *sets* sein kann und dazu noch *member record* in verschiedenen *sets* sein kann, lassen sich leicht recht komplizierte Strukturen konstruieren (s. Abb.3).

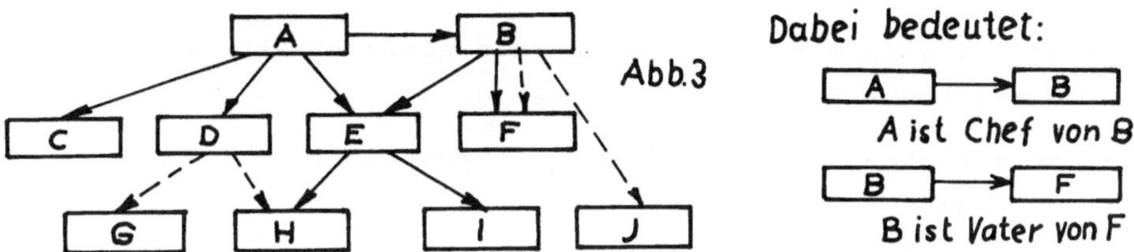

Die entscheidenden Nachteile des CODASYL-Konzepts sehe ich in folgenden Punkten:

1. Der Zugriff zu gesuchten Records ist nur auf sehr eingeschränkte Weise möglich. Man kann einen Record zunächst nur aufgrund seines *keys* finden; von einem gefunden Record kann man sich dann zum nächsten, zum untergeordneten oder übergeordneten Record weiterhangeln *(next member, first member, owner)*. Mengentheoretische Operationen, die anhand gegebener Kriterien zur Selektion bestimmter Records führen, sind nicht möglich.

Zum Beispiel kann man folgende Records nicht auf einfache Weise finden:

a) Alle Patienten mit Diagnose=Herzinfarkt und Medikament=A und Nebenwirkung=X;

b) alle Verbrecher mit Delikt=Bankraub, Haare=schwarz und Alter zwischen 25 und 30;

c) alle Produkte mit Produktart=XYZ und Umsatz>1 Mio.DM.

2. Alle Beziehungen zwischen Records müssen vorher deklariert
    werden und werden bei der Speicherung eines Records durch *pointer*
    realisiert. Das bedeutet, daß man später nur nach solchen Be-
    ziehungen fragen kann, die *vorher* auch datentechnisch schon vor-
    handen waren.

    Alle anderen Beziehungen, sie sonst noch aus logischen oder
    sachlichen Gründen bestehen, sind dem Benutzer nicht zugänglich. [1)]

3. An den Anwendungsprogrammierer werden sehr hohe Anforderungen
    gestellt:

    a) Er muß sich mit der nicht gerade einfachen Logik der
        Datenstrukturen auseinandersetzen;

    b) er muß eine recht komplizierte Programmiersprache
        lernen;

    c) er muß die Attribute (PICTURE) der Felder *(items)*, die er
        benutzen will, richtig beschreiben, obwohl der Compiler
        sich diese Informationen aus der Datenbank holen könnte.

Insgesamt muß man feststellen, daß gerade die schwierigen Probleme
weiterhin den durchschnittlichen Anwendungsprogrammierern zugemutet
werden, also Personen, die nicht einmal in der Lage sind, die Möglichkeiten einer Programmiersprache wie PL/1 voll auszunutzen.

Ein Vorschlag zum Aufbau der Datenbank

Zunächst sollte man versuchen, wie es auch von CODD und anderen An-
hängern des *relational model* gefordert wird[4,5,6,7], die Daten zumindest für die Sicht des Benutzers möglichst in einfacher Form zu
speichern. Ich glaube, es liegt kein Verdienst darin, immer kompliziertere Datenstrukturen dem Benutzer zur Verfügung zu stellen. Der
Ehrgeiz der Datenexperten sollte vielmehr dahin gehen, zu zeigen,
wie man auch mit einfachen Datenstrukturen auskommen kann.

In den meisten Anwendungen kann man sich auf *normalisierte* Records
beschränken[4,6,7] (genauer sogar auf die *dritte Normalform*[6]).

[1)] Dazu empfehle ich auch die Lektüre des satirischen Artikels
"Long Live the Data Administrator" [10] .

Praktisch ausgedrückt sind *normalisierte records* Records, die keine
variable Anzahl von Eintragungen enthalten. Nach Möglichkeit sollte
man auch noch fordern, daß ein Einzel-item nicht variabel lang sein
darf, weil man dadurch dem *software engineer* die Arbeit wesentlich
erleichtert. Bei der Verarbeitung von Dokumenten mit variabel langen
Texten hat man aber mit der letzten Forderung Schwierigkeiten.

In Abb.4 sind diesselben Daten einmal *unnormalisiert* und dann
normalisiert dargestellt.

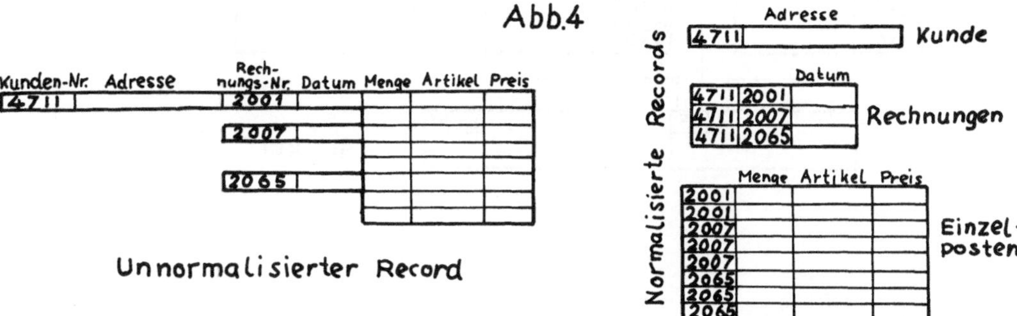

Gleichartige Records sollte man wie in der ganz konventionellen
Datenverarbeitung zu Files zusammenfassen. Die physikalische Reihenfolge der Records ist dabei unwichtig. Aber jeder Record sollte eindeutig identifizierbar sein, und zwar durch ein oder mehrere Felder,
die man zusammen einen *key* nennt. Ohne *keys* hat man beim *Updaten* von
Records Schwierigkeiten.

Von dem *Anwendungsprogrammierer* wird nur verlangt, daß er die File-
namen und die Feldnamen kennt, die er im Augenblick benutzt. Den
Recordaufbau, die Attribute der Felder und die Namen der nicht benötigten Felder braucht er nicht zu kennen. Natürlich muß er die
Bedeutung der benutzten Felder kennen, wenn er mit ihnen sinnvoll
manipulieren will.

<u>Implizite Beziehungen zwischen Records</u>

Trotz der eben geschilderten einfachen Speicherung der Daten, gibt es
auch in einer solchen Datenbank beliebig komplizierte Beziehungen
zwischen einzelnen Records. Es bestehen nämlich auf fast natürliche
Weise logische Beziehungen zwischen Records, die in bestimmten
Feldern den gleichen Wert haben.

In Abb.5 werden durch die Kundennummer Beziehungen zwischen Kunden und den dazugehörigen Rechnungen hergestellt. In Abb.6 werden Beziehungen zwischen Einzel- und Großhändlerrecords, die den gleichen Wohnort und die gleiche Branche haben, hergestellt.

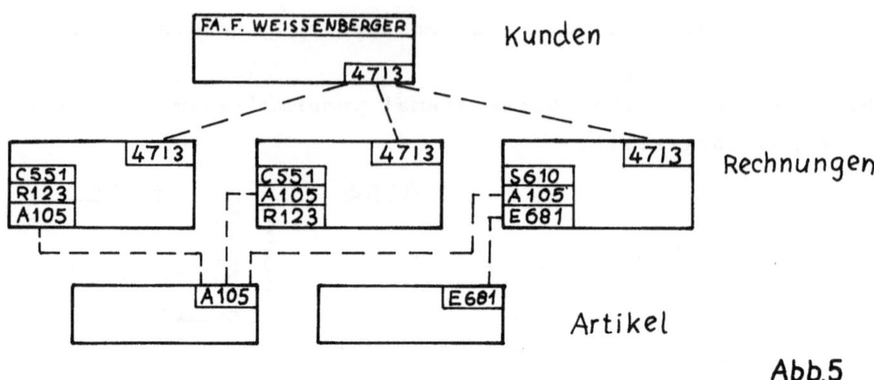

Abb.5

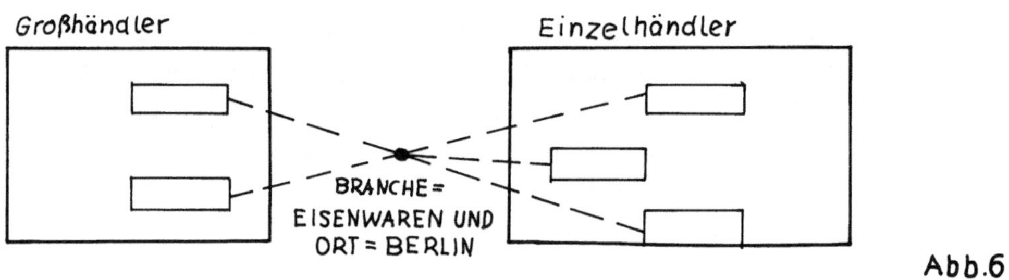

Abb.6

Beziehungen solcher Art könnte man in 3 Klassen aufteilen:

1. Die Records werden einander paarweise zugeordnet. Dieser Fall ließe sich vermeiden, wenn man aus den Paaren gleich einen Record gemacht hätte.

2. Einem Record wird eine unbestimmte Zahl anderer Records zugeordnet (Abb.5). Dies ist der normale Fall. Damit lassen sich schon recht komplizierte Strukturen darstellen (zumindest die von CODASYL untersuchten Strukturen wie *tree, plex, network* [2]).

3. Eine Untermenge von Records wird einer anderen Untermenge aus demselben oder einem anderen File zugeordnet (s. Abb.6).

Verwaltung der Datenbank durch Wörterbücher

Im folgenden möchte ich zeigen, wie man mit Hilfe von *Wörterbüchern* zwei wesentliche Forderungen an eine Datenbank erfüllen kann - nämlich erstens die Möglichkeit zur Bildung von Untermengen anhand gegebener Kriterien und zweitens die Möglichkeit zur Herstellung von Beziehungen zwischen Records. *Wörterbücher* sind seit langem in der Dokumentenverarbeitung als *inverted files* bekannt. Aber seltsamer Weise wird diese Technik in kommerziellen Datenbanken noch sehr wenig angewendet.

Ich möchte hier noch einmal kurz andeuten, wie solche Wörterbücher aussehen:

Ein Wörterbuch ist einem Feld zugeordnet und enthält alle verschiedenen Inhalte dieses Feldes genau einmal[1]. Jedem dieser Wörterbucheintragungen ist eine Liste mit Adressen *(Trefferliste)* zugeordnet, welche auf die zugehörigen Daten zeigen (s. Abb.7).

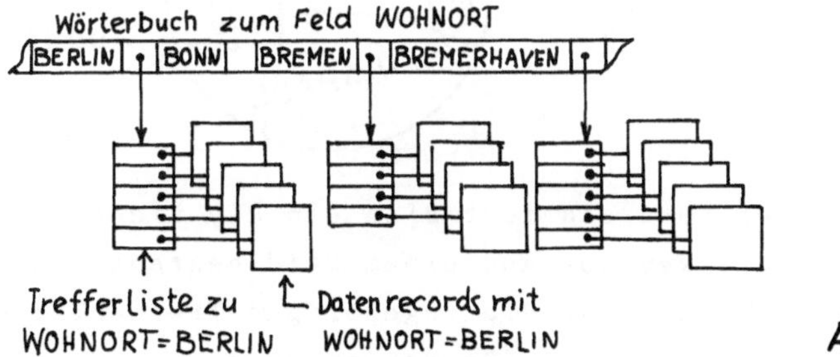

Abb.7

Hat ein Feld (wie in der kommerziellen Datenverarbeitung üblich) pro Record nur eine Eintragung, so werden die Daten durch ein Wörterbuch

---

[1] Über die verschiedenen Techniken, große Wörterbücher so aufzubauen, daß man mit möglichst wenigen Zugriffen zu peripheren Speichermedien auskommt, möchte ich hier nicht reden. Zu diesem Thema empfehle ich die Lektüre von R. Bayer und E. McCreight[1]. Dort ist nach meiner Meinung die bisher brauchbarste Methode beschrieben worden. Diese Techniken habe ich auch in meinem Artikel[9] näher beschrieben.

in disjunkte Mengen unterteilt (Abb.8a und 8b). Bei anderen Anwendungen, wie z.B. bei der Verarbeitung von Dokumenten in Biblio-
theken, kann ein Feld eine variable Anzahl von Werten haben oder
einem Wörterbuch ist eine variable Anzahl gleichartiger Felder zugeordnet. Dadurch werden die Daten in nicht-disjunkte Mengen unterteilt (Abb.9a und 9b). Im ersteren Fall wird man bei der Informations-
suche meist Inhalte verschiedenartiger Felder logisch verknüpfen
(BERUF=BÄCKER UND ALTER<40), im zweiten wird man verschiedene gleichartige Werte verknüpfen (SEGELN UND SKI UND NICHT SCHWARZARBEIT).
Um die relevanten Records zu finden, braucht man nur die Durch-
schnittsmenge der zugehörigen Trefferlisten zu bilden.

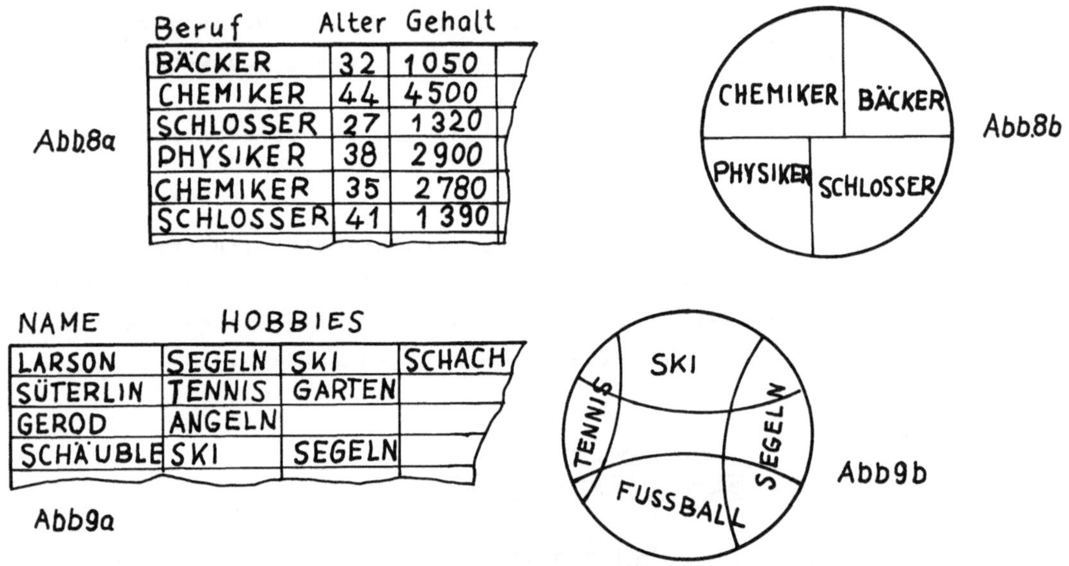

Vom Wörterbuchkonzept her unterscheidet sich ein *key* nicht von
anderen Feldern. Falls der key nur aus einem Feld besteht, zeichnet
er sich höchstens dadurch aus, daß die zugehörigen Trefferlisten nur
eine Eintragung haben. Das bedeutet für den *software engineer*, daß er
auf die Trefferliste verzichten kann und gleich die Adresse des
Records in das Wörterbuch eintragen kann. Eventuell kann er ganz auf
das Wörterbuch verzichten, falls aus dem key der Ort des Records be-
stimmbar ist (z.B. bei index-sequentiellen Dateien). Für den Benutzer
dagegen ist ein key ein Suchkriterium, das einen gesuchten Record
eindeutig kennzeichnet.

Durch das bisher Gesagte soll klar sein, daß man mit Hilfe von
Wörterbüchern leicht Untermengen einer Datei anhand gegebener
Kriterien herausholen kann.

Aber ebenso klar ist, wie man mit Hilfe von Wörterbüchern die oben
beschriebenen impliziten Beziehungen zwischen Records (Abb.5 und 6)
realisiert. Es waren ja Beziehungen, die sich dadurch ergaben, daß
bestimmte Felder von verschiedenen Records den gleichen Inhalt hatten.
Man braucht also nur im Wörterbuch für das betrachtete Feld unter
einem bestimmten Feldwert nachzuschlagen, um alle zusammengehörigen
Records zu finden.

Im Beispiel von Abb.5 müßten Beziehungen über die Kundennummer bzw.
über die Artikelnummer hergestellt werden. In diesem Beispiel werden
die Beziehungen zufällig zwischen *Eigen-* und *Fremdkeys* hergestellt
(im Rechnungsrecord sind z.B. Kundennummer und Artikelnummer *Fremd-*
keys; die Rechnungsnummer wäre dort ein *Eigenkey*). Wie ich durch das
Beispiel von Abb.6 gezeigt habe, können die Beziehungen auch durch
beliebige andere Felder hergestellt werden. Voraussetzung ist nur,
daß für die in Frage kommenden Felder Wörterbücher existieren.

An einem kleinen Beispiel möchte ich zeigen, wie für den Anwendungsprogrammierer der Umgang mit einer Datenbank mit Wörterbüchern aus-
sehen könnte. Als Beispiel bringe ich ein kleines Programm, das alle
Kunden in Bremen und dazu deren unbezahlte Rechnungen ausdruckt. Die
Programmiersprache ist im Augenblick reine Phantasie; die Syntax
wurde PL/1 nachempfunden (bei uns werden die Aufrufe an die Datenbank
noch über CALL-Anweisungen gemacht). Der Kundenfile heiße in dem
Beispiel 'KUNDEN' und der Rechnungsfile 'RECHNUNGEN'. Die Anweisung
FIND ermittelt alle gewünschten Records und liefert zunächst nur die
Anzahl zurück. Durch das GET wird dann erst ein Record nach dem
anderen (oder Teile von Records) geholt.

```
     FIND RECORDS ('KUNDEN') WITH (WOHNORT='BREMEN') QUANTITY(N1)
LOOP1:DO I1=1 TO N1
     GET RECORD ('KUNDEN') ITEMS (NAME,ADRESSE,KUNDEN_NR)
     Drucke NAME, ADRESSE
     FIND RECORDS ('RECHNUNGEN') WITH (KUNDEN_NR=KUNDEN_NR
                              & CODE='N') QUANTITY(N2)
LOOP2:DO I2=1 TO N2
     GET RECORD ('RECHNUNGEN') ITEMS (RECH_NR,DATUM,BETRAG)
     Drucke RECH_NR,DATUM,BETRAG
     END LOOP2
     END LOOP1

/* CODE='N' heißt hier, die Rechnung ist nicht bezahlt. */
```

<u>Schlußbemerkungen</u>

Zum Abschluß möchte ich noch einmal die Vorteile des Wörterbuch-
Konzeptes zusammenfassen:

1. Mengentheoretische Operationen können ohne großen Rechenaufwand
    durchgeführt werden.

2. Alle Daten sind unabhängig von ihrer tatsächlichen physikalischen
    Speicherung bereits implizit nach mehreren Kriterien sortiert;
    nämlich bezüglich aller Felder, für die es Wörterbücher gibt.

3. Beziehungen zwischen Records werden erst bei einer Retrieval-
    anfrage hergestellt. Dadurch ist man sehr flexibel gegenüber
    sich ändernden oder unbekannten Benutzerwünschen.

Die betrachteten Strukturen können durchaus komplizierter sein als
diejenigen beim CODASYL-Vorschlag. Aber niemand braucht explizit
etwas über die Strukturen zu wissen. Der Anwendungsprogrammierer kann
von Fall zu Fall aufgrund der Sachkenntnis *seiner* Daten alle implizit
schon vorhandenen logischen Beziehungen herstellen lassen

<u>Literatur</u>

[1] Bayer,R.,McCreight,E.: Organization and Maintenance of Large
     Ordered Indexes. Acta Informatica 1, No.3, 173-189 (1972)
[2] Codasyl Systems Committee: Feature Analysis of Generalized Data
     Base Management Systems. May 1971
[3] Codasyl Data Base Task Group: April 71 Report
[4] Codd,E.F.: A Relational Model for Large Shared Data Banks.Comm.
     ACM 13 6, 377-387 (1970)
[5] Codd,E.F.: A Data Base Sublanguage Founded on the Relational
     Calculus. ACM SUGFIDET Workshop on Data Description, Access &
     Control, San Diego, Nov. 1971
[6] Codd,E.F.: Further Normalization of the Data Base Relational
     Model. Courant Computer Science Symposia 6 'Data Base Systems'
     May 1971
[7] Neuhold,E.J.: Informationssysteme. GI 2. Jahrestagung
     Karlsruhe 1972
[8] Skronn,H.J.: Verwaltung einer Datenbank durch eine Hierarchie von
     Wörterbüchern.Angewandte Informatik, Heft 1, 21-24 (1973)
[9] Skronn,H.J.: Methoden der Strukturierung von Datenbanken.
     Angewandte Informatik, Heft 5, 204-210 (1973)
[10] Kurz, R.C.: Long Live the Data Administrator.
     Datamation 19, No. 3, 72-74 (1973)

REDUCTION OF RETRIEVAL COSTS FOR ON-LINE RETRIEVAL SYSTEMS

Donald B. Crouch

INTRODUCTION

The objective of on-line information retrieval systems is the retrieval of information residing in the system's data base which is relevant to a query of the system. A query is specified as a set of attributes and the system is expected to retrieve only the information described by (or relevant to) the query. Such systems are being utilized in a variety of applications including medical information systems, automatic document retrieval, computer aided instruction, management information systems, banking systems, and inventory control.

The growing popularity of on-line information retrieval systems and the increasingly frequent appearance of large scale data bases in information retrieval applications are producing major information storage management problems. As the data collection becomes inordinately large, the number of operations necessary to retrieve the desired information often becomes excessive, resulting in reduced system efficiency. This problem is compounded by the fact that most large data bases are dynamic in nature; that is, the collection is constantly subject to a great number of updating and deleting operations. Consequently, in order to minimize the time spent retrieving and updating information in the collection (that is, in order to minimize retrieval costs), a storage management scheme which provides a strategy for optimizing the location of information in secondary storage is needed. The optimization of the storage is necessarily time-dependent.

Although no such strategy exists for large scale information retrieval systems, the essential requirements of such a strategy are evident. The storage management strategy must provide a dynamic file structure for large data bases, a memory hierarchy for multi-level storage of the data, and an algorithm which ensures efficient use of the hierarchy.

The factors to be considered in the design of such a strategy differ from those of traditional approaches. In retrieval systems information growth and the usage pattern of the information are the primary factors which degrade system performance rather than the amount of user activity. If the most active portion of the data base has the most growth, then the system is degraded to a greater extent than if the growth occurred in a less frequently accessed area of information. In addition to the usual considerations of such factors as response time (service time), storage device characteristics and cost of servicing a query, the storage management scheme must also take into account data base characteristics (for subdivision of the collection), collection growth characteristics, patterns of use of the data base, characteristics of user groups including usage growth rate, and collection retirement. The last factor is not meant to imply necessarily a complete loss of an item but merely its reallocation to a remote, limited access, level of storage in the memory hierarchy. Since a priori knowledge of the arrival patterns of queries is not assumed, the additional collection characteristics and user characteristics must be taken into account in order to form a basis of expectations concerning the queries. This basis affects the allocation of information to the secondary storage.

The factors which influence the design of a storage management strategy for large-scale, on-line, information retrieval systems for dynamic data bases indicate that the strategy must necessarily incorporate a data organization capable of handling excessively large collections of data and flexible enough to permit dynamic reorganization of the data structures as changes occur in the information collection. Such an organization must have an associated search strategy which takes advantage of its flexible structure in order to minimize retrieval costs. This emphasis of minimization of costs must not result in a strategy which degrades the ability of the system to retrieve all relevant information in response to a query.

This paper discusses a file organization which satisfies the requirements of the storage management scheme necessary for on-line retrieval systems.

A DYNAMIC FILE STRUCTURE

File organizations and search techniques used in conventional retrieval systems are inadequate for on-line retrieval systems requiring response times of sufficient speed to support a large number of terminals. Essential ingredients of future on-line retrieval systems affecting the file structure include feedback searches and file reorganization methods. Feedback searches are retrieval strategies which incorporate the user in the retrieval process in order to increase search effectiveness. Such strategies include procedures for automatically revamping the search request based on user supplied responses to initial search activities. This technique aids the user who needs certain information residing in the data base but who, due to inexperience or lack of knowledge of the data base, has difficulty formulating his request to obtain the desired information. For example, such a situation frequently occurs in automated document retrieval systems.

The primary requirement which is necessary in order to incorporate a query modification scheme efficiently into a retrieval system is the maintenance of a viable file organization. However, the use of such methods is not the only reason for developing file reorganization procedures for information systems. An even more important motive is the normal collection growth process inherent in a dynamic environment (a major characteristic of many retrieval applications). Although developers of information retrieval systems have generally been aware of the problems created by collection growth, such retrieval systems have not been designed specifically for dynamic collections. Consequently, the file organizations generally used in existing, operating retrieval systems do not provide the necessary flexibility required in an automatic on-line information retrieval system.

If conventional approaches are not suitable for large scale retrieval systems requiring numerous reorganization operations while maintaining fast response times, what type of file organization is most applicable? A file system which has been shown to possess the necessary attributes is the clustered file organization. This system automatically partitions the collection into subsets (clusters) and restricts a search of the data base to that information contained within a select set of clusters. A comparison of conventional file organizations and clustered file organizations indicates that the clustered file is more economical of storage and permits more flexible searches [2].

CLUSTER ANALYSIS

Cluster analysis is rapidly assuming a major role in computerized information retrieval systems. The result of applying a clustering algorithm to an information collection is a set of overlapping "homogeneous" groups or clusters, each containing a subset of the items in the original collection. Homogeneity within clusters implies that the items contained within a common cluster possess similar information or relate to a common idea. Clustering strategies generally may be classified according to the degree of homogeneity among clusters. A bibliography of clustering techniques is contained in [1].

Each item of information in the system is assumed to be represented by an information vector, the components of which may be either binary or weighted. A binary vector indicates merely the absence or presence of particular information in an item, whereas a weighted vector indicates the degree of contribution of each vector component to the information contained in the item. A cluster of items is generally represented by a "centroid vector", the sum of the set of **all** vectors contained within the cluster.

Retrieval of information from a clustered file is performed by comparing each query of the system with the file of centroid vectors. The information vectors contained within the clusters exhibiting a sufficiently high correlation with the query are next compared with the query vector. The resulting set of items is then ranked according to correlation values and returned to the user as the response of the system to the query. Such a search is referred to as a two-level search.

Retrieval costs of information systems utilizing a clustered file organization are primarily affected by the time to perform the correlation calculations and the time to retrieve from external memory the set of clusters considered relevant to the query on the basis of the first-level correlations. The latter time factor can be reduced if the clusters to be retrieved are arranged a priori in an optimal fashion in memory; that is, if clusters of similar homogeneity reside in proximity in secondary storage, the time to retrieve a set of clusters during the secondary search may be reduced. The development of such a multi-level storage technique, a major component of the proposed storage management strategy for large scale systems, does not exist. However, a process for reducing the costs involved in the first time factor has been developed.

REDUCTION OF CENTROID VECTOR LENGTH

A centroid vector normally contains several hundred unique components. Vectors of this length are undesirable for several reasons, namely, high storage costs, increased retrieval time due to correlation calculations, and sensitivity of correlation measures to length. In order to reduce the length of a centroid vector and consequently to reduce retrieval costs, a process is needed for deleting from the centroid vectors those components contributing least significantly to the information contained in the items defining a cluster.

Previous reduction processes generally delete a specified percentage of the centroid components of lowest weight and lowest frequency of occurrance [3]. These processes which yield at most an 80 percent reduction sometimes exclude significant components due to their restrictive selection procedure. To overcome this disadvantage, a statistical reduction procedure which reveals the dominant features of the cluster by extracting those components exhibiting strong inter-relationships within a cluster has been developed.

The centroid reduction process selects components based on the coefficient of variation, defined as the standard deviation divided by the mean value. This measure indicates on an elementary basis the discriminatory power of a component. Consequently, a significant component of the index space of a cluster is considered to be one with a low coefficient value.

In order to reduce the centroid vector, the coefficient of variation is calculated for each unique component in the index space of the cluster. The components exhibiting the lowest coefficient values are selected as representative of the information content of the cluster. The reduced centroid vector is obtained from the original centroid vector by discarding all other coefficients. The number of components to select per cluster may be specified externally. The procedure initially attempts to select this number of components. However, if additional components have the same coefficient value as the largest value of the selected components, then a minimum number of additional components or a maximum number of fewer components is chosen.

Experiments on a data base consisting of document vectors indicate a 95 to 98 percent reduction in the centroid vector lengths using this reduction process. The reduced vectors require substantially less storage space and significantly decrease the time to generate correlation values during the search process. Furthermore, retrieval effectiveness with the reduced vectors is essentially equivalent to that of the full centroid vectors.

SUMMARY

This paper describes the characteristics of a storage management strategy for large scale, on-line information retrieval systems. In order to achieve realistically feasible retrieval from large collections with response times fast enough for an on-line environment, a storage strategy must provide a dynamic file structure for large data bases, a memory hierarchy for multi-level storage of the data, and an algorithm which ensures efficient use of the hierarchy.

The clustered file organization provides the necessary flexibility required in an automatic on-line retrieval system. With the reduction process described in this paper, such a file organization assumes an even more appealing structure for large data bases.

REFERENCES

[1] Crouch, Donald B. "Cluster Analysis: Bibliography." SIGIR Forum, 6 (Fall, 1971), 11-14.

[2] Murray, D. M. "Document Retrieval Based on Clustered Files." Unpublished Ph. D. Dissertation, Cornell University, 1972.

[3] Salton, Gerard. "Dynamic Document Processing," Comm. ACM 15, 7 (July, 1972), 658-68.

DATENSTRUKTUREN UND Q-SYSTEME - EINE MATHEMATISCHE STUDIE

H.-D. Ehrich

1. Einleitung

Beim Entwurf verallgemeinerter Datenbanksysteme spielt die strukturelle Unabhängigkeit der Daten eine große Rolle: die Organisation der gespeicherten Daten soll (bis zu einem gewissen Grade) unabhängig sein von der logischen Beschreibung der Daten auf der Benutzerebene. Wenn der Benutzer nicht mit der aktuellen Speicherorganisation befaßt ist, kann er in seinen Programmen und Anfragen auch nicht auf diese Bezug nehmen. Das heißt, er kann sich nur formal auf Daten, Beziehungen zwischen Daten und Operationen auf Daten beziehen. Es ist dann Aufgabe des Systems, die Daten und die Beschreibung der Daten zentral zu verwalten und die Operationen wie Suche, Änderung etc. zentral zu steuern.

Damit das System diese Aufgaben wahrnehmen kann, müssen die Daten, die Beziehungen zwischen Daten, die Operationen auf Daten und die Abbildungen zwischen verschiedenen Darstellungen formal beschrieben werden.

In dem vorliegenden Beitrag wird ein mathematisches Modell für Datenstrukturen und Anfrageoperationen untersucht. Nach der Definition und Erläuterung dieses "Attribut-Modells" im nächsten Abschnitt werden im Abschnitt 3 dessen Beziehungen zum Relationen-Modell von Codd [1] untersucht. Dann werden im Abschnitt 4 "Q-Systeme", das sind kombinierte Systeme (Datenstrukturen, Anfrageoperationen), definiert,und deren Relevanz für die Untersuchung praktischer Speicher- und Zugriffsorganisationen wird erörtert. Auf der Grundlage eines plausiblen Äquivalenzbegriffs für Q-Systeme werden zum Schluß äquivalente Umformungen von Q-Systemen betrachtet.

2. Das Attribut-Modell

Die Grundkonzeption des Datenstrukturmodells, welches hier präzisiert werden soll, findet sich mehrfach in der Literatur. Insbesondere sei auf den "relational data file" von Salton [6] und die Datenstruktur der assoziativen Sprache LEAP von Feldman und Rovner [2,5] hingewiesen.

<u>Definition 2.1.</u>: Eine <u>Datenstruktur</u> ist ein Quadrupel $D=(\Omega, A, V, \rho)$, wobei Ω, A und V endliche Mengen von Objekten, Attributen bzw. Werten sind. ρ ist eine dreistellige Relation auf Ω, A und V : $\rho \subset \Omega \times A \times V$. Folgende Bedingungen werden gefordert:

$$1.\ pr_1(\rho)=\Omega \qquad 2.\ pr_2(\rho)=A \qquad 3.\ pr_3(\rho)=V$$

Hierbei bezeichnet $pr_i(\rho)$ die Projektion der i-ten Komponente von ρ, $i=1,2,3$, also die Menge der Elemente, die in der i-ten Komponente von ρ vorkommen.

Die Beziehung $(\omega, a, v)\epsilon\rho$ wird folgendermaßen interpretiert:

"Das Attribut a des Objekts ω hat den Wert v"

oder

"Das Objekt ω hat die Eigenschaft (a,v)"

<u>Beispiel 1</u> :

(Karl	, arbeitet an	, Entwurf	)
(Fritz	, arbeitet an	, Programmierung	)
(Hans	, leitet	, Dokumentation	)
(Emil	, arbeitet an	, Dokumentation	)
(Emil	, arbeitet unter	, Hans	)

....

Alle Eigenschaften eines festen Objekts fassen wir zu einem Satz zusammen.

<u>Definition 2.2.</u>: Sei $D=(\Omega, A, V, \rho)$ eine Datenstruktur und $\omega\epsilon\Omega$. Der <u>Satz von ω</u> ist

$$R_\omega := \{ \ (a,v) \mid (\omega, a, v)\epsilon\rho \ \}$$

Durch die Äquivalenzrelation $\omega\equiv\omega'$ $:\Longleftrightarrow pr_1(R_\omega)=pr_1(R_{\omega'})$ wird eine Klasseneinteilung $K=\{\Omega_1, \ldots \Omega_p\}$ auf Ω definiert, in der Objekte mit "gleichem Satzformat" zu Äquivalenzklassen zusammengefaßt werden:

$$\Omega = \bigcup_{i=1}^{p} \Omega_i \ , \quad \Omega_i \cap \Omega_j=\emptyset \ \text{für} \ 1\leq i<j\leq p$$

Wegen der Bedingung 1 der Definition 2.1. ist $pr_1(R_\omega)\neq\emptyset$ für alle $\omega\epsilon\Omega$, und aufgrund der Definition der Äquivalenzrelation $\equiv$ können wir jeder Objektklasse Ω_i, $1\leq i\leq p$, eindeutig die Attributmenge $A_i:=pr_1(R_\omega)$ für $\omega\epsilon\Omega_i$ zuordnen. Wegen der Bedingung 2 der Definition 2.1. ist dann

$$A = \bigcup_{i=1}^{p} A_i \ .$$

Damit können wir die Relation ρ in p paarweise disjunkte Relationen

$$\rho_i \subset \Omega_i \times A_i \times V$$

zerlegen, sodaß gilt:

$$\rho = \bigcup_{i=1}^{p} \rho_i \quad , \quad \rho_i \cap \rho_j = \emptyset \text{ für } 1 \leq i < j \leq p$$

Für die Einschränkungen ρ_i von ρ gilt dann, daß es zu jedem Paar (ω,a) $\epsilon \Omega_i \times A_i$ einen Wert $v \epsilon V$ gibt, so daß $(\omega,a,v) \epsilon \rho_i$ ist.

Wir unterscheiden zwischen "einfachen" und "komplexen" Datenstrukturen. Auf der Grundlage der obigen Überlegungen definieren wir folgendes:

Definition 2.3.: Eine Datenstruktur $D=(\Omega,A,V,\rho)$ heißt **einfach**, wenn die Teilrelationen ρ_i für $1 \leq i \leq p$ Funktionen der Form

$$\rho_i : \Omega_i \times A_i \rightarrow V$$

sind.

Einfache Datenstrukturen sind demnach diejenigen, in denen zu jedem Attribut jedes Objektes höchstens ein Wert gehört. Der Zweck der obigen Überlegungen wird im nächsten Abschnitt deutlich, in dem die Beziehungen zum Relationen-Modell von Codd [1] näher untersucht werden. Damit wird an einem Beispiel gezeigt, wie andere Darstellungen von Datenstrukturen aus dem Attribut-Modell formal hergeleitet werden können.

3. Zusammenhang mit dem Relationen-Modell

Zur Unterscheidung in diesem Abschnitt nennen wir die Datenstrukturen des Attribut-Modells "A-Strukturen" und diejenigen des Relationen-Modells "R-Strukturen", und wir präzisieren Codd's Modell folgendermaßen:

Definition 3.1.: Eine R-Struktur ist ein Paar $D^*=(\mathcal{W},\mathcal{R})$, wobei gilt:

1. $\mathcal{W} = \{V_1,\dots,V_n\}$ ist eine endliche Menge von Wertebereichen (attribute sets in [1]).

2. $\mathcal{R} = \{R_1,\dots,R_p\}$ ist eine endliche Menge von Relationen,

$R_i \subset V_{i1} \times V_{i2} \times \cdots \times V_{ik_i}$ für $i=1,\dots,p$ und $V_{ij} \epsilon \mathcal{W}$ für $j=1,\dots,k_i$

3. Die folgende Bedingung ist immer erfüllt:
$$\bigcup_{i=1}^{n} V_i = \bigcup_{i=1}^{p} \bigcup_{j=1}^{k_i} pr_j(R_i)$$

Die letztere Bedingung besagt, daß es in einer R-Struktur keine überflüssigen Werte gibt, die in keiner Relation vorkommen.

Zunächst fällt auf, daß sich A-Strukturen als spezielle R-Strukturen auffassen lassen:

$$D=(\Omega,A,V,\rho) \;\; \hat{=} \;\; D^*=(\{\Omega,A,V\} , \{\rho\})$$

Umgekehrt läßt sich aber auch jede R-Struktur unter bestimmten, kaum einschränkenden Bedingungen durch eine spezielle, nämlich einfache

A-Struktur darstellen. Um dies zu zeigen, führen wir zwei Transformationen

$$\phi : \{R\text{-Strukturen}\} \to \{\text{einf. A-Strukt.}\}$$
$$\psi : \{\text{einf. A-Strukt.}\} \to \{R\text{-Strukturen}\}$$

ein:

I.   Sei $D^* = (\mathcal{W}, \mathcal{R})$ gegeben. Dann definieren wir

$$\phi(D^*) = D = (\Omega, A, V, \rho)$$

folgendermaßen:

$$\Omega := \{ (r, R) \mid r \epsilon R \epsilon \mathcal{R} \}$$

Jedem Wertebereich $V_i \epsilon \mathcal{W}$ ordnen wir ein Attribut $a(V_i)$ zu:

$$A := \{a(V_1), \ldots, a(V_n)\}$$

Für die Wertemenge V setzen wir

$$V := \bigcup_{i=1}^{n} V_i$$

Die Tripelmenge ρ definieren wir folgendermaßen: ist $\omega = (r, R_i)$ und gehört
zur j-ten Komponente der Relation R_i der Wertebereich V_{ij} sowie zur
j-ten Komponente des k_i-Tupels $r \epsilon R_i$ der Wert $v \epsilon V_{ij}$, genau dann ist

$$(\omega, a(V_{ij}), v) \; \epsilon \; \rho$$

Da in jeder Komponente jeder Relation der R-Struktur D^* nur ein Wert
steht, ist $\phi(D^*)$ offenbar eine einfache A-Struktur.

II.   Sei $D = (\Omega, A, V, \rho)$ eine einfache A-Struktur. Dann definieren wir

$$\psi(D) = D^* = (\mathcal{W}, \mathcal{R})$$

folgendermaßen: jedem Attribut $a_j \epsilon A$, $j = 1, \ldots, n$, ordnen wir den Wertebereich

$$V(a_j) := \{ v \epsilon V \mid \exists \omega \epsilon \Omega : (\omega, a_j, v) \epsilon \rho \}$$

zu. Wir setzen

$$\mathcal{W} := \{V(a_1), \ldots, V(a_n)\}$$

Sei $K = \{\Omega_1, \ldots, \Omega_p\}$ die im vorigen Abschnitt auf Ω eingeführte Klasseneinteilung, und sei

$$A_i = \{a_{i1}, \ldots, a_{ik_i}\} \quad , \quad i = 1, \ldots, p \quad ,$$

die zu Ω_i gehörige Attributmenge (s.o.). Sei ferner

$$\rho_i(\omega, a_{ih}) = v_{ih}$$

für alle $\omega \epsilon \Omega_i$, $i = 1, \ldots, p$ und $h = 1, \ldots, k_i$. Dann setzen wir für $i = 1, \ldots, p$

$$R_i := \{(v_{i1}, \ldots, v_{ik_i}) \mid \exists \omega \epsilon \Omega_i \; \forall h = 1, \ldots, k_i : \rho(\omega, a_{ih}) = v_{ih}\}$$

Es ist $R_1 \subset V(a_{11}) \times \cdots \times V(a_{1k_1})$, und wir setzen

$$\mathcal{R} := \{R_1, \ldots, R_p\}$$

Dann ist $\psi(D) = D^* = (\mathcal{W}, \mathcal{R})$ eine R-Struktur.

Diese Transformationen ϕ und ψ hängen auf folgende Weise zusammen:

Ist D^* eine R-Struktur, in der zwei verschiedene Relationen niemals für alle entsprechenden Komponenten gleiche Wertebereiche haben, so ist

$$\psi(\phi(D^*)) \approx D^*$$

(Die Isomorphie $\approx$ bedeutet wie üblich die Gleichheit bis auf eineindeutige Bezeichnungsänderungen.)

Ist umgekehrt D eine einfache A-Struktur, in der verschiedene Objekte immer verschiedene Sätze haben, so ist

$$\phi(\psi(D)) \approx D$$

Beispiel 2 : Sei D^* gegeben durch folgende Relationen:

PERS	Name	Vater	Beruf
	Karl	Kurt	Lehrer
	Emil	Kurt	Arzt

TEIL	Teilnr.	verw.in	Anz.
	1oo746	XQR2	5

D sei folgende A-Struktur:

$$(X , Name , Karl)$$
$$(X , Vater , Kurt)$$
$$(X , Beruf , Lehrer)$$
$$(Y , Name , Emil)$$
$$(Y , Vater , Kurt)$$

$$(Y , Beruf , Arzt)$$
$$(T , Teilnr. , 1oo746)$$
$$(T , verw.in , XQR2)$$
$$(T , Anz. , 5)$$

Dann ist $\phi(D^*) = D$ und $\psi(D) = D^*$.

4. Q-Systeme

Retrieval-Operationen sind in gewissem Sinne grundlegend für eine ganze Reihe weiterer Operationen auf Datenstrukturen. Die Formalisierung von Retrieval-Operationen in diesem Abschnitt geht mehr von der Sicht des Implementierers aus als von der des Benutzers. Es besteht nicht die Absicht, hiermit eine Grundlage zu schaffen für die Konstruktion einer benutzerorientierten Anfragesprache. Vielmehr wird angestrebt, ein allgemeines Konzept für die Darstellung von Speicher- und Zugriffsorganisationen zu entwickeln. Komplexe Benutzeranfragen werden in der Regel in eine Reihe von Einzelzugriffen aufgelöst, und es sind diese Einzelzugriffe, welche hier untersucht werden sollen.

Sei $D=(\Omega, A, V, \rho)$ eine Datenstruktur.

<u>Definition 4.1.</u>: Eine <u>Frage</u> ist eine zweistellige Relation $q \subset A \times V$. Die <u>Antwort</u> auf q in D ist

$$\alpha_D(q) := \{ \, \omega \varepsilon \Omega \mid q \subset R_\omega \, \}$$

Die <u>Länge</u> von q ist $|q|$, und Fragen der Länge 1 heißen <u>Elementarfragen</u>.

Fragen sind also Kombinationen von Eigenschaften, und die Antwort besteht aus allen Objekten, welche alle geforderten Eigenschaften haben. Fragen sind Mengen und lassen sich als solche durch Mengenoperationen verknüpfen. Für die Vereinigung und den Durchschnitt von Fragen gelten folgende Gestze:

<u>Lemma 4.1.</u>: Sei $D=(\Omega, A, V, \rho)$ eine Datenstruktur. Für alle Fragen $q, q' \subset A \times V$ gilt:

$$1. \quad \alpha_D(q \cap q') \supset \alpha_D(q) \cup \alpha_D(q')$$
$$2. \quad \alpha_D(q \cup q') = \alpha_D(q) \cap \alpha_D(q')$$

<u>Beweis:</u> 1. $\omega \varepsilon \alpha_D(q) \cup \alpha_D(q') \Rightarrow q \subset R_\omega \vee q' \subset R_\omega \Rightarrow q \cap q' \subset R_\omega \Rightarrow \omega \varepsilon \alpha_D(q \cap q')$

2. $\omega \varepsilon \alpha_D(q \cup q') \Longleftrightarrow q \cup q' \subset R_\omega \Longleftrightarrow q \subset R_\omega \wedge q' \subset R_\omega \Longleftrightarrow \omega \varepsilon \alpha_D(q) \cap \alpha_D(q')$

Aufgrund der zweiten Beziehung läßt sich die logische Konjunktion von Fragen als Vereinigung der Fragen darstellen.

Im folgenden sollen kombinierte Systeme, bestehend aus Datenstrukturen und zugehörigen Mengen von "Standardfragen", im Zusammenhang betrachtet werden.

<u>Definition 4.2.</u>: Ein <u>Q-System</u> ist ein Paar $\mathcal{A} = (D, Q)$, wobei $D=(\Omega, A, V, \rho)$ eine Datenstruktur und $Q \subset \mathcal{P}(A \times V)$ eine Menge von <u>Standardfragen</u> ist.

Für Probleme der Implementierung von Q-Systemen sind die folgenden speziellen Eigenschaften von Bedeutung:

<u>Definition 4.3.</u>: Ein Q-System $\mathcal{A} = (D, Q)$ heißt

    1. <u>Tabelle</u> $:\Longleftrightarrow \forall q, q' \varepsilon Q : pr_1(q) = pr_1(q')$

    2. <u>elementar</u> $:\Longleftrightarrow \forall q \varepsilon Q : \quad |q| = 1$

    3. <u>boolesch</u> $:\Longleftrightarrow V \subset \{0,1\} \wedge pr_2(Q) \subset \{1\}$

Hierbei ist $pr_2(Q) := \bigcup\limits_{q \varepsilon Q} pr_2(q)$.

Elementare Tabellen sind unmittelbar der Implementierung durch herkömmliche und bekannte Methoden zugänglich, wie z.B. sequentielle und index-sequentielle Organisation durch Ordnung der Sätze nach den Werten

des Schlüsselattributs, auf das sich alle Fragen beziehen. Ferner kommen
hier Streuspeicherung (hash coding), Suchbäume etc. in Frage. Ein Spei-
cher- und Zugriffssystem mit invertierten Files für einige Attribute
läßt sich als elementares Q-System auffassen. Es gibt fortgeschrittenere
Organisationsmethoden, wie sie z.B. von Ray-Chaudhury [4] und anderen
dort zitierten Autoren beschrieben wurden, die sich als boolesche
Q-Systeme interpretieren lassen. Die Methode der kombinierten Indizes
von Lum [3] gibt Beispiele für Q-Systeme, welche weder Tabellen noch
elementar noch boolesch sind.

Wir wollen untersuchen, ob und ggf. wie sich Q-Systeme umformen lassen,
um sie u.U. in eine für die Implementierung bessere Form bringen zu
können. Für die Untersuchung solcher Umformungen benötigen wir einen
plausiblen Äquivalenzbegriff.

<u>Definition 4.4.</u>: Zwei Q-Systeme $\mathcal{Q}_1 = (D_1, Q_1)$ und $\mathcal{Q}_2 = (D_2, Q_2)$ heißen
<u>äquivalent</u>, in Zeichen $\mathcal{Q}_1 \sim \mathcal{Q}_2$, genau dann, wenn folgendes gilt
$(\alpha_1 := \alpha_{D_1}$, $i=1,2)$:

$$1. \quad \alpha_1(Q_1) \cup \alpha_2(Q_2) \subset \Omega_1 \cap \Omega_2$$

$$2. \quad \exists \kappa : Q_1 \twoheadrightarrow Q_2 \; \forall q_1 \varepsilon Q_1 \; : \; \alpha_1(q_1) = \alpha_2(\kappa(q_1))$$

Hierbei ist $\alpha(Q) := \bigcup_{q \varepsilon Q} \alpha(q)$.

Grob gesagt sind Q-Systeme äquivalent, wenn auf gleiche Fragen gleiche
Antworten gegeben werden. Auf der Grundlage dieses Äquivalenzbegriffs
erhalten wir folgende Ergebnisse:

<u>Satz 4.1.</u>: Zu jeder Tabelle $\mathcal{T} = (D, Q)$ gibt es eine äquivalente Tabelle
$\mathcal{T}^* = (D^*, Q^*)$, deren Attributmenge höchstens ein Attribut enthält (welche
also insbesondere elementar ist) .

<u>Beweis</u>: Sei $D = (\Omega, A, V, \rho)$ und $A = \{a_1, \ldots, a_n\}$. Ist $Q = \emptyset$, so ist die leere
Tabelle $\mathcal{T}^* = ((\emptyset, \emptyset, \emptyset, \emptyset), \emptyset)$ äquivalent zu $\mathcal{T}$. Ist $Q = \{\emptyset\}$, so ist
$\mathcal{T}^* = ((\Omega, \emptyset, \emptyset, \emptyset), \{\emptyset\})$ äquivalent zu $\mathcal{T}$. Q enthalte nun mindestens eine
nichtleere Frage, und o.B.d.A. sei $pr_1(q) = \{a_1, \ldots, a_p\}$, $1 \leq p \leq n$, für alle
$q \varepsilon Q$. Dann setzen wir $a^* := (a_1, \ldots, a_p)$ und ordnen jeder Frage $q \varepsilon Q$,
$q = \{(a_1, v_1), \ldots, (a_p, v_p)\}$, das Paar $\kappa(q) := \{(a^*, v^*)\}$ zu, wobei
$v^* := (v_1, \ldots, v_p) \; \varepsilon V^p$ ist. Sei

$$Q^* := \{ \kappa(q) \mid q \varepsilon Q \}$$
$$\rho^* := \{ (\omega, a^*, v^*) \mid \forall i = 1, \ldots, p : (\omega, a_i, v_i) \varepsilon \rho \}$$
$$\Omega^* := pr_1(\rho^*)$$
$$V^* := pr_3(\rho^*)$$

Dann ist die Tabelle $\mathcal{T}^* = (D^*, Q^*)$ mit $D^* = (\Omega^*, \{a^*\}, V^*, \rho^*)$ äquivalent zu $\mathcal{T}$. Denn mit $\alpha := \alpha_D$ und $\alpha^* := \alpha_{D^*}$ gilt:

$$\alpha(Q) = \{\ \omega\varepsilon\Omega\ |\ \exists q\varepsilon Q : q \subset R_\omega\ \}$$
$$\subset \{\ \omega\varepsilon\Omega\ |\ \forall i=1,\ldots,p\ \exists v_i\varepsilon V\ :\ (\omega, a_1, v_1)\varepsilon\rho\ \}$$
$$= \Omega^*$$

Offenbar ist $\alpha^*(Q^*) \subset \Omega^*$ und $\Omega^* \subset \Omega$, so daß die erste Bedingung für die Äquivalenz erfüllt ist.

Für alle $q\varepsilon Q$, $q=\{(a_1, v_1), \ldots, (a_p, v_p)\}$ ist $\kappa(q) = \{(a_1, \ldots, a_p), (v_1, \ldots, v_p)\}$, und es gilt:

$$\alpha(q) = \{\ \omega\ |\ q \subset R_\omega\ \} = \{\ \omega\ |\ \forall i=1,\ldots,p : (\omega, a_1, v_1)\varepsilon\rho\ \}$$
$$= \{\ \omega\ |\ (\omega, (a_1, \ldots, a_p), (v_1, \ldots, v_p))\varepsilon\rho^*\ \}$$
$$= \{\ \omega\ |\ \kappa(q) \subset R_\omega^*\ \}$$
$$= \alpha^*(\kappa(q))$$

Hierbei ist R_ω^* der Satz von ω in D^*. Daß κ eine bijektive Abbildung ist, ist klar, so daß auch die zweite Bedingung für die Äquivalenz erfüllt ist.

<u>Satz 4.2.</u>:   Zu jedem Q-System $\mathcal{A} = (D, Q)$ gibt es ein äquivalentes Q-System $\mathcal{A}^* = (D^*, Q^*)$, welches elementar und boolesch ist, und dessen Datenstruktur D^* einfach ist.

<u>Beweis</u>:   Sei $\alpha := \alpha_D$ und $\alpha^* := \alpha_{D^*}$. Wir setzen $\Omega^* := \alpha(Q)$, $A^* := Q$ und $V^* := pr_3(\rho^*)$, wobei gilt:

$$\rho^* := \{\ (\omega, q, 1)\ |\ q\varepsilon Q,\ \omega\varepsilon\alpha(q)\ \}$$
$$\{\ (\omega, q, 0)\ |\ q\varepsilon Q,\ \omega\varepsilon\Omega^*\dot{-}\alpha(q)\ \}$$

Offenbar ist ρ^* eine Funktion von $\Omega^* \times A^*$ in V^*, d.h. die Datenstruktur $D^* = (\Omega^*, A^*, V^*, \rho^*)$ ist einfach.

Wir setzen nun $Q^* := \{\{(q, 1)\}\ |\ q\varepsilon Q\}$ und definieren die bijektive Abbildung $\kappa : Q \rightarrowtail Q^*$ durch $\kappa(q) := \{(q, 1)\}$. Setzen wir nun $\mathcal{A}^* := (D^*, Q^*)$, so ist $\mathcal{A}^*$ elementar und boolesch, und es ist $\mathcal{A} \sim \mathcal{A}^*$. Denn einerseits ist $\alpha(Q) = \Omega^* = \alpha^*(Q^*)$ und $\Omega^* \subset \Omega$, und andererseits gilt die folgende Äquivalenz:

$$\omega\varepsilon\alpha(q) \iff (\omega, q, 1)\varepsilon\rho^* \iff \omega\varepsilon\alpha^*(\kappa(q))\ .$$

<u>Literatur</u>

1. Codd, E.F.: A relational model of data for large shared data banks. Comm. ACM 13 (1970), 377-387.

2. Feldman, J.A.-Rovner, P.D.: An ALGOL-based associative language. Comm. ACM 12 (1969), 439-449.

3. Lum,V.Y.: Multi-attribute retrieval with combined indexes.
         Comm. ACM 13 (197o), 66o-665.

4. Ray-Chaudhury,D.K.: Combinatorial information retrieval systems for
         files.   SIAM J. Appl. Math. 16 (1968), 973-992.

5. Rovner,P.D.-Feldman,J.A.: The LEAP language and data structure.
         Proc. IFIP 68, A.J.H.Morrell (ed), North-Holland,
         Amsterdam 1969 , pp. 579-585.

6. Salton,G.: Automatic information organization and retrieval.
         McGraw-Hill, New York 1968.

LOSE KOPPLUNG IN INFORMATIONSSYSTEMEN

HORST WEDDE

Abstract

A new formal concept is presented to describe the behaviour of information systems. It takes into account only the mutual restrictions in the behaviour of the components. First steps are made to formalize properties of systems which guarantee the possibility of transitions and freedom of deadlocks. Solutions are given with special respect to the design of information systems.

1. Einleitung

Bei Einrichtung und Betrieb eines Rechenbetriebes, auch eines großen Datenbanksystems, wirft das fehlerhafte Verhalten von Teilsystemen - etwa

- Fehlerhaftes Funktionieren von Programmen;
- Zusammenbruch von Teilsystemen;
- Datenübertragungsfehler -

in einem bestimmten Aspekt besondere Probleme auf: Eine Fehlerbeschreibung kann wegen der Komplexität der Systeme oft genug keinen Hinweis auf die Ursache oder Entstehungsgeschichte des Fehlverhaltens geben, sie hat dann also höchstens lokal Bedeutung: Eine Fehlfunktion eines Moduls kann evtl. nur bzgl. der Wechselbeziehungen zu direkt benachbarten Moduln konstatiert werden. Daher muß man damit rechnen, daß Fernwirkungen von Korrekturmaßnahmen in unkontrollierter Weise sogar zu unerwünschten Systemzuständen führen, die ohne die Korrektur nicht hätten eintreten können.

Die Behandlung von deadlock-Situationen, also Vorgängen des gegenseitigen Blockierens paralleler (Teil-) Prozesse, kann hier als Beispiel dienen. DIJKSTRA [2] hat ja zur Verhinderung von deadlocks einen Synchronisationsmechanismus angegeben. Je komplizierter jedoch Synchronisationsoperationen werden - zur systematischen Behandlung damit zusammenhängender Verhaltensfragen siehe auch GENRICH und LAUTENBACH [3] -, desto unübersichtlicher in Bezug zum Gesamtsystem ist dem Systementwerfer ihre Wirkungsweise.

HOARE [7] und HANSEN [6] gehen nun, wie bei GÖLLER [4] bemerkt, dazu über, das Synchronisationsprinzip auch für Synchronisationsoperationen zu benutzen. Das geschieht auf der Grundlage, daß Synchronisationen sich gegenseitig ausschließen können. Eben diese Basis soll für den Ansatz der Losen Kopplung auch gewählt werden. Da das hier beschriebene Modell sehr stark auf Bedürfnisse des Planens und Entwerfens von Systemen ausgerichtet ist, wird der Forderung nach formaler Übersichtlichkeit besonders Rechnung getragen. Daher wird nur die Kenntnis der wechselseitigen Störung von Teilsystemen für den formalen Aufbau herangezogen, nicht aber eine innere Struktur der Teilsysteme. Zur Erhaltung der Übersichtlichkeit geht man weiter auch davon aus, daß das modellhaft zu erfassende System modular aufgebaut ist oder entworfen werden soll.

Nach der Einführung der Grundbegriffe und -beziehungen sollen folgende Fragestellungen präzisiert werden:

1) Angenommen, ein Teilsystem M könnte, für sich genommen, einen Zustand Z einnehmen. Behält es dieses Funktionsmerkmal, wenn Verhaltensbeschränkungen von M durch andere Teilsysteme und deren wechselseitige Einflüsse aufeinander mit eingeplant werden?

2) Angenommen, in M kann ein Zustandsübergang $Z_1 \longrightarrow Z_2$ stattfinden. Unter welchen Bedingungen kann dieser auch unter globalen Gesichtspunkten, also unter Berücksichtigung der Einflüsse aller Teilsysteme aufeinander, noch stattfinden?

Eine Antwort auf solche Fragen muß natürlich zu finden sein, ohne daß man auf die Kenntnis aller Gesamtzustände oder -übergänge zurückgreift. Bei der Angabe von Lösungen wird aus Platzgründen auf Beweise verzichtet. Diese stehen in [9] .

Schließlich wird eine Anwendung der angegebenen Sätze im Bereich des computer-gestützten Planens und Entwerfens besprochen, unter Heranziehung eines bereits gebräuchlichen Entwurfsverfahrens. -

Das Konzept der Losen Kopplung geht auf eine Idee von C. A. PETRI zurück. Es wurde im Institut für Informationssystemforschung der Gesellschaft für Mathematik und Datenverarbeitung ausgearbeitet.

2. Grundbegriffe und -beziehungen

Bei dem Versuch, die Wechselbeziehungen zwischen den Teilsystemen ohne Berücksichtigung innerer Verhältnisse dieser Komponenten zu erfassen, liegt es nahe, jedes Teilsystem im wesentlichen mit der Menge der <u>Phasen</u> p zu identifizieren, in denen Störeinflüsse von anderen Teilsystemen wirken oder auf sie ausgeübt werden. Es sei weiter davon ausgegangen, daß zwei Phasen eines Teilsystems sich gegenseitig ausschließen. Einem Teilaspekt der Modularität folgend, seien die Komponenten des Systems voneinander getrennt gedacht. Um verschiedenen Begriffsbildungen in Anwendungsfällen entgegenzukommen, seien die Komponenten neutral als <u>Bereiche b</u> bezeichnet. Man hat also eine Phasenmenge P und eine Bereichsmenge B mit folgenden Eigenschaften:

$$\bigwedge_{b \,\in\, B} : b \subseteq P \; ; \qquad \bigwedge_{b_i,\, b_j \,\in\, B} : (b_i \neq b_j \implies b_i \cap b_j = \varnothing).$$

Die Störeinflüsse des Bereichs b_i auf den Bereich b_j $(i \neq j)$, die hier eine Rolle spielen, werden interpretiert als Unverträglichkeiten (Verbot gleichzeitigen Bestehens) von Phasen von b_i mit solchen von b_j. Sie werden beschrieben durch eine zweistellige Relation $K_{ij} \subseteq b_i \times b_j$ mit:

$$\bigwedge_{b_i,\, b_j \,\in\, B} : (i \neq j \implies K_{ij} = K_{ji}^{-1}).$$

K_{ij} wird unverträgliche Kopplung oder kurz <u>Kopplung</u> zwischen b_i und b_j genannt. Entsprechend hat man eine "lokale" oder <u>gegebene Verträglichkeit</u> L_{ij} zwischen b_i und b_j mit:

$$L_{ij} \subseteq b_i \times b_j \quad \text{und} \quad L_{ij} := b_i \times b_j \setminus K_{ij} \;\; (i \neq j).$$

Aus dem Phasencharakter (s. o.) ist dann motiviert:

$$\bigwedge_{b_i \,\in\, B} K_{ii} := b_i \times b_i \setminus \mathrm{id}_{b_i} \; ; \quad L_{ii} := \mathrm{id}_{b_i} .$$

Zur Abkürzung sei festgelegt:

$$K := \bigcup_{b_i,\, b_j \,\in\, B} K_{ij} \; ; \quad L := \bigcup_{b_i,\, b_j \,\in\, B} L_{ij} .$$

Den Gesamtsituationen eines Systems entsprechen mit den gerade aufgestellten Begriffen Phasenteilmengen $c \subseteq P$ mit:

a) $\bigwedge_{b \,\in\, B} \quad |c \cap b| = 1$; b) $\bigwedge_{p_1, p_2 \,\in\, c} : (p_1, p_2) \in L$.

Dieser Situationsbegriff ist zeitunabhängig formuliert, die Mengen c seien mit dem von A.W. HOLT eingeführten Namen <u>case</u> bezeichnet. Sie bilden die Menge C. Das Quadrupel (P, B, C, K) heißt ein <u>Kopplungssystem</u>. Bei der formalen Behandlung der in 1. gestellten Fragen spielt schließlich eine Kopplungsgrobstruktur der Bereiche eine wichtige Rolle. Wir definieren deshalb für $b_1, b_2 \in B$:

$(b_1, b_2) \in vs(K) \quad :\Longleftrightarrow \quad b_1 \neq b_2 \wedge K_{12} \neq \emptyset$.

Zur Verdeutlichung sei nun ein Grundproblem der Synchronisation, die Betriebsmittelsynchronisation (vgl. $[4]$), an folgendem Beispiel dargestellt:

Die Prozesse $T_1, \ldots, T_4$ benötigen ein Betriebsmittel R, aber höchstens drei davon können es gleichzeitig benutzen. Wir setzen $T_1, \ldots, T_4$ als Bereiche an, von denen jeder eine Phase p_i enthält, in der T_i nicht auf R warten muß. Zur Darstellung der Synchronisationsbedingung führt man einen fiktiven Bereich R' ein, der gerade 4 Phasen enthält, und man zeichnet folgendes Bild von der Kopplungsrelation K :

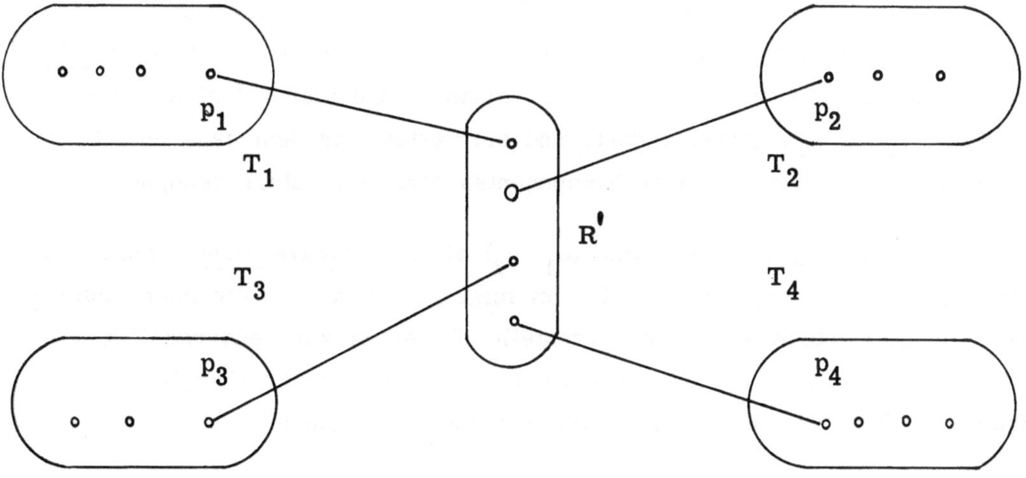

Es gibt cases, die z.B. p_1, p_2, p_3 enthalten, aber keiner von diesen kann p_4 enthalten. - Es ist leicht zu sehen, daß alle Synchronisationsbedingungen obiger

Art nach der angedeuteten Methode darstellbar sind.

In Kopplungssystemen werden Ereignisse definiert auf dem Hintergrund der folgenden Axiome:

a) Ein Ereignis wird beschrieben durch Angabe von Phasenübergängen. Es kann eintreten, wenn die betreffenden Übergänge nicht verboten sind. Über Initialisierung, Ablauf, Dauer und Beendigung eines Ereignisses wird nichts gesagt.

b) Es gibt Elementarereignisse, das sind Ereignisse, in die man sich jedes Ereignis zerlegt denken kann derart, daß das Eintreten eines Teilereignisses das Eintreten keines anderen unmöglich macht (concurrency oder Nebenläufigkeit).

Die Existenz von Elementarereignissen ist eine sehr wichtige Forderung für eine vollständige Erfassung des Verhaltens: Es gibt Modelle, in denen Ereignisse stets weiter zerlegt gedacht werden können (Physik) oder nicht erkennbar oder explizit sind auf der Betrachtungsebene (Simulationssprachen). Stehen im zweiten Fall solche Ereignisse im Konflikt derart, daß eins durch Eintreten dem anderen die Möglichkeit dazu nimmt, so kann der Benutzer des Simulators, weil er von einer Konfliktentscheidung nichts wahrnimmt, sich über die Aussagekraft einer Simulation kein klares oder sicheres Bild machen.

Die Idee zur Definition der Elementarereignisse in Kopplungssystemen beruht auf dem Prinzip, daß die Komponenten aller technischen Systeme gegeneinander einen gewissen Spielraum haben müssen, anders ausgedrückt: stets lose gekoppelt sein müssen. Es wird nämlich hier verlangt, daß sich bei einem Elementarereignis genau eine Phase ändert, und ein System, in dem es solche Ereignisse nicht gäbe, wäre in seinen Komponenten danach zu starr gekoppelt.

Für $c_1, c_2 \in C$ repräsentiert also (c_1, c_2) ein Elementarereignis genau dann, wenn $|c_1 \setminus c_2| = |c_2 \setminus c_1| = 1$. Im folgenden Bild wird ein sehr einfacher Ablauf von Elementarereignissen dargestellt. Dabei ist zur besseren Erkennbarkeit der cases nicht die Kopplungsrelation K, sondern ihr Komplement L gezeichnet. (Das gilt auch für alle weiteren Darstellungen.)

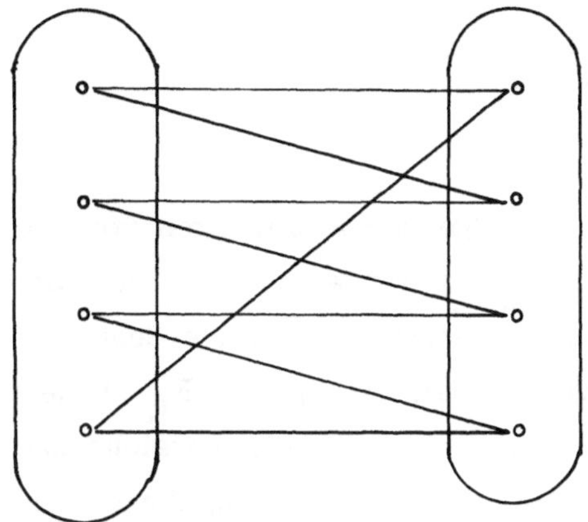

Da es nur zwei Bereiche gibt, sind L-Kanten und cases identisch. In jedem der
beiden Bereiche ist nun ein zyklischer einfacher Phasenablauf möglich von der
gleichen Art. Man hat also im wesentlichen die Funktionsweise einer Uhr mit
4 Phasen dargestellt. (Merkwürdigerweise braucht man dazu mehr als einen
Bereich.)

3. Fragen der Funktionsfähigkeit

Im Abschnitt 1. waren schon Fragen nach gewissen Aspekten der Funktionsfähig-
keit eines Informationssystems in informaler Weise gestellt worden, zunächst
nach Funktionsbeschränkungen einer Systemkomponente durch Ankopplung von
weiteren. Mit den in 2. gewonnenen Begriffen denken wir uns nun ein Kopp-
lungssystem $M = (P, B, C, K)$ und einen case $c \in C$. Faßt man M als Teilsystem eines größeren Systems auf, dann ist eine wesentliche Frage, ob c sich
zu einem case c' des umfassenden Systems fortsetzen läßt. Wir wollen uns hier
auf die Untersuchung des Falles beschränken, in dem $|B| = 2$ ist. Die Frage
ist dann gerade, ob für zwei Phasen p_1 und p_2 aus Bereichen b_1 bzw. b_2 mit
$(p_1, p_2) \in L_{12}$ ein gemeinsamer case existiert. Wir setzen dabei zur Abkürzung für $p_1, p_2 \in P$; $b_i, b_j \in B$:

$$(p_1, p_2) \in G :\Longleftrightarrow \bigvee_{c \in C} : p_1 \in c \wedge p_2 \in c \; ; \quad G_{ij} := G \cap (b_i \times b_j) \; .$$

Es leuchtet sofort ein, daß i.a. $L_{ij} \neq G_{ij}$ ist. Immerhin wäre ein effizienter
Algorithmus zu suchen, der die eben gestellte Frage entscheiden könnte. Dazu
setzt man wie folgt an: Seien $b_i, b_j \in B$. Dann sei

$$F_{ij} := \bigcap_{\substack{n \in \mathbb{N} \\ 1 \longmapsto i_1}} \in A(n,B,i,j) \qquad \bigcup_{k=1}^{n} L_{i_{k-1} i_k} \quad ,$$

wobei $A(n,B,i,j)$ die Menge der Abbildungen von $\{0, \ldots, n\}$ in $\{1, \ldots, |B|\}$ ist mit $i_0 = i$, $i_n = j$ und wobei man sich die Bildung des Relationenprodukts gerade in der anderen Reihenfolge denkt, als sie bei Verkettung von Funktionen gebräuchlich ist. $(p_1, p_2) \in F_{ij}$ bedeutet also, daß, gleichgültig welchen Weg man von b_i über andere Bereiche nach b_j wählt, man stets eine Kette von L-Kanten findet, die p_1 und p_2 längs dieses Weges verbinden.

Um die formale Betrachtung durchsichtiger zu machen, fordert man:

3.1 <u>Axiom</u>: $\qquad \bigwedge_{b_i \in B} F_{ii} = id_{b_i}$.

<u>Bem.</u>: Für die Behandlung der in 1. gestellten Fragen ist das Axiom keine Einschränkung der Allgemeinheit, da man sich leicht davon überzeugt, daß eine Phase, die obiger Bedingung nicht genügt, keinem case angehören kann.

Als erste Folge von 3.1 hat man die

3.2 <u>Proposition</u>: Zur Bestimmung von F_{ij} brauchen nur solche Wege von b_i nach b_j herangezogen zu werden, die längs Kanten der vs(K)-Relation (siehe 2.) verlaufen.

Schließlich noch den

3.3 <u>Satz</u>:
$$F_{ij} = \bigcap_{\substack{n \in \mathbb{N} \\ 1 \longmapsto i_1}} \in I(n,B,i,j) \qquad \bigcup_{k=1}^{n} L_{i_{k-1} i_k} \quad ,$$

wobei $I(n,B,i,j)$ gerade die injektiven Elemente von $A(n,B,i,j)$ enthält.

Da für die auf der rechten Seite der Gleichung stehende Relation 3.2 entsprechend gilt (wegen 3.1), kann man sagen, daß die Bestimmung von F_{ij} deutlich weniger Aufwand verursacht als die direkte Berechnung von G_{ij} durch Berechnung von cases. Da andererseits $G_{ij} \subseteq F_{ij}$ ist, stellt sich hier die Frage, wann $F_{ij} = G_{ij}$ gilt. Dazu als Teilantwort der

<u>3.4 Satz:</u> Sei der Graph der vs(K)-Relation zyklenfrei.

Dann gilt: a) $(b_i, b_j) \in vs(K) \implies G_{ij} = L_{ij}$

b) $(b_i, b_j) \notin vs(K) \implies G_{ij} = F_{ij}$

<u>Bem.:</u> Die Aussage $G_{ij} = F_{ij}$ gilt auch noch unter schwächeren Voraussetzungen. I. a. ist sie jedoch falsch, wie das folgende Gegenbeispiel klarmachen kann. Wie schon vorher ist der Graph der Phasen und L-Kanten gezeichnet:

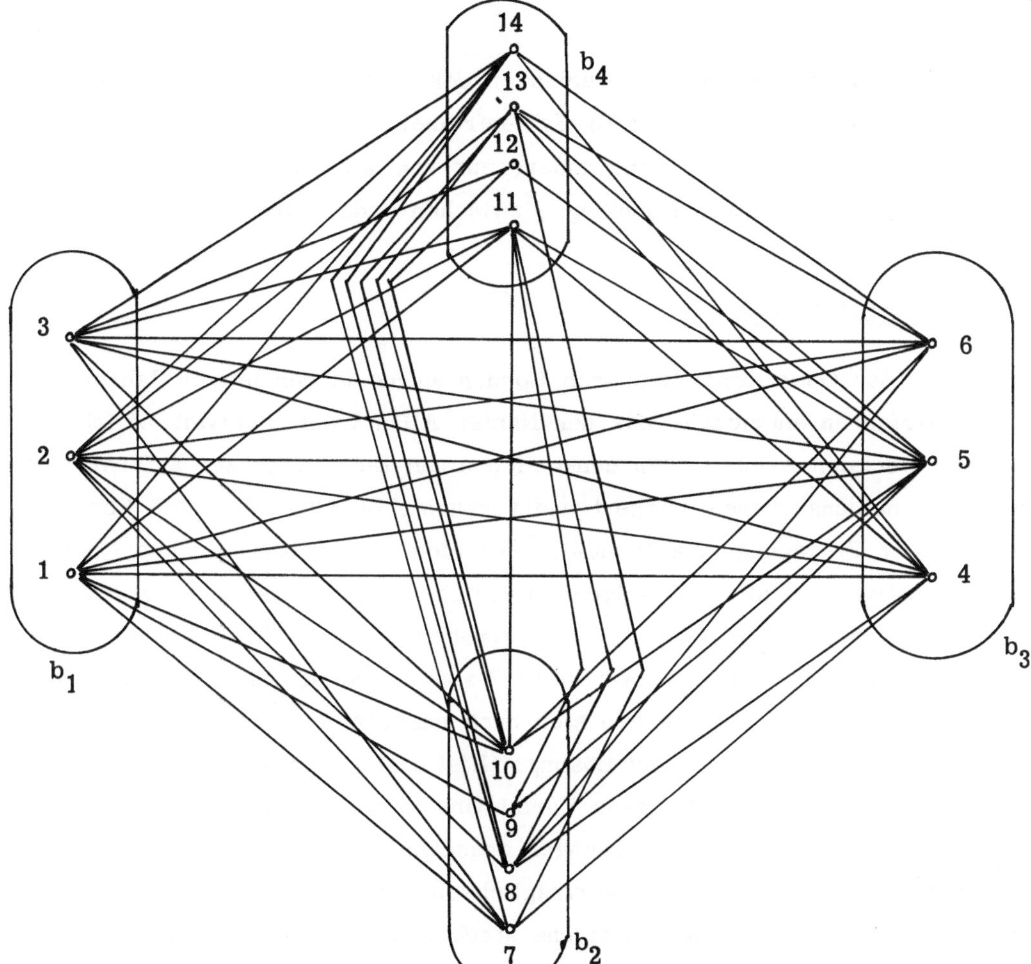

Man rechnet nach, daß $(3, 6) \in F_{13}$, aber $(3, 6) \notin G_{13}$. -

Aus dem Fragenkomplex in 2., der sich mit der Übergangsbeschränkung durch Ankopplung von Teilsystemen beschäftigt, sei hier der folgende Aspekt herausgegriffen: Sei $b_i \in B$, seien $p_1, p_2 \in b_i$. Man setzt:

$$(p_1, p_2) \in R_i :\iff \bigvee_{c_1, c_2 \in C} : c_1 \setminus c_2 = p_1 ; \quad c_2 \setminus c_1 = p_2 .$$

Es existiert also ein elementarer Übergang von p_1 nach p_2 (vgl. 2.). Insbesondere gilt die folgende Beziehung:

$$(p_1, p_2) \in UL_i := \bigcap_{j \neq i} L_{ij} \circ L_{ji} \ .$$

Ist nun $|B| = 2$, so gilt sicher $UL_i = R_i$ (vgl. auch das Beispiel der Uhr in 2.).
Allgemeiner hat man den

3.5 Satz: Enthält der Graph der vs(K)-Relation keine Zyklen, so ist für
$b_i \in B$: $R_i = UL_i$.

Bem.:   Zwar wird der Satz bei Weglassen der Voraussetzung i. a. falsch, immerhin jedoch erhält man bei vs(K)-Zyklenfreiheit, daß die globalen Übergangsmöglichkeiten einer Phase in eine andere nur von der direkten Kopplung dieser
Phasen abhängen, nicht von Kopplungen zwischen anderen Bereichen.

4.   Anwendungsbeispiel

Im Institute for Operational Research London wurde in den letzten Jahren ein
Entwurfsverfahren entwickelt, das den Namen AIDA trägt (Analysis of Interconnected Decision Areas). Man denkt sich einen Entwurfsprozeß auf verschiedenen Entscheidungsebenen gelagert und versucht, für die relevanten Ebenen
eine disjunkte Zerlegung in Entscheidungsbereiche anzugeben, die aus Entscheidungsalternativen bestehen. Aus jedem Bereich ist eine Alternative zu wählen
nach Maßgabe von Verknüpfungen von Alternativen, die in Form von Unverträglichkeiten beschrieben werden. Auf diese Weise bekommt man eine Lösung des
Entwurfsproblems. Es entsprechen sich nach unseren Ausführungen die Begriffe
Phase und Alternative, case und Lösung. (Historisch sind übrigens beide Ansätze parallel.) Die Anwendung dieses Verfahrens in der Bauplanung zeigte, daß
gerade das Prinzip, Wechselbeziehungen zwischen Gestaltungsalternativen durch
Unverträglichkeiten, nicht durch Verträglichkeiten zu beschreiben, viel über-
sichtlichere, weil weniger umfangreiche Strukturen lieferte. Mit wachsender
Problemgröße wird aber das Ziel des AIDA-Programms, alle Lösungen zu ermitteln oder evtl. durch vorher festgelegte Prioritäten eine kleinere Teilmenge
zu bestimmen, immer illusorischer, weil die Lösungsmenge sehr schnell un-
überschaubar wird.
Die Sätze 3.4 und 3.5 geben nun aber Anlaß, die Grundidee von AIDA in neuer
Weise bei der Planung zu verwirklichen: Die Ermittlungen von G_{ij} und R_i sind
offenbar elementare Probleme innerhalb eines Entwurfsprozesses, bei dem die
entsprechenden Daten und Grundbeziehungen in einem Rechner abgespeichert

sind, aber im Dialogbetrieb bearbeitet werden können. Das gilt natürlich besonders, wenn die Bereichs- oder Alternativenmenge so groß ist, daß die Kenntnis von Lösungen keinen echten Anteil mehr liefert zur Übersicht über den Planungsprozeß, außerdem über die Relevanz von Unverträglichkeiten unterschiedliche Annahmen gemacht werden können. (Unter diesem Aspekt ist dann z.B. die Voraussetzung der vs-Zyklenfreiheit nicht mehr so einschneidend.) Im übrigen bewirkt eine derartige Umorientierung, daß Entwurfsverfahren dieser Art auch in anderen Bereichen des computer-aided design stärker Eingang finden können.

Literatur

1 COURTOIS, P.J.; HEYMANS, F.; PARNAS, D.L.: Concurrent Control with "Readers" and "Writers"; Communications of the ACM 14 (1971), 667 - 668

2 DIJKSTRA, E.W.: Cooperating Sequential Processes, in: Programming Languages, Ed. F. Genuys; Academic Press, London 1968

3 GENRICH, H.J.; LAUTENBACH, K.: Synchronisationsgraphen; Acta Informatica (erscheint 1973)

4 GÖLLER, R.: Verallgemeinerung und Implementierung von Synchronisationsoperationen; Springer Lecture Notes in Economics and Mathematical Systems; Bd. 78 (1973)

5 HABERMAN, A.N.: Prevention of System Deadlocks; Communications of the ACM 12 (1969), 373 - 385

6 HANSEN, P.B.: A Comparison of Two Synchronizing Concepts; Acta Informatica 1 (1972), 190 - 199

7 HOARE, C.A.R.: Towards a Theory of Parallel Programming; International Seminar on Operating System Techniques; Belfast / Northern Ireland 1971

8 LUCKMAN, J.: An Approach to the Management of Design; Operational Research Quarterly, Bd. 18 (1967), 345 - 358

9 WEDDE, H.: Lose Kopplung in Informationssystemen; Interner Bericht, Gesellschaft für Mathematik und Datenverarbeitung, Bonn 1972

PROZESSRECHNER

PROBLEME BEI DER SIGNALDETEKTION MIT EINEM PROZESSRECHNER

Johann F. Böhme

Zusammenfassung

Diese Arbeit diskutiert heuristische Lösungsmöglichkeiten für ein
Detektionsproblem, bei dem zwischen zwei stationären Gaußschen
Rauschsignalen zu unterscheiden ist. Die beiden Signale werden
additiv stark durch ein sich langsam in seiner Klangfarbe änderndes
Gaußsches Rauschen gestört. Die Detektion soll mit Hilfe eines
Prozeßrechners durchgeführt werden. Bekannt sind nur die Leistungs-
dichten der Signalprozesse bis auf deren Leistung, die für beide
Signale gleich sei.

1. Einleitung

Die Aufgabe bestehe für einen Operateur darin, mit Hilfe eines Prozeßrechners aus einem endlich langen Stück eines empfangenen Zeit-
signals herauszufinden, welches von zwei möglichen Rauschsignalen
in dem Beobachtungszeitraum gesendet worden ist. Das gesendete Signal sei additiv durch ein Rauschen sehr stark gestört. Die folgende
Abbildung beschreibt die Versuchsanordnung.

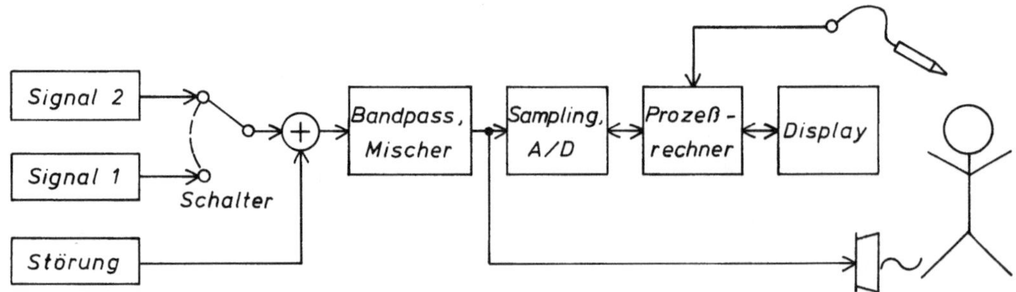

Es sei vorausgesetzt, daß die Geräusche hinreichend genau durch
statistisch voneinander unabhängige Gaußsche Prozesse mit dem Erwartungswert Null beschrieben werden können. Die Signalprozesse
sollen stationär sein und der Störprozeß soll sich langsam im Vergleich zur Beobachtungszeit in seiner Struktur verändern, wie es
zum Beispiel für das Geräusch eines Flugzeuges zutrifft, das in

größerer Höhe vorbeifliegt. Zusätzlich möge man über einige Beob-
achtungszeiträume hinweg das Störgeräusch als ein Stück aus einem
stationären Prozeß ansehen können. Weiter wird angenommen, daß der
Schalter in Zeiträumen, die groß gegen einen Beobachtungszeitraum
sind, umgeschaltet wird, daß der Schalter im Mittel mindestens 10 mal
länger zum Signal 1 als zum Signal 2 zeigt und daß der Schalter
während einer Beobachtung nicht umgeschaltet wird. Schließlich sollen
die spektralen Leistungsdichten der Signalprozesse existieren und
dem Operateur bis auf die Leistung selbst, die für beide Signale
gleich ist, bekannt sein.

Wenn der Operateur die Kovarianzfunktion der Störung und die Signalleistung auch noch kennt, so ist es bekanntlich möglich, optimale
Detektionsstrukturen zur Minimierung z.B. der mittleren Irrtumswahr-
scheinlichkeit anzugeben, die mit hinreichender Genauigkeit auf
einem Prozeßrechner realisiert werden können, falls der Beobachtungszeitraum nicht zu lang wird. Schon wenn nur die Signalleistung unbe-
kannt ist, gibt es keine optimale Detektionsstruktur mehr (s.a. [6]).

Für die vorliegende Aufgabe wird eine heuristische Lösung entworfen
und diskutiert. Der resultierende Detektor berechnet für ein empfan-
genes Geräuschstück angenäherte Maximum-Likelihood-Schätzungen des
Signal-zu-Stör-Leistungsverhältnisses unter den Hypothesen Signal 1
oder Signal 2. Die Differenz der für das Geräuschstück berechneten
maximalen Werte der beiden Likelihood-Funktionen wird mit einer
Schwelle verglichen, wodurch die Detektionsentscheidung getroffen
wird. Der Detektor berechnet die Likelihood-Funktionen durch eine
nicht-real-time-Struktur mit Hilfe eines an den Rechner angeschlossenen Feldtransformationsprozessors.

Um die Likelihood-Funktionen angenähert berechnen zu können, muß der
Frequenzgang eines linearen zeitinvarianten Filters aus dem zeitlich
vor dem Detektionsversuch empfangenen Geräusch geschätzt werden.
Dies kann geschehen, indem man unter der Annahme angenäherter "momen-
taner" Stationarität entweder eine Leistungsdichteschätzung vornimmt
und aus der Schätzung die gewünschten Größen berechnet, oder den Frequenzgang des Filters direkt, z.B. über stochastische Approximation,
schätzt. Der Operateur entscheidet an Hand der Änderung des Geräusch-
klanges, wann sich der Rechner wieder an das Störgeräusch adaptieren
muß.

Eine zweite heuristische Lösung der Aufgabe, die auf eine real-time-Struktur hinzielt, wird angedeutet. Dieser Detektor benutzt diskrete Kalman-Filter, die auf externen Matrizenprozessoren simuliert werden könnten. Jedoch bereitet diese Lösung bei einer Realisierung große Schwierigkeiten, die kurz erläutert werden.

2. Nicht kausale Detektoren

Abgesehen von Digitalisierungsrundungen sollen die empfangenen Geräusche am Eingang des Rechners folgendermaßen beschrieben werden: Sei ζ ein reeller stochastischer Prozeß über der Menge der ganzen Zahlen. Es gebe zwei Hypothesen für ζ , nämlich
$$H_1 : \zeta = \delta_1 + \nu \quad \text{und} \quad H_2 : \zeta = \delta_2 + \nu .$$
δ_1 , δ_2 und ν seien dabei statistisch voneinander unabhängige stationäre Gauß-Prozesse mit dem Erwartungswert 0 und den Kovarianzfunktionen k_{δ_1} , k_{δ_2} und k_ν .

Die Aufgabe, die ein Detektor lösen soll, besteht darin, an Hand der Beobachtung $z = (z(0), \ldots, z(T))$ einer Realisierung von ζ zu den Zeiten $t = 0, \ldots, T$ zu entscheiden, welche Hypothese die Erzeugung von z kontrolliert hat.

Setzt man voraus, daß für den Entwurf des Detektors die Funktionen k_{δ_1} , k_{δ_2} und k_ν bekannt sind, so beherrscht man die Wahrscheinlichkeitsmaße P_1 und P_2 , die die stochastischen Prozesse unter den Hypothesen H_1 und H_2 beschreiben. In diesem Fall ist es möglich, die Entscheidung mit Hilfe der Likelihood-Funktion
$$l(z) = \ln \partial P_1 / \partial P_2 \big|_z$$
zu treffen:
Entscheide H_1 , wenn $l(z) \geqq c$, sonst H_2 .
$\partial P_1 / \partial P_2$ ist Dichte von P_1 relativ zu P_2 und c eine Konstante, die davon abhängt, in welchem Sinne die Entscheidungsregel optimal sein soll. Z.B. kann man durch geeignete Wahl von c das folgende Optimierungsproblem lösen: Minimiere durch Wahl der Entscheidungsregel die Wahrscheinlichkeit einer Fehlentscheidung, wenn die Hypothese 1 vorliegt, unter der Nebenbedingung, daß die Wahrscheinlichkeit einer Fehlentscheidung unter der Hypothese 2 nicht größer als eine vorgegebene Zahl c_0 wird (s.a. [6]).

z ist Realisierung des Zufallsvektors $(\zeta(0), \ldots, \zeta(T))$ der die Kovarianz-Matrix K_ζ mit den Elementen $K_\zeta(t_1, t_2) = k_\zeta(|t_1 - t_2|)$ besitzt.

Dann ergibt sich in Matrizen-Schreibweise

$$(0)\quad 2l(z) = z\left[(K_\nu + K_{\delta_2})^{-1} - (K_\nu + K_{\delta_1})^{-1}\right]z' + \ln\det(K_\nu + K_{\delta_2}) - \ln\det(K_\nu + K_{\delta_1}),$$

wobei K_α $(\alpha = \delta_1, \delta_2, \nu)$ analog zu K_ζ definiert ist.

$l(z)$ auf diese Art und Weise exakt zu berechnen ist für große T praktisch unmöglich. Man sucht daher Approximationen, die leicht, z.B. mit Hilfe der diskreten Fourier-Transformation, berechnet werden können. Eine solche liefert folgende Vorstellung: Setzt man $(\zeta(0),\dots,\zeta(T))$ periodisch zu einem stochastischen Prozeß $\tilde\zeta$ fort, so daß $\tilde\zeta(t + t'(T+1)) = \zeta(t)$ für ganze t' ist, dann stimmen die Realisierungen von ζ und $\tilde\zeta$ für $t = 0,\dots,T$ überein. Jedoch besitzt $\tilde\zeta$ eine Kovarianzfunktion mit der Periode $T+1$ in den Argumenten t_1 und t_2, die für $t_1, t_2 = 0,\dots,T$ die Werte

$$(1)\quad k_{\tilde\zeta}(|t_1 - t_2|) = k_\zeta(|t_1 - t_2|) + \frac{|t_1 - t_2|}{T+1}\left[k_\zeta(T+1 - |t_1 - t_2|) - k_\zeta(|t_1 - t_2|)\right]$$

annimmt. Definiert man die Matrix $K_{\tilde\zeta}$ durch die Elemente $k_{\tilde\zeta}(|t_1 - t_2|)$ für $t_1, t_2 = 0,\dots,T$ und ersetzt in (0) die Matrizen K_α durch die entsprechenden Matrizen $K_{\tilde\alpha}$ $(\alpha = \delta_1, \delta_2, \nu)$, dann erhält man einen approximativen Ausdruck für l. Die Matrizen $K_{\tilde\alpha}$ sind zirkulare Matrizen. In welchem Sinne die Matrizen $K_{\tilde\alpha}$ und K_α für große T asymptotisch äquivalent sind, wird in [4] untersucht. Bis zum Ende dieses Abschnittes wird nur noch mit den angegebenen zirkularen Matrizen gerechnet, wobei "$\sim$" zur Abkürzung fortgelassen wird. $l(z)$ kann dann mit Hilfe des folgenden Ausdrucks berechnet werden:

$$2l(z) = \frac{1}{T+1}\sum_{f=0}^{T}\frac{\left[W_{\delta_1}\left(\frac{f}{T+1}\right) - W_{\delta_2}\left(\frac{f}{T+1}\right)\right]|r\left(\frac{f}{T+1}\right)|^2}{\left[W_\nu\left(\frac{f}{T+1}\right) + W_{\delta_1}\left(\frac{f}{T+1}\right)\right]\left[W_\nu\left(\frac{f}{T+1}\right) + W_{\delta_2}\left(\frac{f}{T+1}\right)\right]} - \sum_{f=0}^{T}\ln\frac{W_\nu\left(\frac{f}{T+1}\right) + W_{\delta_1}\left(\frac{f}{T+1}\right)}{W_\nu\left(\frac{f}{T+1}\right) + W_{\delta_2}\left(\frac{f}{T+1}\right)}$$

Hierbei sind

$$(2)\quad r\left(\frac{f}{T+1}\right) = \sum_{t=0}^{T} z(t)\exp\left(-j2\pi\frac{ft}{T+1}\right),$$

$$W_\alpha\left(\frac{f}{T+1}\right) = \sum_{t=0}^{T} k_\alpha(t)\exp\left(-j2\pi\frac{ft}{T+1}\right)$$

die diskreten Fourier-Koeffizienten der periodisch fortgesetzten Vektoren $z = (z(0),\dots,z(T))$ bzw. $(k_\alpha(0),\dots,k_\alpha(T))$. W_α kann als Leistungsspektrum des Prozesses α interpretiert werden.

In der ursprünglich zu lösenden Aufgabe stehen dem Detektor nicht die exakten Leistungen $P_\nu = k_\nu(0)$ und $P_\delta = k_{\delta_1}(0) = k_{\delta_2}(0)$ von Störung und Signal zur Verfügung. Es ist nur bekannt, daß das Signal-zu-Stör-Leistungsverhältnis $v = P_\delta/P_\nu$ nicht größer als eine Zahl v_0 werden kann. Wie schon erwähnt ist für diesen Fall kein optimaler Detektor (uniformly most powerful test) bekannt. Deshalb wird hier ein heuristisch motivierter Detektor vorgestellt und im Folgenden erläutert.

Offensichtlich kann man schreiben

$$l(z) = \ln \left. \partial P_1/\partial P_2 \right|_z = \ln \left. \partial P_1/\partial P_0 \right|_z - \ln \left. \partial P_2/\partial P_0 \right|_z ,$$

wobei P_0 das Wahrscheinlichkeitsmaß ist, das dem Prozeß ν zugeordnet ist. Dann ist

$$(3)\ 2 l_i(z) = 2 \ln \left. \partial P_i/\partial P_0 \right|_z = \frac{1}{T+1} \sum_f \frac{W_{\delta_i} |r|^2}{W_\nu [W_{\delta_i} + W_\nu]} - \sum_f \ln \frac{W_{\delta_i} + W_\nu}{W_\nu} .$$

Mit $l_i(z)$ kann man optimal das Detektionsproblem

$$H_i : \zeta = \delta_i + \nu \quad \text{und} \quad H_0 : \zeta = \nu$$

lösen. Selbstverständlich wird in dieser Untersuchung vorausgesetzt, daß die Tests nicht singulär sind, daß also z.B. $W_\nu(f) \neq 0$ und $W_{\delta_i}(f) > 0$ für kein f gilt. Wenn P_ν bekannt ist aber P_δ nicht, d.h. v nicht, dann liefert

$$(4)\ \hat{l}_i(z) = \max_{v \leq v_0} l_i(z, v)$$

einen optimalen Detektor für das letzte Detektionsproblem, wobei

$$l_i(z, v) = \frac{v}{T+1} \sum_f \frac{\overline{W}_{\delta_i} |r|^2/P_\nu}{\overline{W}_\nu [v \overline{W}_{\delta_i} + \overline{W}_\nu]} - \sum_f \ln \left(1 + v \frac{\overline{W}_{\delta_i}}{\overline{W}_\nu} \right)$$

und $W_\alpha = P_\alpha \overline{W}_\alpha$ ist. Mit $\hat{l}_i(z)$ wird zunächst aus z der wahrscheinlichste Wert für das Signal-zu-Stör-Leistungsverhältnis v bestimmt und anschließend dieser Wert als der richtige in der ursprünglichen Formel (3) für die Detektion benutzt. Der heuristische Detektor für die Unterscheidung der Hypothesen H_1 und H_2 benutzt als Testfunktion

$$(5)\ \hat{L}(z) = \hat{l}_1(z) - \hat{l}_2(z)$$

und vergleicht die Funktionswerte mit einer geeigneten Schwelle.

Wenn angenommen wird, daß dem Detektor nur die Spektren $\overline{W}_{\delta_1}$, $\overline{W}_{\delta_2}$ und W_ζ unter der Hypothese H_1 bekannt sind, dann ist $W_\zeta = P_\zeta (\overline{W}_\nu + v \overline{W}_\zeta)/(1+v)$

mit v als unbekanntem und $P_\zeta = \rho_\nu(1+v)$ als bekanntem Parameter. Wenn $W_\zeta = P_\zeta \overline{W}_\zeta$ ist, folgt

$$2 l_i(z,v) = \frac{v(1+v)}{T+1} \sum_f \frac{\overline{W}_{\delta_i}\,|r|^2/P_\zeta}{[\overline{V}_\zeta(1+v)-v\,\overline{W}_{\delta_1}][\overline{W}_\zeta(1+v)-v(\overline{W}_{\delta_1}-\overline{W}_{\delta_2})]} - \sum_f \ln\left[1+\frac{v\,\overline{W}_{\delta_i}}{\overline{W}_\zeta(1+v)-v\overline{W}_{\delta_1}}\right].$$

Falls zusätzlich $v \ll 1$ und die Spektren $\overline{W}_\alpha$ im interessierenden Frequenzband hinreichend "wenig zerklüftet" sind, dann kann man $l_i(z,v)$ in eine Reihe nach v entwickeln:

$$(6)\quad 2 l_i(z,v) = \sum_{m=0}^{\infty} (-1)^m a_{im}(z)\, v^{m+1}$$

mit

$$a_{im}(z) = \frac{1}{T+1} \sum_f \left(y_i^{m+1} - y^{m+1} + y^m - y_i^m\right)|r|^2/W_\zeta - \frac{1}{m+1}\sum_f\left(y_i^{m+1} - y^{m+1}\right),$$

wobei $y_i = y + \overline{W}_{\delta_i}/\overline{W}_\zeta$ und $y = 1 - \overline{W}_{\delta_1}/\overline{W}_\zeta$ gesetzt worden sind. Eine Maximierung von $l_i(z,v)$ über $0 \le v \le v_0$ kann nun durch eine einfache, leicht programmierbare Kurvendiskussion erreicht werden, wenn z.B. nach der dritten Potenz von v abgebrochen wird.

In der Einleitung war angenommen worden, daß dem Detektor nur $\overline{W}_{\delta_1}$ und $\overline{W}_{\delta_2}$ bekannt seien. Wenn es also gelingt, vor einem Detektionsversuch das Spektrum W_ζ hinreichend genau zu schätzen, dann kann mit der Annahme der starken Störung der Signale das zuletzt erläuterte Verfahren $[(2)\rightarrow(6)\rightarrow(4)\rightarrow(5)\rightarrow(\text{Schwellwertvergleich})]$ zur Detektion auf dem Prozeßrechner realisiert werden. Das Verfahren ist so entworfen worden, daß ein an den Rechner angeschlossener Feldtransformationsprozessor mit Vorteil anwendbar ist. Ein solcher Prozessor kann u.a. schnell die diskrete Fourier-Transformation eines Feldes, das Produkt und die Summe zweier Felder ausführen oder ein Feld aufsummieren.

Schätzen des unbekannten Leistungsspektrums

In der ursprünglichen Bezeichnungsweise muß also $W_{\tilde{\gamma}}$ geschätzt werden. $W_{\tilde{\gamma}}$ ist das Leistungsspektrum des periodischen Prozesses $\tilde{\gamma} = \tilde{\nu} + \tilde{\delta}_1$. Sei einmal angenommen, die Hypothese H_1 liege vor, d.h. eine Realisierung des stationären Prozesses $\gamma = \nu + \delta_1$ wird empfangen. Nach bekannten Verfahren (s.a. [1]) ist es dann möglich, die spektrale Leistungsdichte W_ζ von ζ hinreichend genau zu schätzen. Im Folgenden wird zunächst angedeutet, wie man eine Schätzung für W_ζ und daraus eine solche für $W_{\tilde{\gamma}}$ erhalten kann.

Sei $M < T$ eine natürliche Zahl, dann ist

$$(7) \quad W_{\mathfrak{z}}^{M,T}(f') = \sum_{t=-M}^{M} e^{-j2\pi f't}\, q\!\left(\frac{t}{M}\right) a_z^T(t)$$

eine Schätzung von $W_{\mathfrak{z}}$, wenn $z = (z(0), \dots, z(T))$ beobachtet worden ist. Hierbei ist

$$a_z^T(t) = \frac{1}{2(T+1)^2} \sum_{f=0}^{2T+1} exp\!\left(j2\pi \frac{ft}{2(T+1)}\right)\Big| \sum_{t'=0}^{T} exp\!\left(-j\,2\pi \frac{ft'}{2(T+1)}\right) z(t')\Big|^2 \quad (|t| = 0, \dots, T)$$

die Autokorrelierte von z und q eine Fensterfunktion mit den Eigenschaften: $q(x) \geqq 0$, $q(0) = 1$, $q(x) = 0$ für $|x| \geqq 1$ und $q(x)$ ist stetig. Z.B. kann q das Parzen-Fenster sein:

$$q(x) = \begin{cases} 1 - 6x^2 + 6|x|^3 & , \text{ wenn } |x| \leq 1/2 \\ 2(1 - |x|)^3 & , \text{ wenn } 1/2 < |x| < 1 \\ 0 & \text{ sonst.} \end{cases}$$

Wenn q_1 die größte natürliche Zahl mit $\lim_{x \to 0} [q(x) - 1]/x^{q_1} < \infty$ ist, $M = \gamma\, T^{1/(2q_1+1)}$ gesetzt wird und $W_{\mathfrak{z}}$ hinreichend glatt ist, dann hat $W_{\mathfrak{z}}^{M,T}(f')$ die Eigenschaft, daß die erwartete quadratische Abweichung von $W_{\mathfrak{z}}^{M,T}(f')$ und $W_{\mathfrak{z}}(f')$ eine Funktion $O\!\left(T^{-2q_1/(2q_1+1)}\right)$ für große T wird. (7) liefert also eine vernünftige Schätzung für $W_{\mathfrak{z}}$. $W_{\mathfrak{z}}^{M,T}\left(f/(2(T+1))\right)$ $(f = 0, \dots, 2T+1)$ kann mit Hilfe eines Feldtransformationsprozessors im Prozeßrechner ohne Schwierigkeiten berechnet werden. Die Feldlänge ist in diesem Fall $2(T+1)$ und nicht $T+1$ wie beim Detektieren. Eine Schätzung von $W_{\mathfrak{z}}$ findet man nun, indem gesetzt wird

$$W_{\tilde{\mathfrak{z}}}^{M,T}\left(f/(T+1)\right) = W_{\mathfrak{z}}^{M,T}\left(f/(T+1)\right) \quad (f = 0, \dots, T).$$

Man benutzt also nur jeden zweiten Wert von $W_{\mathfrak{z}}^{M,T}$. Eine diskrete Fourier-Rücktransformation des Feldes $W_{\tilde{\mathfrak{z}}}^{M,T}\left(f/(T+1)\right)$ $(f = 0, \dots, T)$ liefert dann eine Kovarianzfunktion der Gestalt (1).

In der Einleitung wurde vorausgesetzt, daß sich der Geräuschklang der Störung nur langsam im Vergleich zum Beobachtungszeitraum ändern würde. Also liefert eine Schätzung der eben beschriebenen Art für einen gewissen Zeitraum vernünftige Werte für $W_{\mathfrak{z}}$, wenn die Hypothesen nicht umgeschaltet werden. Die zusätzliche Annahme, daß die Hypothese H_1 ungefähr zehn mal länger als H_2 eingeschaltet ist, motiviert folgende Vorgehensweise zum Schätzen des Spektrums von $\tilde{\mathfrak{z}} = \tilde{v} + \tilde{b}_1$: Betrachte einen Zeitraum der ungefähr einer Schaltperiode entspricht. Berechne zehn Spektren nach obiger Methode aus Beobachtungsintervallen die gleichmäßig über den betrachteten Zeitraum verteilt sind.

Eine geeignete Mittelung liefert das gewünschte Spektrum. "Geeignet mitteln" heißt, unter Ausnutzung von a priori Kenntnissen über die Schaltpunkte oder von "Monotonie"-Eigenschaften des Störgeräusches o.ä. zu mitteln. In der Regel wird der durch diese Vorgehensweise induzierte systematische Fehler größenordnungsmäßig dem praktisch auftretenden zufälligen Schätzfehler gleichen.

Zur Berechnung der Werte $\hat{l}_i(z)$ wird $1/w_\zeta$ benötigt. Es bietet sich daher an, $h = 1/w_\zeta$ direkt zu schätzen, z.B. über stochasitsche Approximation der Lösung der Gleichung $w_\zeta h - 1 = 0$. Im Zeitbereich sind entsprechende Ansätze z.B. in [3] behandelt worden. Eine spezielle Untersuchung, ob die dort angeregte Technik für den vorliegenden Fall Vorbild werden könnte, steht noch aus.

Kausale Detektoren

Die im vorletzten Abschnitt behandelten Detektoren besitzen die Eigenschaft, nicht mit Hilfe von kausalen (oder realisierbaren) digitalen Filtern aufgebaut werden zu können. Die gesamte Beobachtung muß erst in den Detektor eingelaufen sein, ehe dieser seine Berechnung beginnen kann. Dadurch ist, insbesondere bei großen Beobachtungszeiten T, real-time-Verarbeitung unmöglich. Bei kausalen Detektoren ist es anders: jeder einlaufende Wert $z(t)$ der Beobachtung wird sofort verarbeitet. Nach dem Einlauf von $z(T)$ und seiner Verarbeitung kann ohne weitere Rechenschritte die Entscheidung getroffen werden. Kausale Detektoren lassen real-time-Verarbeitung zu.

Nach [5] sind die Funktionen $l_i(z,v)$ für festes v kausal berechenbar:

$$2 l_i(z,v) = \sum_{t=0}^{T} \left[(z(t) - e_0(t))^2 / q_0(t) - (z(t) - e_i(t))^2 / q_i(t) - \ln q_i(t) + \ln q_0(t) \right].$$

Hierbei ist $e_m(t)$ $(m = 0,1,2)$ der Erwartungswert von $\zeta(t)$ unter der Hypothese, daß $z(0), \ldots, z(t-1)$ bekannt ist und daß die Hypothese H_m vorliegt. q_m ist die erwartete quadratische Abweichung von $\zeta(t)$ und $e_m(t)$. Wenn man annimmt, daß die zugrunde liegenden stochastischen Prozesse durch stabile lineare dynamische Systeme endlicher Ordnung mit weißem diskreten Rauschen am Eingang erzeugt worden sind, dann kann man die bedingten Erwartungen durch Kalman-Filter, die mit Hilfe von Matrizen-Prozessoren auf dem Prozeßrechner simuliert werden können, kausal berechnen (s.a. [5], [2]) und die Zahlen $q_m(t)$ ergeben sich als Beiprodukt. Jedoch muß $l_i(z,v)$ über v maximiert werden, und man benötigt eine Bank von Kalman-Filtern, um das

Maximum angenähert bestimmen zu können. Ganz abgesehen von den Schwierigkeiten, die Parameter der dynamischen Systeme aus dem Störgeräusch zu schätzen, scheidet diese Lösungsmöglichkeit aus Aufwandsgründen aus. Vereinfachungen, wie sie bei nicht kausalen Detektoren die Maximierung ermöglichten, scheinen bei kausalen Detektoren nicht offensichtlich zu sein.

Bemerkungen

Die Detektorstruktur , $\hat{l}(z)$ mit einer Schwelle zu vergleichen, die nicht mehr von der Struktur der Geräusche abhängig ist, ist eine heuristische Lösung des Detektionsproblems. Vorhersagen über das Verhalten dieses Detektors sind daher sehr schwierig zu gewinnen. Im Wesentlichen bleiben nur allgemeine Aussagen über die statistische Robustheit bei nicht genauer Kenntnis eines Spektrums bzw. von Parametern. Diese Aussagen haben jedoch wenig Gewicht für das konkrete Detektionsproblem. Simulationen mit echt gemessenen Geräuschen müssen daher wie bei den meisten Mustererkennungsproblemen die gewünschten Auskünfte liefern.

Es ist schon angedeutet worden, daß der nicht kausale Detektor unter den definierten Voraussetzungen auf einem Prozeßrechner mit einem angeschlossenen Feldtransformationsprozessor realisiert werden kann. Die Leistungsfähigkeit eines Detektors wächst monoton mit der Beobachtungszeit T. Daher wird man T gleich der maximal zulässigen Feldlänge des Prozessors setzen (in der Regel 2^{11} oder 2^{12}). In diesem Fall läßt sich eine pseudo-real-time-Verarbeitung realisieren: In Abhängigkeit von der Rechengeschwindigkeit können Geräuschstücke mit mehr oder weniger grossen Abständen untereinander verarbeitet werden. Die Detektionsentscheidung ist mit einer Zeitverzögerung, die der Rechenzeit entspricht, nach dem Eintreffen des letzten samples zu erwarten.

Sollten die Geräusche am Eingang des Rechners schmalbandig sein, so könnte man vorteilhaft mit den komplexen Modulationsprozessen der stochastischen Prozesse rechnen und würde dabei die Abtastrate reduzieren. In Formel (6) müßten die $a_{im}(z)$ entsprechend berechnet werden. Diese Technik lohnt sich jedoch nur, wenn der Feldtransformationsprozessor die Verarbeitung von komplexwertigen Feldern allgemein zuläßt. Andernfalls liefert die Mischung des Empfangsgeräuschbandes auf eine Mittenfrequenz, die nur wenig größer als die halbe Bandbreite ist, das beste Ergebnis.

<u>Literatur</u>

[1]   Anderson, T. W.: <u>The statistical analysis of time series.</u>
      J. Wiley, New York (1971)

[2]   Kalman, R. E.: A new approach to linear filtering and pre-
      diction problems. <u>Trans. ASME, Journ. of Basic Engineering</u>,
      82 (1960), 35-45

[3]   Macchi, C.: Iteration stochastique et detection. <u>Troisième
      colloque sur le traitment du signal et ses applications</u>,Nice
      (1971), proc. No. 33.

[4]   Pearl, J.: On coding and filtering stationary signals by dis-
      crete Fouriertransforms. <u>IEEE Trans., IT-19</u> (1973), 229-232

[5]   Schweppe, F.: Evaluation of likelihood functions for Gaussian
      signals. <u>IEEE Trans. IT-11</u> (1965), 61-70

[6]   Van Trees, H.L.: <u>Detection, estimation, and modulation theory,</u>
      part I and III. J. Wiley, New York (1968 and 1971)

Verfahren zur Nachrichtenreduktion bei der Systemsicherung mit Prozeßrechnern

H. Steusloff, R. Grimm

Zusammenfassung

Die fortschreitende Automatisierung technischer Systeme erfordert eine entsprechend automatisierte Systemsicherung mit dem Prozeßrechner als Hilfsmittel. Eine zentrale Aufgabe bei der Systemsicherung ist die Sammlung von Systemdaten, die wegen des begrenzten Speicherplatzes in Prozeßrechensystemen weitgehend redundanzfrei sein müssen. Aufgrund der durch diese Problemstellung gegebenen Anforderungen werden redundanzreduzierende Verfahren untersucht. Drei Verfahren erweisen sich jeweils als vorteilhaft bezüglich der Leistungskriterien Wiedergabetreue, Reduktionsfaktor und Rechenzeitbedarf.

Einführung

Mit wachsender Komplexität technischer Systeme steigen die Wahrscheinlichkeit für das Auftreten gestörter Systemzustände sowie die durch Systemstörungen verursachten Kosten. Die Funktion der Sicherung technischer Systeme gegen Ausfälle kann der Mensch schon wegen der Menge und Geschwindigkeit des Datenanfalles immer weniger erfüllen. Entsprechend der fortschreitenden Automatisierung technischer Systeme muß daher auch die Systemsicherung automatisiert werden.
Ein sehr flexibles Hilfsmittel für diese Aufgabe ist der frei programmierbare Prozeßrechner. Er hat aufgrund seiner Prozeßlenkungsfunktionen Zugriff zu allen für die Systemsicherung wichtigen Systemgrößen /1/. Eine zentrale Aufgabe des Prozeßrechners im Rahmen der Systemsicherung ist die Datensammlung. Sie ist aufgrund der begrenzten Speicherkapazität nur dann effektiv durchführbar, wenn das Speichern redundanter Datenmengen weitgehend verhindert wird. Dies geschieht durch Verfahren zur Nachrichtenreduktion, die im Hinblick auf ihren Einsatz bei der Systemsicherung besonderen Anforderungen genügen müssen.

Konzept einer Systemsicherung

Die Teilaufgaben einer Systemsicherung sind nach Bild 1 die Systemüberwachung, die Störungsanalyse, die Störungsdiagnose und die Störungsbeseitigung /2/. Je nach dem für die Systemsicherung möglichen Aufwand werden diese Teilaufgaben durch den Menschen oder den Prozeßrechner ausgeführt. Wesentlich ist, daß am Beginn der Systemsicherung die Datensammlung steht, die dem Prozeßrechner vorbehalten ist, da sie den Menschen überfordert.
Die gesammelten Systemdaten dienen sowohl zum fortlaufenden Überwachen des aktuellen Systemzustandes als auch zur Analyse der Entstehung von gestörten Systemzuständen. Dazu müssen Systemgrößen über einen möglichst langen Zeitraum abgespeichert vorliegen; vom Informationsgehalt dieser gespeicherten Datenmenge hängen Erfolg und

Vollständigkeit von Systemüberwachung und Störungsanalyse ab. Um die in einem gegebenen Speicherraum ablegbare Information möglichst groß zu machen, bedient man sich der Nachrichtenreduktionsverfahren für zeitlich veränderliche Systemgrößen.

<u>Entstehung redundanter Systemdaten</u>

Im Sinne der Informationstheorie stellt der zeitliche Verlauf einer Systemgröße eine Nachricht dar mit den Komponenten "Information" und "Redundanz". Derjenige Teil einer Nachricht, der eine Unsicherheit beim Nachrichtenempfänger beseitigt, ist Information; alle weiteren Teile der Nachricht sind Redundanz.

Nachrichtenempfänger bei der Systemsicherung mittels Prozeßrechnern sind die Programme zur Überwachung und Analyse der Systemdaten. Die Nachrichten gelangen aus dem System über Meßumformer, Übertragungskanäle, Abtaster und Wandler in den Prozeßrechner. Auf diesem Wege entsteht an verschiedenen Stellen Redundanz. Wir wollen hier eine besondere Art von Redundanz betrachten, die durch den Einsatz des Prozeßrechners begünstigt wird und als "Abtastredundanz" bezeichnet sei.

Da Prozeßrechnerprogramme die Systemgrößen nur sequentiell und in Digitalform verarbeiten können, ist ein Abtaster und ggf. ein Analog-Digitalwandler an der Verbindungsstelle von System und Rechner unerläßlich. Abtastredundanz entsteht dabei dann, wenn die Abtastfrequenz für eine Systemgröße höher ist als die doppelte obere Grenzfrequenz des abgetasteten Signals. Vermeidung von Abtastredundanz ist möglich, wenn die obere Signalgrenzfrequenz bekannt und stationär ist.

In realen technischen Systemen ist die obere Grenzfrequenz der Signale selten bekannt und ändert sich oft, insbesondere bei Störungen im System. Wenn man die bisher wenig gebräuchlichen Verfahren zur Anpassung der Abtastfrequenz an die Signaleigenschaften /3/ nicht anwenden kann, ist man bei der Wahl der Abtastfrequenz auf Schätzwerte angewiesen. Um auch nicht normale Signalzustände genügend schnell und genau zu erfassen, verwendet man eine Abtastfrequenz von z.B. dem 20-fachen der oberen Signalgrenzfrequenz im Normalzustand des Signals. Dadurch enthält jedoch die abgetastete Datenmenge im Normalfall einen großen Redundanzanteil, die Abtastredundanz.

Diese redundante Datenmenge belastet den Speicherraum des Prozeßrechners bei der Datensammlung unnötig; sie muß vor der Abspeicherung eliminiert werden. Eine Verringerung der Abtastfrequenz wäre gerade für die Systemsicherung ungünstig, da sich Systemstörungen oft durch eine Erhöhung der Signalgrenzfrequenzen ("Signalaktivität") bemerkbar machen.

Eine weitere Art von Redundanz entsteht bei der Analog-Digitalwandlung von Systemsignalen. Die hier festzulegende Auflösung, d.h. die Zahl der Bitstellen des gewandelten Digitalwertes, ist abhängig von der Problemstellung. Für manche Programme ist eine hohe Auflösung erforderlich, während für andere Programme ein Teil der Bitstellen Redundanz darstellt. Diese Art von Redundanz sei "Auflösungsredundanz" genannt.

Wirkung redundanzreduzierender Verfahren

Die im folgenden beschriebenen Verfahren zur Nachrichtenreduktion werden bei der Datensammlung für die Systemsicherung eingesetzt, um die beiden oben beschriebenen Arten von Redundanz zu verringern. Für die Telemetrie wurden Verfahren entwickelt, die Prädiktoren und Interpolatoren, welche aufgrund vorgegebener Toleranzdaten Abtastwerte als redundant kennzeichnen, solange sie innerhalb eines Toleranzbereiches liegen. Diese Verfahren sind auch für die Systemsicherung geeignet; Einzelheiten folgen bei der Beschreibung spezieller Verfahren.

Das Ergebnis eines redundanzreduzierenden Algorithmus ist eine Folge von zeitlich nicht mehr äquidistanten, nichtredundanten Abtastwerten eines Signals. Um den ursprünglichen Signalverlauf rekonstruieren zu können, ist zusätzlich zu dem nichtredundanten Abtastwert noch eine Zeitdifferenzangabe (Adresse, run length code) abzuspeichern; diese Angabe belegt also zusätzlichen Speicherplatz.

Speicherung redundanzreduzierter Datenmengen

Im Gegensatz zur Telemetrie, deren Aufgabe die bitserielle Übertragung von Nachrichten ist, sollen bei der Systemsicherung Nachrichten wortweise gespeichert werden. Während daher die Notwendigkeit der Zeitdifferenzangabe bei der Telemetrie den Erfolg der Redundanzreduktion verringert, ist es bei der Datenspeicherung im Prozeßrechner oft möglich, die Zeitdifferenzangabe im selben Rechnerwort unterzubringen, wie den zugehörigen Abtastwert /4/. Dies gilt insbesondere für abgetastete Analogsignale (11 Bit für 0,1% Auflösung) und die in letzter Zeit sich durchsetzende Wortlänge von 16 Bit bei Prozeßrechnern. Auf diese Weise wird der Erfolg der Redundanzreduktion nicht verringert und gleichzeitig die Auflösungsredundanz beseitigt, indem die nicht für den Abtastwert benötigten Bitstellen mit der Zeitdifferenzinformation belegt werden.

Ist bei wortweise anfallender Nachricht (z.B. Digital-Eingabe-Register) für die Zeitdifferenzangabe ein weiteres Rechnerwort notwendig, so ist eine Redundanzreduktion nur sinnvoll, wenn im Mittel mindestens die Hälfte der Nachricht redundant ist. Enthält die Nachricht über längere Zeit nur redundante Daten, so sind besondere Maßnahmen notwendig, um das Überlaufen der Bitstellen zur Speicherung der Zeitdifferenzangabe zu verhindern. In diesem Falle wird der nächste Abtastwert gespeichert, um die Kontinuität der Zeitaufzeichnung zu sichern. Dies führt zur Speicherung an sich redundanter Abtastwerte und verringert den Erfolg der Redundanzreduktion.

Anforderungen und Leistungsmaße für redundanzreduzierende Verfahren

1. Bruttoreduktionsfaktor

Der Bruttoreduktionsfaktor ist ein Maß für den Erfolg der Redundanzreduktion.

$$F_{RB} = \frac{Z_N}{Z_I + Z_O} \qquad (1)$$

Mittlere Zahl der Abtastwerte pro Zeiteinheit: der Nachricht $=Z_N$, der Information $=Z_I$, aufgrund von Zeitdifferenzüberläufen zusätzlich gespeichert $=Z_O$.

2. Hohe Wiedergabetreue

Die Signalverläufe vor und nach der Redundanzreduktion und Rekonstruktion sollen gut
übereinstimmen. Als Maß werden die mittlere quadratische Abweichung und der Spitzenfehler gewählt.

3. Geringe Rechnerbelastung

Als Maß für die Rechnerbelastung dient die Ausführungszeit der Algorithmen, da der
Speicherplatzbedarf der Algorithmen nicht erheblich unterschiedlich ist und gegenüber dem Speicherplatz für die Datenspeicherung nicht ins Gewicht fällt.

Spezielle Redundanzreduktionsverfahren

Von den Verfahren zur Redundanzreduktion werden nur die Prädiktoren und Interpolato-
ren erläutert und einem Leistungsvergleich unterworfen, da die Transformations- und
Codierungsverfahren bei erheblich größerem Rechenaufwand keine wesentlich besseren
Reduktionsfaktoren liefern /5/, /6/.

Polynomprädiktoren Nullter und Erster Ordnung

Aus der Fülle der bekannten Prädiktorverfahren werden im Rahmen dieser Arbeit nur
einige behandelt(zu den Bezeichnungen siehe Bemerkung am Schluß des Beitrages):

- (a) Zero-Order Predictor Fixed Aperture (ZOP,I);
- (b) Zero-Order Predictor Floating Aperture (ZOP,II), Abb.5;
- (c) First-Order Predictor, Methode I (FOP,I);
- (d) First-Order Predictor, Methode II (FOP,II), Abb.6.

Zur Abkürzung der Schreibweise werden die Verfahren im Text mit den in Klammern stehenden Kurzbezeichnungen angesprochen.

Für den Prädiktor nullter Ordnung (ZOP) gilt (Steigung = 0):

$$\hat{y}_t = y_{t-1} \tag{2}$$

mit

$\hat{y}_t$ = vorhergesagter Abtastwert zur Zeit t

y_{t-1} = tatsächlicher Abtastwert, um eine Abtastperiode zurückliegend.

Beim ZOP,I wird der gesamte Aussteuerbereich in Toleranzintervalle der Breite 2K unterteilt. Liegen der neue und der vorherige Abtastwert in dem gleichen Toleranzintervall, wird er als redundant erkannt, fällt der neue Wert aus dem Toleranzintervall
des vorherigen Wertes heraus, wird die Mitte dieses Toleranzstreifens zur Rekonstruktion der Kurve verwendet.

Beim ZOP,II wird der Extrapolationsbereich mit der Breite 2K symmetrisch um den
letzten Abtastwert gelegt (Abb.5). Sämtliche folgenden Werte, die innerhalb der Toleranzgrenzen liegen, sind redundant. Liegt ein neuer Abtastwert außerhalb dieses
Bereiches, wird er als nichtredundant erkannt und die Toleranzgrenzen werden symmetrisch zu diesem neuen Wert angeordnet. Bei diesem Verfahren ist somit der vorherge-
sagte Wert gleich dem letzten übertragenen Abtastwert und weicht maximal um $^{\pm}$K von
dem tatsächlichen Wert ab.

Für den Prädiktor erster Ordnung (Steigung linear) gilt die Vorhersagebeziehung

$$\hat{y}_t = 2y_{t-1} - y_{t-2}.\tag{3}$$

FOP,I: Zu Beginn werden die ersten beiden Abtastwerte als nichtredundant angesehen und durch die Extrapolationsgerade miteinander verbunden. Um diese Gerade wird ein Toleranzbereich der Breite 2K gelegt. Der nächste Wert wird nach Gl.(3) vorhergesagt. Liegt der tatsächliche Abtastwert innerhalb des Extrapolationsbereiches (ist die Abweichung kleiner $\pm$K), ist er redundant. Das Auftreten eines nichtredundanten Wertes (der außerhalb der Toleranz liegt) erfordert einen neuen Extrapolationsbereich, der aus der Steigung der Verbindungsgeraden zwischen dem nichtredundanten und dem davorliegenden Abtastwert und der Toleranz $\pm$K berechnet wird. Bei der Rekonstruktion werden die nichtredundanten Abtastwerte linear miteinader verbunden, wodurch der Fehler $\varepsilon > |K|$ werden kann.

Zur Verminderung des großen Fehlers wird ein modifiziertes Verfahren vorgeschlagen /7/, FOP,II: Statt des nichtredundanten Wertes wird der letzte innerhalb des Toleranzbereiches liegende (redundante) Abtastwert übertragen und zur Rekonstruktion verwendet (Abb.6). Der bei der Rekonstruktion maximal mögliche Fehler ε ist kleiner $|K|$. Diese Fehlerbetrachtungen beziehen sich jeweils nur auf die Abtastpunkte, nicht auf den dazwischenliegenden Signalverlauf.

Polynominterpolator Nullter und Erster Ordnung

Die Prädiktionsmethoden arbeiten nur dann effektiv, wenn das Signal mit genügend hoher Frequenz abgetastet wird, d.h. wenn die Daten zwischen zwei Abtastwerten relativ konstant sind. Bei Signalen, die durch hochfrequentes Rauschen gestört sind, kann ein größerer Reduktionsfaktor erzielt werden, wenn bei der Reduktion sowohl zukünftige als vergangene Abtastwerte berücksichtigt werden. Hiervon machen Interpolationsverfahren Gebrauch /5/. Zwei Interpolatoren O. Ordnung finden am häufigsten Anwendung:

    (a) Zero-Order Interpolator, Methode I (ZOI,I);

    (b) Zero-Order Interpolator, Methode II (ZOI,II), Abb.7.

Bei dem ZOI,I wird um den ersten Abtastwert ein Toleranzstreifen $\pm$K gelegt und so lange horizontal projiziert, bis ein Abtastwert außerhalb dieses Streifens liegt. Dann wird der letzte noch innerhalb des Streifens liegende Abtastwert gespeichert, um später zur Rekonstruktion des Signals herangezogen zu werden, während um den ersten außerhalb des Toleranzstreifens liegenden Abtastwert eine neue Toleranzgrenze $\pm$K gelegt wird.

Beim ZOI,II wird der Toleranzstreifen nach jedem weiteren Abtastwert vertikal so verschoben, daß eine größtmögliche Anzahl von Abtastwerten innerhalb dieses Toleranzstreifens liegt. Zur Rekonstruktion wird die Mitte des Streifens verwendet. Somit belegt das Signal die gesamte Breite 2K, und die maximale Abweichung zwischen rekonstruierter und ursprünglicher Kurve ist stets <K (Abb.7).

Bei den Interpolatoren 1. Ordnung (FOI) soll wiederum der Signalverlauf durch Geraden größter Länge angenähert werden, ihre Steigung ist jedoch variabel. Man unterscheidet

Verfahren mit 2 oder 4 Freiheitsgraden, wobei der Anfangs- und Endpunkt der Interpolationsgeraden beweglich sind (4 Freiheitsgrade) oder der Anfangspunkt der Interpolationsgeraden mit dem Endpunkt der vorherigen Geraden verbunden wird (2 Freiheitsgrade).

Eine ausführliche Beschreibung der einzelnen Interpolationsalgorithmen 1. Ordnung ("fan method") sowie des ZOP,III und Kombinationen verschiedener Redundanzreduktionsalgorithmen (seriell oder parallel) findet sich in /5/,.../9/.

Leistungsvergleich der Polynomprädiktoren und -interpolatoren

Eine Redundanzreduktion wurde mit den Polynomprädiktoren und -interpolatoren an drei Signaltypen vorgenommen, von denen die bei je einem Signal erzielten Bruttoreduktionsfaktoren F_{RB} in Abhängigkeit von der Toleranzbreite K in den Abb.2-4 dargestellt sind. Die Toleranzbreite wird als prozentuales Verhältnis zur Maximalamplitude aufgetragen. Da der Reduktionsfaktor stark signalabhängig ist, wie M.M. Bruce in /10/ an einem Prädiktor 1. Ordnung bei verschiedenen Signalen gezeigt hat, wurde der Bruttoreduktionsfaktor als Verhältnis zu dem beim ZOP,II bei der größten untersuchten Toleranzbreite erzielten Bruttoreduktionsfaktor aufgetragen, so daß ein direkter Vergleich der Verfahren ohne Umrechnung der Absolutwerte möglich ist. Die Verschiebungen bei dem ZOP,III und FOI,III betragen 1/3, 1/2 und 4/5 der Toleranzbreite.

Bei einem Signalverlauf mit geringer Datenaktivität und nur kleinen Steigungsänderungen in bestimmten Bereichen zeigt sich, daß Verfahren 1. Ordnung (Kurven 6 und 9 in Abb.2) schon bei kleinen Toleranzbreiten hohe Reduktionsfaktoren erzielen. Mit zunehmendem K steigt die Anzahl der beim Amplitudenanstieg im Toleranzschlauch liegenden Abtastwerte, bis sämtliche Werte erfaßt sind und eine weitere Zunahme des Reduktionsfaktors nicht möglich ist.

Das Einknicken von Kurve 5 (ZOP,III$_{V3}$) bei K=16% rührt von einer zunehmenden Anzahl von Zeitüberläufen her, der entsprechende Nettoreduktionsfaktor F_R ist gegenüber K=14% konstant.

Abb.3 stellt die Reduktionsfaktoren bei Anwendung der Algorithmen auf ein tiefpaßgefiltertes stochastisches Signal mit Gaußscher Amplitudenverteilung dar. Die Zeitkonstante des RC-Filters ist um den Faktor 20 größer als das Abtastzeitintervall. Die Verfahren 1. Ordnung liefern mit zunehmender Toleranzbreite wesentlich geringere Reduktionsfaktoren als der ZOI,II und der ZOP,II, sowie der bezogen auf den F_{RB} nahezu gleichwertige ZOI,I. Dies ist auf die häufig (auch im Vorzeichen) wechselnde Signalsteigung zurückzuführen.

Abb.4 zeigt den Verlauf des Reduktionsfaktors bei einem Signal mit unterschiedlich langer Impulsdauer, wobei auch die Amplitude der Impulse variiert. Dieses Signal simuliert den Verlauf bei zufällig auftretenden Störungs- oder Führungssprüngen. Verfahren Nullter Ordnung liefern wiederum die höchsten Reduktionsfaktoren, wobei besonders mit dem ZOI,II wie bei den vorherigen Signalverläufen das beste Ergebnis erzielt werden kann.

Eine Untersuchung der zur Signalreduktion benötigten Zeit zeigt, daß der ZOP,II die
kürzeste Zeit beansprucht, während der ZOI,II wegen der notwendigen Vertikalverschie-
bung der Toleranzgrenzen je nach Signal im Mittel zwischen etwa 40 und 47% langsamer
ist. Der ZOI,I ist gleichschnell dem ZOP,II, liefert aber
einen geringeren Reduktionsfaktor als dieser.

Ein Vergleich der Signalkurven mit den nach der Redundanzreduktion rekonstruierten
Kurven zeigt, daß bezüglich des mittleren Fehlerquadrats der FOP,II die besten Werte
liefert, wohingegen der ZOI,II bei hoher Datenaktivität (Signal 3) deutlich abfällt.
Bei einer Systemsicherung mit Prozeßrechnern muß eine hohe Wiedergabetreue gewährleistet sein. Diese Forderung erfüllt der FOP,II insbesondere bei geringer Datenaktivität (Signal 1) am besten, bei den beiden anderen Signaltypen werden, vor allem
beim Spitzenfehler, nicht so gute Ergebnisse erzielt. ZOP,II und ZOI,II sind hier bei
allen Signaltypen nahezu gleichwertig.

Die genannten Ergebnisse sind in Tabelle 1 wiedergegeben:

Tabelle 1   Vergleich von ZOP,II, FOP,II und ZOI,II

	relativer Brutto-Reduktionsfaktor bei K=10%			relativer mittlerer Rechenzeitbedarf			relat. mittl. Fehlerquadrat bei K=10%			relativer Spitzenfehler bei K=10%		
	S_1	S_2	S_3	S_1	S_2	S_3	S_1	S_2	S_3	S_1	S_2	S_3
ZOP,II	0,583	0,284	0,499	1,000	1,000	1,000	1,000	1,000	1,000	1,000	1,000	1,000
FOP,II	1,120	0,150	0,304	1,297	1,541	1,546	0,379	0,802	0,722	0,275	1,528	1,875
ZOI,II	0,965	0,542	0,764	1,468	1,404	1,401	1,043	1,168	1,570	1,001	1,000	1,003

S_1: Rampe mit quadratischem Anstieg

S_2: Tiefpaßgefiltertes Gaußsches Rauschen

S_3: Impulsrauschen

Bei der Auswahl eines der drei Verfahren, die von den 10 untersuchten bezüglich der
hier angegebenen Leistungskriterien die besten Ergebnisse liefern, muß man von den
an das Verfahren gestellten Anforderungen ausgehen:
Soll der mittlere quadratische Fehler möglichst gering sein, muß man sich für den
FOP,II entscheiden, dessen erzielter Bruttoreduktionsfaktor bei hoher Datenaktivität relativ klein ist bei größerem Rechenzeitbedarf.
Steht neben anderen Aufgaben des Prozeßrechners genügend Zeit für die Redundanzreduktion zur Verfügung, wird man sich für den FOI,II entscheiden, der den größeren
Bruttoreduktionsfehler gegenüber dem ZOP,II liefert bei nahezu gleichem Spitzenfehler. Bei Zeitknappheit bietet sich der ZOP,II an, der einen guten Kompromiß bezüglich Reduktionsfaktor und Fehler darstellt.

<u>Literatur</u>

/1/ Syrbe, M.:   Messen, Steuern und Regeln mit Prozeßrechnern.
                   Akadem. Verlagsgesellschaft, Frankfurt, 1972

/2/ Steusloff, H.: Automatische Systemsicherung in prozeßrechnergeführten Systemen.
                   IITB-Bericht vom 26.2.1973

/3/ Schwier, W.:   Direkte digitale Regelung mit signalabhängiger Abtastperiode.
                   Diss. Karlsruhe 1970

/4/ Steusloff, H.: Systemüberwachung und Störungsanalyse mit Prozeßrechnern.
                   IITB-Mitteilungen 1970, S.15-22

/5/   The special issue on redundancy reduction.
                   Proc. IEEE <u>55</u> (1967), Nr. 3, S.251-406

/6/ Grimm, R.:   Verfahren zur Nachrichtenreduktion und ihre Anwendbarkeit bei
                   der Systemüberwachung mit Prozeßrechnern.
                   IITB-Bericht vom 12.10.72

/7/ Lippmann, R.: Nachrichtenreduktion (Data compression) -
                   Literaturbericht über ausgewählte praktische Verfahren.
                   Deutsche Luft- und Raumfahrt, Mitteilung 68-01, Dezember 1968

/8/ Musmann, H.G.: Angewandte Verfahren der Nachrichtenreduktion.
                   Nachrichtentechn. Zeitschr. (NTZ) <u>21</u> (1968), H.9, S.521-527

/9/ Blerkom, R.van: An adaptive compositive data compression algorithm with reduced
    Schwarz, G.R.: computation requirements.
    Ward, R.J.:   Proc. 1968, Nat. Telemetry Conf., S. 90-95

/10/ Bruce, M.M.   An analysis of a first-order polynomial predictor for data
                   compression.
                   NASA, Washington, D.C., Tech. Note D-3866, März 1967, 29 Seiten

/11/ Grimm, R.:   Leistungsvergleich von Redundanzreduktionsalgorithmen in Hinblick
                   auf Systemsicherung mit Prozeßrechnern.
                   IITB-Bericht (in Vorbereitung)

<u>Bemerkung:</u>
Die Prädiktor- und Interpolatorverfahren werden hier mit den amerikanischen Bezeichnungen eingeführt, die auch in der deutschen Literatur verwendet werden. Vor allem erklären sie die ebenfalls in der deutschen Literatur verwendeten Kurzbezeichnungen der Verfahren.

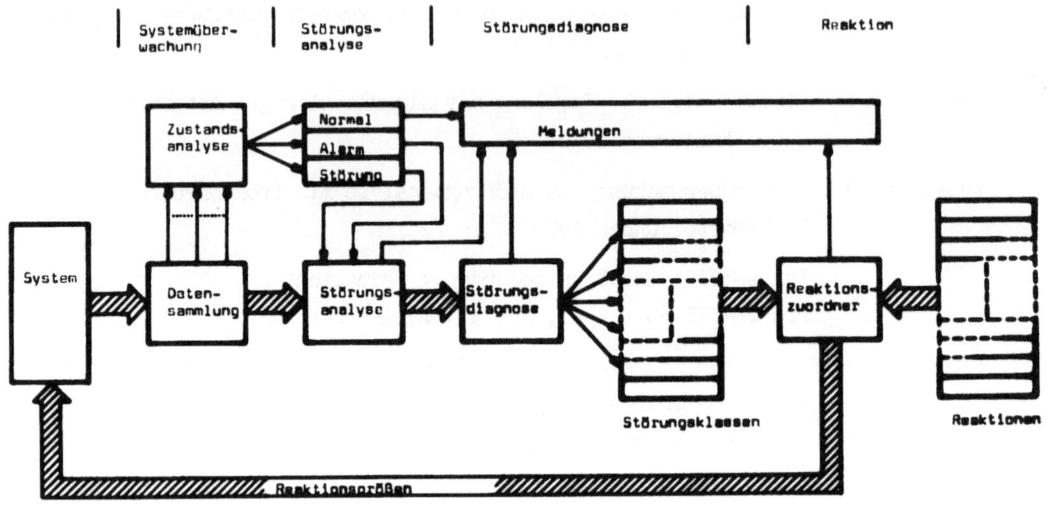

Bild 1 Gesamtkonzept Systemsicherung

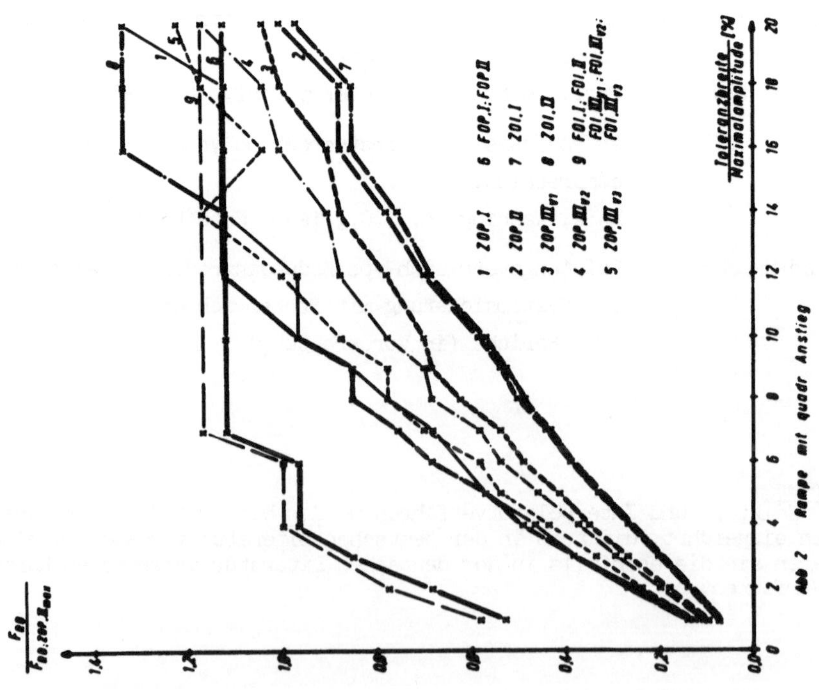

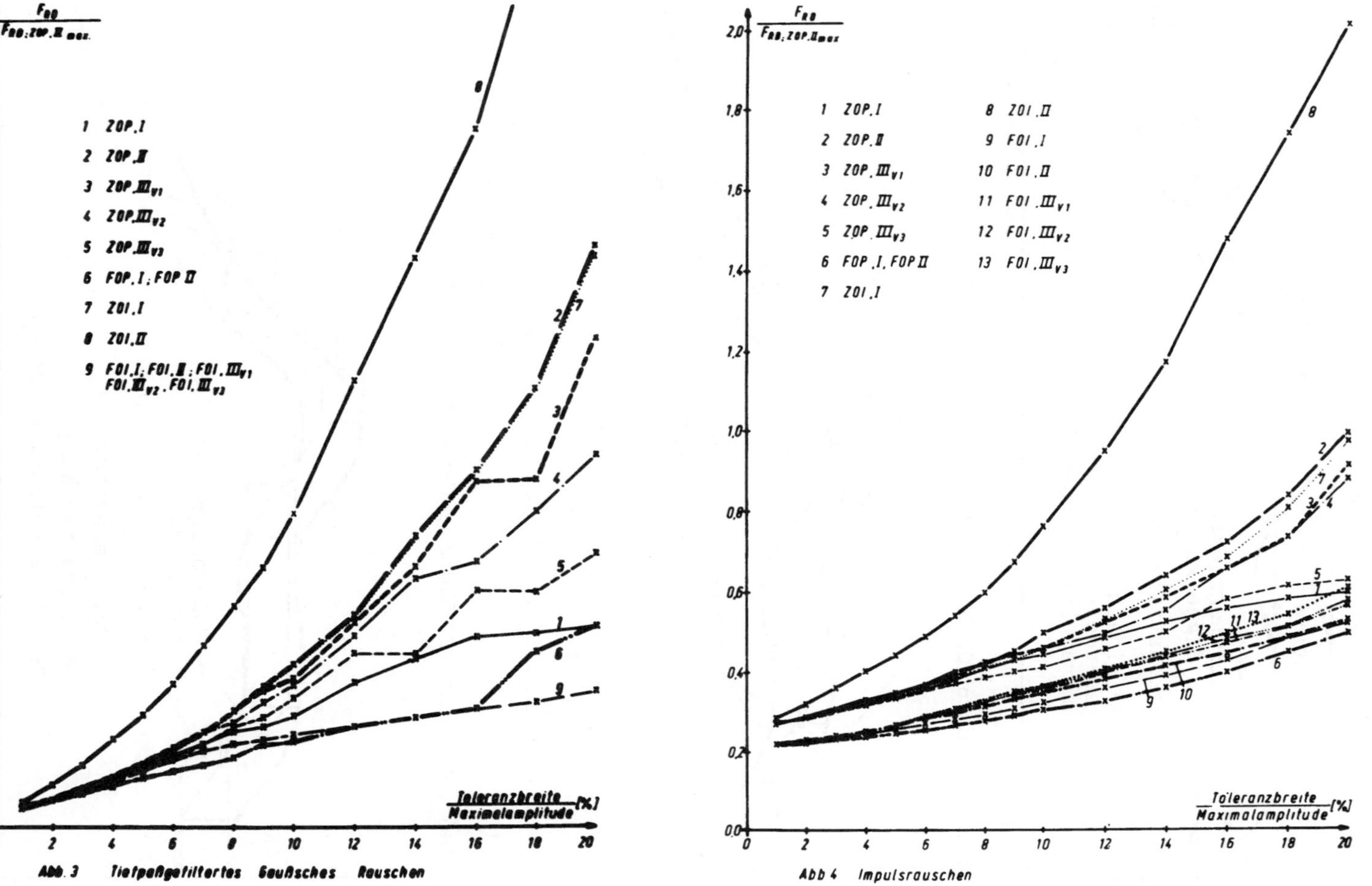
$\dfrac{F_{BB}}{F_{BB;ZOP.II_{max}}}$
1 ZOP.I
2 ZOP.II
3 ZOP.III$_{V1}$
4 ZOP.III$_{V2}$
5 ZOP.III$_{V3}$
6 FOP.I;FOP II
7 ZOI.I
8 ZOI.II
9 FOI.I;FOI.II;FOI.III$_{V1}$, FOI.III$_{V2}$,FOI.III$_{V3}$
Toleranzbreite / Maximalamplitude [%]
Abb. 3 Tiefpaßgefiltertes Gaußsches Rauschen
$\dfrac{F_{BB}}{F_{BB,ZOP.II_{max}}}$
1 ZOP.I   8 ZOI.II
2 ZOP.II   9 FOI.I
3 ZOP.III$_{V1}$ 10 FOI.II
4 ZOP.III$_{V2}$ 11 FOI.III$_{V1}$
5 ZOP.III$_{V3}$ 12 FOI.III$_{V2}$
6 FOP.I,FOP II   13 FOI.III$_{V3}$
7 ZOI.I
Toleranzbreite / Maximalamplitude [%]
Abb 4 Impulsrauschen

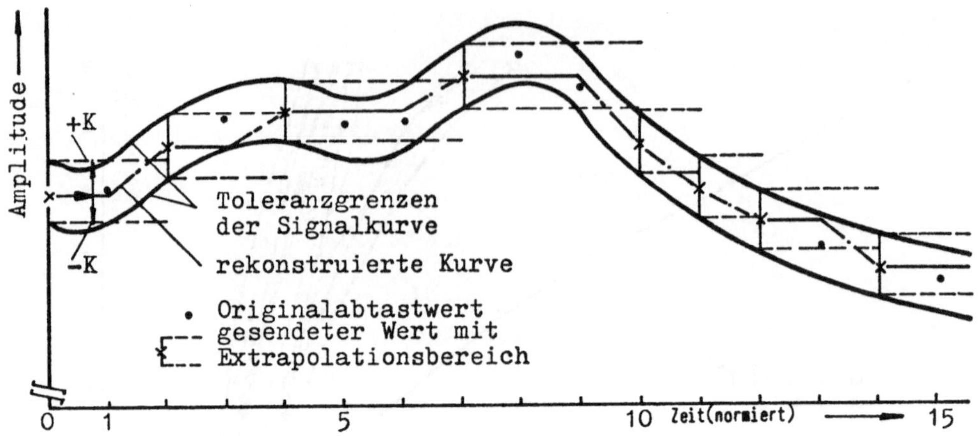

Abb.5   Prädiktor 0. Ordnung (Methode II) nach /7/

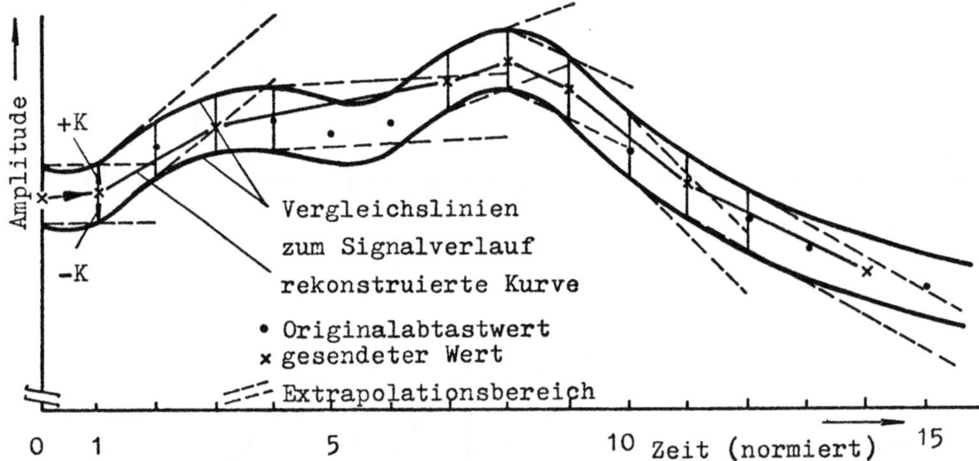

Abb.6   Prädiktor 1. Ordnung (Methode II) nach /7/

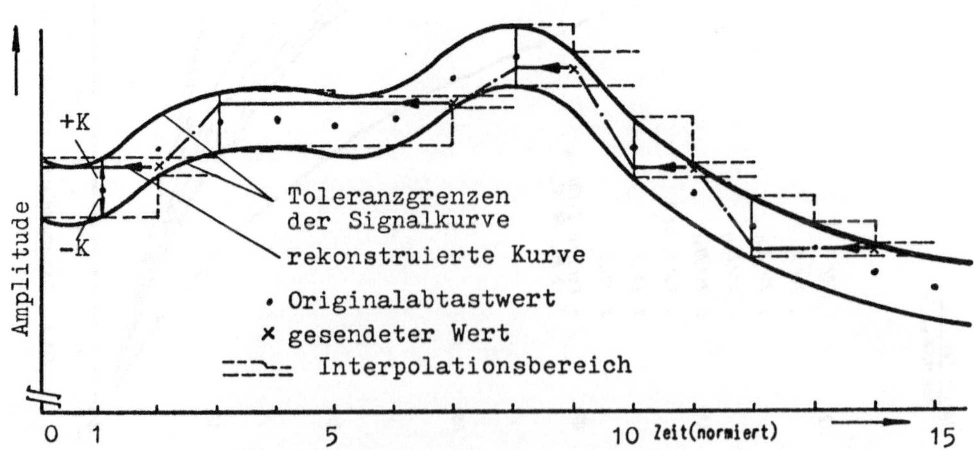

Abb.7   Interpolator 0. Ordnung (Methode II) nach /7/

DIE ANWENDUNG DES PRINZIPS DER MIKROPROGRAMMIERUNG AUF DAS EIN-/AUSGABESYSTEM EINES PROZESSRECHNERORGANISATIONSPROGRAMMS

Winfried Blumann

1. Einführung des Grundgedankens

Prozeßrechner müssen für den Anschluß vieler Gerätetypen geeignet sein. Die verschiedenen Gerätetypen lassen sich in drei Klassen aufteilen.

Zur Klasse 1 zählen konventionelle Geräte mit einer Datendarstellung auf Papier, magnetischen Medien oder Bildschirmen.

Die Klasse 2 umfaßt alle Arten gebräuchlicher Prozeßsignalformer: Alarmeingaben, Impulszähler, Echtzeituhren, Digitaleingaben, Digitalausgaben, momentane und integrierende Analogeingaben, Analogausgaben, Spektrographen u.a.

Zur Klasse 3 gehören Experimental- und Werkzeugmaschinensteuerungen, systemfremde Geräte und Geräte der Klassen 1 oder 2, wenn sie in unüblicher Art und Weise betrieben werden sollen.

Das Ein-/Ausgabesystem löst bei jedem Ein-/Ausgabeaufruf an ein beliebiges Gerät folgende Probleme:
- Die zeitliche Koordination der Zugriffe vieler Benutzer auf jeweils ein Gerät
- Die Transformation von Benutzerparametern in Parameter für den Ein-/Ausgabeprozessor oder das Gerät
- Die Mitteilung von Ablaufbesonderheiten an den Benutzer
- Die Betreuung des Informationsaustausches zwischen Zentrale und Peripherie über die Ein-/Ausgabeschnittstelle.

Die genormten Eigenschaften von Ein-/Ausgabeschnittstellen beschränken unabhängig von dem vielfältigen Charakter der angeschlossenen Geräte die Methoden des Informationsaustausches zwischen Zentrale und Peripherie. Es ist sinnvoll, diesen festen Bezugspunkt der genormten Schnittstelle als Ausgangspunkt für Überlegungen zur Realisierung eines Ein-/Ausgabesystems zu wählen.

Die Organisation des Informationsaustausches über Ein-/Ausgabeschnittstellen (/LEI/) stützt sich auf drei elementare Steuermechanismen:
- Die zentrale Anforderung zur Ausgabe von Geräteparametern

- Die periphere Unterbrechungsanforderung zur Einleitung von
  Programmunterbrechungen
- Die periphere Datenanforderung zur Steuerung von Haupt-
  speicherzugriffen nach dem Prinzip des "cycle stealing".

Diese Steuermechanismen bilden durch Kombination insgesamt
7 Betriebsarten zur Abwicklung von Ein-/Ausgabeverkehr. Die
leistungsstärkste und am häufigsten anzutreffende Betriebsart
ist die blockweise befehlsgesteuerte Datenübertragung. Sie wird
eingeleitet durch 1....n_1 Gerätebefehle. Danach folgen als
Ausführungskern n_2 Datenanforderungen ($n_2 \geqq m$) zur Übertragung von
m Daten. Den Abschluß bilden 1....n_3 Unterbrechungsanforderungen.
Die Anzahl der Betriebsarten ist zwar klein, aber wie das gerade
ausgeführte Beispiel zeigt, sind innerhalb jeder Betriebsart
Variationen in der Aufeinanderfolge der Steuermechanismen
"unbegrenzt" möglich.

Diese Sachverhalte der Ein-/Ausgabeschnittstelle bestimmen
elementare Teilfunktionen des Ein-/Ausgabesystems:
- Koordinierung der Zugriffe zu Geräten
- Aufbau von Kanalprogrammen
- Erzeugung von Ein-/Ausgabebefehlen
- Zuordnung von Unterbrechungsanforderungen zu Aufrufen.
Bei jedem Ein-/Ausgabeaufruf an ein beliebiges Gerät läuft also
im Ein-/Ausgabesystem zwangsläufig eine Folge beliebiger Teil-
funktionen aus einem beschränkten Spektrum an Teilfunktionen ab.

Diese Tatsachen lassen sich in folgender Weise ausnutzen:
Der Benutzer übergibt dem Ein-/Ausgabesystem mit dem Ein-/
Ausgabeaufruf ein "Ablaufmodell" und variable "Ablaufmodell-
parameter". Das Ablaufmodell beschreibt im Detail die aufgerufene
Betriebsart des Gerätes und die Zugriffskoordinierung am Gerät
in Form von "Anweisungen". Diese Anweisungen bestimmen Typ und
Reihenfolge der notwendigen Teilfunktionen. Sie werden vom Ein-/
Ausgabesystem nacheinander bearbeitet. Die variablen Ablauf-
modellparameter sind identisch mit aktuellen Aufrufparametern
wie zum Beispiel Adressen von Datenfeldern.

Das geschilderte Verfahren stellt die Anwendung des Prinzips der
Mikroprogrammierung (/DAV/, /SPE/) auf das Ein-/Ausgabesystem
eines Organisationsprogrammes dar. In einer mikroprogrammierten
Zentraleinheit läuft an Stelle eines Befehls ein aus Mikro-
befehlen bestehendes Mikroprogramm ab. Die schrittweise

Ausführung dieses Programms wird über ein Mikrobefehlsadreßregister gesteuert. Die Gesamtheit der Mikroprogramme ist im Mikroprogrammspeicher der Zentraleinheit abgelegt. In Analogie dazu wird in einem mikroprogrammierten Ein-/Ausgabesystem an Stelle eines Ein-/Ausgabeaufrufs ein aus Anweisungen bestehendes Ablaufmodell abgearbeitet. Die schrittweise Bearbeitung des Modells wird durch ein Anweisungsadreßregister verwaltet. Die Gesamtheit der Ablaufmodelle steht im "Ablaufmodellspeicher" des Ein-/Ausgabesystems. Programmtechnisch sind Ablaufmodelle Datendefinitionen.

Aus ökonomischen Gründen empfiehlt sich die Einführung von drei Typen an Ablaufmodellspeichern. Der Ablaufmodellspeicher des Ein-/Ausgabesystems besteht aus zwei Speicherbereichen. Der eine enthält "öffentliche", der andere "genossenschaftliche" Ablaufmodelle. Zusätzlich sind noch Ablaufmodellspeicher für "private" Ablaufmodelle in Benutzerprogrammen definiert. Unabhängig von der Wahl des Speichertyps stehen die variablen Ablaufmodellparameter stets im Benutzerprogramm.

Öffentliche Ablaufmodelle stellt die Herstellerfirma des Rechners für alle von ihr zu Standardprodukten erklärten Geräte und Gerätefunktionen zur Verfügung. Dem Benutzer bleibt das Vorhandensein eines mikroprogrammierten Ein-/Ausgabesystem verborgen. Der Hersteller hat den entscheidenden Vorteil, daß die Prozeduren des Ein-/Ausgabesystems unabhängig von der Anzahl der angeschlossenen Gerätetypen sind. Die Neueinführung jedes Gerätes als Standardprodukt ist schnell und aufwandsarm möglich. Das Ein-/Ausgabesystem muß lediglich durch neue Ablaufmodelle, die als Datendefinitionen leicht formulierbar sind, erweitert werden.

Private Ablaufmodelle sind für solche Geräte notwendig, die der Hersteller nicht oder noch nicht zu Standardprodukten erklärt hat oder auch für solche Standardprodukte, die der Benutzer in spezieller Art und Weise zu betreiben wünscht. Dem Benutzer steht über das private Ablaufmodell die mikroprogrammierte Struktur des Ein-/Ausgabesystems voll zur Verfügung. So wie in einer mikroprogrammierten Zentraleinheit "fremde Befehle" emulierbar sind, so sind in dem mikroprogrammierten Ein-/Ausgabesystem "fremde Aufrufe" emulierbar. Das ist insbesondere dort von Bedeutung, wo Prozeßrechner mit Geräten vielseitiger Herkunft als Experimentalrechner eingesetzt werden.

Genossenschaftliche Ablaufmodelle sind private Modelle, die der
Benutzer in das Ein-/Ausgabesystem eingegliedert hat. Diese
Eingliederung läßt die Vorteile privater Ablaufmodelle bestehen,
erlaubt aber zusätzlich die simultane Mehrfachausnutzung durch
mehrere Benutzer.

Mit den geschilderten Mitteln kann der Benutzer seinen Ein-/
Ausgabeverkehr sehr flexibel und leistungsfähig gestalten. Er
darf sogar "gleichzeitig" an einem Gerät mit öffentlichen,
privaten und genossenschaftlichen Ablaufmodellen arbeiten.

Ein verfahrenstechnischer Nachteil läßt sich auch durch geschickte
Auswahl des Modellspeichers nicht vermeiden. Die Dekodierung der
Anweisungen verzehrt Laufzeit. Wie die Erfahrung mit einem
realisierten Ein-/Ausgabesystem gezeigt hat, ist der Laufzeit-
verlust gegenüber gerätespezifischen Prozeduren von erträglicher
Größe und wird von den beschriebenen Verfahrensvorteilen leicht
aufgewogen.

2. Anweisungsliste

Das zentrale Problem beim Entwurf und bei der Realisierung eines
mikroprogrammierten Ein-/Ausgabesystems ist die Auswahl einer
ausgewogenen Anweisungsliste. Sie sollte ein möglichst einfaches
Programmieren in der Anweisungsebene erlauben. Diesem Ziele
dient die Berücksichtigung zweier übergeordneter Gesichtspunkte.

Die einzelnen Anweisungen müssen elementar und eindeutig und in
einsichtiger Weise Teilfunktionen zugeordnet sein. Der elementare
Charakter der Anweisungen ermöglicht es, mit einer kleinen
Anweisungsliste auszukommen. Das wird in Einzelfällen sicher
bedeuten, daß ein Ablaufmodell umfänglicher ist, als es beim
Vorliegen von Anweisungen, die auch zusammengesetzte elementare
Teilfunktionen aufrufen, sein müßte. In solchen Fällen macht
sich die Möglichkeit des simultanen Zugriffs auf öffentliche und
genossenschaftliche Ablaufmodelle durch mehrere Benutzer vorteilhaft bemerkbar.

Der zweite übergeordnete Entwurfsgesichtspunkt ist die Verwandtschaft der Anweisungsliste mit der Befehlsliste. Dieser Gesichtspunkt wird nicht auf alle Anweisungen direkt anwendbar sein.
insofern zwangsläufig nicht alle Anweisungen funktionelle
Äquivalente auf Befehlsebene haben können.

Zur Realisierung der genannten Vorsätze ist es nützlich, die Anweisungen entsprechend ihrem Leistungscharakter in Klassen zu unterteilen. Die Klasse der ein-/ausgabebezogenen Anweisungen bedarf aus ökonomischen Gründen der Ergänzung durch eine Anweisungsklasse zur Strukturierung von Ablaufmodellen.

Diese Strukturierung bedeutet die Einführung von Anweisungen zur "Unterablaufmodelltechnik" und zur Bildung von "Anweisungsschleifen". Eine praktische Angleichung an die funktionsäquivalenten Befehle "Unterprogrammsprung" und "Dekrementieren und Springen" verlangt zum Beispiel bei einer Zentraleinheit mit frei adressierbaren allgemeinen Registern zwei Eigenschaften in der Anweisungsebene. Das Ein-/Ausgabesystem stellt frei adressierbare "fiktive Register" zur Verfügung. Sie dienen im Rahmen des genannten Beispiels zur Aufnahme des Rücksprungortes bzw. des Schleifenzählers. Daneben können die Sprungziele als symbolische Adressen auswählbar sein. Es bietet sich an, fiktive Register bei der Mehrzahl der Anweisungen einzusetzen.

Bei den ein-/ausgabebezogenen Anweisungen steht der Gesichtspunkt ihrer jeweiligen elementaren Leistung im Vordergrund. Dieser Gesichtspunkt läßt sich am Beispiel der Anweisungsgruppe zur Koordinierung der zeitlichen Zugriffe vieler Benutzer auf ein Gerät verdeutlichen.

Eine Ein-/Ausgabeschnittstelle zeigt ihre volle Leistungsfähigkeit erst durch Ergänzung mit einem universellen Ein-/ Ausgabeprozessor. In dieser Struktur können "zu einer Zeit" an einem Anschluß der Schnittstelle Unterbrechungsanforderungen unterschiedlicher Qualität eintreffen. Im komplexesten Falle überlagern sich Unterbrechungsanforderungen als Folge von Alarmen und Anforderungen zum Abschluß simultan laufender blockweise befehlsgesteuerter Datenübertragungen mit peripherer Verwaltung von Hauptspeicheradressen. Das bedeutet, daß das Ein-/Ausgabesystem die Zuordnung von Unterbrechungsanforderungen zu Aufrufen über eine Zuordnungswarteschlange und die Steuerung der Zugriffe zu Geräten über eine Zugriffswarteschlange verwalten muß. Diese beiden Verwaltungsvorgänge stellen elementare Teilfunktionen dar, denen individuelle Anweisungen zugewiesen werden. Darüber hinaus ist es im Hinblick auf eine optimale Alarmbearbeitung günstig, wenn Anmeldungen und Abmeldungen in der Zuordnungswarteschlange mit unabhängigen

Anweisungen aufgerufen werden können. Das gestattet es dem
Benutzer, sich bei Bedarf als permanenter Empfänger bestimmter
Alarme anzumelden. Beim Eintreffen der Alarme veraltet lediglich
die Fortsetzadresse des Benutzers, die dieser dann zyklisch im
Rhythmus der eintreffenden Alarme neu installieren muß.

Die Zuordnung jeweils einer Unterbrechungsanforderung über die
e-stellige Zuordnungswarteschlange zu $1 \ldots e_1$ aus e Empfangs-
aufrufen ($e_1 \leq e$) bedarf der Erläuterung. Der Anweisung zur
Anmeldung der Zuordnung, welche eine Unterbrechungsstelle in
der Bearbeitung von Ablaufmodellen darstellt, folgen Anweisungen
zur Entscheidung über die Zuordnung. Diese Anweisungen vergleichen
den "Istdeskriptor", die Anzeigen zur genauen Identifikation der
aufgetretenen Unterbrechungsursache, mit dem "Solldeskriptor",
den Anzeigen zur genauen Spezifizierung der erwarteten
Unterbrechungsursache. Die Zuordnung findet bei einem positiven
Vergleich statt. Der zuvor formulierte Analogiegesichtspunkt
verlangt bei einer entsprechenden Befehlsliste, daß bestimmte
Anweisungen "Anweisungsanzeigen" als Ergebnisausweis setzen,
und daß diese Anzeigen mit bedingten Sprunganweisungen abgefragt
werden können.

Diese Ausführungen mögen genügen, um anzudeuten, welche Probleme
beim Entwurf einer Anweisungsliste auftreten, und welche
Leistungen einzelnen ausgesuchten Anweisungen zuzuweisen sind.
Die hier zugrunde gelegte realisierte Anweisungsliste umfaßt
insgesamt ca. 30 Anweisungen. Die folgende Aufstellung ist ein
Auszug aus dieser Liste:
- Lade fiktives Register
- Ein-/Ausgabebefehl
- Zuordnungsanmeldung
- Zugriffsanmeldung
- Zuordnungsabmeldung
- Zugriffsabmeldung
- Deskriptorvergleich
- Deskriptortransfer ins aufrufende Benutzerprogramm
- Einbinden eines Maschinenbefehls
- Dekrementieren und Springen
- Springen nach Unterablaufmodell
- Springen bedingt
- Kanalbefehl Eingabe eines Byteblockes
- Kanalbefehl Ausgabe eines Byteblockes

- Kanalbefehl mit peripherer Verwaltung von Hauptspeicheradressen und Übertragungsrichtungen.

Die realisierte Anweisungsliste ist logisch vollständig. Es
lassen sich Aufrufe mit vielfältigen Leistungen an alle Geräte,
die die Konventionen der Ein-/Ausgabeschnittstelle einhalten,
formulieren. Zum Beispiel könnte eine Alarmanmeldung die Art
und Weise der Alarmbildung und -übertragung stets so berücksichtigen, daß sich die Anmeldung auf Einzelalarme, Gruppen-
alarme (physikalische Gruppen), logische Verknüpfungen von
Einzelalarmen oder Gruppenalarmen bezieht.

3. <u>Erfahrungen mit einem mikroprogrammierten Ein-/Ausgabesystem</u>

Die Grundlage für diesen Bericht bildet ein im Rahmen der
Organisationsprogramme der Siemens Prozeßrechner 320 und 330
(/HER/) realisiertes mikroprogrammiertes Ein-/Ausgabesystem.
Dieses System wird zur Zeit nur neben einem konventionellen
Ein-/Ausgabesystem, pro Gerätetyp eine gerätespezifische
Prozedur, angeboten.

Die Verfügbarkeit beider Systeme ermöglicht Laufzeitvergleiche
zwischen den beiden Verfahrenstechniken. Als Richtwert für die
Laufzeitverlängerung durch das mikroprogrammierte Verfahren gilt
der Faktor 2. Die Verlängerung schwankt um diesen Richtwert in
Abhängigkeit von der Länge des Ablaufmodelles. Angesichts der
"Gewinne", die das mikroprogrammierte Verfahren sowohl für den
Hersteller als auch den Benutzer bietet, sind die "Laufzeit-
kosten" alles in allem unterproportional.

Das derzeitige Nebeneinander zweier Ein-/Ausgabesysteme darf
keineswegs so verstanden werden, als sei das mikroprogrammierte
System allein keine tragfähige Basis. Zunächst ist dieser
Sachverhalt nur als kluge und vorsichtige Entwicklungspolitik
zu werten. Neue Verfahren lösen alte erst ab, wenn sie sich
theoretisch und praktisch ausreichend bewährt haben. Diese
Ablösung ist dadurch offen gehalten, daß Aufrufe an das
konventionelle System jederzeit durch einen Makroübersetzerlauf
in funktionsgleiche Aufrufe an das mikroprogrammierte System
umgewandelt werden können.

Eine solche Entwicklung wäre dann auf einem Teilgebiet ein
Schritt hin zu einer rationellen Softwareproduktion. Es darf
vermutet werden, daß rationelle Produktion (/BRO/, /HAS/)
innerhalb eines Organisationsprogrammes oder gar eines
Betriebssystems nicht durch Einsatz eines einzigen Verfahrens
möglich ist, sondern daß vielmehr von Teilgebiet zu Teilgebiet
die Verfahrenstechnik zwischen Mikroprogrammierung, Programmierung
in höheren Sprachen, Programmierung unter Einsatz vorgefertigter
Funktionsmodule, Unterprogramme oder Makroaufrufe, variiert
werden muß.

Literatur

/BRO/   P.J. Brown:
         Using a macro processor to aid software implementation,
         The Computer Journal Vol. 12 (1969) S. 327 - 331

/DAV/   P.M. Davies:
         Readings in microprogramming,
         IBM System Journal No. 1, 1972

/HAS/   A. Hassit, J.W. Lageschulte, L.E. Lyon:
         Implementation of a High Level Language Machine,
         Communications of the ACM Vol. 16, No. 4, April 1973

/HER/   K. Herzog:
         Organisationsprogramm für den Prozeßrechner 330,
         Siemens Zeitschrift 47 (1973), H.5

/LEI/   K. Leipold, H. Spreen:
         Organisation des Nachrichtenverkehrs zwischen Zentral-
         einheiten und peripheren Einheiten in Datenverarbeitungs-
         systemen,
         Elektronische Rechenanlagen 11 (1969), H.3

/SPE/   Special Issue on Microprogramming,
         IEEE Transactions on Computers Vol. C-20, No.7, July 1971

LINGUISTISCHE UNTERSUCHUNGEN

AUTOMATISCHE INDEXIERUNG DURCH LINGUISTISCHE SYNTAXANALYSE

Stephan Braun

Eine der Hauptaufgaben bei der automatischen Literatursuche
("Dokumentation") ist die Zuordnung von Stichwörtern zu Dokumenten
("Indexierung"), wobei die Stichwörter den sachlichen Inhalt des
Dokuments soweit charakterisieren sollen, daß das betreffende Doku-
ment bei Vorliegen einer Suchfrage nach Dokumenten des betreffenden
Inhalts durch einen Algorithmus wiedergefunden werden kann, der
Stichwortmengen miteinander vergleicht.

Das einfachste und in der Praxis häufig angewandte Verfahren
zur automatischen Indexierung besteht darin, manuell eine Liste der
für ein Fachgebiet vermutlich wichtigen Stichwörter zu erstellen, den
Originaltext eines Dokuments dann maschinell auf das Vorkommen dieser
Stichwörter zu durchsuchen und dem Dokument die Menge aller so gefundenen Wörter zuzuordnen.

Hierbei ist es häufig notwendig, nicht nur einzelne Stichwörter,
sondern Stichwortgruppen zu verwenden, vor allem dann, wenn ein zur
Inhaltsbeschreibung wichtiger Begriff durch mehrere Wörter dargestellt wird derart, daß die einzelnen Wörter den sachlichen Inhalt
wesentlich weniger genau beschreiben würden. Dies trifft speziell für
Fachtexte, z.B. aus dem Gebiet der Mathematik oder der Informatik zu,
wie das Beispiel des Begriffes "Funktion einer reellen Variablen"
zeigt. Für weniger spezielle Dokumentensammlungen scheint die Verwendung von Wortgruppen zur Indexierung weniger bedeutsam zu sein
(Salton 1968). Im folgenden wird die Verwendung von Wortgruppen zur
Indexierung am Beispiel deutschsprachiger mathematischer Fachtexte
betrachtet.[1] Eine Erweiterung der Untersuchung auf andere als
deutschsprachige Texte ist sicher, eine Erweiterung auf allgemeinere
naturwissenschaftlich-technische Texte wahrscheinlich möglich.

Wortgruppen zur Indexierung treten in der Praxis auf, z.B. bei
den Artikeln der Zeitschrift "Communications of the ACM". Bei solchen
Wortgruppen handelt es sich, linguistisch gesehen, in der Regel um
Nominalphrasen (NP), allerdings nur um gewisse einfache Typen. Im
wesentlichen treten auf

---

1) Die Arbeiten wurden im Rahmen des Sonderforschungsbereichs "Elektronische Rechenanlagen und Informationsverarbeitung" der
   Deutschen Forschungsgemeinschaft durchgeführt.

a) ein Substantiv mit ein oder mehreren Adjektivattributen

   Beispiel: endlicher stochastischer Automat

b) ein Substantiv mit Genitiv- oder Präpositionalobjekt

   Beispiel: Übergangshalbgruppe eines Automaten,
             Automat mit Ausgabe

c) eine Kombination der genannten beiden Fälle

   Beispiel: endlicher Automat mit Ausgabe

Fig.1 gibt eine (kontextfreie) Grammatik G für Nominalphrasen zur Indexierung. G erzeugt im simpelsten Fall ein einzelnes Substantiv; eine kompliziertere durch G erzeugt NP wäre " die abzählbare, geordnete Menge der symmetrischen Zeichenreihen über einem endlichen Alphabet A". Jede von G erzeugte NP möge "Standard-NP" heißen.

$$
\begin{aligned}
\text{NP::=} \quad &\text{ASmArt / ASmArt Ergz}\\
\text{ASmArt::=} \quad &\text{AttrSubst / Art AttrSubst}\\
\text{AttrSubst::=} \quad &\text{Attr Subst / Subst}\\
\text{Attr::=} \quad &\text{Adj / Adj Adj / Adj C Adj}\\
\text{C::=} \quad &\text{und / , / d.h. / oder}\\
\text{Ergz::=} \quad &\text{GenAttr Rest / Rest}\\
\text{GenAttr::=} \quad &\text{ArtGen AttrSubst}\\
\text{ArtGen::=} \quad &\text{der / des}\\
\text{Rest::=} \quad &\text{Praep Symbol / Praep ASmArt / Praep ASmArt Symbol}\\
&\text{/ GenAttr / GenAttr Symbol}
\end{aligned}
$$

Adj:Adjektiv, Art:Artikel, ArtGen:Artikel im Genitiv,
ASmArt:Attributiertes Substantiv mit Artikel, Attr:Attribut,
AttrSubst:Attributiertes Substantiv, C:Konjunktion,
Ergz:Ergänzung, GenAttr:Genitivattribut, Praep:Präposition,
Subst:Substantiv

Fig.1. Grammatik G für Standard-NP

Die Zuordnung von NP zu einem mathematischen Text kann nicht nur darin bestehen, die durch G erzeugten Standard-NP im Text aufzufinden. In manchen Fällen kann der sachliche Inhalt eines Textes auch dann durch eine Standard-NP beschrieben werden, wenn zwar alle Bestandteile der NP im Text auftreten, jedoch nicht in der durch G festgelegten Reihenfolge sondern eingebettet in größere syntaktische Strukturen. Z.B. ist der sachliche Inhalt der Aussage "eine Matrix A wird symmetrisch genannt, wenn..." offenbar darstellbar durch die Standard-NP "symmetrische Matrix", die jedoch im Text nicht auftritt. Damit stellt sich die Aufgabe, in den Sätzen des Originaltextes gewisse syntaktische Strukturen aufzufinden, aus denen sich Standard-NP gewinnen lassen.

Speziell für Fachtexte der Mathematik und auch der Informatik tritt darüberhinaus das Problem auf, daß der sachliche Inhalt nicht in natürlicher Sprache sondern durch Symbole oder Formeln dargestellt sein kann, die zur Indexierung nicht unmittelbar verwendbar sind. Ein Spezialfall dieses Problems besteht darin, daß ein Begriff im Text teils durch ein Wort bzw. eine Wortgruppe, teils durch ein Symbol bezeichnet werden kann. Falls z.B. in einem mathematischen Text von einer"Gruppe G" die Rede ist, kann später eine Aussage wie "falls G abelsch ist..." auftreten. Will man hier die Standard-NP "abelsche Gruppe" erkennen, so muß vorher eine Zuordnung des Symbols "G" zum Wort "Gruppe" erfolgen. Dazu kann man benutzen, daß diese Zuordnung häufig im Text explizit erfolgt, wenn auch nicht in formalisierter Weise.

Sowohl zur Erkennung von Standard-NP als auch zur Symbolzuordnung ist eine linguistische syntaktische Analyse des Originaltextes notwendig, allerdings in vereinfachter Form, da ja keine komplette Analyse gesucht wird. Für eine solche vereinfachte Analyse bietet sich die Technik des von SNOBOL her bekannten "Mustervergleichs" für "Muster mit Alternativen" an (Griswold 1968). Ein SNOBOL-Muster ist eine Menge von Strings, dargestellt durch einen String oder einen aus Mustern durch die Operationen "Konkatenation" und "Alternation" aufgebauten Ausdruck, z.B. A (B|C) D für die Menge {ABD,ACD} als Konkatenation von A, der Alternative (B|C) und D. Beim Mustervergleich eines Musters m mit einem vorgegebenen String x wird x von links nach rechts daraufhin durchsucht, ob einer der Strings aus m als Teilstring in x auftritt. Dazu werden zunächst alle in Konkatenation auftretenden Alternativen durch Abkürzungen ersetzt, wobei eine Menge von Mustern entsteht; im Beispiel entsteht m = A y D und y = B|C. Dann werden Muster m und String x von links nach rechts zeichenweise verglichen, beginnend im Muster beim ersten Zeichen und im String bei einem Anfangszeichen, das zunächst das erste Zeichen ist. Bei Zeichengleichheit wird das jeweils nächste Zeichen in m und x verglichen; falls das Muster-Zeichen eine Abkürzung ist, wird es vorher durch die erste Möglichkeit der betreffenden Alternative ersetzt. Bei Ungleichheit der Zeichen wird an der momentan betrachteten Stelle des Musters oder links davon die nächste noch unausgenutzte Alternativmöglichkeit verwendet, wobei ggf. auch im String nach links zurückgegangen werden muß, und der Vergleich beginnt von neuem. Falls keine solche Möglichkeit existiert, ist der Mustervergleich jedenfalls für das momentan betrachtete Anfangszeichen des String erfolglos, und der gesamte Vergleich beginnt erneut bei dem auf das bisherige Anfangszeichen im

String folgende Zeichen. Das Muster "paßt" auf den String, falls es nach erfolgreichen Einzelvergleichen vollständig abgearbeitet wurde, und es "paßt nicht" in allen anderen Fällen.

Dieser Algorithmus läßt sich mit nur zwei wesentlichen Abänderungen für eine linguistische syntaktische Analyse verwenden. Die Änderungen sind

1. Statt einer Kette von Symbolen hat man im Originaltext eine Kette von Wörtern und im Muster eine Kette von "Angaben".

   Als Angaben kommen dabei in Frage

   (a) ein einzelnes deutsches Wort

   (b) ein Satzzeichen

   (c) die Bezeichnung einer Wortart (z.B.SUBST oder ADJ)

   (d) eine Bezeichnung für "irgendein Wort" oder eine nichtleere Folge irgenwelcher Wörter (Notation: ANY)

   (e) eine Bezeichnung für "irgendein Wort oder eine nichtleere Folge von Wörtern, wobei bestimmte Wörter oder Wortarten nicht auftreten dürfen". (Beispiel: ANY-SUBST für "kein Substantiv")

   (f) eine Bezeichnung für "Wort einer Wortart, ausgenommen spezielle Wörter dieser Wortart".(Beispiel: SUBST-THEOREM für "Substantiv, ausgenommen das Wort ,Theorem' ")

   Ferner ist eine Kurzschreibweise für ein- oder mehrfaches Auftreten einer Angabe zweckmäßig, z.B. (1:3)ADJ für "ein bis drei Adjektive".

   Ein Beispiel für ein solches linguistisches Muster wäre

   $$m = \big[(0{:}2)ADJ/ADJ \;\; [und/oder] \;\; ADJ\big] \; SUBST$$

mit Konkatenation von zwei Angaben: einer Alternative mit den beiden Möglichkeiten (0:2)ADJ ("null bis zweiAdjektive") und ADJ [und/oder] ADJ (zwei Adjektive, dazwischen "und" oder "oder"), und der Wortartangabe SUBST. m paßt auf einfache NP wie z.B. "Matrix", "reelle und symmetrische Matrix" usw.

2. Statt der Prüfung beim Mustervergleich, ob die jeweils nächsten Zeichen in Muster oder String gleich sind, hat man zu prüfen, ob die jeweils nächste Angabe im Muster zum jeweils nächsten Wort im Satz paßt. Im einfachsten Fall — falls die Angabe ein einzelnes deutsches Wort oder ein Satzzeichen ist - ist dieses Passen die Gleichheit zweier Strings. Im allgemeinen benötigt man jedoch ein Wörterbuch, in dem zu jedem Wort die Wortart angegeben ist.

   Das im vorliegenden Fall verwendete Wörterbuch wurde manuell erstellt und enthält z.Zt. ca. 700 Einträge. Wie üblich, enthält es

nicht alle flektierten Formen, sondern für Substantive und Adjektive
meist eine, gelegentlich zwei "Normalformen". Diese Normalformen sind
so gewählt, daß der Eintrag im Wörterbuch stets linker Teilstring einer Wortform des Textes ist; für das Wort "Atom" gibt es somit nur
eine Normalform, für "Verband" existieren VERBAND und VERBAENDE als
Normalformen. Die Reduktion flektierter Formen auf die Normalform ist
damit extrem simpel, kann allerdings auch zu Fehlern führen (z.B.
Reduktion von ALGEBRAISCH zu ALGEBRA, sofern ALGEBRAISCH kein eigener
Eintrag ist), die aber in Kauf genommen werden, zumal sich eine bessere, dann allerdings aufwendigere Reduktion jederzeit einbauen ließe.
Für Verben werden sämtliche flektierten Formen ins Wörterbuch aufgenommen, da zum einen die Reduktion z.B. infolge eingeschobener Zei-
chenfolgen aufwendig werden kann und zum anderen in mathematischen
Texten nur relativ wenige Verbformen auftreten. Wortarthomographen,
z.B. FOLGEN als Verb oder Substantiv, werden mit je einem Eintrag
pro Wortart aufgenommen. Das Wörterbuch ist alphabetisch geordnet,
der Zugriff erfolgt über eine Binärsuche.

Die Analyse erfolgt mit Hilfe eines Programmpakets, geschrieben
in FORTRAN unter Verwendung von Codeprozeduren für den verwendeten
Rechner TR440 zur Stringmanipulation, das eine extern vorzugebende
kontextfreie Grammatik (ohne rekursive Symbole) mit den genannten
"Angaben" als terminalen Symbolen verarbeitet. Dabei wird zunächst
die Satzmenge der Grammatik in Form eines Musters dargestellt und
dieses Muster wird anschließend nach dem angegebenen Algorithmus auf
einen Satz des Originaltextes angewendet. Der Originaltext wird dabei
anhand von Trennzeichen wie Komma oder Blank in Wörter zerlegt. Als
Ergebnis des Mustervergleichs erhält man, falls das Muster paßte,
diejenige Wortfolge aus dem Satz, auf die es paßte, sowie die erfolg-
reiche Variante des Musters. Ferner besteht die Möglichkeit, anhand
einer an die Angaben des Musters anzufügenden Numerierung Wörter oder
Wortfolgen aus dem Abschnitt des Satzes, auf den das Muster paßte,
zur weiteren Verwendung herauszugreifen. Z.B. paßt das Muster

m = ART SUBST:2 ANY-VERB VERB ADJ:1 , [wenn/falls]

auf "eine Matrix A heißt symmetrisch, wenn" und greift die Wörter
"symmetrisch" (unter Nr.1) und "Matrix" (unter Nr.2) heraus. Auf
diese Weise können Standard-NP erzeugt werden.

Der beschriebene Algorithmus zum Mustervergleich ist, wie man
leicht sieht, einer links-rechts-top-down-Analyse im Sinne von
Knuth (Knuth 1971) gleichwertig. Als mögliche Vorteile der Technik
des Mustervergleichs gegenüber den herkömmlichen Techniken zur syntaktischen Analyse formaler Sprachen wären zu nennen

1. Der Mustervergleich stützt sich statt auf das Produktionensystem auf die Satzmenge einer Grammatik. Er eignet sich daher vor allem für empirisch gewonnene, endliche Satzmengen, die, wenigstens zunächst, wenig Regelmäßigkeit im Satzbau zeigen, sodaß das Aufstellen eines Produktionensystems (noch) nicht lohnend erscheint.

2. Der Mustervergleich ist nicht auf das Vorliegen spezieller Eigenschaften des Analysekontextes, wie sie etwa bei LR(k)-Grammatiken ausgenutzt werden, angewiesen.

3. Die Technik des Mustervergleiches ist an den Wunsch angepaßt, Abschnitte eines Satzes zu analysieren, ohne die Lage der Abschnitte im Satz vorher zu kennen und ohne eine Grammatik für den vollständigen Satz zu besitzen. Mit Hilfe des Musterangaben vom Typ (d) oder (e) können ferner unzusammenhängende Abschnitte eines Satzes analysiert werden.

Ergebnisse des Verfahrens liegen bisher für die Symbolzuordnung vor. Hierfür wurden die folgenden Muster aufgestellt und getestet (die Zuordnungen sind durch Pfeile ausgedrückt, F bedeutet "Symbol", ε ist der Nullstring, NP ist durch die Grammatik G aus Fig.1 definiert):

1. NP $[ε/mit/als]$ F

   Beispiele: symmetrische Matrix A

   falls wir die Matrix mit A bezeichnen

2. NP VERB $[ε/PERSPRON]$ $[mit/als]$ F   (PERSPRON: Personalpronomen)

   Beispiele: die Koeffizientenmatrix bezeichnen wir mit K

   die Koeffizientenmatrix sei mit K bezeichnet

3. VERB F $[ε/als]$ NP

   Beispiel: sei x eine Zeichenkette über dem Alphabet A

   sei A als Matrix darstellbar

4. F VERB $[ε/als]$ NP

   Beispiel: A sei eine Matrix

   Dieses Muster paßt allerdings auch z.B. auf den Satz

"Jedes Ideal aus S̲ ist eine Potenz des Primideals q"

mit der falschen Zuordnung von "S" zu "Potenz". Dieser Fehler kann vermieden werden, wenn man beachtet, daß "S" hier zur Präpositionalphrase "aus S" gehört.

5. C F [ε/als] NP

    Beispiel: A sei eine Matrix und K̲ ein Körper

Nach den bisherigen Tests dürften mit diesen Mustern die wichtigsten syntaktischen Strukturen erfaßt sein, durch die in mathematischen Texten die Symbolzuordnung ausgedrückt wird.

Ferner ergab sich, daß einem Symbol auch innerhalb desselben Textes im allgemeinen mehrere NP zugeordnet werden. Z.B. werden im Text (Hasse 1931)

" Die Elemente A aus S mit einer Ordnungszahl a > O bilden ein zweiseitiges Ideal q. q ist Primideal. q ist Hauptideal"

dem Symbol q nacheinander zugeordnet "zweiseitiges Ideal", "Primideal" und "Hauptideal". Diese verschiedenen Begriffe für q hängen, wie das Beispiel zeigt, semantisch eng zusammen. Unter der Voraussetzung, daß ein Autor nicht dasselbe Symbol für völlig verschiedene Begriffe verwendet, könnte die Symbolzuordnung damit einen Zugang zur automatischen Erkennung begrifflicher Beziehungen in mathematischen Texten eröffnen.

LITERATUR

Griswold 1968   R.E.Griswold, J.F.Poage, I.P.Polonsky, The SNOBOL4 Programming Language, Chap.2 ("Pattern matching"). Prentice-Hall, Englewood Cliffs, N.J., 1968

Hasse 1931   H.Hasse, Über p-adische Schiefkörper und ihre Bedeutung für die Arithmetik hyperkomplexer Zahlsysteme. Mathematische Annalen 104, S.495, 1931

Knuth 1971   D.E.Knuth, Top-Down Syntax Analysis. Acta Informatica 1, S.79-110, 1971.

Salton 1968   G.Salton, Automatic Information Organization and Retrieval. McGraw-Hill, New York, 1968.

LINGUISTISCHE ALGORITHMEN ZUR DEFLEXION ALS MITTEL ZUM AUTOMATISCHEN

INDEXIEREN IM DEUTSCHEN

Gerda Schott

Das automatische Indexieren von Texten gehört trotz aller schon geleisteten Vorarbeiten immer noch zu den unzureichend gelösten Problemen der nichtnumerischen Datenverarbeitung. In den verschiedenen Sprachen sind die Problemstellungen vom linguistischen Standpunkt aus jeweils verschieden je nach Flexionsreichtum, Wortbildungsmorphologie und Syntax. Bisher gibt es in keiner der gängigen europäischen Sprachen eine verläßliche und zugleich effiziente Methode zum automatischen Indexieren auf linguistischer Grundlage und zwar aus folgenden Gründen:

1. Noch verfügen wir über kein Verfahren der automatischen Wortartenbestimmung, um möglichst schnell zu den potentiell wichtigsten Informationsträgern zu kommen.

2. Es fehlt bisher an einer verläßlichen Syntaxanalyse, bei der auf umfangreiche Informationen aus einem Wörterbuch verzichtet werden könnte.

3. Statistische Verfahren entbinden nicht von der aufwendigen Arbeit, einen Thesaurus zusammenzustellen.

Die hier beschriebenen Algorithmen lösen ein Teilproblem des automatischen Indexierens, die Deflexion der deutschen Substantive unter Annahme folgender Voraussetzungen:

1. Substantive enthalten von allen Wortarten potentiell die meiste sachliche Information.

2. Bis zu einer möglichen Abschaffung der Großschreibung lassen sich im Deutschen Substantive leicht und schnell automatisch erfassen und zwar

   a) bei bereits in Groß- und Kleinschreibung auf Datenträgern vorliegenden Texten auf direktem Wege.

   b) bei noch nicht auf Datenträgern vorliegenden Texten durch ein Kennzeichen für die Großschreibung, das bei späterer Umstellung auf Kleinschreibung oder bei evtl. Einsatz von Beleglesern ignoriert werden kann.

Durch die sofortige Erfassung der Substantive lassen sich die im Deutschen vorkommenden Überschneidungen der Flexive ER, ES, E, EN bei den zahlenmäßig häufigsten Wortarten (Substantiv, Adjektiv, Verb, Pronomen) ausscheiden und es kann damit eine nicht zu unterschätzende Zahl von Wortartenhomographen vom Typ Zahl/en - zahlen, Folge/n - folgen, Laut/en - laut/en von vornherein ausgeschlossen werden.

Je nach Arbeitsziel, erwarteten Ergebnissen und Effizienzwünschen lassen sich verschiedene Algorithmen formulieren. Alle zu beschreibenden Algorithmen haben zum Ziel, die flektierten Substantive auf ihre Standardform (Nominativ Singular) zurückzuführen.

Algorithmus I

Dieser Algorithmus ist auf Vollständigkeit angelegt, d.h. er erfaßt alle Wörter der deutschen Sprache einschließlich Ausnahmen und Fremdwörtern [1]. Folgende Teile werden dazu benötigt:

a) Ein Wörterbuch

b) Ein Reduktionsalgorithmus, durch den ein Wort schrittweise auf seine Nominativform reduziert wird.

c) Eine Prüftabelle zur Verhinderung von falschen Reduktionen.

Die Ziele dieses Algorithmus lassen sich in 3 Punkten zusammenfassen:

a) Eine eindeutige und richtige Reduktion flektierter Substantive auf ihre Standardform.

b) die Zahl der erforderlichen Wörterbuchvergleiche so niedrig wie möglich zu halten

c) die automatische Erkennung von Homographen im Flexionsbereich z.B. Polen - Pole/n - Pol/en.

d) die Verhinderung von falschen Reduktionen

Als Ergebnisse erhält man die Information,

a) ob ein im Wörterbuch in seiner Standardform enthaltenes Wort flektiert oder unflektiert in einem beliebigen Text vorkommt oder nicht.

b) in welchen Kasus ein reduziertes oder nichtreduziertes gefundenes Wort syntaktisch verwendet sein kann.

c) daß im Wörterbuch nicht gefundene Wörter in der Regel auf die Nominativform reduziert sind.

Wörterbuch: Ein von einem Fachmann für sein Spezialgebiet zusammengestelltes Wörterbuch kann dazu verwendet werden, entsprechende Fachtexte auf das Vorkommen der darin verzeichneten Wörter zu prüfen. Die ohne Deflexion zu erwartenden Wörterbucheinträge liegen zwischen 2 und 5 Formen pro Wort. Die richtige automatische Reduktion der flektierten Wortformen bedeutet eine Platz- und Arbeitsersparnis bei der Zusammenstellung eines Wörterbuches. Außerdem wird es übersichtlicher, da andernfalls die zu einem Wort gehörigen flektierten Wortformen an voneinander entfernten Stellen stehen können, was eine Handhabung durch den Benutzer erheblich erschweren würde, vor allem bei gewünschten Neueinträgen.

Das Wörterbuch enthält neben der Standardform mindestens 2, maximal 4 Informationen, die den Flexionstyp des betreffenden Wortes charakterisieren. Es genügen 2 flektierte Formen, der Genitiv Singular und der Nominativ Plural, um alle anderen flektierten Wortformen abzuleiten. Aufgrund des Zusammenfalls verschiedener Kasus in einer Wortform ließen sich für den Singular und Plural getrennt jeweils verschiedene Flexionstypen aufstellen, in denen alle Wörter der deutschen Sprache erfaßt werden können. Die Flexionstypen ergeben sich aus den Flexiven und deren Verteilung in den einzelnen Kasus, wie aus folgender Tabelle zu ersehen ist:

T a b e l l e 1

Tabelle der Substantivflexive:

SINGULAR:

Wort	Dat	Akk	Gen	FTS
Ort	ø	ø	(E)S	1
Verhältnis	ø	ø	SES	2
Knabe	N	N	N	3
Mensch	EN	EN	EN	4
Zeitung	ø	ø	ø	5
Buchstabe	N	N	NS	6
Interessante	N	ø	N	7
Herz	EN	ø	ENS	8
Ferien				0

PLURAL:

Wort	NAG	DAT	FTP
Garten	ø	ø	1
Auto	S	S	2
Muskel	N	N	3
Zeitung	EN	EN	4
Arbeiterin	NEN	NEN	5
Segel	ø	N	6
Tag	E	EN	7
Verhältnis	SE	SEN	8
Leib	ER	ERN	9
Fossil	IEN	IEN	10
Eisen			0

Erklärungen:

FTS = Flexionstyp Singular
FTP = Flexionstyp Plural
NAG = Nominativ/Genitiv/Akkusativ
Dat = Dativ
Der Nominativ Singular ist stets durch das Null-Morphem (ø) charakterisiert.
Bei den Pluralflexionstypen 1, 6, 7, 9 kann Umlaut (vgl. Gärten, Äpfel, Drähte, Wälder), bei den Pluralflexionstypen 7 und 9 Wechsel von ß - SS auftreten (vgl. Riß - Risse).

Ein Wörterbucheintrag für ein Wort hat folgende grammatische Information:

1. Angabe über den Flexionstyp im Singular (FTS), max.8, s.Tabelle 1
2. Angabe über den Flexionstyp im Plural (FTP), max.10
3. Angabe über den flexionsbedingten Umlaut (U), Beispiel: Betrag-Beträge
4. Angabe über den Wechsel (W) von ß - SS, Beispiel: Paß - Pässe

Ist ein Wort in nur einem Numerus (Singularetantum, Pluraletantum) vorhanden, so wird nur der vorhandene Flexionstyp angegeben, der fehlende Flexionstyp vertritt den fehlenden Numerus. Das Schema, nach dem die Wörter im Wörterbuch kodiert werden, sieht folgendermaßen aus:

Wort	FTS	FTP	U	W
Buch	1	9	1	
Paß	1	7	1	1
Ferien		1		
Eisen	1			
Thema	1	11		
Themata	11	1		

Wörter aus anderen Sprachen, Fremdwörter vornehmlich aus dem Griechischen und Lateinischen oder unregelmäßige Pluralbildungen von der Art Saal - Säle werden kodiert, indem die vom allgemeinen Schema abweichende Pluralform mit einem entsprechenden Vermerk ins Wörterbuch aufgenommen wird. Dadurch werden gerade für die wissenschaftliche Sprache unentbehrliche Fremdwörter vom Typ Matrix - Matrices, Genus - Genera, Numerus - Numeri erfaßt, bei denen sich aus ökonomischen Gründen keine Einordnung in das allgemeine Schema empfahl.

Der Reduktionsalgorithmus:

Der Reduktionsalgorithmus setzt sich aus folgenden Teiloperationen zusammen, auf deren Ergebnisse im Verlauf der Reduktion immer wieder zurückgegriffen wird.

1. Wörterbuchsuche (binär)
2. Umlauterkennung und Umlautreduktion
3. Trennung eines oder mehrerer Buchstaben vom Analysewort
4. Anhängung von Buchstabenfolgen an ein vorher reduziertes Wort
   zur Herstellung der Standardform

Der Reduktionsvorgang beginnt mit dem Wörterbuchvergleich, bei negativem Ausgang der Wörterbuchsuche wird vorhandener Umlaut reduziert und zwar bis zum 5. Buchstaben vom Wortende gerechnet. Aufgrund der morphophonologischen Bildungsgesetze des Deutschen ist ein flexionsbedingter Umlaut nur bis zum maximal 5.Buchstaben vom Wortende der Standardform gerechnet zu erwarten (Äpfel). Alle vor dieser Position liegenden Umlaute sind nicht flexionsbedingt und für die Reduktion ohne Bedeutung. Liegt kein Umlaut vor oder war nach reduziertem Umlaut die Wörterbuchsuche ohne Erfolg, wird der Reduktionsvorgang buchstabenweise bei der Flexionsendung fortgesetzt. Für eine Reduktion der Flexive kommen nur 4 Buchstaben in Frage:S, E, R, N.

Folgendes Flußdiagramm soll den Ablauf verdeutlichen:

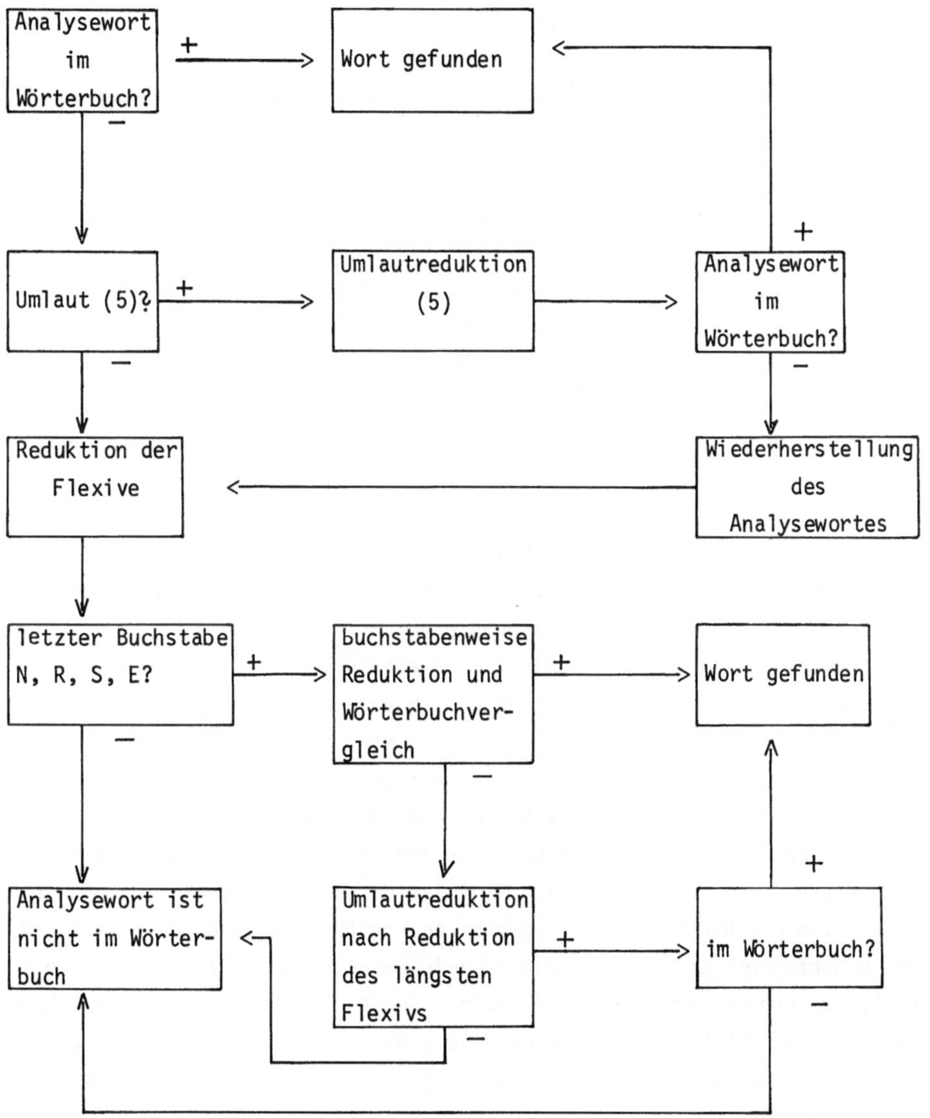

Für die Reduktion der Flexive entstehen folgende Bäume:

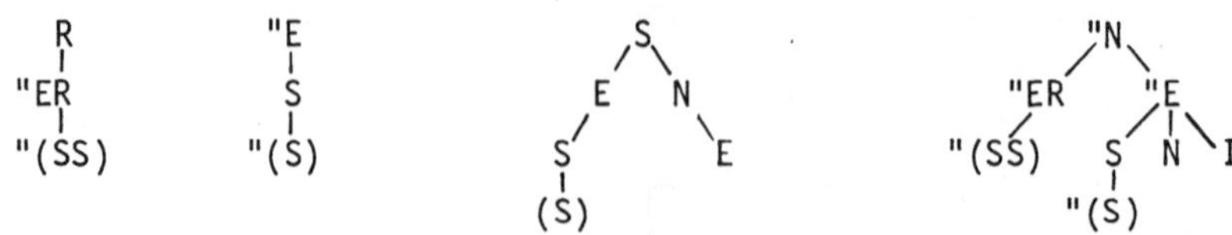

<u>Zur Notation</u>: Das Zeichen " bedeutet, daß bei Wörtern mit den angegebenen Teilbäumen Umlaut auftreten kann. Auf die in Klammern stehenden Grapheme S bzw. SS wird nur abgeprüft, sie werden nicht reduziert.

Fremdwörter vom Typ Radius-Radien, Gremium-Gremien, Basis-Basen, Epos-Epen, Thema-Themen werden durch Reduktion des Flexivs EN und durch Anhängen der Graphemfolgen US, UM, IS, OS, A, O reduziert. Die maximale Zahl der Wörterbuchvergleiche beträgt 10, wenn die genannten Arten von Fremdwörtern durch den Reduktionsalgorithmus behandelt werden. Wenn dagegen die Pluralform solcher Wörter ins Wörterbuch aufgenommen wird, liegt die maximale Zahl der Wörterbuchvergleiche bei 4, der Durchschnitt bei ca. 1,6 (je nach Art des Textes) infolge der in Texten häufigen Nominativform und den mit dieser identischen Kasūs.

<u>Die Prüfung auf Richtigkeit der Reduktion</u>:

Je größer der Wortschatz ist, umso größer wird auch die Wahrscheinlichkeit von Fehlreduktionen, da die natürliche Endung eines Wortes mit einem Flexiv zusammenfallen kann. So könnte Zähler auf Zahl, Kurs auf Kur, Schlösser auf Schlosser, Buche auf Buch reduziert und in einem Wörterbuch gefunden werden. Über die Verschiedenartigkeit und Häufigkeit theoretisch möglicher fehlerhafter Reduktionen bei gleichzeitigem Auffinden des Restwortes im Wörterbuch vor allem beim Umgang mit großen Textmengen sollten keine Illusionen entstehen. Daher empfiehlt sich eine Prüfung auf Richtigkeit der erfolgten Reduktion mit Hilfe von 2 Kasuskombinationstabellen. Diese Tabellen, jeweils nach Singular und Plural getrennt, haben als Parameter das durch die Reduktion einer gegebenen Wortform abgetrennte Flexiv und den bei dem im Wörterbuch gefundenen Wort verzeichneten Flexionstyp. In richtig analysierten Fällen ergibt sich die Kasusbombination des Suchwortes, d.h. jene Kasūs des Singular und/oder des Plural, in denen eine gegebene Wortform bei entsprechender syntaktischer Verwendung vorkommen kann. In falsch analysierten Fällen ergibt sich keine Kasuskombination.

T a b e l l e   2

Kasuskombinationstabellen:

SINGULAR:

FT \ FLX	ø	(E)S	N	EN	NS	SES	ENS
1	6	2					
2	5			3			2
3	6					2	
4	1		7				
5	1			7			
6	8						
7	5		9				
8	1		4		2		
0	Pluraletantum						

PLURAL:

FT \ FLX	ø	S	N	EN	E	ER	SE	SEN	NEN	ERN	IEN
1	8										
2		8									
3			8								
4				8							
5									8		
6	0		3								
7				3	0						
8							0	3			
9						0				3	
10											8
0	Singularetantum										

Die sich ergebenden Kasusiombinationen sind:

0 Nominativ/Genitiv/Akkusativ
1 Nominativ
2 Genitiv
3 Dativ
4 Dativ/Akkusativ
5 Nominativ/Akkusativ
6 Genitiv/Dativ
7 Genitiv/Dativ/Akkusativ
8 Nominativ/Genitiv/Dativ/Akkusativ
9 Genitiv/Dativ

Die Behandlung von Sonderfällen:

1. Homographen der Standardform bei verschiedenem Plural (Bank-Bänke-Banken) werden
   durch Doppelanalyse und Umlautprüfung richtig analysiert.

2. Satzanfänge, die aufgrund der Großschreibung als potentielle Substantive aufgefaßt werden, können anhand einer Negativliste (bestehend aus den gängigen Präpo-
   sitionen, Artikeln, Konjunktionen) fast restlos ausgeschaltet werden. Wo dennoch
   ein anderes Wort als ein Substantiv reduziert wird (Kein/er, Ander/e), entstehen
   keine Fehlreduktionen.

3. Der in keine Regel zu fassende alternative Gebrauch von ES und S im Genitiv Singular, wird als ein den Genitiv markierendes Flexiv aufgefaßt. Die Reduktion jedoch erfolgt buchstabenweise, wodurch ein sonst nötiger 2. Wörterbucheintrag vermieden wird.

4. Homographen im Flexionsbereich, die nicht durch die Kasuskombinationstabelle erfaßt werden, können durch Doppelanalyse der Flexive ER, ERN, E, EN vollständig
   reduziert und damit automatisch erfaßt werden. Beispiele:
   Fächern - Fächer/n - Fäch/er/n   Kasten - Kaste/n

Solcher Art Homographen sind äußerst selten und wegen ihrer semantischen Entfernung voneinander für Indexierungszwecke praktisch ohne Bedeutung.

5. Das Flexiv E des rudimentären Dativ bleibt wegen seiner Bedeutungslosigkeit für Indexierungszwecke unberücksichtigt. Der Algorithmus wurde anhand von Beispielen aus dem rückläufigen Wörterbuch von Mater [2] getestet. Er wurde in FORTRAN IV kompatibel programmiert. Die Rechenzeit lag für 1000 Wortformen bei 28 sec.[1] (Fußnote s.S.10)

Algorithmus II:

Der 2.Algorithmus ist eine vereinfachte Form des beschriebenen Algorithmus, bei dem Effizienzerwägungen und Fehlersicherheit im Vordergrund stehen. Fehlersicherheit, Effizienz, Übersichtlichkeit und Wartung des Programms sind bei Algorithmen, die für praktische Zwecke Verwendung finden sollen, von erheblicher Bedeutung. Wie im Algorithmus I enthält das Wörterbuch Substantive in der Standardform mit den beschriebenen Eintragungen. Der Reduktionsalgorithmus kann wie folgt vereinfacht werden:

a) Doppelanalyse zur Auffindung verborgener Homographen kann wegen des äußerst seltenen Vorkommens derselben entfallen.

b) Fremdwörter, deren Standardform nicht allein durch Reduktion von Flexiven, sondern auch durch Anhängen verschiedener Graphemfolgen erhalten wird, werden aufgrund der zeitraubenden Operationen nicht algorithmisch behandelt, vielmehr wird die Pluralform dieser Wörter ins Wörterbuch aufgenommen, was eine nur unwesentliche Erweiterung des Wörterbuches bedeutet. Da solche Pluralformen auf -EN enden und dieses Flexiv zugleich das häufigste in der Substantivflexion darstellt, müßte jedes auf das Graphem -EN endende und nicht im Wörterbuch enthaltene Wort einer Reihe zeitraubender Operationen unterworfen werden, bevor man die Information erhält, daß das Suchwort nicht im Wörterbuch verzeichnet ist. Je größer also die zu erwartende Zahl der nicht im Wörterbuch stehenden reduzierten Wörter ist, umso größer muß das Interesse sein, den Reduktionsalgorithmus kurz zu halten.

c) Der Reduktionsalgorithmus wird vereinfacht, wenn man sich von vornherein auf die Schreibung SS statt ß einigt. Damit entfällt auch ein Kodierungsmerkmal im Wörterbuch.

d) Im Plural umlautende Substantive sind im Fachwortschatz seltener und können ebenfalls ins Wörterbuch als volle Form nach dem gleichen Verfahren aufgenommen werden wie die Fremdwörter und Ausnahmen. Damit entfällt ein weiteres Kodierungsmerkmal.

e) Die Prüfung auf Richtigkeit der Reduktion wird durch den Verzicht auf Kasuskombinationen vereinfacht, da diese für Zwecke des automatischen Indexierens oder andere Retrievalmethoden ohne Belang sind und allenfalls für automatische Syntaxanalyse benötigt werden können.

Nach Reduktion des Suchwortes und dem Auffinden des reduzierten Wortes im Wörterbuch wird anhand der reduzierten Flexive und der für diese zulässigen Flexionsty-

pen eine Prüfung auf Richtigkeit vorgenommen. Danach sind jeweils für den Singular
und Plural bei den einzelnen Flexiven folgende Flexionstypen zugelassen:

<u>SINGULAR:</u>

<u>Flexive</u>	<u>Flexionstyp</u>
* $\emptyset$	1,2,5,7,8
s	1
* ses	2
n	3,6,7
en	4,8
* ns	6
* ens	8

<u>PLURAL:</u>

<u>Flexiv</u>	<u>Flexionstyp</u>
* $\emptyset$	1,6
s	2
n	3,6
en	4,7
* nen	5
e	7
* se	8
* sen	8
er	9
ern	9
* ien	10

Bei den mit * bezeichneten Flexiven erübrigt sich nach bisherigen Beobachtungen
eine Prüfung auf Richtigkeit der Reduktion, weil in diesen Fällen m.E. keine Fehlreduktionen auftreten können. Die Effizienz des Reduktionsalgorithmus wird dadurch erhöht, der Ausdruck wesentlich vereinfacht.

<u>Algorithmus III:</u>
Dieser Algorithmus entstand aus der Überlegung, eine Deflexion der Substantive
durchzuführen, ohne sich der Mühe unterziehen zu müssen, ein Wörterbuch mit gramma-
tischen Angaben zu versehen. Das Wörterbuch besteht in diesem Falle nur aus Substan-
tiven in der Standardform. Die Kriterien zur Auffindung des richtigen Wortes sind:
1. Reduktion des Suchwortes um ein mögliches Endungsmorphem
2. Reduktion des Suchwortes um vorhandenen Umlaut
3. Gleichzeitiges Auffinden des Restwortes im Wörterbuch
Der Reduktionsalgorithmus ist im Vergleich zu den zuvor beschriebenen um 2/3 kürzer,
wesentlich übersichtlicher und einfacher. Beobachtungen an dem zu erwartenden Wortschatz bei Spezialgebieten berechtigen zu der Annahme, daß mit dem Wegfall der Ko-
dierungsarbeit und somit auch der Prüfungsmöglichkeit auf Richtigkeit der Reduktion
im Vergleich zum Algorithmus I theoretisch die Fehleranfälligkeit größer ist, praktisch aber so niedrig liegen dürfte, daß sie nicht ins Gewicht fällt. Die Ergebnisse
des Testlaufs an 1500 getesteten Wörtern aus der Mathematik und Informatik waren
fehlerfrei. 1000 Wörter wurden in 17 sec. reduziert, wobei programmiertechnische Ef-
fizienzüberlegungen noch weitere Verbesserungen der Rechenzeit erwarten lassen.

<u>Verwendungsmöglichkeiten der Algorithmen:</u>
Die Algorithmen können je nach Arbeitsziel in Informationssystemen verwendet werden,
da sich überall bei nichtnumerischer Datenverarbeitung das Problem der Deflexion
stellt.
1. Prüfung eines Textes (z.B. Abstract, Zeitschriftenartikel, Gesetzestext) auf das
   Vorkommen einer gegebenen Liste von Stichwörtern. Die flektierten Substantive

werden richtig reduziert, die nicht als Stichwörter im Text vorkommenden Substantive werden überwiegend automatisch auf die Standardform reduziert.

2. In gleicher Weise wie eine Stichwortliste von Fachwörtern kann eine Liste von substantivischen Trivialwörtern von der Weiterverarbeitung eines Textes ausgeschlossen werden. Der danach verbleibende Wortschatz wird die meisten potentiellen noch nicht als Stichwörter erfaßten Fachtermini enthalten.

3. Da die Reduktion der in keiner Liste enthaltenen Wörter meist auf die Standardform erfolgt, können die so erhaltenen Substantive zum Aufbau eines Thesaurus verwendet werden, imdem relevante Fachwörter von einem menschlichen Bearbeiter (am besten im on-line-Verfahren) angegeben werden. Die gelegentlich über die Standardform hinaus reduzierten Wörter lassen sich durch einige phononogische Regeln auf ein Minimum beschränken und zur richtigen Ergänzung schnell erfassen.

4. Die Algorithmen können mit einem weiteren Algorithmus zur automatischen Kompositazerlegung verwendet werden, da Komposita selbstverständlich auch flektiert vorkommen, wobei mindestens eines ihrer Bestandteile gewöhnlich bereits als Stichwort in einer Stichwortliste enthalten ist.

5. Noch wichtiger sind in der Fachsprache die Folgen von Adjektiv(en) und Substantiv. Die Algorithmen können zur schnellen Erkennung von bestimmten häufigen Arten von Stichphrasen vom Typ $\left\{ {Adjektive \atop Substantiv} \right\}_{Kasus} \cdot \{Artikel, Präposition\} \cdot Substantiv_{Kasus}$ verwendet werden.

Literatur

[1] G.SCHOTT, Automatic Analysis of Inflectional Morphemes in German Nonns. Acta Informatica 1, 360-374 (1972)

[2] E.MATER, Rückläufiges Wörterbuch der deutschen Gegenwartssprache. Leipzig 1965

[3] D.MAAS, Homographie und maschinelle Sprachübersetzung. Beiträge zur Linguistik und Informationsverarbeitung, Heft 21 (1971) S.7-35

[4] V.G.ADMONI, Stroj sovremennogo nemeckogo jazyka (Der deutsche Sprachbau) 2.Auflage. Moskau, Leningrad 1966

[5] G.SALTON, Automatic Information, Organization and Retrieval, Mc Graw Hill 1968

[6] G.SALTON, Recent Studies in Automatic Text Analysis and Document Retrieval. Journal of the Association for Computing Machinery, Vol.20, No.2, April 1973, S.258-78

[7] G.LUSTIG, Probleme der Textverarbeitung bei der automatischen Indexierung. Bericht über die Tagung im Rahmen der 100-Jahr-Feier der Rheinisch-Westfälischen Technischen Hochschule Aachen. Hrsg.Helmut Schanze, S.130-142

[8] G.LUSTIG, Methoden der automatischen Indexierung. In: Sprachliche Ansätze im Informations- und Dokumentationsbereich. Arbeitstagung des Komitees Automation der Deutschen Gesellschaft für Dokumentation. Frankfurt/M. 1970. Nachrichten für Dokumentation, Beiheft 20, (1970), S.108-117

[9] H.H.ZIMMERMANN, Zur Auflösung von Mehrdeutigkeiten bei einer maschinellen Analyse des Deutschen. Beiträge zur Linguistik und Informationsverarbeitung, Heft 21 (1971) S.36-49.

[10] J.ERBEN, Abriß der deutschen Grammatik, München 1966, 9.Auflage

[11] DONNA HOLMBERG-DICKSON, Wortstammretrieval: Eine Studie zur gegenwärtigen Lage in Praxis und Forschung. Telefunken Computer GmbH, Best.-Nr.440. ZZ.12, Konstanz 1972

---

[1] Diese Version wurde von Herrn Mok-Kong Shen vom Leibniz-Rechenzentrum der Bayerischen Akademie der Wissenschaften, München, programmiert.

KOMPETENZ- ODER PERFORMANZMODELLIERUNG?
<u>EINIGE PSYCHOLINGUISTISCHE VORÜBERLEGUNGEN</u>
<u>ZUR KONSTRUKTION VON DIALOGSYSTEMEN UND -SPRACHEN</u>

Peter Schefe

Hinter der Fragestellung verbirgt sich ein Komplex von Problemen, deren Diskussion mit vielen Mißverständnissen verbunden war. Eine Lösung
aller dieser Probleme kann hier nicht gegeben werden. Ziel dieses Bei-
trags ist, auf bestimmte Tendenzen im Problembereich Informatik - Linguistik - Psychologie und deren Konvergenz hinzuweisen, diese Entwicklung mit eigenen Erfahrungen zu korrelieren und einige allgemeine Fol-
gerungen für die Konstruktion von Dialogsystemen bzw. -sprachen daraus
zu ziehen.

1. <u>Entwicklungstendenzen im Problembereich Informatik - Linguistik -</u> <u>Psychologie</u>

J. Mey sagte 1971 voraus, daß innerhalb der 'Computational Linguistics'
die Syntaxherrschaft der sechziger Jahre abgelöst werde durch eine mehr
semantisch orientierte Modellbildung in den siebziger Jahren. Betrachtet man einige neuere Veröffentlichungen, so scheint sich dieser Trend
sowohl in der Entwicklung der linguistischen Theorie (Lakoff 1960,
McCawley 1968 u.a.) als auch in Implementierungen (Quillian 1969, Winograd 1970, Carbonell 1970, Wexler 1970, Kaplan 1972, Simmons 1972) zu
bestätigen. Während hier der Entwurf semantischer Netzwerke vorwiegend
auf Quillian zurückgeht, entwickelte sich die sogenannte Generative Semantik in der Kritik an Chomskys Generativer Syntax. Diese Hinwendung
zur Semantik scheint nicht ohne Rückwirkungen auf die Konzeption der
Syntax. So ist die Benutzung endlicher Zustandsgrammatiken bemerkenswert.

Dem neuen Trend entspricht eine mehr oder weniger explizite Abkehr von
der Chomskyschen Theorie der Generativen Transformationsgrammatik[1),
die eine Fülle von Publikationen "erzeugt" hat. Die Kritik entzündet
sich vor allem an
   1) Chomskys grundlegender Unterscheidung von Sprachkompetenz(-kennt-
      nis) und Sprachperformanz(-verwendung) sowie der damit korrespon-
      dierenden Unterscheidung von Grammatikalität und Akzeptabilität,

---

1) Vgl. auch M.H. O'Halley, What Do Standard Transformational Grammars
   Produce? - A Computational Study, In: Int.J.Man-Machine Stud. 1973
   (5), S. 137-202.

verbunden jeweils mit der Abwertung des zuletzt genannten als
Forschungsgegenstand und

2) seiner grundlegenden Unterscheidung von syntaktischer Tiefenstruktur, in der die semantische Interpretation lokalisiert wird,
und syntaktischer Oberflächenstruktur, die lediglich phonologisch
relevant ist.

Die Kritik kommt aus verschiedenen Richtungen, sie konvergiert in der
Ablehnung einer isolierten, arbiträren Syntax. Die Beschränkung der linguistischen Aktivitäten auf die Konstruktion prinzipiell arbiträrer Re-
gelsysteme birgt die Gefahr, daß die Sprachwirklichkeit (Kommunikation,
Kognition) vernachlässigt wird.

Zur Untersuchung der Sprache als Mittel der Kommunikation und Kognition
gehört das Studium der Sprache
1. im sozialen Kontext (Labov 1971 u.a.),
2. als psychischer Prozeß:
2.1. mittels psychologischer Tests nach Vorgabe eines theoretischen
Grammatikmodells
2.1.1 im Bereich natürlicher Sprachen (Miller 1964 u.a.)
2.1.2 im Bereich künstlicher Sprachen bzw. Programmiersprachen (Sime et
al. 1973),
2.2. mittels Simulation (Winograd 1970, Kaplan 1972 u.a.)
Ich werde mich im folgenden vornehmlich mit 2.2 beschäftigen.

2. <u>Die Kompetenz-Performanz-Dichotomie</u>

Die Verwirrung in der Kompetenz-Performanz-Diskussion scheint z.T. auf
Chomsky selbst zurückzugehen[2]. Daß ein explizites Regelsystem, welches
Sätzen Strukturbeschreibungen zuordnet, jenseits auch potentieller Be-
wußtheit liegen und gerade deshalb besonders interessant sein soll, wie

---

2) So heißt es in den "Vorüberlegungen" zur Entwicklung seines sogenannten Standardmodells von 1965: "Offenbar hat sich jeder Sprecher einer
Sprache eine generative Grammatik vollständig angeeignet, die seine
Sprachkenntnis ausdrückt. Das will nicht heißen, daß er sich der Regeln der Grammatik bewußt ist, nicht einmal, daß er sie sich bewußt
machen kann, und auch nicht, daß seine Angaben über seine intuitive
Sprachkenntnis notwendig richtig sind. Jede interessante generative
Grammatik wird es größtenteils mit mentalen Prozessen zu tun haben,
die weit jenseits der Stufe aktueller oder selbst potentieller Bewußtheit liegen; es ist weiterhin ganz augenscheinlich, daß die Berichte und Ansichten eines Sprechers über sein Verhalten und seine
Kompetenz irrig sein können. Somit stellt eine generative Grammatik
den Versuch dar, das zu spezifizieren, was der Sprecher wirklich
kennt, und nicht das, was er über seine Kenntnis berichten kann."
(Übersetzung 1969, S. 19f)

Chomsky meint, ist schwer nachvollziehbar. Die Nicht-Stimmigkeit geht
letztlich auf eine idealistische Hypostasierung der generativen Grammatik zurück; die Kompetenz ist in diesem Sinne empirisch nicht überprüfbar. Was der Sprecher "wirklich kennt", kann er offenbar nur dann kommunizieren, wenn er Chomskys Grammatiktheorie "kennt" und akzeptiert.
Eine weitere verwirrende Implikation dieses Ansatzes ist, daß die Grammatik prinzipiell arbiträr konzipiert wird, also keine Simulation des
Sprecher-Hörers liefern soll. So erklärt Chomsky den Satz

"the man who the boy who the students recognized pointed out is a
friend of mine" (1969, S. 22)

für grammatisch, obwohl kein Native Speaker ihn als einen Satz seiner
Sprache akzeptieren würde, weil er die Möglichkeiten des normalen
menschlichen Perzeptionsmechanismus übersteigt. Man kann daraus schließen: er ist lediglich als linguistisches Konstrukt analysierbar und somit einer Kunstsprache zuzurechnen. Nach Chomsky liegt dieser Satz im
Bereich der Sprachkompetenz. Die Kompliziertheit des Sachverhalts erfordert m.E. eine Differenzierung der Kompetenz. Ich unterscheide:

(I) _Performanz_ ist die Verwendung von Sprachstrukturen (Ausdrucksgestalten) in konkreten Situationen.

(II) Die _kommunikative Kompetenz_[3] ist die Fähigkeit, Sprachstrukturen
im Sinne von (I) zu verwenden und ihre kommunikative Adäquatheit
(Akzeptabilität) zu beurteilen. Dies Vermögen kann verschiedene
Grade der Bewußtheit haben.

(III) Die _logische Kompetenz_ impliziert bezüglich der Sprache, daß auch
Sätze wie der oben zitierte, allgemein, Sätze aus Kunstsprachen
produziert und perzipiert (besser: analysiert) werden können[4].

(IV) Die _metasprachliche Kompetenz_ ist das Vermögen, über einer Menge
von Sprachstrukturen Begriffe und Begriffssysteme wie generative
Grammatiken zu explizieren, so daß z.B. der oben zitierte Satz
als linguistisches Konstrukt erkannt werden kann[5].

(V) Die _Spracherlernungskompetenz_ ist die Fähigkeit, (I) - (IV) zu
entwickeln.

Diese Differenzierung ist sicher noch weiter zu verfeinern; sie mag für
den hier verfolgten Zweck genügen.

---

3) Nicht in dem Sinne, wie er meist in der linguistischen Pragmatik verwendet wird.
4) Unter 'Kunstsprachen' verstehe ich hier Konstruktsprachen wie den
Aussagenkalkül, Syntaxnotationssprachen, Programmiersprachen u.ä.
5) (III) und (IV) stehen in engerem Zusammenhang als (III) und (II).

3. Hypothesen zur psychologischen Realität

Chomsky charakterisierte die "Kompetenz" als wesentlich syntaktisches
Vermögen. Obwohl sie nicht mit (II) identisch ist, hat die sprachpsy-
chologische Forschung versucht, die psychologische Realität der Generativen Transformationsgrammatik nachzuweisen. Bei Experimenten ließen
sich Zeit- und Speicherbedarf jedoch eher mit semantischen als mit syntaktischen Faktoren korrelieren (Miller, McKean 1964). Die Versuchser-
gebnisse stützen die Hypothese, daß der Kodierungsprozeß wesentlich von
semantischen Faktoren gesteuert wird, nicht aber die Annahme einer Trennung von syntaktischer Tiefenstruktur und syntaktischer Oberflächenstruktur.

In dieselbe Richtung geht die Kritik im Bereich der linguistischen Modellbildung und Simulation[6]:

1) In der Generativen Semantik wird die Tiefenstruktur durch eine semantische Komponente erzeugt, syntaktische Transformationen überführen sie in die Oberflächenstruktur.

2) In performanzorientierten Simulationen wird die Trennung von Oberflächenstruktur und Tiefenstruktur aufgehoben (Yngve 1960, Winograd
   1970) oder die 'Tiefe' der generativen Syntax beschränkt (Reich
   1969).

Yngve knüpfte an die Forschungen der Informationspsychologie an, die
eine Beschränkung des Kurzzeitgedächtnisses auf fünf bis sieben Einheiten ergeben hatten. Er nahm an, daß demnach der einer normalen kontext-
freien Grammatik zugeordnete Kellerautomat für die Analyse von oben
nach unten auf sieben Speicherplätze zu beschränken sei. Mit diesen einfachen Annahmen versuchte er, einige strukturelle Besonderheiten des
Englischen gegenüber einer Kunstsprache plausibel zu machen. So inter-
pretierte er das Vorkommen diskontinuierlicher Konstituenten einleuch-
tend als Ausdruck des Bestrebens, die Belastung des Kurzzeitgedächtnisses, die mit jeder Verschachtelung zunimmt, gering zu halten. Gegen
Yngves Hypothesen haben Chomsky und Miller (1963) ins Feld geführt, daß
sie ausschließlich die Erleichterung der Kodierung für den Sprecher,
nicht für den Hörer erklären könne. Yngves Modell begünstige ferner die
Konstruktion von Rechtsverzweigungen (-rekursionen) und machte keinen
Unterschied in der Schwierigkeit zwischen Linksverzweigungen (-rekursi-
onen) und Selbsteinbettungen. Chomsky schließt aus der Endlichkeit des

---

6) Unter Modellbildung verstehe ich den Entwurf abstrakter Modelle zur
   Sprachbeschreibung, unter Simulation den Versuch, konkretes Sprecher-
   Hörer-Verhalten nachzubilden.

Gedächtnisses, daß Schachtelungen schwer verständlich, aber nur Selbsteinbettungen von einer bestimmten Tiefe an unverständlich werden. Eine
Bevorzugung von Rechtsverzweigungen liegt zwar im Englischen vor; es
handelt sich jedoch nicht um eine prinzipielle Asymmetrie, da andere
Sprachen Linksverzweigungen stärker entwickelt haben. Dies korreliert
mit dem automatentheoretischen Sachverhalt, daß ein endlicher Transduk-
tor Ketten beliebiger Schachtelungskomplexität mit Ausnahme von Selbsteinbettungen behandeln kann. (Chomsky a. Miller 1963)

Hier setzt Reichs (1969) Kritik an Chomskys Unterscheidung von unendlicher Kompetenz und endlicher Performanz ein. Reich will Sätze wie den
oben zitierten aus der Grammatik einer natürlichen Sprache ausschließen.
Er vertritt die Meinung, daß Selbsteinbettungen in natürlicher Sprache
nicht über eine Tiefe von Eins hinausgehen. Ein Produktions- bzw. Perzeptionsmechanismus kann somit durch ein Netzwerk aus endlichen Automaten simuliert werden, die durch einen Kellerspeicher der Tiefe Eins
erweitert sind.

4. Simulation, Sprachstatistik und Hypothesenprüfung

Wie können solche Hypothesen überprüft werden? Die Konfrontation mit
der Sprachwirklichkeit kann geschehen
1) durch Informantenbefragung über die Akzeptabilität der vom Modell
   generierten bzw. ausgeschlossenen Sätze, durch Lernexperimente u.ä.,
2) durch statistische syntaktische Analyse von Texten, die nicht für
   eine Testsituation konstruiert worden sind, z.B. durch Verwendung
   des Simulationsmodells als Analysemodell.
Für die Untersuchung ist in jedem Fall der Entstehungskontext von Äußerungen sehr wichtig, insbesondere der Unterschied von mündlicher und
schriftlicher Kommunikation, da die Bedingungen hier grundverschieden
sind. Während die Analyse einer gehörten Äußerung augenblicklich im einmaligen Durchgang von links nach rechts erfolgen muß, die Beschränkt-
heit des Kurzzeitgedächtnisses sich also voll auswirkt, kann die Dekodierung bei schriftlichen Texten beliebig viel Zeit beanspruchen und
braucht nicht nur einmal und nicht nur von links nach rechts zu verlaufen. Im Prinzip steht das gesamte Gedächtnis zur Verfügung.

Für die Überprüfung der Tiefenhypothese von Reich ist ein schriftsprach-
licher Text also ein härterer Test, insbesondere ein fachsprachlicher
Text. Die Ergebnisse der von mir durchgeführten statistischen syntaktischen Analyse von Texten der deutschen Wissenschaftssprache (Literatur-

wissenschaft, Medizin, Betriebswirtschaft)[7] scheinen die Hypothese zu bestätigen, die Reich für das Englische behauptet[8].

Für die hier zur Diskussion stehende Thematik ist vor allem die Analyse der deutschen Nominalgruppe (NP) interessant. Sie läßt sich als Kette von Elementen darstellen:

I: (Pränominal)$^+$(Präposition)$^+$(Determinans)((Adverb)$^+$Adjektiv$^+$)$^+$ Substantiv

II: (Pränominal)$^+$(Präposition)$^+$Pronomen [9]

Beispiele, die diesen Mustern entsprechen:

I: "nur von einem gut bekannten Arzt"

II: "nur von ihm"

Die von dieser Grammatik generierten Muster deutscher Nominalgruppen bilden eine reguläre Sprache; sie sind von einem endlichen Automaten akzeptierbar; die erzeugten Ketten haben die Form:

$$\text{PRÄN}^m \text{ PRÄP}^n \text{ DET}^o \text{ (ADV}^{p_i} \text{ ADJ}^{q_j})^r \text{ SUB bzw. PRÄN}^m \text{ PRÄP}^n \text{ PRO} \quad [10]$$

Definition I läßt sich für nachgestellte Attribute erweitern zu:

I': NP (NP)$^+$ mit NP aus Definition I

Die erzeugten Ketten haben dann die Form:

$$(\text{PRÄN}^{m_l} \text{ PRÄP}^{n_k} \text{ DET}^{o_s} \text{ (ADV}^{p_{i_x}} \text{ ADJ}^{q_{j_y}})^{r_z} \text{ SUB})^w \quad [10]$$

---

7) Das 1500 Sätze (ca. 30 000 Wörter) umfassende Korpus wurde als gestreute Stichprobe aus Hochschullehrbüchern und Publikationen in wissenschaftlichen Zeitschriften gezogen.

8) Hauptziel meiner Untersuchung war, das Vorkommen und die Häufigkeitsverteilung von syntaktischen Mustern auf den Ebenen 'Gruppe', 'Subsatz' und 'Gesamtsatz' in verschiedenen Wissenschaftssprachen miteinander zu vergleichen. Dazu wurde ein PL/I-Programm geschrieben, das in Texten, die nach syntaktischen 'Wortarten' kodiert wurden, Muster erkennt, sie in Lexika einträgt sowie verschiedene Sortierungen und statistische Prozeduren durchführt. Eine vollständige Analysegrammatik für das Deutsche zu konstruieren, erfordert mehr Zeit, als zur Verfügung stand. Es wurde eine heuristische Annäherungsgrammatik entworfen, die eine genügend große Zahl der Patterns generiert. Vollständigkeit der syntaktischen Beschreibung ist hier nicht primäres Ziel, da es um einen statistischen Vergleich geht.

9) + bedeutet Iterierbarkeit, () Optionalität eines Elements oder einer Gruppe. Diese Definitionen sind natürlich noch nicht ausreichend; so tritt bei der Kategorie 'Adverb' Mehrdeutigkeit auf, die durch Einführung eines zusätzlichen Zustands beseitigt werden kann; Konjunktionen sind hier der Einfachheit halber weggelassen. Die Erzeugung von Kasuskategorien bleibt unberücksichtigt.

10) mit $m, n, p_i, r, m_l, n_k, p_{i_x}, r_z \in N_o$; $q_j, q_{j_y}, w \in N$; $o, o_s \in \{0,1\}$

Beispiel:

"auch durch Auswahl etwa gleich großer Tiere im gleichen Ernährungszustand"

Die semantischen Beziehungen der einzelnen Untergruppen zueinander lassen sich oft nur aufgrund des semantisch-pragmatischen Vorwissens des Hörers entscheiden, z.B. in:

"mit dem Merckotest für Blutzucker von Merck"

"daß eine solche Reihenfolge der Aufträge auf den Maschinen gefunden wird"[11].

Rechtsverzweigungen in Form nachgestellter Attribute sind in jedem Satz unbeschränkt iterierbar. Dies entspricht sowohl Reichs als auch Yngves Tiefenhypothese. Daß nur in Ausnahmefällen mehr als drei oder vier Verzweigungen vorkommen[12], ist m.E. nicht auf die Komplexität der syntaktischen Analyse zurückzuführen, sondern auf die Notwendigkeit, semantische Einheiten und Relationen zu memorieren und zu behandeln.

Anders liegen die Verhältnisse bei der Erweiterung des vorangestellten Attributs im Deutschen. Hierzu einige Beispiele:

"eine (durch nichts) zu ersetzende Voraussetzung"

"in anderen (von der Krankheit) betroffenen Gebieten"

Solche Strukturen[13] werden in der TG als transformierte Satzeinbettungen interpretiert. Die Schwierigkeit der syntaktischen Analyse wird dadurch aber m.E. nicht befriedigend geklärt, da in der TG jedes Attribut auf eine solche Transformation zurückgeführt wird. Die syntaktische Komplexität wird gerade durch die Selbsteinbettung der nominalen Gruppe (s. Klammerung) entscheidend gesteigert. Erst sie macht die Behandlung der 'Oberflächenstruktur' durch den oben angedeuteten endlichen Automaten unmöglich.

Für die Analyse solcher Strukturen ist dieser Automat um einen Zustand und einen Kellerspeicher der Tiefe Eins zu erweitern. Hier wird die beim Übergang in den Zustand "Einbettung" abgebrochene Matrixkette gespeichert. Nach Abschluß der Analyse des eingebetteten Strings kann dann die der Matrixkette fortgeführt werden. Der so modifizierte Auto-

---

11) In einem Programm mit semantischen Fähigkeiten würde ein System von Relationen, realisiert z.B. in einem semantischen Netzwerk, die Entscheidung zumindest im ersten Beispiel ermöglichen. (Vgl. Winograd 1970, Simmons 1972)
12) Ein längeres Beispiel: "Das Streben nach Sicherung des Betriebs vor den Folgen eines Kaufkraftverfalls".
13) Den statistischen Befund zeigt die Tabelle auf der nächsten Seite.

mat ist ebenfalls finit. Er wird jedoch versagen, sobald eine mehrstufige Selbsteinbettung auftritt.

Dies geschah bei der Analyse des genannten Korpus nur ein einziges Mal,
und zwar in:
    "eine weitere und (durch den (von uns) oben beschriebenen Fall)
    erhärtete Interpretation der Entwicklung eines paradoxen Deszen-
    sus gab Priesl"
Man kann diese 'Ausnahme' als Widerlegung der Tiefenhypothese betrachten; es ist jedoch auch anzunehmen, daß die innere Gruppe als Muster
einheitlich wahrgenommen wird, so daß ein erneuter Prozeduraufruf
nicht erforderlich ist.

TABELLE: Nominalgruppen in Fachtexten

	Tokens	Selbsteinbettungen	%[14]
MEDIZIN (Lehrbuch)	2607	31	0,81
MEDIZIN (Zeitschr.)	3091	37	1,20
LIT.WISS. (Zeitschr.)	2014	21	1,04
BWL (Zeitschr.)	1668	30	1,80
GESAMT	9380	109	1,16

Der statistische Befund sowie die Art der 'Ausnahme' scheinen mir eher
dafür zu sprechen, daß eine mehrfache Selbsteinbettung von Nominalgruppen auch in der wissenschaftlichen Schriftsprache nicht akzeptabel ist.
Dies dürfte auch für die Selbsteinbettungen von Relativsätzen gelten[15].

Das Vermögen des Menschen zur syntaktischen Analyse in 'Echtzeit'
(mündliche Kommunikation, flüssiges Lesen) ist offenbar sehr beschränkt, verglichen mit der Fähigkeit eines rekursiv arbeitenden Compilers. Die 'Komplexität' der Syntax der natürlichen Sprache besteht
demgegenüber in der Vielfalt von Mustern und der Unbestimmtheit, die
erst durch semantische Information aufgehoben wird.

---

14) Signifikante Unterschiede (x^2- Test) bestehen zwischen MEDIZIN(L)/
    BWL sowie LITERATURWISSENSCHAFT/BWL.
15) Das untersuchte Korpus enthält gut 300 Relativsätze, darunter kei-
    ne mehrfache Selbsteinbettung; die Stichprobe ist natürlich viel
    zu klein, um etwas plausibel zu machen.

5. Folgerungen für die Konstruktion von Dialogsystemen und -sprachen

Ein vom Sprechen/Hören weitgehend verschiedener kognitiver Prozeß ist
die Konstruktion/Analyse eines Satzes einer Sprache vom Typ 2 mit unbe-
schränkter Selbsteinbettung, z.B. eines ALGOL-Programms oder eines logischen Ausdrucks. Hier handelt es sich um einen wesentlich bewußteren
und abstrakteren Vorgang, auch wenn es nur um die syntaktische Richtigkeit geht[16]. Dem entspricht die von mir oben vorgeschlagene Unterscheidung von kommunikativer und logischer Kompetenz. Daß Selbsteinbettungen in natürlicher Sprache (Englisch, Deutsch) nur bis zur Tiefe
Eins vorkommen, sollte dennoch bei der Konstruktion von Dialogsystemen
und -sprachen Beachtung finden. Insbesondere Sprachen zur Handhabung
von Operationssystemen im Dialogverkehr dürften Blockstruktur und rekursive Prozeduren nicht angemessen sein. Die Tiefe Eins scheint jedoch auch bei einem auf der Benutzerseite weitgehend 'automatisierten'
Dialog sinnvoll. So sollte man in bestimmten Fällen nach Beendigung
einer Prozedur z.B. die Möglichkeit haben, nicht nur in den Anfangszu-
stand des Monitors zurückzukehren. Die automatische Kellerung des jeweils letzten Monitorbefehls kann die Effizienz des Dialogs erhöhen,
z.B. bei der 'rekursiven' Evozierung eines Compilers vom Editor aus,
wie dies im DEC-SYSTEM-10 möglich ist. Bei größerer Schachtelungstiefe
werden Gedächtnisstützen notwendig. Dialogsprachen liefern diese wie
z.B. APL/360 durch Angabe der Unterbrechungshierarchie oder die Möglichkeit, sich Information über den jeweiligen Zustand zu verschaf-
fen[17]. Beim Verweilen im Dialog wie beim wiederholten Lesen eines Programms wird jedoch die logische Kompetenz wirksam.

Aus der Unfähigkeit des menschlichen 'Kurzzeitprozessors', selbstein-
bettende Konstruktionen unbeschränkt direkt auszuführen, darf nicht
der Schluß gezogen werden, daß bei allen Dialogsprachen auf Schachte-
lung und Rekursion zu verzichten ist. Bei einer empirischen Untersuchung[18] über die Adäquatheit von Konstruktionen mit bedingten Ausdrücken zeigte sich, daß die Blockstruktur der IF-THEN-ELSE-Gruppe für
ein bestimmtes Problem weniger semantische Fehler verursachte als die

---

16) Zum Zusammenhang von syntaktischen Strukturen und semantischen
    Fehlern vgl. Sime et al. 1973.
17) Ich danke diese Information einer pers. Mitteilung von I. Kupka.
18) Sime et al. 1973.

GO-TO-LABEL-Konstruktion. Dies Ergebnis spricht nicht gegen die Tiefenhypothese, sondern macht deutlich, daß die Blockstruktur die logische Kompetenz besser abbildet als die Sprunganweisung[19].

Bei der Auswahl von Sprachstrukturen für den Entwurf von dialogfähigen Programmiersprachen ist die Zweckbestimmung wichtig. Eine Sprache, die für die schnelle Handhabung von Systemen durch Operateure bestimmt ist oder einen Tischrechner ersetzt, wird sich von einer Sprache unterscheiden müssen, die der Ausbildung von Informatikern dient. Während dort die Erreichung einer eng begrenzten kommunikativen Fähigkeit das Ziel ist, wird hier die Erweiterung oder Festigung der logischen Kompetenz angestrebt.

In der neueren Entwicklung kommt auch die metasprachliche Kompetenz ins Spiel, wenn im Dialog über den Dialog, insbesondere die Art der Dialogführung, gesprochen wird[20].

---

19) Dies spricht z.B. gegen die Einführung von BASIC oder FORTRAN als Ausbildungssprache.
20) Persönliche Mitteilung von I. Kupka.

LITERATUR

J.R. Carbonell, AI in CAI: An artificial intelligence approach to computer-assisted instruction, in: IEEE Transactions on Man-Machine Systems 4, (1970), S. 181-189.

Noam Chomsky, Aspekte der Syntax-Theorie, Frkft. (Suhrkamp) 1969.

N. Chomsky, G.A. Miller, Finitary Models of Language Users. In: Handbook of Mathematical Psychology, Vol 2, Eds. R.D. Bruce et al., New York 1963.

Ronald M. Kaplan, Augmented Transition Networks as Psychological Models of Sentence Comprehension, in: Artificial Intelligence 3 (1972), Nr. 2, S. 77-100.

William Labov, Das Studium der Sprache im sozialen Kontext, in: Aspekte der Soziolinguistik, Hrsg. v. W. Klein und D. Wunderlich, Frankfurt 1971, S. 111-194.

G. Lakoff, J.R. Row, Ist Tiefenstruktur notwendig? In: W. Abraham, R. J. Binnick (Hrsg.), Generative Semantik, Frankfurt 1972, S. 66-70, zuerst 1960.

J.D. McCawley, The Role of Semantics in a Grammar, in: Bach and Harms, Universals in Linguistic Theory, N.Y. 1968, S. 125-170.

J. Mey, Computational Linguistics in the Seventies, In: Linguistics 1971, S. 36-61

G.A. Miller, K.O. McKean, A Chronometric Study of Some Relations between Sentences, in: Quart. J. exper. Psychol. 16 (1964), S. 297-308,
auch in: Language, Eds. C. Oldfield, J.C. Marshall, London 1968, S.
213-230.

M.R. Quillian, The Teachable Language Comprehender: A Simulation Program and The Theory of Language, in: CACM 12, 1969, S. 459-476.

Peter A. Reich, The Finiteness of Natural Language, in: Language 45
(1969), Nr. 4, S. 831-834.

M.E. Sime et al., Psychological Evaluation of Two Conditional Constructions Used in Computer Languages, in: Int J. Man-Machine Stud 1973
(5), S. 105-113.

R. Simmons, J. Slocum, Generating English Discourse from Semantic Networks, in: CACM 15 (1972), Nr. 10, S. 891-905.

J.O. Wexler, Information Networks in Generative Computer-Assisted Instruction, in: IEEE Transactions on Man-Machine Systems, Vol. MMS-11
No. 4, Dec. 1970, S. 190-202 = (1970).

T. Winograd, Procedures as a Representation for Data in a Computer Program for Understanding Natural Language, MIT, Cambridge (Mass.) 1970.

V.H. Yngve, A Model and a Hypothesis for Language Structure, in: Proc.
Amer. Philos. Soc., 104 (1960), S. 444-466.

METHODEN DER INFORMATIK FÜR

SPEZIELLE ANWENDUNGEN

SIMWAP AND TETRASIM - TWO EXAMPLES OF APPLICATION ORIENTED SOFTWARE, DEVELOPED ON THE BASIS OF THE SIMULA LANGUAGE

ANDREAS LIE   AND   THOMAS RØGEBERG

1.   INTRODUCTION

SIMULA (1) is a general purpose language, specially oriented towards
the development of user oriented software in various fields. The
language provides the programmer with means (notably the class-subclass
facility) to define concepts relevant to a particular problem - or
problem area. The basic properties of concepts can be collected in a
class definition, which serves as a foundation for further development. Specific characteristics can be added, in the format of lower
level subclass definitions, and this process of progressive refinement
can be repeated as often as required.

Whereas SIMULA itself is not specially oriented towards simulation,
the system class SIMULATION provides concepts to facilitate the production of simulation programs. To make these concepts available in
his program, the user merely has to prefix the program by SIMULATION,
thus:

SIMULATION **begin** <user program> **end**;

This paper is concerned with two application packages constructed with
SIMULA (and SIMULATION) as a basis, namely:

  SIMWAP - aimed at the simulation of warehouses
  TETRASIM - for the simulation of telephone systems.

The two packages are written as subclasses to SIMULATION, thus:

        SIMULATION **class** SIMWAP
        SIMULATION **class** TETRASIM.

To use them, the programmer can apply the class names as prefixes:

    SIMWAP **begin** <warehouse simulation program> **end**;

or

    TETRASIM **begin** <telephone simulation program> **end**;

2. THE SIMULA LANGUAGE

SIMWAP and TETRASIM are based upon the SIMULA language. A reason for
using SIMULA is that this would allow time-true simulations to be performed. This would mean definite advantages in the simulation of
waiting systems compared to roulette methods. Further, the class
facility of SIMULA opens the possibility of defining concepts in close
correspondence to parts of warehouse and telephone systems.

A class definition is a common description of individual objects of a
certain kind. The properties of these objects are contained partly
within the data structure and partly within the operation rule of the
class:

```
class A;  begin <A data>;
                <A procedures>;
                <A statements>;
          end;
```

When such a class has been defined, it is possible to create any
number of objects belonging to this class. A representation of each
individual object is contained within the computer memory. During a
simulation, every object executes its operation rule in parallel with
all the others. Thus a rather direct connection between the physical
system and the simulation model is possible.

3. SIMWAP

In 1967/68 the Norwegian Computing Center cooperated with Industri-
konsulent A/S in the design of a new warehouse. As a result of the
experience gained with this project, an application package called
SIMWAP (SIMulation WArehouse Planning) was developed.

The central elements of a warehouse are its layout, storage equipment,
inventory plan, technical equipment (trucks, pallets, etc.), types of
worker, and its administration and operation.

3.1 Problems associated with warehouse planning

The objective of warehouse planning is to find a configuration which
is effective and yet gives minimum cost operation. The elaboration
of alternative plans requires intensive preliminary study and may be
very time consuming. However, the operation of a large warehouse is
composed of so many mutually interfering sub-tasks that it is difficult
to assess by intuition or rough paper-and-pencil work whether a plan
will function satisfactorily, or if suggested alterations will improve
it. But a plan may be tested by developing a simulation program to
represent it, and then testing that with data describing the desired
material flow into, within and out of it. On the basis of the simulation results, one may decide on alternative plans, revisions of the
operation rules etc. With a modular design, it is relatively simple
to modify a program to reflect these alterations. SIMWAP was developed
with this in mind, in order to reduce the effort spent on implementing
simulation models and testing proposed alternatives.

SIMWAP is based on a simulation model which incorporates properties
common to all warehouses, and does not represent a finished simulation
program in the sense that a plan may be tested directly by merely
running SIMWAP with appropriate data. The user must use the package
components to program details of the particular alternative he wishes
to investigate.

Many of the unique features which the SIMULA language possesses for
the construction of modular programs are applied in SIMWAP. Pre-
written modules are implemented in SIMULA to mirror the behaviour and
structure of concepts which are natural to warehouse designers when
describing the operation of a warehouse. The modules may be extended
by the user or completely fresh modules may be added at will. Since
the pre-written modules serve as a guide, the construction of fresh
modules is usually straightforward.

The user must assess in detail the static components, e.g. layout,
storage equipment etc., as well as the dynamic components, e.g.
administrative and technical processes and procedures, so that the
application of a SIMWAP model for a given alternative demands data
specifying: layout, storage equipment, inventory plan, technical
equipment and material flow into and within the warehouse. The SIMWAP
model includes descriptions of the administrative and technical pro-

cesses of the warehouse. The testing of alternatives with the same
administrative and technical processes then only requires application
of the same program with different sets of data.

3.2 Some concepts of SIMWAP

Using SIMWAP, material flow within the warehouse is described in terms
of the concepts article and order.

An article is characterised by

- article group-number
- order-number
- position in the warehouse; this is evaluated by SIMWAP.

An order is characterised by

- an identifying number
- date and time of the registration of the order
- number of articles comprising this order
- particular type of order.

Three different types of orders are recognised:

- shipment, i.e. lists of articles to be shipped out
  of warehouse
- reception, i.e. lists of articles to be stored
- internal conveyance, i.e. lists of articles to be
  moved within the warehouse.

A warehouse designer wishing articles to have additional characteristics, e.g. weight and price, may extend the SIMWAP definition of an
article to include these extra attributes by prefixing. Any other
SIMWAP definition may be extended in similar fashion. The layout of
a warehouse is described as a set of layout points with coordinates
in a Cartesian system.

All movements in the warehouse follow straight lines between the layout points. Layout points are used to define:

- the passages in the warehouse
- other points in the warehouse at which any change
  of direction may occur, or which may be the start
  or end points of movement

- location of articles or storage places.

It is an essential part of warehouse planning to establish the processes by which working records will be composed, since these are used
by workers for receiving, storing and shipping operations. Thus these
records will determine the way in which any physical layout will be
used. Here we must note:

- priority orders
- that the material handling indicated by the working
  records is in accordance with the directional constraints within the passages
- that the workers are, as much as possible, able to
  move independently of one another in order to reduce
  waiting time in passages in which passing is not
  allowed.

SIMWAP contains a number of useful concepts which the user may employ
when writing his own administrative processes. For example, by using
SIMWAP's sorting procedure, the user may sort the articles according
to ascending/descending passage numbers and, within each passage, the
articles may be sorted in order of increasing/decreasing distance from
the starting point of the passage, etc. Different administrative
routines may thus be tested to find the optimal routines easily for
the particular layout.

3.3 <u>Output from SIMWAP</u>

Output from SIMWAP is divided into three parts:

- An "echo" of the input data, i.e. data characterising
  the static components of an alternative
- Event listing
- Final results.

For the particular alternative, the input "echo" serves as the description of the alternative being simulated.

The event listing is of particular interest when debugging the model.
It shows, among other things:

- whether the workers are functioning according to the
  user specification

- the routing decisions taken by each worker when
  moving from one position to the next
- the technical equipment used.

The final results, which are used to give a quantitative appraisal of
the alternative, include:

- the length of the simulation period.
- histograms giving the distributions of processing
  times for articles and working records, with mean
  handling times and standard deviations.
- the queue distribution for waiting orders.
- the distribution of the processing times broken
  down into transport, waiting and handling time.
- the distribution of idle time and busy time for
  each piece of equipment.

The (SIMWAP) user has access to a ready-programmed foundation upon
which he can build the detailed specifications of the various plans he
wishes to study, since SIMWAP represents know-how on the simulation of
warehouse plans which has been made operative by presenting it as an
application package.

4. TETRASIM

4.1 The background for the project

TETRASIM - abbreviation for TEle-TRAffic-SIMulation, is a project
aimed at the simulation of telephone systems. The project aim is to
make the simulation method more easily available for the analysis of
teletraffic problems.

In the past, simulation has been used as a useful supplement to teletraffic theory, to study effects that would otherwise have been difficult to analyse, for example:

1. Investigation of complicated network configurations
   (gradings).
2. Analysis of the mutual effect of control network
   and speech network.
3. Analysis of large systems - one complete exchange
   or several exchanges.

Previous to the project, members of the TETRASIM group had been engaged in several investigations of type 1 and 2.

It was decided that it would be very useful if simulation could be made available on a more routine basis to users. To avoid having to write every new simulation program from scratch, it was planned to produce "pre-programmed units" corresponding to the basic components of telephone systems. The production of a simulation program would then be a relatively straightforward procedure. Moreover, it seemed feasible to construct complete models for the exchange types most frequently in use in Norway. Simulation of these exchanges would then require preparation of input data only.

The possible application to type 3 problems - large systems - was a major motivating factor.

4.2   The main components of TETRASIM

In accordance with the project aim, TETRASIM contains class definitions on 2 levels:

a.   a "basic" level (1), where the fundamental concepts
     of telephone systems are defined.

b.   a "module" level (2), where complete models
     (e.g. exchange types) are available.

On the basic level, the user has complete freedom to use the class definitions to create almost any system he wants, provided that some rather simple programming rules are obeyed.

An example of such a fundamental class definition is that corresponding to a group of devices. Actual telephone exchanges consist of several such device groups (markers, trunk groups, links, registers, etc.). Every such group is considered an instance of a common class definition.

class teleresource;

Natural attributes to such a class is the number of devices (capacity) and the number occupied. Procedures for testing/updating the status of devices belonging to the group are written as local procedures.

A user who operates on this level may use the tele-resource concept
in the definition of his own system.

Such a user could define any module that is not previously contained
in the TETRASIM library. It might be a part of an exchange or one
whole exchange. The user also has freedom to choose the degree of
detail in the description that is suitable to him. Some groups of
devices (resources) could, for instance, be treated as full availability groups, which is a simplification in most cases.

On "level 2" is contained a predefined set (library) of exchange
models, and, in addition, facilities to make simulation of systems
with more than one exchange possible.

The applicability to the national network has determined the selection
of "library" exchanges. At present, 8B (ITT), ARM and AKK (LME) are
included. Other modules will be added as need arises. In the "library"
exchanges, representation both of control devices and speech network
is maintained.

The "library" module definitions make extensive use of the fundamental
concepts, like teleresources, that are defined on level 1. The exchange definition follows the general scheme.

```
class exchangeX;
begin <attributes defining the device groups (teleresources)
      within the exchange>;
      <procedures for hunting through the different parts
       of the network>;
end;
```

The hunting procedures execute the testing, and eventual occupation of
the device groups in the sequence corresponding to that in the physical
systems.

A user on this level may perform a simulation by selecting the relevant
modules from the exchange library. A simulation of this kind requires
system information in the form of data only. Traffic input to the
system must be specified, as well as routing plans and system information.

To sum up:

A level 1 user:
- applies the fundamental concepts of level 1
  to produce level 2 system modules.

A level 2 user:
-. applies the modules available on level 2
  (exchanges or parts thereof) to define the system
  to be simulated
- provides input information
- performs the actual simulation.

(Fig. 1).

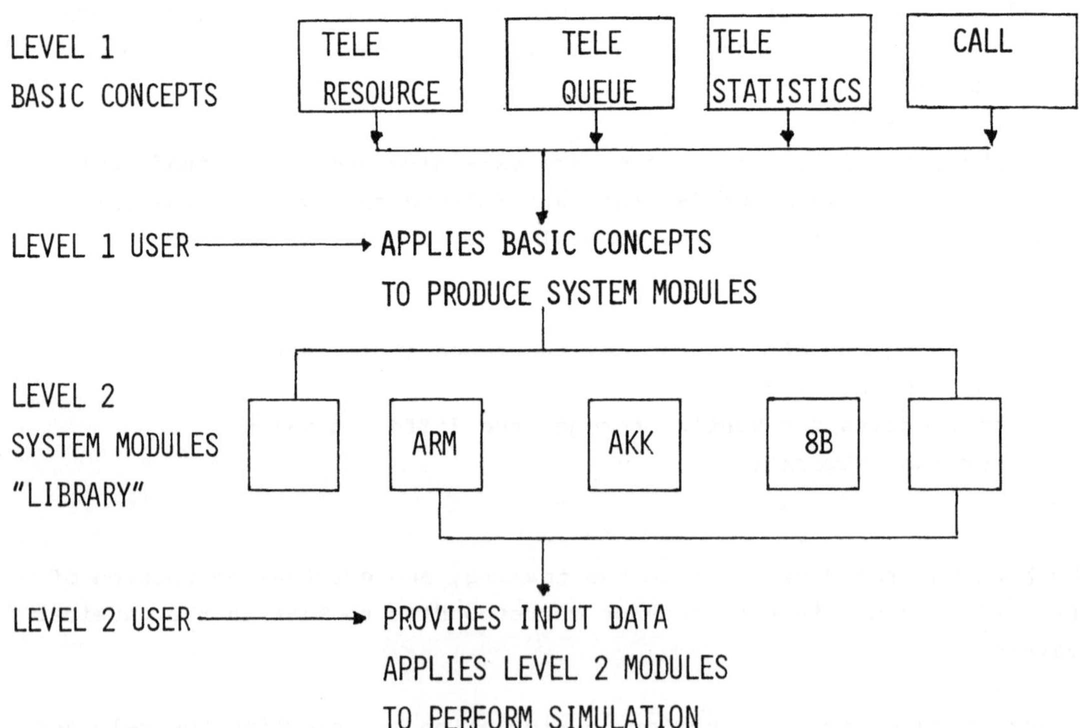

Fig. 1
The two levels of TETRASIM.

4.3 <u>Output information from TETRASIM</u>

Output from a simulation with the TETRASIM system is edited and
printed by a special post-processor. During the simulation itself, a
special output file is prepared. The information on this file consists
of key events, such as the seizure or release of a device, or the inclusion into or removal of a call from a queue. Each event is labelled
by the corresponding value of simulated time. The file may thus be
regarded as a kind of log of the simulation.

The file is used as input to the post-processor, which will prepare
the final output. In principle, complete state distributions for all
resources (device groups) and waiting time distributions are obtainable.
However, it will hardly be desirable or practical to have such detailed
information for all parts of a system. This would amount to something
of the order of 50 histograms for one complete exchange. Therefore
the output is made selectable by options, such that only key figures
(like traffic carried and time congestion) are printed automatically.
The options may be used to select additional information for some of
the more important device groups. This may be done simply by a repeated run with the post-processor, since all the information necessary
is contained in the simulation output file. (Fig. 2).

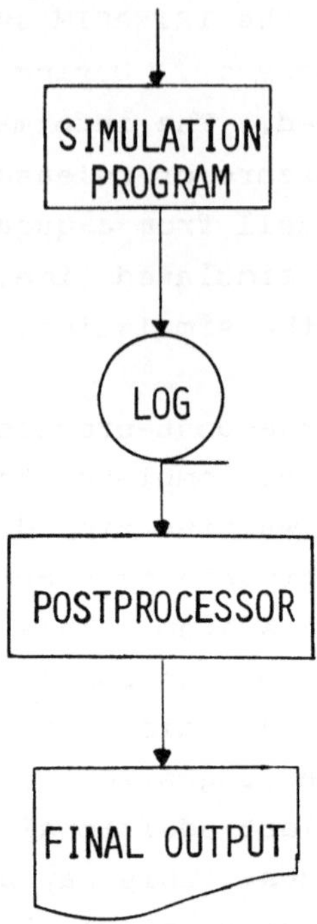

Fig. 2

The simulation program and the postprocessor
communicate via an external memory device ("log").
Input to the simulation is prepared by the
preprocessor (not shown).

Reference to literature:

1)   "SIMULA COMMON BASE LANGUAGE".
     O-J. Dahl, B. Myhrhaug and K. Nygaard
     Norwegian Computing Center, October 1970.

DARSTELLUNGSVERFAHREN FÜR DAS COMPUTERUNTERSTÜTZTE KONSTRUIEREN

Ingolf Grieger [+]

Übersicht :

Der zunehmende Einsatz von Bildschirmgeräten für die verschiedensten Anwendungen erfordert neben der Entwicklung interaktiver Programmsysteme auch das Aufstellen geeigneter mathematischer Methoden. Die Darstellung von Objekten auf einem Bildschirm kann sehr einfach durch entsprechende graphische Transformationen vorgenommen werden. Probleme treten jedoch beim umgekehrten Vorgehen dadurch auf, daß sich auf der zweidimensionalen Bildschirmfläche eine dreidimensionale Information nur über Zusatzbedingungen eingeben läßt. Die entsprechenden mathematischen Beziehungen werden abgeleitet und sind im interaktiven System INGA (Interaktive Graphische Analyse) implementiert. Die elementweise Diskretisierung einer Konstruktion ist ein geeignetes Verfahren, um am Bildschirm interaktiv arbeiten zu können. An einigen typischen Beispielen werden diese Verfahren und das interaktive Arbeiten mit ihnen demonstriert.

1. Einleitung

Das Konstruieren ist ein Vorgang, der sich im allgemeinen nicht völlig automatisieren läßt. Ein großer Teil der Arbeit kann jedoch vom Rechner abgenommen werden und es erscheint daher günstig, den Menschen (Konstrukteur, Designer usw.) in einen Dialog mit dem Computer treten zu lassen. Dieser Dialog kann am besten über ein interaktives Bildschirmgerät, das mit den entsprechenden Eingabevorrichtungen, wie z.B. Lichtstift, Funktionstastatur, ausgestattet ist, erfolgen. Es wird daher hier eine computer-orientierte Methode beschrieben, die es erlaubt, eine Konstruktion, die im allgemeinen aus Baugruppen und vielen Einzelteilen besteht, im Rechner zu implementieren. Den Vorgang des Ersetzens der Konstruktion oder Struktur durch ein Aggregat von diskreten Elementen nennt man idealisieren. Die reale Konstruktion wird durch ein Rechenmodell ersetzt, das um so realistischer ist, je besser die Eigenschaften der Elemente die Art der Konstruktion bzw. Struktur wiedergeben. Allerdings ist das Anfertigen der Idealisierung in allgemeinen Fällen eine zeitraubende Tätigkeit, die durch Verwendung von sogenannten Netzgeneratoren (mesh generators) für bestimmte Klassen von Problemen automatisiert werden kann. Aber auch hier ist die Verwendung interaktiver Verfahren für das Aufstellen der Idealisierung allgemeiner Probleme zweckmäßig. Große Vorteile bietet dieses Modell, wenn außer dem Entwurfsvorgang noch weitere

---

[+] Meinem verehrten Lehrer, Herrn Professor Dr.Dres.h.c.John H.Argyris zum 60.Geburtstag gewidmet.

Untersuchungen (Berechnung von Temperaturverteilungen, statische und dynamische Tragwerksbe-rechnung usw.) erforderlich sind. Die Methode der finiten Elemente ist inzwischen zum allge-meinen Hilfsmittel in den verschiedenen Ingenieursdisziplinen [Argyris,1969] entwickelt worden. Es ist daher naheliegend, entsprechende Annahmen auch für die Darstellung einer Konstruktion [Grieger,1973] zu machen und Verfahren zu entwickeln, die ein interaktives Konstruieren erlau-ben. Zum Ausprobieren der Verfahren werden diese im interaktiven System INGA [Grieger,1973] implementiert, da gerade die Anwendung von verschiedenen Benutzern über die Güte der Verfah-ren entscheidet.

2.   Räumliche Darstellung und ihre Modifikation

Zur Darstellung von beliebigen Objekten auf dem Bildschirm müssen diese im allgemeinen transformiert und in die Bildschirmebene projiziert werden. Die Daten des Benutzers liegen norma-lerweise im kartesischen Benutzerkoordinatensystem vor und müssen in eine andere Ansicht trans-formiert werden, da der Benutzer häufig seine Objekte von verschiedenen Seiten sehen möchte. Die Abbildungstransformation kann bei Verwendung homogener Koordinaten [Roberts,1965] in Matrizenform geschrieben werden.

$$P' = A\,P \tag{2.1}$$

Hierbei ist $P = \{x \quad y \quad z \quad t\}$ der Ausgangspunkt und $P' = \{x'\quad y'\quad z'\quad t'\}$ der abge-bildete Punkt. Die Abbildungsmatrix A besteht aus folgenden Untermatrizen.

$$A = \begin{bmatrix} A_{11}\ (3\times 3) & A_{12}\ (3\times 1) \\ \text{Rotation} & \text{Translation} \\ \hline A_{21}\ (1\times 3) & A_{22}\ (1\times 1) \\ \text{Perspektive} & \text{Maßstab} \end{bmatrix} \tag{2.2}$$

Betrachtet man den hauptsächlich interessierenden Fall der Rotation, so ergeben sich für die Pro-jektion auf den Bildschirm folgende Beziehungen

$$\begin{aligned} x' &= R_{11}\,x + R_{12}\,y + R_{13}\,z \\ y' &= R_{21}\,x + R_{22}\,y + R_{23}\,z \end{aligned} \tag{2.3}$$

Die dritte Beziehung für z' geht leider durch die Projektion auf die zweidimensionale Fläche verloren. Man kann daher für die Rücktransformation nicht einfach die Rotationsmatrix invertie-ren bzw. transponieren,wenn sie orthogonal ist, sondern muß Zusatzbedingungen einführen. Will man beispielsweise mit Nachführkreuz und Lichtstift eine neue Position ansteuern,so empfiehlt sich das Vorschreiben einer bestimmten Ebene in der sich das Nachführkreuz bewegen kann [Hubbold,1970]. Vorzugsweise verwendet man hier ausgezeichnete Ebenen des Koordinaten-systems.

Wählt man beispielsweise die xy –Ebene aus und hält z konstant, so kann man die Gleichungen (2.3) umschreiben

$$\begin{bmatrix} R_{11} & R_{12} \\ R_{21} & R_{22} \end{bmatrix} \begin{bmatrix} x \\ y \end{bmatrix} = \begin{bmatrix} x' - R_{13}\,z \\ y' - R_{23}\,z \end{bmatrix} \tag{2.4}$$

und schließlich nach x und y auflösen.

$$\begin{bmatrix} x \\ y \end{bmatrix} = \frac{1}{R_{11}R_{22} - R_{12}R_{21}} \begin{bmatrix} R_{22} & -R_{12} \\ -R_{21} & R_{11} \end{bmatrix} \begin{bmatrix} x' - R_{13}\,z \\ y' - R_{23}\,z \end{bmatrix} \tag{2.5}$$

Durch zyklisches Vertauschen erhält man die Beziehungen für die beiden anderen Koordinatenebenen.

yz –Ebene (x = konstant):

$$\begin{bmatrix} y \\ z \end{bmatrix} = \frac{1}{R_{12}R_{23} - R_{13}R_{22}} \begin{bmatrix} R_{23} & -R_{13} \\ -R_{22} & R_{12} \end{bmatrix} \begin{bmatrix} x' - R_{11}\,x \\ y' - R_{21}\,x \end{bmatrix} \tag{2.6}$$

zx –Ebene (y = konstant):

$$\begin{bmatrix} z \\ x \end{bmatrix} = \frac{1}{R_{13}R_{21} - R_{11}R_{23}} \begin{bmatrix} R_{21} & -R_{11} \\ -R_{23} & R_{13} \end{bmatrix} \begin{bmatrix} x' - R_{12}\,y \\ y' - R_{22}\,y \end{bmatrix} \tag{2.7}$$

Die Auswahl der Ebene kann vom Benutzer sehr einfach durch Antippen entsprechender Lichtzeichen vorgenommen werden. Hat man Platz für mehrere Ansichten, so kann man auch mit der Dreiseitenansicht arbeiten. Für Probleme, die eine hohe Genauigkeit der Koordinateneingabe erfordern, kann natürlich die Position als Zahlenwert eingegeben werden.

Eine andere Methode ist das Positionieren im Raum unter Verwendung der Interpolationsfunktionen, die den diskreten Geometrieelementen [Grieger, 1973] zugrunde liegen. Als Beispiel dient hier eine räumliche Spirale.

$$x = r\cos\varphi \qquad y = r\sin\varphi \qquad z = c\,\varphi \qquad r > 0, \; c \neq 0 \tag{2.8}$$

Die Spirale ist im Bereich $0 \leq \varphi \leq 2\pi$ mit vier CURVE5-Elementen idealisiert. Das CURVE5-Element basiert auf einer Lagrangeinterpolation 4. Ordnung und hat daher, wie der Name des Elementes sagt, 5 Knotenpunkte. Ein beliebiger Punkt im Element (Matrix x) kann aus den Koordinaten der 5 Knotenpunkte (Matrix x_e) in der folgenden Form dargestellt werden

$$x = \omega\, x_e \tag{2.9}$$

Hierbei setzt sich die Interpolationsfunktion ω aus den Anteilen der einzelnen Knotenpunkte zusammen.

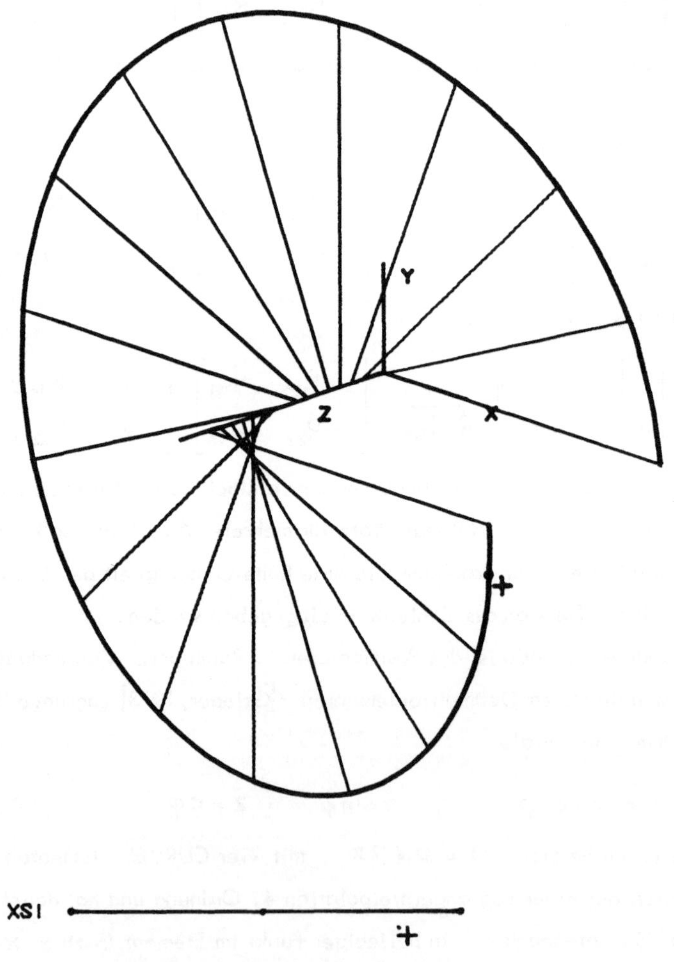

Bild 1   Spirale mit Einheitsskala

$$\omega = \begin{bmatrix} \omega_1 & \omega_2 & \omega_3 & \omega_4 & \omega_5 \end{bmatrix} \qquad (2.10)$$

$$\omega_1 = \tfrac{1}{6}\left(4\xi^4 - 4\xi^3 - \xi^2 + \xi \right)$$

$$\omega_2 = \tfrac{4}{3}\left(-2\xi^4 + \xi^3 + 2\xi^2 - \xi \right)$$

$$\omega_3 = 4\xi^4 - 5\xi^2 + 1 \qquad (2.11)$$

$$\omega_4 = \tfrac{4}{3}\left(-2\xi^4 - \xi^3 + 2\xi^2 + \xi \right)$$

$$\omega_5 = \tfrac{1}{6}\left(4\xi^4 + 4\xi^3 - \xi^2 - \xi \right)$$

Die 5 Knotenpunkte liegen bei $\xi = -1, -0.5, 0, +0.5$ und $+1$. Will man nun einen beliebigen Punkt im Element ansteuern, so benötigt man nur eine Referenzskala für die Eingabe der dimensionslosen Koordinate ξ. Auf dieser Einheitsskala (Bild 1) kann man mit Lichtstift und Nachführkreuz eine beliebige Position ansteuern und über die Interpolationsfunktionen die kartesischen Koordinaten errechnen. Es empfiehlt sich zur übersichtlicheren Darstellung, entsprechend dem Nachführkreuz in der Referenzgraphik auch eine Markierung im tatsächlichen Element im Raume mitwandern zu lassen. Diese Technik kann auch bei Flächen- und Volumenelementen angewandt werden.

3. Flächendefinition mit Finiten Elementen

Ein Hauptproblem des rechnerunterstützten Entwerfens ist das Definieren von Flächen, die nicht oder nicht einfach mathematisch beschrieben werden können. Für die darzustellende Fläche, die im allgemeinen durch eine Reihe von Punkten gegeben ist, sind gewisse Randbedingungen zu erfüllen. Außerdem soll die Fläche auch gewisse Stetigkeitskriterien erfüllen. Diese Forderungen können die sogenannten Minimalflächen [Birkhoff und Garabedian, 1960] erfüllen, wo das Integral

$$\iint \left(w_{xx}^2 + 2\, w_{xy}^2 + w_{yy}^2 \right) dx\, dy \qquad (3.1)$$

ein Minimum sein soll. Es sei daran erinnert, daß im eindimensionalen Fall das Minimalprinzip auf SPLINE-Kurven führt, die physikalisch aus der Minimalisierung der Formänderungsenergie in der Strakleiste hervorgehen. Mathematisch gesehen, ergibt die linearisierte SPLINE-Interpolation kubische Polynome für die einzelnen Segmente.

Im vorliegenden Fall der Flächendefinition entspricht jedoch die Minimalisierung des Integrals der Minimalisierung der Formänderungsenergie einer dünnen Platte. Die Definition von Flächen dieser Art ist also der Biegung einer dünnen Platte äquivalent, bei der die Mittelfläche durch die gegebenen Punkte geht und die Randbedingungen erfüllt werden [Throsby, 1969]. Da diese Flächen im allgemeinen mathematisch nicht einfach faßbar sind, muß man Näherungsmethoden entwickeln. Hier zeigt sich besonders die Stärke und Allgemeinheit der Methode der finiten Elemente in Form der Matrizenverschiebungsmethode [Argyris, 1954] .Die Anwendung dieser Methode erlaubt die Erfüllung der verschiedensten Randbedingungen, wobei die Näherung in großen Bereichen je besser ist, je mehr Elemente zur Diskretisierung benutzt werden.Als Elemente zur Lösung des Plattenbiegeproblems können sowohl Rechtecke als auch Dreiecke in Frage kommen. Die Dreieckselemente sind für viele Zwecke geeigneter, da sie allgemeinere Aufteilungen, wie Verfeinern oder Vergröbern des Rasters, zulassen.

Aus Platzgründen können hier nur einige Grundbeziehungen der Matrizenverschiebungsmethode, die für die Flächendefinition von Interesse sind, aufgezeigt werden.Die Platte, oder allgemein das Tragwerk, wird in eine Anzahl von Elementen aufgeteilt.Jedes Element hat aufgrund seiner geometrischen und elastischen Daten eine Steifigkeit k . Die Eigenschaften des gesamten Tragwerks werden als Summe der Elementsteifigkeiten dargestellt. Durch Akkumulation der einzelnen Elementbeiträge an den entsprechenden Knoten entsteht die Gesamtsteifigkeit K . Diese Transformation kann mit der Zuordnungsmatrix a in Matrizenform dargestellt werden.

$$K = a^t \, k \, a \tag{3.2}$$

Die Gleichgewichtsbeziehung des gesamten Tragwerkes kann in der folgenden Form angesetzt werden

$$R = K \, r \tag{3.3}$$

Hierbei ist R der Belastungsvektor und r der Vektor der unbekannten Verschiebungen.

Zur Lösung des Flächendefinitionsproblems muß man Gleichung (3.3) in lokale (local, Index L) und vorgeschriebene (prescribed, Index P) Freiheitsgrade aufspalten. Die unterdrückten (suppressed) Freiheitsgrade des Randes bzw. der Symmetrieachsen sind hier schon eliminiert. Als Freiheitsgrade werden hier die Koordinaten und Ableitungen der Fläche bezeichnet. Die Aufspaltung ergibt folgende Beziehung

$$\begin{bmatrix} R_P \\ R_L \end{bmatrix} \begin{bmatrix} K_{PP} & K_{PL} \\ K_{LP} & K_{LL} \end{bmatrix} \begin{bmatrix} r_P \\ r_L \end{bmatrix} \tag{3.4}$$

Ausmultipliziert erhält man

$$R_P = K_{PP} \, r_P + K_{PL} \, r_L \tag{3.5}$$

$$R_L = K_{LP} \, r_P + K_{LL} \, r_L \tag{3.6}$$

Hierbei ist r_P der Vektor der vorgeschriebenen Verschiebungen und r_L der Vektor der unbekannten Verschiebungen, die ermittelt werden sollen. Im vorliegenden Fall der Flächendefinition

wird natürlich keine äußere Last **R** aufgebracht, und aus Gleichung (3.6) können die Verschiebungen berechnet werden.

$$\mathbf{r_L} = - K_{LL}^{-1} K_{LP} \mathbf{r_P} \qquad (3.7)$$

Der totale Verschiebungsvektor besteht daher aus den vorgeschriebenen und den zunächst unbekannten Verschiebungen

$$\mathbf{r} = \left\{ \mathbf{r_P} \quad \mathbf{r_L} \right\} \qquad (3.8)$$

Von den globalen Verschiebungen kann durch eine einfache Transformation auf die Element-
ebene übergegangen werden.

$$\boldsymbol{\varrho} = \mathbf{a} \, \mathbf{r} \qquad (3.9)$$

Der Verschiebungsvektor an einer beliebigen Stelle im Element ergibt sich durch Verwendung
der entsprechenden Interpolationsfunktionen

$$w(x,y) = \omega \, \boldsymbol{\varrho} \qquad (3.10)$$

Hierbei ist ω die dem Element zugrundeliegende Matrix der Ansatzfunktionen.

Als Beispiel sei hier die Fläche

$$w = 16\,(x - x^2)(y - y^2) \qquad \text{für den Bereich} \qquad 0 \leq x,y \leq 1 \qquad (3.11)$$

mit dreieckigen Plattenelementen TUBA 3, die durch Eliminierung der Knoten an den Seitenmitten
aus dem allgemeineren Element TUBA 6 [Argyris, Fried, Scharpf, 1968] hervorgehen. Dem
TUBA 3 - Element liegt ein unvollständiger Verschiebungsansatz 5. Ordnung zugrunde. Das Element hat drei Knotenpunkte und folgende Freiheitsgrade

$$w \qquad w_x \qquad w_y \qquad w_{xx} \qquad w_{xy} \qquad w_{yy} \qquad (3.12)$$

Die Netzaufteilung mit den Randbedingungen ist in Bild 2 angegeben. Bei Verwendung von 128
TUBA 3 - Elementen ergeben sich 316 unbekannte Verschiebungen. Die Berechnung wurde mit
dem ASKA - System [ASKA, 1971] auf der CDC 6600 vorgenommen. Aus Platzgründen kann hier
nur eine Darstellung der Fläche auf dem Bildschirm (Bild 3) gezeigt werden. Als Ergebnis erhält
man die ersten und zweiten Ableitungen an den Knotenpunkten und kann über die Vorschrift (3.10)
jeden Punkt im Element interpolieren.

Dieses Verfahren verspricht eine große Anwendungsbreite auch in anderen Gebieten. Man
denke hier zunächst an digitale Geländemodelle, die jedoch in den meisten Fällen nur die Höhen
des Geländes über einem Raster enthalten. In einer weiteren Stufe sind hier auch die Ableitungen

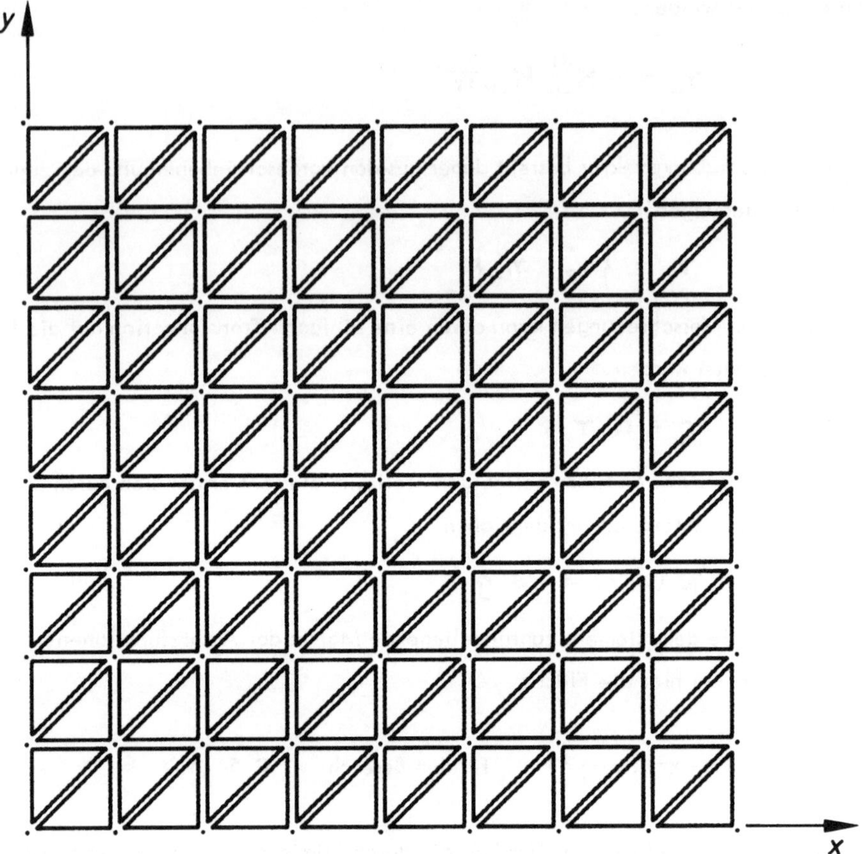

128 TUBA 3 Elemente

81 vorgeschriebene Verschiebungen (w an allen Knoten)

89 unterdrückte Verschiebungen (Randbedingungen)

316 unbekannte Verschiebungen

Randbedingungen : $x = 0$ und $x = 1$: $w_y = 0$, $w_{yy} = 0$

$y = 0$ und $y = 1$: $w_x = 0$, $w_{xx} = 0$

$x = 0.5$ und $y = 0.5$: $w_{xy} = 0$

Bild 2   Flächendefinition mit finiten Elementen
Idealisierung der Fläche $w = 16(x - x^2)(y - y^2)$

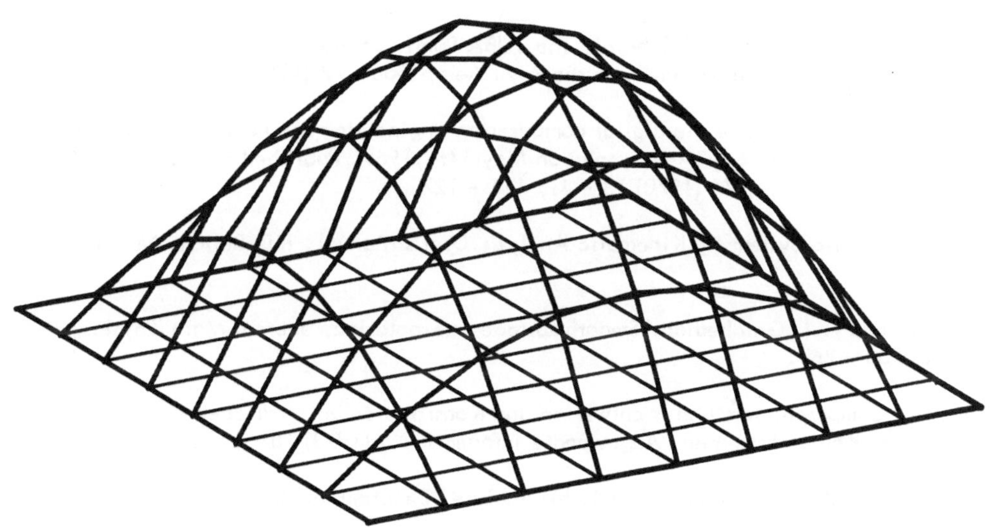

Bild 3   Flächendefinition mit finiten Elementen

Bildschirmdarstellung der Fläche $w = 16(x - x^2)(y - y^2)$

etwa zur Berechnung von Fallinien und Wasserläufen zu berücksichtigen. Aber auch andere Flächen, wie Dachformen von Bauwerken, Formteile aus dem Maschinenbau, Schiffsformen, Flugzeugformen usw., lassen sich in der diskretisierten Form verarbeiten. Das Entwerfen der Form ist Voraussetzung für weitere Berechnungen bzw. kann ohne Betrachtung der Folgeuntersuchungen nicht separat behandelt werden. Hier zeigen sich dann die Vorteile eines Modells, das für die verschiedenen Untersuchungen gleichermaßen gut geeignet ist.

4.   Literatur

[1] J.H.Argyris, Energy theorems and structural analysis, part 1, general theory. Aircraft Engineering, 26 (1954) 347 - 356, 383 - 387, 394. 27 (1955) 42 - 58, 80 - 84, 125 - 134, 145 - 158. Also (Butterworths, London, 1960, 5th Ed. Plenum Press, New York, 1971).

[2] J.H.Argyris, I.Fried and D.W.Scharpf, The TUBA family of plate elements for the matrix displacement method, The Aeron.J. of the Roy. Aeron.Soc., 72 (1968) 701 - 709.

[3] J.H.Argyris, The impact of the digital computer on engineering sciences. 12th Lanchester Memorial Lecture at the Roy.Aeron.Soc. on May 14th, 1969. Published in The Aeron.J. of the Roy. Aeron.Soc., 74 (1970) 13 - 41, 111 - 127.

[4] ASKA - Automatic System for Kinematic Analysis, User's Manual, ISD-Bericht Nr.73, April 1971

[5] G.Birkhoff and H.L.Garabedian, Smooth surface interpolation, Journal Math.Physics, 39 (1960) 258 - 268.

[6] I.Grieger, Computerunterstütztes Entwerfen und Konstruieren mit endlichen Kurven-, Flächen- und Körperelementen, Angewandte Informatik, 3 (1973) 101 - 113.

[7] I.Grieger, INGA - Interaktive Graphische Analyse, Benutzerhandbuch, ISD Bericht Nr. 135, 1973.

[8] R.J.Hubbold, TDD - An interactive three-dimensional drawing program for graphical display and lightpen, Computer Graphics 70 Internat. Symposium, Brunel University, Uxbridge, England, April 1970.

[9] L.G.Roberts, Homogeneous matrix representation and manipulation of n-dimensional constructs, The Computer Display Review, Cambridge, Mass., USA, 1965.

[10] P.W. Throsby, A finite element approach to surface definition, The Computer Journal, 12 (1969) 385 - 387.

EINE WORTSPRACHE ZUR BESCHREIBUNG TECHNISCHER OBJEKTE

Klaus Leinemann, Ulrich Schumann

1. EINLEITUNG

Im Bereich der Konstruktion und Entwicklung technischer Produkte werden in steigen-
dem Maße elektronische Datenverarbeitungsanlagen eingesetzt. Die hierfür verwendeten
Programme und Programmsysteme sind normalerweise auf einen engen Anwendungsbereich
hin orientiert ("produktorientierte Programme") [7]. Schon kleinere prinzipielle
Produktvariationen führen häufig zu umfangreichen Änderungen der Programme und
zugehörigen Dateien. Es liegt nun nahe, nach einem grundsätzlichen Konzept für die
Produktbeschreibung im Bereich der Konstruktionsautomatisierung zu suchen, das gegenüber Konstruktionsvariationen weniger empfindlich ist. Die Arbeit, über die hier
berichtet wird, schlägt auf einem Teilgebiet der Beschreibung technischer Objekte
- nämlich für die Beschreibung ihrer körperlichen Gestalt - ein derartiges Konzept
vor. Diese Arbeit wurde in Zusammenarbeit mit der Firma Siemens, Bereich Datenverarbeitung, durchgeführt und auch durch die in diesem Bereich vorliegenden Erfahrungen mit einem Programmsystem zur automatischen Entwicklung von Leiterplatten für
Digitalrechner angeregt.

2. DIE ZU BESCHREIBENDE DATENMENGE

Wie in [4] ausgeführt, kann die Beschreibung eines technischen Objektes zurückgeführt werden auf die Beschreibung seiner Eigenschaften, seiner Struktur und seiner
Funktion. Dabei enthalten die Eigenschaften Merkmale, die das Objekt ohne jeden Bezug auf andere Objekte besitzt, seine Funktion ist gegeben durch die Menge aller
Relationen zu anderen Objekten, seine Struktur durch die geordnete Menge aller Objekte, aus denen es besteht. Funktion und Struktur laufen auf Systemuntersuchungen
hinaus, wobei einmal das Objekt in einem System und zum anderen selbst als System
betrachtet wird. In der Praxis am vordringlichsten und auch am weitesten fortgeschritten scheint uns die Beschreibung der Eigenschaften und hier vor allem der
geometrischen Eigenschaften, die in sehr vielen Entwurfsphasen eine Rolle spielen.

Eine dem Konstrukteur besonders naheliegende Methode der Darstellung von Körpern
beschreibt Körper als die Vereinigung (evtl. auch Differenz) mehrerer einfacher
Körperelemente. Es wird hier also quasi mit einem Baukasten gearbeitet. Die Körperelemente werden hierbei entweder vorab (a priori) als dem EDV-System bekannte
Elemente dargestellt oder mit einer der in [5] aufgeführten Methode vom Benutzer
definiert.

Diese Methode erlaubt in einfacher Weise den Übergang zu Modellen der Festigkeits-
analyse und der Temperaturberechnung von komplizierten Körpern, da sie der Darstellung von Körpern durch "Finite Elemente" entspricht.

Eine derartige "synthetische" Körperbeschreibung läßt einen geringeren Änderungs-
aufwand erwarten, da die einzelnen Bausteine ihre Individualität behalten, Änderungen sich aber vor allem auf Bausteine beziehen.Aufgrund der Untersuchungen von
Simon [6], wonach 70% der Einzelteile im Maschinenbau durch 16 geometrische
Konstruktionselemente vollständig dargestellt werden, kann man sich auf eine
relativ kleine Menge verschiedener Elementarbausteine beschränken.

3. BESCHREIBUNGSMETHODEN FÜR GEOMETRISCHE EIGENSCHAFTEN

Die Entwicklung der hardware-Einrichtung des Bildschirmgerätes (display) zusammen
mit einem Lichtgriffel (light pen) als Aus- und Eingabegeräte hat die Entwicklung
von rechnergestützten Entwurfssystemen entscheidend beeinflußt. Eine Pionierarbeit
auf diesem Gebiet ist das System SKETCHPAD[9].

Mit dem Lichtgriffel ist es möglich, signalartig gewisse Punkte oder Bereiche
auf dem Bildschirm auszuzeichnen und so direkt graphische Informationen dem Rechner mitzuteilen. Insbesondere kann auf diese Weise auf dem Bildschirm gezeichnet
werden oder auf dem Bildschirm etwas gezeigt werden.

Auf der anderen Seite steht die Entwicklung flexibler problemorientierter Wortsprachen, insbesondere im ICES-System [8]. Hier ist es möglich, benutzergerechte
Wortsprachen so zu definieren, daß der Benutzer sein Problem quasi wie in seiner
Umgangssprache beschreiben kann - allerdings ohne die Hilfsmittel des Skizzierens
und Zeigens auf einer Zeichnung. Programme mit graphischer Eingabe per Wortsprachen
sind z.B. COGO und GRAPHIC [1, 8].

Die Vorteile der Wortsprache gegenüber der graphischen Sprache sind:
- Unabhängigkeit von speziellen hardware-Einrichtungen,
- Genauere Eingabe von Koordinatenwerten u.ä.,
- die Eingabe ist selbstdokumentierend, sie bildet ein verständliches sprach-
  liches Modell des Objektes,
- Änderungen an der Eingabe können im Stapelbetrieb leicht durch Änderung der
  Eingabekarten erreicht werden,
- in der Anwendung vermutlich billiger.

Im Gegensatz zur graphischen Sprache fehlt dagegen der Wortsprache deren natürliche Verwandtschaft zum graphischen Problem. Dies äußert sich insbesondere bei
der Realisierung der Zeigeoperation in der Wortsprache. Hier können bestimmte

Objekte nur durch eine der folgenden Methoden identifiziert werden:

a) durch Namen, die der Benutzer diesen Objekten bei ihrer Erzeugung zugewiesen
   hat und die er entweder kennt oder sich vom Programm auf einer Zeichnung
   zeigen läßt (so realisiert in GRAPHIC),

b) durch funktionale Aussagen; z.B.
   - die linke untere Kante des Objektes 'A',
   - der Schnittpunkt der Linien 'L1' und 'L2'.

Wenn der Benutzer bei Erstellung seiner Wortsprachen-Eingabe schon weiß, welche
Objekte er einzeln ansprechen will, so wird er dies von vornherein mit einem
Namen versehen. Wenn dagegen nachträglich an einer vorliegenden Konstruktion
etwas geändert werden muß, so wird die Methode a) nicht ausreichen und ein mög-
lichst flexibler Satz von Funktionen der Art b) wird erforderlich, wenn nicht
Teile der Konstruktion ganz neu eingegeben werden sollen.

Aufgrund der genannten Vorteile der Wortsprache (insbesondere hardware-Unabhängig-
keit) wird im folgenden Kapitel eine spezielle Wortsprache zur Beschreibung einfacher Körper dargestellt. Diese Festlegung schließt ein interaktives Arbeiten
nicht aus: die Ausgabe kann auf einem Bildschirm erfolgen und die Wortsprache
über eine Tastatur eingegeben werden.

4. SPRACHENTWURF

Die KOSPRA-Wortsprache zur Beschreibung der Geometrie von Konstruktionsobjekten
ist eine Erweiterung von GRAPHIC, einer im Institut für Reaktorentwicklung der
Gesellschaft für Kernforschung entwickelten und implementierten Sprache für den
Umgang mit zweidimensionalen graphischen Objekten (Strichzeichnungen).

Die Verwendung von GRAPHIC als Fundament hat den Vorteil, daß über Implementierungsmöglichkeiten genaue Vorstellungen vorliegen, die Sprache also nicht nur ein
fiktiver Entwurf ist.

Aus der GRAPHIC-Sprache werden insbesondere entnommen:

- graphische Elemente wie Punkt, Text, Polygonzug, Linienzug aus Kreisbögen,
  Approximationskurve, Spline-Kurve, Koordinatenachse, Kreis, Kreisbogen,
  Schraffur;

- logisch-arithmetische Elemente: real, integer, boolean;

- graphische Operationen wie Linie durch zwei Punkte, Tangente von einem Punkt
  an einen Kreis etc.;

- <u>logisch-arithmetische Operationen</u> wie +, -, /, , , =, =;

- Statements zur Darstellung der Programmstruktur: BEGIN, DO, IF...THEN...ELSE, PROCEDURE, CALL.

4.1 Die KOSPRA-Geometrie

Grundelemente dieser Geometrie sind ebene Flächen in einer x-y-z-Ebene des raumfesten kartesischen x-y-z-Systems, beispielsweise Rechtecke und Kreise. Der Übergang in die dritte Dimension erfolgt, indem einer Fläche ein weiterer Parameter, die Körperhöhe, zugeordnet wird. Die Elementarkörper ("Bausteine") dieser Geometrie sind also gerade Zylinder mit parallelen, ebenen Grundflächen, die in der x-y-Ebene liegen.

Zusätzlich existiert eine Menge von Operationen, durch die neue, komplexere Flächen und Körper baukastenartig erzeugt werden können. Hierhin können die bereits definierten Objekte (die Operanden) beliebig im Raum verschoben, jedoch - aus pragmatischen Gründen - nur um eine zur Bezugsebene senkrechten Achse gedreht werden.

4.2 Die KOSPRA-Sprache

4.2.1 Die Definition von Bausteinen

Ein KOSPRA-Statement zur Definition eines geometrischen Objektes hat wie in GRAPHIC die Form

$$\left\{ \begin{array}{l} \text{SETZE} \\ \text{DEFINIERE} \end{array} \right\} \quad \underline{\text{name}} \quad [\left\{ \begin{array}{l} \text{ALS} \\ = \end{array} \right\}] \quad \underline{\text{objektspezifikation}}$$

Die Variante SETZE entspricht einer Zuweisung und bedeutet: "Bearbeite die Objektspezifikation und speichere das Ergebnis als Objekt, das durch <u>name</u> bezeichnet wird." Die andere Variante entspricht etwa einer FORTRAN-statement-function,d.h. bei jeder Referenz auf das Objekt mittels <u>name</u> wird die Objektspezifikation entsprechend den aktuellen Objektdaten ausgewertet.

Bei der Spezifikation eines Objektes wird unterschieden zwischen der Gestalt des Objektes und seiner Lage. Dieses Vorgehen entspricht dem Grundkonzept der Körperbeschreibung durch Elementarkörper (Definition der Gestalt eines Körpers - Verschieben des Körpers - Verschmelzen mit einem anderen Körper), es entspricht wohl auch der Denkweise des Konstrukteurs bei der Synthese von Geräten. Bei einer funktionalen Objektdefinition (z.B.Körper als Füllraum zwischen anderen Körpern) sind Gestalt- und Lageparameter allerdings verknüpft. Auch diese Eingabeart wurde berücksichtigt. Bei Trennung von Gestalt- und Lagebeschreibung können für fehlende Angaben Standard-Werte angenommen werden (z.B.der Koordinatenursprung und die Richtung der positiven x-Achse).

Die Definition einer Fläche oder eines Körpers sieht also so aus:

$$\left\{ \begin{array}{l} \text{DEFINIERE} \\ \text{SETZE} \end{array} \right\} \quad \underline{\text{name}} \quad [\ \left\{ \begin{array}{l} \text{ALS} \\ = \end{array} \right\}\ ]\ \underline{\text{gestalt}} \quad [\underline{\text{lage}}]$$

Beschreibung der Gestalt

Grundlage der Gestaltbeschreibung sind Elementarflächen wie Rechteck, Dreieck, Kreis, Kreissegment, Tangentenfläche und speziell für die Belange der Leiterplattentechnik: der Strich, ein langgestrecktes Flächenelement der Breite B, dessen Mittellinie durch einen Polygon- oder Linienzug gegeben ist.

DEF'DREI1' = DREIECK MIT DEN SEITEN 5. 6. 3.
DEF'RECHT1' = RECHTECK MIT SEITEN 4. 3.
DEF'STRICH1' = STRICH MIT BREITE 4. DEN WINKELN 10. 20. DEM VERLAUF ob.polygonzug
DEF'KREIS1' = KREIS RADIUS 6. CM

Dies sind Spezifikationen für Flächen, deren Lage durch Standard-Werte gegeben ist.

Die Gestaltangabe besteht aus zwei Teilen: dem Teil zur Flächenbeschreibung und einem Teil zur Überführung einer Fläche in einen Körper, wobei der Fläche eine Dicke zugeordnet wird.

DEF   <u>name</u> = <u>flächenbeschreibung</u> <u>art</u> [<u>lage</u>]

wobei <u>art</u>: = (FLAECHE | NKOERPER nh_1 nh_2 | ZKOERPER h_1 h_2 | NZKOERPER nh_1 h_2 |

ZNKOERPER h_1 nh_2)

Die Lage der beiden Grundflächen wird relativ zur Lage der Bezugsfläche angegeben durch Real-Werte oder durch Ebenennummern:

z.B. NKOERPER - 4 3 d.h. die untere Grundfläche liegt 4 Ebenen unter der Bezugsfläche, die oberen 3 Ebenen darüber. Der Standard-Wert für <u>art</u> ist FLAECHE.

Beschreibung der Lage

Grundlage der Lagebeschreibung ist ein raumfestes kartesisches Koordinatensystem, in dem weitere Koordinatensysteme definiert werden können. Koordinatensysteme sind also Objekte der Sprache, ihre Parameter sind: Bezugspunkt, Bezugsrichtung, Umrechnungsvorschriften.

DEF'KOORD1'=KOORDINATENSYSTEM KARTESISCH URSPRUNG 5. 4. RICHTUNG 10 GRAD RASTER 1. 3.

Vorgesehen sind zylindrische und kartesische Systeme mit kontinuierlicher Skala oder Raster, bei denen eine Ortsangabe durch Indizes eines variablen Rasternetzes erfolgt. Der Modifier KOORDINATENSYSTEM in einer Lage-Spezifikation stellt den Bezug zu einem definierten System her.

DEF'RECHT1'RECHTECK SEITEN 1. 2. BEZUEGLICH KOORDINATENSYSTEM 'KOORD1'

Die eigentliche Lagebestimmung geschieht durch die Parameter

$$\underline{lage:} \quad = \quad \underline{ort} \quad \quad \underline{richtung} \quad \quad \underline{ebene}$$

ort und richtung spezifizieren die Lage einer gegebenen Fläche in einer x-y-Ebene, ebene die Lage in der z-Richtung (ebene ist eine z-Koordinate oder eine Ebenennummer. Bei Verwendung beider Versionen wird durch einen Systembefehl die Korrespondenz hergestellt).

DEF 'R1' RECHTECK SEITEN 2. 3. ORT 'P1' RICHTUNG 10. NEBENE 5 KOORD'KOORD1'

Eine Definition einer Fläche oder eines Körpers sieht allgemein so aus:

$$\begin{Bmatrix} DEF \\ SET \end{Bmatrix} \underline{name} \; [\begin{Bmatrix} ALS \\ = \end{Bmatrix}] \; \underline{elementarfläche} \; [\underline{art}] \; [\underline{ort}] \; [\underline{richtung}] \; [\underline{ebene}] \; [\underline{bezugssystem}]$$

$$\longleftarrow \text{Gestalt} \longrightarrow \quad \longleftarrow \text{Lage} \longrightarrow$$

Wesentlich für ein Baukastensystem ist, daß die Lageangaben auch relativ zu anderen Bausteinen möglich sind.

4.2 Operationen mit Objekten

Zwei Operationsgruppen sind hier, entsprechend den beiden Hauptparametern eines Objektes, zu unterscheiden: Operation zur Veränderung der Gestalt und zur Beeinflussung der Lage. Ein Statement hat die allgemeine Form

$$\begin{Bmatrix} DEFINIERE \\ SETZE \end{Bmatrix} \quad \underline{name} \quad [\begin{Bmatrix} ALS \\ = \end{Bmatrix}] \; \underline{operation - angewandt - auf - Objekte}$$

Zu den Gestaltoperationen gehören die Operationen

    VEREINIGUNG   (ob1 [ob2])
    DURCHSCHNITT   (ob1 [ob2])
    DIFFERENZ   (ob1 [ob2])
    KOMPLEMENT   (ob1)

Die Semantik dieser Operationen entspricht der Mengenoperation, die auf die den Flächen bzw. Körpern zugeordneten Punktmengen anzuwenden ist. Neue Objekte können auch aus bereits definierten mittels Vergrößerungs-und Verkleinerungsoperationen erzeugt werden:

DEF 'A1' VERGROESSERUNG UM FAKTOR 2. 3. 4. BEZUEGLICH 'P1' VON 'AO'

Das Objekt AO wird bezüglich des Punktes P1 in x-y-z-Richtung um die Faktoren 2., 3., 4 vergrößert. Entsprechend wird verkleinert. Durch negative Vergrößerungen werden Spiegelungen realisiert.

Die Lage eines Objektes kann durch die <u>Lageoperationen</u> VERSCHIEBUNG bzw. VER-
DREHUNG entsprechend verändert werden. Eine weitere Lageoperation ermöglicht
die implizite Angabe der Verdrehungs- und Verschiebungsparameter durch die Angabe von <u>Bedingungen</u>:

DEF 'A'TRANSPORTIERE SO DASS <u>bedingung</u> [<u>bedingung</u> $_n$] * <u>objekt</u>

Dabei sind folgende Bedingungen möglich:

LA   (ob1   ob2)   "liegt auf"
PA   (ob1   ob2)   "ist parallel zu"
TA   (ob1   ob2)   "ist Tangente zu"
SE   (ob1   ob2)   "ist senkrecht zu"
LI   (ob1   n)   "liegt in Ebene n"

Das Objekt <u>objekt</u> wird dabei solange zunächst verschoben und dann verdreht, bis
alle Bedingungen erfüllt sind oder festgestellt wird, daß die Bedingungen nicht
eingehalten werden können. Diese Operation erscheint uns für den Konstrukteur
besonders hilfreich zu sein.

4.3 Operationen zur Identifikation

In dieser Arbeit gehen die Autoren von der Vorstellung aus, daß die Objekte in
Form von Daten (strukturiert) in einer Bibliothek gespeichert sind. Wie diese
Objektmodelle entstanden sind, ist nicht bekannt, d.h.die Programme zu ihrer
Erzeugung sind nicht verwendbar, nur die den Objekten zugewiesenen Namen stehen
zur Verfügung. In diesem Falle muß die Sprache Möglichkeiten zur Identifizierung
unbenannter Objekte (Elemente) vorsehen.

Sprachlich treten zwei Probleme auf:

- Festlegung eines Bezugselementes- oder -systems. (Festes Koordinatensystem
  oder das als "erstes" abgespeicherte Element eines Objektes etc.)

- Beschreibung der Relation des gesuchten Elementes zu dem Bezugsobjekt ("das
  unterste"; "in der Nähe von").

Als Bezug wird das feste Koordinatensystem oder ein Element eines Objektes verwendet.

DEF 'A' EXTREMELEMENT OBERSTER LINKESTER PUNKT VON 'B'(dabei enthält 'B' das
                                                    Element 'P1')

Außerdem sind Operationen definiert, die das n-te Element einer gegebenen Element-
menge herausgreifen.

4.4 Sonderoperationen

Über die Grundoperationen hinaus sind Operationen nützlich, die Grundoperationen zusammenfassen und Parameter dieser Operationen implizit festlegen. Diese Operationen sind konstruktionsspezifisch.

Der Definition einer räumlich geordneten Objektmenge vorwiegend gleicher Objekte dient die Operation MUSTER.

DEF'A'MUSTER [musterart] [objektanordnung] [rasterwinkel] rasterzahl rasterabstand

[ort] [richtung] [rasterpunkt, ausnahmeobjekt]* regelobjekt

Allen Rasterpunkten wird ein Regelobjekt zugeordnet, mit Ausnahme der Rasterpunkte, denen ein Ausnahmeobjekt zugewiesen wird.

Dem Konstruieren auf einer Mittellinie entspringt die Operation KETTE: Die Lage des folgenden Elements wird jeweils aus der Lage des vorangehenden abgeleitet indem nach jeder Gestaltdefinition das Bezugskoordinatensystem verschoben wird.

$$\text{DEF'A' KETTE ANFANG} \begin{Bmatrix} x \ y \\ \text{ob.punkt} \end{Bmatrix} \text{ob2} \left[\left([\text{RICHTUNG}] \begin{Bmatrix} +X \\ -X \\ +Y \\ -Y \\ N \end{Bmatrix} \right] \begin{bmatrix} \text{VEREINIGUNG} \\ \text{DURCHSCHNITT} \\ \text{DIFFERENZ} \\ \text{REIHE} \end{bmatrix} \text{obi} \right) \right] \text{ENDE}$$

ob2, obi sind Flächen- oder Körperobjekte

Das Objekt ob2 wird in einem Koordinatensystem definiert, dessen Ursprung durch (x, y) gegeben ist.

Durch die Angabe einer Verschiebungsrichtung (RICHTUNG) kann das lokale Koordinatensystem verschoben werden, so daß der Ursprung auf den äußersten Schnittpunkt der bezeichneten Achse mit der Randkurve des vorher definierten Objektes fällt.

Wird für die Richtung N angegeben, so erfolgt keine Verschiebung. Am neuen Ursprung wird das Koordinatensystem gedreht, so daß die y-Achse Tangente zu der Umrandung ist.

In dem verschobenen System wird obi definiert. Es kann mit dem vorher definierten Objekt durch die Operationen VE, DU, DI verknüpft werden, oder aber es wird nur angefügt (RE), wobei das so erzeugte Objekt aus mehreren Einzelkörpern besteht, für die dann allerdings geometrische Bedingungen gelten.

5. SCHLUSSFOLGERUNGEN

Oberstes Prinzip des Sprachenentwurfs war die Anpassung der Sprache und der Sprachfähigkeiten an die Denk- und Arbeitsweise des Konstrukteurs.

Dieser Sprachentwurf zeigt, daß ein Baukastensystem mit einer Menge von Elementarobjekten und einer Menge von Grundoperationen auf den Objekten sich für die

Beschreibung der Geometrie technischer Objekte eignet und eine Realisierung durch eine _Wortsprache_ sinnvoll ist.

Außer für die Sprache existiert ein Entwurf für eine entsprechende Datenstruktur [5], in der die sprachlich eingegebenen Daten gespeichert werden können.

Die bisherige Beschränkung auf geometrische Daten ist prinzipiell unbefriedigend, da in den meisten konstruktiven Problembereichen gleichzeitig viele weitere Daten für einen rechnergestützten Entwurf benötigt werden. In Zukunft sollte man daher nicht noch viel weiteren Aufwand in neue und elegantere Methoden zur Geometriebeschreibung stecken, als vielmehr die Verallgemeinerung auf andere Objektdaten anstreben.

Bisher wurde KOSPRA wegen seiner Abhängigkeit von GRAPHIC (hohe zu erwartende Rechenkosten infolge interpretativer Verarbeitung) und ICES (nicht auf allen Maschinen implementierbar) nicht implementiert. Eine Weiterführung dieser Arbeiten nach der Entwicklung eines EDV-Systems zum rechnergestützten Entwurf (REGENT,[2, 3]) ist vorgesehen.

L I T E R A T U R

[1]   Enderle, G., Schlechtendahl,E.G., Schumann,U., Schuster,R.,
KFK-1722 (Mai 1973)

[2]   Enderle,G., Katz,F., Leinemann,K., Schlechtendahl,E.G., Schnauder,H.,
Schumann,U., Schuster, R.,
KFK-Ext. 8/72-2 (Juni 1972)

[3]   Enderle, G., Leinemann,K., Schlechtendahl,E.G., Schnauder,H., Schumann,U.,
Schuster,R.,
KFK-Ext. 8/72-4 (Oktober 1972)

[4]   Leinemann,K., Schumann,U., _KFK-Ext. 8/72-5_ (Februar 1973)

[5]   Leinemann,K., Schumann,U., _KFK-Ext. 8/72-6_ (Februar 1973)

[6]   Simon,R., _Diss. TH Aachen_ (1968)

[7]   Schlechtendahl, E.G., _Konstruktion_ 25,121-124 (1973)

[8]   Schlechtendahl,E.G., Schumann,U., _KFK-1586_ (Mai 1972)

[9]   Sutherland, I.E., _Spring Joint Computer Conference_, 329-346 (1963)

VERFAHREN ZUR SIMULATION SOZIOÖKONOMISCHER SYSTEME

Peter Hecheltjen

Die zunehmende Aktivität des Staates in der Sozial- und Wirtschaftspolitik, verbunden mit dem Bestreben einer rationalen
Kalkulation des Mitteleinsatzes, stellt immer höhere Anforderungen an die anzuwendenden Planungs- und Prognosetechniken.
Insbesondere besteht ein Interesse an Informationen über die
Auswirkungen alternativer Maßnahmen auf ökonomische und gesellschaftliche Zielvariablen. Der hohe Komplexitätsgrad der zugrundeliegenden Entscheidungsmodelle wird dabei in Zukunft den
Einsatz elektronischer Rechenanlagen unumgänglich machen.

Im Rahmen ihres Forschungsprojektes "Sozialpolitisches Ent-
scheidungs- und Indikatorensystem für die Bundesrepublik
Deutschland" (SPES-Projekt) beschäftigt sich die Sozialpolitische Forschergruppe an der Universität Frankfurt/Main (1)
mit der Entwicklung eines solchen computerunterstützten Ent-
scheidungssystems. Eine der Zielsetzungen besteht darin, einen
Simulator bereitzustellen, mit dem wirtschafts- und sozialpolitische Entscheidungsalternativen durchgespielt werden können.

Neben einer Fülle inhaltlicher Fragen, die sich bei einer Ausgestaltung solcher Systeme ergeben, sind dabei auch verschiedene
Informatik-Probleme zu lösen. Einmal müssen nämlich Verfahren
zur Verwaltung einer Vielzahl sehr unterschiedlicher Datenbe-
stände bereitgestellt werden. Hier kann man allerdings schon
auf recht brauchbare Datenbankkonzepte zurückgreifen. Die noch
zu lösenden Aufgaben sind durchweg inhaltlicher Art und resultie-
ren aus Konsistenzanforderungen, denen das Datenmaterial in seiner Ursprungsform oft nicht genügt.

Aus der Sicht der Informatik dürften die Arbeiten in Zusammenhang mit der Entwicklung eines Simulationssystems von besonderem
Interesse sein. Immerhin sind Simulationstechniken die langfristig wohl wichtigste Anwendung der Informatik im Bereich der

---

(1) Vgl. SOZIALPOLITISCHE FORSCHERGRUPPE, Entscheidungs- und
Indikatorensystem für die Bundesrepublik Deutschland,
Frankfurt 1971.

Sozialwissenschaften (2). Auf diesem Gebiet sind in den letzten
Jahren eine Vielzahl von Entwicklungsarbeiten zu verzeichnen,
wenn auch die sich hier bietenden Möglichkeiten bisher nur wenig
genutzt werden.

Im folgenden soll zunächst versucht werden, die spezifische Struktur von Simulatoren, wie sie in den Sozialwissenschaften gebräuchlich sind, zu skizzieren, anschließend wird zu diskutieren sein,
inwieweit eine Verknüpfung dieser Simulationskonzepte sinnvoll und
realisierbar ist.

1. Die Grundstruktur der Simulationsverfahren

Die Anwendung von Simulationstechniken bedarf heute kaum noch
einer Rechtfertigung (3). Der stetig sich erhöhende Komplexitätsgrad sozioökonomischer Modelle schließt zunehmend die Anwendung der sich alternativ anbietenden analytischen Lösungstechniken aus. Dies liegt einmal an der Begrenztheit der analytischen Lösungstechnik selbst, denn die allgemeine Lösbar-
keit eines konkreten Gleichungssystems ist nur inbestimmten
Fällen gegeben. Aber auch wenn eine geschlossene Lösung theoretisch möglich wäre, braucht es nicht unbedingt von Vorteil zu
sein, diese zu ermitteln. Eine Interpretation der Lösung verlangt
auch hier oft die Berechnung konkreter Einzelfälle, ohne die eine
geschlossene Lösung umfangreicher Systeme nicht mehr überschaubar wäre. Der Nutzen der Anwendung einer analytischen Lösungstechnik läge dann nur noch in einer Erleichterung der Berechnung
von Einzelfällen.

Wenn auch der Einsatz von Simulationstechniken unumstritten ist,
so gilt dies nicht für das jeweils anzuwendende Verfahren. Wenig geeignet für eine Anwendung in den Sozialwissenschaften sind

---

(2) Vgl. H.-J. KRUPP, Artikel "Volkswirtschaft", in: P.MERTENS,
Angewandte Informatik, Berlin 1972.

(3) Vgl. W.MEIßNER, Zur Methodologie der Simulation, in:
ZfgSt, 126(1970),S.385 ff.; H.SIEBERT, Simulation als Infor-
mationsinstrument der Wirtschaftspolitik, in: ZfgSt,126(1970),
S.409

Verfahren der Ereignisfolgesimulation (4). Dies hat vornehmlich
zwei Gründe:

Ereignisorientierte Verfahren sind einmal deshalb meist ungeeig-
net, weil man in sozioökonomischen Modellen oftmals keine Einzelereignisse, sondern Aggregate modellmäßig erfaßt. Solche Modelle
enthalten dann Bestandsgrößen, die Informationen über einen bestimmten Bestand - etwa der Bevölkerung - zu einem bestimmten
Zeitpunkt liefern sowie Stromgrößen, die beispielsweise Aussagen enthalten über monetäre bzw. Güter- und Leistungsströme
in einem Zeitintervall.

Aber auch dort, wo einzelne Ereignisse modellmäßig erfaßt werden,
sind Verfahren der Ereignisfolgesimulation in der Regel wenig geeignet. Meist liegen nämlich die Daten für irgendwelche Einzel-
entscheidungen nur für einen Zeitintervall vor, und man kann dann
lediglich eine Aussage darüber machen, mit welcher Wahrscheinlichkeit ein Ereignis in einem Zeitintervall eintritt bzw. nicht eintritt. Zur Durchführung einer Ereignisfolgesimulation wäre es dagegen erforderlich, jeweils den genauen zeitlichen Abstand zum
nächstfolgenden Ereignis zu kennen. Bei der Ereignisfolgesimulation ergeben sich die Zeitänderungen nämlich dadurch, daß die
Simulationszeit auf den Zeitpunkt des von allen zukünftigen Ereignissen zunächst anstehenden Ereignisses springt.

Die in den Sozialwissenschaften gebräuchlichen Simulationsver-
fahren sind deshalb nahezu alle intervallorientiert. Erforderlich ist jeweils ein Modell, das eine Ausgangssituation zu Beginn
einer Periode mithilfe von Simulationsoperatoren in eine Endsituation am Periodenende transformiert und dabei zugleich die relevanten Stromgrößen bzw. Einzelereignisse in diesem Zeitintervall
bestimmt.

Eine Simulation nur über eine Periode ist allerdings selten. Da
die Endsituation der laufenden Periode wieder als Ausgangssituation
der Folgeperiode betrachtet werden kann, läßt sich dieser Prozeß

---

(4) Siehe hierzu PH.KIVIAT, Simulation Languages, in: TH.H.
NAYLOR (Hrsg.), Computer Simulation Experiments with Models of
Economic Systems, S. 406 ff.

mehrfach wiederholen (vgl. Abb. 1), so daß sich für die einzelnen
Simulationsvariablen Zeitpfade ergeben. Grundsätzlich ist diese

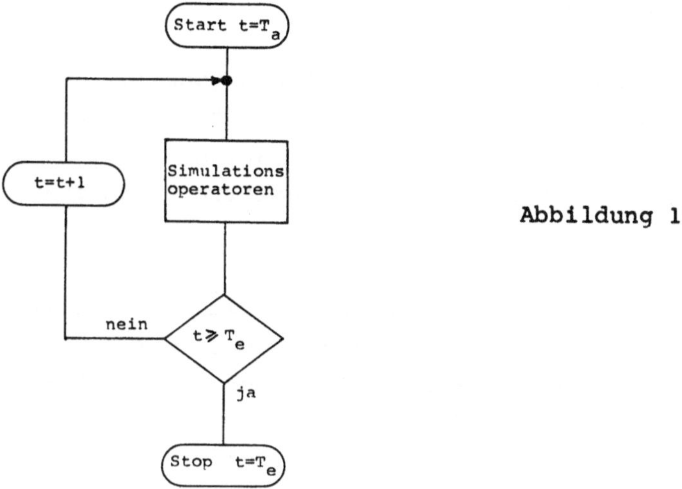

Abbildung 1

Transformation beliebig oft wiederholbar, im Einzelfall hängt die
Anzahl der Wiederholungen vom jeweiligen Prognosehorizont ab.

Ziel dieser Simulationen ist es festzustellen, welche Werte ökonomische oder sonstige gesellschaftliche Zielgrößen in Abhängigkeit von bestimmten politischen Maßnahmen annehmen. Hierzu kann
man einmal die in den Simulationsoperatoren enthaltenen Instrumentvariablen verändern, man kann aber auch die Hypothesen über
das Systemverhalten oder die Daten der Ausgangssituation vari-
ieren.

Meist bietet sich eine Vielzahl von Möglichkeiten an, doch ist
man dann darauf angewiesen, eine Auswahl zu treffen. Sehr rasch
kommt man nämlich, wie die Kombinatorik zeigt, in Größenbereiche,
die nicht mehr verarbeitbar sind. Schon bei 5 Politikinstrumenten
mit je 5 möglichen Parameterwerten wären - wollte man alle sich
hieraus ergebenden Kombinationsmöglichkeiten der Instrumente durch-
spielen - 5^5 = 3125 Durchläufe nötig.

2. Makro-Simulatoren

Wenn auch bisher ein systematischer Einsatz von Simulationsmodellen in der Wirtschafts- und Gesellschaftspolitik noch selten

ist, so hat doch in den sechziger Jahren die Entwicklung von Simu-
lationssystemen sprunghaft zugenommen. Nahezu für alle Industrie-
staaten der westlichen Welt existieren heute zumindest simulations-
fähige ökonometrische Systeme (5).

Durchweg handelt es sich hierbei um Makro-Modelle, in denen eine
Erklärung und Prognose hochaggregierter Daten für eine Volkswirtschaft erfolgt. So wird z.B. in einem solchen System die Gesamt-
summe der Konsumausgaben bzw. der Investitionen in einer Periode
errechnet.

Bei der Entwicklung solcher Simulatoren ist zunächst eine Reihe
inhaltlicher Probleme zu lösen. Voraussetzung für eine Simulation ist nämlich, daß die relevanten Hypothesen in Gleichungsform
gebracht und geschätzt werden, um die Parameter der Verhaltens-
gleichung zu bestimmen. Da in solchen Systemen einige Variablen
sowohl als abhängige wie auch als unabhängige Größen eingehen,
ergeben sich in der Regel zusätzliche Probleme durch die Inter-
dependenz. Dies betrifft einmal die Schätzung der Parameter wi'
auch die Lösungstechnik.

Die Verarbeitung großer interdependenter Systeme bereitet heute
immer noch erhebliche Schwierigkeiten. Man versucht deshalb,
Großsysteme in blockrekursive Grundstrukturen aufzulösen, wofür
es mittlerweile schon recht leistungsfähige Algorithmen (6) gibt.
Eine Simulation solcher Systeme besteht nun darin, mittels der
exogenen bzw. verzögert endogenen, d.h. aller zu Beginn einer
Periode bekannten, Variablen die endogenen Variablen zu bestimmen.

---

(5) Vgl. u.a. W.KRELLE et al., Ein Prognosesystem für die wirt-
schaftliche Entwicklung der Bundesrepublik Deutschland, Meisen-
heim 1969; J.S.DUESENBERRY,G.FROMM,L.R.KLEIN und E.KUH (Hrsg.),
The Brookings Quarterly Econometric Model of the United States,
Amsterdam 1965.

(6) Siehe D.V.STEWARD, Partitioning and Tearing Systems of
Equations, in: J.SIAM Numerical Analysis, Ser.B., 2(1965),
S. 345 ff.

Recht einfach ist dies für den Fall eines linearen Gleichungssystems:

$$A\,y = B\,x$$

läßt sich umformen in

$$y = A^{-1}\,B\,x$$

mit

    y   Vektor der endogenen Variablen

    x   Vektor der exogenen (bzw. der vorherbestimmten) Variablen

    A,B Koeffizientenmatrizen

Die heute gebräuchlichen ökonometrischen Makro-Modelle sind freilich in der Regel nichtlinear. Oft liegt dies daran, daß der Preisindex mit einer preisbereinigten Größe multipliziert wird und beide endogene Variablen sind. Hier hat man nun einmal die Möglichkeit, solche Systeme - etwa mittels Taylor-Reihen - zu linearisieren. Wenn auch gelegentlich von dieser Möglichkeit Gebrauch gemacht wird, so hat sich doch gezeigt, daß dieses Verfahren recht unhandlich und wenig flexibel ist. Jede Veränderung der Spezifizierung erfordert nämlich umfangreiche Umstellungen in dem System. Sieht man einmal von den relativ einfachen Lösungstechniken für lineare Gleichungssysteme ab, so sind heute allgemein Iterationsverfahren gebräuchlich, die nach der Gauss-Seidel-Methode arbeiten. Sie erlauben auch die Lösung nichtlinearer Modelle.

Mittlerweile sind schon mehrere Programmsysteme verfügbar, die relativ leicht eine Simulation von Makro-Modellen ermöglichen. Erwähnenswert ist hier das Programm SIMULATE (7) sowie das Programmsystem TROLL (8). Insbesondere das System TROLL bringt bei einer Simulation von Makro-Systemen eine erhebliche Erleichterung. Neben Routinen zur Simulation von Modellen enthält es nämlich noch Subsysteme zur Schätzung von Gleichungen, zudem erlaubt es Zugriffe auf eine Datenbank.

---

(7) Siehe CH.C.HOLT et al. Program Simulate II, SSRI, Wisconsin 1967.

(8) Siehe M.EISNER, A Researcher's Overview of the TROLL/1 System, NBER Computer Research Center, Cambridge/Mass. 1972.

3. Mikro-Simulatoren

Die ausschließliche Erfassung und Prognose von Makro-Aggregaten
ist in vielen Fällen unbefriedigend. Insbesondere aus der Sicht
der Sozialpolitik, die sich mit der sozialen Lage einzelner Be-
völkerungsgruppen beschäftigt, ist eine Disaggregation wünschenswert. Makro-Modelle können zwar in einem sozialpolitischen Ent-
scheidungssystem wichtige Informationen liefern, soweit sozialpolitische Maßnahmen den üblicherweise der Wirtschaftspolitik
zugerechneten Zielkatalog berühren. Prognosesysteme, die zur
Entscheidungshilfe in der Sozialpolitik herangezogen werden sollen,
müssen jedoch zusätzlich Informationen enthalten über die soziale
Lage von Individuen bzw. sozioökonomischen Elementareinheiten wie
Haushalten und Familien.

Bei diesen Fragestellungen setzt man am zweckmäßigsten Mikro-Simulatoren ein (9). Immerhin besitzt man eine Fülle von Hypothesen
über das Verhalten von Individuen und sozioökonomischen Elementareinheiten, und es liegt daher nahe, dieses Verhalten in einem Simulationsmodell auf der Mikro-Ebene abzubilden. Neben dem Gewinn
an zusätzlichen Informationen ist zu vermuten, daß sich eine Prognose der Entwicklung sozioökonomischer Systeme verbessern läßt,
wenn man nicht nur Makro-Aggregate, sondern auch das Wissen über
das Verhalten der sie beeinflussenden elementaren Entscheidungseinheiten mit in die Vorhersage einbezieht.

Jede dieser Einheiten ist bei der Mikro-Simulation durch eine bestimmte Anzahl meist diskreter Merkmale eindeutig bestimmt. Zu-
grundegelegt ist in der Regel eine Total- bzw. Stichprobenerhe-
bung der Bevölkerung, die durch den Simulationsprozeß periodenwei-
se fortgeschrieben wird. Solch ein Bevölkerungsquerschnitt enthält meist Informationen über einzelne Personen, aber auch über
die Zugehörigkeit dieser Personen zu sozioökonomischen Einheiten,
wie aus Abb. 2 zu ersehen ist. Kleinste Einheit ist die

---

(9) Siehe G.H.ORCUTT et al., Microanalytic Simulation of
Household Behavior, in: Annals of Economic and Social Measurement,
1(1972), S.141 ff.; P.HECHELTJEN, Bevölkerungsentwicklung und
Erwerbstätigkeit, Köln-Opladen 1973.

Einzelperson. Eine oder mehrere dieser Einzelpersonen bilden eine

```
┌─────────────────────────────────────────────────────────────┐
│ Haushalt                                                      │
│ ┌───────────────────────┐ ┌─────────────────────────────────┐│
│ │ Familie 1.            │ │ Familie 2.                      ││
│ │┌──────────┐┌──────────┐│ │┌──────────┐┌──────────┐┌────────┐│
│ ││Person 1.1.││Person 1.2.│ ││Person 2.1.││Person 2.2.││Person 2.3.│
│ │└──────────┘└──────────┘│ │└──────────┘└──────────┘└────────┘│
│ └───────────────────────┘ └─────────────────────────────────┘│
└─────────────────────────────────────────────────────────────┘
```

Abbildung 2

Familie, eine oder mehrere Familien bilden einen Haushalt.

Auf der Mikro-Ebene lassen sich relativ leicht Prozesse wie Geburt,
Tod, Eheschließung und Scheidung simulieren, es ist aber auch möglich, das ökonomische Verhalten der betrachteten Einheiten durch
Zufallsprozesse zu bestimmen. In Abhängigkeit von gegebenen Merk-
malen kann man so etwa den Eintritt von Personen in das Erwerbsleben, ihren Verdienst und eine Reihe anderer interessierender
Variablen ermitteln. In Analogie zu den Makro-Systemen, durch die
Verhaltensannahmen für die gesamte Volkswirtschaft getroffen werden,
werden hier somit Relationen aufgestellt, die das Verhalten einer
sozioökonomischen Einheit beschreiben. Zu beachten bleibt freilich,
daß auf der Mikro-Ebene nicht nur stetige, sondern auch diskrete
Relationen auftreten. So interessiert auf der Makro-Ebene z.B. die
Zahl der in das Erwerbsleben eintretenden Personen, diese Zahl resultiert jedoch aus vielen in den Haushalten getroffenen Alternativ-
entscheidungen, die in dem Mikro-Simulator durch einen stochastischen Prozeß zu erklären sind.

Vergleichsweise einfach kann man bei der Mikro-Simulation Prozesse
erfassen, die die sozioökonomischen Einheiten in ihrer personalen
Struktur unverändert lassen, wie etwa der Eintritt einer Person
in das Erwerbsleben oder der Kauf eines Autos. Einen recht großen Programmieraufwand erfordert dagegen eine Implementation von
Prozessen der Bildung und Auflösung jener Einheiten. Insbesondere
Zuordnungsprozsse, wie sie z.B. bei einer Eheschließung notwendig
werden, stellen hohe verarbeitungstechnische Ansprüche. Immerhin
muß es bei einer Simulation möglich sein, eine Person in der Stichprobe irgendeinem Haushalt aufgrund vorgegebener Merkmale zuzuordnen. Man hat hier die Wahl zwischen dem Aufbau umfangreicher In-
dextabellen oder rechenzeitaufwendigen Sortierprozessen. Welches

der möglichen Verfahren dabei optimal ist, hängt im wesentlichen
von der Anlagenkonfiguration ab und muß deshalb von Fall zu Fall
entschieden werden.

4. Die Verknüpfung von Makro- und Mikro-Simulatoren

Erst aus einer Vereinigung von Makro- und Mikro-Simulatoren ergibt
sich ein leistungsfähiges Simulationssystem zur Analyse und Prognose sozioökonomischer Prozesse. Makroökonomische Modelle sind
zwar eine nützliche Hilfe bei der Analyse von Auswirkungen wirt-
schaftspolitischer Maßnahmen auf Makro-Ziele. Aber auch wenn
diese Makro-Modelle in sehr viele Sektoren unterteilt werden, erlauben sie keinen Einblick in die Verteilungswirkungen dieser Maßnahmen. Andererseits wird das Verhalten sozioökonomischer Entscheidungseinheiten nicht unerheblich auch von dem Verhalten anderer Einheiten beeinflußt. Hier sind Makro-Daten erforderlich, in denen sich
das Verhalten aller übrigen Entscheidungseinheiten widerspiegelt. Wünschenswert sind somit Simulatoren, in denen sowohl Makro- wie auch
Mikro-Prozesse erklärt werden.

Die Sozialpolitische Forschergruppe hat im Rahmen des SPES-Projektes
einen Simulationsansatz entwickelt, in dem beide Simulationsverfah-
ren vereinigt sind. Ein wesentliches Strukturmerkmal dieses Simulators ist sein modularer Aufbau. Wie man aus Abb. 3 entnehmen
kann, besteht das Gesamtsystem aus mehreren Blöcken, die in einer bestimmten Weise miteinander verknüpft sind. Die Simulatoren zur Prognose der Bevölkerungsentwicklung und des sozioökonomischen Status sind
hierbei als Mikro-Simulatoren ausgelegt, die übrigen Simulatoren
sind zunächst als Makro-Simulatoren konzipiert. Langfristig ist
geplant, noch weitere Module durch Mikro-Simulatoren zu beschreiben.

Die Verknüpfung der Module, insbesondere die zwischen Mikro- und Makro-Simulatoren, wirft dabei nicht wenige Probleme auf. Vor einer
Übertragung in den Makro-Teil müssen die Mikro-Variablen nämlich
aggregiert werden. Da der Mikro-Simulationsprozeß vergleichsweise
zeitaufwendig ist, muß zudem auf ein Nachiterieren, wie dies bei
interdependenten Makro-Modellen aufgrund des Einsatzes der Gauss-
Seidel-Lösungstechnik üblich ist, verzichtet werden. Rückwirkungen
der Makro-Aggregate auf die Mikro-Variablen kann man somit erst
mit einer einperiodigen Verzögerung berücksichtigen. Im übrigen

ist dies ein typisches Beispiel dafür, daß zwischen der Formulierung eines Modells und seiner Übertragung in ein Rechenprogramm
ein interdependenter Zusammenhang besteht. Während früher die
Verfügbarkeit über eine analytische Lösungstechnik die Theorie-
bildung erheblich beeinflußte, sind dies heute die technischen
Möglichkeiten der Datenverarbeitung.

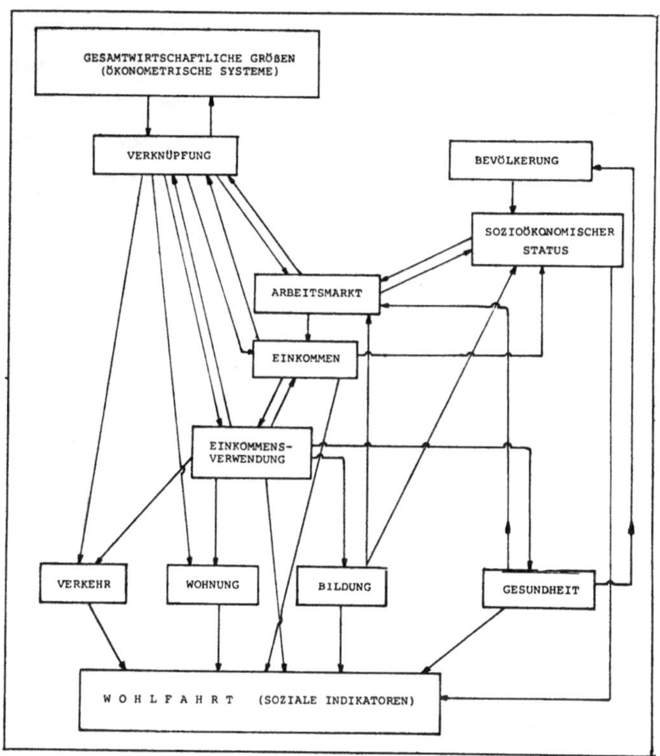

Abbildung 3

Bei der EDV-technischen Implementierung wurde versucht, das System
möglichst flexibel zu halten. Deswegen erfolgte auch eine strikte
Trennung zwischen Programmsegmenten, die der Systemsteuerung dienen,
und Programmsegmenten, in denen die Simulatoren implementiert
sind. In dem Steuerteil wird einmal die gesamte Ablaufsteuerung des Simulationsprozesses, aber auch der Dialog
des Benutzers mit dem Simulator überwacht. Dabei war zu berücksichtigen, daß die Bedienung eines solchen Systems grundsätzlich
keine vertieften EDV-Kenntnisse erfordern sollte. Es wurde deshalb aus Worten der Umgangssprache eine Dialogsprache entwickelt,

die ein relativ einfaches Steuern des Simulationsprozesses von
einer Dialogstation erlaubt. Der Benutzer kann von dort das Gesamtsystem oder Teilsysteme aktivieren. Substrukturen des Simulators relativ leicht verändern, um sie bestimmten Fragestellungen anzupassen, insbesondere kann er aber auch relativ leicht
wirtschaftspolitische Instrumentvariablen eingeben

Die konzeptionellen Arbeiten sowie die technische Implementierung
des Simulators sind mittlerweile abgeschlossen. Der Schwerpunkt
zukünftiger Arbeiten wird im wesentlichen bei der inhaltlichen
Ausgestaltung des Systems liegen, wobei die Datenbeschaffung und
das Testen von Hypothesen noch eine Vielzahl ungelöster Probleme
beinhalten.

Adressen der Autoren

Aguzzi, Gianni; Istituto Matematico, Viale Morgagni 67/A
   I 50134 Florenz
   Mitautoren: F. Cesarini; R. Pinzani; G. Soda; R. Sprugnoli

Beckhoff, Gerhard F.; Computer Science Department
   University of Western Ontario, London, Ontario, Canada N6A 3K7

Beilner, Heinz; Institut für Informatik der Universität
   7000 Stuttgart 80, Pfaffenwaldring 64   .

Bell, C. Gordon; Digital Equipment Corporation
   Maynard, Massachusetts, 146 Main Street, U S A

Blumann, Winfried; Siemens AG
   8000 München 70, Hofmannstr. 11

Böhme, Johann F.; Krupp Atlas-Elektronik
   2800 Bremen, Postfach 44 85 45

Braun, Stephan; Math. Institut der Universität
   8000 München 2, Postfach 20 24 20

Coffman Jr., E.G.; Department of Computer Science
   The Pennsylvania State University
   University Park, Pennsylvania 16802, U S A

Crouch, Donald B.; College of Engineering, University of Florida
   ·Box 1918, Florida 32542, U S A

Culik, Karel; Capkova 31, Bruo, Czechoslovakia

Ehrich, Hans-Dieter; Institut für Informatik und Praktische Mathematik
   der Universität Kiel, 2300 Kiel, Olshausenstr. 40-60

Escher, Wolfgang; Institut für Informatik IV der Universität
   7500 Karlsruhe 1, Postfach 6380

Falkenberg, Eckhard; Institut für Informatik der Universität
   7000 Stuttgart 80, Pfaffenwaldring 64
   Mitautoren: Meyer, Bernd; Schneider, Hans-Jochen

Fleck, M.; IBM Laboratorium
   1010 Wien, Parkring 10
   Mitautor: Oliva, O.

Frick, A.; Fakultät für Physik der Universität
   7800 Freiburg i. Br., Hermann-Herder-Straße 3
   Mitautoren: Bürkle, H.J.; Schlier Ch.

Grieger, Ingolf; Institut für Statik und Dynamik der Luft- und
   Raumfahrtkonstruktionen (ISD) der Universität
   7000 Stuttgart 80, Pfaffenwaldring 27

Grzymala-Busse, Jerzy W.; Department of Electrical Engineering
   Technical University of Poznan
   Pl. M. Sklodowskiej-Curie 2, 60-965 Poznan, Polen

Gschwind, G.; TU Berlin Informatik-Rechnerbetrieb
   1000 Berlin 10, Ernst-Reuter-Platz 8
   Mitautor: Pachaly, J.

Harrison, Michael A.; Department of Computer Science
   University of California, Berkeley, California 94720

Hartenstein, Reiner W.; Institut für Informatik IV der Universität
   7500 Karlsruhe, Postfach 6380

Hecheltjen, Peter; Seminar für Sozialpolitik der Universität
   6000 Frankfurt a.M., Mertonstraße 17-25

Hesse, Wolfgang; Mathematisches Institut der TU
   8000 München 2, Arcisstraße 21
   Mitautoren: Geiselbrechtinger F.; Krieg B.; Scheidig H.

Hoffmann, Hans-Jürgen; Fachbereich Informatik, TH Darmstadt
   6100 Darmstadt, Hochschulstraße 1
   Mitautor: Winkler, G.

Jammel, Alfons; Rechenzentrum der TU München
   8000 München 2, Arcisstraße 21

Kopp, Herbert; Institut für Angewandte Mathematik und Informatik
   der Universität des Saarlandes, 6600 Saarbrücken, Im Stadtwald

Kupka, Ingbert; Institut für Informatik der Universität
   2000 Hamburg 13, Schlüterstraße 70

Langenbach-Belz, Manfred; Institut für Nachrichtenvermittlung
   und Datenverarbeitung der Universität
   7000 Stuttgart 1, Seidenstraße 36

Leinemann, Klaus; Gesellschaft für Kernforschung mbH.
   7500 Karlsruhe, Weberstraße 5
   Mitautor: Schumann, Ulrich

Maurer, Douglas W.; Department of Electrical Engineering and
    Computer Sciences, George Washington University
    Washington, D.C. 20006, U S A

Mersmann, Gerhard; Telefunken Computer GmbH
    7750 Konstanz, Max-Stromeyer-Straße 116

Ovenhausen, Hubert; SCS
    2000 Hamburg 39, Überseering 89

Papert, Seymour; Artificial Intelligence Laboratory
    545 Technology Square, Cambridge, Mass. 02139, U S A

Paul, Wolfgang; Institut für Angewandte Mathematik und Informatik
    der Universität des Saarlandes, 6600 Saarbrücken, Im Stadtwald

Pirotte, Alain; MBLE Research Laboratory,
    B-1170 Brüssel, Avenue EM. van Becelaere 2, Belgien
    Mitautoren: Bouckaert, M; Snelling, M.

Rajlich, Václav; Research Institute of Mathematical Machines
    Luzná ul., Praha 6, Czechoslovakia

Robinet, Bernard J.; Institut de Programmation, Université de Paris VI
    4. place Jussieu, 75230 Paris Cedex 05, Frankreich

Røgeberg, Thomas; Norwegian Computing Center
    Oslo 3, Forskningsvn. 1B, Blindern, Norwegen

Schefe, Peter; Institut für Informatik der Universität
    2000 Hamburg 13, Schlüterstraße 70

Schindler, Sigram; TU Berlin - FB 20 (Kybernetik)
    1000 Berlin 10, Ernst-Reuter-Platz 8
    Mitautor: Wagner, Jochen

Schmitt, Alfred; Fakultät für Informatik der Universität
    7500 Karlsruhe, Postfach 6380
    Mitautoren: Dürre, Karl; Hummel, Helmut

Schneider, H.J.; Lehrstuhl für Informatik II der Universität
    8520 Erlangen-Nürnberg, Egerlandstraße 13
    Mitautor: Weber, Dieter

Schott, Gerda; TU München
    8000 München 2, Arcisstraße 21

Skronn, Hans-Jürgen; 7867 Wehr - 2, Waldmattstraße 27

Smoliar, Stephen W.; 407 Atwood Road
  Philadelphia, Penna. 19118, U S A

Sonnenberg, Walter; Kernforschungszentrum Karlsruhe
  7500 Karlsruhe 1, Postfach 3640

Spaniol, Otto; Fachbereich Angewandte Mathematik und Informatik
  der Universität des Saarlandes, 6600 Saarbrücken, Im Stadtwald

Steusloff, Hartwig; Institut für Informationsverarbeitung
  in Technik und Biologie der Fraunhofer-Gesellschaft e.V.
  7500 Karlsruhe-Waldstadt, Breslauer Straße 48
  Mitautor: R. Grimm

Stiegler, Helmut; Rechenzentrum der TU München
  8000 München 2, Arcisstraße 21

Swoboda, Joachim; AEG-Telefunken
  7900 Ulm, Elisabethenstraße 3
  Mitautor: Rosenbohm, Wilhelm

Tou, Julius T.; Center of Informatics Research, University of Florida
  Gainesville, Florida 32601, U S A

Wedde, Horst; Gesellschaft für Mathematik und Datenverarbeitung mbH.
  5205 St. Augustin 1, Schloß Birlinghoven

Wotschke, Detlef; Department of System Science
  University of California, Los Angeles, California 90024, U S A

INFORMATION SYSTEMS

Julius T. Tou

INTRODUCTION

Several years ago the Sunday New York Times brought up the following two items:
"Will a full week of shorter trading hours bring happiness to brokerage firms whose
back offices are jammed with paper work?" "A professor of psychology at Harvard
University warned that by the year 2000, the limit of man's mind to absorb information may be reached. We may already be nearing some kind of limit for many of the
less gifted among us, and those still able to handle the present level of complexity are in ever increasing demand." Certainly the daily press has little doubt that
information is exploding.

In recent years our very complex and technologically oriented society has created a situation in which more people and organizations have become concerned with
handling information and fewer with handling materials. The need for improved information systems has become more conspicuous, since information in various forms
with different degrees of complexity. One of the major areas in which our society
would face a critical challenge in the 1970's is the explosion of information which
would continue at an accelerated pace.

The information problem could be manifested at a glance of some statistical
data. In 1830, there were about 300 technical and scientific journals in circula-
tion. Today there are over 60,000 journals and 2.5 million articles per year throughout the world in over 50 languages. Each year about 20 billion checks pass through
the banks, with each check being handled four to five times. The major banks in
the United States process more than 25 million pieces of paper per day. The U.S.
Post Office Department is facing a severe mail problem. Today, the U.S. postal system
processes some 27,000 pieces of mail per second or 84 billion pieces per year.
This figure is expected to reach 116 billion by 1980.

Medicine is facing the problem of information explosion similar to that being
faced by many levels of society today. The physicians begin to feel incapable of
effectively handling the tremendous flood of information that must be processed in
medical research and patient care. For proper diagnosis and treatment, the physician
must interview and examine the patient, conduct laboratory and other studies, and
record this information. He must select, collate and compare these data with his own

---

Julius T. Tou is with the Center for Informatics Research, University of Florida,
Gainesville, Florida.

This work was supported in part by the Office of Naval Research and the Army Research Office.

previously gained experience and derive a diagnosis which identifies the disease. This diagnosis determines the course of the untreated illness. In both diagnosis and treatment, the doctor is constantly analyzing and processing information toward realizing the goals of medicine. If the physician could routinely capture and store clinical data in a medical information system without undue effort on his part, he could then take advantage of the speed and analytical capabilities of the system to extend his professional abilities.

Industry is confronted with a pressing need for better information flow between businesses. Executives and managers need to know more about the other businesses within their company, more about their own operations, the markets they are serving, and the timely information in order to make the best decision in a rapidly changing business environment. Information systems find increasingly important use in policy decision making, both in government and in business. Managerial decision making will always involve human judgment, but new concepts and computer oriented techniques have been developed that both suggest and evaluate a greater variety of options than the manager could ever seriously consider. The added feature of risk analysis enables the manager to measure the degree of risk involved in a variety of strategies. Information systems will provide the manager with a better insight as to the implications of his decisions.

Municipal governments are actively seeking the utilization of information systems to improve service delivery or to make comprehensive analysis of their problems for daily operation and for long-range planning. Policies by municipal governments on such matters as property tax equalization, land development, and urban planning will require substantially more information than currently exists if they are to be successful and beneficial to taxpayers. This increased availability of data must also be generated at costs lower than ad hoc studies such as the census and with far greater detail. Furthermore, the broad coverage of government programs and the growing complexity of policy making will leave the municipal governments with no choice other than having recourse to sophisticated information systems. Municipal information systems will organize the arrangements and activities for management of data in support of operations, planning, and policy making in municipal government. The state and its agencies will be pressed for the generation of structures within which municipal governments will function in dealing with the emerging problems. Such functions will cause direct increases in government personnel and costs. Public resistance to increased taxation suggests that other ways must be found to increase the productivity and quality of municipal delivery systems without this corresponding increase in cost. It is the municipal government area that can make significant contributions for the betterment of quality of life.

It appears that we are entering an era in which man and his information system, in a new partnership, can undertake much more complex tasks than ever before. The new partnership will make human society more productive and human life more satisfying. The steady growth in the magnitude and complexity of information systems necessitates the development of new theories and techniques for solving these information problems. We demand instant access to previously recorded information for decision making, and we require efficient methods for entry, analysis, storage, retrieval, editing, recognition, and display of data and information. This paper reviews some of the significant techniques and discusses various important facets of information systems.

PRINCIPAL ELEMENTS OF INFORMATION SYSTEMS

The basic functions of an information system are to enable the user to get quick access to recorded information, to enter data of various forms into the system by both manual and automatic means, to perform speedy data analysis with the aid of the system, to display the desired information for visual inspection or permanent record, and to edit and modify the displayed information as needed. Thus, an information system will be composed of functionally the following principal elements: data entry, data display, data file, data analysis, and data access.

The data entry sub-system serves as the input device for reading data in the form of characters, waveforms, graphs, maps, and pictures into the information system. The data entry may be done manually by teletype, light pen or graph pen, and it can be performed automatically by OCR device or other sophisticated pattern recognition equipment. Some data entry device can be used for graphical and alphanumeric input into the computer system simultaneously as the information is recorded onto a document. Sophisticated data entry sub-system is indeed a kind of information system itself.

The data display sub-system serves as the output device for exhibiting and recording printed materials or graphics. Among the commonly used output devices are line printers, data plotters,cathode-ray tube, and interactive graphics which are capable of performing query, transfer, deleting and editing. The main categories of data plotters are drum plotter, flatbed plotter, CRT plotter, raster scanner, electrostatic printer plotter, micro-scanner plotter, and Laser image processing scanner. For the drum plotter, the material on which plotting is made moves along one axis as the writing instrument is moved along the other axis to generate the two-dimensional movement. The plotting material of a flatbed plotter remains stationary, while the marking instrument moves in both x and y directions; and the fundamental recording material in the CRT system ends up being film. The raster scanner has to create a binary image of the entire plot before the plotting can be done, which requires disk storage. The Laser image processing scanner developed by CBS Laboratories is a high resolution scanner, computer interface and plotter. The trend is to design intelligent graphics terminals which combine facilities with the ability to perform a considerable amount of local processiing, to relieve the main computer of large amounts of I/O for low-level interaction, and to provide the user with immediate response to simple data analysis and symbol manipulation requests. An intelligent graphics terminal is considered as an important element of the information system.

The data file system, also known as the database system, is the major element of an information system. Data consists of numbers, names, codes, and symbols. Each of these items is often referred to as a data element. A database may be defined as an integrated collection of accessible interrelated data. A database comprises simple items,which are called attributes or fields,and compound items which are files, records and links. A file is a compound item made up of an arbitrary number of records, each record having the same logical structure. A link or pointer is a reference to an item that relates to another item which may be physically remote. In an information system, there are two different types of data elements: physical and logical. Physical data elements are the storage cells, addressable by either hardware or software, and usually connoted by such words as bit, byte, block, and segment. On the other hand, logical elements refer to the information carrying items and their relationship to one another. Such terms as files, arrays, records and fields refer to logical data elements. The major requirements for a database are; (1) to permit extremely rapid access to its contents, (2) to provide interactive query and editing capability, (3) to facilitate data analysis and manipulation, and (4) to place no software limitations on database size by obtaining space from secondary storage as it is needed.

In early computer applications in engineering and science, data storage presented few structural problems to the programmer since data were usually organized in a manner similar to the address structure of the physical storage media of the computer. Applications to non-numerical data processing, such as pattern recognition, artificial intelligence, and information retrieval, have revealed that interpretive systems were often slow and cumbersome, and sophisticated users needed new computer storage organizations which were more compatible with highly structured data. Early non-numerical computer applications pointed out that a database not only has information in its contents, but also contains as much information (sometimes even more information) in its structure.

An information system is a very complex and sophisticated communication system which emphasizes not only the physical aspects but also the semantic aspects of information communication and data analysis. Conventional communication systems involves a very simple retrieval scheme, i.e., channel selection. Each channel is precisely specified by a code number, and the number of available channels are small. However, an information system involves a very complex and sophisticated retrieval scheme for data access. The media of communication are the files. Unlike a telephone system, the major complexity lies not in the switching of lines among various subscribers, but in the provision of file structures as central media of communication through which relatively complicated information processing takes place. The generated information is transmitted via documents, which may include monographs, books, reports, letters, memos, charts, graphics, and pictures. Data elements are stored in an information system in an organized manner to preserve interrelationships and to provide access from one data element to another. This organization of data is often referred to as a data structure. In information systems, all data structures can be built up from four basic schemes: sequential structure, random structure, list structure, and hierarchical structure. THe data access techniques are dependent upon the type of data structures which will be discussed in the following sections.

To summarize the above discussion, we may conclude that the principal elements of an information system are data entry, data display, data file, data analysis, and data access. The functional block diagram is shown in Figure 1. In the design of an information system we need to study how to communicate the user's problem with the system; we need to analyze the functional characteristics of the information system; we need to understand the structural descriptions of the information system; and we need to specify the physical properties of the information system.

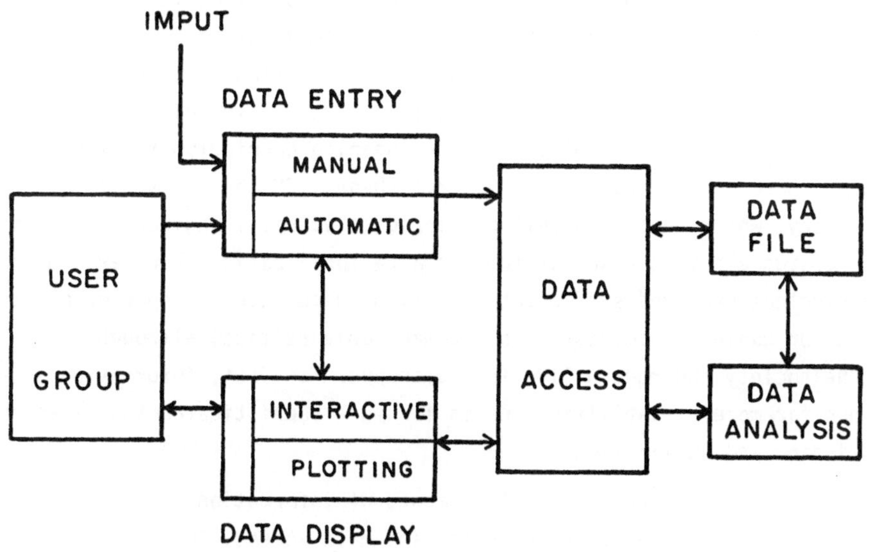

Figure 1. Functional Block Diagram of an Information System.

INFORMATION SYSTEMS THEORY

The design of information systems is not a new subject matter. During the past
ten years a nember of information systems have been developed by computer manufac-
turers and software houses. These systems are aimed toward specific applications
for airline reservations, inventory control, accounts receivable, library retrieval,
hospital operation, medical records, management information, municipal administration — to name a few. Practically all the current information systems are designed
with brute-force techniques on ad hoc basis, simply because of the lack of well-for-
mulated information systems theory. In order to make significant progress in information systems, we must have a much firmer scientific foundation. In fact, before a
new subject matter can be fully developed, we must have a firm theoretical foundation for the subject. It appears that first of all we should lay the groundwork for
the development of a firm theoretical base for information systems.

Information systems today bears some resemblance to electric power systems at
the turn of this century. Let us make a comparative study of these two fields.
Electric power systems deal with the transmission, distribution, and utilization
of electric energy; while information systems are concerned with the entry, storage,
analysis, transformation, retrieval, and display of information. The complexity,
diversity and utility of information are far beyond that of electric energy. The
design elements for electric power systems are schematic diagrams, circuit diagrams,
layouts, etc. By contrast, the design elements of information systems are programs,
flow charts, languages, compilers, algorithms, files, etc. Electric power systems
have been an important subject in electrical engineering curriculum for more than
half a century. Based upon circuit theory, wave theory, EM theory, switching theory,
and control theory, which have been well developed, electrical engineers find no
difficulty to design electric power systems on a rational basis. However, information systems have not received sufficient attention in computer science or electrical engineering or business administration at many universities, although its
impact upon the society and modern life is tremendous. In fact, information systems design has far more variabilities and is far more sophisticated than electric
energy transmission and utilization.

We have discussed that the principal elements of information systems are data
entry, data display, data file, data analysis, and data access. Consequently, to
develop informations systems theory, we must understand the basic principles underlying the above five elements. These principles include data structure, pictorial
data representation, pattern recognition, symbol manipulation, programming languages, interactive graphics, file organization, database management, computer systems, and information retrieval. At the University of Florida, we are teaching
these subjects to our students with interest in information systems. We understand

that at present the courses we are offering may not be coherent with respect to information systems design. However, in the years to come, we will attempt to integrate the contents of these subject matters to form a unified theoretical foundation for information systems and to develop a "language" for communicating the user's problem, specifying the structural descriptions and analyzing functional characteristics of information systems. We hope that such a "language" for information systems will be the counterpart of Maxwell's equations in electrical engineering.

PATTERN PROCESSING

Automatic data entry for an information system will involve pattern recognition process when the data are in the form of characters, speeches, graphics, maps, or pictures. In the design of an automatic pattern recognition system we are concerned with five major problems. The first problem deals with the representation of input data which can be measured from the objects or scenes to be recognized. Each measured quantity describes a characteristic of the pattern, which can be represented by an n-dimensional pattern vector, or by a pattern point in an n-dimensional space or by a string of symbols. The second problem is concerned with the extraction of characteristic features or attributes from the received input data and the reduction of the dimensionality of measurement vectors.

The third problem determines the optimum decision procedures which are needed in the identification and classification process. The pattern recognition machine may be trained to learn the recognition functions which assign the input pattern to an appropriate class. In solving the preprocessing and feature extraction problem, there is generally involved a set of parameters to be estimated and optimized. This gives rise to the parameter estimation problem. Furthermore, it is conceiveable that both the feature extraction process and the decision process may be considerably improved by making use of contextual information in the patterns. Contextual information may be measured by contingent probabilities, language statistics and neighboring variations. In some applications, contextual information is indispensable in making accurate recognition.

The design concepts for automatic pattern recognition are often motivated by how pattern classes are characterized and defined. When the pattern class is characterized by a roster of its members, the recognition scheme may be designed by the membership-roster approach. The set of patterns belonging to the same pattern class is stored in the recognition system. When an unknown pattern is shown to the system it is compared with the stored patterns one by one. The recognition system classifies this input pattern as a member of a pattern class if it matches one of the stored patterns belonging to that pattern class. Such recognition schemes are inexpensive and can work satisfactorily under the condition of perfect pattern samples.

When the pattern class is characterized by common properties shared by all of its members, pattern recognition schemes may be designed by the common-property approach. The basic assumption in this method is that patterns belonging to the same class possess certain common properties or attributes which reflect similarities among these patterns. The common properties are stored in the pattern recognition system. When an unknown pattern is observed by this system, its features are extracted and compared with the stored features. The recognition scheme will classify this new pattern as belonging to the pattern class with the same features. This approach excels the membership-roster approach in many respects. The storage requirement for features of a pattern class is much less than that for the patterns in the class. Since features of a pattern class are invariant, comparison of features allows variation in individual patterns.

When a pattern class is defined by the cluster in the pattern space, the recognition scheme may be designed by the clustering approach via partitioning of the pattern space. Since patterns belonging to the same class tend to flock together, pattern space partitioning would be an effective approach. When the patterns belonging to two different classes form non-overlapping clusters in the pattern space, the recognition and classification problem becomes the problem of generating a partition boundary which separates these two pattern classes.

Characterization of patterns by primitive elements, sub-patterns, and their relationships suggests automatic pattern recognition by the linguistic or syntactic description approach. The pattern is described by a hierarchical structure of sub-patterns analogous to the syntactic structure of languages. This permits application of language theory to the analysis of patterns. A pattern grammar is considered as consisting of finite sets of elements called variables, primitives, and productions. The rules of production determine the type of grammar. The essence in this approach lies in the selection of pattern primitives, the assembling of the primitives, and their relationships into pattern grammars, and the analysis and recognition in terms of the grammar. This approach is particularly useful in dealing with patterns which cannot be conveniently described by numerical measurements or which are so complex that local features cannot be identified and global properties must be used.

Feature selection has been recognized as an important process in automatic pattern recognition. It is one of the most difficult problems. Very little theory is currently available to guide the selection of features for the characterization of a pattern class. To facilitate the analysis of this problem, we may classify the features into four different kinds: (1) physical features, (2) geometrical features, (3) statistical features, and (4) linguistic features. Since human sensory organs are trained to recognize physical and geometrical features, it is natural to use these as the basis for recognition. When machines are designed to recognize patterns, the discriminative features should not be limited to physical and geometrical forms. Since the pattern recognition machine lacks human sensory organs, the physical and geometrical features may not be the most efficient means for classification and recognition. On the other hand, machines may be designed to extract mathematical, statistical or linguistic features of patterns which the human may have some difficulty to determine without the aid of a machine.

Last decade has witnessed considerable interest and rapid advances in research and development in automatic pattern recognition and machine learning. Examples of automatic pattern recognition systems exist in abundance. Successful attempts have been made to design or program machines to read printed or type-written characters, to screen electrocardiograms, to recognize spoken words, to identify bank checks, to analyze cancer cells, and to interpret photographs. Other applications include recognition of hand-written characters and words, general medical diagnosis, classification of seismic waves, detection of targets, prediction of weather, identification of faults and defects.

A simple practical example of automatic pattern classification is found in optical character recognition devices such as the machines which read the code characters in ordinary bank checks. The stylized character set found on most United States bank checks today is the familiar American Bankers Association E-13B font character set, consisting of fourteen characters. These characters are usually printed in ink which contains very finely ground magnetic material. If the character is being read by a magnetic device, the ink is magnetized prior to the reading operation in order to accentuate the presence of the characters and thus facilitate the reading process. When a character comes in for recognition it matches its waveform with the prestored waveforms for the fourteen character set and recognizes the character according to the closest match. Most stylized font character readers in the market today operate on this feature matching principle.

In early pattern recognition studies, we have been concerned with mathematical and statistical approaches making use of distance functions, potential functions, likelihood functions, and stochastic approximation. Emphasis has been placed upon numerical measurements and local features. Recent work in pattern recognition makes use of concepts from formal language theory. This approach is often referred to as syntactic pattern recognition, although terms such as linguistic pattern recognition, structural pattern recognition, and the like, appear in the literature. The basic difference between syntactic pattern recognition and the classical approaches is that the former explicitly utilizes the structure of patterns in the recognition process. Mathematical and statistical approaches on the other hand, deals with patterns on a strictly quantitative basis, thus largely ignoring interrelationships between various components of a pattern. Syntactic approach, which emphasizes structural relationships and global properties, has been thus far largely confined to pictorial patterns which are characterized by recognizable shapes, such as characters, chromosomes, blood cells, tissue sections, graphics, and topographic maps.

In present information systems developed for current use, the aspects of automatic pattern recognition have been given little attention. However, it can be anticipated that pattern processing, which is essential to sophisticated automatic data entry and data display, will soon become an integrated part of modern information systems. Furthermore, pattern recognition principles can be applied to the design of interactive information retrieval system.

INFORMATION SYSTEMS CHARACTERIZATION

Information systems may be categorized, in the main, into two types: (1) storage-retrieval information system, and (2) decision-control information system. The first category includes document referral system, data retrieval system, record-keeping system, automated library system, automated banking system, inventory system, reservation system. Examples of the second category are command control system, management information system, picture processing system, and economic forecast system.

In characterizing an information system, it is necessary to consider the following aspects. The system is capable of communicating with a language in expressing the logical data structures to be constructed and processed. The system is capable of allocating elements of logical data structure to storage structure and managing the use of free space within the storage structure. The system is capable of allocating elements of storage structure to internal and external storage media. The system is capable of maintaining a favorable trade-off between the types of output and responsiveness needed in data access, and the frequency and time allowed for updating the data. An information system usually involves two major types of functions. One type of function is performed by an _operating system_ which manages the allocation, movement, and protection of blocks or segments among various levels of storage. The other type is performed by a _data management system_ which controls the access, manipulation, and protection of the logical data elements within the blocks, making use of the services of an operating system.

In an ordinary storage-retrieval information system, to retrieve an item of information from a file, it is necessary to state what is desired, in which records and files this item will be found, and how to tell when the desired information has been found. The basic requirements for information retrieval are comparison of information needed with information stored and physical recovery of the desired

information. The statement of desired information is conveyed to the files by the
query which is matched against the stored information to determine whether the
stored record contains the type of information specified by the query and to measure its degree of relevance to the query.

Three types of retrieval schemes are in common use. They are data retrieval
system, document retrieval system, and information retrieval system. A data retrieval system involves the retrieval of a string of symbols in response to a query.
A document retrieval system consists of a set of deoument references or names, document surrogates or representation for the members of the document set, and mechanisms
for the generation of responses to queries. Such a system usually involves a two-
step operation, the retrieval of data (such as a call number) followed by a very
large symbol string which describes the document. Since the response is a set of
documents, there is the additional issue of the physical storage and retrieval of
the required documents. An information retrieval system is concerned with the
retrieval of the information contents other than simple data or documents in response to a query. Consequently the three basic types of retrieval schemes are
presented in order of increasing complexity and capability.

The decision-control information system is capable not only of performing the
basic storage and retrieval functions but also providing sophisticated data analysis
and intelligent information processing. Such information systems will be able
to keep the user to make good decisions by automatically correlating appropriate
records, retrieving analyzed data, and generating the desired tables, charts, sum-
maries, maps, graphs, or even alternative recommendations. This type of information
system is in great demand for military operations, business management, and
government administration. A great challenge exists today in the development of
municipal information system.

FILE STRUCTURE AND DATA ACCESS

The major elements in information systems are data files and data access which
have received considerable attention in information system design. These two elements play a central role in data management problems. A number of data management
systems have been introduced during the past few years, all of which possess the
capability of storing, retrieving and up-dating data. Such systems may be considered
as an essential subset of information systems and in many cases data management is
the core of information system design. Figure 2. illustrates the organization of
a data management system, in which DML denotes data manipulation language, and
DDL represents data description language.

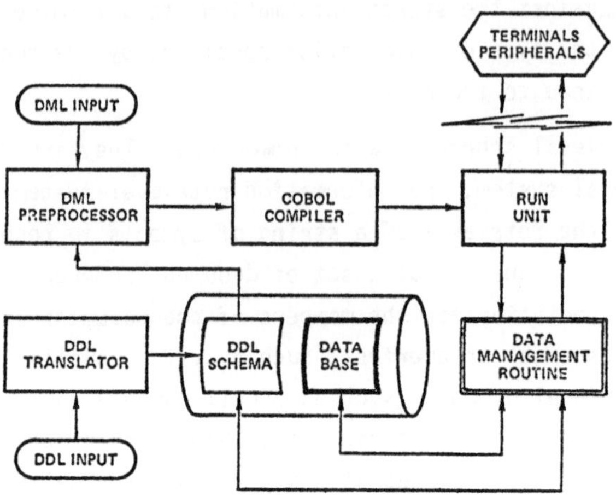

Figure 2. Organization of a Data Management System.

A data base may be considered, in an abstract sense, as a collection of en-coded representations of certain data sets S_1, S_2, ...S_n, associated with certain mappings g_1,g_2, ...,g_n. The data sets form the files of the data base. The mappings will assign attributes, whose meaning is external to the data base itself, to one or another of their sets S_k. Symbolically, this functional operation may be expressed as

$$g: S_k \rightarrow A$$

where A is the range of attributes defined by the mapping g. Since certain mappings will assign elements of one set S_j to elements of another set S_k. Such operation may be written as

$$g: S_k \rightarrow S_j$$

In general, the mapping of g will assign more than one element of data set S_j to certain elements of data set S_k. From the above set-theoretic model of data base, we observe that simple combinations of such basic operations as union, intersection, counting, subset extraction, optimization are only required in data base processing. Such concepts may lead us to the development of basic languages and access algo-rithms.

A file structure is a formatted organization of data records for assignment and distribution in mass storage devices so that the information system may be en-abled to store, retrieve, update, manipulate, and process data with great efficiency. Although many different file structures for data management have been designed, marketed, and described in the literature, all of them are designed on the basis of four fundamental schemes: sequential, random, list, and hierarchical. Among the well publicized commercially available information systems are DM-1,

Data Manager - 1 (Auerbach), TDMS, Time-shared Data Management System (SDC), IDS, Integrated Data Store (GE), GIS, Generalized Information System (IBM). The file structures in these systems are built up from the above four basic schemes and with some variations to meet certain specific requirements. The basic criteria for file structure and accessing are (1) minimization of the space required by the file, (2) minimization of file access, (3) ability to reconstruct the data base after a failure, and (4) ability to transfer record from one device to another when desired. Shown in Figure 3. is a sample file structure illustrating a simplified segment file in a municipal information system. Figure 4. describes a linkage schematic for the street segment file. A DM-1 data pool structure is shown in Figure 5, and a TDMS file structure is exemplified in Figure 6.

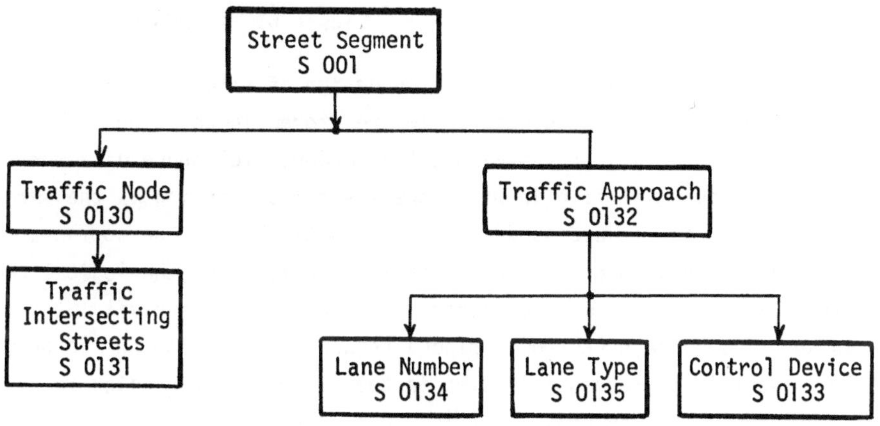

Figure 3. Street Segment File in a Municipal Information System.

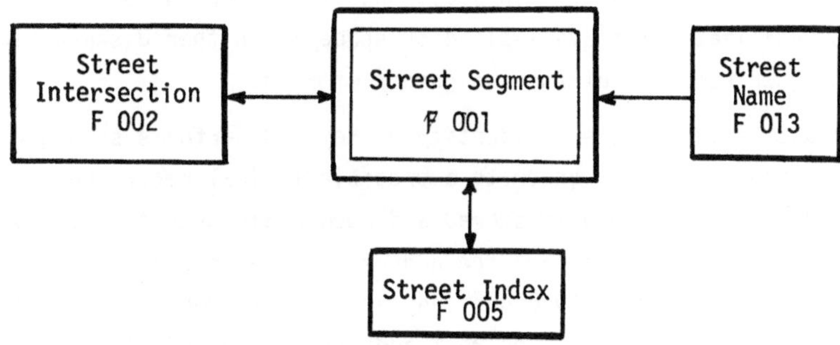

Figure 4. Linkage Schematic for a Street Segment File.

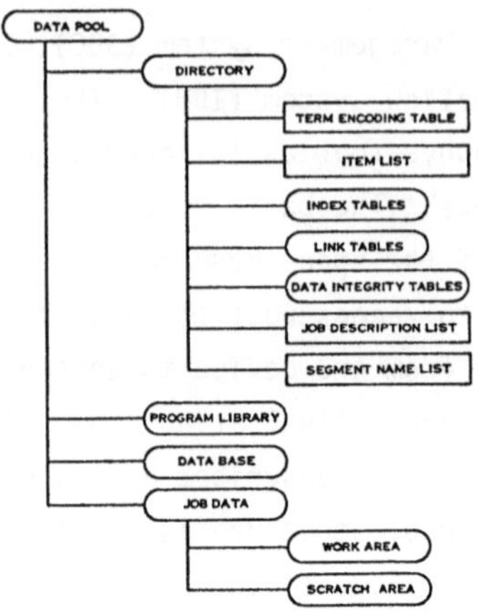

Figure 5. A DM-1 Data Pool Structure.

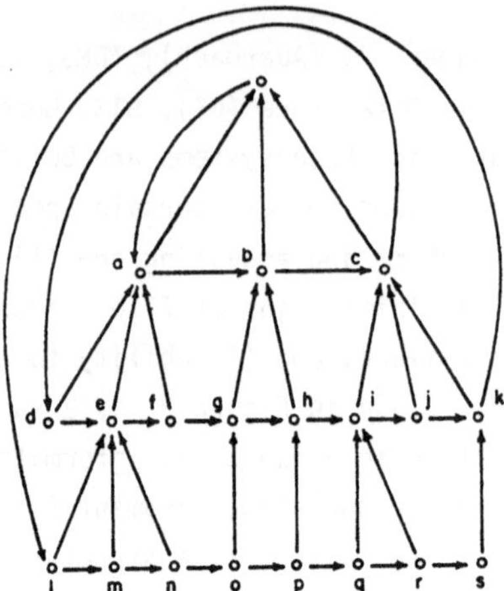

Figure 6. A TDMS File Structure.

Sequential file is perhaps the best known design of file organization for data management. The records in a sequential file are stored in positions relative to other records in accordance with a pre-specified order. Telephone directory is a common example of sequential file in which the key for sequencing is the surname data item of the record. To access data in a sequential file, one common attribute of the records is chosen, which may be a data item or field of the logical record and is called a key. Records may be stored in order of their arrival into the system. In such cases, each record is placed sequentially following the preceding record. The advantage of sequential files is the minimization of disk access required to locate a logical record, resulting in fast access per relationship during retrieval. With the records stored in sequence on a direct access medium or in high speed memory, a binary search can be made. A sequential file has the disadvantage that it makes database expansion difficult unless a link to an additional record of information is created. In addition, it does not allow for transfer for records. Poor utilization of available disk space is another disadvantage unless the system designer can control the assignment of keys.

A random data file takes some identifying key and performs some algebraic or logical manipulation that will generate a probable logical record number. The address is used when the record is stored and used again when the record is retrieved. The relationship between the key and the address of the record is of great importance in dealing with randomly organized data. The commonly used data access techniques are direct addressing, indirect addressing, and dictionary look-up. Direct addressing is used when the programmer knows the record's direct address. Indirect addressing, the logical record number can be derived from some function of a field or key within the record. In a dictionary look-up scheme, a record's direct address is determined prior to storage or retrieval, and both the record's key and direct address are stored in the dictionary. During storage or retrieval, the key is looked up in the dictionary and the associated direct address is used to store or retrieve the record. A random data file can minimize disk accesses. However, it does not allow for transfer of records and wastes file space if the number of overflows is kept to a reasonable level.

A list file structure makes use of pointers to handle the overflow problem and to make the logical organization independent of the physical structure. By contrast, the next logical record in a sequential file is also the next physical record. A pointer links records together for accessing by a key which is relevant to all of the linked records. The major types of list file structure are on-way pointer list structure and doubly-linked list structure. The one-way pointer list structure is simple but is very difficult for the programmer to remember where it came from. The doubly-linked list structure offers a major improvement over the one-way pointer list structure because it is circular in nature. It can start from any item in the list; it can move a record forward and back-forward or to a different place in the list with ease; it can readily insert or delete a record at any point from the list. In case of a failure while updating a list structure, we can use the backward pointers to reconstruct the file. To delete a record it will require five logical disk accesses. The main disadvantage of the list file structure is the space overhead caused by the pointers.

An hierarchical file structure may be considered as a more general linked-list structure. It permits the storage and retrieval mechanisms of a data management system to start with any record in the file and move up or down the hierarchy. One of the most popular techniques for data access is the directory approach that involves one or more levels, or hierarchies, of tables in which a record can be looked up on a particular key. This technique offers many advantages. It saves disk space since the file can be densely packed. Records can be moved around from place to place or from device to device by changing an entry in the appropriate directory. We can move a dead or dormant record to magnetic tape and make rapid file accessing on one key. A prime disadvantage of this approach is its vulnerability to failure.

A variation of the hierarchical file is the category file. Data items of the same category are clustered to form records, and the same data items may belong to different records. The file is designed in an hierarchical structure. The group of data items forms a pattern which possesses certain features. Pattern recognition techniques can be used to retrieve information and up-date the file. The category file is particularly useful in the design of interactive information retrieval system. The SEFIRE system developed at the Center for Informatics Research is built upon a flexible category file which is organized according to information contents and data relations. The category file can be automatically updated and enlarged via man-machine interaction.

Other variations of the basic file structures include tree structure, network structure, multilist file, indexed sequential file, inverted file, relational file, and partially inverted list. The inverted file is an extreme case of the multiple directory system which allows us to access a record on more than one key. Each field in a record will have its own directory or hierarchy of directories. It offers great use in information retrieval applications. However, it combines some of the disadvantages of the directory approach and the linked-list approach. Because every directory must be updated whenever a record is inserted or deleted, its maintenance is awkward. Furthermore, large overhead is required to keep track of the directories themselves. It has been generally agreed that data independence is an important goal of the database designer. By data independence we mean the insensitivity of various application programs to restructure the data when a common database is used. The fundamental advantage of the relational file is the greater degree of data independence it provides.

CONCLUSIONS

This paper presents some of the significant techniques and discusses various important facets of information systems. The principal elements of information systems are data entry, data display, data file, data analysis, and data access. We have discussed the problem of data entry, display, and pattern processing, and have reviewed several basic techniques for the design of data files and data access. Information systems may be categorized, in the main, as storage-retrieval information system and decision-control information system. Because of the shortage of space, such topics as storage devices, physical organization, and programming languages for information systems have not been covered. It appears that there lacks a unified information systems theory and the design of information systems has been done primarily on an ad hoc basis. We hope that in the next few years academicians at various universities throughout the world will be able to develop a theoretic foundation by integrating and extending the principles of pattern processing, file organization, data description, and information retrieval.

BIBLIOGRAPHY

1. Cheng, G.C., et.al., (Eds.), _Pictorial Pattern Recognition_, Thompson Books, Washington, D.C., 1968.

2. Fu, K.S., (Ed.), _Pattern Recognition and Machine Learning_, Plenum Press, New York, N.Y., 1972.

3. Kaneff, S., (Ed.), _Picture Language Machines_, Academic Press, New York, N.Y., 1970.

4. Knuth, D.E., _The Art of Computer Programming, Vol.1_, Addison-Wisley, Reading, Mass., 1968.

5. Lefkovitz, D., _File Structure for On-Line Systems_, Spartan Books, New York, N.Y., 1969.

6. Meadow, C.T., _The Analysis of Information Systems: A Programmer's Introduction to Information Retrieval_, Wiley, New York, N.Y., 1967.

7. Newman, W.M. and Sproull, R.F., _Principles of Interactive Computer Graphics_, McGraw-Hill, New York, N.Y., 1973.

8. Tou, J.T., (Ed.), _Advances in Information Systems Science, Vol.1_, Plenum Press, New York, N.Y., 1968.

9. ____, _Advances in Information Systems Science, Vol.2_, Plenum Press, New York, N.Y., 1969.

10. ____, _Advances in Information Systems Science, Vol.3_, Plenum Press, New York, N.Y., 1970.

11. ____, _Advances in Information Systems Science, Vol.4_, Plenum Press, New York, N.Y., 1971.

12. ____, _Advances in Information Systems Science, Vol.5_, Plenum Press, New York, N.Y., 1973.

13. ____, _Information Systems_, Plenum Press, New York, N.Y., 1973.

14. ____, _Software Engineering - 1_, Academic Press, New York, N.Y., 1970.

15. ____, _Software Engineering - 2_, Academic Press, New York, N.Y., 1971.

16. Tou, J.T. and Gonzalez, R.C., _Principles of Automatic Pattern Recognition_, (to be published in 1974).

17. Waite, W.M., _Implementing Software for Non-Numeric Applications_, Prentice-Hall, Englewood Cliffs, N.J., 1973.

18. Watanabe, S., (Ed.), _Methodologies of Pattern Recognition_, Academic Press, New York, N.Y., 1969.

19. Yourdon, E., _Design of On-Line Computer Systems_, Prentice-Hall, Englewood Cliffs, N.J., 1972.

20. Aron, J.D., "Information Systems in Perspective," ACM Computing Surveys, December, 1969.

21. Balm, G.J., "An Introduction to Optical Character Reader Considerations," Pattern Recognition Journal, September, 1970.

22. Cheng, G.C., "Pictorial Pattern Recognition," Pattern Recognition Journal, March, 1969.

23. Childs, D.L., "A Description of a Set-theoretic Data Structure," Proc. FJCC, Pt.1, 1968.

24. Clemenson, W.D., "File Organization and Search Techniques," in _Annual Review of Information Science and Technology_, Vol.1, (edited by C. Cuadra), Wiley, New York, N.Y. 1966.

25. CODASYL Systems Committee, "A Survey of Generalized Data Base Management Systems," Technicial Report, ACM, May, 1969.

26. CODASYL Systems Committee, "Feature Analysis of Generalized Data Base Management Systems," Technical Report, ACM, May, 1971.

27. Codd, E.F., "A Relational Model of Data for Large Shared Data Banks," Comm. ACM, July, 1970.

28. Coffman, E.G. and Eve, J., File Structures Using Hashing Functions." Comm, ACM, July, 1970.

29. Cotton, I. and Greatorex,F.S., "Data Structures and Techniques for Remote Computer Graphics," Proc. FJCC, Pt.1, 1968.

30. Dixon, P.J. and Sable, J., "DM-1 - A Generalized Data Management System," Proc. AFIPS, Vol. 30, 1967.

31. Dodd, G.G., "Elements of Data Management Systems," ACM Computing Surveys, June, 1969.

32. Early, J., "Toward an Understanding of Data Structures," Comm.ACM, October, 1971.

33. Feder, J., "Languages of Encoded Live Patterns," Information and Control, Vol. 13, 1968.

34. Firschein, O. and Fischler, M.A., "Describing and Abstracting Pictorial Structures," Pattern Recognition Journal, November, 1971.

35. Hsiao, D. and Harary, F., "A Formal System for Information Retrieval from Files," Comm. ACM, February,1970.

36. Hunter, L.W., "A Data Representation Code for Text Processing Systems." International Journal of Computer and Information Sciences, Vol.1, March, 1972.

37. Johnson, C.I., "Principles of Interactive Systems," IBM System Journal, Vol.7, 1968.

38. Lowe, T.C., "The Influence of Data-Base Characteristics and Usage on Direct Access File Organization," Journal of the ACM, October, 1968.

39. McGee, W., "File Structures for Generalized Data Management," Proc. IFIP Congress, Vol.2, North-Holland Publishing Company, 1968.

40. Miller, W.F. and Shaw, A.C., "Linguistic Methods in Picture Processing - A Survey," Proc. FJCC, 1968.

41. Minker, J. and Sable, J., "File Organization and Data Management," in <u>Annual Review of Information Science and Technology</u> Vol.2 , (edited by C.A. Cuadra), Wiley, New York, N.Y,1967.

42. Mori, K.I., et.al., "Microgram Controlled Pattern Processing in a Handwritten Mail Reader-sorter," Pattern Recognition Journal, September, 1970.

43. Morris, R., "Scatter Storage Techniques," Comm. ACM, January, 1968.

44. Narasimhan,R. and Reddy, V.S.N., "A Syntax-aided Recognition Scheme for Hand-printed English Letters," Pattern Recognition Journal, November, 1971.

45. Patton, P.C., "Trends in Data Organization and Access Methods," Computer, November, 1970.

46. Price, C.E., "Table Lookup Techniques," ACM Computing Surveys, June, 1971.

47. Ross, D.T., "The AED Free Store Package," Comm.ACM, August, 1967.

48. Salton, G., "Data Manipulation and Programming Problems in Automatic Information Retrieval," Comm.ACM, March, 1966.

49. Shaw, A.C., "Parsing of Graph Representable Pictures," Journal of the ACM, Vol. 17, 1970.

50. Shoshani, A. and Bernstein, A.J., "Synchronization in a Parallel-Accessed Data Base," Proc. FJCC, Vol.27, 1965.

51. Simon, J.C. and Guiho, G. "On Algorithms Preserving Neighborhood to File and Retrieve Information in a Memory," International J. of Computer and Information Sciences, Vol.1, March, 1972.

52. Strnad, A.L., "The Relational Approach to the Management of Data Bases," Proc. IFIP Congress, North-Holland Publishing Company, 1971.

53. Sussenguth, E.H.," Use of Tree Structures for Processing Files," Comm. ACM, May 1963.

54. Tou, J.T. and Gonzalez, R.C., "Automatic Recognition of Handwritten Characters via Feature Extraction and Multi-level Decision," International J. of Computer and Information Sciences, Vol.1, March, 1972.

55. Van Dam, A., "Some Implementation Issues Relating to Data Structure for Interactive Graphics," International J. of Computer and Information Sciences, Vol.1, December, 1972.

56. Van Dam, A. and Rice, D.E., "On-Line Text Editing: A Survey," ACM Computing Surveys, September, 1971.

57. Williams, R., "A Survey of Data Structure for Computer Graphics Systems," ACM Computing Surveys, March, 1971.

<u>Appendix</u> to the paper "Hierarchy of Interprecters for Modelling Complex digital
          Systems" by R. Hartenstein

A few weeks after submitting the text of the paper to meet the deadline for printing
the proceedings, I listened to the presentation of 3 other papers /15-17/, relating
very closely to subjects out of my paper. In my paper I introduced the criteria of
"structured hardware" and "tricky hardware" for classifying machine organizations
with respect to engineering philosophy. The criteria are defined in terms of the HIM
scheme. From these new papers, I've been listening to after submitting my paper, I
learned some other characterizations of contemporary machine designs. These give
excellent definitions of subsets from the set of "tricky hardware" structures. That's
why I am giving this "post scriptum" as an appendix to my paper for briefly surveying
parts out of those other papers.

R.F. ROSIN discovers 4 "rules of thumb", unconsciously established and unfortunately
used by many computer system designers /15/.

<u>Rule 1:</u> "in case of doubt, sacrifice a design concept to preserve cycle time."

<u>Rule 2:</u> "some facilities are cheap"

<u>Rule 3:</u> "Design constraints don't allow the realization of some otherwise good ideas"

<u>Rule 4:</u> "If it looks nice, it must be beautiful".

The meaning of ROSIN's "rules of thumb" could briefly be explained as follows. Rule 1
refers to an unreasonable short-sighted MIPS-squeezing, neither regarding efficiency
of the instruction set, nor the hardware/software cost ratio. Rule 2 refers to hardware links not intended in the original plan, introduced for adding "extra features
with no extra cost". The design constraints in rule 3 are those, imposed by a unreasonable set of preconceived components. Rule 4 remembers to features, which are
"monuments to the cleverness of the designer" /15/.

For features, which could be results of the application of rule 2 or 4, G.G. SCARROT
uses the name "parasitic cross links", when he says /16/: "Present systems incorporate many logically unnecessary links between subcomponents. Each delaborate modification therefore necessitates so many consequential changes due to the "parasitic
cross links" between subelements so that it is difficult to evolve a system to match
the changing requirements."

Now it is time for a change. A majority in the community of computer architects seems
to be ready to recognize the necessity for a change. E.g. see /16/ for the following
statements: "Computers also became complex and incomprehensible because it is difficult to formulate general simplifying theorems concerning computer design and operation ... In 1973 we are at last beginning to see our way through this jungle."
M.J. MARCUS demands: "There is a need for a consistant architectural form." /17/

WEINBERG discusses the virtues of "ego-less" programming /18/. There is no reason
not to extend this idea to cover the design of machine organisations or overall
system design (see /15/). Such virtues will be very important for getting away from
"tricky hardware" and for succeeding in steps towards "structured hardware".

<u>References</u> (continued)

/15/ Rosin, R.F.   "The Significance of Microprogramming"
                             to be presented at the International Computing
                             Symposium, Davos, Sept. 4 - 7, 1973.

/16/ Scarrot, G.G.   "System Design Objectives for the 70's"
                             Intl. Workshop on Computer Architecture.
                             Grenoble, June 26 - 28, 1973.

/17/ Marcus, M.J.   "A Final Horizontal Architectural Form for
                             Information Processing"
                             Intl. Workshop on Computer Architecture,
                             Grenoble, June 26 - 28, 1973.

/18/ Weinberg, G.   "The Psychology of Computer Programming",
                             von Nostrand Reinhold, New York 1971.

Lecture Notes in Economics and Mathematical Systems

Vol. 48 M. Constam, Fortran für Anfänger. VI, 143 Seiten. 1971. DM 16,–

Vol. 65 W. Everling, Exercises in Computer Systems Analysis. VIII, 184 pages. 1
DM 18,–

Vol. 68 J. Loeckx, Computability and Decidability. An Introduction for Studer
Computer Science. VI, 76 pages. 1972. DM 16,–

Vol. 75 GI-Gesellschaft für Informatik e. V. Bericht Nr. 3. 1. Fachtagung über
grammiersprachen. München, 9.–11. März 1971. Herausgegeben im Au
der Gesellschaft für Informatik von H. Langmaack und M. Paul. VII,
Seiten. 1972. DM 24,–

Vol. 78 GI-Gesellschaft für Informatik e. V. 2. Jahrestagung, Karlsruhe, 2.–4
tober 1972. Herausgegeben im Auftrag der Gesellschaft für Informati
P. Deussen. XI, 576 Seiten. 1973. DM 36,–

Vol. 81 Advanced Course on Software Engineering. Edited by F. L. Baue
545 pages. 1973. DM 32,–

Vol. 83 NTG/GI-Gesellschaft für Informatik, Nachrichtentechnische Gesells
Fachtagung „Cognitive Verfahren und Systeme", Hamburg, 11.–13.
1973. Herausgegeben im Auftrag der NTG/GI von Th. Einsele, W.
und H.-H. Nagel. VIII, 373 Seiten. 1973. DM 28,–